Advances in Psychological Assessment

Volume 4

Paul McReynolds

Editor

ADVANCES IN
PSYCHOLOGICAL
ASSESSMENT

Volume 4

Jossey-Bass Publishers

San Francisco • Washington • London • 1978

ADVANCES IN PSYCHOLOGICAL ASSESSMENT, VOLUME 4
by Paul McReynolds, Editor

Copyright © 1977 by: Jossey-Bass, Inc., Publishers
433 California Street
San Francisco, California 94104
&
Jossey-Bass Limited
28 Banner Street
London EC1Y 8QE

Library of Congress Catalogue Card Number LC 68-21578

International Standard Book Number ISBN 0-87589-355-4

Manufactured in the United States of America

JACKET DESIGN BY WILLI BAUM

FIRST EDITION

Code 7803

The Jossey-Bass
Social and
Behavioral Science Series

Preface

This volume, like its predecessors, brings together a group of original papers in the field of psychological assessment. For readers encountering the *Advances in Psychological Assessment* series for the first time with this volume, a few general comments on the aims and organization of the series are in order.

The general purpose of this series is to identify, describe, and evaluate significant new developments in assessment and thus to provide both professionals and students with an informed understanding of the progress and movement taking place in the field. The plan of the series calls for a new volume containing about a dozen chapters on relevant topics every two or three years.

Each volume includes chapters written from several different perspectives. In some instances, the focus is on a single test instrument or evaluative procedure—either a newly developed technique that appears to have outstanding potential or a standard instrument or procedure that has accumulated considerable new data. In other cases, the emphasis is on surveying and evaluating the various assessment devices and techniques available in important applied or research areas; such "area approaches" may center on particular clinical problems, educational topics, or research themes. In addition, certain special subjects, including methodological treatments and historical surveys relevant to assessment, are included in the series on occasion.

This fourth volume in the series includes twelve chapters on a variety of topics, such as the presentation of a new personality inventory, the elaboration of a film technique for assessing nonverbal communication skills, and surveys of the evaluation of depression and the measurement of curiosity. All of the chapters are written by authorities and will, I believe, be of distinguished utility for practitioners and researchers.

This book is, of course, the product of many authors, and all of them deserve credit for the overall quality of the finished work. As editor, I wish to express my appreciation to all of the contributors for the care and enthusiasm with which they prepared their respective chapters. For secretarial and clerical assistance, I am indebted to Katherine Beauchamp, Linda Gorelangton, Joann Hambacher, and Beverly Rapp. Finally, I am deeply grateful to my wife, Billie, for her invaluable support and assistance throughout the development of this volume.

Reno, Nevada   Paul McReynolds
October 1977

Contents

Preface   ix

Contributors   xiii

Introduction
    Paul McReynolds   1

1. Review of Minnesota Multiphasic Personality
    Inventory Special Scales
    John R. Graham   11

2. Interpreter's Guide to the Jackson
    Personality Inventory
    Douglas N. Jackson   56

3. Assessment of the Actualizing Person
    Robert R. Knapp, Everett L. Shostrom,
    Lila Knapp   103

4. Environmental Dispositions:
    Concepts and Measures
    George E. McKechnie   141

5.   Profile of Nonverbal Sensitivity
         Judith A. Hall, Robert Rosenthal,
         Dane Archer, M. R. DiMatteo,
         Peter L. Rogers   179

6.   Use of Improvisational Techniques in
         Assessment
         Paul McReynolds, Susan DeVoge   222

7.   Nature and Assessment of Self-Disclosing
         Behavior
         Gordon J. Chelune   278

8.   Assessment of Assertiveness
         James R. Hall   321

9.   Assessment of Depression
         Johanna M. Mayer   358

10. Clinical Assessment of Memory
         Moyra Williams   426

11. Assessment of Cognitive Style
         Kenneth M. Goldstein, Sheldon Blackman   462

12. Nature and Assessment of Human Curiosity
         Wallace H. Maw, Ethel W. Maw   526

     Name Index   573

     Subject Index   591

Contributors

DANE ARCHER, *College Five, University of California, Santa Cruz, California*

SHELDON BLACKMAN, *Research and Evaluation, St. Vincent's North Richmond Community Mental Health Center, Staten Island, New York*

GORDON J. CHELUNE, *Division of Clinical Psychology, University of Colorado Medical School, Denver, Colorado*

SUSAN DEVOGE, *Department of Psychology, University of Nevada, Reno, Nevada*

M. R. DIMATTEO, *Department of Psychology, University of California, Riverside, California*

KENNETH M. GOLDSTEIN, *Research and Development, Staten Island Children's Community Mental Health Center, Staten Island, New York*

JOHN R. GRAHAM, *Department of Psychology, Kent State University, Kent, Ohio*

JAMES R. HALL, *Department of Psychology, University of Tennessee, Chattanooga, Tennessee*

xiii

JUDITH A. HALL, *Department of Psychology, Johns Hopkins University, Baltimore, Maryland*

DOUGLAS N. JACKSON, *Department of Psychology, University of Western Ontario, London, Ontario, Canada*

LILA KNAPP, *EdITS/Educational and Industrial Testing Service, San Diego, California*

ROBERT R. KNAPP, *EdITS/Educational and Industrial Testing Service, San Diego, California*

GEORGE E. MCKECHNIE, *Oakland, California*

PAUL MCREYNOLDS, *Department of Psychology, University of Nevada, Reno, Nevada*

ETHEL W. MAW, *Department of Education and Child Development, Bryn Mawr College, Bryn Mawr, Pennsylvania*

WALLACE H. MAW, *Department of Educational Foundations and Department of Individual and Family Studies, University of Delaware, Newark, Delaware*

JOHANNA M. MAYER, *Department of Psychology, University of Nevada, Reno, Nevada*

PETER L. ROGERS, *School of Public Health, Harvard University, Cambridge, Massachusetts*

ROBERT ROSENTHAL, *Department of Psychology and Social Relations, Harvard University, Cambridge, Massachusetts*

EVERETT L. SHOSTROM, *Institute of Actualizing Therapy, Santa Ana, California*

MOYRA WILLIAMS, *Department of Clinical Psychology, Cambridge Area Health Authority, Cambridge, England*

Advances in Psychological Assessment

Volume 4

When we speak of a mental test we have in mind the experimental determination of some phase of mental capacity, the scientific measurement of some mental trait. . . . The purposes for which mental tests have been developed are, of course, varied, but roughly speaking, we may distinguish a theoretical interest on the part of laboratory psychologists and a practical interest on the part of those who are concerned with mind at work in everyday life. . . . We may hope that the skillful study of mental functions by the test method may supply us with a satisfactory account of the nature and interrelations of mental functions, just as the typical introspective experiment has been able to furnish an account of the structural makeup of mind.

Guy Montrose Whipple (1910)

Introduction

PAUL McREYNOLDS

Both scientific and applied psychology rely heavily on advances in assessment for their continued progress. In psychological research, the role of measurement is obvious and crucial, and the adequacy of a study is rarely greater than the precision of its included measures. In applied psychology, the place of assessment is equally clear and equally central; indeed, it is in the more practical applied areas that assessment technology—in such forms as tests and special interview techniques—has had its greatest impact.

Psychological practitioners and behavioral scientists need to keep abreast of new developments in assessment techniques and new perspectives on older techniques. The twelve chapters that follow serve this purpose. As an aid to the reader, I will comment briefly on each chapter and on its relation to the contemporary scene in assessment. But first let me offer several observations on recent and current movements in the field.

My first observation concerns the changing role of assessment in clinical psychological practice. Despite the general validity of my comment above on the place of assessment in the applied areas, the fact is that acceptance of the importance of assessment—at least in its formal, systematic sense—has by no means been universal among clinicians. Although many of the standard personality tests were developed or inspired by clinicians, certain key approaches in clinical practice have traditionally minimized, if not actually eschewed, the use of assessment devices on the grounds that they are of little use. Two major movements in clinical psychology that adopted this view were Rogerian nondirective therapy and behavior modification. To be sure, neither of these orientations was ever completely opposed to assessment. Rogerians were interested from the beginning in techniques for assessing therapeutic progress, and the early behavior modifiers were concerned with identifying specific areas for desensitization in clients. Nevertheless, these two important clinical approaches tended to deprecate the use of systematic assessment to provide more knowledge of the individual case. This led many graduate clinical psychology training programs to greatly deemphasize teaching assessment skills.

I think the situation just described is rapidly changing— indeed, the change that I discern has been going on for several years and only lacks general acknowledgment. I am not suggesting that either the humanistic wing (which is largely the descendant of the earlier nondirective orientation) or the behavioral wing of the clinical scene has suddenly reverted to a commitment to traditional assessment technology; rather, my point is that these theoretical orientations have been developing their own assessment approaches. There is a growing rapprochement among the different clinical orientations regarding assessment, with a subsequent enrichment of the whole field.

Let me be more specific. Although there is still some criticism of assessment in the humanistic camp (Brown, 1972), there is also increasing recognition that assessment can be performed in accordance with values important to psychotherapy (Craddick, 1972). The most significant trend concerning assessment within the humanistic movement is undoubtedly the development of certain personality tests, such as the Personality Orientation Inventory (POI) (Shostrom, 1975; Knapp, Shostrom, and Knapp, Chapter Three, this volume), which provide meaningful evaluations of self-actualization and other variables central to humanistic theory.

It is in behavior modification, however, that concerted

attention to assessment has been most prominent recently. The earliest discussions of behavioral assessment were the chapter by Weiss (1968), in the first volume of the present series, and articles by Cautela (1968) and Goldfried and Pomeranz (1968). Today the surge of interest in behavioral techniques of assessment has reached avalanche proportions with a number of recent books (Ciminero, Calhoun, and Adams, 1977; Cone and Hawkins, 1977; Gambrill, 1977; Goldfried and Sprafkin, 1974; Hersen and Bellack, 1976; Mash and Terdal, 1976) and articles (Bijou and Peterson, 1971; Dickson, 1975; Goldfried, 1976; Goldfried and Kent, 1972; Wolff and Merrens, 1974) on the subject. As Ciminero, Calhoun, and Adams (1977, p. ix) have noted, "Behavioral assessment is undoubtedly one of the most rapidly growing topics in the contemporary field of behavior therapy." Although behavioral assessment techniques are in some respects quite different from the more traditional evaluative methods employed in personology and clinical practice, the similarities between the two orientations are much greater than the differences. Both approaches deal with similar practical problems—such as anxiety, depression, and social skills—and with such common problems of measurement as standardization, reliability, validity, and utility.

The overall role of assessment in applied psychology has been increasing in recent years, partially because of a growing emphasis on evaluative procedures among behaviorally and humanistically oriented psychologists. As a consequence, assessment orientations with different assumptions and goals have gained greater respect for each other; the entire field has become less fractionated. This broader, more inclusive approach to assessment is reflected in two recent general texts, Maloney and Ward's *Psychological Assessment: A Conceptual Approach* (1976) and Sundberg's *Assessment of Persons* (1977).

My second observation concerns the increasing emphasis on environmental assessment. As is generally recognized, a person's behavior is a combination of the characteristics of the person and of the situation in which the behavior occurs. Accordingly, it is desirable, as I have insisted in previous introductions to volumes in this series, to account for both intrapersonal and situational (or environmental) factors in assessment. In the past, psychological assessment has focused on the evaluation of individuals, but in recent years great progress has been made in the development of environmental assessment (see Craik, 1971; Moos, 1975; Moos and Insel, 1974; Stern, 1970), and this trend is continuing. For the most part, however, these newer developments in situational assessment have not been coordinated with complementary methods in the assessment of people; missing are specific assessment packages designed to evaluate *both* the intrapersonal and situational factors involved in predicting the behavior of individuals in relevant real-life situations. Contemporary psychological assessment needs to develop a technology permitting systematic application to individual cases of the formulation that behavior is a joint function of intrapersonal and situational factors.

The third trend that I wish to identify is the increasing use in assessment of action-based methods, which predict a subject's future behavior in a given setting from samples of the subject's actual behavior in a similar setting. The behavior sample in this approach is typically obtained through an improvisational or roleplaying procedure, by a direct simulation of the behavior under consideration, or by the presentation of a problem situation requiring overt action. Filmed or videotaped samples of behavior may also be employed. The focus is on samples of natural behavior, in order to minimize the transformations necessary in drawing inferences from test data to real-life behavior. The growing interest in action-based methods of assessment parallels an increased use of action-based techniques in psychotherapy (Greenwald, 1967), as with the diverse procedures of modeling, behavior rehearsal, psychodrama, and various Gestalt techniques.

The three trends I have discussed are reflected in the present volume in varying degrees. With respect to the first trend, concerning the broadening role of assessment in clinical practice, Chapter Three describes several important instruments that measure key variables in the humanistic framework. Although no single chapter deals with behavioral assessment, this orientation is represented in three chapters (Chapters Six, Eight, and

Nine); each includes different assessment approaches organized around common themes. The second trend, concerning the continuing professional interest in environmental assessment, is represented in this volume in Chapter Four on the measurement of environmental dispositions. The third trend, regarding the increasing use of action-based methods of assessment, is covered by Chapter Six, which is devoted exclusively to the use of improvisational techniques, and Chapter Eight, which reviews a number of roleplaying procedures; additionally, Chapter Five presents a method for evaluating sensitivity to nonverbal cues based on filmed segments of actual behavior.

Besides reflecting the three trends highlighted previously, this volume includes a number of other contributions, of equal importance and interest, concerned with assessment techniques in special areas or with newer developments in traditional areas. The twelve chapters can be roughly divided into two groups: the first six chapters are concerned with specific assessment tests and techniques, while the last six chapters shift the perspective to particular clinical and research areas, with examinations of the evaluative procedures currently available in each area.

In the first four chapters the spotlight is on pencil and paper inventories. Of these, the first three deal with personality inventories in the traditional sense, and the fourth focuses on environmental assessment.

Chapter One, by John R. Graham, is a survey and critical review of a number of special Minnesota Multiphasic Personality Inventory (MMPI) scales. So many MMPI scales have been developed in addition to the basic clinical scales that it is difficult for the average test user to keep track of them, let alone evaluate the more important ones. However, there are times when a certain special scale can add greatly to the usefulness of the instrument. The wide circle of clinicians and researchers employing the MMPI will find this chapter extremely useful.

Douglas N. Jackson, the author of the highly respected Personality Research Form (PRF), presents a newly developed test for personality evaluation, the Jackson Personality Inventory (JPI) in Chapter Two. The JPI measures different personality variables; its construction, like that of the PRF, is based on a careful rationale and on rigorous test technology. The chapter provides a wealth of practical information for users of this new instrument.

The third chapter, by Robert R. Knapp, Everett L. Shostrom, and Lila Knapp, addresses the important problem of measuring key variables in humanistic theory. The theme of self-actualization is, of course, one of the central constructs in modern psychology, and Shostrom and his colleagues, through the Personal Orientation Inventory (POI) and other instruments, are the acknowledged leaders in the attempt to bring this and related constructs under the rein of accurate measurement techniques. Here the authors survey and assemble in one convenient place a wide range of up-to-date information for those workers interested in assessing actualization variables.

Chapter Four is concerned with environmental psychology. George E. McKechnie, the author of two recent instruments in this area—the Environmental Response Inventory (ERI) and the Leisure Activities Blank (LAB)—focuses on the nature and measurement of the various ways in which individuals conceive and relate to different aspects of their physical environments. This chapter constitutes an important contribution in psychology's continuing attempt to metricize man-environment relations.

The fifth chapter, by Judith A. Hall, Robert Rosenthal, Dane Archer, M. R. DiMatteo, and Peter L. Rogers, is unique in two respects. First, it deals with assessment in the area of nonverbal behavior, a concern of great importance and topicality; second, it approaches this problem in an innovative way by having the subject judge meanings conveyed by a filmed model. The chapter summarizes and interprets a massive amount of material on the Profile of Nonverbal Sensitivity (PONS), a fascinating technique developed by the authors. Readers will find the presentation of this impressive new instrument both instructive and interesting.

The method Susan DeVoge and I describe and evaluate in Chapter Six—improvisational assessment—is similar to the PONS method in that both are based on direct samples of actual behavior. However, in the PONS method the subject is the judge, and in improvisational techniques the subject is the actor. As noted earlier in this introduction, the use of improvisational, roleplaying techniques in assessment has been expanding rapidly in recent years; nevertheless, the extent of utilization of this interesting action-based approach, as revealed in Chapter Six, may surprise the reader. In our judgment the improvisational method is extremely powerful and adaptable to a wide range of behavioral variables.

With Chapter Seven the perspective shifts from the examination of particular techniques to a survey of methods available in given areas. The chapter by Gordon J. Chelune concerns the assessment of self-disclosing behavior. The degree to which individuals reveal information about themselves, and the manners in which they do so, comprise a fascinating research area with considerable clinical and social psychological significance. Chelune examines the conceptual bases of disclosing behavior and then reviews the various techniques—including two of his own—developed for assessment of the key variables in self-disclosure. The coverage and critical approach of this contribution will make it extremely helpful to researchers.

James R. Hall offers a critical review of the procedures available for assessing assertive behavior in Chapter Eight. These methods, he points out, divide naturally into two groups: self-report techniques and roleplaying techniques. This chapter, because of its quality and coverage and the current wide interest in the concept of assertiveness, will, I am sure, prove highly useful.

Chapter Nine, by Johanna M. Mayer, is on the assessment of depression. This pervasive and socially disabling affliction is the ongoing focus of a major international research effort. A central facet of this research is the problem of evaluating the degree and manifestations of depression. Mayer's balanced approach provides a highly useful survey, for both practitioners and investigators, of the available techniques for systematic description and measurement of depression.

Another important clinical area—the evaluation of disturbances in memory—is treated in Chapter Ten. Moyra Wil-

liams, the author, has an international reputation in neuro-
psychology and is particularly interested in clinical and theoretical issues associated with memory. Her contribution benefits
from her extensive clinical and research experience in dealing
with problems of memory and constitutes a veritable manual of
procedures in this crucial area. This chapter's significance is
given added weight by the fact that clinical problems of memory, although quite frequent, have rarely been covered systematically.

Chapters Seven through Ten concern topics of primarily a
clinical nature while Chapters Eleven and Twelve deal with
theoretical concepts of more general theoretical interest. Kenneth M. Goldstein and Sheldon Blackman take up the problem
of assessing cognitive style variables in Chapter Eleven. The
many-faceted concept of cognitive style is a central construct in
modern cognitive and personological theory, and during the
past three decades a large number of relevant measurement
techniques have been introduced. Goldstein and Blackman survey this broad field, introduce a useful conceptual scheme, and
provide critical and helpful data on the various instruments.

The final chapter considers the nature and assessment of
curiosity, one of the most active and interesting areas in contemporary motivational psychology. The authors, Wallace H.
Maw and Ethel W. Maw, are widely recognized as leading authorities on curiosity. They bring their wide experience to bear
on a critical examination of the area; their coverage includes an
analysis of the concept of curiosity and a survey of the available
measures. Because of its breadth of coverage and the general
interest in curiosity, Chapter Twelve furnishes a strong and fitting conclusion to the volume.

References

Bijou, S., and Peterson, R. F. "Functional Analysis in the As-
    sessment of Children." In P. McReynolds (Ed.), *Advances
    in Psychological Assessment*. Vol. 2. Palo Alto, Calif.: Sci-
    ence and Behavior Books, 1971.
Brown, E. C. "Assessment from a Humanistic Perspective."

Psychotherapy: Theory, Research and Practice, 1972, *9,* 103-106.

Cautela, J. R. "Behavior Therapy and the Need for Behavioral Assessment." *Psychotherapy: Theory, Research and Practice,* 1968, *4,* 175-179.

Ciminero, A. R., Calhoun, K. S., and Adams, H. E. (Eds.). *Handbook of Behavioral Assessment.* New York: Wiley-Interscience, 1977.

Cone, J. D., and Hawkins, R. P. (Eds.). *Behavioral Assessment: New Directions in Clinical Psychology.* New York: Brunner/Mazel, 1977.

Craddick, R. A. "Humanistic Assessment: A Reply to Brown." *Psychotherapy: Theory, Research and Practice,* 1972, *9,* 107-110.

Craik, K. H. "The Assessment of Places." In P. McReynolds (Ed.), *Advances in Psychological Assessment.* Vol. 2. Palo Alto, Calif.: Science and Behavior Books, 1971.

Dickson, C. R. "Role of Assessment in Behavior Therapy." In P. McReynolds (Ed.), *Advances in Psychological Assessment.* Vol. 3. San Francisco: Jossey-Bass, 1975.

Gambrill, E. D. *Behavior Modification: Handbook of Assessment, Intervention, and Evaluation.* San Francisco: Jossey-Bass, 1977.

Goldfried, M. R. "Behavioral Assessment." In I. B. Weiner (Ed.), *Clinical Methods in Psychology.* New York: Wiley-Interscience, 1976.

Goldfried, M. R. and Kent, R. N. "Traditional Versus Behavioral Personality Assessment: A Comparison of Methodological and Theoretical Assumptions." *Psychological Bulletin,* 1972, *77,* 409-420.

Goldfried, M. R., and Pomeranz, D. M. "Role of Assessment in Behavior Modification." *Psychological Reports,* 1968, *23,* 75-87.

Goldfried, M. R., and Sprafkin, J. N. *Behavioral Personality Assessment.* Morristown, N. J.: General Learning Press, 1974.

Greenwald, H. (Ed.). *Active Psychotherapy.* New York: Atherton, 1967.

Hersen, M., and Bellack, A. S. (Eds.). *Behavioral Assessment: A Practical Handbook.* Elmsford, N.Y.: Pergamon Press, 1976.

Maloney, M. P., and Ward, M. P. *Psychological Assessment: A Conceptual Approach.* New York: Oxford University Press, 1976.

Mash, E. J., and Terdal, L. G. *Behavior-Therapy Assessment.* New York: Springer, 1976.

Moos, R. H. "Assessment and Impact of Social Climate." In P. McReynolds (Ed.), *Advances in Psychological Assessment.* Vol. 3. San Francisco: Jossey-Bass, 1975.

Moos, R. H., and Insel, P. M. *Issues in Social Ecology.* Palo Alto, Calif.: National Press Books, 1974.

Shostrom, E. L. *Actualizing Assessment Battery: Interpretation Brochure.* San Diego: Educational and Industrial Testing Service, 1975.

Stern, G. C. *People in Context.* New York: Wiley, 1970.

Sundberg, N. D. *Assessment of Persons.* Englewood Cliffs, N.J.: Prentice-Hall, 1977.

Weiss, R. L. "Operant Conditioning Techniques in Psychological Assessment." In P. McReynolds (Ed.), *Advances in Psychological Assessment.* Vol. 1. Palo Alto, Calif.: Science and Behavior Books, 1968.

Wolff, W. T., and Merrens, M. R. "Behavioral Assessment: A Review of Clinical Methods." *Journal of Personality Assessment,* 1974, *38,* 3-16.

I

Review of Minnesota Multiphasic Personality Inventory Special Scales

John R. Graham

Since the Minnesota Multiphasic Personality Inventory (MMPI) was first published (Hathaway and McKinley, 1940), its item pool has been used to generate a large number of additional scales. In their two-volume *An MMPI Handbook,* Dahlstrom, Welsh, and Dahlstrom (1970, 1975) listed well over five hundred scales in addition to the original validity and clinical scales. These additional scales vary considerably in terms of what they are supposed to measure, the manner in which they were constructed, their reliabilities, the extent to which they have been cross-validated, the availability of adequate normative data, and the amount of additional validity data that has been generated. They also vary in terms of how frequently they have been utilized in clinical and research settings. Some scales appear to have been used only by their constructors, while others have been employed extensively in research studies and are used routinely in clinical interpretation of the MMPI.

11

The typical user of the MMPI cannot be aware of all of these additional scales and does not have the wide technical information required to evaluate their adequacy and potential utility. The purpose of this chapter is to call to the reader's attention a relatively small number of the additional MMPI scales that, in the author's opinion, have the greatest potential usefulness in research and clinical practice. Because of space limitations, it is not possible to provide an exhaustive review of the literature for each scale discussed. Rather, the approach will be to present a summary of each scale's construction, reliability, validity, and normative data, and also to suggest additional sources of information to readers who want to learn more about a particular scale.

While the decision about which of the many scales to include in this chapter had to be somewhat subjective, several general criteria were used in making the selection. First, it was required that a scale be intended to assess characteristics that are of interest to the typical researcher or clinician. Second, a body of literature must exist that is large enough to permit meaningful conclusions about the usefulness or potential usefulness of the scale.

Harris and Lingoes Subscales

Rationale and Construction. Because the standard clinical scales of the MMPI were constructed empirically with little attention given to scale content, the item content of the scales is quite heterogeneous. The same raw score on a clinical scale can represent different combinations of responses to individual items in the scale. Some investigators have suggested that analysis of the subgroups of items according to content can be helpful in interpreting an MMPI protocol. The subscales developed by Harris and Lingoes (1955, 1968) represent a systematic effort to take into consideration the meaningful subgroups of items within the standard MMPI clinical scales. Harris and Lingoes developed subscales for six of the standard ten clinical scales (D, Hy, Pd, Pa, Sc, Ma). Each subscale was constructed logically by grouping together items in the standard scale that seemed to be similar in content or to reflect a single attitude or trait. The content of items in a subscale was examined, and a label was assigned to reflect the content. Thirty-one subscales were constructed in all, but of these, three summary scales typically are not used in clinical interpretation of the MMPI. The MMPI booklet numbers and scoring directions for each Harris and Lingoes subscale can be found in Volume 1 of *An MMPI Handbook* (Dahlstrom and others, 1970) and in *The MMPI: A Practical Guide* (Graham, 1977). The subscale names for each of the six standard clinical scales are as follows:

Scale 2 (Depression): D1—Subjective Depression; D2—Psychomotor Retardation; D3—Physical Malfunctioning; D4—Mental Dullness; and D5—Brooding.

Scale 3 (Hysteria): Hy1—Denial of Social Anxiety; Hy2—Need for Affection; Hy3—Lassitude-Malaise; Hy4—Somatic Complaints; and Hy5—Inhibition of Aggression.

Scale 4 (Psychopathic Deviate): Pd1—Familial Discord; Pd2—Authority Problems; Pd3—Social Imperturbability; Pd4A—Social Alienation; and Pd4B—Self-Alienation.

Scale 6 (Paranoia): Pa1—Persecutory Ideas; Pa2—Poignancy; and Pa3—Naivete.

Scale 8 (Schizophrenia): Sc1A—Social Alienation; Sc1B—Emotional Alienation; Sc2A—Lack of Ego Mastery, Cognitive; Sc2B—Lack of Ego Mastery, Conative; Sc2C—Lack of Ego Mastery, Defective Inhibition; and Sc3—Bizarre Sensory Experiences.

Scale 9 (Hypomania): Ma1—Amorality; Ma2—Psychomotor Acceleration; Ma3—Imperturbability; and Ma4—Ego Inflation.

Harris and Lingoes (1955, 1968) reported high intercorrelations among subscales and between subscales and parent scales. The considerable item overlap among the scales may account, at least in part, for these high intercorrelations.

Reliability. No test-retest reliability data have been published for the Harris and Lingoes subscales, but Gocka (1965) reported internal-consistency reliability values for the subscales.

The values ranged from 0.04 to 0.85. The brevity of many of the subscales may account in part for some of the very low internal-consistency values.

Norms. In their 1968 mimeographed paper, Harris and Lingoes reported descriptive statistics for a group of psychiatric patients. Gocka and Holloway (1963) presented similar data for male Veterans Administration psychiatric patients. The most comprehensive normative data for the subscales can be found in Volume 1 of *An MMPI Handbook* (Dahlstrom and others, 1970), where T-score conversions for each Harris and Lingoes subscale raw score are presented separately for males and females in the original MMPI standardization sample.

Validity. While the Harris and Lingoes subscales have been widely used clinically since their development, disappointingly little empirical research relevant to the subscales has been published. Graham (1977) compared the Harris and Lingoes subscales with groupings of items based on factor-analytic procedures (Comrey, 1957a, 1957b, 1958a, 1958b, 1958c; Comrey and Margraff, 1958). While there were some marked differences between the rationally derived Harris and Lingoes subscales and the groupings of items derived using factor analysis, the Comrey data include some groupings of items similar to some of the Harris and Lingoes subscales. In an attempt to determine the factor structure of the MMPI, Lingoes (1960) factor-analyzed scores on the Harris and Lingoes subscales and on the subtle-obvious subscales developed by Wiener (1948). He concluded that there are more dimensions in the MMPI than the six suggested by the standard clinical scales included in the analysis and fewer than the thirty-six suggested by the Harris and Lingoes subscales and the subtle-obvious subscales. Calvin (1974) factor-analyzed scores on the five Harris and Lingoes subscales of Scale 2 (Depression) and concluded that four of the subscales appeared to be unidimensional, while one subscale was two-dimensional.

Harris and Christiansen (1946) found that some of the Harris and Lingoes subscales were useful in differentiating successful and unsuccessful psychotherapy patients, and concluded that the subscale information leads to a better understanding of how the successful therapy patient views himself and the environment in which he lives. Gocka and Holloway (1963) reported that the Harris and Lingoes subscales were related to measures of social desirability, introversion-extraversion, and dissimulation, but unrelated to such demographic variables as intelligence, occupational level, and marital status. Only two Harris and Lingoes subscales were related to competency status at the time of hospital admission, and no subscale was related significantly to length of hospitalization. Panton (1959) found a number of significant differences on the Harris and Lingoes subscales between black and white prisoners and between prison inmates and psychiatric patients. Calvin (1975) attempted to identify empirical behavioral correlates for the Harris and Lingoes subscales for a sample of psychiatric patients. While he found reliable correlates for ten of the twenty-eight subscales, he concluded that in most of the cases in his study, subscales did not add significantly to analyses based on the standard clinical scales.

Conclusion. The Harris and Lingoes subscales represent a systematic way to take into account the content of items within the standard clinical scales of the MMPI. While validity data relevant to the subscales are limited, they tend to support the use of the subscales as an additional way of analyzing MMPI protocols. The scales may be especially useful in understanding what kinds of items a test subject endorsed in obtaining a high score on a standard clinical scale.

Masculinity-Femininity (Mf) and Social Introversion (Si) Subscales

Rationale and Construction. When Harris and Lingoes (1955, 1968) reported subscales for the standard MMPI clinical scales, they did not include subscales for the Masculinity-Femininity (Mf) and Social Introversion (Si) scales. Recently, Serkownek (1975) utilized the data from factor analyses of the Mf and Si scales (Graham, Schroeder, and Lilly, 1971) to develop subscales for these two clinical scales. Items loading higher than 0.30 on each factor in the analyses were selected for a scale to assess that factor, and each subscale was labeled by examining the content of its items. The MMPI booklet numbers and scoring directions for the Mf and Si subscales can be found in *The MMPI: A Practical Guide* (Graham, 1977). The labels of the subscales for these two clinical scales are as follows:

Masculinity-Femininity (Mf): Mf1—Narcissism-Sensitivity; Mf2—Stereotypic Feminine Interests; Mf3—Denial of Stereotypic Masculine Interests; Mf4—Heterosexual Discomfort-Passivity; Mf5—Introspective-Critical; and Mf6—Socially Retiring.

Social Introversion (Si): Si1—Inferiority-Personal Discomfort; Si2—Discomfort with Others; Si3—Staid-Personal Rigidity; Si4—Hypersensitivity; Si5—Distrust; and Si6—Physical-Somatic Concerns.

Reliability and Validity. Although no reliability data have been published for the Mf and Si subscales, it is likely—because of the factor-analytic basis for scale construction—that the subscales have a high level of internal consistency. And while no validity data have been published yet for the subscales, Graham (1977) has offered some preliminary interpretive statements for each subscale based on examination of the content of items in each subscale.

Norms. Serkownek (1975) provided norms for the Mf and Si subscales for a group of normal subjects. Graham (1977) used Serkownek's data to report T-score conversions for subscale raw scores for males and females.

Conclusion. Although these subscales have been developed very recently and no reliability or validity data are yet available, they represent a potentially useful addition to the Harris and Lingoes subscales. They are described here in the hope that researchers and practicing clinicians will be stimulated to investigate their reliability and validity.

Wiggins Content Scales

Rationale and Construction. When the MMPI was first published, little attention was given to the content of individual items. In fact, many MMPI users seem to feel that consideration of the content of an individual's responses to the items detracts from the validity of the test. However, some investigators (Hase and Goldberg, 1967; Jackson, 1971; Goldberg, 1972; Koss and Butcher, 1973) have suggested that examination of item content can add significantly to test interpretation. The Wiggins content scales represent a systematic approach to the analysis of the content of an examinee's responses to the MMPI items.

Initially, Wiggins (1966) grouped MMPI items together according to twenty-six content categories, listed by Hathaway and McKinley (1940), to demonstrate the breadth of the item pool. A score was obtained for each category by keying items in the direction least often chosen by normal subjects in the original MMPI standardization sample. Using data from normal college students, Wiggins refined the scales by eliminating some items, reassigning items from one scale to another, eliminating some scales, collapsing other scales, and adding new scales. These procedures resulted in a final set of thirteen content scales judged by Wiggins to be mutually exclusive, internally consistent, moderately independent, and representative of the major content dimensions of the MMPI item pool. The MMPI booklet numbers and scoring directions for items in the content scales can be found in Wiggins's (1966) original article, in *The MMPI: A Practical Guide* (Graham, 1977), and in Volume 2 of *An MMPI Handbook* (Dahlstrom and others, 1975). The labels of the content scales are as follows: Social Maladjustment (SOC), Depression (DEP), Feminine Interests (FEM), Poor Morale (MOR), Religious Fundamentalism (REL), Authority Conflict (AUT), Psychoticism (PSY), Organic Symptoms (ORG), Family Problems (FAM), Manifest Hostility (HOS), Phobias (PHO), Hypomania (HYP), Poor Health (HEA).

Cohler, Weiss, and Grunebaum (1974) developed abbreviated content scales to match the Wiggins scales and demonstrated their equivalence with the full-length Wiggins content scales.

Reliability. Wiggins (1969) has published the only reliability data for his content scales. He reported internal-consistency estimates (coefficient alpha) for several samples of college students and Air Force enlisted men. The coefficients ranged from 0.505 to 0.872, suggesting that the content scales have a high degree of internal consistency.

Norms. Fowler and Coyle (1969) have presented normative data for Wiggins's content scales for a sample of students at
a southern university. Wiggins, Goldberg, and Applebaum
(1971) have reported normative data for a university sample
and for subjects from the original Minnesota normative group.
Tables for converting raw scores on the content scales to T-
scores based on the Minnesota normative data have been constructed by Wiggins (1971) and published by Graham (1977).

Validity. Wiggins and others (1971) correlated content
scale scores with scores from the Edwards Personal Preference
Schedule, the California Psychological Inventory, the Adjective
Check List, and Masculinity and Femininity scales from the
Strong Vocational Interest Blank. They concluded that the resulting intercorrelations offered evidence that the content scales
measure the personality characteristics suggested by their labels.
There also are data indicating that self-report via the content
scales is related to other forms of self-report (Taylor, Ptacek,
Carithers, Griffin, and Coyne, 1972). Data from studies by
Payne and Wiggins (1972) and Boerger (1975) also suggest that
there are reliable and meaningful nontest correlates for the content scales.

While the content scales can differentiate between normal
and psychiatric samples and are systematically related to traditional diagnostic categories (Wiggins, 1969; Kammeier, Hoffman, and Loper, 1973; Loper, Kammeier, and Hoffman, 1973;
Hoffman, Loper, and Kammeier, 1974; Mezzich, Damarin, and
Erickson, 1974; Cohler and others, 1974), Wiggins concluded
that the content scales do not offer measures of degree of
psychopathology, as this term is used traditionally. A factor
analysis of scores on the thirteen Wiggins content scales (Wiggins, 1969) yielded five important dimensions: anxiety prone-
ness versus ego resiliency; impulsivity versus control; health concern; social desirability role playing; and feminine interests.
Based on the content of items in the scales and the limited
amount of validity data available, Wiggins (1966, 1969) and
Graham (1977) generated some preliminary interpretive statements for each of the content scales.

Conclusion. The Wiggins content scales are psychometrically sound measures of the major content dimensions in the MMPI item pool. Content scale scores are related to important nontest behaviors different from the ones assessed by the standard clinical scales. When used in conjunction with the standard clinical scales, the content scales can add significantly to an understanding of an examinee's personality and behavior.

Tryon, Stein, and Chu (TSC) Cluster Scales

Rationale and Construction. The Tryon, Stein, and Chu (TSC) Cluster scales (Stein, 1968) represent a systematic effort to develop scales for assessing the major dimensions or factors tapped by the MMPI item pool. Tryon and his colleagues (Tryon and Bailey, 1965; Chu, 1966; Tryon, 1966; Stein, 1968) developed cluster-analytic procedures and programs and applied them to the item responses of 70 male Veterans Administration outpatients diagnosed as schizophrenic, 150 male Veterans Administration outpatients diagnosed as anxiety reactions, and 90 normal military officers. These procedures yielded seven clusters of items that were judged to be homogeneous both statistically and in terms of content meaning. Scales were developed to assess the clusters by selecting MMPI items that had high loadings for each cluster, and labels were assigned to the scales by examining the content of items included in each scale. The labels of the seven cluster scales are as follows:

   I Social Introversion
  II Body Symptoms
 III Suspicion and Mistrust
 IV Depression and Apathy
  V Resentment and Aggression
 VI Autism and Disruptive Thoughts
VII Anxiety, Worry, Fears

The MMPI booklet numbers and scoring directions for items in the cluster scales can be found in Stein's (1968) article, in *The MMPI: A Practical Guide* (Graham, 1977), and in Volume 2 of *An MMPI Handbook* (Dahlstrom and others, 1975).

Reliability. Because of the cluster-analytic procedures used in constructing the cluster scales, one would expect the scales to have a high degree of internal consistency. Data presented by Tryon (1966) revealed that these expectations are confirmed. Internal-consistency (alpha) coefficients ranged from 0.85 to 0.94. No test-retest reliability data have been published for the TSC scales.

Norms. Stein (1968) presented normative data for the TSC scales for twenty male and thirteen female samples that included normal subjects, medical patients, and psychiatric outpatients and inpatients. Graham (1977) used Stein's descriptive data for composite samples of normal males and females to generate T-score conversions for raw scores on each of the cluster scales. Stein presented data indicating that scores on the TSC scales are not related to age, education, family size, or grade point average for normal college students. However, more intelligent persons tended to score lower than less intelligent persons on all of the cluster scales.

Validity Data. Stein (1968) reviewed studies that correlated scores on the TSC scales with scores from the standard MMPI scales, the Omnibus Personality Inventory, the Edwards Personal Preference Schedule, and the Strong Vocational Interest Blank. Stein interpreted these data as offering strong support for the construct validity of the cluster scales. Graham (1977) interpreted Stein's data as indicating that some of the cluster scales, such as Social Introversion, Body Symptoms, and Depression and Apathy, seem to be measuring characteristics that also are reflected by scores on the standard MMPI scales, while other cluster scales, such as Suspicion and Mistrust, are tapping characteristics not assessed by the standard MMPI scales.

Stein (1968) also compared the TSC scale scores of a number of different criterion groups. In general, these comparisons indicated that more pathological and poorly adjusted groups tend to score higher on the cluster scales. Boerger (1975) identified groups of psychiatric patients who scored high and low on each TSC scale and attempted to identify empirical, extratest correlates for high and low scores. While he was successful in identifying such correlates for high scores on the scales, very few correlates were identified for low scores on the scales. Graham (1977) utilized the results of the studies of Stein and Boerger, along with subjective analysis of content of items in each cluster scale, to generate preliminary and tentative interpretive statements for high and low scores on each of the TSC scales.

Conclusion. The TSC scales are psychometrically sound measures of the major factor or cluster dimensions tapped by the MMPI item pool. Sufficient validity data exist to permit at least tentative interpretations of high scores on the scales. When used in conjunction with the standard MMPI validity and clinical scales, the TSC scales can add significantly to the interpretation of MMPI protocols.

Welsh Anxiety (A) Scale

Rationale and Construction. Welsh (1956) developed the Anxiety (A) scale to assess one of the two major dimensions (anxiety and repression) that have emerged consistently from factor-analytic studies of the standard MMPI scales. Based on data from male Veterans Administration psychiatric patients, Welsh selected items with high loadings on a factor that he originally called "general maladjustment," and through internal-consistency procedures he refined the scale. MMPI booklet numbers and scoring directions for the thirty-nine items included in the final A scale can be found in Volume 2 of *An MMPI Handbook* (Dahlstrom and others, 1975) and in *The MMPI: A Practical Guide* (Graham, 1977). The items in the scale are keyed in such a way that higher scores indicate more psychopathology.

Reliability. The A scale has adequate reliability to justify its use in research and clinical assessment. A split-half reliability coefficient of 0.88, an internal-consistency (Kuder-Richardson 21) coefficient of 0.94, and a four-month test-retest reliability coefficient of 0.94 were reported for the scale (Welsh, 1956; Gocka, 1965).

Norms. Welsh (1956) reported descriptive statistics for

various groups of normal and clinical subjects on the A scale. The most comprehensive normative data for the A scale can be found in Volume 2 of *An MMPI Handbook* (Dahlstrom and others, 1975), where T-score conversions for A scale raw scores are reported for normal males and females in the original MMPI standardization sample.

Validity. Graham (1977) has recently reviewed validity studies relevant to the A scale. He cites research indicating that there are important nontest correlates of scores on the A scale. High scorers on the scale tend to be anxious and uncomfortable, pessimistic, apathetic, unemotional, unexcitable, shy and retiring, hesitant and vascillating, inhibited and overcontrolled, defensive, overly accepting of authority, conforming, submissive, compliant, suggestible, cautious, fussy, cool, distant, and uninvolved. In addition, they have a slow personal tempo, lack confidence in their own abilities, are influenced by diffuse personal feelings, rationalize and blame others for difficulties, and lack poise in social situations. They also tend to become confused, disorganized, and maladaptive under stress and are uncomfortable enough to be motivated to change in psychotherapy. Low A scores can be characterized as extraverted, competent, confident, and somewhat impulsive. Although people with low scores are not likely to be experiencing severe emotional discomfort, they may or may not have serious adjustment problems. There also is evidence that A scale scores tend to decrease during psychiatric hospitalization (Lewinsohn, 1965).

Conclusion. The A scale is a reliable variable that has a number of important behavioral and personality correlates. While anxiety and discomfort are among these correlates, Welsh's original label of "general maladjustment" seems to describe what this scale measures better than does the current label of "anxiety."

Manifest Anxiety Scale (MAS)

Rationale and Construction. The Manifest Anxiety scale (MAS) was developed by Taylor (1951, 1953) to assess emotional responsiveness, one of the determinants of generalized drive state (D) as posited in Hull-Spence learning theory. Originally the scale was used to identify experimental subjects with high and low emotional responsiveness in order to test hypotheses stemming from Hullian theory. Subsequent research studies have examined the relationships between manifest anxiety and numerous aspects of human behavior.

The MAS was rationally constructed. Five clinical psychologists were given a definition of manifest anxiety based on Cameron's (1947) description of chronic anxiety reactions and were asked to select from a pool of 200 MMPI items those that indicated manifest anxiety according to the definition provided. Sixty-five items, for which there was 80 percent agreement or better, were chosen for the preliminary scale. These items and neutral buffer items were administered to a college student sample, and their responses provided the basis for internal-consistency analyses to refine the scale. The 50 items that correlated most highly with the total score on the scale were selected for the final scale and were mixed with 175 buffer items. Although subsequent revisions of the MAS have been attempted, the 50 anxiety items from the 225-item scale constitute the MAS as it is usually scored. In spite of Taylor's (1953) caution to the contrary, the MAS usually is scored from a standard administration of the entire MMPI. The MMPI booklet numbers and scoring directions for the MAS items can be found in Volume 2 of *An MMPI Handbook* (Dahlstrom and others, 1975) and in *The MMPI: A Practical Guide* (Graham, 1977). The items are keyed so that higher scores indicate greater anxiety.

The MAS has been criticized by Edwards (1957) and others on the grounds that MAS scores are so confounded with social desirability response sets that high scores mean little more than a willingness to admit to socially undesirable characteristics and behaviors. Edwards reported a correlation of -0.84 between MAS scores and scores on his MMPI social desirability scale. While MAS scores are undoubtedly related to social desirability, the magnitude of the relationship probably is not as great as Edwards suggested. The correlation that he reported was spuriously high because the two scales that he used have twenty-one common items. Suinn (1967, 1968) found significant associations between MAS item responses and college students' ratings of social desirability for only eleven MAS items in one study and only one item in another. Farber (1964) pointed out that two scales that are highly correlated do not necessarily measure the same thing. Block (1965) suggested that the tendency to admit socially undesirable characteristics and behaviors should be treated as one of many important characteristics of persons who score high on the MAS and some other MMPI scales.

Reliability. Gocka (1965) reported a Kuder-Richardson 21 (internal consistency) value of 0.92 for the MAS for male Veterans Administration psychiatric patients. Taylor (1953) reported test-retest reliability coefficients, based on college student data, of 0.89, 0.82, and 0.81 for intervals of three weeks, five months, and seven to nineteen months, respectively. Thus, it would appear that the MAS has adequate temporal stability and internal consistency to justify its use in research and clinical practice.

Norms. Graham (1977) used Taylor's (1953) data for a large sample of college students to generate T-score conversions for MAS raw scores. Normative data also have been reported for male and female psychiatric patients (Newton, 1968), male and female medical patients at the Mayo Clinic (Swenson, Pearson, and Osborne, 1973), and normal males and females in the original MMPI standardization sample (Dahlstrom and others, 1975). Taylor's original data for college students suggested a nonsignificant tendency for females to score higher than males on the MAS. Subsequent normative data have indicated significantly higher MAS scores for females than males and for younger subjects than older subjects.

Validity Data. Spence and Spence (1966) summarized the predictions made by Hullian theory concerning the relationship between learning and drive level as assessed by the MAS. Basically, one would expect that high MAS scorers would do better than low scorers on simple learning tasks and worse on more complex tasks. Byrne (1974) and Spielberger (1966a) concluded that most empirical data have supported the hypothesized relationship. However, it has become obvious that the relationship between anxiety and learning is not simple and that other variables, such as degree of perceived stress, must be taken into account. Spielberger systematically investigated the relationship between MAS scores and academic achievement. While anxiety and academic achievement were not strongly related across all ability levels, for students of middle-level ability MAS scores and grades were negatively correlated. Further, at all except the very highest ability levels, college dropout rates were nearly four times as great for high anxious as for low anxious subjects.

Reviews of the MAS literature by Byrne (1966, 1974), and Graham (1977) indicated that scores on the MAS are related to other important behaviors. High MAS scorers tend to score high on other anxiety scales, show greater physiological reactivity to real and imagined threat, and be related high on anxiety by observers. In addition, high scorers tend to be more emotionally maladjusted and to report more medical and psychiatric symptoms. The MAS scores tend to decrease during psychotherapy and psychiatric hospitalization. High MAS scorers perceive their environments as threatening and uncontrollable and are less able than low scorers to control autonomic reactions to stress situations. High scorers also are likely to focus on the present rather than the future and to rely on recent past experiences in developing expectations. Spielberger (1966b) differentiated between trait anxiety, which refers to relatively stable, acquired tendencies to respond in an anxious manner in a variety of stressful situations, and state anxiety, which refers to temporary feelings of tension and apprehension and activation of the autonomic nervous system that are situational in nature. He concluded that the MAS measures trait rather than state anxiety.

Conclusions. The MAS is a reliable scale for assessing emotional responsiveness in stress situations. There are validity data suggesting that scores on the MAS are related to a variety of learning tasks and to other important personality characteristics and behaviors. While scores on the scale are related to other anxiety measures, the MAS seems to be assessing general, or trait, anxiety rather than situational, or state, anxiety.

College Maladjustment (MT) Scale

Rationale and Construction. The College Maladjustment (MT) scale was constructed to discriminate between emotionally adjusted and maladjusted college students (Kleinmuntz, 1960b). The MT scale items were selected from the MMPI item pool by comparing responses of forty adjusted male and female students and forty maladjusted male and female students. The adjusted students had contacted a university clinic to arrange for a routine mental health screening examination as part of teacher certification procedures, and none of them admitted to a history of psychiatric treatment. The maladjusted students had contacted the same clinic for help with emotional problems and had remained in psychotherapy for three or more sessions. Item-analytic procedures yielded forty-three items that discriminated between the adjusted and maladjusted students. The MMPI booklet numbers and scoring directions for the MT scale items can be found in Volume 2 of *An MMPI Handbook* (Dahlstrom and others, 1975). Items are keyed so that higher scores are more indicative of maladjustment. Kleinmuntz (1961) found that scores on the forty-three-item scale administered separately corresponded quite well to MT scale scores derived from a standard MMPI administration.

When the MT scale was scored for the original adjusted and maladjusted criterion groups, the maladjusted group was significantly higher than the adjusted group. The MT scale then was administered to fifty new female students designated as maladjusted and twenty-one new male and female students designated as adjusted. Again, the maladjusted students scored significantly higher than the adjusted students. A cut-off score of 15 on the MT scale correctly classified 91 percent of the subjects in the original criterion groups and 89 percent of subjects in the cross-validational groups.

Reliability. When Kleinmuntz (1961) administered the MT scale to college students twice with an interval of three days, a test-retest reliability coefficient of 0.88 was obtained. No other reliability data have been published for the MT scale.

Norms. MT scale normative data have been reported for several different samples of emotionally adjusted and maladjusted college males and females (Kleinmuntz, 1960b, 1961, 1963a; Parker, 1961) and for normal males and females in the original MMPI standardization sample (Dahlstrom and others, 1975). In his 1961 paper Kleinmuntz presented T-score conversions for MT scale raw scores for normal college males and females. Females tend to score higher than males on the MT scale. The MT scale scores of adjusted and maladjusted college students vary considerably from one college setting to another and among divisions within each college. This variation indicates that separate norms and cut-off scores should be established for each specific setting where the MT scale is used.

Additional Validity Data. Kleinmuntz (1961) studied a group of college students who completed the MT scale when they entered school and who later sought out either "vocational-academic" or "emotional" counseling. While the emotional counseling group scored significantly higher than the vocational-academic counseling group, the mean MT scale score of the former group was considerably lower than had been reported previously for other maladjusted groups. Using an MT scale cut-off of 15, Parker (1961) was able to classify correctly 74 percent of maladjusted students who completed the MT scale at the time that they sought counseling but only 46 percent when the MT scale was completed as part of a test battery administered at the time of college admission. Parker's data and his own led Kleinmuntz to conclude that the MT scale is more accurate when used to identify existing emotional problems than to predict future emotional problems. In relation to his efforts to develop MMPI decision rules for the identification of college maladjustment, Kleinmuntz (1963a, 1963b) reported data from several different universities suggesting that maladjusted students score higher than adjusted students on the MT scale. Kleinmuntz (1960b) examined the content of the MT scale items and concluded that the high MT scale scorer presents himself as "an ineffectual, pessimistic, procrastinating, anxious, and worried person who tends to somatize and who finds that much of the time life is a strain" (p. 210).

Conclusion. The MT scale is related to emotional maladjustment among college students. Because of variability of scores from one setting to another, specific norms and cut-off scores should be established in each setting where the scale is used. While the scale has the potential for identifying concurrent maladjustment, its ability to predict future maladjustment has not been established.

Emotional Disorder (Ed) Scale

Rationale and Construction. Recognizing the need for a brief, objective measure of emotional disorder that could be used in community surveys and similar endeavors, Dahlstrom (Dahlstrom and others, 1975) developed the Emotional Disorder (Ed) scale. The scale was patterned after the Health Opinion Survey (HOS), a brief scale usually administered orally in door-to-door interviews in order to determine the prevalence of emotional disorders (Langer, 1962). The twenty-two HOS items were examined, and items were selected from the MMPI item pool that had content similar to that of the HOS items. Closely matching MMPI items were found for twenty of the twenty-two HOS items; one HOS item had no counterpart in the item pool, and one MMPI item matched the content of two HOS items. The Ed scale items are keyed so that higher scores indicate emotional disorder. The MMPI booklet numbers and scoring directions for the Ed scale items can be found in Volume 2 of *An MMPI Handbook* (Dahlstrom and others, 1975).

Reliability. No reliability data have been published for the Ed scale.

Norms. Dahlstrom and others (1975) have presented Ed scale normative data, including T-score conversions, for normal males and females in the original MMPI standardization sample and for a large sample of male and female psychiatric patients. As expected, the psychiatric patients scored much higher than normals on the Ed scale. In general, females tend to score higher than males on the Ed scale, and less educated persons score higher than better educated persons. There are small racial differences on the Ed scale, with white males scoring higher than nonwhite males and nonwhite females scoring higher than white females.

Validity. When Dahlstrom and others (1975) correlated Ed scale scores with standard MMPI validity and clinical scale scores for psychiatric patients, they found that the Ed scale was positively related to the F scale and negatively related to the L and K scales. The highest correlations between the Ed scale and the clinical scales were for Scale 2 (Depression), Scale 7 (Psychasthenia), and Scale 8 (Schizophrenia). Correlations between the Ed scale and the characterological scales (Psychopathic Deviate, Hypomania) were not great. Dahlstrom and his colleagues concluded that the Ed scale is most sensitive to emotional distress, anxiety, guilt, and self-alienation, and least sensitive to sexual, antisocial, and nondepressive affective disorders.

Conclusion. While the Ed scale may have the potential to serve as a brief screening measure of emotional disorder, more validity data are needed before its actual utility can be determined. The scale may not be sensitive to characterological and nondepressive affective conditions.

Low Back Pain (Lb) Scale

Rationale and Construction. Hanvik (1949, 1951) developed the Low Back Pain (Lb) scale to differentiate between two kinds of patients with chronic low back pain—those for whom there is a clear physical basis for the pain and those for whom no organic etiology can be established. The twenty-five items in the Lb scale were selected from the MMPI item pool by comparing the responses of thirty patients whose pain was diagnosed as due to a protruding intervertebral disk and thirty patients for whom comparable pain was diagnosed as not likely to be of organic origin. The items are scored in such a way that high scores suggest functional pain and low scores suggest pain with organic etiology. The MMPI booklet numbers and scoring directions for items in the Lb scale can be found in Volume 2 of *An MMPI Handbook* (Dahlstrom and others, 1975) and in *The*

MMPI: A Practical Guide (Graham, 1977). After establishing an optimal cutting point of 11 for the original groups, Hanvik cross-validated the scale on a new sample consisting of twenty patients with organic low back pain and twenty patients with functional low back pain. The cut-off score of 11 correctly identified 80 percent of the forty patients.

Reliability. Gocka (1965) reported an internal-consistency reliability (Kuder-Richardson 21) coefficient of only 0.22 for the Lb scale for 220 male Veterans Administration psychiatric patients. Obviously, the internal consistency of this scale is highly questionable and should be investigated further with additional samples.

Norms. Swenson and others (1973) reported means and standard deviations on the Lb scale for fifty thousand male and female medical patients at the Mayo Clinic. Dahlstrom and others (1975) presented T-score conversions of Lb scale raw scores for normal males and females in the original MMPI standardization sample.

Additional Validity Data. Very few validity data are available for the Lb scale beyond the cross-validational work of Hanvik (1949). Dahlstrom (1954) reported that the Lb scale was useful for identifying patients with chronic low back pain of functional origin. He also found that high scores on the Lb scale suggested less satisfactory recovery following surgery for known physical defects. Lewinsohn (1965) found that Lb scale scores of psychiatric patients were lower at the time of hospital discharge than at admission. Graham (1977) examined the content of items in the Lb scale and suggested that high scorers are likely to experience physical discomfort in addition to back pain, and they tend to feel restless and dysphoric. In addition, high scorers say that they are comfortable in social situations and rarely get angry or irritated with other people. In general, it appears that high scorers on the Lb scale try to cover up inadequacies and insecurities.

Conclusions. While the Lb scale addresses an important clinical problem, its reliability is questionable and relatively few validity data are available. The scale is generally of limited utility with normal or psychiatric patients, but with individuals having chronic low back pain it can provide additional data for use with traditional clinical criteria in differentiating organic and functional patients.

MacAndrew Alcoholism (MAC) Scale

Rationale and Construction. While many MMPI scales have been developed to identify alcoholics and individuals who are prone to alcoholism, most of them have been successful in differentiating alcoholics from normal subjects but unsuccessful in separating alcoholics from nonalcoholic psychiatric patients. Concluding that these scales assess maladjustment in general rather than alcoholism specifically, MacAndrew (1965) set out to develop an MMPI scale that would differentiate alcoholics from nonalcoholic psychiatric patients.

MacAndrew's Alcoholism (MAC) scale was constructed by contrasting the MMPI responses of two hundred male alcoholics seeking treatment at an outpatient clinic with those of two hundred male nonalcoholic psychiatric outpatients from the same facility. The subjects were quite heterogeneous with respect to age, education, occupation, and income, but they were almost all Caucasians. The MMPI booklet numbers and scoring directions for the fifty-one items that differentiated the alcoholic and nonalcoholic subjects can be found in MacAndrew's original article (1965) and in *The MMPI: A Practical Guide* (Graham, 1977). Two of the items (215, 460) that deal directly with excessive drinking behavior were eliminated from the final scale. Most subsequent studies with the scale also have used the resulting forty-nine-item scale, but some have used all fifty-one items.

Using a cut-off score of 24, the scale correctly classified 81.75 percent of the alcoholic and nonalcoholic subjects used in scale construction (8.75 percent false negatives and 9.50 percent false positives). Using new samples of one hundred male alcoholics and one hundred male nonalcoholic psychiatric patients from the same populations used for scale construction, a cut-off score of 24 produced a classificatory accuracy of 81.5 percent (8.5 percent false negatives and 10.0 percent false positives). Thus, the MAC scale showed virtually no validity shrink-age on cross-validation.

Reliability. While no short-term test-retest or internal-consistency reliability coefficients have been reported for the MAC scale, there is some evidence about stability available from studies that report scores before and after treatment programs. In several studies, MAC scale scores did not change significantly during treatment programs ranging in length from sixty-nine to ninety days or during a one-year follow-up period after treat-ment (Rohan, Tetro, and Rotman, 1969; Rohan, 1972; Chang, Caldwell, and Moss, 1973; Huber and Danahy, 1975). Hoffman and others (1974) examined the MMPIs of male alcoholics, ad-ministered at the time of treatment for alcoholism and thirteen years earlier when they had entered college, and found no dif-ferences in MAC scale scores over this extended period. Thus, it would appear that MAC scale scores are quite stable over time.

Norms. Descriptive statistics for the MAC scale have been reported for alcoholics, nonalcoholic psychiatric patients, drug addicts, persons charged with criminal acts, medical patients, college students, and job applicants (MacAndrew, 1965; Whisler and Cantor, 1966; Rhodes, 1969; Rich and Davis, 1969; Rohan and others, 1969; Uecker, 1970; Vega, 1971; Williams, McCourt, and Schneider, 1971; Kranitz, 1972; Rohan, 1972; Hoffman and others, 1974; Apfeldorf and Huntley, 1975; Fowler, 1975; Ruff, Ayers, and Templer, 1975). In addition, Dahlstrom and others (1975) reported means and standard devi-ations for normal males and females in the original MMPI stan-dardization sample. While most studies with the MAC scale have used only male subjects, those that have reported data sepa-rately for the sexes have indicated that males tend to score higher than females. MacAndrew (1965) and Rosenberg (1972) reported that MAC scale scores were not related to age for their subjects, but Apfeldorf and Huntley reported correlations vary-ing from -0.25 to -0.61 between MAC scale scores and age.

Additional Validity Data. Some investigators (Rich and Davis, 1969; Rhodes, 1969; Uecker, 1970; Vega, 1971; Williams and others, 1971; Rohan, 1972; Rosenberg, 1972; Apfeldorf and Huntley, 1975) reported successful replication of MacAndrew's (1965) finding that the MAC scale can effectively separate alcoholics from nonalcoholic psychiatric patients. These studies report classification rates ranging from 69.5 percent to 85.0 percent. When the MAC scale was used in a domiciliary setting with older patients, the classification rates were 61.5 percent and 62.0 percent. In two studies suggesting that drug addicts score high on the MAC scale, heroin addicts (Kranitz, 1972) and opiate addicts (Fowler, 1975) scored significantly higher than psychiatric patients, but not significantly different from alcoholics. These findings prompted some writers to conclude that the MAC scale may be useful as a measure of an addictive personality in general (Fowler, 1975; Graham, 1977). In a well-executed longitudinal study, Hoffman and his colleagues (1974) located MMPIs administered thirteen years previously (upon entering college) to alcoholic males then in treatment. When the MAC scale scores of these males were compared with those of their classmates who did not become alcoholics, significant differences were found. There also are data suggesting that persons who drink excessively but are not alcoholics score higher on the MAC scale than persons who do not drink excessively (Williams and others, 1971; Apfeldorf and Huntley, 1975). Thus, it would seem that the MAC scale can identify individuals who overuse alcohol but who have not been diagnosed as alcoholics, and also perhaps persons who eventually will become alcoholics. Ruff and others (1975) offered some preliminary data suggesting that the MAC scale may reflect acting-out tendencies in general, and not specifically a tendency to abuse alcohol. While several factor-analytic studies of the MAC produced somewhat inconclusive results, they do suggest that high scorers on the MAC scale tend to be asocial persons with a tendency to manifest acting-out behavior of various kinds (MacAndrew, 1967; Finney, Smith, Skeeters, and Auvenshine, 1971).

Conclusion. The MacAndrew scale is a very reliable instrument that can effectively differentiate between alcoholics and nonalcoholics. It also may be sensitive to drug abuse and other acting-out behaviors. Since it tends not to change over time or as a result of treatment programs, one may infer that it is tapping some important, nonsituational aspects of personality and behavior. Further investigation of the scale may shed important light on the dimensions that differentiate alcoholics from nonalcoholics.

Ego Strength (Es) Scale

Rationale and Construction. Barron (1953) constructed the Ego Strength (Es) scale to predict the response of neurotic patients to individual psychotherapy. Items were selected for the Es scale from the original MMPI item pool by contrasting the responses of seventeen patients whose conditions were judged as improved after six months of individual psychotherapy with the responses of sixteen patients whose conditions were judged as unimproved after six months of individual psychotherapy. The MMPI booklet numbers and scoring directions for the sixty-eight items included in the Es scale can be found in Volume 2 of *An MMPI Handbook* (Dahlstrom and others, 1975) and in *The MMPI: A Practical Guide* (Graham, 1977). Barron cross-validated the Es scale by comparing scores on the scale with ratings of improvement for three groups of patients involved in individual psychotherapy. For all three groups, patients rated as more improved obtained higher Es scale scores.

Reliability. Barron (1953) reported an odd-even reliability coefficient of 0.76 and a three-month test-retest reliability coefficient of 0.72 for the Es scale. In addition, Gocka (1965) reported a Kuder-Richardson 21 (internal consistency) value of 0.78 for the scale. Thus it appears that the Es scale has adequate reliability to justify its use in research and clinical assessment.

Norms. Although descriptive statistics for the Es scale have been reported for many different groups, the most extensive normative data can be found in Volume 2 of *An MMPI Handbook* (Dahlstrom and others, 1975). These authors presented T-score conversions for Es scale raw scores separately for normal males and females in the original MMPI standardization sample. More intelligent and better-educated persons tend to score higher on the Es scale (Wirt, 1955; Tamkin and Klett,

1957). The data concerning the relationship between Es scale scores and age are inconsistent. Males tend to score higher on the Es scale than females; originally this fact was interpreted as indicating a greater willingness of females than of males to admit to problems and complaints (Taft, 1957; Getter and Sundland, 1962; Distler, May, and Tuma, 1964). However, a more reasonable explanation of the sex difference is that males score higher because the Es scale contains some items dealing with masculine role identification (Holmes, 1967).

Additional Validity Data. Graham (1977), after reviewing subsequent validity studies with the Es scale, concluded that attempts by other investigators to cross-validate the Es scale as a predictor of change in psychotherapy have yielded inconsistent results. In some studies higher Es scale scores have been associated with a more positive change in treatment, while in other studies no systematic relationship has been found between Es scale scores and changes in treatment. The Es scale seems to work well when used to predict the response of neurotic patients to individual, psychoanalytically oriented psychotherapy, and less well when other kinds of patients or other kinds of treatment are involved. Dahlstrom and others (1975) suggested that high Es scale scores for persons who obviously have difficulties but do not admit them may not predict a favorable treatment outcome, while high Es scale scores for persons who do admit emotional problems may suggest a favorable outcome.

There also are data indicating that the Es scale can be viewed as a measure of general psychological adjustment, higher scorers being better adjusted. Psychiatric patients tend to score lower than nonpatients (Quay, 1955; Taft, 1957; Gottesman, 1959; Kleinmuntz, 1960a; Himelstein, 1964; Speigel, 1969), and psychotic patients tend to score lower than neurotic patients (Tamkin, 1957; Tamkin and Klett, 1957; Hawkinson, 1962; Rosen, 1963). In addition, high Es scale scorers tend to be more aware of internal conflicts (Himelstein, 1964). There are inconsistent data concerning changes in Es scale scores as a function of treatment (Barron and Leary, 1955; Lewinsohn, 1965).

Conclusion. While the Es scale predicts response to

psychotherapy when neurotic patients and individual, psychoanalytically oriented therapy are involved, it probably is not
very useful for predicting response to other kinds of treatment
or for other kinds of patients. The scale is related to emotional
adjustment and may indicate the strength of psychological resources available for dealing effectively with stress.

Overcontrolled-Hostility (O-H) Scale

Rationale and Construction. Megargee and his associates
(Megargee and Mendelsohn, 1962; Megargee, Cook, and Mendelsohn, 1967; Megargee, 1973) suggested that persons who com-
mit acts of extreme physical aggression, such as homicide, can
be divided into two major types. Habitually aggressive (undercontrolled) persons have failed to develop appropriate controls
against the expression of aggression, so that when they are pro-
voked they respond with aggression of an intensity proportional
to the degree of provocation. Chronically overcontrolled persons, by contrast, have very rigid inhibitions against the expression of any form of aggression. Most of the time they do not
respond appropriately to instigation, but occasionally, when the
instigation is great enough, they may act out in an extremely
aggressive manner.

The original Overcontrolled-Hostility (O-H) scale was the
most promising of six provisional scales developed to differentiate assaultive and nonassaultive criminals (Megargee and others, 1967). Items were selected for the scale from the MMPI
item pool by comparing response frequencies of four groups of
male subjects: (1) extremely assaultive prisoners convicted of
murder, voluntary manslaughter, mayhem, or assault with a
deadly weapon; (2) moderately assaultive prisoners convicted of
battery; (3) prisoners convicted of nonviolent crimes; and (4)
men who had not been convicted of any crime. To be included
in the scale, items had to differentiate between assaultive and
nonassaultive men but not between nonviolent prisoners and
men who had not been convicted of any crime.

When a cut-off score of 22 was used for the original fifty-
five-item O-H scale, all of the extremely assaultive, twenty-five

of the twenty-eight moderately assaultive, and forty of the forty-four nonviolent criminals used to select items were correctly identified. The scale then was cross-validated on new groups of extremely assaultive, moderately assaultive, and nonviolent male prisoners. The three cross-validational groups differed significantly on the O-H scale, with extremely assaultive prisoners scoring higher than moderately assaultive and nonviolent prisoners, but with the two latter groups not differing significantly from each other. The item responses of the cross-validational groups on the original O-H scale were analyzed, and items that did not discriminate between the assaultive and nonassaultive groups were eliminated. MMPI booklet numbers and scoring directions for the thirty-one items included in the final O-H scale can be found in the original article by Megargee and others (1967) and in Volume 2 of *An MMPI Handbook* (Dahlstrom and others, 1975).

Reliability. Megargee and others (1967) reported a coefficient of internal consistency (Kuder-Richardson 21) of 0.56 for the O-H scale for a combined group of criminals and college students. While this coefficient is lower than for most of the other scales included in this chapter, Megargee and his colleagues pointed out that it was comparable to the median split-half reliability of the nine standard clinical scales of the MMPI.

Norms. In their original article on the O-H scale, Megargee and his associates (1967) presented T-score conversions for O-H scale raw scores for male and female college students. Lane (1976) summarized normative data for twenty-eight samples including college students, Peace Corps volunteers, and prison inmates. Dahlstrom and others (1975) reported O-H scale means and standard deviations for males and females in the original MMPI standardization sample. While the relationship between O-H scale scores and demographic variables has not been studied extensively, it appears that blacks score higher than whites and that females score higher than males.

Additional Validity Data. Megargee and his associates (1967) found that overcontrolled male prisoners scored higher on the O-H scale than did undercontrolled prisoners. Other investigators reported that the O-H scale successfully differentiated severely assaultive and nonassaultive prisoners (Deiker, 1974; Fredericksen, 1976). The Deiker study used male subjects, while Fredericksen used females. In some studies the O-H scale did not differentiate violent criminals with a history of violence from violent criminals with no such history (Fisher, 1970; Mallory and Walker, 1972), individual extreme assaulters, group extreme assaulters, and nonassaultive prisoners (Rawlings, 1973); nor did it differentiate child molesters with a history of such activity from child molesters with no such history (McCreary, 1975). Lane (1976) suggested that some of these negative findings could be due to a confounding of race and the assaultiveness criterion and to the manner in which the O-H scale was administered. While no data were presented to support the contention, Lane stated that the O-H scale must be administered in the context of the entire MMPI.

Some data indicate that scores on the O-H scale are related to other important nontest behaviors. High scorers tend to be more impunitive, report fewer angry feelings, and express less verbal hostility in reaction to frustration than low scorers, but high and low scorers do not differ in their tendencies to model aggressive behavior or in such physiological indices as galvanic skin response, heart rate, and blood pressure (White, 1970a, 1970b; Vanderbeck, 1973). In addition, high scorers on the O-H scale tend to have higher thresholds for violent than for neutral pictures presented in a tachistoscope; the difference in thresholds was greater for high scorers than for low scorers, but not significantly so (Wheeler, 1971). Lester, Perdue, and Brookhart (1974) predicted that from a psychoanalytic point of view overcontrolled murderers should be more depressed than undercontrolled murderers, but data from their study did not support such a relationship. Likewise, Kissinger (1973) failed to find O-H scale differences between female psychiatric patients who had attempted suicide, those who had threatened but not attempted suicide, and those who did not make suicidal threats.

Data from several studies have contributed to a description of the typical high scorer on the O-H scale (White, McAdoo, and Megargee, 1963; Megargee, 1969; Blackburn, 1972; Haven, 1972; Fredericksen, 1976). In addition to being

less overtly aggressive in a variety of situations, high scorers
tend to be more adequately socialized, responsible, and able to
present a socially acceptable facade than low scorers. They have
strong needs to achieve and excel, and their attitudes tend to be
conservative. They are emotionally mature, and they have
strong emotional controls. They tend to be dependent on other
people and are generally trustful. The family backgrounds of
high O-H scale scorers have been characterized as nurturant and
supportive. While adequate discipline was present in the families
of high scorers, they were able to talk over problems with parents. For males, an adequate male model was likely to have
been present in the home.

   Conclusion. The research generated by the development
of the O-H scale supports the construct of overcontrolled hostility. While there are some data indicating a relationship between
O-H scale scores and assaultiveness, the validity and reliability
of the scale have not been sufficiently demonstrated to permit
its use for making individual predictions about assaultive behavior. Further research is needed to delineate more clearly the
relationship between O-H scale scores and assaultive acts and to
identify mediating variables. Nevertheless, the scale should be
useful to the practicing clinician in understanding the dynamics
of aggressive control and expression in some individual patients.

Repression-Sensitization (R-S) Scale

   Rationale and Construction. The repression-sensitization
construct had its origin in the perceptual defense research conducted at Harvard University in the late 1940s (Bruner and
Postman, 1947). One important conclusion of these studies was
that individuals fall along a continuum in terms of how they
react to threatening stimuli. At one end are persons who tend to
try to avoid, deny, or repress such stimuli (repressors); at the
other end are those who tend to utilize approach behaviors,
such as intellectualization and obsessive rumination, in trying to
cope with stress (sensitizers).

   Byrne constructed the Repression-Sensitization (R-S)
scale to provide an objective, paper-and-pencil measure of this

repression-sensitization dimension. Altrocchi, Parsons, and Dickoff (1960) developed a measure of the dimension based on scores on six MMPI scales (L + K + Hy − D − Pt − Welsh A). Byrne recognized that since some items appear in more than one of these scales, they are weighted more than other items in the index. The original R-S scale suggested by Byrne (1961) was made up of all items comprising the six scales in the Altrocchi index, but each item was scored only once. In addition, items scored in different directions on the scales were eliminated. Originally, the R-S scale items were randomly mixed with 26 buffer items and printed on a separate questionnaire. Byrne, Barry, and Nelson (1963) used internal-consistency item-analysis procedures to revise the original R-S scale. Using a large sample of college student subjects, they identified items in the scale that had the highest correlations with total R-S scale scores. These analyses yielded the 127 scored items and 55 buffer items that constitute the present R-S scale, on which high scores suggest sensitization and low scores suggest repression. The MMPI booklet numbers and scoring directions for these items are presented by Byrne and others (1963) and in Volume 2 of *An MMPI Handbook* (Dahlstrom and others, 1975).

Reliability. Byrne and others (1963) reported an internal-consistency coefficient of 0.94 (with Spearman-Brown correction) for fifty-eight male and seventy-six female college students. They also found a test-retest reliability coefficient of 0.82 with a three-month interval between testings. An odd-even reliability coefficient of 0.91 (corrected by the Spearman-Brown formula) for ninety-two college student subjects was reported by Bernhardson (1967). Thus it appears that the R-S scale has sufficient reliability to warrant its use in research and clinical assessment.

Norms. Normative data for the R-S scale have been reported for large samples of college students (Byrne and others, 1963), black and white prisoners (Fisher, 1969), medical patients at the Mayo Clinic (Schwartz, 1972), and the original MMPI standardization sample (Dahlstrom and others, 1975). While no sex differences were found for the college student subjects, females scored higher (toward the sensitization end of the

continuum) than males in the medical patient and MMPI standardization samples. Chabot (1973) reported that sex interacts
with R-S scale scores in predicting behaviors such as responses
to sexual stimuli, self-evaluative behavior, and various indices of
adjustment. While Fisher found no differences between black
and white prisoners on the R-S scale, Evans and Alexander
(1970) reported that black college students scored significantly
lower (toward the repression end of the dimension) than
Byrne's normative data for white college students. Both
Schwartz and Fisher reported a moderate positive relationship
between age and R-S scale scores.

    Validity. Byrne (1964) and Bell and Byrne (in press) have
summarized the voluminous research literature generated by the
R-S scale. Based on these reviews, it appears that the R-S scale is
a valid measure of the repression-sensitization dimension and
that scores on the scale are related to a number of meaningful
nontest behaviors. There is consistent evidence that persons
scoring high on the scale tend to utilize primarily approach reactions to stress, while low scorers tend to use avoidance reactions. In addition, high scorers tend to be more dogmatic,
have lower self-esteem and perceive a more external locus of
control. While high scorers (sensitizers) verbalize more emotional reactivity to stress situations, low scorers (repressors)
actually show more physiological reactivity in such situations.
High scorers attribute more hostility to other people and to
themselves, and low scorers are perceived by others as more
aggressive than they believe themselves to be. High scorers respond to attack with counteraggression, they are more responsive to sexual stimuli, and they associate positive affect with
sexual arousal.

    While Byrne (1961) originally hypothesized a curvilinear
relationship between the R-S scale and emotional adjustment,
with middle scorers being better adjusted than high or low
scorers, most data indicate a linear (negative) relationship. Using
a variety of measures of adjustment, low scorers (repressors)
tend to be better adjusted than high or middle scorers. While
they are incomplete and somewhat inconsistent, there are some
data concerning the relationship between R-S scale scores and

psychotherapy process and outcome variables (Thelen, 1969; Mayo, Walton, and Littmann, 1971; Pengel, 1971; Pellegrine, 1971; Segal, 1971; Tanley, 1973; Baldwin, 1973, 1974). Sensitizers, when compared with repressors, tend to have different attitudes about, expectations from, and behaviors during counseling and psychotherapy. The relationship between R-S scale scores of therapists and clients and treatment outcome has not been delineated clearly in the existing literature.

Conclusion. The R-S scale is a reliable measure of an important personality dimension. A large body of research literature suggests that there are important personality and behavioral correlates of R-S scale scores. While more research is needed to clarify some of the preliminary and inconsistent findings in the literature, the scale should be quite useful to researchers who require an objective measure of defensive style in reaction to stress and to the clinician who wants to understand how clients react to stress and threat.

Concluding Remarks

The reader may be surprised, and perhaps disappointed, that such a small number of scales were judged suitable for discussion in this chapter. Why did so many scales fail to meet the criteria for inclusion? Many of the scales listed by Dahlstrom and others (1970, 1975) were constructed by graduate students as part of degree requirements and were never published. Other scales were quickly abandoned when cross-validational efforts were unsuccessful. Still other scales dealt with such esoteric constructs or behaviors that they never captured the interest of clinicians or researchers. While the literature contains some potentially useful scales for which relevant evaluative data are not yet available, it is unlikely that many of them will prove to be worthwhile.

It is unrealistic to expect that a pool of items that was assembled originally for the development of scales related to clinical diagnosis would be suitable for the construction of scales as diverse as those found in the MMPI literature. Many important constructs and behaviors simply are not represented adequately in the MMPI item pool. It is very difficult to construct good scales from bad items. While there are definite advantages in developing new scales that can be scored from an existing instrument like the MMPI, better scales probably can be constructed by developing new, relevant items for each construct or characteristic to be assessed.

Despite these rather sobering comments, there are a number of highly useful special MMPI scales, as this review has made evident. If used with suitable selectivity and clinical judgment, these scales can add considerably to the overall utility of the MMPI.

References

Altrocchi, J., Parsons, O. A., and Dickoff, H. "Changes in Self-Ideal Discrepancy in Repressors and Sensitizers." *Journal of Abnormal and Social Psychology*, 1960, *61*, 67-72.

Apfeldorf, M., and Huntley, P. "Application of MMPI Alcoholism Scales to Older Alcoholics and Problem Drinkers." *Journal of Studies on Alcohol*, 1975, *36*, 645-653.

Baldwin, B. A. "Generalization of Self-Discrepant Information as a Function of Defensive Style." *Journal of Counseling Psychology*, 1973, *20*, 235-239.

Baldwin, B. A. "Self-Disclosure and Expectations for Psychotherapy in Repressors and Sensitizers." *Journal of Counseling Psychology*, 1974, *31*, 455-456.

Barron, F. "An Ego Strength Scale Which Predicts Response to Psychotherapy." *Journal of Consulting Psychology*, 1953, *17*, 327-333.

Barron, F., and Leary, T. "Changes in Psychoneurotic Patients with and Without Psychotherapy." *Journal of Consulting Psychology*, 1955, *19*, 239-245.

Bell, P. A., and Byrne, D. "Repression-Sensitization." In H. London and J. E. Exner (Eds.), *Dimensions of Personality*. New York: Wiley, forthcoming.

Bernhardson, C. S. "The Relationship Between Facilitation-Inhibition and Repression-Sensitization." *Journal of Clinical Psychology*, 1967, *23*, 448-449.

Blackburn, R. "Dimensions of Hostility and Aggression in Abnormal Offenders." *Journal of Consulting and Clinical Psychology*, 1972, *38*, 20-26.

Block, J. *The Challenge of Response Sets: Unconfounding Meaning, Acquiescence and Social Desirability in the MMPI*. New York: Appleton-Century-Crofts, 1965.

Boerger, A. R. "The Utility of Some Alternative Approaches to MMPI Scale Construction." Unpublished doctoral dissertation, Kent State University, 1975.

Bruner, J. S., and Postman, L. "Emotional Selectivity in Perception and Reaction." *Journal of Personality*, 1947, *16*, 69-77.

Byrne, D. "The Repression-Sensitization Scale: Rationale, Reliability, and Validity." *Journal of Personality*, 1961, *29*, 334-349.

Byrne, D. "Repression-Sensitization as a Dimension of Personality." In B. A. Maher (Ed.), *Progress in Experimental Personality Research*. Vol. 1. New York: Academic Press, 1964.

Byrne, D. *An Introduction to Personality: A Research Approach*. Englewood Cliffs, N.J.: Prentice-Hall, 1966.

Byrne, D. *An Introduction to Personality: Research, Theory, and Applications*. Englewood Cliffs, N.J.: Prentice-Hall, 1974.

Byrne, D., Barry, J., and Nelson, D. "Relation of the Revised Repression-Sensitization Scale to Measures of Self-Description." *Psychological Reports*, 1963, *13*, 323-334.

Calvin, J. "Two Dimensions or Fifty: Factor Analytic Studies with the MMPI." Unpublished manuscript, Kent State University, 1974.

Calvin, J. "A Replicated Study of the Concurrent Validity of the Harris Subscales of the MMPI." Unpublished doctoral dissertation, Kent State University, 1975.

Cameron, N. *The Psychology of Behavior Disorders: A Bio-Social Interpretation*. Boston: Houghton-Mifflin, 1947.

Chabot, J. A. "Repression-Sensitization: A Critique of Some Neglected Variables in the Literature." *Psychological Bulletin*, 1973, *80*, 122-129.

Chang, A. F., Caldwell, A. B., and Moss, T. "Stability of Personality Traits in Alcoholics During and After Treatment as Measured by the MMPI: A One Year Follow-Up Study." *Proceedings of the 81st Annual Convention of the American Psychological Association,* 1973, *8,* 387-388.

Chu, C. "Object Cluster Analysis of the MMPI." Unpublished doctoral dissertation, University of California, Berkeley, 1966.

Cohler, B. J., Weiss, J. L., and Grunebaum, H. V. " 'Short-Form' Content Scales for the MMPI." *Journal of Personality Assessment,* 1974, *38,* 563-572.

Comrey, A. L. "A Factor Analysis of Items on the MMPI Depression Scale." *Educational and Psychological Measurement,* 1957a, *17,* 578-585.

Comrey, A. L. "A Factor Analysis of Items on the MMPI Hysteria Scale." *Educational and Psychological Measurement,* 1957b, *17,* 586-592.

Comrey, A. L. "A Factor Analysis of Items on the MMPI Hypomania Scale." *Educational and Psychological Measurement,* 1958a, *18,* 313-323.

Comrey, A. L. "A Factor Analysis of Items on the MMPI Paranoia Scale." *Educational and Psychological Measurement,* 1958b, *18,* 99-107.

Comrey, A. L. "A Factor Analysis of Items on the MMPI Psychopathic Deviate Scale." *Educational and Psychological Measurement,* 1958c, *18,* 91-98.

Comrey, A. L., and Margraff, W. "A Factor Analysis of Items on the MMPI Schizophrenia Scale." *Educational and Psychological Measurement,* 1958, *18,* 301-311.

Dahlstrom, W. G. "Prediction of Adjustment After Neurosurgery." *American Psychologist,* 1954, *9,* 353.

Dahlstrom, W. G., Welsh, G. S., and Dahlstrom, L. E. *An MMPI Handbook.* Vol. 1. *Clinical Interpretation.* Minneapolis: University of Minnesota Press, 1970.

Dahlstrom, W. G., Welsh, G. S., and Dahlstrom, L. E. *An MMPI Handbook.* Vol. 2. *Research Developments and Applications.* Minneapolis: University of Minnesota Press, 1975.

Deiker, T. E. "A Cross-Validation of MMPI Scales of Aggression on Male Criminal Criterion Groups." *Journal of Consulting and Clinical Psychology,* 1974, *42,* 196-202.

Distler, L. S., May, P. R., and Tuma, A. H. "Anxiety and Ego Strength as Predictors of Response to Treatment in Schizophrenic Patients." *Journal of Consulting Psychology,* 1964, *28,* 170-177.

Edwards, A. L. *The Social Desirability Variable in Personality Assessment and Research.* New York: Dryden, 1957.

Evans, D., and Alexander, S. "Some Psychological Correlates of Civil Rights Activity." *Psychological Reports,* 1970, *26,* 899-906.

Farber, I. E. "A Framework for the Study of Personality as a Behavioral Science." In P. Worchel and D. Byrne (Eds.), *Personality Change.* New York: Wiley, 1964.

Finney, J., Smith, D., Skeeters, D., and Auvenshine, D. "MMPI Alcoholism Scales: Factor Structure and Content Analysis." *Quarterly Journal of Studies on Alcohol,* 1971, *32,* 1055-1060.

Fisher, G. "The Repression-Sensitization Scale: Effects of Several Variables and Two Methods of Obtaining Scores." *Journal of General Psychology,* 1969, *80,* 183-187.

Fisher, G. "Discriminating Violence Emanating from Over-Controlled Versus Under-Controlled Aggressivity." *British Journal of Social and Clinical Psychology,* 1970, *9,* 54-59.

Fowler, R. "A Method for the Evaluation of the Abuse Prone Patient." Paper presented at the meeting of the American Academy of Family Physicians, Chicago, October 1975.

Fowler, R. D., and Coyle, F. A. "Collegiate Normative Data on MMPI Content Scales." *Journal of Clinical Psychology,* 1969, *25,* 62-63.

Fredericksen, S. J. "A Comparison of Selected Personality and History Variables in Highly Violent, Mildly Violent, and Nonviolent Female Offenders." Paper presented at 11th annual MMPI symposium, Minneapolis, Minn., March 1976.

Getter, H., and Sundland, D. M. "The Barron Ego Strength Scale and Psychotherapy Outcome." *Journal of Consulting Psychology,* 1962, *26,* 195.

Gocka, E. "American Lake Norms for 200 MMPI Scales." Unpublished manuscript, Veterans Administration Hospital, American Lake, Wash., 1965.

Gocka, E., and Holloway, H. "Normative and Predictive Data on the Harris and Lingoes Subscales for a Neuropsychiatric Population." Technical Report No. 7. Veterans Administration Hospital, American Lake, Wash., 1963.

Goldberg, L. R. "Parameters of Personality Inventory Construction: A Comparison of Prediction Strategies and Tactics." *Multivariate Behavioral Research Monographs*, 1972, 7.

Gottesman, I. I. "More Construct Validation of the Ego-Strength Scale." *Journal of Consulting Psychology*, 1959, 23, 342-346.

Graham, J. R. *The MMPI: A Practical Guide.* New York: Oxford University Press, 1977.

Graham, J. R., Schroeder, H. E., and Lilly, R. S. "Factor Analysis of Items on the Social Introversion and Masculinity-Femininity Scales of the MMPI." *Journal of Clinical Psychology*, 1971, 27, 367-370.

Hanvik, L. J. "Some Psychological Dimensions of Low Back Pain." Unpublished doctoral dissertation, University of Minnesota, 1949.

Hanvik, L. J. "MMPI Profiles in Patients with Low Back Pain." *Journal of Consulting Psychology*, 1951, 15, 350-353.

Harris, R., and Christiansen, C. "Prediction of Response to Brief Psychotherapy." *Journal of Psychology*, 1946, 21, 269-284.

Harris, R., and Lingoes, J. "Subscales for the Minnesota Multiphasic Personality Inventory." Mimeograph. The Langley Porter Institute, San Francisco, 1955.

Harris, R., and Lingoes, J. "Subscales for the Minnesota Multiphasic Personality Inventory." Mimeograph. The Langley Porter Institute, San Francisco, 1968.

Hase, H. D., and Goldberg, L. R. "Comparative Validity of Different Strategies of Constructing Personality Inventory Scales." *Psychological Bulletin*, 1967, 67, 231-248.

Hathaway, S. R., and McKinley, J. C. "A Multiphasic Personality Schedule (Minnesota): I. Construction of the Schedule." *Journal of Psychology*, 1940, 10, 249-254.

Haven, H. J. "Descriptive and Developmental Characteristics of Chronically Overcontrolled Hostile Prisoners." *FCI Research Reports,* 1972, *4,* 1-40.

Hawkinson, J. R. "A Study of the Construct Validity of Barron's Ego Strength Scale with a State Mental Hospital Population." *Dissertation Abstracts International,* 1962, *22,* 4081.

Himelstein, P. "Further Evidence of the Ego Strength Scale as a Measure of Psychological Health." *Journal of Consulting Psychology,* 1964, *28,* 90-91.

Hoffman, H., Loper, R., and Kammeier, M. "Identifying Future Alcoholics with MMPI Alcoholism Scales." *Quarterly Journal of Studies on Alcohol,* 1974, *35,* 490-498.

Holmes, D. S. "Male-Female Differences in MMPI Ego Strength: An Artifact." *Journal of Consulting Psychology,* 1967, *31,* 408-410.

Huber, N., and Danahy, S. "Use of the MMPI in Predicting Completion and Evaluating Change in Long-Term Alcoholism Treatment Program." *Journal of Studies on Alcohol,* 1975, *36,* 1230-1237.

Jackson, D. N. "The Dynamics of Structured Tests: 1971." *Psychological Review,* 1971, *78,* 239-249.

Kammeier, M. L., Hoffman, H., and Loper, R. G. "Personality Characteristics of Alcoholics as College Freshmen and at Time of Treatment." *Quarterly Journal of Studies on Alcohol,* 1973, *34,* 390-399.

Kissinger, J. R. "Women Who Threaten Suicide: Evidence for an Identifiable Personality Type." *Omega,* 1973, *4,* 73-84.

Kleinmuntz, B. "An Extension of the Construct Validity of the Ego Strength Scale." *Journal of Consulting Psychology,* 1960a, *24,* 463-464.

Kleinmuntz, B. "Identification of Maladjusted College Students." *Journal of Counseling Psychology,* 1960b, *7,* 209-211.

Kleinmuntz, B. "The College Maladjustment Scale (MT): Norms and Predictive Validity." *Educational and Psychological Measurement,* 1961, *21,* 1029-1033.

Kleinmuntz, B. "MMPI Decision Rules for the Identification of

College Maladjustment: A Digital Computer Approach." *Psychological Monographs*, 1963a, *77*, No. 577, 1-22.

Kleinmuntz, B. "Personality Test Interpretation by Digital Computer." *Science*, 1963b, *139*, 416-418.

Koss, M. P., and Butcher, J. N. "A Comparison of Psychiatric Patients' Self-Report with Other Sources of Clinical Information." *Journal of Research in Personality*, 1973, *7*, 225-236.

Kranitz, L. "Alcoholics, Heroin Addicts, and Non-Addicts: Comparisons on the MacAndrew Alcoholism Scale of the MMPI." *Quarterly Journal of Studies on Alcohol*, 1972, *33*, 807-809.

Lane, P. J. "Annotated Bibliography of the Megargee et al.'s Overcontrolled-Hostility (O-H) Scale and the Overcontrolled Personality Literature." Unpublished manuscript, Florida State University, 1976.

Langer, T. S. "A Twenty-Two Item Screening Scale of Psychiatric Symptoms Indicating Impairment." *Journal of Health and Human Behavior*, 1962, *3*, 269-276.

Lester, D., Perdue, W. C., and Brookhart, D. "Murder and the Control of Aggression." *Psychological Reports*, 1974, *34*, 706.

Lewinsohn, P. M. "Dimensions of MMPI Change." *Journal of Clinical Psychology*, 1965, *21*, 37-43.

Lingoes, J. "MMPI Factors of the Harris and Weiner Subscales." *Journal of Consulting Psychology*, 1960, *24*, 74-83.

Loper, R. G., Kammeier, M. L., and Hoffman, H. "MMPI Characteristics of College Freshman Males Who Later Became Alcoholics." *Journal of Abnormal Psychology*, 1973, *82*, 159-162.

MacAndrew, C. "The Differentiation of Male Alcoholic Outpatients from Non-Alcoholic Psychiatric Outpatients by Means of the MMPI." *Quarterly Journal of Studies on Alcohol*, 1965, *26*, 238-246.

MacAndrew, C. "Self Reports of Male Alcoholics—A Dimensional Analysis of Certain Differences from Non-Alcoholic Male Psychiatric Patients." *Quarterly Journal of Studies on Alcohol*, 1967, *28*, 43-51.

McCreary, C. P. "Personality Differences Among Child Moles-
     ters." *Journal of Personality Assessment,* 1975, *39,*
     591-593.
Mallory, C. H., and Walker, E. C. "MMPI O-H Scale Responses
     of Assaultive and Nonassaultive Prisoners and Associated
     Life History Variables." *Educational and Psychological
     Measurement,* 1972, *32,* 1125-1128.
Mayo, P. R., Walton, H. J., and Littmann, S. K. "Relevance of
     Repression-Sensitization to Neurotic Patients in Milieu
     Treatment." *Psychological Reports,* 1971, *28,* 794.
Megargee, E. I. "Conscientious Objectors' Scores on the MMPI
     O-H (Overcontrolled-Hostility) Scale." *Proceedings of the
     77th Annual Convention of the American Psychological
     Association,* 1969, *4,* 507-508.
Megargee, E. I. "Recent Research on Overcontrolled and Under-
     controlled Personality Patterns Among Violent Offend-
     ers." *Sociological Symposium,* 1973, No. 9, 37-50.
Megargee, E. I., Cook, P. E., and Mendelsohn, G. A. "Develop-
     ment and Validation of an MMPI Scale of Assaultiveness
     in Overcontrolled Individuals." *Journal of Abnormal
     Psychology,* 1967, *72,* 519-528.
Megargee, E. I., and Mendelsohn, G. A. "A Cross-Validation of
     Twelve MMPI Indices of Hostility and Control." *Journal
     of Abnormal and Social Psychology,* 1962, *65,* 431-438.
Mezzich, J. E., Damarin, F. L., and Erickson, J. R. "Compara-
     tive Validity Strategies and Indices of Differential Diag-
     nosis of Depressive States from Other Psychiatric Condi-
     tions Using the MMPI." *Journal of Consulting and
     Clinical Psychology,* 1974, *42,* 691-698.
Newton, J. R. "Clinical Normative Data for MMPI Special
     Scales: Critical Items, Manifest Anxiety, and Repression-
     Sensitization." *Journal of Clinical Psychology,* 1968, *24,*
     427-430.
Panton, J. "The Response of Prison Inmates to MMPI Sub-
     scales." *Journal of Social Therapy,* 1959, *5,* 233-237.
Parker, C. A. Letter to the editor. *Journal of Counseling
     Psychology,* 1961, *8,* 88-89.
Payne, F. D., and Wiggins, J. S. "MMPI Profile Types and the

Self-Report of Psychiatric Patients." *Journal of Abnormal Psychology,* 1972, *79,* 1-8.

Pellegrine, R. J. "Repression-Sensitization and Perceived Severity of Presenting Problem of Four-Hundred Forty-Four Counseling Center Clients." *Journal of Counseling Psychology,* 1971, *28,* 332-336.

Pengel, J. E. "The Repression-Sensitization Scale as a Predictive Measure of Certain Client and Counselor Behavior in the Initial Interview." *Dissertation Abstracts International,* 1971, *32* (1-A), 187-188.

Quay, H. "The Performance of Hospitalized Psychiatric Patients on the Ego-Strength Scale of the MMPI." *Journal of Clinical Psychology,* 1955, *11,* 403-405.

Rawlings, M. L. "Self-Control and Interpersonal Violence: A Study of Scottish Adolescent Male Severe Offenders." *Criminology,* 1973, *11,* 23-48.

Rhodes, R. "The MacAndrew Alcoholism Scale: A Replication." *Journal of Clinical Psychology,* 1969, *25,* 189-191.

Rich, C., and Davis, H. "Concurrent Validity of MMPI Alcoholism Scales." *Journal of Clinical Psychology,* 1969, *25,* 425-426.

Rohan, W. "MMPI Changes in Hospitalized Alcoholics." *Quarterly Journal of Studies on Alcohol,* 1972, *33,* 65-76.

Rohan, W., Tetro, R., and Rotman, S. "MMPI Changes in Alcoholics During Hospitalization." *Quarterly Journal of Studies on Alcohol,* 1969, *30,* 389-400.

Rosen, A. "Diagnostic Differentiation as a Construct Validity Indication for the MMPI Ego Strength Scale." *Journal of General Psychology,* 1963, *69,* 65-68.

Rosenberg, N. "MMPI Alcoholism Scales." *Journal of Clinical Psychology,* 1972, *28,* 515-522.

Ruff, C., Ayers, J., and Templer, D. "Alcoholics' and Criminals' Similarity of Scores on the MacAndrew Alcoholism Scale." *Psychological Reports,* 1975, *36,* 921-922.

Schwartz, M. S. "The Repression-Sensitization Scale: Normative, Age, and Sex Data on 30,000 Medical Patients." *Journal of Clinical Psychology,* 1972, *28,* 72-73.

Segal, B. "Further Investigation of Personality Correlates of the

A-B Scale." *Psychotherapy: Theory, Research and Practice*, 1971, *8*, 37.

Serkownek, K. "Subscales for Scales 5 and 0 of the Minnesota Multiphasic Personality Inventory." Unpublished manuscript, 3134 Whitehorn Road, Cleveland Heights, Ohio 44118, 1975.

Speigel, D. E. "SPI and MMPI Predictors of Psychopathology." *Journal of Projective Techniques and Personality Assessment*, 1969, *33*, 265-273.

Spence, J. T., and Spence, K. W. "The Motivational Components of Manifest Anxiety: Drive and Drive Stimuli." In C. D. Spielberger (Ed.), *Anxiety and Behavior*. New York: Academic Press, 1966.

Spielberger, C. D. "The Effects of Anxiety on Complex Learning and Academic Achievement." In C. D. Spielberger (Ed.), *Anxiety and Behavior*. New York: Academic Press, 1966a.

Spielberger, C. D. "Theory and Research on Anxiety." In C. D. Spielberger (Ed.), *Anxiety and Behavior*. New York: Academic Press, 1966b.

Stein, K. B. "The TSC Scales: The Outcome of a Cluster Analysis of the 550 MMPI Items." In P. McReynolds (Ed.), *Advances in Psychological Assessment*. Vol. 1. Palo Alto, Calif.: Science and Behavior Books, 1968.

Suinn, R. M. "Social Desirability and the Taylor Manifest Anxiety Scale, the General Anxiety and Test Anxiety Scales." *Educational and Psychological Measurement*, 1967, *27*, 1119-1120.

Suinn, R. M. "Removal of Social Desirability and Response Set Items from the Manifest Anxiety Scale." *Educational and Psychological Measurement*, 1968, *28*, 1189-1192.

Swenson, W. M., Pearson, J. S., and Osborne, D. *An MMPI Sourcebook: Basic Item, Scale and Pattern Data on 50,000 Medical Patients*. Minneapolis: University of Minnesota Press, 1973.

Taft, R. "The Validity of the Barron Ego-Strength Scale and the Welsh Anxiety Index." *Journal of Consulting Psychology*, 1957, *21*, 247-249.

Tamkin, A. S. "An Evaluation of the Construct Validity of Bar-
    ron's Ego-Strength Scale." *Journal of Consulting Psychol-
    ogy,* 1957, *13,* 156-158.
Tamkin, A. S., and Klett, C. J. "Barron's Ego-Strength Scale: A
    Replication of an Evaluation of Its Construct Validity."
    Journal of Consulting Psychology, 1957, *21,* 412.
Tanley, J. C. "Use of Personality and Interest Measures in Pre-
    dicting Crisis Phone Counselor Effectiveness." *Disserta-
    tion Abstracts International,* 1973, *33* (8-B), 3964.
Taylor, J. A. "The Relationship of Anxiety to the Conditioned
    Eyelid Response." *Journal of Experimental Psychology,*
    1951, *41,* 81-92.
Taylor, J. A. "A Personality Scale of Manifest Anxiety." *Jour-
    nal of Abnormal and Social Psychology,* 1953, *48,*
    285-290.
Taylor, J. B., Ptacek, M., Carithers, M., Griffin, C., and Coyne,
    L. "Rating Scales as Measures of Clinical Judgment: III.
    Judgments of the Self of Personality Inventory Scales and
    Direct Ratings." *Educational and Psychological Measure-
    ment,* 1972, *32,* 543-557.
Thelen, M. H. "Repression-Sensitization: Its Relation to Adjust-
    ment and Seeking Psychotherapy Among College Stu-
    dents." *Journal of Consulting and Clinical Psychology,*
    1969, *33,* 161-165.
Tryon, R. C. "Unstructured Cluster and Factor Analysis with
    Application to the MMPI and Holzinger-Harmon Prob-
    lems." *Multivariate Behavioral Research,* 1966, *1,* 229-
    244.
Tryon, R. C., and Bailey, D. (Eds.). *User's Manual of the BC
    TRY System of Cluster Analysis.* Berkeley: University of
    California Computer Center, 1965.
Uecker, A. E. "Differentiating Male Alcoholics from Other
    Psychiatric Inpatients." *Quarterly Journal of Studies on
    Alcohol,* 1970, *31,* 379-383.
Vanderbeck, D. J. "A Construct Validity Study of the O-H
    (Overcontrolled-Hostility) Scale of the MMPI, Using a So-
    cial Learning Approach to the Catharsis Effect." *FCI
    Research Reports,* 1973, *5,* 1-18.

Vega, A. "Cross-Validation of Four MMPI Scales for Alcoholism." *Quarterly Journal of Studies on Alcohol,* 1971, *32,* 791-797.

Welsh, G. S. "Factor Dimensions A and R." In G. S. Welsh and W. G. Dahlstrom (Eds.), *Basic Readings on the MMPI in Psychology and Medicine.* Minneapolis: University of Minnesota Press, 1956.

Wheeler, C. A. "Overcontrolled Hostility and the Perception of Violence." *FCI Research Reports,* 1971, *3,* 1-22.

Whisler, R., and Cantor, J. "The MacAndrew Alcoholism Scale: A Cross-Validation in a Domiciliary Setting." *Journal of Clinical Psychology,* 1966, *22,* 311-312.

White, W. C. "Selective Modeling in Youthful Offenders with High and Low O-H (Overcontrolled-Hostility) Personality Types." *FCI Research Reports,* 1970a, *2,* 1-31.

White, W. C. "Validity of the Overcontrolled-Hostility (*O-H*) Scale: A Brief Report." *Journal of Personality Assessment,* 1970b, *39,* 587-590.

White, W. C., McAdoo, W. G., and Megargee, E. I. "Personality Factors Associated with Over- and Undercontrolled Offenders." *Journal of Personality Assessment,* 1963, *37,* 473-478.

Wiener, D. W. "Subtle and Obvious Keys for the MMPI." *Journal of Consulting Psychology,* 1948, *12,* 164-170.

Wiggins, J. S. "Substantive Dimensions of Self-Report in the MMPI Item Pool." *Psychological Monographs,* 1966, *80,* No. 630, 1-42.

Wiggins, J. S. "Content Dimensions in the MMPI." In J. N. Butcher (Ed.), *MMPI: Research Developments and Clinical Applications.* New York: McGraw-Hill, 1969.

Wiggins, J. S. "Content Scales: Basic Data for Scoring and Interpretation." Unpublished manuscript, University of Illinois, 1971.

Wiggins, J. S., Goldberg, L. R., and Applebaum, M. "MMPI Content Scales: Interpretive Norms and Correlations with Other Scales." *Journal of Consulting and Clinical Psychology,* 1971, *37,* 403-410.

Williams, A., McCourt, W., and Schneider, L. "Personality Self-Descriptions of Alcoholics as Heavy Drinkers." *Quarterly Journal of Studies on Alcohol*, 1971, *32*, 310-317.

Wirt, R. D. "Further Validation of the Ego-Strength Scale." *Journal of Consulting Psychology*, 1955, *20*, 123-124.

II

Interpreter's Guide to the Jackson Personality Inventory

DOUGLAS N. JACKSON

The Jackson Personality Inventory (JPI) (Jackson, 1976) was designed for use with nonpsychiatric, nonclinical populations of average or above average intelligence and education. A good deal of attention was placed on development of the scales and the choice of scale names having clear, readily understood meanings and definitions so as to facilitate scale interpretation. But like any personality assessment development, it is important for the user to be trained and experienced not only in the general. field of psychological testing but also with the specific constructs employed in the test and the unique way in which the test assesses these variables of personality. It is the purpose of this chapter, like the one appearing in the first volume of this series on the California Psychological Inventory (CPI) (Gough, 1968), to introduce the JPI and familiarize the reader with both the approach employed in JPI scale construction and the interpretation of JPI scales and scale configurations.

Although some readers might be acquainted with the author's Personality Research Form (PRF) (Jackson, 1974) in its various formats, it is appropriate to emphasize that the JPI is entirely distinct, sharing no items with the PRF and having no substantive scales with the same scale names. (One validity scale, Infrequency, also appears in the PRF, but the items for these two scales are different.) What the two tests do share is a similar scale construction strategy and rationale, and, of course, being authored by the same individual.

The JPI is comprised of 320 true-false items, divided equally into sixteen 20-item scales. Reusable booklets with directions printed on the cover are employed. The answer sheet, in which true and false responses are made by placing an X in boxes arranged in thirty-two columns, provides a convenient basis for hand scoring. A single template is used for scoring all sixteen scales. Total scores are obtained by summing two columns for each scale and recording the total at the bottom of the answer sheet. Totals are then transferred to a profile expressed in terms of T-scores, with a mean of 50 and a standard deviation of 10. The respondents' task is simply to answer true or false, based on whether they consider the item true of themselves or agree with its content. For each of the sixteen scales one-half of the items are keyed true and one-half are keyed false. Typically college students complete the JPI in a little more than a half hour, but because there is a wide range in individual completion times, it is usually wise to allow fifty to sixty minutes for group administration. The JPI can, of course, also be administered individually. Although it is best to administer the JPI under supervised conditions, for most populations there is no problem in administering it without close supervision—or even administering it through the mail.

Norms for the JPI are based upon the responses of two thousand male and two thousand female students drawn from a total of forty-three North American colleges and universities. Thirty-four of these were randomly selected from a publication of the U.S. Office of Education listing postsecondary schools and colleges, with the remaining colleges chosen to round out the geographical representativeness of the sample and to include data from three Canadian universities. The profile is based on these data. In addition, high school norms for males and females are also available. Although normative data are not available at the present time for individuals below high school age or for adults, item content of the JPI is appropriate for these populations. Of course, for individual interpretation of individuals drawn from noncollege populations, relevant normative data are required. The reading level of the JPI is such that it could be administered down to about the seventh grade without undue difficulty, although, as with any reading task, individuals with reading difficulties might require help.

Rationale for Scale Construction

The choice of a scale development strategy for the JPI emphasized defining carefully the constructs that underlie the JPI scales and representing these constructs faithfully in item writing. Scale construction, begun some fourteen years before JPI publication, involved six general steps: (1) selection of constructs for measurement, (2) development of scale definitions, (3) item writing and editing, (4) administration to large samples of respondents and application of multistage item-analytic procedures, (5) final item selection and assembly of the JPI booklet, and (6) validity and norming studies. An overall philosophy of psychological measurement is apparent in the decisions made at various stages. Although the author has expressed this point of view in some detail elsewhere (Jackson, 1970, 1971, 1974, 1975), its development has been extended further with the JPI. A recapitulation of these views might be useful.

Although originally directed at fact gatherers in biology, there is reason to believe that T. H. Huxley's observation that "those who don't go beyond fact rarely get as far as fact" applies equally in personality assessment. The alternative to careful construct definition in personality scale construction is either intuitively based work, where the ideas behind the scale are not communicated (if in fact they exist), or scales based on item differentiation of criterion groups, as, for example, in the development of a scale by contrasting the responses of carpenters with those of men in general. The proponents of the latter strategy sometimes argue that it is "rigorous" because human judgment is not allowed to intrude at any stage of scale construction. I view it as an alternative to clear thinking, frequently resulting in scales so replete with response bias and so devoid of substantive validity that they usually lack usefulness even for the modest goal of predicting the particular criterion upon which scale construction depended. Users are rarely interested in the literal prediction of particular criteria. Rather interest usually is focused on *understanding* a person and identifying his or her location on a construct dimension. It is therefore commonplace for such scale developers to assign broad construct names and even scale definitions to scales developed from particular criteria on the basis of their intuitive grasp of the psychological characteristics possibly underlying criterion performance. This shifts the validation problem from that of predicting a criterion to that of validating a construct and requires evidence for scale homogeneity and freedom from sources of irrelevant variance, evidence of which is rarely proffered.

If one's goal is to measure a psychological construct of general import, it is necessary both to define it broadly enough to be relevant to a variety of situations and to sample systematically in item content the facets relevant to the dimension. In order to find items that meet these conditions, it is necessary to exercise care in item writing, be sensitive to the relevance of items written for inclusion in a scale (as well as to their distinctiveness from other scales), write a substantially larger item pool than ultimately required (Loevinger, 1957), and avoid item content implicating extreme levels of evaluative bias. In JPI scale construction, a number of empirical item-selection strategies were employed, designed to foster homogeneity as well as item discrimination and freedom from response bias. But even without elaborate empirical item-selection procedures, there is evidence that even naive item writers, employing a construct-oriented approach, can produce reliable and valid personality scales. In response to a challenge (Jackson, 1971) to compare the criterion-oriented external strategy with a construct approach, both Ashton and Goldberg (1973) and Jackson (1975) reported superior peer-rating validities for personality scales developed using the construct approach to those obtained for like-named, empirically derived California Psychological Inventory scales.

After a large item pool had been prepared, items were edited and culled so that there was a total of about 100 to 120 items for each of the sixteen scales. Items for each scale were assembled into one of seven booklets comprising two or three scales, plus a desirability scale, and administered to one of seven groups of respondents, each numbering in excess of three hundred. Item analyses were conducted for each scale. Forty items were chosen showing the highest Differential Reliability Index (Jackson, 1970, 1974, 1976), which in this case was designed to identify optimal levels of item reliability and variance, and minimum association with desirability. These items were in turn administered to new large samples of respondents and subjected to an item-analytic procedure (Neill and Jackson, 1976), yielding an Item Efficiency Index, designed to minimize correlations among scales as well as maximize scale homogeneity. The final selection of items was based on the Item Efficiency Index as well as the item's possessing middle-range popularity values (those less than 0.20 or greater than 0.80 were discarded), substantive considerations, and representativeness of item content and wording. Although we consider the key element in JPI scale construction to have been the attention devoted to scale definition and item writing, the empirical procedures employed are perhaps the most elaborate ever applied to personality scale construction.

Concepts Underlying JPI Scales

Henry Murray, whose early experience was in natural and biological science, was impressed by the degree to which students of personality lacked a basic vocabulary for their science. The task of identifying the basic components of personality is hardly appealing; even less appealing is studying other's compendia of such components. It would be so easy if we could settle on one, two, or three basic dimensions. However, in Murray's (1962) words, "If life *is* complex, if an event *is* the concrescence of numberless mutually dependent factors, and if an adequate formulation of it *must* take account of many of them, what then? The answer would appear to be that a student has to set himself to the task of memorizing the elementary anatomy of a science before he can think about the subject at all. The concepts must be so actively alive in him that they pop into consciousness without deliberation, time and time again" (p. 231, italics in original).

The concepts of personality, at least those for which a body of empirical research has developed, are those for which someone has provided usable and convincing measures. The origins of these measures have been derived from a variety of sources—empirical studies (MacKinnon, 1958; compare Wiggins, 1973, p. 544), personality theory (Hall and Lindzey, 1970; Wiggins, 1973, pp. 443-467), and "synthetic" characterizations of criterion performance (Stern, Stein, and Bloom, 1956). But whatever approach is used to generate hypotheses about the nature of personality variables, global, relatively undifferentiated concepts must be defined in a sufficiently clear manner so that other psychologists can agree on measurement operations and item content. This is an essential prerequisite to sound measurement in personality in the author's opinion (Jackson, 1971). Indeed, there is now fairly convincing evidence that if this definitional step can be achieved, one may dispense with the psychologist altogether and depend on novice test constructors (Ashton and Goldberg, 1973; Jackson, 1975).

The concepts selected for inclusion in the JPI are based on the author's judgment of what might be interesting and useful measures of personality. Some of these measures are similar to those defined by others in research studies or personality questionnaires. Others have not had a prominent place in the psychological literature. The reason for including measures that have apparently been adequately measured by others is twofold: the techniques for selecting items and suppressing response biases used in the construction of the JPI were more advanced than those available previously, and a general purpose personality inventory might be considered incomplete if certain personality variables, like Anxiety, Organization, and Social Participation, were omitted altogether. One could debate endlessly about alternative choices, but such debate is fruitless. The range of possible personality dimensions is very large, much larger than can be encompassed reliably in a single personality inventory that can be administered in one hour. Contrary to the beliefs of some psychologists, the contents of personality questionnaires are not interchangeable. The future will undoubtedly bring more specialized personality assessment devices, differentiated in terms of intended target population, reading level, length, degree of differentiation among concepts, and the specificity or generality of the concepts assessed. The evaluation of a personality questionnaire should consider the implicit or explicit target audience. Quite obviously a questionnaire developed for normal people should not be evaluated in terms of its use on psychiatric patients, but neither should one expect that all conceivable normal attributes of personality will be or should be included in a single assessment device. In the next section each of the variables of personality included in the JPI is discussed, together with some of the considerations leading to the present choice of dimensions and the decision to define them in a particular way.

Individual JPI Scales

Personality scale scores should be interpreted in the light of the assumptions and preconceptions guiding their development. Thus, scales developed in terms of the differentiation of some criterion behavior should be interpreted with a clear appreciation of that particular criterion. For example, an interpretation of a score on a personality scale with items differentiating students rated high on integrity by teachers from those rated low would emphasize the reputational component of integrity in a particular situation, rather than a more general interpretation. None of the JPI scales depend on a particular criterion for interpretation. Rather, their interpretation should be based on their definitions as well as known empirical findings regarding the scales. In a sense, this simplifies interpretation. This is true because the scale definition links the characteristic to a broader semantic and implicit psychological network of traits and trait relationships. To the extent that JPI scale definitions are rooted in lay conceptions of personality, one need not look to idiosyncratic psychological definitions or particular criteria to impute meaning to scale scores.

Of course, one cannot rest the psychological case for the utility or interpretability of these variables with their definitions alone; one must seek evidence of validity as well. To be consistent, it is appropriate to seek evidence of convergent and discriminant validity using a variety of methods that permit an evaluation of scale definitions as well as individual scales. This is the acid test for multiscore personality inventories, a test that few survive unscathed.

In this section information will be presented regarding each scale. Following the heading of each section, which gives the scale name and abbreviation, is an illustrative true-keyed item.[1] After presenting and discussing the rationale underlying individual scales, results from multivariate studies of profile configurations will be employed as an aid in interpreting typical profiles.

Anxiety (Anx). I often think about the possibility of an accident. Although the JPI was developed primarily for use with normal rather than psychiatric groups, it is nevertheless true that information about anxiety, one of the most salient and general manifestations of psychopathological disturbance, is often helpful in normal populations.

The JPI Anxiety scale, unlike certain similar scales, is designed primarily to differentiate persons in the normal range of anxiety rather than to uncover severe psychopathology. Persons scoring high on this scale tend to manifest symptoms commonly regarded as being associated with anxiety: worry, apprehension, the condition of being easily upset, preoccupation, fearfulness, and physical complaints associated with tension. Persons low on

---

[1]The JPI items and scale definitions are copyright © 1976 by Douglas N. Jackson and may not be reproduced without permission. Further details regarding the nature of the scales and the validity studies cited are contained in the *JPI Manual* (Jackson, 1976).

Anxiety are able to remain calm even in stressful situations and are described as easygoing, relaxed, composed, and collected. Although the enormous literature on anxiety (for example, McReynolds, 1968; Spielberger, 1966, 1972) precludes a detailed discussion of current theory and research, it should be mentioned that scale construction proceeded with a general awareness of this literature, both in terms of certain pitfalls to avoid and in terms of the strides made in the conceptualization and measurement of anxiety over the past twenty-five years. In particular, I wished to avoid the global and inexplicit definitions of anxiety prevalent in earlier measures of neuroticism and of manifest anxiety. Similarly, although a good deal has been made of the distinction between state and trait anxiety over the past decade (Spielberger, 1972), JPI scale construction proceeded in the belief that measurement should assess enduring characteristics rather than transitory ones. Enduring characteristics are more likely to be predictive of other events in the person's life, to be more general and hence more descriptive of broad aspects of personality, and to be more independent of unique situational events and measurement artifacts. Although not denying the possible utility of obtaining data regarding a person's level of anxiety in a certain situation, I prefer the more general alternative for a multipurpose personality questionnaire. It should be evident, therefore, that the JPI Anxiety scale should not be used to assess short-term changes in anxiety level as a result of brief experimental treatments or otherwise. What it *does* assess is the essentially consistent level of anxiety as it has developed over the course of an individual's lifetime.

Most measures of anxiety are substantially associated with measures of desirability. Although it is a matter of some controversy as to how to interpret this sort of finding, it remains a source of considerable embarrassment to personality assessment specialists. It is difficult to maintain that one is measuring several unique dimensions of personality if all dimensions are substantially associated with desirability. Some have argued that it is the very nature of psychopathological personality dimensions to be highly evaluative and that such characteristics are inevitably confounded conceptually and empirically with measures of desirability. The approach taken with the JPI is that specific dimensions of personality are substantially distinct conceptually from self-evaluation and that measurement efforts should be directed at maintaining this distinctiveness. To what extent was this goal achieved with the JPI Anxiety scale? A group of 116 female university students was administered the JPI together with the Desirability scale from the Personality Research Form, Form E (PRF-E) (Jackson, 1974). The correlation was −0.29, a rather low value considering the correlations reported for the Taylor Manifest Anxiety scale (Jackson and Messick, 1962; Edwards, 1957, 1970).

What is the meaning of a high score on the Anxiety scale? First of all, it implies that the individual experiences the discomfort and symptoms of anxiety—other measures based on self-rating or self-report tend to converge with JPI Anxiety scale scores. The Anxiety scale correlates −0.74 with the Bentler Psychological Inventory[2] Stability scale, 0.71 with a rationally constructed twenty-item adjective checklist, and 0.64 (in two studies) with self-ratings of anxiety. Although these correlations may be interpreted as influenced by method variance, it should be noted that this shared variance is largely unique to the anxiety factor. It would appear to be based on the common source of these scores in the individual's own experiencing and reporting of anxiety. Correlations with peer ratings relevant to anxiety, although lower in magnitude than those reported for self-ratings, are the highest in two studies with the Anxiety scale, when compared with the other fifteen JPI scales. The data thus indicate that there is some correspondence between the individual's reporting and experiencing of anxiety and anxiety as perceived by peers. In addition, the portion of the variance in Anxiety scale scores not predictable from peer ratings is not entirely random error or linked to undesirable responding, but might be interpreted as a function of the unique position that

[2] The Bentler Psychological Inventory (BPI) and the Bentler Interactive Psychological Inventory (BIPI) are two unpublished psychological assessment devices developed by Peter M. Bentler. The BPI is based on self-reports, while the BIPI is based on peer ratings.

an individual has for observing his or her own experience of anxiety.

Breadth of Interest (Bdi). I am very interested in politics. This scale historically has not been given a prominent place as a psychological construct, but it does have a number of antecedents in the psychological literature. It bears more than a casual kinship to Murray's (1962) need Understanding and, indeed, correlates moderately highly with the PRF-E Understanding scale. Also, studies (for example, Barron, 1953a; Gough, 1961) conducted at the Institute for Personality Assessment and Research, University of California, Berkeley, identified a number of correlations between Q-sort ratings of a similar variable and a range of cognitive and personality variables.

Persons high on the Breadth of Interest scale are interested in experiencing and learning about a variety of things and may be described as being attentive, involved, curious, exploring, inquisitive, and interested. People low in Breadth of Interest are described as narrow, unobservant, insular, and having confined tastes. Among the significant correlates of the Breadth of Interest scale are the Jackson Vocational Interest Survey Academic Achievement scale, Sentience and Understanding from the PRF-E, and Art Interest, Perceptiveness, and Travel Interest from the Bentler Psychological Inventory (BPI).

Complexity (Cpx). I enjoy the challenge of reading a complicated novel. Perhaps this scale should have been named Preference for Complexity rather than Complexity. A high score on this scale does not necessarily imply that the individual shows complexity in his or her personality dynamics, but rather that he or she is likely to manifest an interest in intellectual and artistic problems requiring complex analysis or thought processes. It owes its origins to two general lines of research: the first comprises the important work of Barron (1953a) on the personality correlates of preference for complex versus simple artistic productions derived from the Barron-Welsh Art Judgment scale; the second is derived from research in social perception and the perception of personality (for example, Sechrest and Jackson, 1961) springing from the theoretical tradition of Kelly (1955). These studies indicate that there are many different possible interpretations and nuances in defining complexity as a cognitive and personality variable. To foster homogeneity of measurement, it is necessary to be clear about which of these facets one wishes to emphasize. As indicated, my decision was to proceed with a definition and a set of items focusing on a preference for seeking complicated solutions to abstract problems. Item content for Complexity falls largely into three major categories: interpersonal content and motives, artistic judgment and preference, and consideration of and discussion about general topics requiring analysis.

Persons scoring high in Complexity enjoy abstract thought, show an interest in pursuing topics in depth regardless of their difficulty, prefer intricate solutions for problems, and tend to be impatient with oversimplification. Defining trait adjectives include: complex, contemplative, clever, discerning, intellectual, thoughtful, and analytical. Persons scoring low on this dimension tend to prefer concrete to abstract thinking and interpretations, avoid contemplative thought, and generally avoid activity aimed at probing for new insights. Such persons may be described as uncomplicated, straightforward, matter-of-fact, unreflective, and predictable. Important correlates are consistent with the definition. For example, on the Bentler Interactive Psychological Inventory (BIPI), a technique for obtaining ratings of a person from a single individual with whom that person is well acquainted, persons high in Complexity are rated significantly high in Art Interest, Intelligence, and Leadership. Such persons also tend to be higher than average on the MMPI Mf scale, that is, to score in the feminine direction. They also tend to be nominated by peers as high in Complexity.

Conformity (Cny). I try to act in such a way that others will accept me. Research on social conformity, following the classic studies of Asch (1956), has been one of the most prolific areas in social psychology over the past three decades. Personality correlates of social conformity were identified in important studies by Barron (1953b), by Crutchfield (1955), as well as by Linton (1955). This work was followed by literally hundreds of studies seeking to uncover cognitive, situational, and personality determinants of yielding responses. Both Barron and

Crutchfield identified personality items differentiating yielding and conforming groups in their respective experimental conformity situations. Although some of these items dealt directly with reports of conforming or independent behavior, many of the other items were quite heterogeneous. With this sort of situation it is not certain whether one is dealing with sampling peculiarities or legitimate basic personality correlates. It was therefore decided in scale construction to foster homogeneity in the scale and focus on aspects of conforming behavior specifically rather than on the more remote exemplars or correlates of psychological conformity.

Consistent with psychological theorizing about social conformity, persons receiving high scores are likely to be susceptible to social influence and group pressure, to modify their behavior to be consistent with the standards set by others, and to adapt readily to the pressures of group membership. High scorers are defined as being compliant, acquiescent, adapting, accommodating, cooperative, concurring, and emulating. Low scorers are notable for either their independence in thought and action, that is, being unswayed by others' opinions, or by showing anticonformity behavior (Stricker, Messick, and Jackson, 1970), that is, the tendency to act in opposition to the social influence. Such persons are characterized by the following defining trait adjectives: individualistic, self-directed, self-reliant, unyielding, nonconforming, unrestrained, contradicting, and disagreeing.

The patterning of correlations with other assessment devices is consistent with expectations based on the definition of the Conformity scale. It correlates -0.42 with the BPI Invulnerability scale, and 0.69 and 0.63 with PRF-E scales for need for Social Recognition and Succorance, respectively. Of particular interest are the differences between groups of student demonstrators and nondemonstrators as reported by Neill and Jackson (1976). The mean score for the Conformity scale for the demonstrators was 6.0, while the mean for the nondemonstrators was 10.1, which yielded a value of the t statistic of 5.10, a difference that is significant well beyond the 0.001 level. In fact, the difference was so great between the two groups on this one scale that there was relatively little overlap. A fruitful avenue for further research would be to investigate the conditions under which the JPI Conformity scale predicts responses to different kinds of laboratory-based and natural social conformity and obedience conditions.

Energy Level (Enl). I enjoy all kinds of vigorous hobbies. Like most of the other JPI scales, the definition and interpretation of this scale is consistent with the title. Individuals high on the Energy Level scale have resources of energy, impress others as being active and spirited, rarely complain of being tired or fatigued, are capable of intense work or recreational activity for long periods of time, and are generally considered vigorous. Defining trait adjectives include: lively, persevering, industrious, tireless, dynamic, enthusiastic, and eager. A low scorer, on the other hand, tends to tire more easily and quickly, avoid strenuous activities, show low stamina, require a great deal of rest, and be slow to respond. Such persons tend to be described as passive, listless, drowsy, lazy, and languid. Although the characteristics measured by the scale tend to be regarded as desirable, the correlation between the Energy Level scale and the PRF-E Desirability scale is only 0.25. The patterning of the correlations with MMPI scales, particularly those from the "neurotic triad," are as might be expected. Significant negative correlations are found for the MMPI Hypochondriasis, Depression, and Psychasthenia scales. On the other hand, PRF-E scales for Achievement, Endurance, and Understanding correlate significantly positively. As with several of the other JPI scales, the student activist groups in the Neill and Jackson study were significantly higher in Energy Level.

Innovation (Inv). I like to experiment with various ways of doing the same thing. It is important to be clear that there was no attempt in the development of the Innovation scale to identify persons who are creative in some field. In other words, the intent of the scale is not to identify people with the ability or the capacity for creative work, but rather to identify a personality dimension that might predispose an individual to seek novel solutions in a variety of situations. In scale construction it was discovered that many of the items for Breadth of Interest and Innovation were substantially correlated with both scales. In order to prevent the two scales from being highly correlated or confused, a statistical procedure related to the Differential Reliability Inventory Index (Jackson, 1974, 1976) was employed to identify items highly associated with one scale and minimally associated with the alternative scale. This finding does, however, indicate that there is probably an inevitable link between the tendency to have a wide range in interests and proclivity for inventiveness as defined by the Innovation scale.

Persons obtaining high scores are described as individuals who tend towards originality of thought, are motivated to develop novel solutions to problems, value new ideas, and like to improvise. Defining trait adjectives include ingenious, original, innovative, productive, and imaginative. People obtaining low scores report a general lack of creative motivation, conservative thinking, and a preference for routine activities. Low scorers are characterized by the following defining adjectives: unimaginative, deliberate, practical, sober, prosaic, literal, uninventive, and routine.

The Innovation scale is positively correlated in both males and females with PRF-E scales for Autonomy, Change, and Sentience, and negatively correlated with Cognitive Structure and Need for Social Recognition. High-scoring individuals tend to be identified as "persons capable of originality of thought," to prefer the occupation of appliance designer, and to be perceived by others as high in Agility, Art Interest, and Self Acceptance on the Bentler Interactive Psychological Inventory.

It would be rather interesting to explore the degree to which the Innovation scale is related in experimental situations designed to reflect the disposition to seek novel solutions as well as the quality of such solutions. Although the scale was not designed to predict qualitative differences in originality, it remains an open question as to whether these would be found.

Interpersonal Affect (Iaf). I am quite affectionate toward people. The original name for this scale was Interpersonal Warmth. I quickly discovered that the vast majority of people consider themselves warm individuals and that most people receiving low scores complained about the finding. It was therefore decided to employ the term *affect,* which has approximately the same denotative meaning but a more neutral evaluative connotation. The origin of this scale stems from interest in assessing psychopathology as well as a reading of Tomkins (1962). The negative pole of Interpersonal Affect is shallow affect, involving deviant and possibly pathological levels of unresponsivity in situations where most individuals would be responsive. Not only did I observe in certain psychopathological groups that shallow affect was elevated, but also that the measurement of this attribute, even in normal populations, represented a dimension along which individuals could be placed with a high degree of reliability. For example, Jackson and Payne (1963) reported an internal-consistency reliability for a one-hundred-item forced-choice shallow affect scale of 0.96. Furthermore, it was discovered that this scale was predictive of attitudes towards capital punishment as well as other similar attitudes. In a study by Friend (1966) of freedom from speech interference in a stressful interpersonal communication situation, persons high in shallow affect showed less interference. It was therefore considered appropriate to assess this dimension using items designed to separate individuals in the normal range of functioning.

Persons receiving high scores on Interpersonal Affect tend to be described as identifying closely with other people and their problems, valuing close emotional ties with others, and being concerned about others. They are characterized by such defining trait adjectives as emotional, tender, kind, affectionate, demonstrative, warmhearted, sympathetic, and compassionate. Individuals receiving low scores sometimes have difficulty relating to people, being regarded as emotionally unresponsive to others and aloof. Typically, they prefer impersonal to personal relationships and report little concern or compassion for other people's problems. Defining adjectives include: unresponsive, distant, hardhearted, taciturn, unemotional, indifferent, and cold. Persons high on Interpersonal Affect rate themselves as Affectionate and Sympathetic, and are seen by others as "compassionate and warm, tends to identify closely with people, and expresses feelings." They are rated by others in the Bentler

Interactive Psychological Inventory as high in Generosity, a finding consistent with their highest correlation among PRF-E scales with the Nurturance scale. Consistent with earlier findings, one would expect such individuals to display attitudes consistent with compassion and concern for others.

There is a wide variety of research possible with this scale. One possible study is in the area of the psychology of law, where it might be anticipated that individuals high in Interpersonal Affect would be prone to weigh such tangential evidence as social and personal factors in determining a defendant's innocence.

Organization (Org). I do not like to leave things until the last possible moment. This scale has its origins within the Murray system with Murray's definition of need Order, although the JPI conceptualization of Organization is somewhat more cognitive and less concerned with a definition focusing on an orderly environment. Organization thus refers specifically to habits of thought and work rather than to orderliness. It nevertheless is rather highly correlated with the PRF-E Order scale as well as with the PRF-E scale for Cognitive Structure.

Persons receiving high scores on Organization tend to use their time effectively, complete work on schedule, and avoid distractions when concentrating on a job or test. Defining trait adjectives include orderly, disciplined, tidy, consistent, methodical, precise, neat, meticulous, and systematic. Persons receiving low scores on the Organization scale manifest such behavior as procrastination, falling behind schedule, being easily distracted, mislaying objects, and handling events in an unsystematic, unplanned manner. They may be characterized as being disorganized, inefficient, absentminded, and forgetful.

The Organization scale, in addition to the correlates of the PRF given above, is associated with the Bentler Psychological Inventory scales for Deliberateness and Diligence, as well as scales indicating Orderliness and Clothes Consciousness. The JPI Organization scale correlated 0.65 with the peer rating of Orderliness on the Bentler Interactive Psychological Inventory. Further insight into the nature of what is measured by the Organization scale is indicated by certain negative correlations.

Organization correlates negatively with reported nonmedical drug use, tobacco smoking, scales reflecting impulse expression (Performing Arts and Adventure) from the Jackson Vocational Interest Survey, and the JPI Risk Taking scale.

One would anticipate that the Organization scale would generally be predictive of behavior in situations in which impulse control and planning are pitted against impulse expression. Tasks involving a high degree of unpredictability, as well as occupations that do not tend to follow an orderly sequence or routine, should be avoided by persons high in Organization, while those where planning was at a premium, such as accounting, should be preferred.

Responsibility (Rsy). I am very careful not to litter public places. Of all of the JPI scales, Responsibility shows the highest correlation with the Desirability scale (0.39), although this correlation is by no means high when compared with those based on the scales of other personality questionnaires. The behavior assessed by this scale is linked to desirability because it was explicitly designed to measure persons along a dimension of degree of socialization. Nevertheless, every item on the scale correlated more highly with its own scale than it did with the Desirability scale. Persons scoring high on this scale would be expected to experience a strong obligation to be honest and upright as well as a sense of duty to other people. Such people would also possess a strong, inflexible conscience, experiencing genuine guilt for transgressions of moral precepts. Conventionally desirable behavior would be descriptive of high scorers: responsible, honest, ethical, incorruptible, scrupulous, dependable, conscientious, reliable, stable, and straightforward. Low scorers would be expected to be prone to break promises, take little interest in community projects, fail to meet obligations, and avoid being held accountable for their actions. Defining trait adjectives include unreliable, indifferent, unfair, remiss, neglectful, thoughtless, negligent, inconsiderate, self-centered, and careless. Significant validity coefficients include both the self-reporting Bentler Psychological Inventory and the peer-rating Bentler Interactive Psychological Inventory scales for Law Abidance (0.77 and 0.60, respectively), reported church attendance, a Bentler Interactive Psychological Inventory rating of Trustfulness, and a nomination (where judges have chosen the person most characterized by the trait from a group of peers) for "has strong conscience; behaves responsibly." Negative correlations with reported nonmedical drug use, alcoholic use, and two measures of Ethical Risk Taking (Jackson, Hourany, and Vidmar, 1972) have also been reported.

Risk Taking (Rkt). I would enjoy the challenge of a project that could mean either a promotion or the loss of a job. Risk taking is a psychological construct that has received considerable attention in the psychological literature, both as an area of experimental study (Rettig, 1966; Slovic, 1964) and as a variable of personality. Particularly notable is an extensive theoretical and empirical review by Kogan and Wallach (1967), in which they identified a number of potential manifestations of risk taking, including gambling (or more generally, monetary risk taking), physical risk taking, social risk taking, and ethical risk taking. To appraise the degree to which each of these facets represented a common theme of generalized risk taking, Jackson and others (1972) sought to assess each of these facets with a number of distinct methods of measurement: personality inventory, occupational preferences, situational dilemmas (adapted from Kogan and Wallach, 1964), and self-ratings. In addition, a number of additional scales were included for comparison, including the JPI scales for Risk Taking, Self Esteem, and Responsibility. The general result from the study was that each of the four facets demonstrated significant levels of convergent and discriminant validity across methods of measurement and defined its own distinct factor. When these factors were correlated in a higher-order factor analysis, however, a single general risk-taking factor emerged, with which each of the four facets was correlated. Although construction of the JPI Risk Taking scale was initiated before this study was begun, it similarly was designed to sample broadly a number of facets of risk-taking behavior. The substantial correlations between the JPI Risk Taking scale and the individual measures of risk taking in the Jackson, Hourany, and Vidmar study tended to support the validity of the JPI scale as a measure of generalized risk taking.

As employed on the JPI, Risk Taking is defined as a variable of personality in which danger and exposure to uncertain outcomes play a key role. The high scorer enjoys gambling and taking other types of monetary chances as well as adventures having an element of peril. Indeed, the high scorer on Risk Taking may derive gratification from pursuing daring ventures and perhaps actively seeking them. Persons scoring high on this scale are described as bold, reckless, impetuous, intrepid, enterprising, incautious, and rash. Low scorers are cautious about unpredictable situations and unlikely to bet, avoid situations involving personal risk even where great rewards are possible, and generally avoid exposing themselves to any situation with an uncertain outcome, regardless of whether the risks are monetary, physical, social, or ethical. They are described as cautious, hesitant, careful, wary, prudent, discrete, heedful, unadventurous, precautionary, security minded, and conservative.

In addition to the range of correlations with risk-taking measures from the study already described, Risk Taking correlates significantly with Bentler Psychological Inventory measures of Deliberateness (-0.52) and Travel Interest (0.41) and peer ratings from the Bentler Interactive Psychological Inventory measures of Masculinity (0.37), Deliberateness (-0.37), and Thriftiness (-0.34). Risk takers report that they would try marijuana if legalized. The Risk Taking scale correlated significantly with self and peer ratings of risk taking in three separate studies.

Self Esteem (Ses). I am able to talk intelligently to people in a wide variety of occupations. Like many other JPI variables, Self Esteem has a dual ancestry. Its roots can be traced on the one hand to lay or implicit personality theory, and on the other to formal psychological theorizing, particularly in the work of the Yale group (Janis, 1954, 1955). Consistent with the latter, we define Self Esteem as relevant particularly to the individual's relationships with other people. There are many facets to self-esteem (compare Coopersmith, 1967); it can be differentiated with respect to such factors as personal appearance and sexual attractiveness, athletic prowess, intellectual achievement, and socioeconomic or social status. As with risk taking, one might expect a degree of correlation between some or all of these facets. But in the case of self-esteem, such a scale would probably not possess a high degree of homogeneity. For this reason and in order to retain a definition similar to that of the Yale investigations, the decision was made to highlight the social and interpersonal aspects of self-esteem in scale construction.

High scorers on the Self Esteem scale are confident in dealing with others, not easily embarrassed or influenced, and likely to speak out in social situations. They manifest presence and aplomb in interpersonal situations. Alternatively, those scoring low experience feelings of awkwardness among people, especially strangers, negative evaluation of self as a group member, fear of embarrassment, and unpleasantness in a novel social situation.

A group of seventy Stanford University students completed adjective checklist responses to a trait-rating questionnaire in which items had been keyed rationally to be consistent with the definition of Self Esteem. The correlation between the JPI Self Esteem scale and the twenty-item adjective checklist was 0.74. (The median correlation for all fifteen JPI scales was 0.70 with their respective appropriate adjective checklist scales.) High scorers tended to endorse items like self-assured, composed, egotistical, self-possessed, poised, and self-sufficient. Low scorers endorsed items that were quite the opposite—self-deprecating, timid, unassuming, modest, shy, humble, and self-conscious.

Among the significant correlates of the Self Esteem scale are the Bentler Psychological Inventory scales for Attractiveness and Self Acceptance and the PRF-E scales for Exhibition and Dominance. Significant negative correlations were obtained for the MMPI D, Pt, and Si scales. Among peer-rating correlations are the Bentler Interactive Psychological Inventory measures of Extraversion, Leadership, and Self Acceptance, and the nomination for "self-assured; not easily embarrassed by others; self-sufficient." For low scorers, the nomination "experiences feelings of inferiority in dealing with others" was also significantly related. Neill (1968) found correlations ranging between 0.43 and 0.87 for peer and self-rankings and ratings of self-esteem and the JPI Self Esteem scale. The patterning of correlations with other measures indicates that, in addition to correlations already reported with measures closely linked conceptually to Self Esteem, high scorers are seen on the Bentler Interactive Psychological Inventory as high in Agility, Ambition, Attractiveness, Cheerfulness, and Travel Interest. Low scorers are characterized by above average ratings in Law Abidance. On the PRF-E, high scorers reveal their interpersonal interest by scoring above average on Affiliation, Change, and Nurturance for males, and Affiliation, Change, and Play for females.

The psychological literature contains a wide variety of studies on the self-esteem dimension, its antecedents, and its correlates in a variety of experimental situations. One interesting question relates to the degree to which high Self Esteem develops in people as a result of their having been reinforced in the past for generally competent performances. This is a plausible interpretation that may have unexpected implications. For example, League and Jackson (1964), using an earlier version of a self-esteem scale, found that persons low in self-esteem were more conforming in a situation in which they were asked to count the number of pure tones sounded, given a unanimous but erroneous group consensus. This was consistent with previous research. But what had not been investigated previously was the ability of persons high and low in self-esteem to count accurately the number of tones sounded in the absence of information about the reports of others. League and Jackson found that persons low in self-esteem were significantly less accurate in their counting. Hence their conformity was in a sense rational behavior, based on their greater evaluation of the adequacy of others' performance compared with their own. Thus it may be an oversimplification to assume that self-esteem *causes* a certain kind of social or cognitive behavior. Rather, both self-esteem and criterion behaviors may stem from a certain constellation of antecedents. It is a problem for further research to appraise: (1) the degree to which a common factor of general self-esteem is broadly relevant to a variety of different kinds of behavior, (2) the degree to which facets of self-esteem can be differentiated across methods of measurement, (3) the precise role of such important variables as competency and social reinforcement in the development of self-esteem, (4) the degree to which physical attractiveness and self-esteem influence one another from the vantage points of both the actor and the perceiver, and (5) the degree to which the trait of self-esteem is capable of being modified by specific environmental treatments.

Social Adroitness (Sca). I hold my personal feelings in check if they might interfere with my getting what I want from someone. Christie and his collaborators (Christie and Geis, 1970) are responsible for introducing the ideas of Machiavelli, the political philosopher and pragmatist, to contemporary social psychological and personality theory. Starting with prescriptions by Machiavelli gleaned from *The Prince* about governmental operation, Christie developed a pool of items designed to measure what he considered to be the trait of Machiavellianism. Much interesting research has been generated from this line of work, particularly regarding the ability of high Machiavellians to manipulate their environments and other people, as in Singer's (1964) study of grade-getting behavior.

The Social Adroitness scale was influenced by the previous work on Machiavellianism, but the two scales are by no means identical. A perusal of the Machiavellianism scale and factor-analytic studies by Christie and Geis reveals that the Machiavellianism scale is quite complex psychologically, involving what may indeed be distinct aspects of Machiavelli's philosophy—cynicism, values favoring manipulation, and self-reported skill at influencing others. This complexity would not foster scale homogeneity or conceptual simplicity. In addition, the very name of Machiavelli conjures up associations that generally have negative connotations, especially when it is used to describe a personality trait. Our decision, therefore, was to avoid this label in developing the scale and redefine the dimension. Recalling that Machiavelli also wrote the first book on diplomacy, we initially termed this scale Social Intelligence. After some reflection, it was decided that this title perhaps redressed the evaluative balance too much by sounding too positive. Additionally, the term implies more than skill at influencing others— highly socially intelligent persons are expected to be accurate in predicting the behavior of others (Sechrest and Jackson, 1961).

The label Social Adroitness appeared to be both evaluatively more neutral and descriptively more accurate.

The definition for Social Adroitness highlights the essentially interpersonal nature of this construct. Rather than focusing on attitudinal variables like cynicism, our definition describes a more subtle kind of social influence than is involved, for example, in a scale assessing dominance. Persons high in Social Adroitness are skillful at persuading others to achieve a particular goal, often by indirect means. Descriptive adjectives for high scorers include diplomatic, shrewd, sophisticated, tactful, crafty, influential, subtle, persuasive, discreet, and worldly. Low scorers are defined as tactless when dealing with others, socially naive and maladroit, and insensitive to the effects of their behavior on others. Trait adjectives describing the low scorer include direct, straightforward, frank, tactless, candid, unpolished, undesigning, outspoken, impolite, blunt, and naive.

Possibly because of the subtle nature of Social Adroitness, the scale has proved to be the most difficult of any of the JPI scales to validate by self and peer ratings. In the study of seventy Stanford University students, it was the only scale that failed to yield a higher correlation with its appropriate adjective checklist scale than with irrelevant scales. Unlike the significant correlations obtained for the other scales with relevant peer ratings, the correlation of Social Adroitness and the relevant trait name of "diplomatic" was essentially zero. Although peer ratings have occasionally correlated with Social Adroitness, these have not been high. It is safe to conclude that the variables of personality assessed by the Social Adroitness scale are not readily identifiable in self or peer ratings.

There is an alternative to the interpretation that these scales lack convergent validity. It may be that the characteristics assessed by the Social Adroitness scale are too subtle and too remote from implicit or lay conceptions of personality to be readily identifiable by peers. This view is reinforced by the difficulty consistently encountered in finding trait adjectives to describe this dimension. Since Social Adroitness explicitly involves the capacity for using indirect means for influencing others, it is reasonable to suppose that high scorers would not be identified as such. Even individuals rating themselves are prone in this area to misinterpret and to lack insight—how many people would endorse traits like socially unintelligent, undiplomatic, or naive?

What the Social Adroitness scale should predict is the capacity to achieve goals related to interpersonal influence. One such study (Jackson and Buckspan, 1969) investigated the role of Social Adroitness in an experimental bilateral bargaining situation (Siegel and Fouraker, 1960; Fouraker and Siegel, 1963). In this experimental bargaining situation, a single buyer of a specific hypothetical commodity is confronted by a single seller of that commodity. Competitive interests are involved since each party wants to maximize his or her own profit. At the same time, cooperation must exist if an agreement is to be reached at all. Eighty subjects, forty persons high in Social Adroitness scores and forty low, were assigned randomly to one of four conditions: high or low perceived status, and buyer or seller. Whereas Siegel and Fouraker had rigorously controlled such economically irrelevant variables as personality or bargaining ability by avoiding anything but written bids and counteroffers, this study explicitly paired individuals in a face-to-face setting. Results indicated that persons high in Social Adroitness earned significantly more profit than those low in Social Adroitness by the Mann-Whitney U-test, whereas the experimentally manipulated bargaining status had no significant effect. These results are consistent with those reported by Christie and Geis (1970) for the Machiavellian scale. It would appear that studies of bargaining behavior might well employ personality variables, particularly Social Adroitness, in further experimental research.

Another area of relevance to Social Adroitness is that of experimenter influence (Rosenthal, 1967). Canon (1967), following an earlier study undertaken in collaboration with the author, undertook a study in which student experimenters were to study a "well-known illusion." Half were instructed that the illusion resulted in systematic underestimation of the size of a figure, while the other half were given the opposite information. Canon reported that there was indeed a relationship between Social Adroitness and experimenter influence on the outcome of the research, with the persons higher in Social Adroitness showing the greater influence.

Social Participation (Spt). At a social event I try to get around and talk to all of the guests. One of the better-established factors in the personality area is the one sometimes termed *sociability,* and at other times mislabeled as *extraversion.* Stated simply, some persons strongly prefer the company of others, while others do not. Because this is a rather salient dimension in interpersonal activity, a personality inventory aspiring to encompass the interpersonal domain would be deficient if it omitted such a factor. The pertinent JPI scale is termed Social Participation and focuses on social activity for its own sake. Unlike Social Adroitness, there is no ulterior motive implied. Persons scoring high on Social Participation will eagerly join a variety of social groups, seek both formal and informal association with others, value positive interpersonal relationships, and be actively social. Defining trait adjectives include friendly, gregarious, outgoing, convivial, fun loving, extraverted, congenial, cordial, and good-natured. Low scorers are likely to keep to themselves, have a smaller circle of acquaintances, and avoid social activities. Adjectives for a low scorer include nonparticipatory, solitary, unsociable, retiring, uncommunicative, and withdrawn.

The JPI Social Participation scale correlates positively with a number of personality scales, including Extraversion and Cheerfulness from the Bentler Psychological Inventory and Affiliation from the PRF-E. Negative correlations include PRF-E Autonomy and MMPI Si. Peers tend to perceive high scorers as high on Extraversion and Cheerfulness in the Bentler Interactive Psychological Inventory.

Tolerance (Tol). I find it refreshing to discuss my views with someone who strongly disagrees with me. There has been a great deal of research over the past four decades on the nature of ethnic prejudice and tolerance as sociological phenomena, as well as phenomena related to personality and cognition. One of the leading theorists in this period has been Milton Rokeach (1951, 1954, 1960; Rokeach and Fruchter, 1956), who progressively refined his conception of the origins of intolerance and dogmatism. For Rokeach, ethnic attitudes are a special case of more general values and personality dispositions reflecting rigidity, narrow-mindedness, and general dogmatism. These dispositions need not be related to particular attitudes, since leftists and rightists or atheists and religious persons might manifest them to the same degree. Importantly, Rokeach (1973) theorized and supported empirically (Rokeach and Kleijunas, 1972) the idea that belief congruence is more important than race or ethnic background in determining attitudes toward another person. The JPI Tolerance scale was developed to encompass the idea, prominent not only in Rokeach's work but in much contemporary psychological research, that a fundamental aspect of a person liking or disliking other people is the degree of similarity of their beliefs and attitudes. Furthermore, the extent to which this general principle applies will vary from one individual to another. Those who are capable of experiencing views unlike their own without a negative affect, who are capable of liking, admiring, and respecting persons with different values, backgrounds, and behavior may be deemed tolerant; those who are incapable, intolerant.

High scorers on Tolerance are thus expected to accept people even though their beliefs and customs are different from their own, be open to new ideas, be free from prejudice, and welcome dissent. Defining trait adjectives include broad-minded, unprejudiced, receptive, judicious, impartial, dispassionate, lenient, and indulgent. Low scorers would be expected to make quick evaluative judgments about others, feel threatened by persons holding opinions different from theirs, reject persons from different ethnic, religious, cultural, or social backgrounds, and identify closely only with those sharing their beliefs. The following adjectives are characteristic of the low scorer: intolerant, cocksure, dogmatic, opinionated, narrow-minded, prejudiced, and uncompromising.

Gardner and his colleagues at The University of Western Ontario have conducted a large-scale research program on the nature of ethnic stereotyping and prejudice, particularly as they relate to second-language acquisition. In one study Gardner (1973), using a Canadian sample, conducted a factor analysis of a number of variables, including attitudes towards blacks, Negroes (both labels, "blacks" and "Negroes," were used), Jews, and French Canadians, together with the Jackson Personality Inventory. Figure 1 portrays one of Gardner's major find-

Figure 1. Factor Defined by JPI Scales and Positive Attitudes Toward Various Groups.

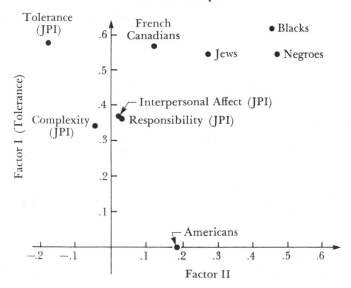

ings, in which Factor I is marked by positive attitudes towards each of the ethnic and racial groups (except Americans) and by the JPI Tolerance scale. (Factor II was not relevant to the JPI.) JPI scales for Interpersonal Affect, Responsibility, and Complexity also loaded this factor. Clearly there is evidence that the Tolerance scale is related to attitudes toward minority groups. Stereotype measures of these groups, on the other hand, define a different factor. Since the nature of ethnic and ideological tolerance and their antecedents are complex, a wide array of studies is possible with the Tolerance scale.

Value Orthodoxy (Vlo). Our censorship laws have proven to be for our own good. The idea of cultural change can be conceptualized along a time continuum. Within any cultural setting there are subcultures manifesting either rapid or slow cultural change. Some groups will reflect the average values of their society as it existed fifty or one hundred years ago, while others exhibit changes in values that the society as a whole will not adopt until some future time. Similarly, individuals may be differentiated with respect to the degree to which they have incorporated values of cultural change or, alternatively, of tradition.[3]

In our own culture, the values notable for the degree to which they are undergoing cultural change are associated with religion, sex, economics, family relationships, patriotism, euthanasia, and abortion. Some of these areas, for example sex and religion, are generally regarded as taboo for personality questionnaires. However, as with most broad dimensions of personality, the choice of item content is not limited to one narrow subject area. It is possible to find items not dealing directly with taboo areas that are quite highly correlated with the total scale. It is also possible to write items dealing with taboo areas in a way that does not arouse defensive reactions. For example, an item like "Some of the current fashions for women are too indecent to be worn in public" assesses attitudes concerning sexual freedom in an indirect manner. A content analysis of the Value Orthodoxy scale reveals the following breakdown: respect for tradition, parents and authority—4 items; suicide and euthanasia—3 items; laws and censorship—2 items; drugs and drinking—2 items; divorce—1 item; patriotism—1 item; individual economics—1 item; dishonesty—1 item; dress—1 item; religious institutions—1 item; and general values—3 items. Had I been guided solely by the item analyses there would also be a representation of items dealing with sex and religion, but these were deleted for the reasons indicated.

The relevance of religion and sex to Value Orthodoxy is apparent from its correlates. Value Orthodoxy correlates positively with the Bentler Psychological Inventory scale for Religious Commitment and negatively with the BPI scales for Lib-

[3]I am indebted to Paul Verden for discussions leading to the development of the Value Orthodoxy scale. An additional theoretical foundation for this scale stems from studies in the psychology of conservatism (Wilson, 1973).

eralness and Sexual Experience. This same pattern of correlations is also reflected in peer ratings from the Bentler Interactive Psychological Inventory; high scorers are seen as high on Religious Commitment and Law Abidance and low on Liberalism. Value Orthodoxy correlates 0.57 with reported frequency of church attendance and 0.75 with a self-rating of "traditional vs. modern in outlook." It is also reflected in attitudes toward drugs, tobacco, and alcohol consumption. High scorers would not try marijuana if legalized, tend not to report present use of marijuana or tobacco, are opposed to legalizing marijuana, and report less use of alcohol. When they do engage in nonmedical drug use, they find it unpleasant to a significantly greater degree than low scorers.

A number of research possibilities exist with the Value Orthodoxy dimension. There is a long-standing controversy regarding the degree to which attitudes predict behavior. To the extent that values are a superordinate construct subsuming other values, it is reasonable to expect that they would be more generally predictive of broader classes of behavior than would more circumscribed attitudes. Judging from the pattern of correlations already obtained, one would expect that the Value Orthodoxy scale would be capable of predicting to some degree any behavior relevant to a dimension of cultural change. Situational and contextual determinants are also relevant, of course, but where the criterion is the frequency of the target behavior over a variety of situations or over a period of time, values would be likely to play a more prominent role. Their greater stability over particular attitudes would also contribute to broader predictive power.

Infrequency (Inf). I have kept a pet monkey for years. The Infrequency scale is included to detect careless or nonpurposeful responding and mistakes in using the scoring key. Some psychologists have questioned the need for such a scale in a personality inventory, arguing that the great majority of respondents are quite serious in their answering. This is true, but evidence for careless responding arises with sufficient frequency to cause concern. On a number of occasions when graduate students have applied computer programs to scoring the JPI, an elevated Infrequency scale score has revealed an error in the students' use of the program or scoring key. In a study by Bentler (1964; Jackson, 1971) the Infrequency scale showed a substantial relationship with an index of test-retest stability of personality-inventory scale scores. On the other hand, our experience has indicated that Infrequency is only elevated slightly in deviant populations, even of psychotic psychiatric patients. For the small number of additional items, the Infrequency scale returns a greater degree of confidence in the remaining fifteen scale scores.

Modal Profiles for the JPI

Concept of a Modal Profile. Although much can be learned about a person by examining his or her individual scale scores, a consideration of the entire configuration of scale scores yields additional insight. Over the past several years my students and I have maintained an active interest in the classification of personality and the implications of employing alternative approaches to classification. Our work in this area (Jackson and Williams, 1975; Skinner, Jackson, and Hoffman, 1974; Skinner, Reed, and Jackson, 1976) has evolved into a formulation and series of analytic steps that Skinner (1977) has termed *modal profile analysis.* Although different types of classification problems involve different assumptions and lend themselves to some classification techniques better than to others, there has been an unfortunate tendency in psychology to assume that one clustering algorithm is as good as another for a particular problem. In personality assessment what one frequently is looking for is a representation of an idealized individual, or "ideal type," indicative of a broader class that shares similar attributes and for which a common set of predictions might be made. This may have the advantage over purely descriptive methods because classification permits the application of psychological laws differentially to different types of persons. Thus, an attempt is made to go beyond purely descriptive work and inductive generalization to the development of concepts representing broader classes of individuals and the development of theoretical systems or models (Hempel, 1965). Each modal profile represents the personality profile and the patterning of behavioral dimensions that is characteristic of the subset of persons in a particular population. In general, individuals will not be perfect representations of a single modal profile but are more likely to be combinations of several. Even so, the modal profile most similar to an individual's observed profile is likely to describe him or her best. By the identification of a variety of modal profiles that appear with some frequency in the population, it is possible to classify a majority of the individuals in terms of their similarities to one of these ideal types. The extent to which this is possible is an empirical matter, but the goal is to reduce the apparently chaotic diversity of individual profiles to a manageable system involving relatively few modal profiles.

An example may clarify this use of modal profiles. Skinner and others (1974) identified eight modal profiles among a large number of alcoholic psychiatric patients who had completed the Differential Personality Inventory, an unpublished structured questionnaire involving twenty-eight content scales of psychopathology developed by the author in collaboration with Samuel Messick. The sixteen types comprising the eight modal profiles generated in this analysis comprise a set of ideal types with different sets of symptoms and different prognoses. On the basis of earlier work in our laboratory (Partington and Johnson, 1969), it might be inferred that there are also a number of demographic characteristics, including education, drinking patterns, and socioeconomic class, that differentiate these types. These results provide a foundation for investigating the extent to which alcoholic patients resembling specific modal profiles have different probabilities for successful treatment under varying programs.

The goal, then, with modal profile analysis is to identify a set of higher-order constructs, each of which implies a specific differential pattern of personality scores and differential probabilities for behavior in a wide variety of situations. Having established the existence of such modal profiles, one is free to investigate: the degree of replicability of these modal profiles in samples drawn from the same and different populations; the degree to which new samples may be sufficiently classified, using various criteria, into the modal profile system; and the evaluation of the different modal profiles as the foundation for predicting different criteria, as well as for studying the differential operation of psychological laws as a function of membership in distinct ideal types (Lorr, 1966).

For a more complete discussion of the method for obtaining modal profiles, the reader is referred to papers by Jackson and Williams (1975) and by Skinner (1977). Briefly, the analysis is predicated on the representation of a data matrix, usually with entities (for example, individuals) as rows and attributes (for example, personality scale scores) as columns. This data matrix can be partitioned into three general components, namely, elevation (the entity mean over the attributes), scatter (the degree of dispersion of each profile), and shape (a measure of correlation or association between each individual's profile and the idealized modal profile). In addition, a certain proportion of the variance is attributable to error.

Having formulated the problem in this way, the first stage is to identify within any given sample the ideal types that underlie the given data set. This may be accomplished by decomposing the data matrix in each of several samples according to the Eckart-Young (1936) theorem and obtaining the left- and right-hand eigenvectors and a diagonal matrix of singular values. After appropriate rotation of the large components, the component scores derived from this analysis describe the projection of each attribute on the principal components of the entity factor space. Thus, one obtains a matrix describing idealized profiles that account for the major components of a larger number of observed profiles. The second stage is to compare the idealized types derived from each of a number of samples. This is accomplished by applying generalized canonical correlation procedures to the separate sets of modal profiles based on different samples. Stated simply, to the extent that the different profile shapes derived from each sample correspond across samples, one has evidence that modal profile types are replicable. The procedures for accomplishing this are in principal similar to procedures proposed for the analysis of multitrait-multimethod matrices (Jackson, 1975), in that they involve the decomposition of a matrix of component score intercorrelations. Normally those profiles replicating across three or more samples are retained for further analysis and interpretation. In the third stage one determines the extent to which one can account for a substantial percentage of the variance in a new sample by employing profiles so derived. This is a test of the generalizability of the modal profiles.

Modal Profiles for the JPI. The procedures briefly outlined above were applied to three groups of 150 males and three groups of 150 females who had completed the JPI as part of the normative group. Following the procedure outlined, the identification of modal profiles took place first within each of the separate groups of males and females. In every one of the three male and three female groups five eigenvalues in the basic structure analysis were found to exceed unity. The decision was thus made to retain five modal profiles within each sex and to compare these across randomly drawn samples. It should be noted that within the separate groups the classification rate was excellent. When individual profiles were compared with the within-group modal profiles using as a criterion a correlation of 0.50 or better, the classification efficiencies (the percentage of individuals who could be assigned to one modal profile) were 78.7, 81.3, and 86.7 for the males, and 82.0, 78.7, and 79.3 for the females. This is unusually high, but it should be recognized that they are based on the derivation samples; these classification efficiencies will be compared with those from new samples.

The next step in the analysis was an evaluation of the replicability of the modal profiles in the sets of male and female groups. Multiple-set factor analysis revealed that there were substantial correlations among implicit component scores. Factor analysis of these implicit component scores, followed by rotation to a univocal varimax criterion (Jackson and Skinner, 1975), indicated that final profiles were well defined by intraset profiles, with median loadings of 0.85 in both the three male and the three female samples. It was thus decided to retain the initially defined five profiles for males and females for further evaluation and research.

Description of JPI Modal Types. Tables 1 and 2 present the five male and five female profiles, respectively. The data are presented as T-scores, with a mean of 50 and a standard deviation of 10, where the standardization is across the fifteen JPI scales within each profile. It should be recognized immediately that each of these profiles is bipolar in the sense that a person may be classified as very similar to the positive pole or the negative pole of the profile. In the case of Modal Profile I+ for males, such a person would tend to have high scores on Organization, Responsibility, and Value Orthodoxy. Another person might possess an opposite pattern of scores, showing high scores on Complexity, Risk Taking, and Social Adroitness and low scores on Organization, Responsibility, and Value Orthodoxy. Such a person would thus be classified as being most similar to the negative pole of Modal Profile I for males. Thus for the five male modal profiles, there are ten modal types, two for each modal profile. Each of these shows a unique pattern of responses, a unique configuration of JPI scores, and a particular set of predictions for nontest behavior.

The bipolarity of modal profiles is illustrated in Figure 2, in which the results for male subject numbers 603 and 486 are presented, exemplars of male Modal Profiles I+ and I−, respectively. Similarly, Figure 3 presents plotted JPI scores with two female respondents classified as representing female Modal Profiles I+ and I−, respectively. It is clear from an inspection of these figures that persons falling within a particular type are characterized by not only certain high score but also a definite configuration that includes extremely low scores and intermediate scores as well. An appropriate interpretation of such a set of configurations of scores is in terms of high, intermediate, and low response probabilities for behavior related to each of the fifteen JPI scales. This is a useful alternative to scale-by-scale interpretation, since knowledge of the respondent's particular modal type alone immediately implies a set of response probabilities with respect to a wide range of behavior.

Table 3 presents the high-scoring scales for each of the modal types for males, and Table 4 presents similar data for females. The low scale points for each modal type may be

Table 1. Modal Profiles for Male JPI Samples.

Modal Profile	Anxiety	Breadth of Interest	Complexity	Conformity	Energy Level	Innovation	Interpersonal Affect	Organization	Responsibility	Risk Taking	Self Esteem	Social Adroitness	Social Participation	Tolerance	Value Orthodoxy
I	47	43	34	58	51	39	50	60	64	36	50	40	58	50	69
II	58	46	53	59	52	38	51	48	39	63	45	34	73	50	43
III	41	40	35	52	54	50	44	57	37	61	65	68	57	38	52
IV	30	57	51	34	60	54	41	49	55	56	62	36	58	61	49
V	55	57	50	48	62	45	36	71	48	62	38	44	36	43	54

Table 2. Modal Profiles for Female JPI Samples.

Modal Profile	Anxiety	Breadth of Interest	Complexity	Conformity	Energy Level	Innovation	Interpersonal Affect	Organization	Responsibility	Risk Taking	Self Esteem	Social Adroitness	Social Participation	Tolerance	Value Orthodoxy
I	40	60	64	36	49	61	51	32	49	57	55	43	50	63	38
II	65	40	56	59	41	45	65	38	37	53	50	54	64	45	37
III	33	45	41	52	58	42	55	47	60	38	62	43	72	53	47
IV	42	46	46	45	61	52	39	60	33	66	63	61	55	42	40
V	62	53	59	43	62	46	56	68	46	40	52	32	47	49	36

Figure 2. Profiles of Two Male Respondents Scoring High and Low on JPI Modal Profile I.

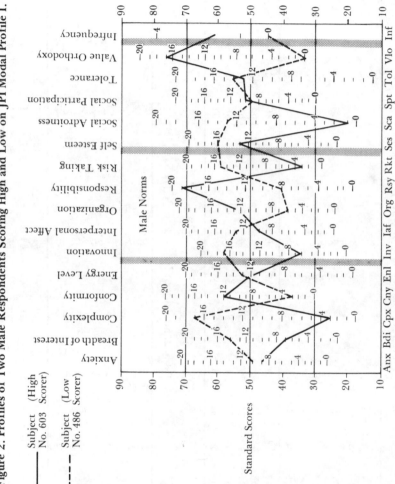

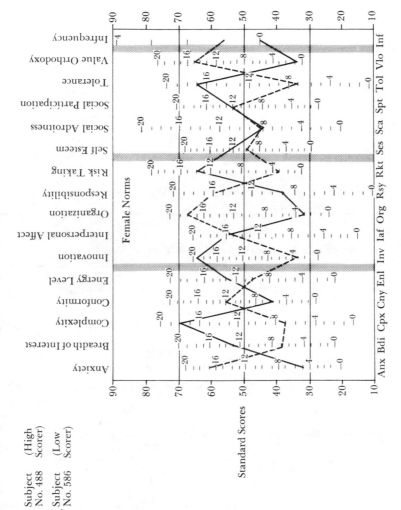

Figure 3. Profiles of Two Female Respondents Scoring High and Low on JPI Modal Profile I.

Subject No. 488 (High Scorer)
Subject No. 586 (Low Scorer)

Table 3. Salient Scales for the JPI Male Modal Profile Types.

Type I+ Organization, Responsibility, Value Orthodoxy	Type I− Complexity, Innovation, Risk Taking
Type II+ Conformity, Risk Taking, Social Participation	Type II− Innovation, Responsibility, Social Adroitness
Type III+ Risk Taking, Self Esteem, Social Adroitness	Type III− Complexity, Responsibility, Tolerance
Type IV+ Energy Level, Self Esteem, Tolerance	Type IV− Anxiety, Conformity, Social Adroitnness
Type V+ Energy Level, Organization, Risk Taking	Type V− Interpersonal Affect, Self Esteem, Social Participation

Table 4. Salient Scales for the JPI Female Modal Profile Types.

Type I+ Complexity, Innovation, Tolerance	Type I− Conformity, Organization, Value Orthodoxy
Type II+ Anxiety, Interpersonal Affect, Social Participation	Type II− Organization, Responsibility, Value Orthodoxy
Type III+ Responsibility, Self Esteem, Social Participation	Type III− Anxiety, Complexity, Risk Taking
Type IV+ Energy Level, Risk Taking, Self Esteem	Type IV− Interpersonal Affect, Responsibility, Value Orthodoxy
Type V+ Anxiety, Energy Level, Organization	Type V− Risk Taking, Social Adroitness, Value Orthodoxy

obtained from its complement. Although the technique used to identify the individual's type in modal profile analysis is to correlate his or her profile with that of the modal profile, in clearcut cases one can simply identify the high and low salients of the individual's profile and compare them with the values in Table 3 or 4.

Comparison of Classification Efficiencies. It will be re-called that classification rates in the first stage of JPI modal pro-file analysis ranged from about 79 percent to 87 percent in the three groups of males and three groups of females. If classifica-tion was based predominantly on chance association of ran-domly occurring profiles, classification rates should be near chance level on a new sample. To test the robustness of these modal types, the JPI was administered to a new sample of 732 males and 750 females. A fairly conservative criterion for inclu-sion in a modal type was set. If a person showed a correlation with a modal profile higher than an absolute value of 0.50, and this was the highest correlation for any of the five, this person was classified in terms of the type related to the modal profile. Using this criterion, the classification percentage was 71 for males and 73 for females. These values are much higher than expectations based on random data, compare very favorably with values reported for MMPI classification systems, and attest to the feasibility of applying the modal profiles derived in our analyses to new samples.

Applications of Modal Typology. The demonstration that individual profiles may be classified reliably under broader cate-gories has a number of implications for research and the use of personality test scores. Four possible applications are note-worthy: in studies of the perception of personality, in occupa-tional classification and vocational counseling, in studies of teaching and learning styles, and in prediction studies.

Research in the perception of personality and clinical judgment (Paquin and Jackson, 1977; Reed and Jackson, 1975; Strasburger and Jackson, 1977) has demonstrated that individ-uals can make reliable predictions about the behavior of persons who are described in terms of modal type. There is some data supporting the view that characterizations inconsistent with modal types yield low reliability. One fruitful avenue for fur-ther study is an investigation of the extent to which the validity of predictions about behavior will vary as a function of the de-gree to which target persons are similar to frequently or infre-quently appearing types.

There is evidence (Siess and Jackson, 1970) that person-ality factors and vocational interest factors can be located within a common space. The question arises about the extent to which persons in different occupations may be differentiated by modal type classification. A similar question arises about the relative success rates of persons in different occupations as a function of their modal type. If such correlations could be established, the possibility of employing these classification procedures for vocational counseling would exist. In a preliminary study, Skinner, Jackson, and Rampton (1976) identified consistently different personality profiles for persons in different military personnel classifications, but data on a wider range of occupations would be informative. One occupation for which there are extensive data bearing on the relevance of personality data and rated performance is teaching (for example, Medley and Mitzel, 1963). Because the majority of JPI scales bear on interpersonal or cognitive dimensions that are relevant to teaching, the modal type classification of teachers or teacher trainees might relate to different teaching styles and different levels of teaching performance. Similarly, membership in particular typal clusters might indicate a preference for certain styles of learning over others. For example, Modal Profile I+ females are characterized by high scores in Complexity, Innovation, and Tolerance, while those at the negative pole are characterized by high Conformity, Organization, and Value Orthodoxy. The former group might learn more effectively in an environment encouraging exploration and individual projects, while the latter group might proceed at a faster pace when working under highly structured, programmed conditions. A study of other modal types will suggest other hypotheses.

There are at least two ways in which the modal profile approach may be relevant to prediction. First, membership in a modal type might serve as a moderator variable with respect to another predictor. Psychological relationships might thus be observed to vary as a function of modal type membership. This is plausible in light of the findings of Kogan and Wallach (1964), who reported such moderated relationships between anxiety and risk taking, two variables of personality defining JPI modal profiles. A second application of modal profiles is in the area of classical prediction. Since a person may be characterized as

being differentially similar to each of the five JPI modal profiles, these indices of similarity may be used as scores in linear
regression studies. The reduced number of variables increases
the degrees of freedom. This can be a decided advantage, especially when the number of individuals is not large. Data from
such analyses will serve to appraise the validity of the configuration of JPI scores rather than individual scales and would support the use of profile information rather than individual scale
information in psychological report writing and research.

Overview

In this chapter I have outlined the rationale, scale construction strategies, scale definitions and correlates, and empirically derived scale configurations for the Jackson Personality
Inventory. Although a great deal of work over several years has
been devoted to the JPI, especially to scale construction, I do
not pretend that it is a completely validated test. Much more
experimental and correlational work needs to be done on the
properties of the scales and their ability to predict socially important behavior in different situations.

References

Asch, S. E. "Studies of Independence and Conformity: I. A
    Minority of One Against a Unanimous Majority." *Psycho-
    logical Monographs,* 1956, *70,* No. 9.
Ashton, S. G., and Goldberg, L. R. "In Response to Jackson's
    Challenge: The Comparative Validity of Personality
    Scales Conducted by the External (Empirical) Strategy
    and Scales Developed Intuitively by Experts, Novices,
    and Laymen." *Journal of Research in Personality,* 1973,
    7, 1-20.
Barron, F. "Complexity-Simplicity as a Personality Dimension."
    Journal of Abnormal and Social Psychology, 1953a, *48,*
    163-172.
Barron, F. "Some Personality Correlates of Independence of
    Judgment." *Journal of Personality,* 1953b, *21,* 287-297.

Bentler, P. M. "Response Variability: Fact or Artifact?" Unpublished doctoral dissertation, Stanford University, 1964.

Canon, L. K. "Relationship of Tendencies Toward Interpersonal Manipulation to Experimenter Bias." *American Psychologist,* 1967, *22,* 560.

Christie, R., and Geis, F. *Studies in Machiavellianism.* New York: Academic Press, 1970.

Coopersmith, S. *Antecedents of Self-Esteem.* San Francisco: W. H. Freeman, 1967.

Crutchfield, R. S. "Conformity and Character." *American Psychologist,* 1955, *10,* 191-198.

Eckart, C., and Young, G. "The Approximation of One Matrix by Another of Lower Rank." *Psychometrika,* 1936, *1,* 211-218.

Edwards, A. L. *The Social Desirability Variable in Personality Assessment and Research.* New York: Dryden, 1957.

Edwards, A. L. *The Measurement of Personality Traits by Scales and Inventories.* New York: Holt, Rinehart and Winston, 1970.

Fouraker, L. E., and Siegel, S. *Bargaining Behavior.* New York: McGraw-Hill, 1963.

Friend, R. "The Effects of Emotional Stimuli on the Speech Behaviour of Persons Differing in Anxiety and Affect." Unpublished master's thesis, University of Western Ontario, 1966.

Gardner, R. C. "Ethnic Stereotypes: The Traditional Approach, a New Look." *The Canadian Psychologist,* 1973, *14,* 133-148.

Gough, H. G. "Techniques for Identifying the Creative Research Scientist." In *Conference on the Creative Person.* Berkeley: Institute of Personality Assessment and Research, University of California, 1961.

Gough, H. G. "An Interpreter's Syllabus for the California Psychological Inventory." In P. McReynolds (Ed.), *Advances in Psychological Assessment.* Vol. 1. Palo Alto, Calif.: Science and Behavior Books, 1968.

Hall, C. S., and Lindzey, G. *Theories of Personality.* (2nd ed.) New York: Wiley, 1970.

Hempel, C. G. *Aspects of Scientific Explanation.* New York: Free Press, 1965.

Jackson, D. N. "A Sequential System for Personality Scale Development." In C. D. Spielberger (Ed.), *Current Topics in Clinical and Community Psychology.* Vol. 2. New York: Academic Press, 1970.

Jackson, D. N. "The Dynamics of Structured Personality Tests: 1971." *Psychological Review,* 1971, *78,* 229-248.

Jackson, D. N. *Personality Research Form Manual.* Rev. ed. Port Huron, Mich.: Research Psychologists Press, 1974.

Jackson, D. N. "The Relative Validity of Scales Prepared by Naive Item Writers and Those Based on Empirical Methods of Personality Scale Construction." *Educational and Psychological Measurement,* 1975, *35,* 361-370.

Jackson, D. N. *Jackson Personality Inventory Manual.* Port Huron, Mich.: Research Psychologists Press, 1976.

Jackson, D. N., and Buckspan, B. "Social Adroitness and Bargaining Behavior." Research Bulletin No. 99. Department of Psychology, University of Western Ontario, 1969.

Jackson, D. N., Hourany, L., and Vidmar, N. J. "A Four-Dimensional Interpretation of Risk Taking." *Journal of Personality,* 1972, *40,* 483-501.

Jackson, D. N., and Messick, S. "Response Styles on the MMPI: Comparison of Clinical and Normal Samples." *Journal of Abnormal and Social Psychology,* 1962, *65,* 285-299.

Jackson, D. N., and Payne, I. R. "Personality Scale for Shallow Affect." *Psychological Reports,* 1963, *13,* 687-698.

Jackson, D. N., and Skinner, H. A. "Univocal Varimax: An Orthogonal Factor Rotation Program for Optimal Simple Structure." *Educational and Psychological Measurement,* 1975, *35,* 663-665.

Jackson, D. N., and Williams, D. R. "Occupational Classification in Terms of Interest Patterns." *Journal of Vocational Behavior,* 1975, *6,* 269-280.

Janis, I. L. "Personality Correlates of Susceptibility to Persuasion." *Journal of Personality,* 1954, *22,* 504-518.

Janis, I. L. "Anxiety Indices Related to Susceptibility to Persuasion." *Journal of Abnormal and Social Psychology,* 1955, *51,* 663-667.

Kelly, G. A. *The Psychology of Personal Constructs.* 2 vols. New York: Norton, 1955.

Kogan, N., and Wallach, M. A. *Risk-Taking: A Study in Cognition and Personality.* New York: Holt, Rinehart and Winston, 1964.

Kogan, N., and Wallach, M. A. "Risk Taking as a Function of the Situation, the Person, and the Group." In G. Mandler, P. Mussen, N. Kogan, and M. A. Wallach (Eds.), *New Directions in Psychology.* Vol. 3. New York: Holt, Rinehart and Winston, 1967.

League, B. J., and Jackson, D. N. "Conformity, Veridicality and Self-Esteem." *Journal of Abnormal and Social Psychology,* 1964, *68,* 113-115.

Linton, H. "Dependence on External Influence: Correlates in Perception, Attitudes, and Judgment." *Journal of Abnormal and Social Psychology,* 1955, *51,* 502-507.

Loevinger, J. "Objective Tests as Instruments of Psychological Theory." *Psychological Reports,* 1957, *3,* 635-694.

Lorr, M. *Explorations in Typing Psychotics.* Oxford, England: Pergamon Press, 1966.

MacKinnon, D. W. *An Assessment Study of Air Force Officers: Part V. Summary and Applications.* Wright Air Development Center Technical Report No. 91(V). Personnel Laboratory, Lackland Air Force Base, Lackland, Tex., December 1958.

McReynolds, P. "The Assessment of Anxiety: A Survey of Available Techniques." In P. McReynolds (Ed.), *Advances in Psychological Assessment.* Vol. 1. Palo Alto, Calif.: Science and Behavior Books, 1968.

Medley, D. N., and Mitzel, H. E. "Measuring Classroom Behavior by Systematic Observation." In N. L. Gage (Ed.), *Handbook of Research on Teaching.* Chicago: Rand McNally, 1963.

Murray, H. A. *Explorations in Personality.* New York: Science Editions, 1962. (Originally published 1938.)

Neill, J. A. "Development and Evaluations of Four Types of Structured Personality Tests." Unpublished doctoral dissertation, University of Western Ontario, 1968.

Neill, J. A., and Jackson, D. N. "Minimum Redundancy Item Analysis." *Educational and Psychological Measurement,* 1976, *36,* 123-134.

Paquin, M. J., and Jackson, D. N. "Labelling Effects in Clinical Judgments of Psychopathology." *Journal of Clinical Psychology,* 1977, *33,* 109-115.

Partington, J. T., and Johnson, F. G. "Personality Types Among Alcoholics." *Quarterly Journal of Studies on Alcohol,* 1969, *30,* 21-34.

Reed, P. L., and Jackson, D. N. "Clinical Judgment of Psychopathology: A Model for Inferential Accuracy." *Journal of Abnormal Psychology,* 1975, *84,* 475-482.

Rettig, S. "Group Discussion and Predicted Ethical Risk Taking." *Journal of Personality and Social Psychology,* 1966, *3,* 629-633.

Rokeach, M. " 'Narrow-Mindedness' and Personality." *Journal of Personality,* 1951, *20,* 234-251.

Rokeach, M. "The Nature and Meaning of Dogmatism." *Psychological Review,* 1954, *61,* 194-204.

Rokeach, M. *The Open and Closed Mind.* New York: Basic Books, 1960.

Rokeach, M. *The Nature of Human Values.* New York: Free Press, 1973.

Rokeach, M., and Fruchter, B. "A Factorial Study of Dogmatism and Related Concepts." *Journal of Abnormal and Social Psychology,* 1956, *53,* 356-360.

Rokeach, M., and Kleijunas, P. "Behavior as a Function of Attitude-Toward-Object and Attitude-Toward-Situation." *Journal of Personality and Social Psychology,* 1972, *22,* 194-201.

Rosenthal, R. "Covert Communication in the Psychological Experiment." *Psychological Bulletin,* 1967, *67,* 356-367.

Sechrest, L., and Jackson, D. N. "Social Intelligence and Accuracy of Interpersonal Perception." *Journal of Personality,* 1961, *29,* 167-182.

Siegel, S., and Fouraker, L. E. *Bargaining and Group Decision Making.* New York: McGraw-Hill, 1960.

Siess, T. F., and Jackson, D. N. "Vocational Interests and Personality: An Empirical Integration." *Journal of Counseling Psychology,* 1970, *17,* 27-35.

Singer, J. E. "The Use of Manipulative Strategies: Machiavellianism and Attractiveness." *Sociometry,* 1964, *27,* 128-150.

Skinner, H. A. "The Eyes That Fix You: A Model for Classification Research." *Canadian Psychological Review,* 1977, *18,* 142-151.

Skinner, H. A., Jackson, D. N., and Hoffman, H. "Alcoholic Personality Types: Identification and Correlates." *Journal of Abnormal Psychology,* 1974, *83,* 658-666.

Skinner, H. A., Jackson, D. N., and Rampton, G. M. "The Personality Research Form in a Canadian Context: Does Language Make a Difference?" *Canadian Journal of Behavioral Science,* 1976, *8,* 156-168.

Skinner, H. A., Reed, P. L., and Jackson, D. N. "Toward the Objective Diagnosis of Psychopathology: Generalizability of Modal Personality Profiles." *Journal of Consulting and Clinical Psychology,* 1976, *44,* 111-117.

Slovic, P. "Assessment of Risk-Taking Behavior." *Psychological Bulletin,* 1964, *61,* 220-233.

Spielberger, C. D. (Ed.). *Anxiety and Behavior.* New York: Academic Press, 1966.

Spielberger, C. D. (Ed.). *Anxiety: Current Trends in Theory and Research.* New York: Academic Press, 1972.

Stern, G. G., Stein, M. I., and Bloom, B. S. *Methods in Personality Assessment.* New York: Free Press, 1956.

Strasburger, E. L., and Jackson, D. N. "Improving Accuracy in a Clinical Judgmental Task." *Journal of Consulting and Clinical Psychology,* 1977, *45,* 303-309.

Stricker, L. J., Messick, S., and Jackson, D. N. "Conformity, Anticonformity, and Independence: Their Dimensionality and Generality." *Journal of Personality and Social Psychology,* 1970, *16,* 494-507.

Tomkins, S. S. *Affect-Imagery-Consciousness.* New York: Springer, 1962.

Wiggins, J. S. *Personality and Prediction: Principles of Personality Assessment.* Reading, Pa.: Addison-Wesley, 1973.

Wilson, G. D. (Ed.). *The Psychology of Conservatism.* London: Academic Press, 1973.

III

Assessment of
the Actualizing Person

ROBERT R. KNAPP, EVERETT L. SHOSTROM, LILA KNAPP

The publication of the *Personal Orientation Inventory* (Shostrom, 1963) marked the beginning of systematic research based on the theory of actualizing, which may be defined as "the process of being what one is and of becoming more of what one can be." The process of actualizing has been the subject of numerous articles and books and serves as the basis for a series of tests collectively referred to as the Actualizing Assessment Battery (Shostrom, 1975). This chapter will attempt to trace the major directions of research stimulated by the availability of these new measurement instruments, summarize some of the major findings available to date, and suggest major avenues for related study.

Actualizing may be seen as an expression of fulfillment in two basic contexts: within the individual (*intra*personal) and in the individual's relations with others (*inter*personal). The Personal Orientation Inventory (POI) and the Personal Orientation Dimensions (POD) (the latter presented as a refinement and extension of the POI) are primarily measures of intrapersonal actualizing. Two other inventories developed by Shostrom, the

103

Caring Relationship Inventory (CRI), first published in 1966, and the Pair Attraction Inventory (PAI), which appeared in 1970, primarily measure aspects of interpersonal actualizing. These four inventories represent the assessment dimension of actualizing therapy and are collectively termed the Actualizing Assessment Battery (AAB).

The inter- and intrapersonal aspects of being are represented schematically in Figure 1. The top portion of the figure (Figure 1a) shows two individuals existing in states of withdrawal or independence, without reference to any specific other. These individuals, however, are still in contact with their

Figure 1. Rhythm of Relating.

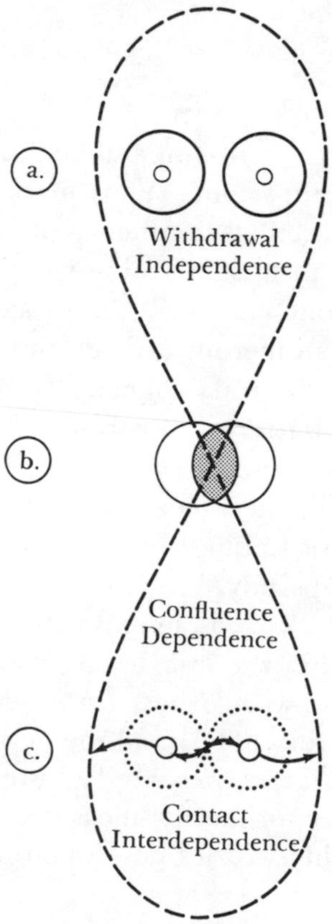

inner cores. Actualizing theory holds that this state of being is important, because individuals must be in touch with themselves and at peace with themselves before they can cope with the world. This intrapersonal state of being is the concern of both the POI and the POD.

The PAI and the CRI, on the other hand, measure a person's interpersonal being in reference to a specific other; for in addition to being in touch with oneself, actualizing involves the capacity to interrelate with others in a rhythmic and harmonious manner. Figure 1b symbolizes two people in intimate contact in a state of confluence or dependence, as would exist in a close sexual relationship or in a situation involving high intimacy, such as mutual empathy or sorrow. Figure 1c presents a third alternative—two people in a state of contact, or interdependence, where the permeable membranes of their facades are touching; but each person is also in contact with his or her own core and in contact with others at his or her facade, or periphery.

The instruments and research based on concepts of intrapersonal actualizing assess the relationship between outside variables and personal well-being and fulfillment. This was the beginning point of research into the actualizing person. It was first necessary to establish that what was being measured indeed reflected concepts commonly agreed on as representative of actualizing persons before moving on to the more complex measurement tasks represented in assessment of interpersonal actualizing.

Intrapersonal Actualizing:
The Personal Orientation Inventory

The Personal Orientation Inventory was the first published instrument developed specifically to measure concepts of self-actualizing—concepts that include Maslow's (1968, 1971) hypotheses about self-actualization; Riesman, Glazer, and Denny's (1950) system of inner- and other-directedness; May, Angel, and Ellenberger's (1958) as well as Perls's (1947; Perls, Hefferline, and Goodman, 1951) conceptualization of time orientation; and Bach and Goldberg's (1974) theories of acceptance of aggression.

The POI consists of 150 two-choice comparative value-judgment items reflecting constructs drawn from the theoretical formulations of Maslow, Riesman, Rogers, Perls, and others. In particular, it is designed to measure the process of actualizing as presented by Maslow (1968) and as extended by Shostrom, Knapp, and Knapp (1976). Sample items are:

10. a. I live by values which are in agreement with others.
    b. I live by values which are primarily based on my own feelings.
73. a. Man is naturally cooperative.
    b. Man is naturally antagonistic.

In responding to the POI, the participants are asked to select the statement in each pair that is most true of themselves. Items are logically grouped into two major scales and ten subscales that are used to compare the responses with normative samples. One of the major scales, Inner-Direction (I), is interpreted in terms of a support ratio, which measures other-directedness versus inner-directedness. The support ratio defines autonomy by assessing a balance between other-directedness and inner-directedness. The other major scale of the POI, Time Competence (T_c), is interpreted in terms of a time ratio, which assesses the degree to which one is reality oriented in the present and is able to bring past experiences and future expectations into meaningful continuity.

The subscales of the POI are designed to tap values important in the development of the actualizing individual. The Self-Actualizing Value (SAV) scale measures the affirmation of primary values held by self-actualizing people. The Existentiality (Ex) scale measures the ability, situationally or existentially, to react without rigid adherence to principles. The Feeling Reactivity (Fr) scale measures sensitivity of responsiveness to one's own needs and feelings. The Spontaneity (S) scale measures freedom to react spontaneously. The Self-Regard (Sr) scale measures affirmation of self-worth or strength. The Self-

Acceptance (Sa) scale measures affirmation or acceptance of oneself in spite of one's weaknesses or deficiencies. (It is probably more difficult to achieve self-acceptance than self-regard, though actualizing requires both.) The Nature of Man (Constructive) (Nc) scale measures the degree of one's constructive view of the nature of man. (A person with a constructive view sees man as essentially good, and can resolve the good-evil, feminine-masculine, selfish-unselfish, spiritual-sensual, and other extreme dichotomies in the nature of man.) The Synergy (Sy) scale measures the ability to be synergistic—to transcend dichotomies on a broad basis. (The synergistic person sees that work and play are not necessarily different and that lust and love, selfishness and unselfishness, and similar "dichotomies" are not really opposites at all.) The Acceptance of Aggression (A) scale measures the ability to accept one's natural aggressiveness, as opposed to acting with defensiveness, denial, and repression of aggression. The Capacity for Intimate Contact (C) scale measures the ability to develop intimate-contact relationships with other individuals, unencumbered by expectations and obligations.

Research Applications. Among the most important of the early studies with the POI are those that concentrated on accumulating evidence for the validity of the instrument. In the initial validation study reported by Shostrom (1964), several prominent psychologists nominated criterion samples of "self-actualizing" and "nonactualizing" persons, who subsequently completed the POI. The POI scale differences between these samples were statistically significant for the major POI concepts of Time Competence (T_c) and Inner-Direction (I). In addition, nine of the ten POI subscales significantly differentiated these clinically nominated groups. (Profiles for these criterion groups are presented in Figure 2.) Thus, these inventory scores provided classifications corresponding to observations by highly skilled therapists based on knowledge of behavior gained over long periods of time. Subsequent studies demonstrated that the instrument differentiated hospitalized psychiatric patients from nonhospitalized and normal samples (Fox, Knapp, and Michael, 1968) and that POI scores are rather highly correlated (up to $r =$

Figure 2. POI Profiles for Nominated Actualizing and Nonactualizing Samples.

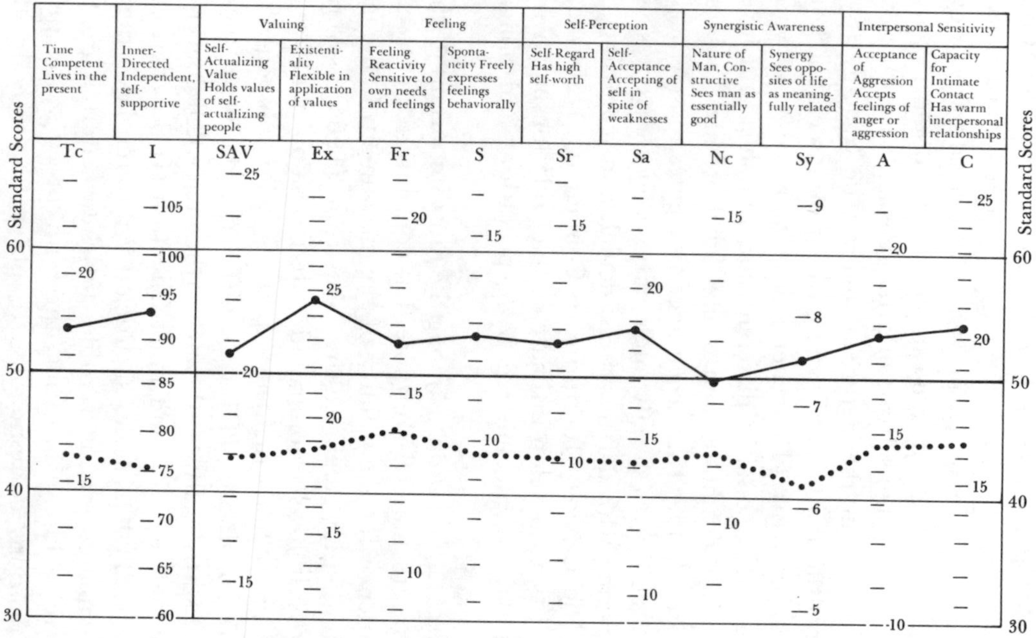

	Tc	I	SAV	Ex	Fr	S	Sr	Sa	Nc	Sy	A	C
Actualizing (—) (N=29)												
m	18.9	92.9	20.7	24.8	16.3	12.7	12.9	18.9	12.3	7.6	17.6	20.2
σ	2.5	11.5	3.6	3.5	2.8	2.9	1.9	3.5	2.2	1.2	3.1	3.4
Non-Actualizing (- - -) (N=34)												
m	15.8	75.8	18.0	18.9	14.3	9.8	10.2	14.2	11.3	6.2	14.7	16.5
σ	3.6	16.2	3.7	5.4	3.8	3.4	3.3	4.0	2.0	1.9	3.5	4.3

Source: Shostrom (1964).

0.69) with experts' ratings of self-actualization (McClain, 1970; Jansen, Bonk, and Garvey, in press). Most of the evidence for the validity of the POI is presented in the *Handbook for the Personal Orientation Inventory* (Knapp, 1976) and will not be repeated here. Beyond these studies, much of the major research with the POI might be classified into the effects of individual therapy and the effects of group therapy on intrapersonal actualizing as reflected in POI scores.

Effects of Individual Therapy. Evidence of the effectiveness of the POI in measuring changes during individual therapy has been demonstrated through repeated administration of the inventory during the course of therapy (Shostrom and Knapp, 1966). Although there are few studies in this area, the evidence available thus far shows an increase in POI scores as the length of time in therapy increases.

In a study concerned with outpatients, Shostrom and Knapp (1966) found that all POI scales significantly differentiated a sample of outpatients just beginning therapy from those in advanced stages of the therapeutic progress. Profiles for these groups are presented in Figure 3. In this same study POI scales were intercorrelated with MMPI scales for the male and female outpatient samples. Correlations ranged in magnitude from 0.00 to −0.67, the latter being in the male sample between the POI Spontaneity scale and the MMPI Social Introversion scale (Si). More significant relationships (twelve out of twenty-four r's of 0.40 or greater, $p > 0.01$) were obtained with the Si scale than with any other MMPI scale. The Si scale is presented not as a clinical scale (in the sense of being chiefly for use with hospitalized patients) but is purported to be widely used in counseling and guidance work. The comparatively high magnitude of correlations of POI scales against this scale (the average r being −0.41) appears to support the contention that the POI is measuring attributes important in the development of harmonious interpersonal relationships within "normal" populations. The next greatest number of significant correlations was against the MMPI Depression scale (D), where eleven out of twenty-four r's were above 0.40 and an average correlation of −0.38 was obtained. Highest relationships with the Depression scale were

Figure 3. POI Profiles for People in Beginning and Advanced Outpatient Therapy.

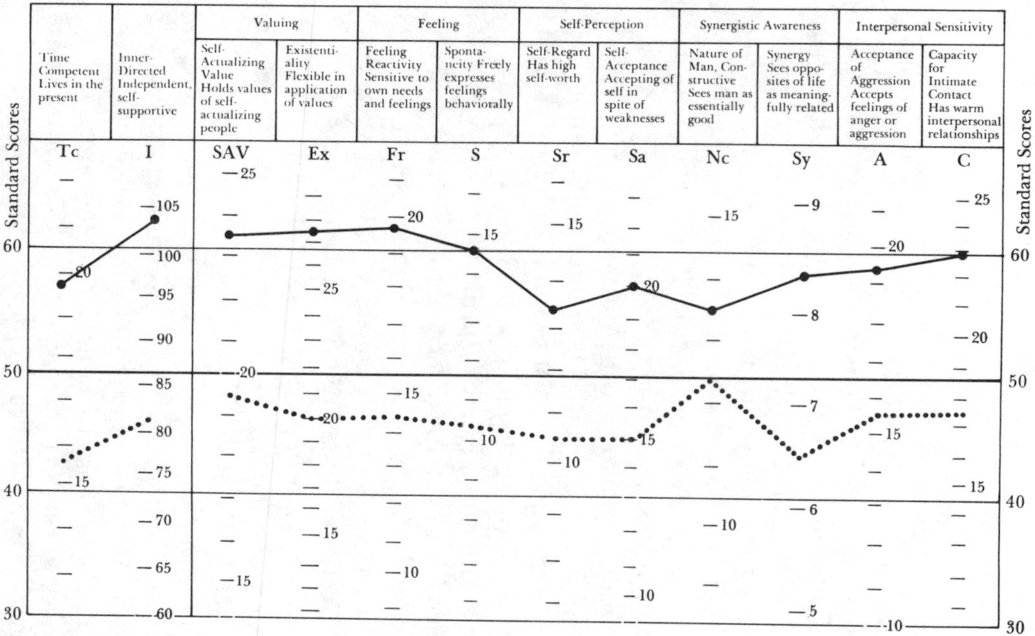

	Tc	I	SAV	Ex	Fr	S	Sr	Sa	Nc	Sy	A	C
Advanced (—) (N=39)												
m	19.7	104.2	23.3	27.2	19.6	14.8	13.5	20.0	13.6	8.3	19.4	23.0
σ	1.9	8.4	1.9	3.2	2.0	1.8	1.6	3.5	1.6	.8	3.0	2.7
Beginning (- - -) (N=37)												
m	15.6	81.2	19.6	20.1	14.5	10.7	10.7	15.0	12.4	6.7	15.6	17.8
σ	3.7	13.4	3.1	9.9	3.4	3.2	3.0	3.6	2.1	1.3	3.6	4.0

Source: Shostrom and Knapp (1966).

negative and against the POI scales of Inner-Direction, Acceptance of Aggression, and Self-Regard. These relationships support the contention that POI scales are tapping areas of "emotional morale," or psychological well-being.

Effects of Group Therapy. The measurement of the effects of group therapy (encounter group) on dimensions measured by the POI represents the single largest body of data available from research into the actualizing person and thus, perhaps, represents the most fruitful content area for evaluation of the effectiveness of the POI in measuring the processes of actualizing.

As was the case with the validity studies of the POI, the various studies concerned with the effects of group therapy are given extensive coverage in the *Handbook for the Personal Orientation Inventory* (Knapp, 1976) and need not be enumerated in detail here. An example of use of the POI in evaluating the effects of group therapy is that by Foulds and Hannigan (1976). That study represents the most recent effort in a series of researches by the authors of the effects of a brief group workshop experience on the level of self-actualization. Results based on a carefully controlled design investigated the immediate and long-term effects reflected in POI scores. Experimental and control groups were formed by the random assignment by sex of seventy-two college student volunteers to these groups. Subjects in the experimental groups participated in a twenty-four-hour continuous Gestalt workshop and completed the POI before the workshop, five days later, and six months later. Findings revealed significant positive pre-post changes ($p < 0.01$) on an overall measure of self-actualization and on ten of twelve subscales. A comparison of posttest and six-month follow-up scores disclosed that the achieved gains persisted over time and that additional significant positive change ($p < 0.05$) occurred on the overall measure of self-actualization and on two subscales. The nontreatment control group completed only pre- and posttests and demonstrated no significant changes. These results provide additional confirmation for the hypothesis that the Gestalt marathon workshop is an effective method for fostering psychological development and self-actualization in volunteer, growth-seeking college students. The number of studies that have been conducted to date point to the effectiveness of the POI as a measure of actualizing. The results of some of the more important of these studies are summarized in Table 1.

Although the composition of the samples and nature of the treatment experience varies greatly among the group therapy studies, a fairly consistent picture emerges when viewed in terms of the summary in Table 1. The overwhelming preponderance of significant increases in POI scores occurred within the experimental groups, with only a few significant increases occurring in control samples. Of the nine studies considered in which treatment results were compared with a control sample not involved with encounter training, fifty-six significant increases were observed in the experimental group, while only four increases reached significance in the control samples. Eight of nine studies reported significant increases on the major Inner-Direction scale. In terms of subscales, eight studies demonstrated increases in Spontaneity. Other frequently observed increases were in the subscales of Existentiality, Acceptance of Aggression, and Capacity for Intimate Contact. The subscales of Self-Actualizing Value and Self-Acceptance demonstrated increases in five and six of the nine studies, respectively. Increases in other scales reached significance in less than half of the studies and thus may be considered to be relatively less subject to change under the conditions imposed and the techniques generally employed in group experiences.

Empirical Verification of Theoretical Constructs of Self-Actualizing. It would appear natural that the POI and the more recently developed POD would be the chosen instruments for researchers interested in empirical investigations of humanistic concepts of self-actualizing. Developed in consultation with Maslow, the POI covers many of the concepts encompassed in his theory of the self-actualizing person. As Maslow noted about the POI in his last published book (1971), "[The POI] correlates well with external variables of various kinds, and keeps on accumulating additional correlational meanings. As a result, I feel heuristically justified in *starting* with my 'determined naivete.' Most of what I was able to see intuitively, directly, per-

Table 1. Significant Pre-Post Increases for POI Scales in Major Encounter Group Studies.

POI Scales	Studies with Control Group (Experimental Group)									Without Control				
	Alperson, Alperson, and Levine (1971)	Byrd (1967)	Foulds and Hannigan (1976)	Guinan and Foulds (1970)	Kimball and Gelso (1974)	Seeman, Nidich, and Banta (1972)	Treppa and Fricke (1972)	Walton (1973)	Young and Jacobson (1970)	Bammen and Capelle (1972)	Bebout and Gordon (1972)	Culbert, Clark, and Bobele (1968)	Knapp and Fitzgerald (1973)	Reddy (1973)
Time Competence (Tc)	**	**	**											**
Inner Directed (I)	**	*	**	**	**	**	*	**		**	**	**	**	**
Self-Actualizing Value (SAV)	*	*	**	**	**	*	*				**	**		*
Existentiality (Ex)	*		**	**	**		**	*	**	**	*			**
Feeling Reactivity (Fr)	*	**	**	**						**	*		**	**
Spontaneity (S)	*	**	**	**	**	**	*	*			**		**	**
Self-Regard (Sr)	**		**	**	**	**	*					*	**	
Self-Acceptance (Sa)	**		**	**	*		**	*		**				**
Nature of Man (Constructive) (Nc)		*			*									
Synergy (Sy)	*						*					*		*
Acceptance of Aggression (A)	*	**	**	*		**				**	**		**	
Capacity for Intimate Contact (C)	*		**	**		*				**	**	*		**

Table 1 (Continued)

POI Scales		Studies with Control Group									Without Control				
		Alperson, Alperson, and Levine (1971)	Byrd (1967)	Foulds and Hannigan (1976)	Guinan and Foulds (1970)	Kimball and Gelso (1974)	Seeman, Nidich, and Banta (1972)	Treppa and Fricke (1972)	Walton (1973)	Young and Jacobson (1970)	Bamen and Capelle (1972)	Bebout and Gordon (1972)	Culbert, Clark, and Bobele (1968)	Knapp and Fitzgerald (1973)	Reddy (1973)
Time Competence	(Tc)														
Inner Directed	(I)														
Self-Actualizing Value	(SAV)														
Existentiality	(Ex)	*													
Feeling Reactivity	(Fr)							*							
Spontaneity	(S)														
Self-Regard	(Sr)														
Self-Acceptance	(Sa)														
Nature of Man (Constructive)	(Nc)							**		**					
Synergy	(Sy)														
Acceptance of Aggression	(A)														
Capacity for Intimate Contact	(C)														

*Significant at the .05 confidence level.
**Significant at the .01 confidence level.

Source: Knapp (1973).

sonally, is being confirmed now with numbers, tables and curves" (p. 28).

Among the early applications of the POI bearing on confirmation of Maslow's theory was a study (Knapp, 1965) in which self-actualizing as measured by the POI was shown to be negatively related to the concept of neuroticism as measured by the Eysenck Personality Inventory (EPI) (Eysenck and Eysenck, 1963). When divided, on the basis of EPI scores, into samples of comparatively "neurotic" (High Neurotic) and "emotionally stable" (Low Neurotic) college students, the emotionally stable students were higher on all POI scores, as illustrated in Figure 4. As noted by Hilgard and Atkinson (1967) these results "would support Maslow's contention that he was describing mentally healthy people" (p. 160). A number of subsequent studies have related POI scores to concepts of adjustment represented in other instruments. Examples are: (1) the data of Shostrom and Knapp (1966), in which the POI was shown to be negatively related to measures of pathology obtained from the MMPI; (2) the evidence, presented by Knapp and Comrey (1973), of a high relationship between a factorial measure of emotional stability obtained from the Comrey Personality Scales (Comrey, 1970) and self-actualizing as measured by the POI; and (3) the study by Mattocks and Jew (1974), in which the POI was shown to be positively related to the concept of the "well-adjusted person" as defined by a Q-Sort adjustment scale.

Verification of hypotheses generated from Maslow's theory of self-actualization provided the basis of a study by Hekmat and Theiss (1971). Maslow's maxim of the self-actualizing individual's "resistance to enculturation" was studied through a social-conditioning technique. The hypothesis was that persons with low POI scores would respond more to reflection of feeling as a reinforcer for affective self-disclosures than would those with moderate or high scores. The POI was administered to sixty subjects, who were assigned, on the basis of their scores, to one of four groups: highly self-actualizing, moderately self-actualizing, low self-actualizing, and control. Conditioning consisted of reflective statements by the experimenter to every self-disclosure comment made by each subject during interviews.

Figure 4. POI Profiles for "High" Neurotic and "Low" Neurotic College Samples.

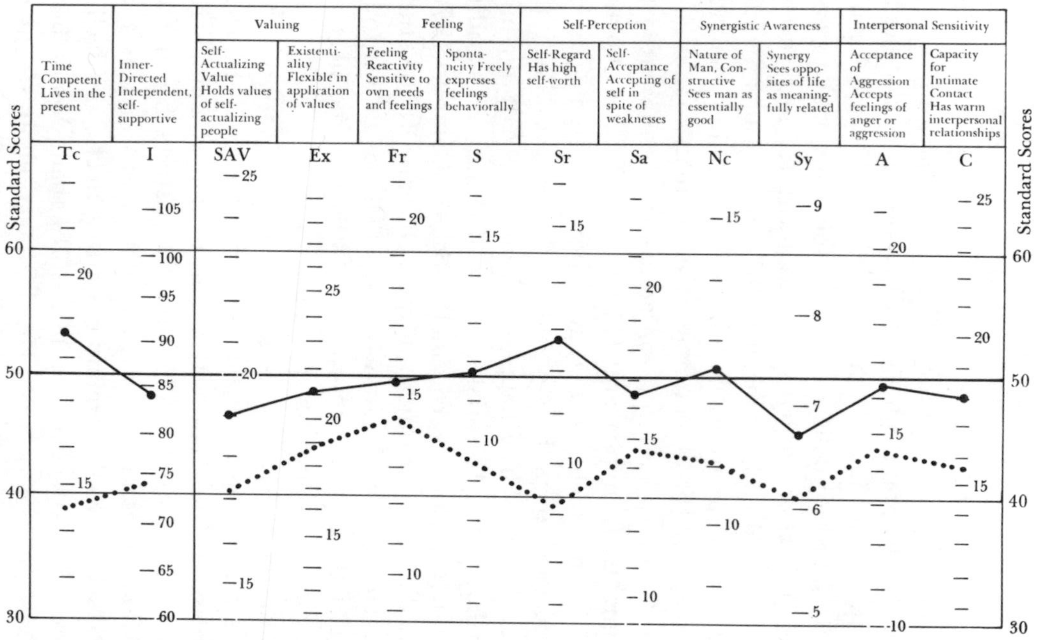

	Tc	I	SAV	Ex	Fr	S	Sr	Sa	Nc	Sy	A	C
Low Neurotic (–) (N=38)												
m	18.2	84.1	19.0	21.1	15.3	11.7	12.8	16.5	12.5	6.8	16.2	18.0
σ	2.2	8.3	2.8	3.1	2.7	2.3	1.6	2.9	1.6	1.1	3.3	3.2
High Neurotic (- - -) (N=38)												
m	14.4	74.0	17.1	19.0	14.2	9.2	9.3	14.7	11.0	6.1	14.9	15.9
σ	2.8	9.3	2.6	3.7	2.9	2.2	2.3	3.8	1.9	1.3	3.1	3.5

Source: Knapp (1965).

The results indicated that prior to conditioning the highly self-actualizing individuals displayed a significantly higher rate of affective self-disclosures than did the moderately or low self-actualizing group. During conditioning, however, the highly self-actualizing individuals showed a significantly lower degree of responsiveness to social reinforcement compared with the low and moderate self-actualizers. Thus, analysis of adjusted scores indicated that the low self-actualizing group had the highest rate of conditioning. The highly self-actualizing individuals showed a nonsignificant gain in rate of affective self-disclosures during conditioning. Results were interpreted as providing empirical support for Maslow's assertion that highly self-actualizing individuals are "resistant to enculturation."

As Hekmat and Theiss (1971) note, a goal of psychotherapy may be to help the client achieve "intrinsic learning (becoming)" through reflection. As they further note, their results suggest that "as an individual moves toward self-actualization, the locus of effective reinforcement may move from the external to the internal source and the traditional therapeutic technique thus becomes less effective" (p. 105). Hekmat and Theiss speculate that the highly self-actualizing individual responds more to the therapist as a model than as a dispenser of reinforcement. They further suggest that therapists with high levels of genuineness, authenticity, and self-disclosure may achieve the most effective behavior modification with highly self-actualizing clients. These results add significantly to previous findings concerning the relationship of self-actualization to counseling effectiveness.

Maslow's (1970) conjecture that conformity would be negatively related to self-actualizing received experimental support from a study reported by Crosson and Schwendiman (1972). POI Inner-Direction scale scores were used as the measure of self-actualizing, and conformity was measured under social pressure by a Crutchfield apparatus with perceptual-discrimination judgments consisting of matching the lengths of lines and choosing the largest relative area of geometrical figures. Thus, as the authors note, design of the study extends the construct validity of the POI to objective, behavioral predictions and adds to the number of verifications of the nomological network extending from the self-actualizing model. Conformity behavior in a group setting is of theoretical moment to the concept of self-actualizing. Maslow has described the actualizing person as one who would feel no constraint to yield to social influences. This independence from social pressures should hold for pressure to conform to the expectations of the group and for the use of others' responses as information. Thus it was hypothesized that relatively self-actualizing individuals would exhibit independent behavior in a conformity situation. The obtained correlation of -0.28 between the Inner-Direction scale scores and the conformity behavioral score was significant beyond the 0.025 confidence level and was accepted as supporting the hypothesis of a negative relationship between self-actualizing and conformity. Although significant, the obtained correlation is low, which may be due to the restricted range of the POI scores. Subjects in this study were introductory psychology students, among whom there are comparatively few self-actualizing individuals, a fact further supported in this study by the observation that the distribution of the Inner-Direction scores had a slight positive skewness, with most subjects falling in the nonactualizing range.

In a related study, Zimmerman, Smith, and Pedersen (1970) found low but generally positive correlations between a measure of conformity and POI scales in each of three treatment groups ranging in size from thirty-five to forty-six. One correlation, that between Spontaneity scale scores and conformity behavior, reached significance at the 0.05 confidence level ($r = 0.27$). Due to the inconsistent pattern of correlations in the three treatment groups, no overall conclusion could be reached concerning the relationship of POI scales to conformity behavior. Doyle (1975), in a sample of 150 subjects, reported that nine of the twelve POI scales were significantly correlated with the field-independent perceptual style as measured by Witkin's rod-and-frame test.

Findings from investigations among college student samples are, in fact, consistent with the observation made by Maslow (1970), who after searching a college campus for self-actualized subjects stated, "I had to conclude that self-actualization of the sort I had found in my older subjects perhaps was not possible in our society for young, developing people" (p. 150). In comparison to adult samples, high school and early college mean scores fall generally in a T-score range of 40 to 45.

Results from a number of studies have been interpreted as providing support for the conceptualization of actualizing in terms of an educational model of personal development. The model of actualizing (Shostrom and others, 1976a) upon which the Actualizing Assessment Battery is based is considered to be an educational model. A fundamental assumption is that social behavior is learned and that changes in behavior follow the learning process. Thus psychotherapy is viewed as an *educational* problem, dealing mostly with normal persons who have problems of living. For example, Leib and Snyder's (1967) interpretation of the beneficial effect of special treatment on both achievement and self-actualizing of underachievers supports Maslow's concept of the development of self-actualization. Such treatment is hypothesized as providing the special attention that meets needs of belongingness, love, and esteem, releasing these individuals for further personal development. Similarly, Pearson (1966) interpreted the increases in self-actualizing resulting from a group-directed form of guidance as reflecting an increased self-acceptance generated by the confidence placed in students' ability to find effective solutions to problems. Such process, when viewed as part of the psychological "chain reaction" described by Rogers (1951, pp. 481-533) in his theory of personality and behavior, gives theoretical credence to the application of the actualizing model in educational situations.

Intrapersonal Actualizing:
The Personal Orientation Dimensions

In an effort to look to the future, Shostrom and his colleagues have introduced a new research instrument called the Personal Orientation Dimensions (Shostrom, 1974). The POD differs from the POI in that it is a refinement and extension of dimensions of actualizing reflected in the POI. The extensive research with the POI has given impetus to the development of a more comprehensive measure of concepts of actualizing, which the POD now fulfills. It contains more items than the POI (260 as compared with 150) and includes some concepts of actualizing not previously measured.

The scales of the POD can be divided into four major categories: Orientation, Polarities, Integration, and Awareness. The Orientation scales include measures of Time Orientation (the capacity to live primarily in the present with full feeling-reactivity rather than blaming one's past or depending on future plans) and Core Centeredness (the tendency to trust one's feelings within as a criterion for behavior rather than looking to "shoulds" or "oughts" from authorities outside oneself).

The scales in the Polarities section of the POD measure Strength (the capacity to experience and express a personal sense of power, security, worth, adequacy, or competence), Weakness (the capacity to experience and express one's humanness, vulnerability, hurt, or helplessness—accepting one's occasional impotence and inadequacy to cope with life), Anger (the capacity to experience and express one's feelings of anger in mild or more intense ways, as appropriate to the situation or in accordance with one's reactions to a situation), and Love (the capacity to experience and express feelings of warmth, tenderness, or affection to different persons in different ways).

The Integration category of the POD includes the Synergistic Integration scale and the Potentiation scale. Synergistic Integration is the understanding that commonly held opposites (strength-weakness, anger-love) are not really opposites, but rather are mutually complementary—their power as a whole exceeds their summated power as parts. Potentiation refers to the understanding that no one principle, such as honesty or fairness, can control one's life, but that additional principles, such as humanness and being oneself, can augment, amplify, and empower one's philosophy.

The final category of the POD, Awareness, includes scales to measure Being, Trust in Humanity, Creative Living, Mission, and Manipulation Awareness. Being refers to an orientation to life that includes the willingness to be or express whatever one feels, thinks, or senses within (such as joy, sorrow, helplessness, or boredom), as opposed to a "doing" orientation, which seeks to impress others by striving and pleasing. Trust in Humanity is the ability to constructively view the nature of man as trustworthy and essentially good. Creative Living is the capacity to be effective and innovative and to become excited about decisions, judgments, or tasks. It also refers to the utilization of unique or individual ways of problem solving. The Mission scale measures sense of dedication to a life task or mission, including a belief in the importance of developing one's highest potentialities. Finally, Manipulation Awareness is the capacity to recognize common manipulative, or controlling, patterns in others and also to admit that one has a tendency, as do others, to manipulate from time to time.

Initial development of the POD followed from the extensive clinical and research use of the POI. Item analyses and construct validity against a variety of external criteria provided detailed item data and scale validity information for concepts measured by the POI. Research based on the use of the POI, as summarized by Knapp (1976), provided a major source of construct and item validation in development. Further theoretical development of concepts describing actualizing persons represented another cornerstone for POD construction. In addition, the results of the published item factor-analytic studies of the POI by Lorr and Knapp (1974) and Silverstein and Fisher (1974) were considered.

Based on these studies and the further theoretical writing of Maslow (1971) and Shostrom and others (1976b), a new pool of 370 items was developed and administered to a number of samples. Among these was an entering college-freshman sample of 402 reported by David Sundberg (personal communication, 1974). Results from this sample were submitted to monotonicity analysis, a technique described by Bentler (1971), in which the input is analogous to that of factor analysis except that the former takes a matrix of monotonicity coefficients rather than the matrix of correlations. Items submitted to analysis included 338 whose endorsement values were 95 percent or less. Thirteen

hypothesized factors were extracted. Table 2 presents a sample
item from the highest loading items on each factor. This factor

Table 2. Sample Items from Among Highest Loading in Analysis
with Factor Loadings.

POD Scale	Sample Item	Magnitude of Factor Loading (Absolute)
Time Orientation	*For me the future usually seems most hopeful. For me the future often seems most hopeless.	0.51
Core Centeredness	I feel that I have a right to expect others to do what I want of them. *I do not feel that I have a right to expect others to do what I want of them.	0.57
Strength	I am bothered by fears of being inadequate. *I am not bothered by fears of being inadequate.	0.51
Weakness	*It is easy for me to admit I have some personal weaknesses. I do not have to admit to personal weaknesses.	0.82
Anger	*I have no objection to getting angry. Anger is something I try to avoid.	0.53
Love	*I can share deep emotional feelings with another. I avoid deep emotional involvements.	0.59
Synergistic Integration	For me, selfishness and unselfishness are clearly opposites. *For me, selfishness and unselfishness need not be opposites.	0.40
Potentiation	I follow diligently the motto "Don't waste your time." *I do not feel bound by the motto "Don't waste your time."	0.46
Being	*I sometimes feel the need to withdraw from people. I never feel the need to withdraw from people.	0.67
Trust in Humanity	*I feel that people are more basically good than bad. I feel that people are more basically bad than good.	0.78
Creative Living	*I respond well to challenge. I do not respond well to challenge.	0.46
Mission	*I have found a mission in life to which I am dedicated. I have no mission in life to which I feel especially dedicated.	0.50

Table 2 (Continued)

POD Scale	Sample Item	Magnitude of Factor Loading (Absolute)
Manipulation Awareness	*I believe that many people play persecuted to get their way. I do not believe that many people play persecuted to get their way.	0.49

Note: Asterisk indicates direction of factor loading.

structure thus represents the total sphere of a person's psychological being in terms of the concepts of actualizing measured by the POD.

Based upon and extending the work of the POI, POD items are stated both positively and negatively. Thus, the particular continuum or end poles of the dichotomy in question are made explicitly clear. While other similar inventories have assumed that the examinee knows the opposite of the statement, Perls (1947, p. 17), following Roget, made it very clear that such is often not the case. Instead, opposites are dictated not by words but by context. Thus, the same word often has several correlated terms according to the context in which it is considered. For example, both *receiving* and *taking* are opposite to the word *giving*. The first correlated term refers to the persons concerned in the transfer, while the second term relates to the mode of transfer. *Old* has both *new* and *young* as opposites, depending on whether it applies to living beings or to things. In reviewing this item format, Coan (1972, p. 293) concluded, "The use of double-statement items makes the test seem a little monotonous, but it often provides the subject with a more clearly delineated choice than he would otherwise have. Its advantages seem to outweigh its shortcomings." In terms of interpretive usefulness it has been proven useful to explicitly state the conceptual continuum in question, particularly in therapy.

Encouraging results from preliminary research with the POD have been obtained from a wide variety of populations, including samples taken from college students, church congregations, delinquents, alcoholics, teachers, hospitalized psychotics, and nominated actualizing persons. Many of the validating techniques refined through the development of the POI have been applied to the POD, and among the most important of these are the use of the clinically nominated samples and the comparison of these samples to independently identified samples corresponding to the various levels of actualizing, such as hospitalized psychiatric patients. The initial validating studies for the POD, reported and summarized by Shostrom and others (1976b), show that the POD scales differentiate clinically nominated actualizing persons from nonactualizing persons and that institutionalized alcoholics (Jansen, Knapp, and Knapp, 1976) and institutionalized psychiatric patients (Rofsky and others, in press) score significantly lower than actualizing and other noninstitutionalized samples.

Interpersonal Actualizing:
The Caring Relationship Inventory

Although research with the POI and the POD has been concerned with intrapersonal as well as interpersonal actualizing and has included the measurement of content areas having personal and social implications, research with the Caring Relationship Inventory (Shostrom, 1966) as well as the Pair Attraction Inventory (Shostrom, 1970) has concentrated primarily on establishing validity of the instruments in terms of interpersonal actualizing criteria.

The CRI is a measure of the essential elements of love or caring in human relationships. The guidelines used in the initial development of this inventory were based, in part, on the theoretical writings of Fromm, Lewis, Maslow, and Perls. The CRI consists of eighty-three items concerning feelings and attitudes of one member of a male-female pair toward the other member. Responses of either "true" or "false" are made to each of the items, first as applied to the other member of the couple (spouse, fiance, or sweetheart), and second as applied to an ideal mate. Two forms of the CRI are used, one for the male's rating of the female and one for the female's rating of the male.

Development of the CRI was based on responses of criterion groups of successfully married or actualizing couples and of nonactualizing couples—troubled couples in counseling and non-actualizing, divorced individuals.

Items on the CRI are grouped into five major scales—Affection (or Agape) (A), Friendship (F), Eros (Er), Empathy (Em), and Self-Love (SL)—and two subscales—Being Love (BL) and Deficiency Love (DL).

Affection, or Agape, reflects the capacity of a person to feel a sense of unconditional love for others in a manner similar to the way God is said to feel for mankind. It is a charitable, altruistic form of love in which one feels deeply for the other individual as another unique human being. It involves compassion, appreciation, and tolerance and has been defined as caring for the needs of another person as a parent does for a child. The danger, expressed through excessive affection, is that parents may begin to feel that they "own" the child. Likewise, in a marriage the same principle holds. One marriage partner never owns the other.

Friendship is a helping, nurturing form of love. It involves unconditional acceptance characterized by the love of another's personhood. Friendship is a love of equals based on an appreciation of the other person's talents and worth. Friendship may become manipulative, however, when one begins to exploit or use other people rather than to appreciate them.

Eros is a romantic, sexual, or erotic form of love. It develops in the relationship between mother and child, in which there is much skin contact and feeling by both. Any sexual relationship may become manipulative and be referred to as *seduction*. Seduction means using the other person's body physically without appreciating the total spiritual nature of the other person.

Empathy is a form of love reflecting the capacity of a person to feel for another. It develops as one begins to learn peer and sex roles. In later life empathy becomes a peer love based on appreciation of common interests and respect for each other's equality. Manipulative empathy is called *pharisaism* in that one says one thing and does another.

Self-Love is the ability to accept one's own weaknesses as well as appreciate one's individual, unique sense of personal worth. It includes the acceptance of one's full range of positive and negative feelings toward one's partner. Self-love may become manipulative when a person treats the self as an object or thing rather than as something to be respected.

Being Love (B-Love) is the love of another solely for his or her being as a person without conditions or reservations. It is an admiring, respectful love—an end in itself.

Deficiency Love (D-Love) is the love of another for what that person can do for one. It is an exploiting, manipulating love of another as a means to an end.

In describing the CRI and contrasting it with earlier work, Kelley (1974) has stated, "A more promising approach is found in the Caring Relationship Inventory developed by Everett L. Shostrom. . . . Shostrom's careful work may well lay the foundation for a more accurate measurement and understanding of the elusive quality of love. . . . With such a test, we can begin to answer the question of what love means and how stable and lasting it is" (pp. 220-221).

Validity of the CRI. In an investigation of the validity of the CRI (Shostrom, 1966), the inventory was administered to samples of actualizing couples, troubled couples, and divorced individuals. The seventy-five actualizing couples had been married at least five years and indicated that they had worked through any marital difficulties they might have had. The fifty troubled couples were receiving marital counseling. The divorced sample consisted of 108 individuals who responded to the CRI in terms of their divorced spouse. Profiles for these samples plotted against the CRI norms based on successfully married couples are shown in Figure 5.

Mean differences between the successfully married sample and samples of troubled or divorced individuals were significant for all CRI scales. The greatest differences were obtained on the CRI Friendship scale. Thus it might appear from results of the CRI that faltering marriages reflect a lack of appreciation of common interests rather than a lack of romance, sex, or other aspects of love. Clinically, it has been felt that the one

Figure 5. Comparison of Actualizing Couples, Troubled Couples, and Divorced Individuals on the CRI.

	Affection	Friendship	Eros	Empathy	Self-Love	D-Love	B-Love	
60	13	15		15	14			60
		12				8	15	
	12	14	11	14	13			
					12	7	14	
		13	— 10 —					
50	—11			13				50
	Actualizing Married Couples	9		11	6			
	10	12	8	12	10	5	13	
	9	11	7	11	9	4	12	
40			6		8		11	40
	8	10	5	10	7	3	10	
	7	9	4	9	6	2		
30			3				9	30
	6	8	2	8	5	1		
		7	1	7	4	0	8	
	5				3			
20			0	6				20

Standard Scores (left and right axes)

- - - - Troubled Couples   ———— Divorced Individuals

form of loving divorcees most desire from a second mate is that of friendship. Results from the CRI support this contention. In particular, divorcees seem to want a buddy, not just a sweetheart.

Bustanoby (1974) recommended the use of the CRI as a device for measuring caring in pair relationships, especially for evaluation in "marriage enrichment programs." R. P. Travis and P. Y. Travis (personal communication, 1975) have presented results from the application of the CRI in a program of this kind (the Pairing Enrichment Program), showing that such programs result in significant positive changes on the CRI from pre- to posttesting. In the preliminary analysis, data showed that all scales were significantly increased between pre- and postadministration of the CRI. We believe that the new emphasis on such programs of enrichment will benefit from research utilizing an instrument like the CRI, which measures caring dimensions. Although the CRI is being widely used in a number of other similar settings, the resulting data are just now becoming available.

In the most recent and perhaps most carefully controlled application of the CRI in research, Huber (1976) investigated three sequential marriage encounter weekend workshops held at Mission San Luis Rey in Oceanside, California. There, Huber conducted three testing sessions with an experimental group of seventy-one couples and a control group of thirty-one couples. Using identical time spans, Huber administered the CRI to members of these married couples singly. Huber compared the responses of the experimental and the control groups at the beginning of the weekend encounter, at the end of the weekend, and again after a six-week consolidation period. In the case of the experimental group couples, the change agent was, of course, the actual encounter process, to which the control group had not been exposed.

The encounter itself provided information on an idealized concept of marriage, representing it as a social institution viewed by the religious community to be based on biblical precepts. It also provided psychological definitions of feelings and the importance of expressing these to the spouse, as well as a series of practicum periods. During these periods, each spouse recorded his or her own feelings that each theretofore had been reluctant to admit to himself or herself and even more fearful of divulging to the partner. During these periods couples, in the privacy of their quarters, shared these feelings and discussed them in the form of a "dialogue," during which they attempted to resolve inconsistencies. The intent of the program, therefore, was twofold—to open up a healthy form of interspouse communication and to provide a sense of self-hood or personal identity derived from contributing to the fulfillment of a deific plan for humanity in general.

The effectiveness of this undertaking, as measured by the CRI, was significantly positive. Table 3 provides actual measurement data relating to the score means of both groups for each scale of the CRI, and the associated profiles (Figure 5) graphically portray the variations that occurred in the means of both

Table 3. Analysis of Variance on the Caring Relationship Inventory.

Scale or Subscale	Pretest		Posttest		Follow-Up		F
	M	SD	M	SD	M	SD	
Affection							
Experimental	10.3	2.4	12.1	1.8	11.7	2.1	10.9[a]
Control	10.6	2.7	10.4	2.8	10.4	3.2	
Friendship							
Experimental	12.1	3.1	14.0	2.2	13.9	2.6	3.4
Control	12.3	3.1	12.8	3.3	12.8	3.2	
Eros							
Experimental	10.3	3.3	11.6	3.0	11.8	3.2	7.5[b]
Control	10.0	3.5	10.3	3.5	10.2	4.2	
Empathy							
Experimental	12.3	2.5	14.0	1.9	14.1	1.8	11.1[a]
Control	12.1	2.4	12.0	2.7	13.0	2.9	
Self-Love							
Experimental	9.5	2.9	10.5	2.9	10.4	3.0	0.6
Control	9.7	2.9	10.1	3.0	10.7	3.4	
Deficiency Love							
Experimental	6.5	2.1	6.5	2.2	6.8	2.2	3.4
Control	6.1	2.0	6.6	2.0	6.4	2.1	
Being Love							
Experimental	13.0	2.7	15.2	1.8	14.9	2.0	4.1[c]
Control	13.1	2.8	13.1	2.9	13.7	3.2	

[a]Significant at the 0.001 level.

[b]Significant at the 0.01 level.

[c]Significant at the 0.05 level.

groups, as correlated with the impact, or lack of it, of the marriage encounter weekend.

An examination of the pretest data clearly shows that initially there was relatively little difference between the experimental group and the control group. However, the posttest scores of the experimental group are markedly higher than those of the control group, although the scores of the latter are indeed somewhat higher than their pretest scores. What seems of greater importance, however, is the differential comparison of the means of these two groups, that is, the sizes of the increases in both cases. Evidently with the experimental group there is a major shift in Affection following the experience of the weekend, with its risk-involving dialogues. A comparable increase is also seen in the Friendship means as well as those of Eros, Empathy, and B-Love. While the D-Love shifts for both groups are of the same order of magnitude, oddly enough a reversal occurs in the Self-Love scale scores, the control group means being greater than those of the experimental group.

Whatever the reasons for the various shifts, it is clear that the CRI is an instrument highly sensitive both to one-time feelings of caring and to changes in these feelings with time in response to directed experiences of openness between marriage partners.

Interpersonal Actualizing: The Pair Attraction Inventory

The psychological determinants of lover and mate selection pose problems of both theoretical and practical concern to marriage counselors and therapists. In his pioneering book *Mate Selection* (1958), Winch postulates that men and women are attracted to one another because of complementary needs. It is the differences that are attractive, each partner complementing the differences perceived in the other. However, the more recent research of Lederer and Jackson (1968) supports the opposite hypothesis: Men and women are attracted to each other because of symmetry of interests and personality.

The emergence of such apparently contradictory points of view and the consequent need for an operationally defined statement of the variables underlying mate selection led to development of the Pair Attraction Inventory (PAI) (Shostrom, 1970), which is designed to measure both complementarity and symmetry in pair relationships. Research upon which the PAI is based has suggested that these two apparently contradictory concepts are compatible, and indeed, research with the PAI has indicated that actualizing couples are, in a rhythmical manner, both complementary and symmetrical.

The theory upon which the PAI is based is derived in part from research conducted at the Institute of Personality Assessment at Berkeley by Leary, Barron, MacKinnon, and Coffey (Leary, 1957), in which the scores representing a large sampling of personality characteristics were found to be aligned on two basic polarities: anger-love and strength-weakness. The theories of Winch (1958) fit the same general scheme.

Recent research with the PAI (Shostrom, 1970) compares scores from divorced spouses as opposed to lovers. The data collected thus far suggest that with the divorced person the tendency is to select a complementary partner when the original mate is symmetrical, and vice versa. This finding may have implications for a study of unfaithfulness in marriage. Boredom, or routine, is perhaps an important cause of this problem and this boredom is temporarily alleviated by the choice of a different kind of lover, inside or outside of marriage.

The theory underlying the development of the PAI suggests that there are seven basic kinds of unconscious mate choices that operate in selecting a marriage partner:

1. The nurturing relationship: the mother-son pattern. This unconscious choice is suggested in the writings of Freud. The mother-son relationship permits a man to remain a child and to behave much as he did at home while growing up. It permits a woman simply to imitate the role that her own mother played and requires no creative adjustment to mature adulthood. The weak sonlike husband has unconsciously chosen his opposite, the strong motherlike woman.

2. The supporting relationship: the daddy-doll (father-daughter) pattern. The writings of Henrik Ibsen, especially *A Doll's House*, suggest the presence of this pattern in our culture. The father-daughter relationship is the reverse of the mother-son relationship: The man plays the role of strength and the woman that of weakness. Each represents a kind of cultural distortion of masculinity and femininity. The man appears to be strong, and the woman plays a childlike role in response to him.

3. The challenging relationship: the bitch-nice guy (shrew-nice guy) pattern. The writings of James Thurber have cleverly lampooned this pattern, which has become a prototype of the unhappy American marriage. The shrewlike woman has exaggerated her expression of anger and denies her vulnerability. The nice guy has exaggerated his expression of love and denies his assertiveness. This pattern is often referred to as a matriarchal marriage.

4. The educating relationship: the master-servant (tyrant-nice gal) pattern. The tyrant-nice gal relationship is immortalized in Shaw's *Pygmalion,* wherein Professor Henry Higgins transforms a servant girl into a lady. In this pattern a strong husband educates and trains a weak, servile wife. The nice gal lacks identity and projects her powers onto the tyrannical master in idolatrous love.

5. The confronting relationship: the "hawks" pattern. This relationship is illustrated in Edward Albee's play, *Who's Afraid of Virginia Woolf?* It is often called *competitive marriage* and occurs when a top dog marries another top dog, with each geared for battle. Competition replaces love in this power play relationship. The overt hostility is, in reality, a muffled and unacknowledged cry of deep pain.

6. The accommodating relationship: the "doves" pattern. C. S. Lewis, in his classic *Screw-Tape Letters,* writes tellingly of the dove relationship, insisting that a young couple need only be convinced that they should spend a lifetime struggling to please each other. We call this the nothing-nothing relationship: two underdogs with no substance or identity. Doves are passive manipulators and use guilt as their primary weapon to control one another.

7. The actualizing relationship: the rhythmic pattern. In contrast to each of the above, the rhythmic relationship is like the ebb and flow of the tides or the revolving motion of the seasons. Actualizing couples are able to be strong and weak, angry and loving, and to respond with freedom and creative rhythm. Rather than an institution rigidified in roles, the actualizing relationship is a workshop for growth. The actualizing relationship synthesizes in rhythm all of the relationships above.

Validity of the PAI. A recent study conducted by F. L. Shostrom (1973) and reported by F. L. Shostrom and Knapp (1977) compared predictions of trained therapists, based on their knowledge through client interviews, with results on the PAI for the same subjects. The thirty therapists participating in the study were drawn from the fields of marriage and family counseling, psychiatry, psychiatric social work, pastoral counseling, and psychology. Each therapist selected two or more clients. Altogether 150 clients were rated. After familiarization with the PAI categories, each therapist selected the one scale that best described each client and the client's relationship to his or her partner. The administration of the PAI followed the therapist's diagnosis. Client profiles were plotted for each of the seven PAI scales and compared with the judgment of the therapist. Analysis of the data yielded a high correlation between therapist diagnosis and client score on the PAI for five of the seven PAI categories; two categories, Accommodating Relationship and Supporting Relationship, failed to achieve significant correlations. The five categories that correlated significantly suggest that the PAI is a valid therapeutic tool, and the results seem to show that the PAI facilitates identification of problem areas in interpersonal relationships. It appears that the PAI might be successfully utilized in nontherapeutic settings, such as premarital counseling, and presents an interesting opportunity for long-term research along these lines.

As with the CRI, the PAI is currently being used in a number of research studies, but the data are just becoming available. Because both the CRI and PAI are interpersonal instruments that have been more recently devised, data are less available than on the POI, which has a longer history and is a measure of intrapersonal actualizing.

Summary and Future Directions

Validity data available to date for the inventories comprising the Actualizing Assessment Battery support the validity of the individual instruments for a number of applications. Particularly important among the lines of evidence available are the relationships established between clinical observation and test scores on each of the four instruments and the sensitivity of the instruments to change following various educational, or treatment, experiences.

As evidenced by the wide variety of topics considered in the studies available, concepts measured by the POI have stimulated research into a broad spectrum of values and behavior that are considered important in the development of the actualizing person. The availability of a quantitative measure of such concepts has contributed greatly to the clarification and testing of theoretical hypotheses in this field of human behavior. The CRI and PAI are newer instruments and consequently fewer studies are available, yet the evidence from the studies is positive.

Major consideration contributing to the wide applicability of the Actualizing Assessment Battery instruments, particularly the POI, certainly have been the objectivity of measurement, the positive and nonthreatening nature of the concepts measured, the resistance to faking, the relevant "in the now" statements of items and description of the constructs, and, in general, the usefulness of the results to clients, therapists, and researchers. As Maslow (1971) observed with respect to the POI, "Self-actualization can now be defined quite operationally, as intelligence tests used to be defined, that is, self-actualization is what that test tests" (p. 28). The wide use of the instruments in the Actualizing Assessment Battery as an integral part of the evaluation of the effects of psychotherapeutic intervention represents a major advance in psychological assessment. Most impressive perhaps are the substantial number of studies, including the most recent research, such as that of Foulds and Hannigan (1976), which demonstrates the sensitivity of the POI to changes resulting from group therapy techniques.

Of major interest in the design of future studies will be the differential predictive usefulness of the many concepts developed by Shostrom as well as the differential usefulness of these concepts in predicting diverse outside criteria. In particular, further construct validation of the newer concepts measured by the POD as well as those interpersonal dimensions measured by the CRI and PAI are anticipated. Beyond the use of these instruments in measuring the overall effectiveness and the relative effectiveness of treatment procedures, it is anticipated that further attention will be given to matching a client with the type of treatment.

A number of studies have also been concerned with the effects of institutional supportiveness on levels of actualizing of the group members. Assuming that personal actualizing is a goal affecting institutional policy, other studies should be undertaken to determine the effect of various policies on levels of intra- and interpersonal actualizing of institutional members. The relationships presented by Andrew Greeley (personal communication, 1970) between encyclicals of the Catholic Church and levels of actualizing of priests are examples of evidence that might be used in weighing effects of institutional policy. Results of applying this method in educational and industrial organizations are eagerly awaited.

In summary, a more sophisticated set of measurement concepts and techniques has evolved as evidenced by the research briefly outlined in this chapter. These instruments, based as they are on an explicitly stated theoretical base with a broad research foundation, should prove eminently useful for clinical and educational as well as research applications.

References

Alperson, B. L., Alperson, E. D., and Levine, R. "Growth Effects of High School Marathons." Experimental Publications System. Washington, D.C.: American Psychological Association, 1971.

Bach, G. R., and Goldberg, H. *Creative Aggression*. Garden City, N.Y.: Doubleday, 1974.

Banmen, J., and Capelle, R. "Human Relations Training in Three Rural Manitoba High Schools: A Three-Month Follow-Up." *Canadian Counsellor*, 1972, *6*, 260-270.

Bebout, J., and Gordon, B. "The Value of Encounter." In L. N. Solomon and B. Berzon (Eds.), *New Perspectives on Encounter Groups*. San Francisco: Jossey-Bass, 1972.

Bentler, P. M. "Monotonicity Analysis: An Alternative to Linear Factor and Test Analysis." In D. R. Green, M. P. Ford, and G. B. Flamer (Eds.), *Measurement and Piaget*. New York: McGraw-Hill, 1971.

Bustanoby, A. "The Pastor and the Other Woman." *Christianity Today*, August 30, 1974, pp. 7-10.

Byrd, R. E. "Training in a Non-Group." *Journal of Humanistic Psychology*, 1967, *25*, 296-299.

Coan, R. W. "Review of the Personal Orientation Inventory." In O. K. Buros (Ed.), *The Seventh Mental Measurements Yearbook.* Highland Park, N.J.: Gryphon Press, 1972.

Comrey, A. L. *Comrey Personality Scales.* San Diego: EdITS, 1970.

Crosson, S., and Schwendiman, G. "Self-Actualization as a Predictor of Conformity Behavior." Unpublished manuscript, Marshall University, 1972.

Culbert, S. A., Clark, J. V., and Bobele, H. K. "Measures of Change Toward Self-Actualization in Two Sensitivity Training Groups." *Journal of Counseling Psychology,* 1968, *15,* 53-57.

Doyle, J. A. "Field-Independence and Self-Actualization." *Psychological Reports,* 1975, *36,* 363-366.

Eysenck, H. J., and Eysenck, S. *The Eysenck Personality Inventory.* San Diego: EdITS, 1963.

Foulds, M. L., and Hannigan, P. S. "Effects of Gestalt Marathon Groups on Measured Self-Actualization: A Replication and Follow-Up Study." *Journal of Counseling Psychology,* 1976, *23,* 60-65.

Fox, J., Knapp, R. R., and Michael, W. B. "Assessment of Self-Actualization of Psychiatric Patients: Validity of the Personal Orientation Inventory." *Educational and Psychological Measurement,* 1968, *28,* 565-569.

Guinan, J. F., and Foulds, M. L. "Marathon Group: Facilitator of Personal Growth?" *Journal of Counseling Psychology,* 1970, *18,* 101-105.

Hekmat, H., and Theiss, M. "Self-Actualization and Modification of Affective Self-Disclosures During a Social Conditioning Interview." *Journal of Counseling Psychology,* 1971, *18,* 101-105.

Hilgard, E. R., and Atkinson, R. E. *Introduction to Psychology.* New York: Harcourt Brace Jovanovich, 1967.

Huber, J. W. "The Effects of Dialogue Communication upon the Interpersonal Marital Relationship." Unpublished doctoral dissertation, United States International University, 1976.

Jansen, D. G., Bonk, E. C., and Garvey, F. J. "Relationships between Personal Orientation Inventory and Shipley-Hartford Scale Scores and Supervisor and Peer Ratings of Counseling Competency for Clergymen in Clinical Training." *Journal of Community Psychology,* in press.

Jansen, D. G., Knapp, R. R., and Knapp, L. "Measurement of Personality Change in an Alcoholic Treatment Program: Further Validation of the Personal Orientation Dimensions." *Educational and Psychological Measurement,* 1976, *36,* 505-507.

Kelley, R. K. *Courtship, Marriage, and the Family.* New York: Harcourt Brace Jovanovich, 1974.

Kimball, R., and Gelso, C. J. "Self-Actualization in a Marathon Group: Do the Strongest Get Stronger?" *Journal of Counseling Psychology,* 1974, *31,* 38-42.

Knapp, R. R. "Relationship of a Measure of Self-Actualization to Neuroticism and Extraversion." *Journal of Consulting Psychology,* 1965, *29,* 168-172.

Knapp, R. R. *Handbook for the Personal Orientation Inventory.* San Diego: EdITS, 1976.

Knapp, R. R., and Comrey, A. L. "Further Construct Validation of a Measure of Self-Actualization." *Educational and Psychological Measurement,* 1973, *33,* 419-425.

Knapp, R. R., and Fitzgerald, O. R. "Comparative Validity of the Logically Developed Versus 'Purified' Research Scales for the Personal Orientation Inventory." *Educational and Psychological Measurement,* 1973, *33,* 971-976.

Leary, T. *Interpersonal Diagnosis of Personality.* New York: Ronald Press, 1957.

Lederer, W. J., and Jackson, D. D. *The Mirages of Marriage.* New York: Norton, 1968.

Leib, J. W., and Snyder, W. U. "Effects of Group Discussions on Underachievement and Self-Actualization." *Journal of Counseling Psychology,* 1967, *14,* 282-285.

Lorr, M., and Knapp, R. R. "Analysis of a Self-Actualization Scale: The POI." *Journal of Clinical Psychology,* 1974, *30,* 355-357.

McClain, E. W. "Further Validation of the Personal Orientation Inventory: Assessment of Self-Actualization of School

Counselors." *Journal of Consulting and Clinical Psychology,* 1970, *35,* 21-22.

Maslow, A. H. *Toward a Psychology of Being.* (2nd ed.) New York: Harper & Row, 1968.

Maslow, A. H. *Motivation and Personality.* (2nd ed.) New York: Harper & Row, 1970.

Maslow, A. H. *The Farther Reaches of Human Nature.* New York: Viking, 1971.

Mattocks, A. L., and Jew, C. C. "Comparison of Self-Actualization Levels and Adjustment Scores of Incarcerated Male Felons." *Educational and Psychological Measurement,* 1974, *34,* 69-74.

May, R., Angel, T., and Ellenberger, H. *Existence.* New York: Basic Books, 1958.

Pearson, O. "Effects of Group Guidance upon College Adjustment." Unpublished doctoral dissertation, University of Kansas, 1966.

Perls, F. *Ego, Hunger and Aggression.* London: Allen & Unwin, 1947.

Perls, F., Hefferline, R., and Goodman, P. *Gestalt Therapy.* New York: Julian, 1951.

Reddy, W. B. "The Impact of Sensitivity Training on Self-Actualization: A One-Year Follow-Up." *Small Group Behavior,* 1973, *4,* 407-413.

Riesman, D., Glazer, N., and Denny, R. *The Lonely Crowd.* New York: Doubleday, 1950.

Rofsky, M., and others. "Assessing the Level of Actualizing of Psychiatric In-Patients: Validity of the Personal Orientation Dimension." *Educational and Psychological Measurement,* 1977, in press.

Rogers, C. *Client-Centered Therapy.* Boston: Houghton Mifflin, 1951.

Seeman, W., Nidick, S., and Banta, T. "Influence of Transcendental Meditation on a Measure of Self-Actualization." *Journal of Counseling Psychology,* 1972, *19,* 184-187.

Shostrom, E. L. *Personal Orientation Inventory.* San Diego: EdITS, 1963.

Shostrom, E. L. "A Test for the Measurement of Self-Actualization." *Educational and Psychological Measurement,* 1964, *24,* 207-218.

Shostrom, E. L. *Caring Relationship Inventory.* San Diego: EdITS, 1966.

Shostrom, E. L. *Pair Attraction Inventory.* San Diego: EdITS, 1970.

Shostrom, E. L. *Personal Orientation Dimensions.* San Diego: EdITS, 1974.

Shostrom, E. L. *Actualizing Assessment Battery: Interpretation Brochure.* San Diego: EdITS, 1975.

Shostrom, E. L., and Knapp, R. R. "The Relationship of a Measure of Self-Actualization (POI) to a Measure of Pathology (MMPI) and to Therapeutic Growth." *American Journal of Psychotherapy,* 1966, *20,* 193-202.

Shostrom, E. L., Knapp, L., and Knapp, R. R. *Actualizing Therapy: Foundations for a Scientific Ethic.* San Diego: EdITS, 1976a.

Shostrom, E. L., Knapp, R. R., and Knapp, L. "Validation of the Personal Orientation Dimensions: An Inventory for the Dimensions of Actualizing." *Educational and Psychological Measurement,* 1976b, *36,* 491-494.

Shostrom, F. L. "A Validity Study of Shostrom's Pair Attraction Inventory." Unpublished master's thesis, United States International University, 1973.

Shostrom, F. L., and Knapp, R. R. "Relationship Between Clinical Ratings and Inventory Measures of Intrapersonal Styles: Validity of the Pair Attraction Inventory." *Educational and Psychological Measurement,* 1977, *37,* 541-543.

Silverstein, A. B., and Fisher, G. "Cluster Analysis of Personal Orientation Inventory Items in a Prison Sample." *Multivariate Behavioral Research,* 1974, *9,* 325-330.

Treppa, J. A., and Fricke, L. "Effects of a Marathon Group Experience." *Journal of Counseling Psychology,* 1972, *19,* 466-467.

Walton, D. R. "Effects of Personal Growth Groups on Self-Actualization and Creative Personality." *Journal of College Student Personnel,* 1973, *14,* 490-494.

Winch, R. F. *Mate Selection.* New York: Harper & Row, 1958.
Young, E. R., and Jacobson, L. I. "Effects of Time-Extended Marathon Group Experiences on Personality Characteristics." *Journal of Counseling Psychology,* 1970, *17,* 247-251.
Zimmerman, S. F., Smith, K. H., and Pedersen, D. M. "The Effect of Anticonformity Appeals on Conformity Behavior." *Journal of Social Psychology,* 1970, *81,* 93-103.

IV

Environmental Dispositions: Concepts and Measures

GEORGE E. McKECHNIE

This chapter focuses on issues and problems involved in extending the traditional personality assessment paradigm to a new field of psychological research, environmental psychology, which is the study of man-environment relationships. Specifically of concern here are *environmental dispositions,* that is, individual differences in personality as it functions in relation to the everyday physical environment (Craik, 1970, 1976).

In the first section of this chapter, the origins of the notion of environmental dispositions are identified and related to developments in traditional areas of personality theory and research. In the second section, tentative boundaries for this new domain are offered, along with a survey of recent research on environmental dispositions. Then, two new standardized instruments resulting from the application of assessment technology to environmental psychology are presented. The development of the Environmental Response Inventory (ERI) (McKechnic, 1974a) is described in the third section. The fourth section analyzes the psychological structure of recreation and leisure phenomena as measured by the Leisure Activities Blank (LAB) (McKechnie, 1975). In the fifth section, research applications of the ERI and LAB are summarized, and comments are offered on the future directions of environmental dispositions research.

A New Domain for Personality Research

Personality theory and assessment traditionally have focused on two domains of the psychological functioning of the individual: intrapsychic and interpersonal (Searles, 1960; Craik, 1969). The former domain is concerned with how the person relates to his own impulses and inner life and includes such traits as self-acceptance, self-control, and self-punishment. The interpersonal, or social, domain refers to how the individual relates to other persons in his social environment and involves such traits as dominance, responsibility, and friendliness. Recent advances in the discipline of environmental psychology (Craik, 1973; Proshansky, Ittelson, and Rivlin, 1970) underscore the potential theoretical importance and applied utility of a third domain for personal research, which is concerned with how a person relates to the physical aspects of his everyday environment. It is this domain to which the term *environmental dispositions* refers.

Historically, it was the psychoanalytic theorists—mainly Freud, Jung, and Adler—who bore and nurtured the notions of intrapsychic psychology. To be sure, their theories recognized the interpersonal aspects of life and their relevance to intrapsychic functioning. The *person* in early psychoanalytic theory was no solipsist. One may indeed read social and even environmental factors into Freud's personality theory, yet little may be gleaned from his work that is directly relevant to the description and analysis of individual differences in the ways the individual relates to other persons and to objects in his life space. Although Freud's man related to parents, then siblings, and ultimately to family surrogates, these interpersonal relationships were but pale shadows of the theories of interpersonal functioning that would subsequently be developed.

The roots of interpersonal psychology, though implicit in

and traceable to the writings of the early psychoanalysts, are divergent and may be unearthed in several fields. Ego psychology, with its emphasis on the conscious, executive functions of the ego (in its quest to balance the impulses of the id and the demands of the superego with the requirements of the social environment), provided a clear extension of psychoanalytic theory to contemporary interpersonal psychology. Other historical branches are found in the work of the social psychoanalysts (Fromm, Horney, Klein, and Sullivan) and in the field theory of Lewin (1935) and the need-press conception of Murray (1938). These theorists inextricably tie the person to the social milieu within which he lives and through which he defines his humanity.

It was not until the second half of the century, however, that the functioning of personality in relation to the everyday *physical* environment began to attract attention in its own right. Balint (1955) in Britain and Searles (1960) in the United States provided important conceptualizations. Balint contributed vivid case histories of two environmental personality types, the *philobat* (who regards the environment as a friendly expanse) and the *ocnophil* (who fears the environment's horrid empty spaces). Searles, working also from the psychoanalytic perspective, developmentally traced the significance of the nonhuman environment in both normals and schizophrenics. In France, Bachelard (1964) explored the phenomenology of space in his book *The Poetics of Space*. These were the beginnings of an interest in the personality of man as it relates to the physical aspects of everyday life.

Although it encapsulates what are necessarily complex and multidetermined movements in the history of psychology, the foregoing sketch traces a clearly discernible trend in personality from an interest in intrapsychic to interpersonal to environmental phenomena. In one sense, this conceptual growth has been achieved merely by redefining personality to refer to an increasingly broad and encompassing domain—the composite environment in which the person lives and functions. (In the language of field theory, this trend may be represented as an increased differentiation of the life space.) To the extent that

man is a social animal, no disposition can be thought of as purely intrapsychic. Nor, because of the implicitly social nature of
the man-made environment, can any environmental disposition
be devoid of interpersonal meaning. Under this interpretation,
intrapsychic dimensions are—in the adult personality at least—
inextricably intertwined with interpersonal functioning. Likewise is interpersonal psychology an important component of
man-environment relationships. Backpackers seek the wilderness
not only to experience nature but also to get away from people!
Nevertheless, it is conceptually useful to delineate as precisely
as possible these three domains of personality functioning.
Craik's (1972a) conceptual framework for human psychology
helps us to do so.

This framework distinguishes three major systems: the
personality system, the *social system,* and the *environmental
system.* The personality system consists of "the skills, cognitive
capacities, values, dispositions, and psychodynamics of the individual agent" (Craik, 1972a, p. 72). The social system refers to
"the institutional structures, regulatory principles, technological
capabilities, and adjustment mechanisms of society" (p. 73).
The environmental system consists of "the dynamic linked network of physical, chemical, and biological subsystems" (p. 74).

The personality system may be subdivided into three
component parts. The first component is self-reflective, referring to how the person deals with his own personality structure
and dynamics. Although it is true (for all but the most genetic
of personality theorists) that personality differentiation results
from interaction of the person with the social and environmental systems, these interactions are not of interest in themselves at this level of analysis, but only in the sense and to the
extent that they influence the structuring of intrapsychic aspects of the personality system. The second and third components refer to the personality system as it reflects and is differentiated by the social and environmental systems,
respectively.

In everyday life, interactions between the various systems
may occur quite rapidly in reciprocal and multifaceted ways,
making conceptual distinctions of this sort rather difficult to

sustain. Nevertheless, in the context of discovery (Reichenbach, 1938) such distinctions serve a useful dialectic function.

Personality in the Everyday Physical Environment

The everyday physical environment provides a myriad of behavioral options for man. Many of these alternatives have both significant psychological implications for the person and ecological implications for the environment in which he or she behaves. Some activities bring physical security to the actor; others give him aesthetic pleasure. Many environmental behaviors pollute the environment and consume resources; others are self-consciously directed toward conservation. Two contexts of environmental behavior—recreation and migration—illustrate the diverse implications of environmental dispositions.

Within a given class of recreational activity—camping or boating, for example—various forms of environmental behavior are possible. For some vacationers, proper camping involves a heavy backpack, spartan meals and bed, and long distances on foot. For others, the camping ritual requires a mobile home packed with beer and a TV set and parked at the nearest vacant lot. Boaters, too, differ in their environmental life-styles. Some enjoy canoeing, others rowing; some people sail, still others prefer yachting. Some activities involve minimum consumption of resources, whereas others are extravagant. Some allow maximum interaction with and appreciation of the natural environment, yet others effectively insulate man from the primitive forces of the earth.

A second example of the vast range of individual differences in relating to the environment is that of geographic migration and the large number of environment-related decisions involved (Craik, 1972b). To what part of the country docs the person migrate and for what reasons? Does he choose to buy a home or rent one? Perhaps he selects a condominium or townhouse rather than a flat or split-level home. Does he prefer the inner city or a suburban location? Does he locate within walking distance to work, or will he commute by auto or public transportation? Is he more concerned with the conveniences of the kitchen or the quietness of the neighborhood? Does he require a shop for tinkering or a library for study? These are some of the individual differences to which the term *environmental dispositions* refers.

By this point, the reader may have begun to question whether any of the above individual differences reflect specifically environmental dispositions rather than interpersonal or intrapsychic ones. Because of the newness of the concept and the present lack of cumulative research, it is not yet known to what extent environmental dispositions possess explanatory and predictive power that goes beyond that tapped by the more traditional areas of personality. For some individuals the environmental component of personality is relatively undeveloped and thus lacks salience. Yet because of their broad and all-encompassing focus, environmental dispositions may in the long run demonstrate great explanatory and predictive powers.

At stake here are two technical aspects of validation, competitive and incremental validity. How well do environmental-personality variables compare with more traditional measures in accounting for interesting environment-related behaviors? Also, to what extent do measures of environmental dispositions add to the data provided by traditional personality approaches? These are empirical questions for which adequate data are not yet available: *Ergo caveat lector.*

Indeed, a number of traditional measures of personality do appear to relate to everyday environmental behaviors. These have recently been reviewed by Craik (1969). Included among these are several measures of stimulus (or arousal) seeking behavior (Zuckerman, Kolin, Price, and Zoob, 1964; Penny and Reinehr, 1966; Garlington and Shimota, 1964; Howard, 1961). Conceptual analyses of this research area have been reported recently by Zuckerman (1971) and Mehrabian and Russell (1973). Closely related is the need-change scale of the Adjective Check List (Gough and Heilbrun, 1965). Also of importance are the dichotomous scales of the Myers-Briggs Type Indicator (Myers, 1962), based on Jung's theory of types: extraversion/introversion, sensation/intuition, thinking/feeling, and judging/perceiving.

Other recent research has focused on the notion of environmental dispositions and has developed concepts (and in some cases measurement scales) for relating these variables to behavioral environmental criteria. Kluckhohn and Strodtbeck (1961), in their book *Variations in Value Orientations,* identified three distinct environmental value orientations among American Indian tribes: man over nature, man in harmony with nature, and man subject to nature. Sonnenfeld (1969) claims that there are four basic environmental dispositions: sensitivity to the environment, mobility in the environment, control over the environment, and risk taking in the environment. Little (1973) has developed the Person-Orientation and Thing-Orientation scales to measure two fundamental dimensions of personality: the extent to which the individual relates to the social and physical environments, respectively. Marshall (1969) developed a ninety-three-item Privacy Preference Scale. Six components of the disposition to privacy were uncovered by factor analysis: neighboring, visual and auditory seclusion, solitude, intimacy, anonymity, and self-disclosure. A methodologically similar study by Hendee, Catton, Marlow, and Brockman (1968) identified seven components of the "wildernism" disposition: spartanism, antiartifactualism (for example, a dislike of plumbing in campsites), primevalism (enjoyment of pure wilderness features, such as waterfalls), humility, outdoorsmanship, aversion to superfluous symbolic interaction (for example, naturalist talks), and escapism. Mehrabian and Russell (1973) have recently reestablished the arousal-seeking dimension within the realm of environmental dispositions. They developed a forty-item scale to measure arousal-seeking tendency. When responses to these items were factor analyzed, five factors emerged: arousal from change, arousal from unusual stimuli, arousal from risk, arousal from sensuality, and arousal from new environments. More recently, an entire issue of the journal *Environment and Behavior* was devoted to research on environmental dispositions (see Craik and McKechnie, 1977).

Additional studies of this sort may help to further demarcate the domain of environmental dispositions. The remainder of this chapter describes two systematic attempts to survey its dimensions and boundaries. First, details of the development of the Environmental Response Inventory are presented; then similar information is provided for the Leisure Activities Blank. Finally, research examples from areas in which these two instruments have been (or may be) used are outlined, concluding with comments on the potential utility of environmental disposition measures for research in traditional areas of human psychology.

Development of the Environmental Response Inventory

The Environmental Response Inventory (ERI) is a broadbandwidth multiscale personality inventory (Cronbach and Gleser, 1957) designed to measure an array of environmental dispositions. Development and refinement of the ERI was carried out over a period of about five years and employed a complex, multimethod test-construction sequence. The following steps were involved: identification of a general set of environmental themes, creation of a general item pool to tap these themes in their various facets, explanatory factor analysis of subject responses to that pool of items, identification and evaluation of the resulting scales, revision of the item pool to tap more adequately the empirically derived dimensions, multijudge rational assignment of the new items to the dimensions, statistical iteration of the scales to maximize item scale intercorrelations, shortening of the resulting scales, and a confirmatory factor analysis of the reduced item pool.

Developers of comprehensive multiscale personality inventories measuring the traditional domains of intrapsychic and interpersonal dispositions have determined what dimensions to measure (Goldberg, 1972) by appealing to explicit classificatory theories—such as those of Kraepelin, Spranger, Jung, or Murray —or to some implicit linguistic (Cattell, 1957) or cross-cultural (Gough, 1957) trait-selection strategy. These options were not available in the case of the ERI because previous psychological writing had not provided an adequate set of concepts for describing man-environment interactions. Thus it was necessary to develop a search strategy that promised to yield a reasonably representative set of themes and from which a stable set of underlying factors could be extracted. This search made use of the cumulative insight of many generations and cultures by identifying man-environment themes relative to personality contained in the scientific, cultural, and philosophical writings of the past.

A preliminary set of man-environment themes was generated for the ERI using this critical humanistic survey method. Surveyed literature included the following: *Traces on the Rhodian Shore* (Glacken, 1967), *The Machine in the Garden* (Marx, 1964), *The Intellectual Versus the City* (White and White, 1962), *Man on Earth* (Charter, 1962), *The Human Habitat* (Huntington, 1928), *The Poetics of Space* (Bachelard, 1964), *The Nonhuman Environment* (Searles, 1960), *Personal Space* (Sommer, 1969), *Variations in Value Orientation* (Kluckhohn and Strodtbeck, 1961), "Environmental Psychology" (Craik, 1970), "America's Changing Environment" (Fall 1967 issue of *Daedalus*), "Man's Response to the Physical Environment" (October 1966 issue of *Journal of Social Issues*), and sundry miscellaneous articles and chapters, including those by Zuckerman and others (1964) and Balint (1955). On the basis of these readings, the following themes were selected: conservation, pastoral ideals, urban life, rural life, science and technology, stimulus preferences and aversions, cultural life, recreation and leisure activities, geographic preferences, architectural preferences, environmental memories, and ecological knowledge. From these themes, 218 personality test items were generated, named the Environmental Reaction Survey, to which respondents answered true or false.

This preliminary version of the ERI was administered to 814 subjects. Their responses were then intercorrelated and factor analyzed (described in McKechnie, 1969). Six factors were found, corresponding approximately to the first six scales of the final version of the ERI, all nine of which are described in Table 1. Two of these dimensions, Environmental Adaptation and Stimulus Seeking, appear to be closely related to psychological concepts previously reported in the general psychological literature: man over nature (Kluckhohn and Strodtbeck, 1961) and sensation seeking (Zuckerman and others, 1964). The remaining

Table 1. ERI Scales and Descriptions.

Scale	Major Themes	Sample Items
PA (Pastoralism)	opposition to land development; concern about population growth; preservation of natural resources, including open space; acceptance of natural forces as shapers of human life; sensitivity to pure environmental experiences; self-sufficiency in the natural environment	"Our natural forests should be preserved in their natural state, with roads and buildings prohibited." "Birth control practices should be accepted by everyone." "Natural resources must be preserved, even if people must do without." "It is good for man to submit to the forces of nature." "The idea of walking into the forest and 'living off the land' for a week appeal to me."
UR (Urbanism)	enjoyment of high density living; appreciation of unusual and varied stimulus patterns of the city; interest in cultural life; enjoyment of interpersonal richness and diversity	"I would enjoy riding in a crowded subway." "I like the variety of stimulation one finds in the city." "The cultural life of a big city is very important to me." "Cities bring together interesting people."
EA (Environmental Adaptation)	modification of the environment to satisfy needs and desires and to provide comfort and leisure; opposition to governmental control over private land use; preference for highly designed or adapted environments; use of technology to solve environmental problems; preference for stylized environmental details	"A person has a right to modify the environment to suit his needs." "There should [not] be a law against anyone owning more than a thousand acres of land." "I like to go to shopping centers where everything is in one place." "Making rain by artificially 'seeding' clouds is a great technological advance." "I like crystal chandeliers."
SS (Stimulus Seeking)	interest in travel and exploration of unusual places; enjoyment of complex and intense physical sensations; breadth of interests	"I would enjoy traveling around the world on a sailing ship." "I like to ride on roller coasters." "I like experimental art." "I would enjoy driving a racing car." "Alleys are interesting places to explore."

Table 1 (Continued)

Scale	Major Themes	Sample Items
ET (Environmental Trust)	general environmental openness, responsiveness, and trust; competence in finding one's way about the environment vs. fear of potentially dangerous environments; security of home; fear of being alone and unprotected	"Sometimes I'm afraid of too much stimulation—from sounds, colors, odors, etc."[a] "I shudder at the thought of finding a spider in my bed."[a] "I feel most secure when I am working around the house."[a] "I'd be afraid to live in a place where there were no people nearby."[a] "I often have trouble finding my way around a new area."[a]
AN (Antiquarianism)	enjoyment of antiques and historical places; preference for traditional vs. modern design; aesthetic sensitivity to man-made environments and to landscape; appreciation of cultural artifacts of earlier eras; tendency to collect objects for their emotional significance	"Modern buildings are seldom as attractive as older ones." "I enjoy browsing in antique shops." "I am quite sensitive to the 'character' of a building." "It would be fun to own some old-fashioned costumes." "I enjoy collecting things that most people would consider junk."
NP (Need for Privacy)	need for physical isolation from stimuli; enjoyment of solitude; dislike of neighboring behavior; need for freedom from distraction	"There are often times when I need complete silence." "I am happiest when I am alone." "I get annoyed when people drop by without warning." "I am easily distracted by people moving about."
MO (Mechanical Orientation)	interest in mechanics in its various forms; enjoyment in working with one's hands; interest in technological processes and basic principles of science; appreciation of the functional properties of objects	"I enjoy tinkering with mechanical things." "I would enjoy the work of an architect." "I usually save spare nuts and bolts." "I would like to work with computers." "I like things that have precision parts."
CO (Communality)	A validity scale tapping honest, attentive, and careful test-taking attitude; response	"I like to visit historic places." "As a child, I was taught respect for all living

(continued on next page)

Table 1 (Continued)

Scale	Major Themes	Sample Items
	to items in statistically modal manner.	things." "I have vivid memories of where I lived as a child." "Traveling isn't really worth the effort."[a] "I seldom pay attention to what I eat."[a]

[a]An answer of false was a positive answer in scoring.

Source: Adapted from the *Manual for the Environmental Response Inventory.* Copyright 1974 by Consulting Psychologists Press. Used by permission.

four dimensions contain themes tapped in previous research but represent essentially new formulations.

On the basis of these findings, the ERI item pool was revised, reworked, and expanded to 330 items in an effort to tap more adequately the dimensions found empirically in the initial item pool. Also included in the expanded item pool were items written to measure two dimensions that were selected for inclusion in the final version of the test but had not been represented in the initial item pool, Need for Privacy and Mechanical Orientation, in recognition of the work of Marshall (1969) and Little (1973), respectively, on these two topics. Finally, a 5-point response format was adopted: 5 = strongly agree; 4 = agree; 3 = neutral or don't know; 2 = disagree; 1 = strongly disagree.

The 330-item version of the ERI was then administered to a new sample of 1,334 respondents, of whom 939 were undergraduate students at ten universities in the United States and Canada, 255 were a representative adult sample of Marin County, California, residents, and the remaining 140 were members of environmental interest groups. An iterative rational scaling procedure was then employed as follows: A panel of nine judges independently assigned each of the 330 ERI items to one of the eight environmental dispositions concepts. On the basis of these nominations, a tentative rational scaling of the ERI was made, leaving unassigned those items for which agreement was low. The 1,334 respondents were then scored on each scale, and item-scale correlations computed for the matrix of eight scales by 330 items. This matrix was then examined to identify any item that correlated higher with a scale to which it was not assigned than with the scale to which it was. In these cases, the item was reassigned to the scale with which it correlated the highest, and the subject sample rescored accordingly. A new Scale X Item matrix was computed and inspected for additional errant items, which were again reassigned. This iterative process was continued through four complete cycles, at which point no further reassignments were necessary. The scales resulting from this procedure ranged in length from twenty-one to fifty-seven items.

In an effort to reduce the length of the scales, items were eliminated that had extreme endorsement rates, low variance, or content that overlapped with other items. As a result, scales were pruned to nineteen to twenty-two items each. When these brief scales were compared with their respective long versions, a high degree of congruence was found: The correlations ranged from 0.93 to 0.99. Descriptions of the major themes tapped by the final versions of the ERI scales are given in Table 1.

A validity scale (Communality) was constructed by selecting those items having extreme endorsement rates and scoring them in the modal response direction. A scale having a negatively skewed frequency distribution was thus constructed. Random response to these items yields a score on Communality that is three standard deviations below the mean. This scale thus may identify a possibly invalid protocol.

The final version of the ERI contains 184 items, 165 of which comprise the eight shortened dispositional scales. Because of the complex sequence by which the final item pool and scales evolved, a confirmatory factor analysis was performed (on 150 of the 165 items, the computer program limit) to determine if the original factor structure had been preserved and if the Need for Privacy and Mechanical Orientation concepts, selected a priori, would emerge as independent factors. The results of this analysis, presented in detail in McKechnie (1972), indicate that the research goals had largely been achieved. The items for the rational scales of Pastoralism and Antiquarianism combined in the factor analysis to yield a derivative dimension, tentatively identified as Environmental Nostalgia. This factor was found to correlate 0.72 with Pastoralism and 0.88 with Antiquarianism. Each of the remaining six rational scales, however, was virtually identical to its factor counterpart, the correlations ranging from 0.94 to 0.99.

Validation of the ERI scales was undertaken in two related studies. In the first, the environmental life-styles of Marin County, California, residents were studied (McKechnie, 1972). The ERI scales were correlated with environmentally relevant demographic variables, environmental attitudes, and recreation patterns (using the Leisure Activities Blank described below). In the second study (McKechnie, 1975), personality correlates of ERI scales were identified in a subsample of fifty subjects (twenty-five males, twenty-five females) selected from the life-style study as examples of various leisure-activity types. Because of the small sample size in the second study relative to the total N, a comparison was made of the variances of the ERI variables for the subsample with those for the entire sample. This comparison revealed only slight, nonsignificant differences in means and variances, indicating that little restriction of range on the ERI variables had occurred as a result of this selection method.

These data corroborate the interpretations made earlier on the basis of the manifest content of the scale items and also suggest important psychological implications of the scales. The following summary for the Urbanism scale is illustrative.

People who score high on Urbanism: (1) tend to participate in intellectual activities like visiting museums, playing bridge, attending plays and lectures, and traveling abroad, but tend not to engage in such outdoor recreation as playing baseball, fresh water fishing, or horseshoes; (2) in response to environmental attitude statements, tend to be concerned about an adequate housing supply and urban transit, but are unconcerned about local population density; (3) tend to be highly educated and hold high-status, high-income jobs; and (4) on the Strong Vocational Interest Blank, tend to score high on the Supervisory/Administrative scales (for example, personnel director or school superintendent) and low on the Mechanical/Technical scales (for example, dentist, carpenter, or printer). Also, (5) assessment staff Q-sort descriptions of high scorers on Urbanism emphasize their cognitive and verbal abilities, as does a positive correlation of the scale with the California Psychological Inventory (CPI) Intellectual Efficiency. For fuller details on the validity of the ERI scales, the reader is referred to the *Manual* (McKechnie, 1974a).

Reliability data for the ERI are also given in the *Manual*. Test-retest reliabilities range from 0.90 to 0.81 for the eight substantive scales; split-half reliabilities range from 0.74 to 0.87 in one study and 0.71 to 0.86 in another.

In its present form the 184 items of the ERI require an administration time of twenty-five to thirty minutes for college students, and up to forty minutes among unselected adults. The inventory is appropriate for persons fifteen years of age and older, of average or higher than average intelligence.

The Psychology of Recreation and Leisure

In the U.S. and other technologically advanced societies, the luxury of ample time to do what one wants to do, unconstrained by job, chores, or other nondiscretionary obligations, has become a way of life. Although social scientists of various persuasions now raise serious doubts about our psychological preparedness for the increasing amounts of leisure provided by industrialization (Burch, 1971; Clawson, 1966; Wolf, 1970; Martin, 1969; Hartlage, 1969) and forecast social crises resulting from our lack of knowledge about the psychology of leisure, psychologists have been somewhat reluctant to study leisure behavior and to help meet this social need (McKechnie, 1974c). Too often, this topic has been approached from the perspective of remedying the unfortunate consequences of mismanaged leisure (such as drug use, alcoholism, and juvenile delinquency), rather than of understanding leisure behavior as a positive psychological phenomenon worthy of scientific analysis in its own right.

From the perspective of environmental dispositions, leisure behavior is of considerable theoretical interest for a number of reasons. It is an abundant, naturally occurring (rather than experimentally induced) behavior that is relatively un-restrained by life circumstances. Because of this lack of con-straint, enormous individual differences exist in the ways people use leisure time. Furthermore, the regularity and distinctiveness of different sorts of leisure activity allow the psychologist to infer the personal implications of the behavior (such as the use of cognitive processes, interpersonal skills, and sensorimotor abilities) and the environmental implications (for example, pol-lution, conservation, appreciation, and avoidance) as well. Indeed, the individual's behavior in unstructured periods of leisure time is a continuing projective test that displays many of the themes likely to be important in environmental dispositions.

Two aspects of the psychology of leisure are important to environmental dispositions: identifying the main types of lei-sure activity patterns and determining the personality correlates of participation in these patterns. Although it is possible—as in the case of dispositional measurement—to construct recreation categories rationally (for example, passive or active pastimes, games, and water sports), an empirical strategy is more likely to sample the domain of leisure activities representatively. The Leisure Activities Blank was developed with the above two goals in mind.

The LAB consists of a list of 120 common leisure activi-ties, which evolved from a list developed by the author and sub-sequently modified on the basis of suggestions by colleagues at the Institute of Personality Assessment and Research. For each activity, the respondent indicates the extent of past participa-tion (1 = never; 2 = once or a few times; 3 = once regularly, but now not regularly; 4 = regular current participation) and future intentions (1 = don't expect to do it; 2 = uncertain; 3 = expect to do it). Due to space limitation, only results of the past por-tion of the LAB ("LAB–past") are presented here.

The subject sample upon which the LAB was developed consisted of 288 adult residents of Marin County, California, selected (using age, sex, and residence location quotas) to be representative of the entire county. Marin County was chosen for study because its distinct geographical boundaries (Pacific Ocean to the west, San Francisco Bay to the south and east, twenty miles of relatively uninhabited farmland to the north) form an ecological niche and because of the recreation-mindedness of its relatively affluent population and its favorable geography and climate. In the author's opinion, the clearest understanding of the psychology of leisure was to be found in a subject population having recreation opportunities unrestricted by climate, geography, or insufficient leisure time or disposable income.

Factor analyses of LAB-past responses (described in detail in McKechnie, 1972) yielded the six scales summarized in Table 2. The first scale, Mechanics, includes a variety of traditionally masculine pastimes and emphasizes mechanical activities. The second scale, Crafts, is the feminine counterpart to Mechanics and includes a number of traditionally female pastimes. The third scale, Intellectual, shows a configuration of urban culture, intellectual interests, and community involvement. The appearance of backpacking, hiking-walking, and conservation-ecology on this dimension is consistent with the findings of other researchers (for example, Hendee, 1969) that wilderness users tend to be highly educated urban residents. The fourth scale, Slow Living, includes both passive (watching movies, social drinking, and sunbathing) and commonplace (reading newspapers and magazines, watching television) pastimes. The fifth scale, Sports, included the neighborhood sports of adolescence. The sixth scale, Glamour Sports, clusters the sporting activities that require special and often expensive equipment and a specific geographic locale (such as mountains, lakes, or the ocean).

A sampling of the various interrelationships of the LAB activities are graphically illustrated in the "SPAN diagram" (Tryon and Bailey, 1970), presented in Figure 1. By plotting psychological similarity in terms of spatial distance on the surface of a sphere, this diagram provides a psychological map of leisure. Activities that are plotted close together are highly intercorrelated and by inference are psychologically similar, whereas those that appear well separated are uncorrelated or even negatively correlated (McKechnie, 1974b). Noteworthy also are the general spatial configurations of the clusters.

Table 2. LAB-Past Scales and Descriptions.

Scale	Representative Activities	Description	
		High Scorers	Low Scorers
ME (Mechanics)	auto repair, billiards, boxing, carpentry, hunting, marksmanship, mechanics, woodworking	ambitious, coarse, confident, extraverted, fickle, hard-headed, masculine, methodical, opportunistic, practical, realistic, robust, self-accepting, shy, sociable	aesthetically responsive, affectionate, appreciative, confused, feminine, introverted, irritable, mannerly, prudish, responsible, trusting, understanding
CR (Crafts)	ceramics, cooking, designing clothes, flower arranging, jewelry making, knitting, needlework, weaving	affectionate, careless, compassionate, defensive, distractible, emotional, fickle, frivolous, flexible, independent-minded, spunky, tolerant	calm, deliberate, dignified, formal, intolerant, logical, mannerly, masculine, persevering, planful, precise, stolid, unemotional
IN (Intellectual)	attending concerts, civic organizations, going to plays, political activities, reading books, visiting museums, writing poetry or stories, conservation organizations	active, assertive, dominant, efficient, gloomy, impatient, intellectual, intelligent, interests wide, selfish, sophisticated, unrealistic	cautious, commonplace, conservative, easygoing, friendly, jolly, leisurely, mild, opportunistic, patient, quiet, retiring, simple
SL (Slow Living)	gardening, going to movies, social drinking, sunbathing, talking on telephone, visiting friends, window shopping, writing letters	attractive, business minded, efficient, energetic, extrapunitive, healthy, independent, persevering, planful, self-accepting, serious, severe, well-adjusted	awkward, contented, dull, generous, intrapunitive, jolly, slipshod, self-denying, self-deprecating, self-pitying, spineless, undeserving
SP (Sports)	badminton, baseball, basketball, football, jogging, squash, table tennis, volleyball	aggressive, ambitious, confident, dominant, forceful, having initiative, masculine, outgoing, persevering, restless, sociable, spontaneous	artistic, confused, despondent, fearful, feminine, fussy, ingenious, introverted, self-pitying, slow, worrying
GS (Glamour Sports)	archery, canoeing, horseback riding, motorboating, motorcycling, mountain climbing, sailing, skiing, tennis	attractive, daring, efficient, flexible, healthy, highbrow, intelligent, loyal, optimistic, psychologically minded, resilient, resourceful, spontaneous, tolerant	bitter, blustery, despondent, fearful, foolish, gloomy, preoccupied, self-denying, unexcitable, weak, withdrawn

Source: Adapted from the *Manual for the Leisure Activities Blank.* Copyright 1975 by Consulting Psychologists Press. Used by permission.

Mechanics forms a tight cluster relative to Slow Living, for example, whereas the Crafts pastimes are dispersed almost to the point of forming a bridge between the two other clusters. Marginal activities suspended between two clusters are interpretable as psychologically intermediate. Observe also the psychological contours that exist within a cluster. The "slow living" end of the Crafts cluster contains the "feminine" crafts of flower arranging and home decorating, whereas the "mechanics" region of the same cluster contains the "masculine" crafts of sculpture and leatherwork.

The psychological aspects of participation in these leisure activities was explored by using the same subject samples involved in the validation of the ERI as described above. Personality characteristics of high and low scorers on the six LAB scales, based upon Adjective Check List assessment staff descriptions, are given in Table 2. Notice that descriptions of high scorers are similar for several scales, as are those for low scorers. These similarities seem to reflect a general activity syndrome (Smith, 1964) associated with leisure behavior. Clinically speaking, persons who are depressed or otherwise psychologically impaired tend to have few leisure interests, and thus score low on all of the LAB scales.

On the basis of these data, preliminary interpretations of the LAB scales have been prepared and are given below. These musings are speculative, and should be regarded as tentative. Because of their underlying similarities, Mechanics and Crafts have been considered together.

As recreation modes, Mechanics and Crafts may play comparable roles in the personal functioning of sex-appropriate participants. Several features of these patterns are striking: (1) they are generally sex-exclusive; (2) they involve specific interaction with the nonsocial world and often culminate in the production of goods, trophies, or other tangible rewards; (3) they allow for "parallel play" activity, in which the participant is sociable without direct interpersonal involvement; and (4) they require the learning of sensorimotor skills. Heavy involvement in Crafts or Mechanics activities may indicate a repudiation of interpersonal involvement. The person who habitually retires to

Figure 1. Mechanics, Slow Living, and Crafts Clusters.

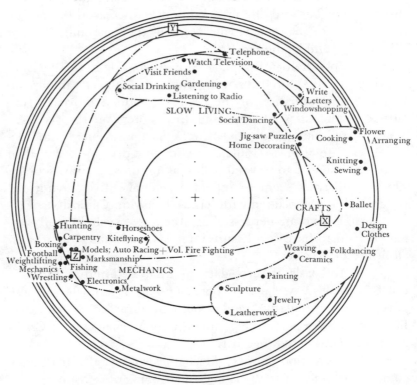

Note: This is one of five SPAN diagrams needed for a statistically exhaustive graphic representation of the data matrix.

shop or sewing room to attend an important project is opting out of interpersonal family involvement or other possibly threatening circumstances by displacing onto the inanimate world emotional energy that for one reason or another cannot be given to another human being. In effect, the very high scorer on Crafts or Mechanics has chosen to specialize in objects rather than people (Little, 1973). For persons whose involvement reaches moderate levels, these activities offer opportunities for creativity that they feel may be missing elsewhere in their lives. These pastimes were typically learned early in life and are continued later in life without critical reflection.

High scores on the Intellectual scale imply a cathexis of matters of the mind. In work or play, such a person's approach to life is an analytic one. Facts and experience are sought, either for their own sake or to provide a basis for political, social, or other symbolic (rather than physical) action. Intellectual activity has consequences beyond self-entertainment. The motivation underlying action may be political, aesthetic, or the communication of human experience. Sometimes it may merely be stimulation of the mind for its own sake (as with chess). The unit of leisure for the intellectual cluster is typically the meeting of an organization, the performance of a play or concert, or the practice of a skill (playing a musical instrument, darkroom technique, or writing poetry). These activities have in common a concern with and reflection upon man as a psychological entity. They are seldom competitive (chess is an exception), can be enjoyed alone or with others, and in most sectors of society both men and women participate, although among lower-class groups some may be regarded as unmanly or unwomanly.

People who lead full, active, perhaps hectic lives, who are heavily involved in their career or in family raising, occasionally need a change of pace, a chance to slow down and relax. This is what Slow Living is all about. For these people, the slowly paced activities of watching television, window shopping, or talking to friends on the telephone are a refreshing respite and a well-earned reward. Persons scoring high on this cluster are planful, efficient, energetic individuals who work hard and play easy. They indulge themselves in the simple but satisfying everyday pleasures that allow for relaxation and an expression of autonomy.

Sports activities are the outdoor recreation energy consumers. They tend to be highly action oriented, allow for competition (either with oneself or against others), and often involve situations which offer much stimulation for the senses. A clean-cut youthfulness and vigor pervades the activities constituting the Sports cluster. The natural unit for the pastimes is the "game" or "match," and the typical motivation is to compete and win (or prevail). The underlying themes are achievement, dominance, and sensuous pleasure in using one's body at its optimal level of performance.

The Glamour Sports cluster includes outings or events from which the participant derives status and recognition. Each involves the person "making the scene." The activities are usually prestigious and of the sort likely to be featured in vacation advertisements. They usually require specialized and expensive equipment and consequently have a socioeconomic status component. They constitute what the average citizen considers to be "the good life."*

Validity data for the scales are provided in the LAB manual (McKechnie, 1975). They are based on the same set of variables available for the ERI validation and thus tend to focus on the psychological implications of the scales (see above) rather than the certification of participation or interest in a given recreational activity or cluster per se. The following summary for the Glamour Sports scale is illustrative.

People who score high on Glamour Sports tend: (1) on the ERI scales, to express an interest in interacting with the environment (that is, Pastoralism, Stimulus Seeking, and Environmental Trust scales); (2) to show social ascendancy, intellectual ability, and psychological resourcefulness on the CPI; and (3) to be intuitive, as measured by the Myers-Briggs Type Indicator. For details on the personality correlates of the LAB scales, the reader is referred to the *Manual* (McKechnie, 1975).

---

*These interpretive summaries are adapted from the *Manual for the Leisure Activities Blank*. Used by permission.

Reliability data for the LAB are also provided in the *Manual* (McKechnie, 1975). Test-retest reliabilities were found to range from 0.71 to 0.92 for the six substantive LAB-past scales and from 0.63 to 0.93 for the eight LAB-future scales. Corresponding split-half reliabilities ranged from 0.81 to 0.93 and from 0.76 to 0.94, respectively.

In its present form, the LAB can be completed by most subjects in under twenty minutes. It has been used with subjects as young as fifteen years of age, of average or greater intelligence. Because of the unpsychological nature of the items and response format, the LAB may be of special value in situations where standard personality tests provide material that is too reactive or too subject to dissimulation.

Applications of the Environmental Dispositions Paradigm

Although both the ERI and LAB may be employed as "subtle" measures of personality to be employed in traditional areas of psychological research, to date the two instruments have found application largely in two new fields. The LAB is now being employed in a number of ongoing studies of the therapeutic recreation counseling process, a new and rapidly growing health specialty (McKechnie, 1974b). Because most of this research is still in progress, it is not possible to report findings here. The interested reader is referred to the *Manual for the Leisure Activities Blank* (McKechnie, 1975) and the *Therapeutic Recreation Journal* (for example, McKechnie, 1974b) for further information.

The ERI, in contrast, has been employed in diverse areas of the interdisciplinary field of man-environment relations and is likely to be used in several others. These include migration, family planning, environmental planning, client assessment in architecture, resolution of conflict among environmental interest groups, recreation, environmental perception and cognition, and environmental attitudes.

Migration. Human migration has taken on an increasingly discretionary quality in recent years. As migrants have become motivated more by internally defined motivation rather than the external forces of ecology or economy, social scientists have begun to look beyond demographic variables to personality constructs in explaining the psychological dimensions of migration (Gough, 1972b). Kegel-Flom (1976) administered the ERI along with several other psychological tests to fifty-nine graduates of the School of Optometry at the University of California, Berkeley, twenty-seven of whom had set up practice in an urban area and thirty-two in a rural area (see Table 3). The urban optometrist group scored significantly higher on the Urbanism scale of the ERI than did the rural optometrist group ($t = 2.93$; $p > 0.01$). On the remaining ERI scales, the two groups were not found to be significantly different, thus demonstrating good discriminant validity for the scales as a set (Campbell and Fiske, 1959.)

Table 3. Scores on ERI Urbanism Scale of Optometrists from Different Locations in Three Geographic Regions.

Geographic Region	Rural			Suburban			Urban			Inner City		
	N	$\overline{X}$	SD	N	$\overline{X}$	SD	N	$\overline{X}$	SD	N	$\overline{X}$	SD
West	59	52.3	9.6	12	54.8	17.6	18	63.8	11.7	6	67.8	11.5
Midwest	47	52.8	8.1	15	57.7	7.2	19	63.5	10.8	9	55.7	4.7
South	39	53.9	9.8	9	54.7	10.3	16	60.7	9.4	14	63.5	10.1

Note: These data were obtained on Health Professions Special Project Grant #5D08PR0237-02, awarded to the School of Optometry, University of California, Berkeley, California 94720. The author wishes to thank Penelope Kegel-Flom for permission to report these data here.

In subsequent investigations, the Urbanism scale continued to differentiate the optometrists by the location of their practice (Kegel-Flom, 1976). These findings replicate for three different geographic locations: the West (California, Washington, and Oregon), the Midwest (Illinois and Indiana), and the South (Alabama, Arkansas, Louisiana, Mississippi, and Tennessee). Scores on Urbanism increase with increasing urbanness of location for all three geographic regions with the single exception of the midwestern inner city group.

Family Planning. Because of the failure of several classic attempts to relate pronatalist attitudes to personality variables (Fawcett, 1970), psychologists have largely ignored the potential contributions of personality assessment measures to the understanding of fertility patterns. In previous studies, pronatalist values have been shown to relate to social custom, economic necessity (in old age), or religious teachings. But as cultural values become more modern and secular (Gough, 1976), such factors as ecological concerns about overpopulation, the psychological importance of privacy, interests in new life-styles, and attitudes toward various contraceptive methods undoubtedly become prominent. Environmental disposition measures tap these sources of variance. Gough's (1972a) concept of modernity promises to be a key moderator variable in this research area: Environmental dispositions may be related to individual differences in childbearing patterns only for persons who are modern (rather than traditional) in their personal outlook. An investigation under way by the author (with Joann LeMaistre) seeks to relate ERI measures with choice and successful use of contraceptive methods among women of childbearing age. We hypothesize that such variables as Pastoralism, Environmental Trust, and Need for Privacy will be more significantly related to pronatalist attitudes among persons scoring high on Gough's Modernity scale than among low scorers on this dimension.

Assessment of Architectural Clients. The present-day architect is called upon to design for diverse groups of clients. Often he knows little about their environmental needs and preferences, yet is expected to produce design solutions that take these factors into account. One response to this dilemma, advocacy planning, places the architect in the role of environmental clinician, who interviews and interacts informally with the client in an effort to uncover environmental values and preferences that typically are latent at best. Unfortunately, this approach has been no more successful than the clinical prediction paradigm in personality assessment (Wiggins, 1973). What the architect needs is an actuarially based prediction system.

The ERI and other measures of environmental dispositions would fit well into a research program designed to provide satisfactory housing for persons who have not previously stated their environmental preferences and values or to match designer and client on such personal factors. For example, multiple-regression prediction equations for various housing forms (such as a separate single-family dwelling, cluster development, or an apartment) or particular styles (such as California modern, colonial, or adobe). Also, the ERI could be used as a didactic tool by the architect to help him compensate for differences in environmental values, much like the use of the didactic analyses in clinical training.

Environmental Decision Making. The implicit, extraprofessional values and beliefs of persons in positions of authority often influence their professional decision making. Environmental decision makers are not immune to such influences. Sewell (1971) has reported that sanitation engineers and public health officials having joint jurisdiction over the same environmental problem recommend solution strategies that reveal values implicit in their respective professional socialization: The engineers want to solve problems by building treatment plants and sewer systems, while the public health officials advocate the implementation of health standards and their enforcement through fines and threats of closure. Under such circumstances, it is unclear how the public interest may be best served.

In the context of environmental decision making, two general types of value clashes are of interest: those among collaborating professionals having different areas of expertise and those among environmental special interest groups with conflicting goals.

Several research applications illustrate the use of the ERI for understanding the policy stance of environmental specialists in terms of personality factors. One set of data derives from the development of the ERI itself (McKechnie, 1974a). Four professional groups of potentially overlapping jurisdictions have been disaggregated from the final ERI norming sample (total N = 1,334): graduate students in city and regional planning at the University of California, Berkeley ($N = 34$), undergraduate geography students at the University of Victoria in Canada ($N = 20$), students in a recreation resource class at the University of Massachusetts ($N = 21$), and a group of wilderness recreation researchers associated with the U.S. Department of Agriculture North Central Forest Experiment Station, Ely, Minnesota ($N =$

21). Mean profiles for each of these groups are given in Figure 2. Because it is not possible at present to control for possible geographical (regional) effects on ERI scores, no formal comparisons will be made. Nevertheless, it is not difficult to imagine a decision situation on wilderness management in which geographers, regional planners, experts in recreation resource management, and wilderness recreation researchers fail to reach a consensus. In such a case, heterogeneities in implicit values and beliefs concerning such variables as privacy, the value of cultural artifacts, and carrying capacity might well cause dissent and perhaps even open hostility.

A second use of the ERI in the planning arena focuses upon differences in environmental dispositions that exist *within* a profession. Charns (1973) related ERI scale scores of professional planners and planning students to their policy stance (recorded on a 5-point scale of relative support) on important California environmental issues. Cross-validated multiple regression equations are given in Table 4 for several of these issues (Charns, 1973). For each of several dozen criterion statements, multiple regression equations were computed using the nine ERI scale variables. A double-split cross-validation design was employed. Under other circumstances, these policy issues might be regarded as mere attitudinal items. In the present case, however, they serve as a work sample for the planners. These equations thus demonstrate the potential contribution of ERI disposition measures to the professional decision making of planners.

Clashes among environmental interest groups are of special interest because they typically involve a sampling of the opinions actually operating within a given ecological niche (O'Riordan, 1971). The author recently studied one such niche (McKechnie, 1972). A comparison was made of various environmental interest groups operating in Marin County, California, including members of the Sierra Club ($N = 24$), the county planning department ($N = 12$), and a local rod and gun club ($N = 4$). Although the numbers are too small to allow a definitive analysis of the data, the mean profile differences given in Figure 3 are striking. The rod and gun club members seem noticeably differ-

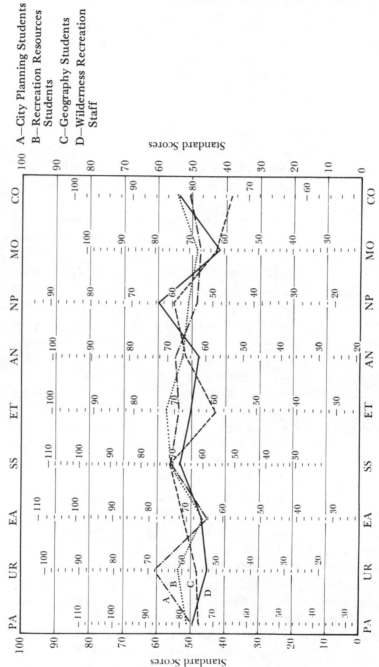

Figure 2. Mean ERI Profiles for Four Environmental Professions.

A—City Planning Students
B—Recreation Resources
   Students
C—Geography Students
D—Wilderness Recreation
   Staff

Table 4. Multiple Regression Prediction of Planning Policy Stance
from ERI Scales.

1. *Criterion:*	"Electricity should be rationed to conserve natural resources and reduce pollution from generating plants."
	$R = .64 \; (.63)$[a]
Equation:	$C = 3.689 - .045 \; EA + .034 \; PA$
2. *Criterion:*	"Some people advocate increased governmental regulation of coastline development, whether the land is publicly or privately owned."
	$R = .47 \; (.47)$
Equation:	$C = 5.112 - .038 \; EA + .013 \; UR + .012 \; SS$
3. *Criterion:*	"Many state and national parks that build roads, picnic areas with restroom facilities, boating docks, etc., should continue this type of development because it increases accessibility and allows full utilization of the park."
	$R = .57 \; (.52)$
Equation:	$C = .414 + .052 \; EA - .012 \; SS + .031 \; AN - .019 \; PA$

[a]Initial multiple R coefficient (cross-validated multiple R coefficient).

ent from the more similar planning department and Sierra Club groups, scoring nearly two standard deviations higher on Environmental Adaptation and scoring well below them on Urbanism, Stimulus Seeking, and Environmental Trust. Unlike the groups shown in Figure 2, the people represented here can—and do—regularly attend the same planning hearings to voice their opinions. No wonder such meetings often end in a stalemate.

Another focus of this study was an evaluation of the comparative utility of ERI disposition scales, demographic variables, recreation behavior scales, and recreation intention scales (McKechnie, 1972) in accounting for a number of environmental attitudes toward issues of great importance in Marin County. Multiple regression analysis was used for this purpose. Equations for twenty-seven environmental attitude criteria were computed, using the nine ERI scales, fourteen LAB scales, and fourteen environment-related demographic variables, such as commuting distance. Once again, a double-split cross-validation design was employed. Sample findings are given in Table 5. ERI variables were found to contribute substantial common-factor

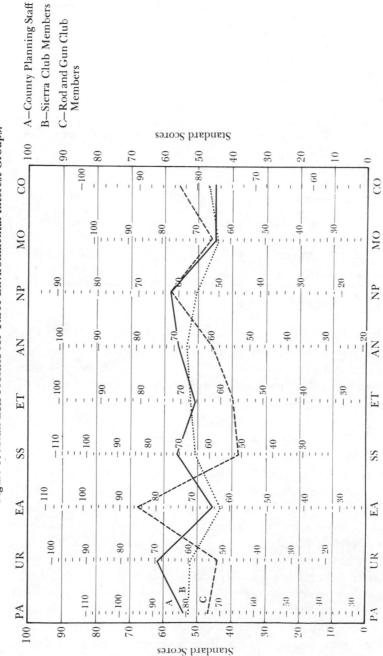

Figure 3. Mean ERI Profiles for Three Environmental Interest Groups.

A–County Planning Staff
B–Sierra Club Members
C–Rod and Gun Club
      Members

Note: The profile sheet is reproduced from the Manual for the Environmental Response Inventory. © Copyright 1974, by Consulting Psychologists Press, Inc.

Table 5. Multiple Regression Prediction of Environmental Attitudes from ERI Scales and Other Variables.

1. *Criterion:*	Checking of statement "Compared to Marin County, an ideal county would have fewer houses." (check = 1; no check = 2)
	$R = .49 \ (.36)$
Equation:	$C = 2.1694 - .145 \ PA + .169 \ UR - .101 \ ET + .520$ Commute distance to work.
2. *Criterion:*	Rating of statement "If the population here were to double within ten years, I would leave." (yes = 1; uncertain = 2; no = 3)
	$R = .53 \ (.33)$
Equation:	$C = 3.9991 - .326 \ PA + .116 \ UR - .352$ Ego Recognition (Scale of Leisure Activities Blank) $+ .135$ Education level.
3. *Criterion:*	Rating of statement "Zoning and other development controls should increase." (more = 1; present level ok = 2; less = 3)
	$R = .46 \ (.33)$
Equation:	$C = 2.5409 + .150 \ EA + .193 \ AN - .686$ Amount of yearly vacation time $- .181$ Education level.
4. *Criterion:*	Ranking in importance of conservation of open space as a community issue.
	$R = .52 \ (.44)$
Equation:	$C = .70357 - .357 \ PA + .527 \ EA - .697 \ AN - .203$ Commute distance to work.

variance to the stepwise multiple regression equations. Although no foolproof procedure was available for ensuring that the selection of predictor variables was not biased in favor of one or another class of variables, it is noteworthy that the ERI variables fared well in the comparisons.

Concluding Remarks

A number of years ago, Block (1965) decried the preoccupation of so many test constructors with personality test items in the tradition of the Bernreuter, MMPI, and CPI, and called upon researchers to explore other pools of test variance. By expanding personality assessment to the realm of environmental dispositions, the ERI and LAB necessarily depart from the traditional item pool. (The latter, in fact, abandons as well the traditional item format, substituting instead self-report of past behavior and self-prediction of future behavior.) Holding aside for the present some interesting questions of assessment technique (for example, its immunity from response styles and sets), the fundamental issues of competitive and incremental validity remain: To what extent do the ERI and LAB (and other measures of environmental dispositions) provide substantial new sources of personality variance, sources inadequately measured by traditional assessment instruments? In the absence of data demonstrating their uniqueness and usefulness, devotees of the parsimony principle will dismiss environmental dispositions as an unnecessary complication of an already complex field. Unfortunately, little data are available at present to address these issues other than the correlations of ERI and LAB scales with such standard tests as CPI, MMPI, Strong Vocational Interest Blank, Myers-Briggs Type Indicator, and Allport, Vernon and Lindzey Study of Values reported in the ERI (McKechnie, 1974a) and LAB (McKechnie, 1975) manuals. In this writer's opinion, this research question is not likely to be addressed directly in the near future and will be resolved only gradually as findings accumulate.

From the perspective of environmental psychology and the allied man-environmental disciplines, however, the question of utility in relation to intrapsychic and interpersonal dispositions is irrelevant. Here, the question of interest is this: To what extent do individual differences in environmental dispositions relate to significant environmental behaviors? From this viewpoint, the utility of environmental dispositions measures seems self-evident and parsimonious. Thus, it is in these research areas where the most frequent applications of the instruments are being made—and with good success. Although presently modest in number, these studies suggest the diverse applications to which a broad-bandwidth instrument such as the ERI might be employed in psychological research.

References

"America's Changing Environment." *Daedalus,* Fall 1967, *69.*

Bachelard, G. *The Poetics of Space.* New York: Orion Press, 1964.

Balint, M. "Friendly Expanses—Horrid Empty Spaces." *International Journal of Psychoanalysis,* 1955, *36,* 225-241.

Block, J. *The Challenge of Response Sets.* New York: Appleton-Century-Crofts, 1965.

Burch, W. R., Jr. "Images of Future Leisure: Continuities in Changing Expectations." In W. Bell and J. A. Mau (Eds.), *The Sociology of the Future.* New York: Russell Sage Foundation, 1971.

Campbell, D. T., and Fiske, D. W. "Convergent and Discriminant Validation by the Multitrait-Multimethod Matrix." *Psychological Bulletin,* 1959, *56,* 81-105.

Cattell, R. B. *Personality and Motivational Structure and Measurement.* New York: World, 1957.

Charns, H. "Personality, Preference and Planning." Unpublished master's thesis, University of California, Berkeley, 1973.

Charter, S. P. R. *Man on Earth: A Preliminary Evaluation of the Ecology of Man.* Sausalito, Calif.: Contact Editions, 1962.

Clawson, M. "Economics and Environmental Impacts of Increasing Leisure Activities." In F. F. Darling (Ed.), *Future Environments of North America.* Garden City, N.Y.: Natural History Press, 1966.

Craik, K. H. *Assessing Environmental Dispositions.* Paper presented at the 82nd annual meeting of the American Psychological Association, Washington, D.C., September 4, 1969.

Craik, K. H. "Environmental Psychology." In K. H. Craik and others, *New Directions in Psychology IV.* New York: Holt, Rinehart and Winston, 1970.

Craik, K. H. "An Ecological Perspective on Environmental Decision-Making." *Human Ecology,* 1972a, *1,* 69-80.

Craik, K. H. "The Individual and the Physical Environment: Assessment Strategies in Environmental Psychology." In W. M. Smith (Ed.), *Behavior, Design and Policy: Aspects of Human Habitats.* Green Bay: University of Wisconsin, 1972b.

Craik, K. H. "Environmental Psychology." In P. H. Mussen and M. R. Rosenzweig (Eds.), *Annual Review of Psychology.* Vol. 24. Palo Alto, Calif.: Annual Reviews, 1973.

Craik, K. H. "The Personality Research Paradigm in Environmental Psychology." In S. Wapner, S. B. Cohen, and B. Kaplan (Eds.), *Experiencing the Environment.* New York: Plenum, 1976.

Craik, K. H., and McKechnie, G. E. "Editor's Introduction: Personality and the Environment." *Environment and Behavior,* 1977, *9* (2), 155-168.

Cronbach, L. J., and Gleser, G. C. *Psychological Tests and Personnel Decisions.* Urbana: University of Illinois Press, 1957.

Fawcett, J. T. *Psychology and Population.* New York: Population Council, 1970.

Garlington, W. K., and Shimota, H. E. "The Change Seeker Index: A Measure of the Need for Variable Stimulus Input." *Psychological Reports,* 1964, *14,* 919-924.

Glacken, C. J. *Traces on the Rhodian Shore: Nature and Culture in Western Thought from Ancient Times to the End of the Eighteenth Century.* Berkeley: University of California Press, 1967.

Goldberg, L. R. "Some Recent Trends in Personality Assessment." *Journal of Personality Assessment,* 1972, *36,* 547-560.

Gough, H. G. *Manual for the California Psychological Inventory.* Palo Alto, Calif.: Consulting Psychologists Press, 1957.

Gough, H. G. *Manual for the Personal Values Abstract.* Palo Alto, Calif.: Consulting Psychologists Press, 1972a.

Gough, H. G. "Some Possible Contributions of Personality Testing to the Understanding of Human Migration." Paper presented at the International Conference on Migration, Rome, June 1972b.

Gough, H. G. "A Measure of Individual Modernity." *Journal of Personality Assessment,* 1976, *40,* 3-9.

Gough, H. G., and Heilbrun, A. B. *The Adjective Check List Manual.* Palo Alto, Calif.: Consulting Psychologists Press, 1965.

Hartlage, L. C. "The Scientific Management of Leisure Time." *Journal of Clinical Psychology,* 1969, *25,* 226-228.

Hendee, J. C. "Appreciative Versus Consumptive Uses of Wildlife Refuges: Studies of Who Gets What and Trends in Use." *Transactions of the Thirty-Fourth North American Wildlife and Natural Resources Conference.* 1969.

Hendee, J. C., Catton, W. R., Jr., Marlow, L. D., and Brockman, C. G. "Wilderness Users in the Pacific Northwest: Their Characteristics, Values, and Management Preferences." USDA Forest Service Research Paper PNW-61. 1968. Washington, D.C.: U.S. Department of Agriculture Forest Service, 1968.

Howard, K. I. "A Test of Stimulus-Seeking Behavior." *Perceptual and Motor Skills,* 1961, *13,* 416.

Huntington, E. *The Human Habitat.* New York: D. Van Nostrand, 1928.

Kegel-Flom, P. "Identifying the Potential Rural Optometrist." *American Journal of Optometry and Physiological Optics,* 1976, *53,* 479-482.

Kluckhohn, F. R., and Strodtbeck, F. L. *Variations in Value Orientations.* New York: Harper & Row, 1961.

Lewin, K. *A Dynamic Theory of Personality.* New York: McGraw-Hill, 1935.

Little, B. R. *Person-Thing Orientation: A Provisional Manual for the T-P Scale.* Windsor, Canada: National Foundation for Educational Research Publishing Company, 1973.

McKechnie, G. E. "The Environmental Response Inventory: Preliminary Development." Unpublished manuscript, Institute of Personality Assessment and Research, University of California, Berkeley, 1969.

McKechnie, G. E. *A Study of Environmental Life Styles.* Unpublished doctoral dissertation, University of California, Berkeley, 1972.

McKechnie, G. E. *Manual for the Environmental Response In-*

ventory. Palo Alto, Calif.: Consulting Psychologists Press, 1974a.

McKechnie, G. E. "Psychological Foundations of Leisure Counseling: An Empirical Strategy." *Therapeutic Recreation Journal,* 1974b, *8* (1), 4-16.

McKechnie, G. E. "The Psychological Structure of Leisure: I. Past Behavior." *Journal of Leisure Research,* 1974c, *6,* 1.

McKechnie, G. E. *Manual for the Leisure Activities Blank.* Palo Alto, Calif.: Consulting Psychologists Press, 1975.

"Man's Response to the Physical Environment." *Journal of Social Issues,* October 1966, *22* (entire issue).

Marshall, N. "Orientations Toward Privacy: Environmental and Personality Components." Unpublished doctoral dissertation, University of California, Berkeley, 1969.

Martin, A. "Idle Hands and Giddy Minds: Our Psychological and Emotional Unpreparedness for Free Time." *American Journal of Psychoanalysis,* 1969, *29* (2), 147-156.

Marx, L. *The Machine in the Garden: Technology and the Pastoral Ideal in America.* New York: Oxford University Press, 1964.

Mehrabian, A., and Russell, J. A. "A Measure of Arousal Seeking Tendency." *Environment and Behavior,* 1973, *5,* 315-334.

Murray, H. A., and others. *Explorations in Personality.* New York: Oxford University Press, 1938.

Myers, I. B. *Manual for the Myers-Briggs Type Indicator.* Princeton, N.J.: Educational Testing Service, 1962.

O'Riordan, T. "Public Opinion and Environmental Quality: A Reappraisal." *Environment and Behavior,* 1971, *3,* 191-214.

Penny, R. K., and Reinehr, R. C. "Development of a Stimulus-Variation Seeking Scale for Adults." *Psychological Reports,* 1966, *18,* 631-638.

Proshansky, H. M., Ittelson, W. H., and Rivlin, L. G. (Eds.). *Environmental Psychology: Man and His Physical Setting.* New York: Holt, Rinehart and Winston, 1970.

Reichenbach, H. *Experience and Prediction: An Analysis of the*

Foundations and Structure of Knowledge. Chicago: University of Chicago Press, 1938.

Searles, H. F. *The Nonhuman Environment, in Normal Development and in Schizophrenia.* New York: International Universities Press, 1960.

Sewell, W. R. D. "Environmental Perceptions and Attitudes of Engineers and Public Health Officials." *Environment and Behavior,* 1971, *3* (1), 23-59.

Smith, D. H. "Evidence for a General Activity Syndrome: A Survey of Townspeople in 8 Massachusetts Towns and Cities." *Proceedings of the 77th Annual Convention of the American Psychological Association,* 1964, *4,* 453-454.

Sommer, R. *Personal Space: The Behavioral Basis of Design.* Englewood Cliffs, N.J.: Prentice-Hall, 1969.

Sonnenfeld, J. "Personality and Behavior in the Environment." *Proceedings of the Association of American Geographers,* 1969, *1,* 136-140.

Strong, E. K., Jr. *Vocational Interests of Men and Women.* Stanford, Calif.: Stanford University Press, 1943.

Tryon, R. C., and Bailey, D. E. *Cluster Analysis.* New York: McGraw-Hill, 1970.

White, M., and White, L. *The Intellectual Versus the City: From Thomas Jefferson to Frank Lloyd Wright.* Cambridge, Mass.: Harvard University/M.I.T. Press, 1962.

Wiggins, J. S. *Personality and Prediction: Principles of Personality Assessment.* Reading, Mass.: Addison-Wesley, 1973.

Wolf, W. "Dealing Constructively with Our Increased Leisure Time." *American Journal of Psychotherapy,* 1970, *24* (3), 440-449.

Zuckerman, M. "Dimensions of Sensation-Seeking." *Journal of Consulting and Clinical Psychology,* 1971, *36,* 45-52.

Zuckerman, M., Kolin, E. A., Price, L., and Zoob, I. "Development of a Sensation-Seeking Scale." *Journal of Consulting Psychology,* 1964, *28,* 477-482.

V

Profile of Nonverbal Sensitivity

JUDITH A. HALL, ROBERT ROSENTHAL, DANE ARCHER,
M. R. DiMATTEO, PETER L. ROGERS

In this chapter we describe the development and construct validity of an audiovisual test designed to measure the ability to decode nonverbal cues conveyed by the face, body, and tone of voice.[1] This test is called the Profile of Nonverbal Sensitivity, or PONS.

Although nonverbal communication plays a central role in human behavior, it remains far from well understood. We have just begun to learn about the ways in which our nonverbal behavior affects other people, about differences among people in their abilities to understand and convey nonverbal messages, and about the ways in which such differences matter in people's lives.

[1] The research reported here was supported by grants from the National Science Foundation and the Milton Fund of Harvard University to Robert Rosenthal and is reported in more detail in Rosenthal, Hall, DiMatteo, Rogers, and Archer (1978). Order of authorship on the present chapter reflects our respective contributions to the preparation of this particular manuscript and not necessarily to the research program as a whole. (Note: Judith A. Hall was formerly Judith H. Koivumaki.)

179

There are several reasons why our knowledge about non-verbal behavior is so incomplete. One has to do with the strong verbal orientation of our society. For example, schools in our culture teach children that communication is equivalent to the successful use of words. There are other, more subtle reasons for our lack of formal knowledge about nonverbal behavior. Different types of nonverbal communication are so embedded in our daily lives that we use nonverbal messages without being aware of them. When we form an opinion of what someone is like, for example, the opinion is probably based in part upon a complex analysis of nonverbal information. When we conclude that someone we have just met is angry or jealous or anxious to leave, we may have determined this as much by listening to the person's tone of voice or observing how agitated the person's movements were as by interpreting what was actually said.

Even though we use nonverbal cues every time we meet or talk with someone, we are generally unable to describe the cues we use. Instead, if asked why we reached an opinion about someone, we are likely to say that it was just a "feeling" or that there was "something" about the way the person acted. And yet we are intuitively aware that we perceive (often accurately) an enormous number of nonverbal messages. This "tacit knowledge" (Polanyi, 1962) paradox of being able to use nonverbal cues that we cannot describe was what the anthropologist Edward Sapir had in mind when he said that people could understand gestures because of "an elaborate and secret code that is written nowhere, known by none, and understood by all" (Sapir, 1949).

These factors have limited the discussion of the role of nonverbal behavior in everyday life and have also contributed to neglect of this area in social science research. The scientific study of nonverbal communication has in addition met substantial methodological barriers. Unlike attitudes or other types of verbal behavior, nonverbal communication has in the past been very difficult to record, code, analyze, and reproduce. The development and diffusion of film and videotape technology have recently generated a marked increase in investigation of this area.

The study of the decoding of nonverbal cues is not new, however. Many efforts have been made in the past to assess the accuracy of judgments of nonverbal cues defined both broadly and narrowly. Research on social intelligence (Walker and Foley, 1973), empathy (Campbell, Kagan, and Krathwohl, 1971), judging personality (Cline, 1964), and person perception (Tagiuri, 1969) involves decoding of nonverbal cues to varying degrees. Such decoding is often mixed to an unknown extent with other skills and behaviors, such as the ability to judge contextual or situational cues, knowledge of personal dispositions, wisdom in choosing the right social responses, and various motivational states. Decoding of strictly nonverbal cues also has a long history of study; in fact, it is one of the oldest traditions in social psychology (for example, Allport, 1924). We hope our own research adds something new by emphasizing individual differences and systematically attempting to develop and validate an instrument for assessing these individual differences.

We feel an important obstacle in investigating nonverbal communication has been the absence of standardized measures of individual accuracy in interpreting and conveying nonverbal cues in various modalities, or *channels*. Obviously, well-validated measures of decoding and encoding skills would make it much easier to study such issues as individual differences in nonverbal skills and in the use of different channels of communication, sex differences in nonverbal abilities, nonverbal abilities in special groups and occupations, and cultural differences. Researchers interested in these kinds of questions have had to make up their own measuring instruments, often without the time and resources necessary for establishing their validity. The absence of standard measures has also, of course, made it hard to study the correlates of these skills. Without such measures, it is hard to learn whether people with well-developed nonverbal skills differ from other people and, if so, in what ways. It would be important to know, for example, whether those who are better at sending or receiving nonverbal cues are more successful, better liked, more intelligent, better leaders, or more artistic.

Actually, the PONS test grew not only out of our interest in individual differences but also out of a desire to understand the variables that may moderate interpersonal outcomes of many sorts. The immediate context of this interest was research on the effect of teachers' expectations on the performance of their pupils and the effect of experimenters' expectations on the behavior of their research subjects (Rosenthal, 1967, 1971, 1976; Rosenthal and Jacobson, 1968). This research has shown that one's expectations for the behavior of other people can unintentionally influence those people to change their behavior in the direction of those expectations; that is, expectations can become a self-fulfilling prophecy.

Although the processes by which these expectations operate is not well understood, there is some reason to think that the effect is mediated by various types of nonverbal communication (Adair and Epstein, 1968; Duncan and Rosenthal, 1968; Rosenthal, 1969; Rosenthal and Fode, 1963; Troffer and Tart, 1964; Zoble and Lehman, 1969). A teacher might communicate high expectations for a pupil, for example, in the tone of voice used when speaking to him or her in class. Unless the pupil is sensitive to the nonverbal qualities of the teacher's voice, of course, the unintended message may go unnoticed. But if the pupil is sensitive to paralanguage, he or she may be influenced to change his or her performance to conform to the teacher's expectation (Conn, Edwards, Rosenthal, and Crowne, 1968; Rosenthal, 1971, 1974).

Teachers undoubtedly vary, like other people, in the clarity of their nonverbal encoding in different nonverbal channels, just as pupils vary in their decoding ability or sensitivity to nonverbal communication in different channels. Variations in these nonverbal abilities might determine the outcome of an interaction between two people. It might be, for example, that teachers whose best encoding channel is vocal would be most effective with pupils whose best decoding channel is auditory. Similarly, teachers who are most expressive in the facial channel might be most effective with pupils who are best at decoding faces. Teachers might be relatively less effective if their best encoding channel did not correspond to a pupil's best decoding channel.

Ultimately, then, what we would want would be a series of accurate measurements for each person, describing his or her relative ability to send and receive in each of a variety of channels of nonverbal communication. It seems reasonable to suppose that if we had this information for two or more people we would be better able to predict the outcome of their interaction, regardless of whether the focus of the analysis was on the mediation of interpersonal expectations or on some other interpersonal transaction.

Our model envisages people moving through their "social spaces" carrying two vectors, or profiles, of scores. One of these vectors describes the person's differential clarity in conveying messages through various channels of nonverbal communication. The other vector describes the person's differential sensitivity in receiving messages conveyed through these same various channels of nonverbal communication.

Thus, the scores on channels of sending by the sender can be correlated with the scores on channels of receiving by the receiver. A higher correlation reflects a greater potential for accurate communication between the dyad members, since the receiver is then better at receiving the channels that are more accurately encoded by the sender. The mean (arithmetic, geometric, or harmonic) of the correlations between the vectors of one person and those of another reflects how well the dyad members understand or decode each other's communications. That mean correlation need not reflect how well the dyad members like each other, however, only that they should understand each others' intended and unintended messages more quickly, including how they feel about one another. Although a high mean correlation of channel scores may be an indication of a high degree of efficiency in dyadic communication, excellent communication could also take place between people who show little profile similarity but who may be uniformly good senders and receivers of nonverbal cues.

The original idea for the PONS test grew out of this framework. We believed that our predictions about the outcome of an interaction between two people, whether in an expectancy situation or some other setting, would be improved if we had information about the decoding and encoding abilities of the participants.

Design and Development of the PONS Test

The Profile of Nonverbal Sensitivity (PONS) is a forty-seven-minute black and white 16-mm film and soundtrack composed of 220 two-second auditory and visual segments. The 220 segments are a randomized presentation of twenty short scenes portrayed by a young woman, each scene represented in eleven different channels of nonverbal communication. The test taker's task is to view the film and to circle the label that correctly describes the scene enacted in each segment. The test taker makes this choice from two alternative labels printed on an answer sheet containing 220 such pairs of descriptions. Each segment is followed by a pause long enough for the decision to be made and recorded.

This chapter will be devoted almost entirely to describing and summarizing results obtained with the 220-item, or full PONS test. Several short forms have been developed, as well as several short forms based on the PONS format but employing different senders. These short tests are described in the appendix at the end of the chapter. Although several important validational results were obtained using these short forms of the PONS, for the sake of brevity, simplicity, and robustness of findings we only summarize two of them here: results for deaf and blind samples, since these people had no option but to judge only certain channels of the PONS, and results using the Brief Exposure PONS, since this form addresses the question of length of communication exposure and is thus more than just a short, alternate form of the PONS.

Channels. The eleven channels in the PONS are made up of various kinds of auditory and visual information sent by the portrayer. These channels can be thought of as falling into two types. The first five channels are pure channels: (1) face alone, no voice; (2) body from neck to knees, no voice; (3) face and body down to thighs (called "face plus body" or "figure"), no voice; (4) electronically filtered voice (called "CF" for "content filtered"), no picture; and (5) randomly spliced voice (called "RS"), no picture. The remaining six channels are mixed channels, made by combining the pure channels: (6) face plus randomly spliced voice; (7) face plus electronically filtered voice; (8) body plus randomly spliced voice; (9) body plus electronically filtered voice; (10) figure plus randomly spliced voice; and (11) figure plus electronically filtered voice. Table 1 displays the eleven channels arranged in a two-way table of four levels of video by three levels of audio, as well as the pooled channels or marginals that are also often used in data analysis.

Table 1. Number of Test Items in Each Channel of the PONS Test.

	Video Cue Type				
Audio Cue Type	None	Face	Body	Figure[a]	Marginals
None	—[b]	20	20	20	Video 60
Randomly Spliced	20	20	20	20	RS 80[d]
Content Filtered	20	20	20	20	CF 80[e]
Marginals	Tone 40	Face 60	Body 60	Figure 60	Total 220
		Face 120[c]	Body 120[c]		

[a]Face and body.

[b]Empty cell in design. In statistical analyses, this cell is frequently filled in with a chance-level score for each person in order to allow for a fully crossed repeated-measures analysis.

[c]Includes figure items.

[d]RS = Randomly spliced voice.

[e]CF = Electronically content-filtered voice.

Voice Content Masking. Until relatively recently, researchers interested in eliminating the verbal content of utterances had to use a method known as "standard content." In this method, the speaker would recite either standard, meaningless material, such as the alphabet or numbers, or some standard, meaningful, but affectively neutral or ambiguous material, usually a word, a phrase, or a sentence or two. In each of these cases the speaker would recite the same material over and over (or several speakers would recite the same material), varying the mood or voice tone to suit the emotion being sent. The listener can understand the words, but the words do not help the listener to identify the emotion.

Several masking techniques have been developed that seem to improve on the standard content method. In these newer methods the speaker is free to use whatever words are appropriate for the emotion or situation, since the words are made unintelligible afterwards by altering the voice recording in various ways. The advantage of this approach is in increasing the spontaneity and authenticity of the original portrayals. It also allows for the masking of voices recorded unobtrusively—a clear advantage over the standard content method.

The randomized splicing technique (Scherer, 1971) requires the audio tape to be physically cut into small pieces, reordered randomly, and reassembled. The length of the pieces depends on the speed of tape transport; in the PONS the tape speed was 7½ inches per second and the pieces were two inches long. When the spliced tape is played back, the voice sounds natural in many ways, but of course the words cannot be understood because they are scrambled.

The electronic filter used in making the PONS was modeled on the one reported in Rogers, Scherer, and Rosenthal (1971). It removes selected bands of frequencies and clips the audio signal so that the voice sounds muffled and slightly distorted. By carefully adjusting the various controls, the intonation, rhythm, tempo, and loudness of the voice can be kept the same, while speech intelligibility is lost.

The decision to use two kinds of speech masking—randomized splicing and electronic filtering—where one kind might have sufficed was based on the findings of Scherer, Koivumaki, and Rosenthal (1972), which suggested that these two techniques affect the voice in different ways. The randomized splicing seems to make the voice seem more pleasant and peaceful than ordinary speech as rated by judges in the study cited above. The electronic filter seems to make the voice sound easier, calmer, and steadier than ordinary speech. The randomized splicing retains the acoustic properties of the voice while altering the correct sequence of the communication, whereas the electronic filtering does just the reverse: It noticeably changes some acoustic properties of the voice but keeps the sequence intact. In a sense, then, the two methods are complementary.

Portrayal of the Scenes. The portrayals in the PONS test were done by a member of our research group. She was Caucasian, from the northeastern United States, and was age twenty-four when the test was made. After it had been decided not to use a professional actress in order to avoid a stereotyped enactment, our portrayer was selected for convenience and because her continued participation in the group assured the possibility of gathering additional information on her if the need arose. She was not chosen on the basis of her nonverbal sending skill or other nonverbal characteristics, about which little was known.

Thirty-five scenes were videotaped. At no time was a script rigidly adhered to, but rather the exact wording often changed with each repetition of the scene. This flexibility of wording was intended to enhance the genuineness of the feelings expressed, which was hoped to reflect the natural style of the portrayer and not be artificial, memorized, or self-conscious. Naturalistic expression was the focus, not the specific words.

The thirty-five videotaped scenes were chosen on the basis of certain broad criteria. The first interest was to represent a wide variety of situations and emotions, both strong and mild, positive and negative. In addition, a special attempt was made to find interactive situations. Since the purpose of the test was to measure the ability to understand cues sent by another person, it made sense to concentrate on cues sent in interaction.

Final Selection of the Scenes. The twenty scenes used in the final version of the PONS were chosen by eight people who knew the portrayer (including the portrayer herself), who as a group viewed the figure (face plus body) "takes" of all scenes in their full length (averaging 5.5 seconds) without any content masking of the voice. For each scene each rater did the following: (1) ordered the several takes according to overall personal preference, (2) gave the most favored take a score of 0 to 100 on the basis of how well the scene conveyed the intended emotion or situation, (3) rated the sender's behavior in the most favored take on a scale from 1 to 7 for each of three dimensions: friendliness (positivity), interpersonal dominance, and intensity of feeling.

For the thirty-five final takes (see below), the correlation of median positivity rating with median dominance rating was -0.05. Intensity was correlated 0.35 with dominance ($p <$ 0.05, two-tailed), and -0.50 with positivity ($p < 0.005$, two-tailed). Intensity ratings were subsequently ignored for being significantly related to the other two rating dimensions.

The final best take for each scene was the one having the lowest sum of the ranks given by the eight raters (a scene with more first choices would have a lower sum of ranks than a scene with more second and third choices). The scenes were then categorized on the positivity and dominance dimensions: high positive, low positive, high dominant, and low dominant. Finally, from each of the quadrants formed by the intersection of the positivity and dominance dimensions, five scenes were selected; in general, these were the five having the highest score on the 0-100 rating for success in conveying the intended emotion or situation (some scenes were also excluded due to technical flaws).

Table 2 shows the final selection of scenes and their positions in the four quadrants formed by the positivity and dominance dimensions. For these twenty scenes, the correlation of

Table 2. PONS Scenes Arranged in Affective Quadrants.

Positivity	Dominance	
	Submissive	Dominant
Positive	Helping a customer.	Talking about one's wedding.
	Ordering food in a restaurant.	Leaving on a trip.
	Expressing gratitude.	Expressing motherly love.
	Expressing deep affection.	Admiring nature.
	Trying to seduce someone.	Talking to a lost child.
Negative	Talking about the death of a friend.	Criticizing someone for being late.
		Nagging a child.
	Talking about one's divorce.	Expressing strong dislike.
	Returning faulty item to a store.	Threatening someone.
	Asking forgiveness.	Expressing jealous anger.
	Saying a prayer.	

the eight judges' median positivity rating with their median dominance rating was -0.38 ($p = 0.10$, two-tailed).

Data-Analytic Model

The eleven channels and four quadrants can be conceptualized in terms of an analysis-of-variance model so that each person assessed provides five replications (scenarios) in each cell of a 2 X 2 X 11 (positive/negative X dominant/submissive X channels). An even more useful model is based on the assumption of a hypothetical twelfth channel, "no video, no audio." The expected accuracy rate for this channel is 50 percent, but adding it to the model permits a more powerful and more compact analytic model: 2 X 2 X 2 X 2 X 3 (positive/negative X dominant/submissive X face shown/face not shown X body shown/body not shown X no audio/randomly spliced/content filtered).

For each person or for any homogeneous group of persons, this model permits an evaluation of accuracy in nonverbal communication as a function of these five orthogonal factors and two-, three-, four-, and five-way interactions among them. In addition, individuals and groups can be compared with one another on the relative importance to each person or to each group of all five factors taken singly or in interaction.

For some purposes a sixth factor of order or learning is added. Thus, within each combination of channel and scene type there are five scenes that can be arranged for analysis into the order in which they are shown in the PONS test. This order or learning factor with its five levels is fully crossed with the five factors listed above. Individuals and groups can, therefore, be compared on their degree of learning in the course of the test as well as on their level of performance. In addition, one can examine such questions as which channels show greater learning and which content quadrants show greater learning.

It should be noted that our data-analytic model does not make frequent use of all eleven channels or all forty-four combinations of channels and affect quadrants. The model employs all this information but in a more efficient and reliable manner by subdividing parts of the eleven-channel profile into larger subsections than channels based only on twenty scenes each. Thus all scenes employing face can be compared with all scenes not employing face, all scenes employing body can be compared with all scenes not employing body, all scenes employing audio information can be compared with all scenes not employing audio information, and so on. This series of comparisons, or contrasts, is appreciably more reliable and powerful than the simultaneous examination of all eleven channels.

Limitations and Advantages of Approach

Although the PONS test overcomes some problems of previous decoding research, the test is not without its own limitations. In making the PONS test, there were some trade-offs—perhaps inevitable—between experimental control and ecological validity. While trying to make the PONS a reliable measure of decoding in separate channels, we also tried to make its content representative of real-life behavior. It is probably impossible to achieve both fully. For example, the difficulties we would have had if we had filmed behavior occurring in natural settings would have included uncertainty about the proper labels for the emotions exhibited and perhaps even for the psychological context, uneven control over technical quality, and probably giving up the idea of filming and audiotaping all the relevant behavior occurring in different channels simultaneously.

Because of our choice of method, there are a number of ways in which the nonverbal behavior in the PONS film differs from nonverbal behavior in everyday life, and also ways in which the judging is quite different from the kind of judging that people do every day. These differences are intentional design features of the PONS, not unwitting conceptual oversights. These differences are discussed below.

Channel Isolation. In everyday life we generally have multiple channels available for interpretation at the same time. In interacting with someone we can try to decode all of their channels of communication simultaneously. There are some circum-

stances, of course, under which the channels available for interpretation are limited, such as talking on the telephone.

In most face-to-face interaction, however, we have available all the nonverbal cues that the PONS film isolates into
separate channels. In everyday life it might be the case that we
use a hierarchy of channels, starting with the channel easiest to
decode. In trying to judge someone's emotions, for example, it
might be that we tend to prefer the face, and only use other
channels when the face is not visible. The PONS film, however,
isolates nonverbal behavior into different channels and therefore restricts the nonverbal cues available to the decoder in a
manner unlike everyday life, at least for some of its eleven channels. For mixed channels, the stimulus becomes more like everyday life (for example, face, body, and tone).

Absence of Verbal Information. In everyday life most
nonverbal behavior occurs in conjunction with verbal behavior.
When we try to decode a person's emotion in a face-to-face situation, we may be using both these kinds of information in our
interpretation. It could be that nonverbal cues acquire meaning
principally in terms of their reinforcement (or contradiction) of
what the person is saying rather than as a completely independent source of information.

The nonverbal behavior in the PONS film occurs in pure
form; that is, the encoder's verbal (semantic) behavior has been
entirely eliminated. This was of course intentional, since the
PONS was designed to be a measure of nonverbal sensitivity
alone.

Some Nonverbal Cues Not Examined. The PONS film
measures eleven channels of nonverbal behavior, and these channels contain behavior encoded by the face, body, and voice.
There are, however, other types of nonverbal information that
the film does not convey. For example, Argyle (1972) provides
an inventory of ten different headings of nonverbal communication, and Cook (1971) lists fifteen.

Some of the cues on these lists only have meaning when
two or more people interact (for example, proximity, body contact, eye contact, and conversational head nods), and others are
embedded in channels already in the PONS film (for example,

posture, physique, hair style, and clothes). Finally, there are even more types of nonverbal cues, in addition to those listed by Argyle and Cook, that are not in the PONS film, such as olfaction, flushed skin color, and sweating. In choosing channels for inclusion in the PONS film, we tried to select those that seemed most indispensable to the decoding of emotions: the face, the body, and the voice.

Decoding Only. The PONS film provides extensive information about an individual's decoding abilities, but provides no information about the encoding abilities or expressiveness of the person. In face-to-face interaction, a person is both an encoder and a decoder, and both these abilities are likely to be important determinants of the outcome of the interaction. The obstacles involved in creating a standardized test of encoding abilities are at least formidable; at any rate, the PONS is a measure of decoding only.

Posed Criterion. The criterion of accuracy for each item in the PONS test is in part the situation or feeling that the encoder intended to portray. In everyday life, of course, we are more likely to be decoding spontaneous or unposed emotions. The PONS encoder's portrayals were also rated and selected for authenticity, as described earlier. This procedure was followed to ensure that her emotional expressions were not ineffectual, melodramatic, or stereotyped.

The problem of a criterion in researching emotion, however, is complex. A number of researchers have discussed the relative merits of different types of criteria in decoding research (Frijda, 1969; Cook, 1971; Knapp, 1972; Ekman, Friesen, and Ellsworth, 1972; Ekman, 1973). For example, Cook (p. 83) lists five alternate ways of establishing a criterion: (1) face validity (what the encoder intended to send), (2) researcher opinion (the way the researcher labels the emotion), (3) ratings (a panel of judges rate the portrayals), (4) self-description (the encoder evaluates his or her own feelings), and (5) objective or biographical data (independent measures of what the encoder was actually feeling, as in the observation of reactions to experimental or naturally occurring stimuli).

In selecting the portrayals for inclusion in the PONS film,

we used a total of four of these methods: face validity (what our encoder meant to send), researcher opinion (we evaluated the effectiveness of each portrayal), ratings (a panel of judges rated each portrayal), and self-description (the encoder evaluated her own feelings).

These four methods were the only appropriate procedures, given the design of the PONS film. We did not want to use experimental manipulations to induce real emotions, since only a very restricted range of real emotions could have been ethically produced in this manner. As a result, the PONS encoder was not spontaneously experiencing hate, mourning, jealousy, and the other emotions in the film. Since the encoder was portraying but not actually experiencing the emotions in the film, Cook's other criterion procedure was inappropriate. Likewise, it would not have made sense to obtain objective data like physiological measures. In summary, the criterion of accuracy in the PONS film is a combination of the emotion the encoder intended to send and the emotion the researchers, the encoder, and various judges decided she had in fact sent.

On a priori, though not on empirical, grounds we might prefer spontaneous over posed stimuli because it is ultimately the decoding of everyday nonverbal cues about which we want to make inferences. However, it would be a common error of logic to assume that because our ultimate interest is in spontaneous nonverbal cues, a better index of accuracy could be constructed from the use of such stimuli. Surface similarities between models and things modeled are no guarantee of predictive utility. A model's utility lies in our knowing the relationship between the properties of the model and the thing modeled. At the present time we do not know whether real-life stimuli would, for our purposes of assessing individual differences, be better, worse, or no different from the posed stimuli we have employed for the PONS. We do know, however, that in a study by Zuckerman, Hall, DeFrank, and Rosenthal (1976), people who were better at decoding posed facial expressions were also better at decoding spontaneous facial expressions ($r = 0.58, p < 0.001$), and that people who were better at communicating via posed facial expressions were also better at communicating via spontaneous facial expressions ($r = 0.46$, $p < 0.001$). In that study, the spontaneous expressions were obtained by surreptitiously videotaping subjects' faces while they were watching emotion-arousing videotaped scenes, and the posed expressions were obtained by asking the same subjects to reproduce the same facial expressions. In another study using similar methodology (Buck, 1975), children's abilities to communicate facially in spontaneous and posed modes were also positively correlated (median correlation of posed sending accuracy with four measures of spontaneous sending accuracy = 0.35).

Although such methods have been employed to elicit identifiable "spontaneous" nonverbal cues, it is questionable whether such cues are any more like real-life interpersonal communication than are the posed cues used in the PONS. Interpersonal communication probably consists of a mixture of cues that are unknowingly conveyed and cues that are conveyed quite deliberately. To some extent people may be capable of choosing their nonverbal behavior as consciously as they are capable of choosing their words. The posed cues embodied in the PONS may not, therefore, be as unrepresentative of real interpersonal nonverbal communication as one might at first think.

One Encoder. The PONS film contains the nonverbal behavior and expressions of only a single encoder. In everyday life, of course, we are surrounded by large numbers of encoders who probably vary in their expressiveness. However, the available literature on nonverbal communication suggests that good decoders are likely to be more accurate than poor decoders across different encoders. In addition, the various validity studies reported in this paper effectively discount the possibility that the PONS encoder is extremely idiosyncratic in her encoding behavior. It does seem justified, therefore, to generalize from the decoding measured by the PONS test to decoding ability in general, though we could not know at the outset that this would be the case. It is only because of the network of validational findings that we can conclude that the PONS was not, in fact, disadvantaged by the use of a single encoder. In principle, of course, it might well have been.*

---

*Further analysis of a set of fifty-nine encoders sending four scenes in each of three modes (spontaneous, talking, and posed; Zuckerman, Hall,

One Sex. One consequence of employing only one sender was that only one sex could be represented. It was important to ascertain, therefore, the degree to which this fact could affect our results, particularly results having to do with sex differences in decoding. For example, women might be superior to men in decoding a woman sender but not a man sender. A review of numerous decoding studies employing nonverbal judging tasks other than the PONS showed very clearly that the sex of the encoder made no difference either in the number of studies showing female advantage or in the magnitude of the effect (Hall, in press). The literature thus suggests that we suffered no overall loss of generality from employing only one sex.

Lack of Context. The emotional situations in the PONS film are presented without a context. In real life, we are often able to interpret emotions in light of several types of contextual information: the situational antecedents of the emotion or situation at hand (Is the person sad at the loss of a chess game, or sad at the loss of a spouse?), our past history with the encoder (Is the person exceptionally angry, or is this level of agitation an enduring characteristic?), and our knowledge about the onset and duration of an emotion (Is the person exploding into sudden rage, or is the emotion a smoldering anger?).

The PONS items are, of course, presented without context so that we may know better what information is being judged. This kind of decoding is not without a naturalistic counterpart. We are frequently in situations where we form an opinion, after minimal exposure, about the emotion a total stranger is experiencing.

Recognition Versus Interpretation. The PONS test measures whether a decoder can recognize emotions that the encoder is making no effort to disguise. In everyday life we sometimes need to interpret a person's emotions whether or not they

---

DeFrank, and Rosenthal, 1976) showed that the median of the twelve internal consistencies (coefficient alpha) of 0.87 was essentially the same as the internal consistency of the PONS (0.86) when alpha was based on 220 items in both cases. Thus, agreement among different senders is very similar to agreement among different items sent by the single sender of the PONS. The single sender of the PONS evoked no more homogeneous responses to the 220 scenes than would have been evoked by a set of 220 different senders each sending a single scene. (See too Rosenthal and others, in press.)

are manifest. That is, we sometimes need to go beyond a recognition of the manifest "performance" of an emotion to try to see whether this performance conceals greater complexities of emotion within the person.

The PONS test is more a measure of the decoder's ability to recognize the manifest level of emotion than it is a measure of the decoder's ability to draw complex interpretations about the true state of the encoder. Interpretations of this kind are probably based on weighing many different levels and intensities of cues (which may be in concert or in conflict) and are clearly beyond the scope of the PONS test. As the validity studies reported later indicate, however, the PONS test does tap decoding abilities that affect a person's life in the real world.

Summary of Major Findings

Since its development in 1971, the PONS test has been given to over two hundred samples of subjects in the United States and other countries. In addition to the PONS scores and the information on national origins in these samples, we were often able to gather data on other theoretically important variables, such as age, gender, sensory and psychiatric impairment, cognitive ability, psychosocial attributes, and occupation. The present paper offers a summary of what we consider to be some of the important results of these studies as well as some suggestions for future research. All of the summarized findings, along with much more detail on the measures and the samples, are reported in a monograph in preparation (Rosenthal, Hall, DiMatteo, Rogers, and Archer, 1978). The studies reported in that monograph were conducted by us with the help of many generous collaborators in many places, including twenty-two colleges and universities in the United States and eighteen abroad, and fourteen primary and secondary schools in the United States and abroad. Over seven thousand people have been tested in samples that included university students, children and teenagers, teachers and teachers in training, physicians and therapists (in practice and in training), businessmen, mental patients, actors, and married couples. As much as possible, we tried to replicate our findings. However, many gaps are left in our knowledge, and many of our findings are tentative.

As often as possible in the summary that follows, we report effect sizes (in σ units). This effect-size index shows the magnitude of effect for any dichotomous independent variable and enables one to answer the question "How big is the observed difference?" It is defined as the difference between the means of the groups being compared divided by the shared standard deviation of the two groups (Friedman, 1968; Cohen, 1969). One advantage of the effect-size index is that, being expressed in standard units, it greatly facilitates comparison and summary of results from separate studies.

Normative Data. Internal-consistency reliability was computed for the high school norm group of 492 students in three public schools in the eastern, midwestern, and western United States. The KR-20 internal consistency for the PONS test was 0.86, and theta (Armor, 1974) was 0.92. For a group of 200 children in grades three through six in two public schools in the midwestern United States, KR-20 was also 0.86. Retest reliability was 0.69 (median of six samples), and the median retest reliability of the eleven-channel profile based on four samples was 0.41. In general, channels with higher retest reliabilities showed greater internal consistency ($r = 0.43$). These internal consistency and retest reliabilities were quite adequate, reaching the level obtained by standard group-administered tests of intelligence.

Table 3 shows the reliability of the classification of the twenty scenes of the PONS into the quadrants formed by the crossing of the two dimensions of positive-negative and dominant-submissive. When only the physical characteristics of the audio channels were considered, the dominant-submissive dimension was much more clearly differentiated (by frequency and amplitude) than was the positive-negative dimension. When methods of establishing the reliability of scene classification other than the physical characteristics of the audio channels were employed, the median reliabilities tended to be 0.80 or higher for both the positive-negative and dominant-submissive dimensions.

Table 3. Reliability of Classification of Scenes Within Quadrants.

Method of Classification	Positive-Negative	Dominant-Submissive	Four Quadrants
Analysis of Alternatives[a]	0.70	0.91	0.92
U.S. Judges' Ratings	0.97	0.92	—
English Judges' Ratings	0.79	0.67	—
Agreement of U.S. Judges with English Judges	0.88	0.63	—
Agreement Among Ratings of Three Channels (Face, Body, Figure)	0.80	0.85	—
Median	0.80	0.85	—
Audio Analyzer[b]			
Frequency	0.00	0.91	0.77
Amplitude	0.00	0.90	0.77

[a]Medians of four samples.

[b]Medians of randomly spliced, content-filtered, and original unfiltered voice.

Adding information affected PONS accuracy as follows: information from tone of voice, $\sigma = 1.85$; from body, $\sigma = 3.57$; and from face, $\sigma = 6.81$; providing information from dominant rather than submissive scenes, $\sigma = 1.73$; from negative rather than positive scenes, $\sigma = 2.48$. For the PONS test, tone, body, and face cues contribute to accuracy in judging the scenes in the approximate ratios of 1:2:4, respectively.

Table 4 presents the results of the factor analysis of the eleven channels of the PONS. The four factors correspond to the randomly spliced and content-filtered channels taken alone, the three channels showing only the body and the six channels showing the face.

Grouping Samples. In several analyses we attempted to

Table 4. Factor Analysis of Eleven Channels.

Factor	Median Loading	Number of Channels	Number of Items
Face Present	0.68	6	120
Randomly Spliced	0.95	1	20
Content Filtered	0.96	1	20
Body Without Face	0.59	3	60

group samples according to the shapes of their eleven-channel and four-factor profiles. This was done by performing principal-component analysis, using samples as variables and PONS channels or factors as units (Q-type factor analysis).

These analyses, using 142 samples, yielded several factors that we found fairly easy to interpret. These interpretations were made by comparing the characteristics of high and low loading samples on each factor. Following the interpretation, the profile shapes of the high and low loading samples were compared to see if any interpretation of the profiles could be made that made sense in light of the factor interpretations. Interpretations of factors and their associated profile shapes must be seen as tentative and subject to validation.

The strongest factor of the eleven-channel analysis, accounting for 20.3 percent of the variance after rotation, was named the *sophisticated-unsophisticated* factor because one pole was characterized by a relatively large number of college and professional groups, while the other pole was characterized by young samples, mental patients, and "exotic" non-Western samples. The sophisticated samples' profiles showed relatively good performance on video and poorer performance on audio, while the unsophisticated samples' profiles showed the reverse pattern. We suggested that reading tone of voice may be an unsocialized skill compared with reading visual cues.

The analysis of the four-factor profile also revealed a factor that we called sophisticated-unsophisticated, accounting for 41.6 percent of the variance after rotation. The samples loading on the two poles of this factor were similar to those described above, and their profiles showed even more clearly their contrasting performances on tone and visual cues.

From this four-factor analysis there emerged another relatively easily interpreted factor (42.7 percent of variance after rotation). This factor was called the *American—non-American* factor, in accordance with the identities of the high and low loading samples. The American samples showed higher scores on content-filtered (CF) than on randomly spliced (RS) speech, and the non-American samples showed the reverse pattern. We suggest that intonation contours in American-spoken English, which are retained in CF speech, may be more powerful cues to affective meaning for American listeners than for foreigners, and that the reliance placed on such cues by Americans may have hurt their performance on RS speech. Foreigners, on the other hand, may have been misled in their interpretations of CF speech insofar as the American intonation contours differed from those that would be used in their own languages.

In an analysis of variance of 126 samples, in which samples were clustered into fourteen a priori categories, it was found that the categories comprising mental patients, alcoholics, children, and exotic non-Western samples (the unsophisticated) scored relatively better on pure tone channels and relatively worse when video cues were present compared with the remaining samples (effect size = 0.65σ). In addition, the unsophisticated groups performed relatively better on scenes showing positive-submissive affect (effect size = 0.88σ).

Length of Communication Exposure. A forty-item brief-exposure form of the PONS was developed to permit us to study the effects of length of exposure on accuracy in decoding nonverbal cues from the face and body. The twenty face-only and the twenty body-only scenes from the full PONS were each subdivided into four groups of scenes varying in length of exposure. Whereas in the full PONS each film clip is two seconds long (forty-eight frames of film), in this test the four lengths of film clip are 1/24, 3/24, 9/24, and 27/24 second, corresponding to one, three, nine, and twenty-seven frames of film. Thus each presentation of the face or the body is substantially shorter than in the full PONS test.

The results of nine studies of high school and college students and U. S. adults ($N = 506$) were quite consistent in showing accuracy very much greater than chance (and large in magnitude) at even the one-frame length of exposure. Accuracy showed a dramatic increase in going from one to three frames, but no further increase in going from three frames to nine frames or to twenty-seven frames. Mean percent accuracies for one, three, nine, and twenty-seven frames were 56 percent, 74 percent, 73 percent, and 74 percent, respectively. The very dramatic gain in accuracy in going from one to three frames may have been due to the introduction of motion in the longer exposure or simply to the longer visual access to the stimulus materials or to both.

Decreasing exposure length to nine or fewer frames from twenty-seven frames actually increased accuracy for body cues but greatly decreased accuracy for face cues. Perhaps body cues are rapidly processed in high speed exposures in an intuitive, global, nonanalytic manner, with additional small increases in exposure length serving more to confuse than to assist decoding.

Subjects' self-ratings of their relationships with others tended to be negatively correlated with accuracy at high speed exposures. Perhaps those persons most accurate at the fastest speeds have less satisfactory interpersonal relationships because they are able to decode cues they are not intended to decode. The hypothesis is put forward that people who are especially accurate at high speed exposures may "know too much" about others to be socially acceptable.

Gender. The main effects of gender were examined for several age levels. Females were usually more accurate on the PONS test, and Table 5 shows effect sizes (in σ units) for grade

Table 5. Gender Effects at Various Age Levels.

Age Level	N	Effect Size (σ units)[a]
Grade School Norm Group	200	0.62
Junior High Norm Group	109	0.49
12 High School Samples (Weighted Mean)	581	0.57
34 College Samples (Weighted Mean)	1725	0.44
Median	—	0.53[b]

[a]Positive values indicate better performance by females.

[b]The median effect size for all 133 samples available at the time of the analysis was 0.42σ.

school, junior high, high school, and college samples. These effects are of moderate and fairly consistent magnitude across all four age levels and for the entire pool of 133 samples on which relevant data were available at the time of analysis. Consistent with the results of Table 5, several analyses of variance on subsets of samples revealed only small interactions of age and sex, indicating that the gender effect is relatively stable cross-sectionally.

Two interactions of PONS subscales with gender were found for both the grade school and high school norm groups and for a college sample. Females were especially better than males at judging stimuli in which body cues were present (effect sizes = 0.46σ for grade school, 0.26σ for high school, and 0.14σ for college). Females were also especially better than males at judging negative affect cues (effect sizes = 0.45σ for grade school, 0.26σ for high school, and 0.46σ for college).

In four samples the median correlation of the PONS total with the math score on the Scholastic Aptitude Test (SAT) was 0.30 for males and 0.02 for females. The failure of the math SAT to correlate with PONS for females raises the intriguing possibility that the process of judgment may be somewhat different for males and females. We suggest that perhaps an analytic approach profits males on the PONS, whereas for females a more global, intuitive process may be more profitable.

Age. The full-length PONS test was administered to a grade school norm group of two hundred children in grades three through six. The children used an answer sheet that had large type and simplified vocabulary. Internal-consistency reliability (KR-20) for this group was 0.86. Accuracy improved linearly with grade level in this sample (effect size = 0.87σ). In addition, an analysis of age and dimensions of affect showed that the third graders were relatively better at judging negative cues than children in grades four through six ($\eta = 0.21$).

In an analysis of variance of the performance of four age levels (grade school, junior high, high school, and adults), a large linear trend was found (effect size = 3.59σ). The simple correlation between PONS total and mean age in 124 nonpsychiatric samples was 0.34, whereas a more powerful analysis in which samples were blocked into five age levels showed a somewhat larger linear effect ($\eta = 0.49$) and also a quadratic trend ($\eta = 0.47$), showing that performance starts to level off somewhere between twenty and thirty years of age.

It was found that younger samples showed a relative advantage at judging tone as opposed to video cues (ρ between age level and pure video minus pure audio = 0.86). This finding, which fits with some of our other findings as well as with some published results by other researchers, leads to the suggestion that the ability to read vocal cues may be developed prior to the ability to read visual cues, and perhaps may even be unlearned to some degree during socialization.

Cultural Variation. In extensive cross-cultural testing, over two thousand subjects from nearly sixty samples from twenty nations have taken the PONS. Those cultures best able to decode the PONS were independently rated as most similar to American culture (r for thirty samples = 0.70), although every culture tested performed very substantially better than chance. The cultures best able to decode the PONS were also those whose languages were most similar to American language ($r = 0.62$), suggesting the possibility that linguistic similarity may be paralleled by paralinguistic similarity.

Cultures that were more modernized, as defined by per capita steel consumption, automobiles in use, and physician availability, showed greater accuracy on the PONS (median $r = 0.52$), and cultures that were more developed in communications in particular (as defined by per capita energy consumption, newsprint consumption, telephones in use, television sets, and radios) were especially likely to be better decoders on the PONS (median $r = 0.79$). Interestingly, indices of contact with the United States (trade with the United States, tourists from the United States, and foreign mail received) showed a lower median correlation with PONS accuracy ($r = 0.15$). Cultures more developed in communications may have greater experience with and practice in decoding nonverbal cues in the variety of channels tested by the PONS, and they may also be more motivated to understand communications conveyed through various channels.

Within the United States, ethnic and social class correlates of full PONS performance have not been studied extensively. What evidence there is so far suggests no overall difference in PONS performance between whites and nonwhites. For two samples of high school students, we found that girls from higher social class backgrounds scored higher than girls from lower social class backgrounds on the PONS (mean r = 0.26), while boys from higher social class backgrounds scored lower than boys from lower social class backgrounds (mean r = -0.15, differing from the girls' mean r of 0.26 at $p < 0.001$).

Cognitive Correlates. Two kinds of cognitive correlates were examined—performance measures and cognitive style measures. Within the performance category, we can further distinguish general intellectual abilities, for which we would predict a low relationship with PONS, and specific judging abilities in person perception, for which we would predict more substantial correlations with PONS.

Table 6 shows that the relationship between PONS and general intellectual abilities (IQ, SAT, school achievement, and vocabulary) were small, indicating that the PONS test does not merely measure general intellectual ability.

Table 6. Intellectual Performance Correlates of PONS Using High School and College Students.

Variable	Number of Samples	r[a]
IQ	4	0.14
Scholastic Aptitude Test Score	6	0.15
School Achievement	4	0.03
Vocabulary	1	0.18
Median	—	0.14

[a]Median r across N samples of median correlation of PONS subscales with cognitive variable or its subscales.

For several special groups the overall correlations between PONS and intellectual ability were considerably higher. For third graders, reading and math achievement were correlated 0.36 with PONS; for teachers in Singapore the correlation between English proficiency and PONS was 0.60; and for psychiatric patients and alcoholics the correlations of IQ with PONS were 0.26 and 0.52. All of these groups, we would expect, might have difficulty with language. As Table 7 shows, when the samples are subdivided according to their level of performance on the cognitive tests, it is apparent that the substantial correlations occur mainly in the low category. For persons

Table 7. Intellectual Performance Correlates of PONS for
Linguistically Impaired Groups.

	r^a		
Variable (Sample)	*Low*	*Medium*	*High*
Reading and Math (Third graders)	0.40	0.08	0.11
English Proficiency (Singapore teachers)	0.60	0.27	0.14
IQ (Alcoholics)	0.34	0.34	0.33
IQ (Psychiatric patients)[b]	—	0.26	—
Median	0.40	0.26	0.14

[a]Median r of PONS subscales with cognitive variable or its subscales.

[b]Sample not divided into low, medium, and high performance groups.

in the high category, the median correlation with PONS is the same as it was for unimpaired samples ($r = 0.14$).

To explore further the relationship of PONS to intellectual abilities, we performed a principal-components analysis on data from a high school sample for which we had PONS, SAT, and IQ scores. Two factors were derived, one representing PONS and the other representing intellectual ability. The loadings of IQ, verbal SAT, and math SAT on the PONS factor were 0.19, −0.02, and −0.07, respectively. This finding supports our general conclusion that PONS decoding skill is not related in any important way to general intelligence.

The Group Embedded Figures Test, a test of perceptual disembedding, was given to three samples. The median correlation with PONS total was 0.08 for males and 0.28 for females, indicating that for females, at least, field independence (good disembedding) was associated with higher PONS scores.

Table 8 shows correlations between the PONS and skill in person perception, and between the PONS and two dimensions of cognitive style. The Programmed Cases task measures ability to judge personality from verbal information. The four nonverbal decoding tasks (each given to a different sample of subjects) involved judging emotions from visual or auditory cues, judging the pleasantness of the sender's mood, or judging personality or other personal facts from minimal verbal-plus-nonverbal cues. As the table shows, both of these kinds of judging tasks were correlated positively with the PONS total.

Table 8. Other Cognitive Correlates of PONS.

Variable	Number of Samples	r^a
Person Perception		
Assessing programmed cases	1	0.26
Other nonverbal decoding tests	4	0.28
Cognitive Style		
Cognitive complexity	2	0.28
Differential attention	1	—
Face	—	0.48
Body	—	0.72
Tone	—	0.07

[a]Median r across N samples.

"Differential attention" refers to a person's apparent preference for attending to one channel over another (say, face over body). We measured individual differences in preferences for face, body, and filtered speech, and correlated these scores with scores on the PONS. Differential attention was positively associated with PONS video accuracy but not with tone. This and several other of our findings relating to difficulty and learning suggest that accuracy on tone is not as responsive to effort, attention, and practice as are the video channels.

Psychosocial Correlates. In many of our studies, PONS performance was correlated with standard tests of personality, ratings by self, and ratings by others. Table 9 summarizes the results of these studies and shows that PONS performance is somewhat better predicted by standard tests of personality and by judges' ratings than by measures involving self-report.

Subjects scoring higher on the PONS total also scored as better adjusted, more interpersonally democratic and encouraging, less dogmatic, more extraverted, more likely to volunteer for and appear for behavioral research, more popular, and more interpersonally sensitive as judged by acquaintances, clients, spouses, or supervisors. This last result, based on twenty-four studies, of which twenty-one showed positive correlations, provides especially consistent evidence for the validity of the PONS as a measure of interpersonal sensitivity.

Table 9. Median Correlations of PONS Performance with
Psychosocial Measures.

Psychosocial Measure (Scale)	Number of Studies	Median r
Interpersonal Adequacy (Median of 6 CPI scales)	5	0.25
Maturity (Median of 6 CPI scales)	5	0.22
Achievement Potential (Median of 3 CPI scales)	5	0.31
Intellectual and Interest Modes (Median of 3 CPI scales)	5	0.23
Task Orientation (Least Preferred Co-Workers)	1	0.21
Democratic Orientation (Minnesota Teacher Attitude Inventory)	2	0.24
Encouraging Toward Pupils (Observational)	2	0.76
Masculine Therapeutic Style ("A-B" Therapist Variable)	3	0.03[a]
Nondogmatic (Dogmatism)	2	0.20
Low in Need for Approval (Marlowe-Crowne Social Desirability scale, CPI, Personality Research Form)	9	0.07
Low in Machiavellianism (Machiavelli Scale)	4	0.08
Social-Religious Values (Study of Values)	1	0.28
Extraversion (Myers-Briggs Type Indicator, Self-Ratings)	3	0.19[b]
Low in Self-Monitoring (Self-Monitoring Scale)	6	0.08
Self-Reports of Interpersonal Success	10	0.06
Opposite Sex Relationships and Gains in PONS (Self-Ratings and Judges' Ratings)	2	0.62
Self-Report of Nonverbal Sensitivity	28	0.08
Spouse's Report of Nonverbal Sensitivity	2	0.20
Interpersonal Sensitivity (Judges' Ratings)	22	0.22
Popularity (Judges' Ratings)	1	0.15
Volunteering and Appearing for Research (Behavior)	2	0.40
Low in Psychoticism (Psychiatric Patients; 2 Scales)	1	0.30
Median	—	0.22

Note: CPI is the California Psychological Inventory.

[a] For dominant scenes only, median $r = 0.35$.

[b] For randomly spliced speech, median $r = -0.23$.

Impaired Groups. Several samples of psychiatric patients and alcoholic patients have been tested with the PONS. The results were that patients consistently scored below the level of the norm group subjects by a substantial amount—a full standard deviation.

Nevertheless, the performance of the patient groups was dramatically better than chance, and patients were able to profit from the addition of audio cues, body cues, and face cues. Just as for the normals, face cues aided accuracy much more than did body cues, and body cues aided accuracy much more than did audio cues. However, the addition of audio, body, and face cues improved the accuracy of the patient groups less than it improved the accuracy of the normal subjects. In addition, normals benefited more than psychiatric patients in going from pure audio to pure video channels and in going from pure to mixed channels of nonverbal cues. All of these effects, though not large in magnitude, showed patients to be consistently less able than normals to profit from the addition of more nonverbal information.

Further evidence for this relative handicap in benefiting from the addition of channels of nonverbal cues comes from the correlations showing that as the information level of a channel increases, so does the relative disadvantage to the patient groups (median $r = 0.64$). The advantage that accrues from the correct response alternative being paired with an incorrect response alternative from a different quadrant is similarly smaller for the patients than for the normals. Finally, psychiatric patients profit substantially less than normals from the practice obtained in going from the first half to the last half of the PONS. The size of this disadvantage is a full standard deviation.

Although, in general, correlations between PONS performance and self-ratings of sensitivity to nonverbal cues tend to be very small, an interesting exception occurred with a sample of Australian psychiatric patients, who showed a large positive correlation ($r = 0.50$) between total PONS performance and a composite self-rating of interpersonal sensitivity.

For some of the psychiatric patients, scores on two measures of psychoticism were available, and scores on these scales were correlated with scores on the total PONS. Patients scoring as less psychotic on the two scales scored higher on the PONS (median $r = -0.30$), and this relationship was only slightly decreased by partialing out the effects of intellectual ability (median $r = -0.24$).

A group of blind students took the forty-item original sender audio test, with no clear evidence of any overall difference in the performances of the blind and the sighted comparison groups. However, the blind students age seventeen or less performed better than the sighted students age seventeen or less. Among students older than seventeen, the performance of the sighted was better than the performance of the blind unless mental age was partialed out.

A group of deaf students (ages ten to fifteen) took the video-only portion (sixty items) of the PONS. Among these students, those whose hearing was more impaired performed substantially less well than did the students whose hearing was less impaired. Interestingly, PONS performance was not related appreciably to skill at reading ($r = -0.13$), lipreading ($r = 0.02$), or IQ ($r = -0.16$). The performance of the deaf students as a group was substantially lower than the performance of the comparison groups of students at all age levels. For a sample of deaf college students, however, we found no significant difference between their PONS performance and that of their hearing comparison groups.

Roles and Relationships. When various U. S. occupational groups were ranked on PONS total, the top three ranks were held by actors (two samples), students of nonverbal communication (three samples), and students of visual arts (three samples). These three groups did not differ significantly among themselves, but together they were significantly higher scoring (effect size = 0.45σ) than the fourth-ranked group, eight samples of clinicians, whose scores were comparable to those of U. S. college students. The eight groups of clinicians did not differ from each other significantly, but together scored better than the fifth- and sixth-ranked groups, teachers (ten samples) and business executives (three samples) (effect size = 0.42σ). These two groups scored similarly to U. S. high school students.

For teachers and clinicians, supervisors' ratings of professional skill were obtained. For teachers, the median correlation between PONS total and teaching skill in three samples was 0.38. For clinicians, the median correlation between PONS total and clinical skill in thirteen samples was 0.20. Hence, rated excellence in these two occupations requiring interpersonal skills was related to PONS decoding, even though on the average these two groups did not perform outstandingly on the PONS.

For both teachers and clinicians, greater professional advancement was associated with *lower* PONS scores (for teachers in one sample, $r = -0.66$; for clinicians, median of four samples, $r = -0.62$). In the absence of longitudinal data, we cannot say whether these persons lose some of their nonverbal sensitivity as they advance, or whether those who achieve greater advancement are less sensitive to begin with.

It was hypothesized that experience with preverbal children might enhance one's sensitivity to nonverbal cues. When two samples of parents of toddlers were compared with two matched samples of nonparents, the parents were shown to be more accurate on the PONS (effect size = 0.50σ). This effect was due mainly to differences between the women who were mothers and those who were not.

Several analyses have been undertaken to begin to explore the effects of similarity-dissimilarity of the PONS profiles of romantic couples. Comparison of real couples with randomly paired opposite-sexed persons showed a tendency for the real couple members to be more *dissimilar* to each other than the members of the artificial couples on both profile shape and overall level of PONS accuracy (median effect size for four samples = 0.28σ). For dating couples, longevity as defined by whether they were still together one year after taking the PONS test was associated with more dissimilarity in overall accuracy of the couple members ($r = 0.33$). Among the same couples, more reciprocal self-disclosure was also associated with more dissimilarity in overall accuracy (median r over three indices of PONS dissimilarity, male-female report, and disclosure received-disclosure given = 0.34). Hence it would appear that it is adaptive for couple members' nonverbal decoding skills not to be too similar, though it is not clear why this should be so.

In a study comparing the PONS performance of friends and family of our PONS sender with the performance of a group of matched strangers, there was no main effect of group but there was an interaction of mode with group: Friends and family performed relatively better on audio, and strangers performed relatively better on video (effect size = 0.43σ). Long-term effects of knowing the sender may have been especially beneficial for the decoding of tone, because the tone channels are so difficult and so resistant to short-term effects of practice, training, and attention.

Practice and Training. There is considerable evidence to suggest that prior experience in taking the PONS serves to improve subsequent performance. For eight samples that were tested twice, the average increase in performance from first to second testing was very large (1.79σ). The gains in performance due to retesting were especially large in the sixty scenes in which only the body was shown. Practice may be more useful to decoding body cues because there is less opportunity in everyday life to decode body cues apart from face cues. An experiment in which subjects were randomly assigned to a pretest or a no-pretest condition yielded essentially the same result as did the earlier cited eight studies. Pretesting yielded a great PONS performance advantage, which was greatest for the sixty scenes showing only the body.

For two samples we correlated the gains in total PONS performance with rated interpersonal success with people of the opposite sex. In both studies those showing greater gains in PONS accuracy reported better relationships with persons of the opposite sex (median $r = 0.62$). Perhaps the ability to profit from experience in assessing nonverbal cues makes it easier to relate to others of the opposite sex.

For one of the samples just referred to, subjects rated their accuracy in receiving through various channels of nonverbal communication. Just as we have usually found, these self-ratings did not correlate very highly with actual PONS performance on the pretest (median r for three self-ratings = 0.19). However, these self-ratings correlated substantially with gains in PONS accuracy (median $r = 0.49$). Perhaps when people rate their sensitivity to nonverbal cues, they are actually evaluating their ability to learn to decode someone they have not met before. A subsequent study obtained results in the same direction but not as large in size of effect ($r = 0.17$).

For an additional set of eight samples we examined the gains in accuracy in going from the first half to the last half of the PONS test. The overall size of the gain was substantial

(0.89σ), but smaller than the size of the gain from an initial to a subsequent administration of the PONS (1.79σ). That result seems understandable, however, in view of there being fewer items to practice on in going from the first to last half compared with going from an initial to a subsequent full PONS testing (110 versus 220 items). Just as was the case for studies of the effects of pretesting, these studies of the single testing situation also showed that the greatest practice effects accrued to the sixty items showing only the body.

A pilot training program was developed to determine whether PONS performance could be improved in a single training session lasting about ninety minutes. The program was administered to a randomly selected subset of mental health professionals, while the remaining professionals served as waiting list controls. The results were promising; those receiving the brief training performed better on the PONS than did the controls (0.58σ). Somewhat surprisingly, the more experienced clinicians showed the greater benefits of training.

Finally, a study was conducted in which meditators and nonmeditators were tested on the PONS, once just after meditating and once after not meditating. The results were very clear; each group performed better on the PONS when it was doing its characteristic task: Meditators gained more after meditating and nonmeditators gained more after not meditating.

Interpersonal Expectancy Effects. Previous research has shown that experimenters in psychological experiments can inadvertently influence the outcome of their research by communicating their expectations to research subjects via subtle nonverbal cues (Rosenthal, 1976). As indicated earlier in this chapter, we hypothesized that nonverbal communication skills may partly determine who might be the most effective communicator in these circumstances and also who might be most influenced by such cues. The study of the role of nonverbal communication skills as a moderator of interpersonal influence was one important reason for the development of the PONS. We have begun to assess the relationship of skill on the PONS to the communication of interpersonal expectancies, one kind of interpersonal influence.

Table 10 shows that in four kinds of study, there was no overall tendency for persons more sensitive to nonverbal cues in

Table 10. Median Correlations of PONS Total with Measures of Susceptibility to Experimenter's Expectancies.

Dependent Variable	Number of Samples	r
Judgments of Success and Failure in Faces	7	−0.00
Achilles Heel Response	1	0.04
EEG Alpha Frequency	1	0.09
EEG Alpha Amplitude	1	0.26
Median	—	0.06

the PONS to be more susceptible to the experimenter's expectancies. Perhaps nonverbally sensitive people can detect subtle biasing attempts and behave so as to counteract or reduce the effectiveness of such subtle communication. Some slight support for this hypothesis came from our analysis of subjects' ability to detect the direction of the experimenter's expectancies in silent films of experimenters interacting with subjects in a role-playing experiment. For seven samples the median correlation of PONS total with subjects' ability to detect bias was 0.13 (median for four college samples = 0.20, median for three adult samples = −0.06). PONS audio scores were more highly related to this ability than were PONS video scores (effect size = 0.92σ).

We would expect that nonverbal decoding skills of the sending member of a pair of interactants might also influence the communication of expectancies. In a study of teacher expectancies, the correlation between teacher's PONS total score and teacher's ability to bias pupils' intellectual performance in the direction of the teacher's expectancy was 0.15, which, though small, does suggest that teacher's decoding skills may play a part in such outcomes.

We would also expect that in a dyad the nonverbal sending skills of the sending member and the nonverbal judging skills of the receiving member should jointly influence the success of interpersonal influence attempts. In one study (Zuckerman, DeFrank, Hall, and Rosenthal, in press), the combined effect of experimenter's sending skill and subject's PONS decoding skill on bias was substantial (effect size = 1.07σ).

Construct Validity

The defining feature of construct validation is that there is no single criterion that will validate the instrument. This makes proper construct validation a long and difficult process. The general problem of construct validation is especially acute when the attribute has not been extensively researched or measured in the past. That was the situation for the PONS test.

All of the relationships reported in this chapter between PONS scores and other variables help to define the construct validity of the PONS. In evaluating these relationships one should keep in mind that the expected magnitudes are not very large. Along these lines, Cohen (1969) notes that the near maximum criterion validity coefficients for personality measures fall around 0.30. The criterion validity coefficients obtained in the PONS research fall close to that upper limit on the average, and the correlations of PONS scores with variables that should be less highly correlated, such as IQ, are suitably low. All in all, then, the PONS test has fared well in terms of criterion validity and discriminant validity, and hence in terms of construct validity.

After establishing the network of relationships between scores on one's instrument and other measures, the question remains of whether the name given to the attribute measured by one's instrument is appropriate. The only test of this is whether any alternative construct fits the observed pattern of relationships better than does the construct originally proposed. In the case of the PONS test we feel that "nonverbal sensitivity" best describes the construct we have been investigating.

Prospectus

Origins of Individual Differences in Nonverbal Sensitivity. Despite the large amount of research we have done, we know little about factors that directly affect nonverbal sensitivity.

Why do people differ in their abilities to "read" various channels and kinds of affect? Some possible determinants and some
avenues of research are suggested here.

To the extent nonverbal sensitivity is an acquired ability,
developmental, especially longitudinal, research is called for.
This would mean developing good decoding tasks for use with
younger age groups than we have so far tested and searching
systematically for correlates and determinants of individual differences in children's nonverbal sensitivity. Such determinants
could be genetic, physiological, and psychological. Psychological
factors might involve a child's response to family characteristics
if, for example, children's profiles of skills grew to resemble
those of their same-sexed or caretaking parent, or if children's
skills developed to compensate for nonverbal decoding or encoding weaknesses on the part of the parent. Other aspects of
early development, such as the quality and quantity of parent-
child interaction, could affect the development of nonverbal
skills. Research among younger children would also enable us to
explore one of our most intriguing unanswered questions: What
accounts for the fact that females at all ages tested so far score
higher than males on the PONS?

To the extent that nonverbal sensitivity can be deliberately changed, research involving various interventions is called
for. Research of this type would help us find out whether, for
example, experience or training in certain occupations, in certain social situations, or with particular others (such as one's
spouse) affects one's ability to decode nonverbal cues. One
might also study what kinds of experiences are conducive to the
further development of nonverbal sensitivity after the age of
thirty and later, when our cross-sectional analyses suggest that
PONS skill typically levels off.

To the extent that individual differences in nonverbal
sensitivity are caused by transient cognitive, motivational, and
situational factors, new ways of measuring nonverbal sensitivity
that take such factors into account could be developed. For
example, judging strategies (for example, analytic, intuitive, and
imagistic) may differ among people (or perhaps between the
sexes) and might account for some variation in level of skill.

Situational and motivational factors affecting decoding ability would include the judge's perception of the consequences of good or bad judging in the particular situation; the judge's willingness to pay attention, which could vary with the judge's liking of the sender or the judge's mood; and the salience of different dimensions of affect for different judges. Other situational factors involving sender characteristics could relate to the sender's sending skill or motivation, interactions of sender-judge characteristics (for example, subculture or gender), and history of the particular sender-judge dyad. In other words, the traitlike skill measured by the PONS is only one component of a person's true nonverbal sensitivity—a sensitivity that varies with shifts in judging strategies, with motivation, with situations, and with stimulus persons.

Implications of Individual Differences in Nonverbal Sensitivity. There are important general theoretical as well as practical implications of the research on individual differences in sensitivity to nonverbal communication. Perhaps the most general implication is that the outcome of interpersonal interactions may be affected in important ways by the interactants' sensitivity to nonverbal cues. Thus in such relatively formal relationships as therapist-patient, physician-patient, counselor-client, attorney-client, teacher-student, experimenter-subject, and employer-employee, the extent to which the goals of the dyad or the dyad members are met may depend to an important degree on the members' sensitivity to nonverbal cues. Similarly, in the more informal relationships found in everyday life, such as the relationships among couples, friends, roommates, acquaintances, and new encounters, the outcomes may depend heavily on the members' sensitivity to one another's nonverbal cues.

It seems reasonable to propose as well that the level of ability to send nonverbal cues in various channels will also contribute importantly to the outcomes of the formal and informal relationships noted above. If for any formal or informal dyad we could specify the accuracy of sending in each nonverbal channel as well as the accuracy of receiving of both the dyad members, we might advance our understanding of interpersonal interaction significantly. We would not only learn more about how to build an adequate theory of interpersonal relations, but we would also learn more that would help us to improve the ability to help others by improving the quality of help-giving dyads, such as physician-patient, therapist-patient, and teacher-student. Learning more about the optimal fit or match between a helper's and a help receiver's profiles of sending and receiving abilities may improve considerably our capacity to provide culturally important interpersonal services.

Matching therapists or physicians or teachers implies selecting them for certain characteristics relative to known characteristics of their patients or students. However, selection can be employed even without a specific knowledge of patient or student characteristics. It may be, for example, that selecting therapists, physicians, or teachers on the variable of sensitivity to nonverbal communication could appreciably improve the level of care or education provided. Even a small correlation between helpers' sensitivity to nonverbal cues and helpers' ability to actually be helpful to others would be of great practical utility in terms of the thousands of help receivers who would be better served over the years. Sensitivity to nonverbal cues appears also to be a very useful basis on which to develop selection instruments for professions and occupations other than the helping professions.

To the extent that sensitivity to nonverbal cues can be improved (and the evidence suggests that it can be), it may be useful to develop a variety of programs designed to improve sensitivity to nonverbal cues. The benefits to the helping professions of such training programs are obvious, but perhaps improved sensitivity to nonverbal cues could also contribute to an improvement in the relationships between the sexes, among ethnic groups and races, and among people in general.

APPENDIX: SHORT PONS TESTS

Visual Mode

Still Photo PONS. The still photo version of the PONS test comes in two forms. One is a set of sixty 4 X 5 inch photographs, the other a set of 35-mm slides made from these photographs, each taken from one of the sixty scenarios comprising the face, body, and figure (face and body) channels in the full PONS. The photo test is administered with an overhead (opaque) projector, and the slide test is administered with a slide projector. The correlation of Still Photo PONS total with full PONS total for fifty-three high school students was 0.53 (p < 0.001).

Photo Booklet PONS. This is a self-paced and self-administered forty-item booklet version, employing the twenty face-only and twenty body-only items from the Still Photo PONS. For two samples, sixty-two teachers and twenty-four business executives, the correlations of Photo Booklet PONS total with full PONS total were 0.64 (p < 0.001) and 0.05.

Face and Body PONS. This film test contains the twenty face-only and twenty body-only items from the full PONS. The correlation of total score on this test with total on the Brief Exposure PONS was 0.50 for 108 high school students.

Brief Exposure PONS. This film employs the twenty face-only and twenty body-only items from the full PONS, but the exposure lengths of the film items are shortened from 2 seconds to 1/24, 3/24, 9/24, or 27/24 seconds. The correlation of Brief Exposure PONS total with full PONS total for fifty-four college students was 0.54 (p < 0.001).

Auditory Mode

Original Sender Audio PONS. This test contains the twenty randomized-spliced-only and the twenty content-filtered-only items from the full PONS.

Male Sender Audio PONS. This test was made on the exact format of the audio sections of the full PONS, but with a twenty-five-year-old Caucasian male from the U. S. as the sender. It has twenty randomized-spliced items and twenty content-filtered items. The median correlation of Male Sender Audio PONS total with the tone-only portions of the full PONS for three samples was 0.30.

Child Sender Audio PONS. This test was made on the

same format as the Original Sender Audio PONS and the Male Sender Audio PONS, but with an eight-year-old Caucasian girl from the U. S. as the sender. A few of the scenes enacted by the portrayer were changed to make them meaningful to a child of her age.

References

Adair, J. G., and Epstein, J. S. "Verbal Cues in the Mediation of Experimenter Bias." *Psychological Reports,* 1968, *22,* 1045-1053.

Allport, F. H. *Social Psychology.* Boston: Houghton Mifflin, 1924.

Argyle, M. "Nonverbal Communication in Human Social Interaction." In R. A. Hinde (Ed.), *Non-Verbal Communication.* Cambridge, England: Cambridge University Press, 1972.

Armor, D. J. "Theta Reliability and Factor Scaling." In H. L. Costner (Ed.), *Sociological Methodology 1973-1974.* San Francisco: Jossey-Bass, 1974.

Buck, R. "Nonverbal Communication of Affect in Children." *Journal of Personality and Social Psychology,* 1975, *31,* 644-653.

Campbell, R. J., Kagan, N., and Krathwohl, D. R. "The Development and Validation of a Scale to Measure Affective Sensitivity (Empathy)." *Journal of Counseling Psychology,* 1971, *18,* 407-412.

Cline, V. B. "Interpersonal Perception." In B. A. Maher (Ed.), *Progress in Experimental Personality Research.* Vol. 1. New York: Academic Press, 1964.

Cohen, J. *Statistical Power Analysis for the Behavioral Sciences.* New York: Academic Press, 1969.

Conn, L. K., Edwards, C. N., Rosenthal, R., and Crowne, D. "Perception of Emotion and Response to Teachers' Expectancy by Elementary School Children." *Psychological Reports,* 1968, *22,* 27-34.

Cook, M. *Interpersonal Perception.* New York: Penguin, 1971.

Duncan, S., and Rosenthal, R. "Vocal Emphasis in Experi-

menters' Instruction Reading as Unintended Determinant
of Subjects' Responses." *Language and Speech,* 1968, *11,*
20-26.

Ekman, P. (Ed.). *Darwin and Facial Expression: A Century of
Research in Review.* New York: Academic Press, 1973.

Ekman, P., Friesen, W. V., and Ellsworth, P. *Emotion in the
Human Face: Guidelines for Research and an Integration
of Findings.* Elmsford, N.Y.: Pergamon Press, 1972.

Friedman, H. "Magnitude of Experimental Effect and a Table
for Its Rapid Estimation." *Psychological Bulletin,* 1968,
70, 245-251.

Frijda, N. H. "Recognition of Emotion." In L. Berkowitz (Ed.),
Advances in Experimental Social Psychology. Vol. 4.
New York: Academic Press, 1969.

Hall, J. A. "Gender Effects in Decoding Nonverbal Cues."
Psychological Bulletin, in press.

Knapp, M. *Nonverbal Communication in Human Interaction.*
New York: Holt, Rinehart and Winston, 1972.

Polanyi, M. "Tacit Knowing: Its Bearing on Some Problems of
Philosophy." *Reviews of Modern Physics,* 1962, *34.*

Rogers, P. L., Scherer, K. R., and Rosenthal, R. "Content-Fil-
tering Human Speech: A Simple Electronic System." *Behavioral Research Methods and Instrumentation,* 1971, *3.*

Rosenthal, R. "Covert Communication in the Psychological Experiment." *Psychological Bulletin,* 1967, *67,* 356-367.

Rosenthal, R. "Interpersonal Expectations: Effects of the Experimenter's Hypothesis." In R. Rosenthal and R. L. Rosnow (Eds.), *Artifact in Behavioral Research.* New York:
Academic Press, 1969.

Rosenthal, R. "Teacher Expectations and Their Effects upon
Children." In G. S. Lesser (Ed.), *Psychology and Educational Practice.* Glenview, Ill.: Scott, Foresman, 1971.

Rosenthal, R. *On the Social Psychology of the Self-Fulfilling
Prophecy: Further Evidence for Pygmalion Effects and
Their Mediating Mechanisms.* Module 53. New York:
MSS Modular Publications, 1974.

Rosenthal, R. *Experimenter Effects in Behavioral Research.*
(enlarged ed.) New York: Irvington, 1976.

Rosenthal, R., and Fode, K. L. "Three Experiments in Experimenter Bias." *Psychological Reports,* 1963, *12,* 491-511.

Rosenthal, R., Hall, J. A., DiMatteo, M. R., Rogers, P. L., and Archer, D. *Sensitivity to Nonverbal Communication: The PONS Test.* Unpublished manuscript, Harvard University, 1978.

Rosenthal, R., Hall, J. A., and Zuckerman, M. "The Relative Equivalence of Senders in Studies of Nonverbal Encoding and Decoding." *Environmental Psychology and Nonverbal Behavior,* in press.

Rosenthal, R., and Jacobson, L. *Pygmalion in the Classroom: Teacher Expectations and Pupils' Intellectual Development.* New York: Holt, Rinehart and Winston, 1968.

Sapir, E. A. "Communication." In D. G. Mandelbaum (Ed.), *Selected Writings of Edward Sapir in Language, Culture, and Personality.* Berkeley: University of California Press, 1949.

Scherer, K. R. "Randomized-Splicing: A Note on a Simple Technique for Masking Speech Content." *Journal of Experimental Research in Personality,* 1971, *5,* 155-159.

Scherer, K. R., Koivumaki, J., and Rosenthal, R. "Minimal Cues in the Vocal Communication of Affect: Judging Emotions from Content-Masked Speech." *Journal of Psycholinguistic Research,* 1972, *1,* 269-285.

Tagiuri, R. "Person Perception." In G. Lindzey and E. Aronson (Eds.), *The Handbook of Social Psychology.* Vol. 3. (2nd ed.) Reading, Mass.: Addison-Wesley, 1969.

Troffer, S. A., and Tart, C. T. "Experimenter Bias in Hypnotist Performance." *Science,* 1964, *145,* 1330-1331.

Walker, R. E., and Foley, J. M. "Social Intelligence: Its History and Measurement." *Psychological Reports,* 1973, *33.*

Zoble, E. J., and Lehman, R. S. "Interaction of Subject and Experimenter Expectancy Effects in a Tone Length Discrimination Task." *Behavioral Science,* 1969, *14,* 357-363.

Zuckerman, M., DeFrank, R. S., Hall, J. A., and Rosenthal, R. "Accuracy of Nonverbal Communication as Determinant of Experimenter Expectancy Effects." *Environmental Psychology and Nonverbal Behavior,* in press.

Zuckerman, M., Hall, J. A., DeFrank, R. S., and Rosenthal, R. "Encoding and Decoding of Spontaneous and Posed Facial Expressions." *Journal of Personality and Social Psychology,* 1976, *34,* 966-977.

VI

Use of Improvisational Techniques in Assessment

PAUL McREYNOLDS, SUSAN DeVOGE

This chapter will review and evaluate a potentially powerful yet generally unheralded approach to personality assessment. This approach is built around the use of improvisational, or roleplaying, techniques. Though the approach is hardly new—it was first proposed in the 1930s and has been employed to some degree ever since—it has advanced considerably in recent years, both in popularity and in technology, and in our judgment it now merits recognition and examination as an important special approach in psychological assessment. The method appears to be especially promising for evaluating interpersonal variables.

In this presentation we will focus on attempts to develop systematic, standardized improvisational assessment techniques. It should be noted, however, that the most widespread current use of improvisations in assessment is in the form of psycho-

The authors are grateful to G. P. Ginsburg, Kenneth Nordin, Sandra Osborne, and Bruce Pither for their helpful comments on various portions of this chapter.

therapists observing roleplays carried out by their clients and then making inferences from these enactments about the personality styles and capacities of the clients. The line between the use of roleplays for therapy and their use for personality evaluation is sometimes a very fine one, and the same enactment may often serve both functions.

It is our hope that the present review and critique will serve not only to bring together and integrate a wide range of work on improvisational techniques but also to help define this area of assessment and stimulate increased interest and research in it.

What Improvisational Assessment Is

The general theme of improvisational assessment, as we will use the term here, is that the subject imagines being in a prescribed environmental situation and then carries out actual behaviors, primarily verbal, in accord with the demands of the situation. Typically the subject is assisted in the imaginary phase of creating the situation by instructions, certain props (such as chairs, a telephone, and the like), and frequently by one or more other persons with whom he or she interacts. During the behavioral phase the subject makes up, or improvises, ongoing behavior as the action proceeds, which is of course the reason that the method can appropriately be referred to as improvisational assessment.

During the behavioral phase the subject's behavior is observed by one or more judges or raters, who assess the subject's behavior and make inferences, either on a broad, intuitive basis or by the use of systematic rating scales or coding procedures, about the subject's personality structure or specific behavioral patterns. In the postbehavioral phase, additional sources of data may be tapped: These include the subject's evaluation of the adequacy of his or her performance, whether the performance seemed typical of his or her real-life behavior, how much stress the performance caused, and so on. The entire improvisation may be videotaped for further, later analysis.

A few words on terminology are in order at this point.

The terms *improvisation* and *roleplaying* are currently used more or less interchangeably in the literature, though roleplaying appears to be the broader, more generic term. Thus, *improvisations* or *improvisational roleplaying* may be defined as a subclass of roleplaying in which the subject, given that he accepts the circumstances with which a roleplay opens, makes up his behavior as he goes along—he is thus simply himself dealing with a somewhat novel problem situation. Contrasting with this is what may be called "controlled roleplaying," in which the subject attempts to behave in such a way as to fulfill the specifications of a given role—for example, an assertive or a caring person. A number of authors (Corsini, 1966; Mixon, 1971; Moreno, 1964; Moreno, 1974; Wohlking and Weiner, 1971) have proposed classifications of roleplaying techniques. Our distinction between improvised roleplaying and controlled roleplaying is somewhat similar to that between the spontaneous and structured roleplaying described by Wohlking and Weiner and can be accommodated to Mixon's taxonomy.

There are a number of therapeutic approaches—psychodrama, Gestalt therapy, assertive training, and others—that utilize roleplaying procedures. It seems preferable, however, to keep these and other applications conceptually separate from the procedures themselves, and for the latter *improvisations* and *roleplaying* are both appropriate terms.

Pioneering Approaches to Improvisational Assessment

Though the use of roleplaying in various culturally ingrained rituals and in drama has a very long history, its use in psychological assessment, even in a preliminary way, is quite recent. In order to understand the present scene, it is essential to review this recent history in some detail. The narrative begins with the development of psychodrama.

Moreno, Psychodrama, and Improvisational Assessment. Early in this century Jacob L. Moreno, a young psychiatrist in Vienna, began experimenting with the possible therapeutic uses of theatrical modalities, a venture that eventually culminated in the systematic procedure to which Moreno gave the name *psychodrama*. Moreno, who was born in 1892 in Rumania and died in the United States in 1974—he had settled in this country in 1925—was a highly creative if somewhat unorthodox therapist and was one of a handful of seminal figures who laid the foundations for the diversity that characterizes modern psychotherapy.

In 1921 Moreno carried out, in the Komedian Haus Theatre in Vienna, what he later considered to have been the first psychodramatic session (Moreno, 1964; Anderson, 1974); this was an attempt, using dramatic expression, to deal with some of the seething political unrest in postwar Vienna. Later in the same year Moreno founded the Spontaneity Theatre (*Das Stegreiftheater*) in a location not far from the Vienna Opera House. It was in this experience, according to Moreno (1959b), that he first became aware of the therapeutic potentialities of spontaneous acting. In the United States he first employed his psychodramatic technique with children at a Sunday school in Brooklyn in 1925 and in the same year gave a demonstration of psychodrama at Mount Sinai Hospital in New York. Interest in psychodrama increased greatly during the 1930s and 1940s, though it remained somewhat outside the mainstream of psychiatry. In 1937 Moreno established the journal *Sociometry*, and in 1947 he founded *Sociatry* (later *Group Psychotherapy*). His most important books were *Psychodrama* (Moreno, 1959a, 1964, 1969) and *Who Shall Survive?* (Moreno, 1953).

The essence of psychodrama is that the subject, or protagonist, enacts certain roles in a theater-like setting as prescribed by, and under the direction of, the director-therapist. The "cast" typically includes one or more other persons, termed *auxiliary egos,* who are either professional personnel or other members of the therapy group, and whose function is to play whatever roles are necessary to permit the protagonist to enact the desired scene. For example, if the protagonist is to perform a role with her parents, then auxiliary egos would be called on to play the roles of her father and mother. The aims of psychodrama are to permit catharsis of emotionally charged issues, to help the client to gain insights, and to provide practice in significant role behaviors. The protagonist, of course, has to improvise his or her behavior, though in line with the general guidelines put forth by the director-therapist.

The primary focus of psychodrama has always been on therapeutic benefits, rather than on assessment. Nevertheless, a number of direct applications to assessment were made by Moreno and his associates in the early period of psychodrama. We will now discuss these briefly. First of all, it should be noted that in standard therapeutic psychodrama sessions the director-therapist routinely makes certain clinical evaluations of the protagonist. Thus, Moreno (1959b), in describing his first psychodrama experiences in 1921, reports how he gained significant clinical insights into the relationship between a young woman and her husband through observations of their psychodramatic portrayals.

A more systematic use of psychodrama in assessment was proposed by Moreno (1953) in the method he termed the "Spontaneity Test." The primary purpose of this procedure was to assess the amount of spontaneity manifested by subjects. The method evidently had at least two versions. In the first application (Moreno, 1953, pp. 337, 347-348; see also Moreno, 1950, pp. 147-148) two subjects are instructed to adopt a given emotion—anger, fear, sympathy, or dominance—with respect to the other; then the two subjects, without prior consultation, are asked to carry out a psychodramatic interaction. In the later and more sophisticated version (Moreno, 1964, pp. 117-129), there is a psychodramatic interaction between the subject and the tester, in which the subject imagines himself in a prescribed situation in interaction with the tester and improvises accordingly. For example, in one situation used in the Spontaneity Test the subject imagines himself driving his car too fast and being stopped by a state trooper, played by the tester. In another one the subject is called into the office of his employer (played by the tester), told that his work has been unsatisfactory, and dismissed. Moreno reported that the spontaneous reactions of subjects to the prescribed situations varied greatly. Thus, Moreno comments, with respect to the state trooper episode, that the reactions ranged "from meekness and subordination . . . all the way to aggressiveness and, even, actual assault and from open recognition of the delinquency to cheating, lying and, finally, attempts at bribery" (1964, p. 127).

It is important, Moreno conceived, that the tester be carefully prepared so that he is able to present the same psychodramatic stimulus to each subject. At the same time the tester must be flexible and versatile in responding to the various courses of action of different subjects.

Two recorders were recommended. One recorder takes notes on all words spoken in the psychodrama, while the other records gestures and motions. Both record certain time values. It was concluded that "our studies to date indicate that spontaneity scales can be constructed which have a great deal of precision, showing the degree with which an individual deviates from the relative norm" (Moreno, 1964, pp. 128-129).

As far as we are aware such scales were never published, and it is unclear how far or how systematically they were developed. Similarly, the exact details of the scenario and the instructions to the subjects are not reported. The practice of the Moreno group was evidently to utilize the same dramatic situation over and over, with different subjects, at a given session. This procedure obviously pointed up individual differences but did not focus on any given person. Nevertheless, it is clear that the main theme of improvisational assessment, in which the subject's behavior in a standard interpersonal situation is systematically evaluated by raters, was clearly stated and used by Moreno. In evaluating the method he wrote that "the spontaneity test is able to uncover feelings in their nascent, initial state. Through it we get a better knowledge of the genuine attitudes an individual may develop in the course of conduct and clinch acts in the moment of their performance" (1964, p. 122).

In a brief later discussion titled "Improvisation for Personality Assessment," Moreno notes that a number of standard psychodramatic situations have been devised that "enable the director and group members to get a profile of the action potential of the individual which paper and pencil tests are unable to uncover" (1969, p. 245). The situation descriptions referred to here are those developed in the OSS program, which we will discuss in the next subsection.

In addition to the paradigm of the Spontaneity Test, in which an individual is faced with a complex problem situation, Moreno (1953, pp. 348-354; see also 1964, pp. 161-176) developed the Role Test. In this procedure the subject is asked to enact a variety of different roles; the aim is to assess the "role range" of the subject. For example, a child might be asked to play the roles of various different vocations, and the number of roles that he is able to enact meaningfully would reveal the degree to which he has assimilated this aspect of his culture.

The OSS, the VA, and Improvisational Assessment. For an examination of the next important step in the development of improvisational assessment we turn our attention to the U.S. Office of Strategic Services (OSS). This organization was set up in 1942 to carry out a variety of special missions, including intelligence activities, during World War II. The importance and taxing nature of the tasks of the OSS meant that personnel had to be selected with great care, and accordingly a special group, under the direction of Henry Murray, then director of the Harvard Psychological Clinic, was set up to develop and carry out personnel selection procedures. The psychologists involved in this procedure included such well-known names—in addition to Murray—as Donald Fiske, Donald MacKinnon, O. H. Mowrer, Percival Symonds, Edward Tolman, Robert Tryon, and Kurt Lewin. A number of interesting and innovative lifelike assessment procedures, including in particular some focusing on the evaluation of behavior under stress, were devised. Our interest here, however, will be limited to one of these tests, titled "Improvisations." So far as we are aware, it is here that the term *improvisation* first comes to be used technically to describe roleplaying behaviors involved in assessment.

The Improvisations test was one of three utilized under the heading of "individual task situations," the other two being one in which the candidate directed two helpers (stooges) in building a wooden structure, and one in which the candidate interviewed a job applicant (stooge). Though both of these tests involved improvised behavior to some degree, we will restrict our attention here to the more significant example, the Improvisations test. The OSS experience with this method is described in the book *Assessment of Men* (OSS Assessment Staff, 1948, pp. 168-177) and in papers by Symonds (1947) and Bronfenbrenner and Newcomb (1948). Though a number of psychologists were involved in the development of the test, the principal figures were apparently Bronfenbrenner, Newcomb, and Symonds. The first two of these, particularly Bronfenbrenner, continued work on the technique after the war, as we will see shortly.

The Improvisations procedure was derived from the work of Moreno and represented an adaptation of psychodrama to the specific needs of the OSS assessment staff. The usual procedure at Station S, the country home in Virginia where the assessment was carried out, was generally as follows. Candidates were tested individually but dealt with in groups, and the entire assessment period covered three days. The improvisations were carried out in the evening of the second day in group meetings of candidates. There were a table and two chairs at the front of the room where the action took place. Candidates performed in pairs. A number of scripts had been prepared from which the candidate could choose. One of the early ones, which it was hoped would be helpful in identifying leadership qualities, was this: "Mr. F. of this organization has been working as an administrative assistant for about two months. He feels that he has been doing a good job. His superior, Mr. G., however, is so dissatisfied with the work of his assistant that he decides to call him into his office. The scene to be enacted is the conversation between Mr. F. and Mr. G." (OSS Assessment Staff, 1948, p. 170).

During the improvisations staff members made careful observations of the behaviors of both candidates, and following the enactments the performance was discussed by the entire group. The original hope—that the procedure would be especially sensitive to the identification of leadership qualities—was not supported by the early work; however, the method proved signally helpful in illuminating general interpersonal characteristics of the subjects, and a number of broader improvisations, many of them specially created for given subjects, were developed. It was concluded that the method works best when the subjects are presented with a natural, meaningful situation representing a problem of interpersonal relations, but are not told how they are to feel or behave or what they are to say. Consequently, "once the situation begins, each person is on his own; he has to improvise. Hence the name by which the procedure was designated" (Bronfenbrenner and Newcomb, 1948, p. 369). Here is an example that illustrates the approach recommended:

> Candidates A and B are told that they have been fellow workers for several months. B has a car; A does not. This morning, as on one or two previous occasions, A arranged to borrow B's car.
> Candidate A is given the following additional data. He had driven B's car for only a block when he overlooked a stop sign and was hit by a truck which damaged the car very severely. A returns to the office to find B.
> Candidate B is given the following additional information. Shortly after A had arranged to borrow B's car, B got a message which requires that he definitely have his car this morning. He looks around for A. Luckily A is just coming in the door [Bronfenbrenner and Newcomb, 1948, pp. 368-369].

Though an early attempt was made to utilize rating scales in connection with the Improvisations test, this was abandoned as incongruent with the subtle aspects of behavior revealed by the technique, and consequently no quantitative data on the test were obtained. It was felt by the assessment team, however, that the insights gained about candidates was greater for Improvisations than for any other assessment procedure except the interview.

In all, 111 different improvisation situations were used in the OSS. These were classified by Symonds (1947, pp. 45-50) into seven different types, as situations concerning: (1) personal criticism; (2) interpersonal conflict of aims, goals, and ideals; (3) situations involving moral issues; (4) interview; (5) rejection; (6) intrapersonal conflict and decision; and (7) authority-subordination.

The next step in the development of improvisational assessment techniques was in a U.S. Veterans Administration (VA) sponsored project concerned with the prediction of performance of clinical psychologists (Kelly, 1947; Kelly and Fiske, 1950, 1951). In this study, carried out by the University of Michigan, several hundred clinical psychology trainees, beginning in 1946, were administered a variety of tests, and the results of these were later compared with criterion ratings of clinical effectiveness in order to evaluate the predictive validities of the tests. One of the consultants on this project, which got underway shortly after the end of the war, was Urie Bronfenbrenner, who—as we have already seen—had been active in the use of improvisations in the OSS. Consequently, when the question arose as to the use of an improvisational approach in the VA project, background material was readily available.

It was concluded (Bronfenbrenner and Newcomb, 1948, p. 373) that unlike the OSS experience, in which a diversity of different roleplays was employed, it would be desirable to develop a standard battery of situations for improvisation that would be applicable to adults in general. Accordingly, a set of six situations was devised. These included two each from the following three areas: (1) the conflict between dependency needs and demands for independence and self-sufficiency; (2) conflicts in authority relationships; and (3) conflicts in relationships with the opposite sex. This appears to have been the first development of a standard improvisational battery in the history of assessment. The general pattern employed in the OSS work—that of having each improvisation enacted by two subjects so that they could both be evaluated—was continued. Each subject was given a slip of paper indicating his or her instructions and did not see the directions given to the other subject. Here are the instructions for one of the six skits (Bronfenbrenner and Newcomb, 1948, p. 375), in this case a heterosexual one (there were two heterosexual situations; each subject—regardless of sex—played the male role in one and the female role in the other):

Participants: Mary and Jim
Directions for Jim: You and Mary have been going together for several months. You feel that

the time has arrived when you must come to an understanding about your relationship. You are sitting with Mary and have a chance to talk about it in private.

Directions for Mary: Same as above.

The research did not include the development of systematic rating scales yielding quantitative data for the improvisations as such, since the authors felt "that such development must wait upon a better understanding of the dimensions of behavior elicited by the technique" (Bronfenbrenner and Newcomb, 1948, p. 376). However, the Improvisations test, as in the OSS experience, was only one of several situations tests, and ratings based on all of these were compared later with criteria of clinical effectiveness. The findings (Soskin, 1949; Kelly and Fiske, 1951), as represented in correlations between criterion data and situation ratings, were generally positive but low (on the order of 0.20, with about half of the values statistically significant). Unfortunately the quantitative results did not reflect directly or specifically on the improvisations technique.

Other Early Studies. The studies reviewed so far were highly innovative, and they strongly suggested that improvisational methods can play a useful role in personality assessment. The great deficiency in the studies was that none of them faced up to the problems of reliability and validity. The latter of these issues is necessarily complex and difficult, but the former is in principle relatively straightforward.

An important study by Rotter and Wickens (1948) was the first to gather systematic reliability data on roleplayed assessment situations. These investigators developed two comparable situations for the evaluation of a variable they termed social aggressiveness (similar to what today is termed assertiveness). Each situation involved an interaction between two subjects, one in a dominant social role (for example, a faculty adviser on the campus newspaper), and the other in a subordinate social role (for example, a student applying for the position as editor). Each of the forty-eight subjects in the study performed in both roleplaying situations, one in the dominant and the other in the subordinate position. Each role portrayal was rated, by several judges, on a five-point scale representing intensity of social aggressiveness displayed by each subject. Interrater reliability coefficients, among two sets of four judges each, ranged from 0.59 to 0.84, with the overall average r (by z transformation) being 0.71. In addition to this result, it was possible, by using two other sets of three judges each, to obtain estimates of the consistency of the rated behaviors. Thus, the correlation between measures of social aggressiveness on the same subjects in the two roleplays, based on data from raters who saw the same subjects in the two enactments, was 0.78, whereas the analogous value was only 0.55 for data from independent ratings of performance in the two roleplays. The difference is indicative, in part, of the influence of having formed an impression of a subject in one improvisation on one's second rating of him. If one thinks of the two roleplays as alternate forms of the same test, then the 0.55 is a measure of test reliability. In view of the fact that rater reliability was only 0.71, the 0.55 value indicates considerable trait consistency.

Moldawsky, in 1951, undertook the comparison of measures of personality rigidity as assessed first by a pencil and paper rigidity measure (R scale), and second by a roleplaying procedure patterned after Moreno's Spontaneity Test. Moldawsky devised a situation in which the subject improvised the behavior of trying to sell Christmas cards to a passerby. The expectation was that flexible subjects would alter their sales approach as necessary and be rated by observers as less rigid. Since five observers (judges) were utilized, it was possible to obtain a measure of interrater reliability; this value, for the raters as a group, was 0.89. There was, however, no significant relationship between the two measures of rigidity. It remained unclear whether this lack of relationship was due to lack of validity of the R scale, of the roleplay employed, or of both, or whether on the contrary both were valid but failed to correlate as a result of the possibility that rigidity is not a general trait, but is situation specific.

Harrow (1951, 1952), in an intensive study of the therapeutic efficacy of psychodrama in the treatment of schizophrenia, devised a special improvisational procedure termed the "Role Test" as part of the assessment battery. This test involved improvisations in three different situations, each with another person. Performances were rated by three judges on each of eight variables: (1) interaction with and responsiveness to others, (2) realism, (3) emotional intensity, (4) affiliative interaction, (5) ability to adapt spontaneously, (5) personal security and comfort displayed in role, (7) ability to take and act out a role, and (8) ability to apprehend and describe a role. Ratings were obtained pre- and posttreatment. The results showed high interjudge reliabilities (average 0.91 for pretest and 0.90 for posttest ratings). Pre- and postratings were in the predicted direction, but only one (realism) approached significance. Two other early studies utilizing a roleplaying approach to assessment were those of Kay (1947) and Kerstetter (1947). The first of these involved the use of roleplays in the selection of medical students, and the second examined the possibility of using roleplaying techniques in the prediction of marital success.

Nature and Rationale of Improvisational Assessment

Before surveying recent and current developments in improvisational assessment, it will be helpful to consider with some care the underlying logical and theoretical bases of improvisational assessment. We will begin with an examination of the different levels of behavior.

Levels of Behavior. It is useful to make a distinction among different classes, or levels, of behavior in terms of the extent to which they are reality oriented. From this perspective four levels can be readily identified, as follows: real-life behavior, pretending behavior, vicarious behavior, and dreaming. Though a rigorous analysis of the characteristics of each of these levels and of the differences among them is beyond the scope of this chapter, the general ordering is obvious and defensible. All four levels are real, in the sense of referring to actual occurrences. They differ, however, in the degree to which the perceptual focus of the experiencing person is constrained by the specifications of objective reality.

In what we are referring to, following customary usage, as *real-life behavior,* the behaving person, from an objective viewpoint, is actually doing what he conceives himself as doing and what he appears to others to be doing. At this level the behavior of the person is severely limited by the constraints of reality, and he has to adapt, insofar as his skills permit, to whatever vicissitudes the real world confronts him with, including not only the laws of physics but also his own competences and the behaviors of other persons whose actions affect him.

By *pretending behavior* we refer to episodes in which the person, for the duration of that episode, consciously suspends his acceptance of one or more perceived constraints of reality and pretends that reality is in certain respects different from what he knows it actually is. These changes in assumptive constraints yield a kind of "as if" behavior. For example, a small boy may stand on a pitcher's mound and pretend that he is a grown-up player in the big leagues. It is important to note that most of the constraints of reality are not altered in pretending behavior: Since the behavior involves overt performance, it is under essentially the same physical limitations of time, space, and causality as is real-life behavior.

The third behavioral level is *vicarious behavior.* In this form the actions are not performed overtly but are purely mental. Such imaginary creations are, of course, not devoid of reality considerations, but they are, or may be, much freer of reality constraints than is real-life or pretending behavior. In particular, the binds of here-and-now reality, physical limitations, and temporal order may be loosened. This is especially true in the case of certain fantasies.

In the fourth level, *dreaming,* the constraints of reality are even looser, so that all manner of fantastic events may seem to occur.

We have, then, a kind of continuum ranging from real-life behavior at one extreme to dreaming at the other. It is, of course, not implied that these different levels are mutually exclusive. On the contrary, individuals often engage in fantasy and real-life behaviors at the same time. Similarly, much everyday behavior involves attempts to present oneself in accord with certain pretended roles, as Goffman (1959) and others have noted. The general ordering proposed here is similar in some respects to a number of earlier formulations, including Lewin's (1936) concept of degrees of irreality and Borgatta's (1950) formulation of levels of behavior. Though psychologists have been interested in all four of the levels we have delineated, most attention has, of course, been given to the prediction and understanding of real-life behavior. In general, the task of psychological assessment has been to predict real-life behavior.

Pretending Behavior. Roleplaying is a straightforward instance of pretending behavior. Of the four suggested levels of behavior, then, our main interest here is in that class. Let us look briefly at the prevalence of pretending behavior in human life. In the experiences of primitive cultures various instances of pretending behavior of the kind that we would call roleplaying —including diverse rituals, ceremonies, celebrations, and reenactments of significant events—often occupy a central place. In some cases the therapeutic procedures employed by tribal medicine men take the form—to use modern terminology—of psychodrama (Harmeling, 1950; Ellenberger, 1970, pp. 28-32), and the communal acting out of cultural myths serves an institutional function. Even in modern societies such culturally sanctioned group roleplays are not uncommon: Witness, for example, the recent reenactments of battles and other events of the Revolutionary period in connection with the American bicentennial.

The concept of pretending behavior leads directly to the notion of drama, which itself is believed to have originated out of earlier mimetic songs and dances, and which in its own right has a very long history. The close relevance of drama to the present discussion is indicated by the fact that the terminology of roleplaying is lifted directly from dramaturgical literature. It is interesting, too, to note that just as in psychological applications the subject may be asked either to enact a carefully prescribed role or to improvise from a set beginning, so in drama there is a history not only of the classical scripted plays, but also of improvisational theater, going back to the commedia dell'arte in the Italian Renaissance and continuing today in various improvisational acting groups.

Perhaps the most common example of pretending be-havior is the make-believe play of children. Recent research (Singer, 1973; Curry and Arnaud, 1974; Bruner, Jolly, and Sylva, 1976; Garvey, 1977) has focused on the development of the capacity in children to take on pretending roles and to im-provise appropriate behaviors. The capacity for make-believe play is developed rather slowly in early childhood. Apparently its development is facilitated by roleplaying models provided by adults (Garvey, 1977).

It is evident from this brief survey that the idea of im-provisational roleplaying is not at all uncommon. Hence when we ask subjects to improvise their behaviors in the assessment setting, we are not asking something of them that is strange and exotic, for which they have no background.

Logic of Improvisational Assessment. We will be con-cerned, in this section, with assessment in the sense of predict-ing real-life behavior. It is generally agreed that the best way to learn how a given person would act in a given situation is to observe her in that situation and see directly how in fact she does act. It is true, of course, that the person may well not behave in the identical way the next time she is in that situation because of subtle changes in the situation or in the person's need or mood states, but there is a good probability that her subsequent behavior will be at least roughly similar. The impli-cation of this analysis is that *the greater the similarity between the behavioral situation from which one is predicting a given person's behavior and the behavioral situation to which the tester is predicting that person's behavior, the greater will be the accuracy of prediction, other things being equal.*

Thus, if an assessor wishes to know how a person, John, behaves when with his supervisor, the assessor can—at least in principle—observe John interacting with his supervisor. Similar statements can be made with respect to how John behaves with his wife, his mother, and so on, or—more broadly—how he be-haves, in terms of given categories such as hostility and sociabil-ity, with people in general. Though it is sometimes possible to arrange for such direct observations—as when an assessor spends a period observing a family at home or a child at school—unfor-tunately this approach generally presents major practical difficulties; when a generalization as to how a person behaves over a variety of different situations is desired, the practical problem of making direct observations becomes, except in rare instances, insurmountable.

Because of the general impracticability of predicting real-life behaviors from direct observations of the subject in other, similar real-life situations, assessment psychologists typically turn to that form of behavior that is most easily tapped in the testing room, that is, vicarious behavior. The subject is, in effect, asked to imagine himself or herself in a variety of situations and to report how he or she would behave or has behaved in those situations. This form of testing takes two typical forms: first, specific inventory questions about the subject's past or potential behavior; and second, freely structured fantasy productions that are assumed to represent, at some level, the subject's real-life behavior. Both inventory and fantasy methods, particularly the former, are highly convenient and have achieved impressive empirical successes. Such approaches, however, are necessarily limited, in terms of the above generalization, by the basic differences between vicarious and real-life behaviors.

The general argument for improvisational assessment is that it is possible, through this form of pretending behavior, to attain a greater degree of similarity between the situations predicted *from* and the situations predicted *to* than by any other feasible method, with a consequent advantage in validity and meaningfulness for the roleplaying approach. The respects in which improvised roleplaying and real-life behavior overlap include these features: Both involve overt actions performed under the constraints of physical and temporal realities; both are present, here-and-now activities; and both require making up one's behavior, in the face of new circumstances, as he or she goes along.

The general point we have just made in a somewhat formal way is, to be sure, not a new one. Corsini (p. 80) stated much the same view in 1966, as follows: "The more similar a test is to the function itself, the better is the degree of validity of measurement. Thus, we test a person's typewriting ability on a typewriter; how well a person swims by his performance in a swimming pool; and how well he handles social situations by observing him in the drawing room. Therefore, if we want to know how a person acts in relation to others, as when they tease him, we quite likely can find out best by a roleplaying test rather than by interviewing him, by asking him to fill out a questionnaire, or by asking him what he sees inkblots to be."

The degrees of relationship between the standard types of tests and real-life behavior as we conceive them is indicated in Figure 1. We suggest that personality inventories are, in prin-

Figure 1. Hypothetical Relations of Three Assessment Methods to Real Behavior.

Fantasy Material	Inventory Responses	Improvised Roleplaying	Real-Life Behavior

ciple, closer to actual behavior than fantasy (projective) devices, because they include more constraints. The ordering proposed is similar to that posited in 1950 by Borgatta (level of reality, roleplaying, interview response, and questionnaire response).

Another way of pointing out the close relationship between improvised roleplaying and real-life behavior is as follows. It is generally accepted that behavior is the resultant of two main classes of determinants, those in the person and those in the situation. In the case of observing real-life behavior, both the person and situational determinants of the behavior that one is trying to understand, as well as the resultant overt behavior itself, are of course present. For roleplayed behavior the person determinants are present, the situational determinants are present in part (for example, if the situation is one of the subject interacting with another person, there is actually another person present), and overt behavior is also present. Though this overt behavior cannot be assumed to be identical to that in real-life behavior, it will approximate it because of the overlap in determinants. In the case of self-report data, however, only the person determinants are the same as in real-life behavior, with both the situational determinants and the resultant behavior being imagined.

The hypothesized close approximation of improvised

roleplaying to real-life behavior is, of course, applicable only to that class of behavior that occurs overtly and can be roleplayed. Thus, it would be difficult to assess a subject's inner states and self-perceptions by roleplaying procedures except in a very inferential way. For these important characteristics various self-report techniques are the instruments of choice. In our view, the improvisational method is best suited for assessing an individual's interpersonal styles, in part because individuals frequently seem to have little insight into this aspect of their functioning. Further, in suggesting that behavioral prediction is enhanced when the situation from which the prediction is made is basically similar to the situation predicted to, we do not mean to imply that this is the only meaningful or useful assessment model. An alternative general approach, with good scientific credentials, is to identify the underlying components of a given kind of behavior, perhaps on the basis of a general theory, and then to base one's prediction on the measurement of these underlying components. In this approach, which requires a high degree of theoretical sophistication, one might, for example, utilize such variables as ego strength, need for achievement, intelligence, and the like. Though we respect such an orientation, we believe that the roleplaying approach, in those areas where it is applicable, offers greater immediate promise.

How "Real" Is Improvised Roleplaying? The previous section has argued that improvised roleplaying is highly similar to real-life behavior. Let us now examine the evidence on this point. Several introductory points should be made. First, it is necessary, in order for improvised behavior to approximate real-life behavior, that the subject be meaningfully involved in it; second, the situation that the subject finds himself or herself in at the beginning of the roleplay must be sufficiently related to the subject's prior experience that he or she can effectively empathize with it; and third, the subject's participation should involve the ongoing improvising of behavior in response to circumstances over which he or she lacks complete control (for example, the behavior of another person in the roleplay).

Borgatta, in two impressive studies in the 1950s, was one of the first to produce substantial evidence on the roleplay-reality issue. In the first study, Borgatta (1951) compared reactions to frustration as assessed on the basis of "actual" behavior, roleplayed behavior, and fantasy behavior. Though low scoring reliability limited the generality of the findings, it was found that data from roleplays were significantly closer to data from "actual" behaviors than were written fantasy data. In a later, extensive follow-up study Borgatta (1955) had 125 Air Force men participate, in groups of three, in a series of sessions in which they first planned two roleplays ("actual" behavior), and then performed them (roleplayed behavior). In addition each subject completed a projective test, the Conversation Study (Borgatta, 1955). Data from all three levels—"actual," roleplayed, and projective—were scored on the Bales (1950) system for coding interpersonal behavior, and compared. The results showed a correlation of 0.76 between "actual" and roleplayed behaviors on the overall Bales score (general activity rate). The analogous correlations were: between roleplays and the projective test, 0.27; and between the projective test and "actual" behavior, 0.34. An analysis of factor structure indicated extensive "parallelism" between "actual" and roleplayed behavior, leading to the conclusion that "roleplaying appears to give the same kinds of information that are available from interaction in actual situations as defined in this study" (Borgatta, 1955, p. 394).

Another study yielding similar results is the intensive project reported by Kreitler and Kreitler (1968). These investigators collected highly detailed information on a wide range of behavior for twenty-five hospitalized psychiatric patients. The data were based on interviews of ward staff familiar with the subjects' activities, and the behavioral areas sampled included performance style, social behavior, work behavior, emotional behavior, biological needs, and pathological behavior. Analogous data were obtained independently on seventeen psychodramatic scenes. Most of these were quite brief enactments, and none involved another person. As an example, here is scene 7: "You come home feeling a strong longing to see your beloved, and you write her/him a letter. Show us what you do and read the letter aloud." On the basis of complex analyses, both real-life and roleplayed descriptive data were transformed into "be-havior items" (BIs). An example of a BI is, "In the course of any action she stops frequently to talk to people about things irrelevant to the action" (Kreitler and Kreitler, 1968, p. 187). The overall results were as follows: 990 BIs were identified in the ward observation data, and 933 in the roleplayed data. Of these, 761 appeared in both sets, and of these 515 (68 percent) were fully concordant in the two sets, 36 (5 percent) were fully contradictory, and 210 (27 percent) were partially concordant. The degree of concordance is highly significant.

The overall findings just reviewed indicate that, generally speaking, subjects draw from the same personal repertoire of possible behaviors in improvised roleplaying that they use in real-life, so that to a very notable degree the former mirror the latter. Indeed, there is considerable evidence that subjects are unable, even if they try, to successfully mask at least some aspects of their personality. Borgatta (1961) divided subjects into high, medium and low assertiveness groups on the basis of observational data, and a year later had the subjects enact prescribed roles differing in assertiveness. The amount of assertiveness shown in the roleplays was a function not only of the prescriptions but also of the underlying dispositional characteristics of the subjects. More recently, Lippa (1976) had subjects previously classified as introverts or extraverts roleplay both of these behavioral styles; in both cases, the underlying dispositional style "leaked" through to uninformed judges. A report by Middleton (in press) is also relevant here. This study found that subjects playing a role congruent with their position on the CPI Dominance scale performed better than those playing a role out of keeping with their typical style.

A study by Leibowitz (1968) assessed subjects in three measures of aggressiveness conceived to differ in "behavioral directness," a variable somewhat similar to the behavioral continuum proposed in Figure 1. The measure of "direct behavior" was the Buss (1961) aggression machine (BAM), a contrived situation in which the subject is led (incorrectly) to believe that he is administering electric shocks to other persons; his willingness to do so is taken as an index of his aggressiveness. The other two measures were the Buss and Durkee (1957) Hostility Inventory, and ratings of the amount of aggression shown on three brief roleplays. The latter two measures intercorrelated 0.36, but neither was significantly related to the BAM scores. The interpretation of this study is somewhat moot. If the BAM is taken as an instance, or index, of real-life behavior, then the findings do not agree with the other studies presented here, which indicate a parallelism between real-life and improvised behaviors. On the other hand, it is quite possible that roleplays are closer approximations to real-life aggression than the BAM is. The interpretation offered by Leibowitz is also plausible— namely, that the BAM assesses the tendency to physical aggression, and the roleplays he used assess the tendency to verbal aggression, so that one would not necessarily expect the two measures to be intercorrelated.

We turn now to a final study that bears more directly and unequivocally on the relation between improvised and real-life behavior. This interesting study, by Stanton and Litwak (1955), was addressed to the question of "whether interpersonal competence exhibited in roleplaying is representative or typical of the subject's interpersonal competence in 'real' life" (p. 668). The general procedure was to compare ratings of autonomy (defined as "the ability to maintain ideal behavior under interpersonal stress" (p. 669) based on three improvised roleplays and real-life behavior. Fifty-two subjects, comprising forty-four foster parents and eight graduate students, were tested. The assays of real-life autonomy were made by informed social workers in the case of the foster parents and by fellow students for the graduate student subjects. In some cases subjects were rated by two judges, and it was possible to derive a list of thirty-five subjects rated by judges who knew them "very well," twenty-six subjects rated by judges who knew them "well," and eight rated by judges who knew them "poorly." The correlations between the roleplay and real-life ratings of autonomy were, respectively, for these three rater groups 0.82, 0.53, and −0.48. Reliability coefficients for the roleplaying test ranged from 0.81 to 0.97, with an average of 0.90.

Taken in their entirety, the studies reviewed above provide very strong support for a close relationship between improvised and real-life behaviors, as argued earlier on theoretical grounds. Further evidence on this point will be presented later in this paper in terms of validity data on certain improvisational tests. It should be noted that the relation of roleplayed to "real" behavior is of interest not only to assessment psychologists but also to social psychologists. Here much of the attention has been focused on the use of roleplaying methods in social psychological research, particularly on the possibility of employing roleplays as an alternative to research methods that involve deceiving the subject (Kelman, 1967; Freedman, 1969; Mixon, 1971, 1972). It is interesting to note that both alternatives in this controversy actually involve pretending behavior—either by the subjects, when it is called roleplaying, or by the experimenters, when it is termed dissimulation (Hamilton, 1976). This entire area—in which a rather large literature has accumulated—has recently been critically examined by Ginsburg (in press), who concludes that "active roleplaying" methods (similar to what we are calling improvised roleplaying) can contribute significantly to social psychological research, provided their nature and limitations are recognized. The reader is also referred to a recent symposium on the topic arranged by Hendricks (1977).

The question of just how similar improvised behavior is to real-life behavior does not have a simple answer, since obviously the degree of similarity varies with a number of factors, including, presumably, the degree to which the subject is involved—both cognitively and affectively—in the improvisations; the extent to which the setting, including in particular other roleplayers, contributes to the sense of reality; and the extent to which the subject is able, on the basis of his prior experience and his view of the world, to meaningfully accept the opening situation as presented. No doubt some subjects are better at improvisations than others, and all are better at some times than at other times. Further, the method, until the subject gets well into it, is somewhat novel, and it is likely that subjects who are apprehensive about new experiences take somewhat longer to get fully involved in improvisational procedures than subjects who welcome novelty.

In any case, the improvisational procedure in which a subject is interacting with another person would seem to call for typical rather than idiosyncratic behavior. As Corsini (1966, p. 83) has put it, "the necessity for immediate responses to complex social stimuli tends to elicit usual rather than prepared behavior. The fact that the individual must think, feel, and act simultaneously tends to lead him to act in his usual rather than in some dissimulative manner."

Each individual, it can be assumed, has a repertoire of behaviors for dealing with various kinds of situations. In any given situation that particular behavior, from the available repertoire, will be employed that seems—at some level of analysis, probably generally automatic or unconscious—to be most suitable. It is thus evident that whatever behavior the subject shows in an improvisational roleplay *necessarily comes from her repertoire, and thus directly tells the assessor something valid about that person.* We know that the subject *can* behave in the way she has, because she has just done so, and we can strongly suspect that the behavior performed has a fairly high response probability in her repertoire hierarchy because it has occurred under conditions that limit the opportunities for deliberative dissimulation.

The question of the similarity between improvisations and real-life behavior is ultimately an empirical one. Nevertheless, it is in part a pseudo-question. This is because the criterion of how one behaves in real-life is itself a very slippery one. Let us suppose that we are trying to predict, through improvisations—or indeed by any method—how you would behave in real-life if you were to go to a cleaning establishment to pick up your coat and found a spot on it that hadn't been there when you took it in. Would you complain? Would you demand to see the manager? Would you refuse to pay? Would you accept their apology? Your response to these questions is, no doubt, that it "all depends"—on the attitude of the clerk at the cleaning establishment, on what he or she says, on the mood you're in that day, on which behavior (of those that you *could* manifest) would seem, in view of the foregoing factors, most effective, and so on. In fact, then, *there is no simple, single way that you would invariably behave in this situation* that could serve as a criterion. Indeed, it is quite possible that there is more heterogeneity in real-life behavior than in roleplayed behavior.

Recent Developments

We will now survey the current scene in improvisational assessment. We will first look briefly at the extensive but relatively informal use of the method as employed by clinicians observing roleplaying carried out by their clients and then making inferences from these enactments about the personality styles and capacities of the clients. Then we will examine, in greater depth, the more systematic, standardized improvisational assessment procedures that are currently available.

Informal Applications of Improvisational Assessment. Practicing clinicians engaged in psychotherapy regularly engage in a process of ongoing assessment of their clients. While some therapists frequently employ standard psychological tests, such as the MMPI, the CPI, or the Rorschach for this purpose, others, either because of time limitations or because of their philosophy of therapy, base their evaluations solely on interview data and on observations of and reports from the client during the therapy sessions. For an increasing number of therapists, in both individual and group situations, the use of roleplaying provides a useful type of assessment. A particularly appealing feature of this approach is that it can be meaningfully integrated into the therapeutic procedures. In fact, it is often difficult, when a particular scene is roleplayed by a client, to say whether it is primarily therapy or assessment, since obviously it is both. The general paradigm is that the client is asked to roleplay a given situation—frequently one specifically devised by the therapist—to point up a given problem area and to gain practice in its solution.

A particularly striking feature of the trend toward the use of roleplays in basically therapeutic contexts is the extent to which it characterizes a broad range of approaches in therapy and behavior change (Boies, 1972; Corsini, 1966; Krasner, 1959; Mann, 1956). First, of course, one thinks of classic psychodrama. Though Moreno recently died, the psychodramatic approach is still widely employed (Blatner, 1973; Greenberg, 1974; Yablonsky, 1976) and routinely includes clinical assessments of client role enactments. An even older approach—Adler's individual psychology—has been combined with psychodrama to yield Adlerian action therapy (Shoobs, 1946, 1956; O'Connell, 1975). In this method improvisational techniques are used to reveal the hidden purposes of disturbed behavior and to point up the life-style of the client.

Another therapeutic orientation that utilizes roleplaying is Kelly's (1955, pp. 360-451; Bonarius, 1970) fixed-role therapy, in which the client acts out a "fixed-role sketch" described by the therapist, with the aim being to change or expand the client's personal constructs. Roleplaying also occupies a central place in Gestalt therapy (Perls, 1971, 1973; Fagan and Shepherd, 1970). This is exemplified in the "empty chair" technique, in which a dialogue is acted out between conflicting parts of the self or with another person in fantasy. Roleplaying methods are also utilized by Gestalt therapists in the analysis of dreams.

Roleplaying methods are widely employed in behavior therapies, particularly in assertiveness training (Adinolfi, McCourt, and Geoghegan, 1976; Field and Test, 1975; Wolpe, 1969), behavior rehearsal (Lazarus, 1966; McFall and Marston, 1970; McFall and Lillesand, 1971; Casey, 1973), and social skills training (Argyle, Bryant, and Trower, 1974; Argyle, Trower, and Bryant, 1974; Goldsmith and McFall, 1975; Maxwell, 1976). Several systematic improvisational assessment procedures have been developed in the behavioral framework; we will consider these presently.

Many family therapy techniques also employ roleplaying procedures that serve both therapeutic and assessment roles. Thus, Satir (1967, 1972), in her use of family sculpturing, assigns family members roles to act out and uses the resultant feedback to assess the family dynamics. Others employing roleplaying methods for clarification of family problems include Zweben and Miller (1968) and Knoblochova and Knoblochova (1970).

It is evident that the use of roleplaying techniques has

become a fairly standard part of the modal psychotherapist's armamentarium. Such techniques, however, are not limited to the clinical setting; on the contrary, they are widely employed in education (Chesler and Fox, 1966; Buchan, 1972; Sarason and Sarason, 1974; Hawley, 1974; Furness, 1976) and industry (Maier, Solem, and Maier, 1957; Corsini, Shaw, and Blake, 1961).

The informal assessment of improvised roleplays that are associated with the various treatment and training programs described above can undoubtedly be very powerful. Such an approach, however, lacks the advantages in rigor and standardization that are characteristic of more formally developed test procedures. We turn now, then, to a look at current directions in this area.

Personnel Evaluations Through Roleplaying. We are aware of four areas—business management, medicine, police work, and counseling—in which systematic improvisational assessment techniques have been developed. It is somewhat surprising that the approach has not been more widely utilized for evaluative purposes in educational and vocational guidance settings; though some efforts have been made along this line (for example, Buchan, 1972, pp. 34-35; Zytowski, 1964), the area appears to be conspicuously open for further development.

Improvisational procedures have been used fairly widely in management for assessment purposes (Corsini and others, 1961, pp. 133-145; Dunnette, 1971), though more in the form of systematic roleplaying exercises that provide data for evaluation than in the form of rigorously standardized tests. In the "in-basket" exercise, the management assessee is provided with materials such as telephone memos and reports and is asked to respond to them. He may then be interviewed, in a roleplaying format, with a member of the assessment team playing the role of his supervisor (Dunnette, 1971; Lopez, 1966). Another procedure is to have several candidates roleplay a decision-making business meeting.

In medicine Levine and McGuire (1968) have developed an attractive improvisational procedure for assessing physician competence in specialty areas. These investigators were faced with the problem that certain aspects of physician competence

—in particular, interviewing, advising, and reassuring patients—
cannot be adequately evaluated by written or oral examinations. In order to deal with the problem they devised a set of
three standardized roleplaying situations.

In the first of these the candidate in the specialty area
carries out a diagnostic interview with a member of the assessment team playing the role of a patient; in the second the candidate, after being provided with the description of the medical
problem of a patient, explains the treatment plan to the patient,
who is again roleplayed by one of the assessment staff; and in
the third five candidates together roleplay a patient management conference. In all three instances the subject's performance was independently rated on adequacy of performance
by the participating staff member and one other judge. A number of different teams of raters were used, and the overall interrater reliabilities were for the first situation 0.73, for the second
situation 0.83, and for the third (group conference) 0.25. There
was evidence that some rater teams used more stringent standards than others; this emphasizes the importance of training
raters carefully. Correlations between ratings and conventional
written examinations of professional competence were low,
indicating that the roleplays were providing new information.
Some evidence of the validity of the technique was afforded by
the fact that residents in higher levels of training scored higher
than less advanced residents (for the first improvisation, $p <
0.001$; for the second, $p = 0.08$).

An improvisational format for use in the selection of police recruits has been carefully developed by Mills (1976). The
problem of assessing competence for police work is an especially difficult one, because of the many different skills and the
high stress levels involved. Most standard psychological instruments, developed for different purposes, are of limited usefulness for identifying the positive features of police candidates. In
order to systematically sample candidates' police-relevant behaviors under conditions of stress, Mills devised a set of roleplays in which two candidates improvise an interaction based on
a prescribed opening situation. In some instances a third person
—a member of the assessment team—also plays a role.

An example of the improvisations employed is the "loitering scene." The opening situation is that some owners in a certain section of the city have complained that a gang of juveniles is hanging around bothering people and perhaps stealing small items. As the patrolman (played by one of the candidates) approaches the scene the gang leader (played by another candidate) walks forward to meet him. In the course of their interaction one of the store owners (played by a staff member) interrupts and agitatedly asks the patrolman to make the gang leave.

Improvisations are performed before a group of candidates, and all participate in the discussion of performances. Assessment team observers evaluate the roleplayed performances, in conjunction with other data, in order to make overall ratings of candidates' suitability for police work.

In the field of counseling improvisational methods have been used as a means of evaluating counselor effectiveness. The general model is that the counselor to be evaluated is observed and rated while he or she is actually performing a counseling session. In order to provide for standardization of counselee problems and personalities in the evaluation of different counselors, members of the assessment staff—referred to as "coached clients"—play the role of the counselee, presenting given problems to the counselor. Kelz (1966) developed a counselor assessment program that included the use of coached clients in two fifteen-minute counselor interviewing situations. Counselor performances were rated by expert judges on eight categories (appearance, expression, relationship, communication, knowledge, perception, interpretation, and termination). The mean interjudge correlations were 0.53 and 0.45 for the two interviewing situations. These relatively low values are in accord with the well-known difficulty of rating counseling skill and do not reflect directly on the use of the roleplayed counselees. The counselee performances received high ratings for realism and consistency.

Research on the use of coached clients has been reviewed by Whiteley and Jakubowski (1969). More recently, Friesen and Dunning (1974), in connection with the program for evaluation of counseling practicum students at the University of Nebraska at Lincoln, have investigated the extent to which minimally coached roleplayed clients do in fact present a consistent, pre-scribed role from counselor to counselor. Two nonprofessional women, each given only one session of pretraining, played a client role for ten counseling sessions. The results indicated very marked roleplaying consistency, in both verbal and nonverbal behaviors, from session to session with different counselors. This finding, though based on only two cases, supports the ra-tionale of utilizing roleplayed clients in counselor assessment.

Evaluations of Assertiveness Through Roleplaying. It is with respect to the assessment of assertive behavior that stan-dardized roleplaying techniques have so far had their greatest development. The tests within this area are reviewed in detail in Chapter Eight of this volume, so it is unnecessary to examine them at length here. It will, however, be helpful to call atten-tion to the major tests and to make some general comments. McFall and Marston (1970; McFall and Lillesand, 1971; McFall and Twentyman, 1973) developed a standardized improvisa-tional procedure referred to as the Behavioral Role-Playing Assertion Test. This technique consists of a number of situa-tions setting the occasion for assertive behavior and presented to the subject on audiotape. Eisler, Miller, and Hersen (1973) constructed the Behavioral Assertiveness Test (BAT), a tech-nique consisting of fourteen situations relating to assertiveness, with each roleplayed by the subject interacting with a model enacted by a member of the assessment staff. More recently, Eisler, Hersen, Miller, and Blanchard (1975) have devised a thirty-two-scene roleplaying procedure focusing on the influ-ence of different situational factors in behavior. The latest im-provisational testing procedure in this area is one devised by Edinberg, Karoly, and Gleser (1977) for the assessment of assertiveness in the elderly.

The main reasons that improvisational techniques have been widely used in assessing assertiveness would seem to be, first, that lack of assertiveness is a frequently seen clinical prob-lem requiring treatment and assessment, and second, that asser-tiveness is by definition an interpersonal problem for which a roleplaying approach is highly suitable. There is no reason, how-ever, to suppose that assertiveness is unique in these respects.

Evaluating Social Skills Through Roleplaying. Weiss (1968), in his studies of interpersonal accord, appears to have been the first investigator to employ a modified roleplaying approach in the systematic assessment of social skills. He had subjects listen to taped monologues under the pretense that they were engaging in a conversation. Instead of replying orally to the recorded voice, however, the subject's task was to press a button on each occasion when he or she would normally make some kind of rapport-maintaining gestural or vocal response. The skill score was the degree to which the subjects' accord responses conformed to normatively defined appropriate places for responses. Weiss found the measure of interpersonal accord to be related to a number of social variables.

Rehm and Marston, in 1968, studied twenty-four college males reporting problems in meeting and dating girls. The treatment consisted of participation in a self-reinforcement therapy group, and adequate controls were provided. A special procedure, called the Situation Test (ST), was developed to measure behavior change. This test consisted of ten social situations presented orally on tape. Each situation was described by a male voice, which was followed by a line of dialogue by a female, to which the subject was to respond. For example, the opening male voice says, "As you are leaving a cafeteria, a girl taps you on the back and says. . . ," and the female dialogue is "I think you left this book." The subjects' responses were taped and later rated by undergraduate women on anxiety, adequacy of response, and likability. Parallel forms of the test were developed, which yielded reliability coefficients of 0.82, 0.67, and 0.72 for the three variables. Under treatment, ratings changed in the direction predicted, though only one of the three (likability) reached significance. Melnick, in 1973, employed a modification of the Rehm and Marston ST in a further study of dating behavior in college men. The major difference was that whereas Rehm and Marston had presented the situations in an audiotaped format, Melnick utilized videotaped situations.

In another investigation of male dating behavior Arkowitz, Lichtenstein, McGovern, and Hines (1975) utilized what they termed the Taped Situation Test (TST). This improvisational procedure, adapted from the Rehm and Marston technique, consists of ten audiotaped heterosexual situations to which the subject responds. In addition, subjects were asked to interact with a female staff member in a roleplaying situation and then roleplayed a telephone call asking for a date. The TST was scored for response latency and number of words, and social skill was measured by ratings of the subject's interaction with the female staff member and also by peer ratings. The TST latency correlated −0.45 with the former variable and −0.33 with the latter.

Three other somewhat similar roleplaying techniques for the assessment of male skill in heterosexual interactions have been developed by Borkovec, Stone, O'Brien, and Kaloupek (1974), Curran (1975), and Twentyman and McFall (1975). The first two of these studies included a three-minute roleplayed interaction between the subject and a female staff member. In Curran's study the roleplays were videotaped and rated for the subject's anxiety and interpersonal skill. The mean interrater reliability coefficients for these two variables were 0.70 and 0.76, respectively.

The improvisational assessment technique devised by Twentyman and McFall is more elaborate. Their test procedure, which has not been given a formal name, includes six three-minute roleplays enacted via intercom between the male subject and a female assistant in an adjoining room and one five-minute roleplay with the two persons in the same room. Here is one of the opening situations (Twentyman and McFall, 1975, p. 386), as described to the subject: "You are on a break at your job. You see a girl who is about your age at the canteen. She works in another part of the store, and consequently you don't know her very well. You would like to talk to her. What would you say?"

Behavioral ratings, focusing on anxiety, were made by two observers through a one-way mirror. Interrater correlations, obtained at two different times, were 0.94 and 0.89. Several other variables, including social skillfulness, were rated later from audiotapes. Interrater correlations for skillfulness were 0.70 and 0.66. Support for the validity of the test was furnished by significant differences between treated and control groups for both anxiety and social skillfulness.

The most sophisticated improvisational test yet developed for evaluating male dating skills is the Role-Played Dating Interactions test (RPDI), developed by Rhyne, MacDonald, McGrath, Lindquist, and Kramer (1974). This test consists of three four-minute simulated dating interactions performed by the subject and a female staff member. Important features of the RPDI are the careful training and programming of the actresses, in order to provide rigorous standardization of the situations, and detailed scoring criteria. The two variables measured are anxiety and dating skill. A detailed test manual is available (Rhyne and others, 1974). For anxiety, interrater reliability coefficients range from 0.85 to 0.90; and for skill from 0.95 to 0.98. Evidence for the validity of the RPDI has been obtained by MacDonald, Lindquist, Kramer, McGrath, and Rhyne (1975); in their study three of four skill training groups, but no control groups, showed significant improvement on RPDI skill scores.

It is evident from the above descriptions, as well as from two excellent reviews (Eisler, 1976; Hersen and Bellack, 1977), that most of the systematic work in social skills assessment to date, other than that on assertiveness, has been concerned with male dating skills. However, the notable success of improvisational approaches in this area strongly indicates that roleplaying methods can be useful in evaluating a variety of interpersonal styles.

In support of this inference we will refer, in closing this section, to an interesting study on social caution carried out by Efran and Korn (1969). The subjects—ninety-three college males—participated in twenty-five-minute leaderless discussion groups devoted to getting to know each other. Subjects who actively participated (AP) in the discussion and those who were socially cautious (SC) were identified by a sociometric procedure. Later each subject took part in seven roleplaying enactments, each of which consisted of making an imaginary telephone conversation in response to a stated opening situation. For example, one instruction was "Today is the birthday of a

friend who lives in California. Call him for a birthday surprise."
All responses were taped and rated on social cautiousness. The
interrater reliability was 0.70, and the biserial r between these
ratings and the sociometric assignments (AP or SC) was 0.63 (p
< 0.001).

　　Evaluating the Expression of Anger Through Roleplaying.
The interrelated topics of anger, hostility, and aggression constitute one of the more widely studied and more socially relevant
areas in contemporary personology, and a number of relevant
assessment instruments have been developed (Megargee and
Menzies, 1971). For the most part, however, these instruments
have been confined to measures of trait variables, such as hostility and aggressiveness, with state variables, such as the arousal
of anger, being more difficult to assess. One of the ways individual differences in this characteristic are sometimes investigated is by noting subjects' reactions to insulting remarks in the
laboratory, but this approach has serious ethical as well as methodological difficulties. Recent developments in the assessment
of provocations to anger through improvisational techniques are
therefore highly welcome.

　　Wagner (1968a) devised the Anger Expressiveness Test
(AE-Test) in order to study the effects of positive and negative
reinforcements on the expression of anger. Alternate forms of
the test, each including twelve potentially anger-provoking situations, were given before and after a roleplaying treatment
program. An example of a test situation (p. 92), which the subject is asked to imagine, is this: "You are sitting in a movie and
you politely ask the woman in front of you to take off her large
hat. She refuses, telling you that it will mess up her hair. I want
you to respond in the same way that you feel you would if you
were in this particular situation. What would you say?" The
subjects' responses were audiotaped and judged for degree of
anger expression. Interrater reliabilities were 0.83 and 0.72 for
pre- and posttest ratings, respectively. The results were that subjects who in the treatment phase had been socially rewarded for
the expression of anger showed stronger anger responses in the
posttreatment testing than did subjects who had been socially
punished, thus providing evidence of construct validity for the

AE-Test. A subsequent study (Wagner, 1968b), using impersonal reinforcers, obtained similar though less significant results.

The therapeutic goal in Novaco's (1975, 1976a, 1976b)
research was the enhancement of anger control in thirty-four
clients whose outbursts of anger constituted a central problem.
Several different treatment modalities were employed and compared. Though several assessment methods were used, the major
one was an improvisational technique developed by Novaco.
For the pretreatment testing three roleplays, one neutral followed by two provocative ones, were used. A different set of
three was employed for posttesting. Unlike the format in the
Wagner studies described above, each roleplay involved an ongoing interaction between the subject and a live actor. In each
improvisation there was first the description of the opening situation and then an introductory dialogue, after which the subject had to improvise. In one roleplay, for example, the situation was that the subject had bought a pair of slacks at a
clothing store the day before and later discovered that they had
a hole in them. He or she is now attempting to return them to
the store. The opening dialogue (Novaco, 1975, p. 99), read by
the subject and the assistant, who plays the role of a sales-
person, is as follows:

Salesperson:	Can I show you something today, sir (ms.)?
Subject:	*Yes, I want to exchange these pants I bought yesterday.*
Salesperson:	Hum, that was one of our sale items. I'm very sorry, sir (ms.), but all sales were final on those items.
Subject:	*But these have a hole in them.*
Salesperson:	That's ridiculous! We don't sell de-fective merchandise, sir (ms.).
Subject:	*Well, they were like this when I got them.*
Salesperson:	Then what did you buy them for?
Subject:	*Because I didn't know they had a hole in them.*
Salesperson:	Don't you look at what you are buying? Most people know what

	they are getting when they buy something.
Subject:	[subject begins improvising]

Self-ratings of anger, plus blood pressure and galvanic skin response (GSR) changes, were recorded. The first, neutral roleplay, served to provide baseline data. The results showed significant reductions in self-ratings of anger for both imagined and roleplayed provocations across treatment groups. There were also significant across-treatment reductions in blood pressure for both modes of provocation; notably, the roleplays produced significantly higher blood pressure elevations than the imagined provocations. Similarly, GSRs in response to provocation were also significantly reduced by treatments; GSRs in response to roleplays were significantly greater than for imagined scenes.

The results of this study indicate that reactions to role-played provocations can serve effectively in the study and assessment of anger. In Novaco's (1975, p. 47) words, "there is absolutely no doubt that the roleplay procedures used in the present study generated anger arousal, as can be seen from the self-report ratings, elevations in blood pressure, and GSR reactivity. Even though subjects recognized the roleplay interaction as such, they at times reported sustained anger from their experience because of the extent of the involvement."

It should be noted that Novaco's study, though the most detailed and definitive in the area, was not the first to investigate the effects on a physiological variable of stress induced by roleplaying. Newton, Paul, and Bovard (1957) earlier had each member in a group of seven student nurses roleplay an interaction in which she was praised by her "employer," while each member in another group of seven improvised an interaction in which she was criticized by her employer. Measures of finger temperature declined significantly more in the stressful (criticizing) enactment than in the positive roleplay.

Evaluating Interpersonal Conflict Through Roleplaying.
Unlike the studies that we have reviewed so far in this section, which focused on the evaluation of individuals, the recent project of Raush, Barry, Hertel, and Swain (1974) was devoted to

the assessment and analysis of married couples. Their important study, lasting over a period of several years, investigated the marital patterns of forty-six couples. Though a number of data-gathering procedures, including interviews and questionnaires, were utilized, the major instrument employed was one termed the "Improvisations." The procedure consisted of four husband-wife roleplays, devised primarily by Blank and Goodrich (Raush and others, 1974, p. 3). An earlier report on the method consisted of a 1962 film by Blank, Flint, and Wells (referred to in footnote 8, Goodrich, Ryder, and Raush, 1968, p. 384).

In each improvisation scene the husband and wife were given somewhat different instructions and then asked to enact the scene together. Standardized instructions were not used; rather, though the general form of each situation was the same for all couples, specific details were modified as necessary to increase the involvement of the subjects.

In the first scene, both husband and wife are informed that it is their first wedding anniversary. Additionally—and separately—the husband is told to imagine that he has secretly arranged to take his wife out to dinner, and the wife is told to imagine that she has prepared a special dinner at home. The scene opens with the husband arriving home from work. The second roleplay opens with a situation in which both the husband and wife each wish to watch very special but different TV programs. The third concerns a situation in which the husband feels the need for emotional distance from his wife, and she feels the need for closeness; the fourth situation is the reciprocal of this, with the wife preferring emotional distance.

All interactions were recorded and analyzed according to a complex coding system that was developed during the course of the study. The unit of analysis was an *act,* defined as "any remark or statement by one spouse between decipherable statements by the other spouse. Thus, it could be a single word or a few sentences" (Raush and others, 1974, p. 110). The coding system eventually employed included six categories—cognitive, resolving, reconciling, appealing, rejecting, and coercive acts—into which all acts were classified by judges. Interrater reliabilities ranged from 0.64 to 0.80. The coded data were analyzed in order to probe into ways in which people who are committed to each other manage the inevitable conflicts that arise in an ongoing relationship.

An examination of the substantive findings of the study is not in order here, and there is no straightforward criterion against which to evaluate the validity of the Raush and others' improvisational testing and coding system; it is evident from their monograph, however, that the coded data were interpretable in a highly systematic and theoretically meaningful way.

The Improvisation Test for Individuals (Impro-I). Of the many improvisational assessment procedures that we have examined so far in this chapter, some were constructed for limited use in an experimental setting, and others were developed to serve as assessment instruments in limited areas of behavior, such as assertiveness or modeling practices. None, however, was specifically designed to serve as a broad-gauged personality test in the sense in which this phrase is usually employed in psychology, that is, to refer to standardized, quantitative, multivariate instruments, including conventional psychometric data along with appropriate instructions for interpretation. In view of the many successful applications of the improvisational approach, as documented in the previous pages, such a broad-based role-playing personality test would seem to have considerable potential.

In this section we will briefly describe a newly devised instrument of the kind just suggested. Since this test is still in the process of development, the summary to be offered here is in the nature of a preliminary report. The Improvisation Test for Individuals (Impro-I) was constructed by McReynolds, DeVoge, Osborne, Pither, and Nordin (1976, 1977; Pither, Osborne, McReynolds, DeVoge, and Nordin, 1977) to provide measures of interpersonal styles in adult subjects of either sex. The test consists of twelve standardized improvisational role-plays and two sets of rating scales. Each roleplay consists of an interaction between the subject and one or two assessment staff, who play standardized roles. At the outset of each roleplay the subject is instructed as to the situation that he or she is to pretend exists at the beginning of the scene. Both the subject and the assessment team actor(s) then read several lines of introductory dialogue designed to lead the subject up to a behavioral choice point that is crucial with respect to the interpersonal dimension being assessed. At this point the subject improvises his or her behavior, with the participating staff member also improvising, though in strict accord with prescribed limits. The improvisation continues until the test administrator feels that the scene has reached closure or is no longer informative. The entire testing usually requires about thirty-five minutes. The subject's performances are rated by the administrator and another observer on two sets of scales, one concerning the effectiveness of the subject's performance on each roleplay separately, and the other referring to specific interpersonal styles as manifested in the entire test.

The Impro-I is designed to sample, to as great an extent as practicable within a single testing session, a broad range of meaningful interpersonal themes. Thus, subjects are given situations that call for them to express, or to deal with another person's expression of, assertiveness, rejection, hurt, sadness, anger, and appreciation. The roleplays are presented in the context of business relationships, friendships, and intimate relationships, and involve interactions with peer and authority figures of both sexes. As an example of the Impro-I approach, the introductory description and opening lines for one of the improvisations, which is concerned with reactions to sadness in a friend of the same sex, is given below. (Another example of the Impro-I roleplays is given in Chapter Eight.)

It's Saturday night and you've been planning to go see a show with your best friend. You go over to pick up your friend, but no one answers the door, so you go around back and find him/her sitting on the porch.

Friend: Oh hi. Was that you at the door?
Subject: *Yeah, how come you didn't answer it?*
Friend: Well, I was afraid it might be my neighbor, and I didn't feel like talking to her. But I'm glad you found me back here.

Subject:	*So am I. Well, are you ready to go?*
Friend:	Go where?
Subject:	*To see the show—don't you remember? Tonight's the last night.*
Friend:	Oh no, I forgot all about that.
Subject:	*Well, hurry up and get ready. I don't want to be late.*
Friend:	Listen, I really don't feel up to going tonight. Would you mind if I just stayed home?
Subject:	*Why, what's the matter? Why don't you want to go?*
Friend:	Well, my cousin was killed this morning. The one I grew up with. It was a head-on collision, and everyone was killed.
Subject:	[subject begins improvising]

Since the Impro-I is still under development, definitive evaluations of the test are not yet available. Interrater reliabilities for the twelve effectiveness scales, based on twenty cases, range from 0.45 to 0.97, with a mean of 0.83. Intercorrelations among the scales and subject evaluations of their own performances in the different roleplays, based on forty-seven cases, have been obtained (McReynolds and others, 1977). On the basis of preliminary experience with the Impro-I in a clinical setting, we believe the test to have considerable potential as a multidimensional assay of interpersonal styles.

The Improvisation Test for Couples (Impro-C). This instrument was devised by Osborne and Pither (1977a, 1977b, 1977c), both of whom were also part of the team that constructed the Impro-I. The purpose of the Impro-C, which is intended as a companion test to the Impro-I, is to provide clinically useful information on the process and style of couple interaction. The test is intended for general use with married couples or with unmarried couples of the same or opposite sex. Like the Impro-I, the Impro-C is a multidimensional instrument and is designed to provide information on a broad range of interactional styles in a variety of lifelike settings. In addition to its relationship to the Impro-I, the Impro-C was modeled in part after the improvisational system developed by Raush and others

(1974), described earlier in this chapter. The underlying rationale of the Impro-C is the systems theoretical approach, in which the emphasis is on the couple as an interacting and interlocking unit, rather than on the traits of two separate individuals.

The Impro-C consists of ten structured roleplays, each performed conjointly by the two members of the couple being assessed; unlike the format with the Impro-I, members of the assessment staff are not involved in the improvisations. Each roleplay is carried out in the following way. As in the Raush and others (1974) procedure, the opening situation is described separately, from his or her own point of view, to each subject, who is unaware of the situation as described to the other subject. The two subjects then interact, improvising their behaviors until the interaction is terminated by the test administrator. Following each improvisation each subject is asked to evaluate the extent to which the subject's own performance and that of his or her partner are typical of their real-life behavior. Observer ratings of the subjects' performances are completed on two sets of scales, one (Communication Scale) concerned with the couple's patterns of communication during each improvisation, and the other (Overall Style Scale) based on all ten roleplays, focusing on specific interactional styles.

The interpersonal themes sampled by the Impro-C include conflict, distance, hurt, anger, stress, appreciation of self, and appreciation of the partner. These themes were selected as being more nearly universal than specific content categories such as household chores or child rearing and more in keeping with a process orientation to therapy. As an illustration of the Impro-C method, the opening situation, as described separately to the two subjects for one of the improvisations—this one a scene inspired by and adapted from Raush and others (1974), and concerned with feelings of distance in a heterosexual couple—is presented below.

Instructions to Man: Imagine that for the last several days (name of partner) has been cold and irritable with you. She doesn't seem to want to talk at all and she hardly even looks at you. You don't know why she's acting this way, and you feel like you have to say something to her about it. Take a moment to imagine how you would feel in this situation. (PAUSE). When you go in, (name of partner) is sitting alone in the living room.

Instructions to Woman: Imagine that for the last several days you have been wanting to be alone a lot. There's nothing in particular happening in your life, but you just don't feel like being with people, (name of partner) included. When you have been around (name of partner) lately, you've felt irritable and haven't wanted to talk. Take a moment to imagine having these feelings. (PAUSE). Right now you are sitting alone in the living room hoping not to be disturbed.

Systematic work on the Impro-C so far has involved thirty-one couples. Reliability data (Osborne and Pither, 1977a) are quite good. On the Communication Scale variables the coefficients of agreement (Robinson's A) between raters generally fell between 0.80 and 0.90, and the interrater agreement on total communication (collapsing separate dimensions) was 0.97. Mean interrater reliability on the Overall Style Scale variables was 0.82 (Robinson's A). Preliminary clinical experience with the test indicates that it may prove extremely useful in work with couples. This is especially true in view of the fact that the Impro-C, unlike many assessment techniques in the area, focuses directly on the processes of partner interaction from a systems-oriented perspective.

Concluding Remarks

The diversity of studies and test procedures reviewed in the foregoing pages demonstrates several points about improvisational techniques: First, such techniques have been used for some time in assessment, at least in a limited way; second, a considerable number of systematic roleplaying assessment procedures, covering a fairly large range of interpersonal behaviors, are currently available; and third, most of the test procedures described have been employed with notable utility in a variety of experimental and clinical studies. We believe, as we indicated at the beginning of this chapter, that the improvisational approach to assessment has now come of age—though we would not say that it has yet reached full maturity, since obviously there is need for further development.

The approach is, of course, not without possible problems. Let us look briefly at some of the questions that may be raised.

Reliability and Validity. The reports reviewed in this chapter, taken in their entirety, would suggest high marks for improvisational techniques on these two criteria. Almost all of the many reliability coefficients reported were moderate to high; similarly, most of the systematic validity data—with the exception of the Leibowitz (1968) study, which is ambiguous in its implications—were quite positive. Though further validity studies are clearly needed, the available psychometric data are very favorable to the roleplaying approach.

Standardization of Test Procedures. Most roleplaying tests—and in our opinion the more promising ones—involve an *in vivo* improvised interaction between the subject and a staff member. The main problem in standardization is in guaranteeing that the behavior of this staff member is consistent, and yet appropriate to the nuances of the ongoing interaction. This is a difficult but not insurmountable problem. Several latest-generation instruments, including the RPDI (Rhyne and others, 1974), the Impro-I (McReynolds and others, 1976), and the Impro-C (Osborne and Pither, 1977b), include specific instructions to the actor on the maintenance of the prescribed role. The study by Friesen and Dunning (1974), reviewed earlier, indicates that satisfactory role standardization can be obtained through careful, though not necessarily extensive, pretraining.

Design of Roleplays. Though a discussion of the guidelines to be used in developing roleplays is beyond the scope of this chapter, it should be emphasized that in order to be effective a roleplay must be carefully designed around the behavioral theme that it is intended to reflect. This statement is supported by the previously discussed Stanton and Litwak (1955) study, in which ratings of autonomy made on scenes specifically designed to highlight autonomy were highly valid, whereas ratings of autonomy made on roleplays designed to highlight empathy and creativity correlated insignificantly (0.16) with the criterion of autonomy.

Observer Ratings. It should be noted that the manner in which improvisational tests attain a level of quantification is by having observers rate (or code) the behavior of the subject(s). Indeed, the generic theme of roleplaying tests is that of bringing lifelike behaviors into the testing room, where they can be systematically observed. It is to be emphasized, then, that the scales used for ratings and the training of raters are key aspects of the improvisational approach.

The Question of Acting Ability. It is probable that some skepticism about the improvisational approach to assessment exists in certain quarters as a result of the feeling that the method is essentially one in which the subject merely "acts" a role, with a consequent advantage given to subjects who are good actors. It is important to emphasize, therefore, that the foregoing interpretation is not the model that we are espousing. The subject in a typical improvisational assessment procedure is not acting a role, except in the metaphorical sense that all of us, much of the time, are enacting given roles in real life (Sarbin and Allen, 1968); rather, the subject is being himself or herself, improvising his or her behavior in a novel and somewhat unpredictable situation, in much the same sense that one improvises ongoing behavior in real life. To be sure, the subject does have to accept, on a pretending basis, the opening situation for a roleplay, and it is possible that the capacity to do this is related to acting ability, but the subject does not thereafter have to pretend a given role. The only real actor—in the usual meaning of this term—in the testing situation is the assessment team member enacting the prescribed role with the subject (in terms of the distinction we made at the beginning of this chapter, the subject's performance is "improvised roleplaying" and that of the actor "controlled roleplaying").

Test Costs. Improvisational tests tend to be quite expensive, since for maximal yield they typically require one or two actors plus one or two raters. Some investigators, as described earlier, have devised less expensive roleplaying tests by audio-taping the opening statement of an actor and limiting the subject's input to his or her first response. This approach has much to commend it, but can hardly be expected to provide the amount of information generated by the more lifelike *in vivo* interactional method. Because of the cost of the latter method, however, it almost certainly will never be widely used in the sense that, say, personality inventories are. Because of their expense, improvisational tests appear most suitable for use when the focus is on individuals, as in a clinic or in research with small samples. In any event, the emphasis should not be solely on the cost of testing. There is a place in the psychological armamentarium for procedures that, though expensive, have high yields. In medicine, many useful tests are quite expensive, and the same is true of certain tests, such as the Reitan-Halstead battery, employed in psychology.

Special Advantages. We commented in the above paragraphs on some of the possible problems in improvisational assessment. In this concluding paragraph we wish to call attention to several relatively unique advantages of the roleplaying approach. First of all, roleplaying tests are generally easy and meaningful for subjects to perform. Though there is typically some uncertainty at first, most subjects quickly get into the spirit of the method and typically find the improvisations more entertaining than boring or threatening. Further, the idea of improvisations as a method of personality assessment makes immediate sense to most subjects and thus enhances their morale and cooperativeness. Second, improvisational tests can be administered to individuals with low verbal skills. Indeed, there is some reason (Riessman, 1964) to believe that roleplaying techniques may be particularly useful in working with educationally and culturally disadvantaged persons. Third, in addition to the formal, quantitative data provided by improvisations, they offer the clinical observer a large bonus of additional idiographic information about the subject, more so probably than any method except the in-depth interview. When the observer is also the individual who must make certain decisions about the subject, this yield of tacit knowledge can be extremely valuable. And finally, improvisational assessment methods have the advantage that they can frequently be integrated directly into ongoing psychotherapy or social skills training: This is true in the sense that roleplays used in assessment may themselves stimulate meaningful discussions in therapy or may be incorporated in part into social skills training programs.

References

Adinolfi, A. A., McCourt, W. F., and Geoghegan, S. "Group Assertiveness Training for Alcoholics." *Journal of Studies on Alcohol,* 1976, *37,* 311-320.

Anderson, W. "J. L. Moreno and the Origins of Psychodrama: A Biographical Sketch." In I. A. Greenberg (Ed.), *Psychodrama: Theory and Therapy.* New York: Behavioral Publications, 1974.

Argyle, M., Bryant, B., and Trower, P. "Social Skills Training and Psychotherapy: A Comparative Study." *Psychological Medicine,* 1974, *4,* 435-443.

Argyle, M., Trower, P., and Bryant, B. "Explorations in the Treatment of Personality Disorders and Neurosis by Social Skills Training." *British Journal of Medical Psychology,* 1974, *47,* 63-72.

Arkowitz, H., Lichtenstein, E., McGovern, K., and Hines, P. "The Behavioral Assessment of Social Competence in Males." *Behavior Therapy,* 1975, *6,* 3-13.

Bales, R. F. *Interaction Process Analysis: A Method for the Study of Small Groups.* Reading, Mass.: Addison-Wesley, 1950.

Bandura, A. *Principles of Behavior Modification.* New York: Holt, Rinehart and Winston, 1969.

Blatner, H. A. *Acting-In: Practical Applications of Psychodramatic Methods.* New York: Springer-Verlag, 1973.

Boies, K. G. "Role Playing as a Behavior Change Technique: Review of the Empirical Literature." *Psychotherapy: Theory, Research and Practice,* 1972, *9,* 185-192.

Bonarius, J. C. P. "Fixed Role Therapy: A Double Paradox." *British Journal of Medical Psychology,* 1970, *43,* 213-219.

Borgatta, E. F. "The Use of Psychodrama, Sociodrama and Related Techniques in Social Psychological Research." *Sociometry,* 1950, *13,* 244-258.

Borgatta, E. F. "An Analysis of Three Levels of Response: An Approach to Some Relationships Among Dimensions of Personality." *Sociometry,* 1951, *14,* 267-316.

Borgatta, E. F. "Analysis of Social Interaction: Actual, Role Playing, and Projective." *Journal of Abnormal and Social Psychology,* 1955, *51,* 394-405.

Borgatta, E. F. "Role-Playing Specification, Personality, and Performance." *Sociometry,* 1961, *24,* 218-233.

Borkovec, T. D., Stone, N. M., O'Brien, G. T., and Kaloupek, D. G. "Evaluation of a Clinically Relevant Target Behavior for Analog Outcome Research." *Behavior Therapy,* 1974, *5,* 503-513.

Bronfenbrenner, U., and Newcomb, T. M. "Improvisations—An Application of Psychodrama in Personality Diagnosis." *Sociatry,* 1948, *1,* 367-382.

Bruner, J. S., Jolly, A., and Sylva, K. *Play: Its Role in Development and Evolution.* New York: Penguin, 1976.

Buchan, L. G. *Roleplaying and the Educable Mentally Retarded.* Belmont, Calif.: Fearon, 1972.

Buss, A. H. *The Psychology of Aggression.* New York: Wiley, 1961.

Buss, A. H., and Durkee, A. "An Inventory for Assessing Different Kinds of Hostility." *Journal of Consulting Psychology,* 1957, *21,* 343-348.

Casey, G. A. "Behavior Rehearsal: Principles and Procedures." *Psychotherapy: Theory, Research and Practice,* 1973, *10,* 331-333.

Chesler, M., and Fox, R. *Role-Playing Methods in the Classroom.* Chicago: Science Research Associates, 1966.

Corsini, R. J. *Roleplaying in Psychotherapy: A Manual.* Chicago: Aldine, 1966.

Corsini, R. J., Shaw, M. E., and Blake, R. R. *Roleplaying in Business and Industry.* New York: Crowell-Collier, 1961.

Curran, J. P. "Case Histories and Shorter Communications." *Behavior Research and Therapy,* 1975, *13,* 65-68.

Curry, N. E., and Arnaud, S. H. "Cognitive Implications in Children's Spontaneous Role Play." *Theory into Practice,* 1974, *13,* 273-277.

Dunnette, M. D. "The Assessment of Managerial Talent." In P. McReynolds (Ed.), *Advances in Psychological Assessment.* Vol. 2. Palo Alto, Calif.: Science and Behavior Books, 1971.

Edinberg, M. A., Karoly, P., and Gleser, G. C. "Assessing Assertion in the Elderly: An Application of the Behavior Analytic Model of Competence." *Journal of Clinical Psychology,* 1977, *33,* 869-874.

Efran, J. S., and Korn, P. R. "Measurement of Social Caution: Self-Appraisal, Role Playing and Discussion Behavior." *Journal of Consulting and Clinical Psychology,* 1969, *33,* 78-83.

Eisler, R. M. "The Behavioral Assessment of Social Skills." In M. Hersen and A. S. Bellack (Eds.), *Behavioral Assessment: A Practical Handbook.* Elmsford, N.Y.: Pergamon Press, 1976.

Eisler, R. M., Hersen, M., Miller, P. M., and Blanchard, E. B. "Situational Determinants of Assertive Behaviors." *Journal of Consulting and Clinical Psychology,* 1975, *43,* 330-340.

Eisler, R. M., Miller, P. M., and Hersen, M. "Components of Assertive Behavior." *Journal of Clinical Psychology,* 1973, *29,* 295-299.

Ellenberger, H. F. *The Discovery of the Mind.* New York: Basic Books, 1970.

Fagan, J., and Shepherd, I. (Eds.). *Gestalt Therapy Now.* Palo Alto, Calif.: Science and Behavior Books, 1970.

Field, G. D., and Test, M. A. "Group Assertive Training for Severely Disturbed Patients." *Journal of Behavior Therapy and Experimental Psychology,* 1975, *6,* 129-134.

Freedman, J. L. "Role Playing: Psychology by Consensus." *Journal of Personality and Social Psychology,* 1969, *13,* 107-114.

Friesen, D. D., and Dunning, G. B. "The Use of the Minimally

Coached Role Playing Client in Training Evaluation." *Canadian Counselor,* 1974, *8,* 46-53.

Furness, P. *Role-Play in the Elementary School.* New York: Hart, 1976.

Garvey, C. *Play.* Cambridge, Mass.: Harvard University Press, 1977.

Ginsburg, G. P. "Role Playing and Role Performance in Social Psychological Research." In M. Brenner, P. Marsh, and M. Williams (Eds.), *The Social Contexts of Method: Readings in the Sociology of Methodology.* London: Croom Helm, in press.

Goffman, E. *The Presentation of Self in Everyday Life.* New York: Anchor Books, 1959.

Goldsmith, J. B., and McFall, R. M. "Development and Evaluation of an Interpersonal Skill-Training Program for Psychiatric Inpatients." *Journal of Abnormal Psychology,* 1975, *84,* 51-58.

Goodrich, D. W., Ryder, R. G., and Raush, H. L. "Patterns of Newlywed Marriage." *Journal of Marriage and the Family,* 1968, *30,* 383-391.

Greenberg, I. A. (Ed.). *Psychodrama: Theory and Therapy.* New York: Behavioral Publications, 1974.

Hamilton, V. L. "Role Play and Deception: A Re-Examination of the Controversy." *Journal for the Theory of Social Behaviour,* 1976, *6,* 233-250.

Harmeling, P. C. "Therapeutic Theatre of Alaska Eskimos." *Group Psychotherapy,* 1950, *3,* 74-76.

Harrow, G. S. "The Effects of Psychodrama Group Therapy on Role Behavior of Schizophrenic Patients." *Group Psychotherapy,* 1951, *3,* 316-320.

Harrow, G. S. "Psychodrama Group Therapy." *Group Psychotherapy,* 1952, *5,* 120-172.

Hawley, R. C. *Value Exploration Through Role-Playing.* Amherst, Mass.: Education Research Associates, 1974.

Hendricks, C. "Role-Playing as a Methodology for Social Research: A Symposium." *Personality and Social Psychology Bulletin,* 1977, *3,* 454.

Hersen, M., and Bellack, A. S. "Assessment of Social Skills." In

A. R. Ciminero, K. S. Calhoun, and H. E. Adams (Eds.), *Handbook of Behavioral Assessment.* New York: Wiley, 1977.

Kay, L. W. "Psychodrama Examines the Doctor." *Sociatry,* 1947, *1,* 35-42.

Kelly, E. L. "Research on the Selection of Clinical Psychologists." *Journal of Clinical Psychology,* 1947, *3,* 39-42.

Kelly, E. L., and Fiske, D. W. "The Prediction of Success in the VA Training Program in Clinical Psychology." *American Psychologist,* 1950, *5,* 395-406.

Kelly, E. L., and Fiske, D. W. *The Prediction of Performance in Clinical Psychology.* Ann Arbor: University of Michigan Press, 1951. (Reprinted New York: Greenwood Press, 1969.)

Kelly, G. A. *The Psychology of Personal Constructs.* Vol. 1. New York: Norton, 1955.

Kelman, H. "Human Use of Human Subjects: The Problem of Deception in Social Psychological Experiments." *Psychological Bulletin,* 1967, *67,* 1-11.

Kelz, J. W. "The Development and Evaluation of a Measure of Counselor Effectiveness." *Personnel and Guidance Journal,* 1966, *44,* 511-516.

Kerstetter, L. "Role Testing for Marriage Prediction." *Sociatry,* 1947, *1,* 220-224.

Knoblochova, J., and Knoblochova, F. "Family Therapy in Czechoslovakia: An Aspect of Group-Centered Psychotherapy." In N. Ackerman (Ed.), *Family Therapy in Transition.* Boston: Little, Brown, 1970.

Krasner, L. "Role Taking Research and Psychotherapy." *Research Reports of VA Palo Alto,* No. 5. Palo Alto, Calif.: VA Hospital, 1959.

Kreitler, H., and Kreitler, S. "Validation of Psychodramatic Behaviour Against Behaviour in Life." *British Journal of Medical Psychology,* 1968, *41,* 185-192.

Lazarus, A. "Behavior Rehearsal vs. Non-Directive Therapy vs. Advice in Effecting Behavior Change." *Behavior Research and Therapy,* 1966, *4,* 209-212.

Leibowitz, G. "Comparison of Self-Report and Behavioral Techniques of Assessing Aggression." *Journal of Consulting and Clinical Psychology,* 1968, *32,* 21-25.

Levine, H. G., and McGuire, C. "Role-Playing as an Evaluative Technique." *Journal of Educational Measurement,* 1968, *5,* 1-8.

Levine, K. *Principles of Topological Psychology.* New York: McGraw-Hill, 1936.

Lippa, R. "Expressive Control and the Leakage of Dispositional Introversion-Extraversion During Role-Played Teaching." *Journal of Personality,* 1976, *44,* 541-559.

Lira, F. T., Nay, W. R., McCullough, J. P., and Etkin, M. W. "Relative Effects of Modeling and Role Playing in the Treatment of Avoidance Behaviors." *Journal of Consulting and Clinical Psychology,* 1975, *43,* 608-618.

Lopez, F. M. "Evaluating Executive Decision-Making: The In-Basket Technique." *AMA Research Study 75.* New York: American Management Association, 1966.

MacDonald, M. L., Lindquist, C. U., Kramer, J. A., McGrath, R. A., and Rhyne, L. D. "Social Skills Training: Behavior Rehearsal in Groups and Dating Skills." *Journal of Counseling Psychology,* 1975, *22,* 224-230.

McFall, R., and Lillesand, D. B. "Behavior Rehearsal with Modeling and Coaching in Assertive Training." *Journal of Abnormal Psychology,* 1971, *77,* 313-323.

McFall, R., and Marston, A. R. "An Experimental Investigation of Behavior Rehearsal in Assertive Training." *Journal of Abnormal Psychology,* 1970, *76,* 295-303.

McFall, R., and Twentyman, C. "Four Experiments on the Relative Contributions of Rehearsal, Modeling, and Coaching to Assertion Training." *Journal of Abnormal Psychology,* 1973, *81,* 199-218.

McReynolds, P., DeVoge, S., Osborne, S. K., Pither, B., and Nordin, K. "Manual for the Impro-I." Mimeograph. Department of Psychology, University of Nevada, Reno, 1976.

McReynolds, P., DeVoge, S., Osborne, S. K., Pither, B., and Nordin, K. "An Improvisational Technique for the

Assessment of Individuals." Unpublished manuscript, Department of Psychology, University of Nevada, Reno, 1977.

Maier, N. R. F., Solem, A. R., and Maier, A. A. *Supervisory and Executive Development.* New York: Wiley, 1957.

Mann, J. H. "Experimental Evaluations of Role Playing." *Psychological Bulletin,* 1956, *53,* 227-234.

Maxwell, G. M. "An Evaluation of Social Skills Training." Paper presented at annual conference of New Zealand Psychological Society, 1976.

Megargee, E. I., and Menzies, E. S. "The Assessment and Dynamics of Aggression." In P. McReynolds (Ed.), *Advances in Psychological Assessment.* Vol. 2. Palo Alto, Calif.: Science and Behavior Books, 1971.

Melnick, J. "A Comparison of Replication Techniques in the Modification of Minimal Dating Behavior." *Journal of Abnormal Psychology,* 1973, *81,* 51-59.

Middleton, P. "A Test of Sarbin's Self-Role Congruency Theory Within a Role Playing Therapy Analogue Situation." *Journal of Clinical Psychology,* in press.

Mills, R. B. "Simulated Stress in Police Recruit Selection." *Journal of Police Science and Administration,* 1976, *4,* 179-186.

Mixon, D. "Behavior Analysis Treating Subjects as Actors Rather than Organisms." *Journal for the Theory of Social Behaviour,* 1971, *1,* 19-32.

Mixon, D. "Instead of Deception." *Journal for the Theory of Social Behaviour,* 1972, *2,* 145-177.

Moldawsky, S. "An Empirical Validation of a Rigidity Scale Against a Criterion of Rigidity in an Interpersonal Situation." *Sociometry,* 1951, *14,* 153-174.

Moreno, J. L. "Group Psychotherapy: Theory and Practice." *Group Psychotherapy,* 1950, *3,* 142-188.

Moreno, J. L. *Who Shall Survive?* (Rev. ed.) New York: Beacon House, 1953. (Originally published 1934.)

Moreno, J. L. *Psychodrama.* Vol. 2. New York: Beacon House, 1959a.

Moreno, J. L. "Psychodrama." In S. Arieti (Ed.), *American Handbook of Psychiatry*. Vol. 2. New York: Basic Books, 1959b.

Moreno, J. L. *Psychodrama*. Vol. 1 (3rd ed.) New York: Beacon House, 1964. (Originally published 1946.)

Moreno, J. L. *Psychodrama*. Vol. 3. New York: Beacon House, 1969.

Moreno, Z. T. "A Survey of Psychodramatic Techniques." In I. A. Greenberg (Ed.), *Psychodrama: Theory and Therapy*. New York: Behavioral Publications, 1974.

Newton, G., Paul, J., and Bovard, E. W. "Effect of Emotional Stress on Finger Temperature." *Psychological Reports,* 1957, *3,* 341-343.

Novaco, R. W. *Anger Control.* Lexington, Mass.: Lexington Books, 1975.

Novaco, R. W. "The Functions and Regulation of the Arousal of Anger." *American Journal of Psychiatry,* 1976a, *133,* 1124-1128.

Novaco, R. W. "Treatment of Chronic Anger Through Cognitive and Relaxation Controls." *Journal of Consulting and Clinical Psychology,* 1976b, *44,* 681.

O'Connell, W. E. *Action Therapy and Adlerian Theory.* Chicago: Alfred Adler Institute, 1975.

Osborne, S., and Pither, B. "The Improvisation Test for Couples (Impro-C)." Paper presented at meeting of the California Psychological Association, Los Angeles, 1977a.

Osborne, S. K., and Pither, B. *The Improvisation Test for Couples (Impro-C): A Preliminary Manual.* Unpublished manuscript, Department of Psychology, University of Nevada, Reno, 1977b.

Osborne, S. K., and Pither, B. "A Systematic Technique for Behavioral Assessment of Couples." Unpublished manuscript, Department of Psychology, University of Nevada, Reno, 1977c.

OSS Assessment Staff. *Assessment of Men.* New York: Holt, Rinehart and Winston, 1948.

Perls, F. S. *The Gestalt Approach and Eyewitness to Therapy.* Palo Alto, Calif.: Science and Behavior Books, 1973.

Perls, F. S. *Gestalt Therapy Verbatim.* New York: Bantam Books, 1971.

Pither, B., Osborne, S. K., McReynolds, P., DeVoge, S., and Nordin, K. "The Improvisation Test for Individuals (Impro-I)." Paper presented at meeting of the Western Psychological Association, Seattle, April 1977.

Raush, H. L., Barry, W. A., Hertel, R. K., and Swain, M. A. *Communication, Conflict and Marriage: Explorations in the Theory and Study of Intimate Relationships.* San Francisco: Jossey-Bass, 1974.

Rehm, L. P., and Marston, A. R. "Reduction of Social Anxiety Through Modification of Self-Reinforcement: An Instigation Therapy Technique." *Journal of Consulting and Clinical Psychology,* 1968, *32,* 565-574.

Rhyne, L. D., MacDonald, M. L., McGrath, R. A., Lindquist, C. U., and Kramer, J. A. "The RPDI: A Method for the Measurement of Male Social Dating Skills." *JSAS Catalog of Selected Documents in Psychology,* 1974, *4,* 42.

Riessman, F. "Role-Playing and the Lower Socio-Economic Group." *Group Psychotherapy,* 1964, *17,* 36-48.

Rotter, J. B., and Wickens, D. D. "The Consistency and Generality of Ratings of 'Social Aggressiveness' Made from Observation of Role Playing Situations." *Journal of Consulting Psychology,* 1948, *12,* 234-239.

Sarason, I. G., and Sarason, B. R. *Constructive Classroom Behavior: A Teacher's Guide to Modeling and Role-Playing Techniques.* New York: Behavioral Publications, 1974.

Sarbin, T. R., and Allen, V. L. "Role Theory." In G. Lindzey and E. Aronson (Eds.), *The Handbook of Social Psychology.* Vol. 1. (2nd ed.) Reading, Mass.: Addison-Wesley, 1968.

Satir, V. *Conjoint Family Therapy.* Palo Alto, Calif.: Science and Behavior Books, 1967.

Satir, V. *Peoplemaking.* Palo Alto, Calif.: Science and Behavior Books, 1972.

Shoobs, N. E. "The Application of Individual Psychology Through Psychodramatics." *Individual Psychology Bulletin,* 1946, *5,* 3-21.

Shoobs, N. E. "Individual Psychology and Psychodrama."

American Journal of Individual Psychology, 1956, *12,* 45-52.

Singer, J. L. *The Child's World of Make-Believe.* New York: Academic Press, 1973.

Soskin, W. F. *A Study of Personality Ratings Based on Brief Observation of Behavior in Standard Situations.* Unpublished doctoral dissertation, University of Michigan, 1949.

Stanton, H. R., and Litwak, E. "Toward the Development of a Short Form Test of Interpersonal Competence." *American Sociological Review,* 1955, *20,* 668-674.

Symonds, P. M. "Role Playing as a Diagnostic Procedure in the Selection of Leaders." *Sociatry,* 1947, *1,* 43-50.

Twentyman, C., and McFall, R. M. "Behavioral Training of Social Skills in Shy Males." *Journal of Consulting and Clinical Psychology,* 1975, *43,* 384-395.

Wagner, M. K. "Reinforcement of the Expression of Anger Through Role-Playing." *Behavior Research and Therapy,* 1968a, *6,* 91-95.

Wagner, M. K. "Comparative Effectiveness of Behavioral Rehearsal and Verbal Reinforcement for Effecting Anger Expressiveness." *Psychological Reports,* 1968b, *22,* 1079-1080.

Weiss, R. L. "Operant Conditioning Techniques in Psychological Assessment." In P. McReynolds (Ed.), *Advances in Psychological Assessment.* Vol. 1. Palo Alto, Calif.: Science and Behavior Books, 1968.

Whiteley, J. M., and Jakubowski, P. A. "The Coached Client as a Research and Training Resource in Counseling." *Counselor Education and Supervision,* 1969, *9,* 19-29.

Wohlking, W., and Weiner, H. "Structured and Spontaneous Role Playing: Contrast and Comparison." *Training and Development Journal,* 1971, *25,* 8-14.

Wolpe, J. *The Practice of Behavior Therapy.* Elmsford, N.Y.: Pergamon Press, 1969.

Yablonsky, L. *Psychodrama: Resolving Emotional Problems Through Role-Playing.* New York: Basic Books, 1976.

Zweben, J., and Miller, R. "The Systems Games: Teaching, Training, Psychotherapy." *Psychotherapy: Theory, Research, and Practice,* 1968, *5,* 73-76.

Zytowski, D. G. "Diagnostic Psychodrama with a College Freshman." *Group Psychotherapy,* 1964, *17,* 123-128.

VII

Nature and Assessment of Self-Disclosing Behavior

GORDON J. CHELUNE

The purpose of this paper is to review and evaluate the concept of self-disclosure and the methods used to assess this important class of behavior. Self-disclosure, the verbal communication of personal information about one's self to another, has been the focus of considerable theoretical and empirical inquiry in recent years. Much of the research interest stems from the role of self-disclosure in theories of psychological adjustment, the psychotherapeutic process, and interactional behavior. In this chapter we will briefly review the conceptual background of self-disclosure and the factors affecting self-disclosing behavior. We will also discuss the basic parameters of the disclosing process, particularly the major approaches and techniques used to study self-disclosing behavior.

Conceptual Background

The concept of self-disclosure is derived primarily from existential and phenomenological theory. To *disclose* means to make known or to show. *Self*-disclosure, therefore, is the

278

process by which we make ourselves known to other persons by verbally disclosing personal information.

Self-disclosure has often been postulated to have important consequences for psychological adjustment and interpersonal functioning. Fromm (1955) has referred to self-disclosure as a means for decreasing both phenomenological distance and alienation from self as well as from others. The concept of self-disclosing behavior plays a central role in Rogers's theory of personality change (1961). For Rogers, self-disclosure is a characteristic of acceptance of self and the means to achieve this end. Mowrer (1961) formulated a theory of psychopathology in which guilt from not disclosing one's perceived transgressions is the underlying cause of emotional disturbance. Only by the disclosure of one's "sins" to another person can one attain emotional health. Jourard (1964, 1968) has been a leading advocate of the positive aspects of self-disclosure. For Jourard, self-disclosure is both a symptom of personality health and a means to achieve "real-self being" and interpersonal effectiveness.

The concept of self-disclosure has also received considerable attention with respect to the psychotherapeutic process. "Most clinical and theoretical descriptions of the psychotherapeutic process have focused upon . . . self-disclosure . . . as one of the central happenings" (Truax and Carkhuff, 1965, p. 3). Both Ellis (1959) and Sullivan (1954) have commented on the therapeutic value of client disclosure and the nontherapeutic value of abstract interactions devoid of personal disclosure. Truax (1961) and Truax and Carkhuff (1964, 1965) have noted that both the client's and the therapist's disclosures play important roles in the successful outcome of therapy. Yalom (1970, p. 271) has suggested that "self-disclosure is a prerequisite for the formation of meaningful interpersonal relationships in a dyadic or in a group situation."

The role of self-disclosure in interpersonal relationships has been examined extensively within the context of social exchange and social penetration theories and has been reviewed by Cozby (1973). According to social penetration theory, the development of an interpersonal relationship is a joint outcome of situational determinants, interpersonal reward/cost factors, and personality characteristics (Altman and Taylor, 1973; Taylor, 1968; Taylor, Altman, and Sorrentino, 1969). Relationships are thought to proceed from nonintimate to intimate areas of exchange via verbal disclosure, activities jointly engaged in, and nonverbal communication (Cozby, 1973). Within relationships the amount of information disclosed to a given individual has been found to be highly correlated with the amount of information received from that person (Jourard, 1959; Jourard and Richman, 1963; Levinger and Senn, 1967; Rivenbark, 1971). This reciprocity or "dyadic effect" has been interpreted as a result of a social exchange process in which self-disclosure functions as a social reward (Certner, 1973; Worthy, Gary, and Kahn, 1969).

Factors Affecting Self-Disclosure

As noted earlier, self-disclosure is the process of making oneself known by verbally communicating personal information, a definition implying a social context. Self-disclosure cannot occur in isolation; another person must be present to receive the disclosure. It is evident, however, that the disclosure of one's feelings of job dissatisfaction to one's spouse, for example, has a different meaning and significance than the same disclosure to one's employer. Intrinsic, therefore, to the assessment and interpretation of self-disclosing behavior is an appreciation of the variables that affect it.

Self-disclosure can be conceptualized as a set of response data, that is, as a product of the context in which it occurs. The meaning of these data is a function of both the input variables (social-situational factors) and the personality characteristics of the discloser. It is beyond the scope and purpose of this paper to give more than a brief overview of these factors. For a more complete discussion, the interested reader should refer to the excellent reviews presented by Cozby (1973) and Goodstein and Reinecker (1974).

Input Variables. One of the major social-situational variables affecting the self-disclosure of personal information is the target person or recipient of the disclosure (Chelune, 1976a;

Jourard and Lasakow, 1958; Panyard, 1973). Also, the relationship between the discloser and the target person (Levinger and Senn, 1967; Pedersen and Higbee, 1969), the verbal and nonverbal behavior of the target (Jourard and Jaffe, 1970; Shapiro, Krauss, and Truax, 1969; Worthy and others, 1969), liking for the target person (Certner, 1973; Jourard, 1964; Worthy and others, 1969), and the sex of the target (Jourard, 1964, 1971; West and Zingle, 1969) have all been found to affect self-disclosing behavior.

Another major class of input variables affecting self-disclosure can be grouped under the term *setting condition,* meaning those conditions in which a social interaction occurs. "A setting condition is, therefore, those aspects of a social situation which are independent of the target person(s) involved. Thus, being on a blind date is a specific setting condition which may vary in terms of the target person(s) involved" (Chelune, 1976c). Unfortunately, very little research has been done in this area. However, in the two studies that have examined the relative influence of various factors on self-report measures of disclosure, setting condition factors were found to account for large proportions of the total observed variance (Chelune, 1976c; Frankel and Powers, 1971). Clearly, further investigation of the influence of setting conditions on self-disclosure is needed.

The final input variable that we will highlight is the content or topic of self-disclosure. Almost all social interactions involve some disclosure of the self to others. While some aspects of the self are rather public and therefore readily disclosed, "there is other information about one's self that is rather private or intimate and is disclosed only under special circumstances" (Goodstein and Reinecker, 1974, p. 51). Early self-disclosure studies using self-report inventories yielded consistent differences in amount of disclosure between topic categories (Jourard, 1964). For example, subjects reported revealing less information on items dealing with such topics as "body" and "personality" than on items concerning "interests" and "work" (Jourard and Lasakow, 1958). Elaborate and extensive scaling of stimulus items according to judged intimacy and topic content have been done (Marshall, 1970; Taylor and Altman, 1966; Worthy and others, 1969) and self-report instruments containing items of known intimacy value have been constructed (Jourard, 1971; Kipnis and Goodstadt, 1970; Knecht, Lippman, and Swap, 1973; Ryckman, Sherman, and Burgess, 1973).

Characteristics of the Discloser. A variety of studies have been conducted to examine the relationship between self-disclosure and demographic and personality characteristics. Sex differences have commonly been reported in the literature; although a number of studies have revealed no sex differences, the overall evidence indicates that females disclose more than males (Cozby, 1973). Differences in disclosure between racial groups (Dimond and Hellkamp, 1969; Jourard and Lasakow, 1958), national groups (Jourard, 1961d; Melikian, 1962; Plog, 1965), and social classes (Mayer, 1967; Tulkin, 1970) have also been reported. Examination of the relationship between birth order and self-disclosure has revealed that "later borns" report higher self-disclosure than firstborns (Dimond and Hellkamp, 1969; Dimond and Munz, 1967). Age is also a variable affecting the pattern of self-disclosure. It appears that disclosure to peers increases with age while disclosure to parents decreases (Jourard, 1961a; Rivenbark, 1971; Skypeck, 1967).

The personality correlates of self-disclosure have been extensively examined; research in this area has been reviewed by Cozby (1973). Correlations between personality measures and self-disclosure scores have generally been low and often equivocal. Altman and Taylor (1973) suggested that the search for relationships between trait disclosure and other personality measures is unrealistic. They proposed that self-disclosure be examined within the context of specific relationships and settings. Several consistencies in the literature are worthy of note, however. From the studies summarized by Cozby (1973) there appears to be a positive relationship between self-disclosure and measures of extraversion and sociability. Studies by Taylor and Oberlander (1969) and Sousa-Poza, Shulman, and Rohrberg (1973) have also found significant positive relationships between self-disclosure and perceptual sensitization and field dependence. A differential relationship between repression-sensitization and self-disclosure for males and females has been reported by Chelune (1975b) and partially replicated in a later study (Chelune, 1975c). Other investigators have demonstrated that sensitizers elaborate more and spend more time verbalizing their emotional experiences than do repressors (Axtell and Cole, 1971; Carroll, 1972; Davis and Sloan, 1974; Kaplan, 1967).

Parameters of Self-Disclosure

A crucial issue to the measurement of any construct is the development of an operational definition of the construct. While we have already defined self-disclosure as the verbal communication of personal information, the extensive self-disclosure literature contains a wide diversity of studies emphasizing different aspects and a variety of techniques for assessing these aspects. As noted by Cozby (1973), self-disclosure is not a unitary construct. As an interpersonal behavior, self-disclosure is thought to include five basic dimensions: (1) amount or breadth of personal information disclosed, (2) intimacy of the information disclosed, (3) rate or duration of disclosure, (4) affective manner of presentation, and (5) flexibility of the disclosure pattern (Chelune, 1975a). Therefore, before reviewing the techniques used to assess self-disclosure, we will briefly review the basic parameters of self-disclosure.

Amount. Amount or breadth of disclosure is simply the number of self-descriptive aspects about the self revealed. Self-report assessment of amount of disclosure has typically involved asking subjects whether they have disclosed certain information to specified target persons (Jourard, 1959, 1961d) or to what degree they have disclosed the information (Jourard and Lasakow, 1958; Panyard, 1971). Behavioral indices of amount have been derived by checking off the number of items revealed in self-introductions (Chittick and Himelstein, 1967; Himelstein and Kimbrough, 1963), counting the number of words used in self-descriptive essays (Burhenne and Mirels, 1970; Pedersen and Breglio, 1968b), and counting the number of self-references from tape-recorded interviews (Chelune, 1975c; Haymes, 1969; Powell, 1968).

Intimacy. As noted previously, early research yielded consistent differences in the amount of disclosure between topic categories. It became evident that the amount of self-reported disclosure varied with the perceived intimacy or ego relevance of the subject matter. Taylor and Altman (1966) developed a pool of 671 items about the self and scaled them for intimacy and topical content. The items have been used to construct several inventories that permit the assessment of both amount and intimacy of reported disclosures (Kipnis and Goodstadt, 1970; Jourard and Resnick, 1970; Marshall, 1970; Strassberg and Anchor, 1975). Behavioral measures of the depth or intimacy of actual disclosure have typically followed a scalar method (Doster, 1971; Pedersen and Breglio, 1968b; Suchman, 1965; Truax and Carkhuff, 1965; Vondracek, 1969a).

Rate and Duration. Duration (the time spent describing aspects of the self) has been a popular behavioral index of self-disclosure and has been used in a number of studies (Bath and Daly, 1972; Doster and Brooks, 1974; Jourard and Jaffe, 1970; Taylor and others, 1969; Vondracek, 1969b). The use of duration as a measure of self-disclosure assumes that the information imparted is proportional to the time spent disclosing it. Although group rankings of members' self-disclosure and participation were found to be highly correlated ($\rho = 0.71$; Goodstein, Goldstein, D'Orta, and Goodman, 1976), the use of duration as a measure of disclosure has been criticized by Block and Goodstein (1971). They state that "the duration of utterances would seem to bear no necessary theoretical or empirical relationship to the quantity or quality of self-disclosure. A single, well-timed word or glance may disclose more about a person than paragraphs of banalities" (p. 596).

An alternative temporal measure of self-disclosure is the rate of disclosure per interval of time, that is, the information or the number of self-descriptive statements given per unit of time. This approach removes the effects of different speaking times. Several studies suggest that rate of disclosure is a meaningful measure. Weintraub and Aronson (1962) found the quality of speech highly correlated with rate of speech. Mehrabian (1971) found statement rate the single most predictive factor in affiliative behavior. The number of self-references per minute has also been used to demonstrate modeling effects (McGuire, Thelen, and Amolsch, 1975) and sex differences (Chelune, 1976a).

Affective Manner of Presentation. Affective manner of presentation has been proposed as a new parameter of self-disclosing behavior (Chelune, 1975a). The parameter has its origins in the more general notion—degree of incongruence—of Rogers's "process continuum" (Walker, Rablen, and Rogers, 1960). As conceptualized by Chelune (1975a), the affective manner of presentation implies that there is an appropriate affective charge that can be attached to the revelation of intimate information, and that this affect plays an important role in communicating information about the self. "While an individual may disclose the facts of his experience to other persons, if he suppresses their affect he cannot become truly known to these others" (Chelune, 1975a, p. 81). Thus, the parameter of affective manner of presentation relies on both the linguistic and paralinguistic aspects of a person's verbal behavior. Suchman (1965) included this paralinguistic aspect in his Revealingness Index but did not measure it independently. The Revealingness Scale has recently been refined by Brooks (1974) to include a rating category for responses reflecting affective involvement in external content. Again, however, affect is not measured independently and is confounded with the intimacy of the content. Other investigators have evaluated affect in verbal behavior (Janofsky, 1971; Salzinger and Pisoni, 1958), with the measures being based on grammatical (the use of *I* or *we*) or linguistic (the use of affect words) constructions. Fischer and Apostal (1975) have demonstrated that unfilled pauses in conversation serve as vocal cues for subsequent high levels of disclosure, pointing further to the importance of paralinguistic factors in determining the perception of self-disclosure. Chelune (1975c) has recently developed a content analysis system that independently assesses the judged degree of congruence between verbal content and affective manner of presentation. This index has successfully demonstrated behavioral shifts in subjects' affective manner of presentation to different target persons (Chelune, 1976a).

Flexibility. The final parameter of self-disclosing behavior, self-disclosure flexibility, is a situational dimension that conceptually stems from the belief that there is an optimal amount of self-disclosure for a particular situation (Jourard, 1964). Too much or too little disclosure in a given social situation is perceived as inappropriate and indicative of maladjustment (Chaikun and Derlega, 1974a, 1974b; Chelune, 1976c). Self-disclosure flexibility, therefore, refers to the ability of a person to modulate his or her characteristic disclosure levels according to the interpersonal and situational demands of various social situations, for example, the topic of disclosure, the target person, and the setting condition (Chelune, 1975a). The ability to accurately differentiate interpersonal and situational variables and the willingness to alter characteristic disclosure patterns accordingly are implicit in the concept of self-disclosure flexibility.

The dimension of self-disclosure flexibility has meaning only within the context of repeated observations on subjects. Chelune (1976c) has constructed a self-report instrument, the Self-Disclosure Situations Survey, that can be adapted to provide a gross index of self-disclosure flexibility. This index of disclosure flexibility was found to be related to two self-report measures that presumably reflect alertness to social and situational demands in the environment (Chelune, 1976c), thereby supporting the construct validity of the instrument. A method for assessing self-disclosure flexibility from behavioral samples of subjects' verbal behavior has also been developed by Chelune (1975c).

Self-Disclosure Assessment Techniques

As noted by Goodstein and others (1976), there are at least three different perspectives from which self-disclosure can be measured. The first is that of the discloser and typically utilizes self-report inventories or self-rating scales. The second perspective is that of the recipient or an observer who rates the discloser along some scalar metric. The final perspective is neutral, using objective measures of self-disclosing behavior. For the purposes of this chapter we will present a selected review of some of the major techniques illustrating each of the above perspectives.

Self-Report Measures

All self-report inventories are to some degree self-disclosure measures, for they represent a record of what a person is willing to reveal about himself to an examiner. Jourard and his colleagues pioneered the development of specific self-report measures of self-disclosure, and Jourard (1971) presented a large compendium of these inventories in his book *Self-Disclosure: An Experimental Analysis of the Transparent Self*. In this section we will examine several of these inventories as well as some of the major modifications and innovations that have been recently made in the self-report assessment of self-disclosure.

Measures of Amount of Disclosure. The earliest self-report instrument is the sixty-item Self-Disclosure Questionnaire (SD-60) developed by Jourard and Lasakow (1958). This widely used instrument (Dimond and Hellkamp, 1969; Dimond and Munz, 1967; Doster and Strickland, 1971; Jourard, 1964; Melikian, 1962; Mulcahy, 1973; Pedersen, 1973; Sousa-Poza and others, 1973; Truax and Whittmer, 1971) measures the amounts of past self-reported disclosure to each of four target persons—the mother, the father, a male friend, and a female friend—by asking subjects to rate each of the sixty items using the following three-point scale (Jourard, 1964, p. 163):

0. Have told the other person nothing about this aspect of me.
1. Have talked in general terms about this item. The other person has only a general idea about this aspect of me.
2. Have talked in full and complete detail about this item to the other person. He knows me fully in this respect, and could describe me accurately.

The sixty items are rationally classified into groups of ten in six general categories: "attitudes and opinions," "tastes and interests," "work," "money," "personality," and "body." Thus, a subject rates each of the ten items in the six topic categories for his or her past disclosure to each of the four target persons. In addition to an overall disclosure score, scores for each target person and each topic category can be obtained.

The general psychometric quality of the SD-60 is considered quite good. Jourard and Lasakow (1958) report an overall odd-even split-half reliability coefficient of 0.94, and Fitzgerald (1963) reports split-half reliability coefficients between 0.78 and 0.99 for the six SD-60 topic areas. Fiske (1966), in discussing the concept of cumulative homogeneity as a measure of test adequacy, also found that the SD-60 compared favorably with a number of widely used tests and questionnaires. Pedersen and Higbee (1968) examined the construct validity of the SD-60, using Campbell and Fiske's (1959) multitrait-multimethod matrices, and found both convergent and discriminative validity for the SD-60.

While the reliability and construct validity of the SD-60 appear sound, the predictive validity of the instrument as a measure of general disclosingness has been seriously questioned. Scores from the SD-60 correlated only 0.10 with the number of items of information revealed during self-introductions in a classroom setting (Himelstein and Kimbrough, 1963). Nonsignificant correlations have also been reported between Jourard's SD-60 and ratings of intimacy in self-descriptive essays (Burhenne and Mirels, 1970; Pedersen and Breglio, 1968a), ratings of disclosure in group settings (Hurley and Hurley, 1969; Lubin and Harrison, 1964), and time spent talking and ratings of intimacy in structured interviews (Vondracek, 1969a, 1969b). While reports of past disclosure did not predict interview behavior, Wilson and Rappaport (1974) did find that self-reported measures of generalized expectancy on the SD-60 for disclosure to a stranger predicted actual interview disclosure to a stranger. Similarly, Simonson and Bahr (1974) found a correlation of 0.78 between self-reported willingness to disclose each item on the SD-60 to a therapist and ratings of actual disclosure to the therapist. Panyard (1973) examined the consensual validity of the SD-60 between friends and found a correlation of 0.63.

These various validity studies, with their somewhat discrepant findings, suggest that the SD-60 is probably a fairly valid measure of past disclosure to specific target persons and, with the appropriate instruction set, for future disclosure to an anticipated target person. The negative results can probably be best accounted for by the dissimilarity between the nature of the SD-60 and the particular disclosure setting in which the independent measures were obtained. In other words, given the importance of the social-situational input variables, it is not surprising to find "that self-report measures of past disclosure to specified individuals or targets are at variance with behavioral measures of on-going self-disclosure within specific situations" (Chelune, 1975a, p. 79).

In addition to the SD-60, Jourard developed two similar self-report inventories, the SD-25 (Jourard, 1961c, 1961d) and the SD-40 (Jourard, 1961a, 1961b, 1971; Jourard and Richman, 1963). The statements in the SD-25 and SD-40 tend to cover the same topic areas as those in the SD-60 but are worded differently and are not explicitly divided into topic areas. The SD-25 retains the same four target persons as the SD-60 but has an abbreviated rating scale. The subject rates each of the twenty-five items for either "have disclosed" or "have not disclosed" to each target person. Jourard (1961d) reports odd-even reliability coefficients of 0.90 or higher for each target subscale on the SD-25. In examining the convergent and discriminative validity of the SD-25, Pedersen and Higbee (1968) conclude that construct validity exists for the SD-25, but that there is some variation between the SD-25 and SD-60 as measures of self-disclosure.

The SD-40 follows the same format as the SD-60 with respect to targets and rating schemata. Odd-even reliability coefficients for each of the targets ranged from 0.75 to 0.90, and 0.85 for the total score (Jourard and Richman, 1963). Test-retest reliability coefficients after six months were established from two samples and were 0.61 and 0.62 for the total score (Jourard and Richman, 1963). Jourard (1961b) found a significant correlation between scores on the SD-40 and Rorschach productivity ($r = .37$, $N = 270$), suggesting that there is some construct validity for the inventory. Results of a factor analysis of the SD-40 were presented by Jourard (1971, pp. 94-100), with eight factors being extracted. The most important of these were: a parent factor, a boyfriend factor, and a girl friend factor. Once again, these results suggest that "openness" or self-disclosure is to some extent dependent on the target person or recipient to whom the disclosure is directed.

A number of researchers have used a modification of either the SD-60 or the general format to develop their own instruments for obtaining self-report data on self-disclosure. Modifications have been made in one or more of the following respects: instruction set, number of items, rating scale, or target persons. Simonson and Bahr (1974) and Wilson and Rappaport (1974) asked subjects to rate the SD-60 items with respect to their willingness to disclose the information referred to in the items, while Sote and Good (1974) asked subjects to rate selected items in terms of frequency of discussion on a four-point never-frequently dimension. The number of original SD-60 items used in modified instruments has varied from fifteen (Sote and Good, 1974) to thirty items (Halverson and Shore, 1969). Rating scales have been equally diverse (Bath and Daly, 1972; Simonson and Bahr, 1974; Sote and Good, 1974). Panyard (1971) extended Jourard's original three-point scale to a six-point scale after she obtained a split-half reliability coefficient of only 0.70 for the SD-60. Using her extended rating scale she was able to improve the reliability to 0.91 and obtain a test-retest reliability coefficient of 0.91 after five months. Rather than Jourard's original four targets (mother, father, male friend, and female friend), the following have all been used as alternative target persons: a stranger, an acquaintance, and a best friend (Halverson and Shore, 1969), the therapist (Simonson and Bahr, 1974), a best friend and the closest family member (Truax and Whittmer, 1971), a same sex friend and the better liked parent (Bath and Daly, 1972), and the best-liked girl and least-liked girl in class (Fitzgerald, 1963). Plog (1965), following the general format of the SD-60, developed a forty-item self-disclosure instrument in which the items are equally divided among eight topic areas. Respondents are asked to rate themselves on a four-point scale with respect to their willingness to disclose each item to six target persons. Split-half reliabilities for this instrument have ranged from 0.89 to 0.94 (Plog, 1965).

Measures of the Intimacy of Disclosure. Initial studies by Jourard and others (Jourard, 1961d; Jourard and Lasakow, 1958; Melikian, 1962; Plog, 1965) revealed consistent differences between topic categories on the SD-60. These differences gave rise to the idea that the amount of disclosure varied with respect to the ego relevance or intimacy content of the items on the questionnaire. Researchers subsequently have developed a number of instruments and methods for assessing the intimacy of disclosure from self-report data. Several of the major approaches will be presented here.

Stemming from their interest in social penetration theory, Taylor and Altman (1966) scaled 671 statements, dealing with aspects of the self, for intimacy by the Thurstone procedure (Thurstone and Chave, 1929) for use in studies of interpersonal relations. Additionally, the statements were sorted into thirteen topical categories according to content. The judgments for intimacy and topical content were made by a sample of college students and a sample of sailors. Correlations between the two samples ranged from 0.76 to 0.94 for the thirteen categories considered individually and 0.90 for the pooled correlations. Use of thirty-five- and seventy-item instruments yielded split-half and alternate form reliabilities of 0.82 to 0.86. It was Taylor and Altman's intent that the items should be used to develop self-disclosure questionnaires with known intimacy and content properties. Kipnis and Goodstadt (1970) used forty-seven of the intimacy scaled items in their study of friendship relations. Similarly, Taylor (1968) constructed a forty-item instrument and reported a split-half reliability of 0.94 for several targets. In a later study, Taylor, Altman, and Wheeler (1973) used a forty-eight-item questionnaire covering twelve topic categories and three levels of intimacy, and reported that the questionnaire scores were significantly related to actual disclosures between pairs of sailors.

Marshall (1970) used the items from the Taylor and Altman (1966) pool to construct a self-disclosure questionnaire containing 144 items scaled for intimacy. The questionnaire covers twelve content areas with 12 items in each. Three levels of intimacy are equally represented among the items in each topic category. Subjects are instructed to rate each item on a three-point scale for how much they have disclosed to their best friend. Intercorrelations among the twelve content categories have ranged from 0.37 to 0.88, while correlations between the total score and each category score vary from 0.61 to 0.87 (Vondracek and Marshall, 1971). The advantages of Marshall's questionnaire over inventories such as the SD-60 are: (1) every item is scaled for intimacy, (2) the questionnaire assesses both intimacy and breadth (amount) of disclosure, and (3) the content areas sampled are more extensive and complete than those of the SD-60 (Vondracek and Marshall, 1971).

Jourard and Resnick (1970) devised an interesting procedure for obtaining self-report data on disclosure in actual interviews. This procedure provides a means for combining amount and intimacy into a single composite score. Subjects initially completed a forty-item questionnaire (compare Jourard, 1971, pp. 227-228) that first asked them to indicate which items they had disclosed fully in the past and then which items they would be willing to discuss fully with a same-sexed partner. On the basis of the pooled scores (past disclosure plus willingness to disclose) on this inventory, twelve high and twelve low disclosers were selected and paired in dyads. Each dyad was given twenty topics selected from Taylor and Altman's (1966) pool and printed on four-by-four-inch cards. Five items were of low intimacy value, five of intermediate, and ten of very high intimacy value (compare Jourard, 1971, p. 229). The members of the dyads were instructed to discuss each topic by taking turns. After each topic was considered by the dyad, the subjects rated their own response for amount of disclosure on a three-point scale (0 = no disclosure, 1 = partial disclosure, 2 = full disclosure). A weighted or composite score was obtained for each item by multiplying the subjects' rating for amount of disclosure by the intimacy value of the topic (1 = low, 2 = intermediate, 3 = high). Jourard and Resnick (1970) did not claim any particular advantage for weighting the disclosure scores in this manner, but on examination of the data the weighted method does appear to separate the high and low dyads more than the amount scores alone. The composite score may be a more sensitive index of self-disclosure than amount or intimacy scores considered individually.

Worthy and others (1969) developed a novel technique for obtaining objective self-report intimacy data. Briefly, their procedure involves the use of seventy questions previously scaled for intimacy according to the Thurstone method of scaling. These seventy questions are equally divided into ten sets of seven questions each, each representing seven different levels of intimacy. Thus, the ten sets of seven questions are comparable on the dimension of intimacy. Questions range in intimacy from those regarding food preferences to those regarding sexual activity. Subjects meet in groups of four and communicate by passing notes. There are ten trials and every subject is given identical sets of seven questions in the trials. The subjects can pick any of the questions to answer. On each trial a subject has to choose which questions to answer and to whom to send it. The subject is not allowed to answer the same question more than once. Disclosure scores are obtained by summing the intimacy levels of the questions answered in each of the ten trials. This procedure has been employed in studies by Gary and Hammond (1970) and Certner (1973) and is lauded by these investigators as a technique for providing objective information about group interactions. A serious flaw in the methodology, however, is that no account is made for what is actually said in the notes. An individual may choose a high intimacy question but answer in a superficial manner, thereby disclosing very little. One might overcome this methodological flaw by rating what is actually said on some scalar metric and then multiplying this value by the intimacy level of the question answered, as was done in the Jourard and Resnick (1970) study.

Child and Adolescent Measures. Most self-disclosure research has focused on late adolescent and young adult subject populations. In order to overcome the limitations of such a restricted age range, several researchers have designed self-report measures of disclosure for younger age groups. West and Zingle (1969) developed a forty-eight-item Self-Disclosure Inventory for Adolescents (SDIA), which divides items equally among the following six content areas: health and physical development, self-centered concerns, boy-girl relations, home and family relations, school concerns, and money status concerns. Subjects rate each item for frequency of discussion on a four-point scale ranging from "never" to "often." The original target persons (West and Zingle, 1969) included the mother, the father, a male friend, a female friend, a teacher, and a counselor. In a later study (West, 1971), only the mother, father, friend of the same sex, and friend of the opposite sex were used. West and Zingle (1969) reported an odd-even split-half reliability of 0.97 for the total disclosure score, and a test-retest reliability coefficient of 0.84. The total SDIA scores correlated 0.52 with Rotter's Revealingness Scale, thus providing some construct validity for the SDIA (West and Zingle, 1969). Further validity data for the SDIA were provided by West (1971). In this study, West obtained SDIA data from eighty adolescent subjects and then independently obtained similar data from the designated target persons. Correlations were computed between the criterion scores obtained from the targets' protocols and each of the subjects. The resulting coefficients ranged from 0.42 to 0.61 for target persons, with an overall validity coefficient of 0.54. West (1971), on examining the validity coefficients by sex, noted that the SDIA may be a more valid measure of self-disclosure among girls than boys.

Several other authors have developed self-report instruments designed to assess self-disclosure in children and adolescents between grades one and six (Skypeck, 1967), grades six and twelve (Rivenbark, 1967, 1971), and grades ten and thirteen (Mulcahy, 1973). These inventories are basically modified versions of Jourard's SD-60. Skypeck (1967) designed a twenty-five-item inventory in which the content and wording would be understandable and relevant to children aged six to twelve (compare Jourard, 1971, p. 201). Rivenbark (1967) and Mulcahy (1973) modified the SD-60 items to make them applicable to older children and adolescents. Results obtained with these instruments generally show that self-disclosure increases with age and that sex-related patterns of disclosure emerge as subjects grow older (Mulcahy, 1973; Rivenbark, 1971; Skypeck, 1967).

Situational Inventories. With the growing evidence that social-situational factors play an important role in determining the level of self-disclosure, there is an increasing need for research that examines the role of these factors (Altman and Taylor, 1973; Chelune, 1976a; Cozby, 1973). Several researchers have addressed this important research issue by developing situationally oriented self-disclosure inventories (Argyle and Little, 1972; Chelune, 1976c; Frankel and Powers, 1971). Two self-report approaches will be presented here as examples.

Frankel and Powers (1971) examined reported self-disclosure within an S-R (stimulus situation-response) framework. Their S-R Inventory of Self-Disclosure (SRISD) presents subjects with nine situations (physical-setting conditions, such as "You arc in a bowling alley") and sixteen topic questions ("Are you superstitious?"). The subjects are to respond to each of the sixteen questions in each of the nine situations. Unfortunately, there is no indication of how the subjects' responses are scored. Data from fifty-three subjects, however, did reveal that 7 percent of the total variation observed on the SRISD was due to subjects, 14 percent due to situations, 25 percent due to the questions, and 28 percent to the interactions between these factors. Clearly, the amount of reported disclosure was significantly affected by the nature of the topic questions and the setting in which the disclosure occurred.

Chelune (1976c) has developed a novel twenty-item self-report measure, the Self-Disclosure Situations Survey (SDSS), that is specifically designed to be sensitive to the social-situational determinants of self-disclosure. The SDSS consists of twenty different social situations aimed at sampling various social interactions in which young adults may be involved. The twenty situations are divided into four groups of five items according to one of four target persons involved: a friend, a group of friends, a stranger, and a group of strangers. The five items within each target class represent five different levels of physical-setting conditions scaled for intimacy. Thus, the SDSS represents a 4 × 5 (target by intimacy of setting condition) matrix of items. Subjects are instructed to imagine themselves in each situation and then to rate on a six-point scale the general level of disclosure that they would be comfortable with in that situation. Odd-even split-half reliability coefficients and test-retest reliability have been computed (Chelune, 1975c,

1976c), with the odd-even reliability coefficients ranging from 0.80 to 0.89 and the test-retest reliability coefficient being 0.75. The validity of the SDSS Stranger subscore in predicting actual disclosure to a stranger in an interview setting has been examined with the results suggesting that there is "concurrent validity for the representativeness of the SDSS Stranger items in reflecting how these individuals (the subjects) evaluate their verbal performances to a stranger" (Chelune, 1976c).

An additional feature of Chelune's SDSS is that it can be adapted to provide a gross index of the parameter of self-disclosure flexibility. As the reader will recall, self-disclosure flexibility requires a person to differentiate interpersonal and situational variables first and then to adapt his or her disclosure pattern accordingly. Since the SDSS presents a subject with twenty different social situations that vary systematically in terms of both an interpersonal (target person) and a situational (setting condition) variable, the amount of variation as measured by a standard deviation among the twenty SDSS situations may serve as a gross index of a person's flexibility. Flexibility scores derived in this manner were found to be positively related to two self-report measures that presumably reflect alertness to social-situational demands in the environment (Chelune, 1976c), suggesting that there is some validity to these scores.

Observational Measures

Self-disclosing behavior involves both a sender and a recipient. Thus far we have examined various procedures and instruments for assessing self-disclosure from the perspective of the sender. We will now examine several of the techniques and metrics by which persons other than the sender—recipients or independent observers—judge the sender's self-disclosing behavior. It is important to keep in mind that judgments made from the observer's perspective "may involve the use of different judgment criteria" than those used by the sender (Goodstein and others, 1976, p. 145).

Projective Techniques. Projective tests have long been

popular methods in psychology for obtaining information about the personal aspects of an individual. Hamshire and Farina (1967) used subjects' responses to TAT cards as a source of data by which to rate the level of openness or self-disclosure of the individual. The level of free, unrestricted communication of personal information is rated on a five-point scale based on a manual that summarizes the story characteristics associated with the five scale points. Interrater reliability coefficients for the TAT cards using this procedure are reported by the authors to be between 0.50 and 0.88. Green (1964), using an incomplete-sentences model, developed the Self-Disclosure Sentence Blank (SDSB), which attempts to standardize the scoring for self-disclosure from an individual's sentence completions. The SDSB (compare Jourard, 1971, pp. 230-234) consists of twenty sentence stems that have a pull for self-disclosure. The subject's responses to each sentence stem is scored for personal disclosure by use of a manual that details five levels of response. Graham (1970) reported an interrater reliability of 0.91 over ten subjects for Green's SDSB.

Peer Nominations. The peer nomination technique has been employed as a means of ranking individuals within a group for self-disclosure (Goodstein and others, 1976; Halverson and Shore, 1969; Himelstein and Lubin, 1965). Typically, each member of the group ranks the other members for perceived amount of self-disclosing behavior. The ranks of the entire group are summed, yielding the group's rank-order nominations for the most disclosing to the least disclosing member. While the peer nomination technique is a popular sociometric method in the study of group behavior, its validity is questionable in large groups, in which interpersonal contacts may become restricted to smaller segments of the group's membership.

Self-Descriptive Essays. Methods for scoring the depth of self-disclosure from self-descriptive essays have been developed by Pedersen and Breglio (1968b) and Burhenne and Mirels (1970). The Self-Disclosure Questionnaire (Pedersen and Breglio, 1968b) consists of five essay questions, each presented at the top of separate sheets of paper. The questions were designed to cover the same content areas as Jourard's SD-60 self-report instrument (Jourard and Lasakow, 1958). A depth-of-disclosure score for the answers to each question is obtained by the independent ratings of two judges using the following three-point scale (Pedersen and Breglio, 1968a, p. 294):

1. Discloses little or nothing of himself.
2. Discloses only on a general level; discloses facts but little or no disclosure of a personal nature.
3. Discloses attitudes and information of a personal nature.

Interrater reliability for the depth-of-disclosure ratings using the above scale is reported at 0.83 by Pedersen and Breglio. Burhenne and Mirels's (1970) procedure is similar to Pedersen and Breglio's. Subjects are presented with five essay topics and instructed to answer each as frankly as possible and to write a minimum of three sentences per topic. Subjects are alloted five minutes for each question. Unlike Pedersen and Breglio, Burhenne and Mirels had the essays rated on a five-point authenticity scale, with values 1, 3, and 5 defined for the raters. Interrater reliability using this scale was established at 0.85 in a previous pilot study.

Rating Systems. The most popular sources of verbal data on which ratings of self-disclosure are made are the interactions that occur in groups or interviews. Numerous scalar methods have been employed that vary in rating steps used (Chaikin, Derlega, Bayma, and Shaw, 1975; Ribner, 1974; Simonson and Bahr, 1974) and in parameters assessed (Chelune, 1975c; Davis and Sloan, 1974; Lubin and Harrison, 1964; Ribner, 1974). The selected scalar methods to be presented here are representative of well-defined rating systems that typically have scoring manuals available.

Before looking at these self-disclosure rating systems, however, two of the precursors of formal self-disclosure scales may be noted. These are the Process Scale (Walker, Rablen, and Rogers, 1960) and the Depth of Intrapersonal Exploration Scale (Truax, 1962b). The Process Scale is based on Rogers's (1961) theory of personality and represents a continuum from fixity and rigidity to looseness and flexibility. This continuum is composed of seven aspects or "strands" that can be assessed on seven ten-point scales from written transcripts. Truax's (1962b) Depth of Intrapersonal Exploration (DX) scale essentially attempts to measure the extent to which an individual engages in self-exploration with weightings given for the disclosure of private material. The ten-point DX scale attempts to define the extent of self-exploration, ranging from no demonstrable intrapersonal exploration to a very high level of self-probing and exploration. Interrater reliability coefficients among six raters using the DX scale have ranged from 0.58 to 0.78 (Truax, 1962a), and the scale has been employed to study both patient and therapist communications in psychotherapy (Truax and Carkhuff, 1964, 1965).

Perhaps the earliest rating scale explicitly designed to assess ongoing self-disclosure in personal interactions is Suchman's (1965) Revealingness (REV) Scale. The REV is similar in design to the aspect "manner of relating" on the Process Scale and attempts to assess both the content and style of communication during an interval of ongoing interaction. The scale consists of six rating levels that reflect a continuum from productions in which "the person talks about external conditions of the world" to "one in which the subject expresses himself with self-involvement and feeling" (Epting, Suchman, and Barker, 1969, p. 5). Suchman (1965) reported interjudge reliability coefficients ranging from 0.53 to 0.76 using four judges, and a correlation of 0.87 with more extensive training of two judges (Suchman, 1966).

The major contribution of the REV scale is that it attempts to take into account the parameter of affective manner of presentation. In a recent study (Brooks, 1974), the REV scale was extended to eight levels of revealingness in order to place additional emphasis on affective involvement. Additionally, verbal segments were rated for modal level of response rather than for the highest level of response, as suggested by Suchman (1965). Interrater reliability for the revised REV scale was reported to be 0.72 over 160 verbal segments. Based on her results using the revised REV, Brooks concludes that past reports of sex differences in self-disclosure may be erroneously based on unidimensional measures of self-disclosure and that perhaps whether males and females differ depends on the parameter measured.

An excellent example of a well-defined rating system is Doster's Self-Disclosure Rating Scale. Doster (1971) has carefully prepared a training manual, complete with guidelines and practice examples, for use with his rating scale. Essentially the scale rates the content of verbal behavior along a seven-step superficial-personal continuum. At the lower values, the subject is judged as focusing on external material and events with little indication of personal involvement. The higher values reflect personal disclosures that focus on aspects of the self and on the impact of external events on the self. Each value is defined and samples are provided. The scale has been widely used in conjunction with several time measures in order to study various aspects of interview behavior (Doster, 1972, 1975; Doster and Brooks, 1974; Doster and Slaymaker, 1972; Doster and Strickland, 1969, 1971; McGuire, Thelen, and Amolsch, 1975). Interrater reliability coefficients for the Self-Disclosure Rating Scale in these studies ranged from a low of 0.62 and 0.71 (Doster and Strickland, 1971) to a high of 0.84 and 0.94 (Doster and Brooks, 1974). A condensed version of the scale was used by Shimkunas (1972) to study the pathological verbalizations of schizophrenics. Shimkunas reported that raters were within one point of agreement on 94 percent to 97 percent of the observations of sixty subjects.

Strassberg and Anchor (1975) developed a scale for rating the intimacy of disclosure on the basis of content alone. The Intimacy Rating Scale (IRS) is a three-point content categorization derived from a rescaling of the items in Taylor and Altman's (1966) study. After deleting items similar to each other in content and with large standard deviations, the authors arrived at a scale consisting of thirty-five categories approximately evenly divided among three intimacy levels: low, medium, and high. The consensual validity of the IRS was examined by Strassberg and Anchor (1975) in the following way: First, they rated twenty-one varied personal statements using the IRS; then, they presented these same statements to a sample of college students, who rated the perceived intimacy of each statement on a three-point scale. A correlation of 0.96 was obtained between the authors' IRS ratings of the statements and the mean intimacy scores of the subjects.

A system for assessing self-disclosing behavior among pre-adolescents was described by Vondracek and Vondracek (1971). On the basis of pilot work, eight categories of response are defined: "family," "friends," "self," "activities," "evaluation of own performance," "transgressions," "tastes and attitudes," and "expressions of feelings." Most of these content areas are scored for two levels of intimacy. The categories "expressions of feelings" and "transgressions" are scored for three levels of intimacy. Scores are based essentially on frequencies observed. Interrater reliability was reported at 0.96 (Vondracek and Vondracek, 1971).

Objective Measures

Two parameters of self-disclosing behavior, amount and duration, readily lend themselves to objective measurement. As the reader will recall, amount of disclosure refers to the number or breadth of the items of information disclosed, whereas duration refers to the time spent disclosing aspects of the self. In this section we will examine some of the objective procedures used to assess these two dimensions.

Measures of Amount. It was noted earlier that self-descriptive essays have been used to yield ratings of depth of disclosure. In addition to ratings of depth, Burhenne and Mirels (1970) and Pedersen and Breglio (1968b) utilized the number of words subjects used to describe themselves as a measure of amount of disclosure. The underlying assumption was that the more words used to describe oneself the greater the information revealed. While this assessment procedure is objective and highly reliable, its conceptual relation to self-disclosure is weak, since the concise, explicit subject is penalized.

The amount or breadth of disclosure, based solely on topical content, has been assessed in vivo during self-introductions by Himelstein and Kimbrough (1963) and from taped introductions by Chittick and Himelstein (1967). Observers simply checkmarked each item of information revealed by a subject within a topic area. The subject's score was the total number of checkmarks or the number of topics covered. Interrater reliabilities using this procedure were 0.75 (Himelstein and Kimbrough, 1963) and 0.99 (Chittick and Himelstein, 1967) using the rank-order method. No provision, however, is made for self-descriptive elaborations on a topic in this procedure. A subject merely receives one check mark per topic. Kohen (1975) overcame this difficulty by defining a unit of disclosure as the smallest segment of verbal behavior to which an observer could assign a classification. In this way, subjects who elaborated on a particular topic received a check mark for each unit of disclosure. Interjudge reliabilities using Kohen's procedure ranged from 0.81 to 0.87.

Content analysis techniques have been widely used to score amount of disclosure from samples of verbal behavior. These procedures divide verbal behavior into units, assign each unit to a category or position on a metric, and summarize the coded units in order to provide a basis for inferential statements (Marsden, 1971). Whalen (1969) developed a content analysis system that provides for the continuous rating of five major verbal response classes with an event recorder. Among the categories scored in this technique are "personal discussion" and "impersonal discussion." Verbal statements of personal self-disclosure, immediate feelings, and personal questions are categorized as "personal discussion." Whalen (1969) reports interrater reliability of 0.75 and above for in vivo scoring of the frequencies of her verbal classes. Whalen's system has also been used to analyze written transcripts of tape-recorded interviews (Rappaport, Gross, and Lepper, 1973; Wilson and Rappaport, 1974). Using written transcripts, Rappaport and others (1973) reported 92-percent agreement between raters over 3,200 statements, and Wilson and Rappaport (1974) 96-percent agreement over 1,500-statement units.

Sousa-Poza and Rohrberg (1976) coded self-disclosure in transcribed protocols of therapy sessions in two ways. The first, "level of disclosure," consists of two mutually exclusive categories, "direct disclosure" and "indirect disclosure." The second, the interaction code, assesses the directionality of disclosure. The authors reported that for 80 percent of the verbal acts there was act-by-act agreement between raters. Other studies (Kraft and Vraa, 1975; Mann and Murphy, 1975) have utilized content analysis procedures that categorize verbal behavior similarly to Sousa-Poza and Rohrberg's level of disclosure.

The concept of self-reference has been a popular unit of self-disclosure in content analysis systems. Rogers (1960, p. 248) has operationally defined a self-reference as "a verbal response by S which describes him in some way, tells something about him, or refers to some affect he experiences." Self-references may be positive, negative, or ambiguous, depending on whether they are favorable, unfavorable, or neutral. The grammatical sentence is the basic unit considered for scoring. Rogers reports interrater reliabilities between 0.83 and 0.95 for all self-reference categories scored from tape-recorded interviews. Powell (1968) reports similar reliability coefficients (0.84 to 0.94) for the self-reference categories, and reliabilities between 0.88 and 0.94 for recoding after one month.

A difficulty with using merely the frequency of self-references as an index of amount of disclosure is that not all subjects verbalize at the same rate: The subject who verbalizes quickly has a greater opportunity to make more self-references than the subject who verbalizes slowly. Chelune (1976c) has presented data supporting this notion. In order to remove this problem, Powell (1968) had each self-reference class expressed as a percentage of the subject's total number of responses. In this way the percentage of self-references or the information density of a subject's verbalizations becomes the index for amount of disclosure. Anchor, Vojtisek, and Berger (1972) used this percentage procedure to examine the effects of sociability upon self-disclosure patterns in groups. Bath and Daly (1972) modified the procedure slightly and used the ratio of frequency of self-references over the frequency of references to other-than-self. They reported an interrater reliability of 0.91 for the numerator and 0.93 for the denominator of their ratio. Chelune (1975c) used the same procedure as Powell for computing the percentage of self-references. However, he refined the basic unit of analysis. Instead of using the sentence as the basic unit, Chelune used the "thought unit" or independent, nonreflexive clause (Dollard and Mowrer, 1947) as the basic scoring unit. Using a detailed scoring manual (Chelune, 1975c), raters achieved pooled reliabilities of 0.98 for scoring the number of thought units, 0.97 for classifying thought units as self-references, and 0.90 for computing the percentage of self-references.

A system for weighting self-references according to whether they are first-person references or reflexive second-person references was developed by Haymes (1969; compare Jourard, 1971, pp. 216-218). Tape-recorded interviews are blocked into thirty-second intervals and a score of 2, 1, or 0 is assigned to the intervals. In any given thirty-second interval only one score is given, which is for the maximally disclosing statement. A score of 2 is assigned to first-person references, a score of 1 to reflexive second-person references in which the word *you* is a substitution for *I*, and a score of 0 to statements of other-than-self. Self-disclosure in this system is defined by four major response classes: (1) expressions of emotions and emotional processes, (2) expressions of needs, (3) expressions of fantasies, strivings, hopes, or dreams, and (4) expressions of self-awareness. Stone and Gotlib (1975) used Haymes's scoring procedure but rated ten-second rather than thirty-second intervals. They reported interrater reliability of 0.87 for scoring over twelve minutes of tape-recorded speech for forty-eight subjects. Chelune (1975c) also used Haymes's scoring schemata, though in a modified form. Instead of assigning one score to an entire thirty-second interval as Haymes did, each self-reference within a thirty-second block of speech was evaluated and given an appropriate weight. A pooled interrater reliability coefficient of 0.97 was obtained using this modification.

Time Measures. The most widely used temporal measure of self-disclosing behavior is duration or time spent talking; it appears in over twenty self-disclosure studies. Speech duration is assumed to be related to self-disclosure output and willingness to disclose (Doster and Strickland, 1971). In several cases, duration has even been used as a measure of amount of disclosure

(Himelstein and Kimbrough, 1963; Vondracek, 1969a, 1969b). The assumption is that the more a person talks, the more disclosing he or she must do. Block and Goodstein (1971, p. 596) have attacked this assumption, stating that "the duration of utterances would seem to bear no necessary theoretical or empirical relationship to the quantity or quality of self-disclosure." In a recent study, however, Goodstein and others (1976) found that group members equated their fellow members' amount of participation with amount of self-disclosure ($\rho = 0.71$). Self-rankings of participation and self-disclosure were not as highly correlated ($\rho = 0.49$), but it is evident that participation time is related in some way to the degree of perceived self-disclosure, particularly from the recipient's point of view.

Several studies reporting intercorrelations between various measures of disclosure and speech duration have shed light on the nature of the relationship between duration and perceived self-disclosure. Duration of speech was found to be unrelated to the percentage of self-references revealed by an individual (Bath and Daly, 1972; Doster and Brooks, 1974). However, moderately high correlations, ranging from 0.42 to 0.55, have been consistently reported between duration and ratings of depth of disclosure (Doster, 1975; Doster and Brooks, 1974; Doster and Strickland, 1971; Vondracek, 1969a). Davis and Sloan (1974) have even reported a correlation as high as 0.79 between speech durations and ratings of intimacy. From these data it appears that speech durations are related not to amount of disclosure, but to the perceived intimacy of the disclosures. The longer an individual speaks on topics regarding the self, the more intimate the disclosures become or are perceived to become.

Rate of disclosure, or the number of self-descriptive statements per unit of time, has been used to control for the effects of different speaking times among subjects (Chelune, 1975c, 1976a; McGuire and others, 1975; Mehrabian, 1971). Rate of disclosure is thought to reflect information rate independently of idiosyncratic speech rhythms. Unfortunately, no data comparing measures of duration and rate of disclosure are presently available.

Two additional time measures, reaction time and the silence quotient, have been used in self-disclosure research, principally by Doster and his colleagues (Doster, 1972, 1975; Doster and Brooks, 1974; Doster and Strickland, 1969, 1971). These objective time measures are similar to those described by Goldman-Eisler (1961) and Matarazzo, Wiens, and Saslow (1965). The reaction time measure is the amount of latency in seconds that a subject takes before responding to an interview topic. Doster (1972, p. 205) considers the reaction time measure "an assessment of silent deliberation about topics before speaking." The silence quotient is obtained by summing all silent pauses over three seconds (excluding reaction time) and then dividing this sum by the total duration of the response to an item. The quotient also assesses amount of silent deliberation and monitoring. Lengthy reaction times and high silence quotients are considered to reflect cautiousness in preparing verbal disclosures. Doster (1975) was able to demonstrate longer reaction times among highly anxious subjects than among less anxious subjects. The data presented by Fischer and Apostal (1975), however, conflict with the interpretation that silences are necessarily a sign of cautiousness. Instead, unfilled pauses in conversations (silences) were found to enhance counselors' perceptions of counselee self-disclosure, suggesting that silent pauses may serve as discriminate cues, warning recipients that a high-level disclosure is to follow. The role silence plays in self-disclosing behavior is probably highly complex and warrants further investigation.

A Multidimensional Assessment Procedure

While we have described numerous methods and procedures for assessing self-disclosing behavior, most of the indices discussed have been unidimensional measures, that is, measures assessing only one parameter of self-disclosure. As the reader will recall, self-disclosure is not a unitary construct but, as a class of behavior, is thought to have five basic dimensions. The independent but simultaneous assessment of each of these parameters is important if self-disclosure, as a total concept, is to be meaningfully and systematically studied as a behavioral process.

Unfortunately, few multidimensional procedures have been developed. Doster (1972, 1975) and his colleagues (Doster and Brooks, 1974; Doster and Strickland, 1971) have typically assessed at least two parameters, intimacy and duration, in their research. Two studies in the literature have reported results in terms of three disclosure dimensions: amount, intimacy, and duration (Doster and Brooks, 1974; McGuire and others, 1975). Recently, Chelune (1975c) developed an explicit, detailed multidimensional procedure, the Self-Disclosure Coding System (SDCS), for coding each of the five self-disclosure parameters from samples of verbal behavior.

The SDCS consists of eleven coding categories and uses both written transcripts and tape recordings for coding. Seven coding categories constitute the core system: (1) amount (A), the number of thought units expressed; (2) self-reference (SR), the number of thought units that describe some quality or aspect of the speaker; (3) self-reference percent (SR%), the basic index of amount of self-disclosure, computed by the formula SR/A; (4) intimacy, the judged depth or ego relevance of the verbal content (rated on a five-point scale); (5) affect, the judged degree of congruence between the verbal content and the affective manner of presentation (rated on a five-point scale); (6) rate, the number of self-references per unit of time; and (7) self-disclosure flexibility, an index of variability in SR% among three or more situations, represented by a standard deviation.

Using a detailed scoring manual (Chelune, 1975c), raters applied the SDCS to seventy-two five-minute interviews obtained from twenty-four subjects. The obtained interrater reliabilities for the above seven variables were 0.98, 0.97, 0.90, 0.79, 0.77, 0.97, and 0.80, respectively. Four additional coding categories supplement the SDCS system and represent a further breakdown of the SR variable. These are: (8) positive self-reference (SR+), a self-reference that describes a positive aspect or quality of the speaker; (9) negative self-reference (SR−), a self-reference that describes an unfavorable aspect or quality of the speaker; (10) neutral self-reference (SRo), a self-reference that cannot be clearly classified as either SR+ or SR—; and (11) self-reference weighted (SRw), a category that weights self-references using Haymes's (1969) system, depending on whether the SR is a first-person reference or a reflexive second-person reference. The obtained interrater reliabilities for these four categories were 0.95, 0.92, 0.81, and 0.97, respectively (Chelune, 1975c).

Chelune (1976a) used the SDCS system to examine the nature of sex and target differences in disclosure. Males and females in his sample did not differ in the percentage of information revealed (SR%), nor were there sex differences in the congruence between verbal content and affective manner of presentation or in self-disclosure flexibility. The females did, however, verbalize more than the males and make more self-references per minute than males. The females' verbal content was also rated as more intimate than the males' verbal content. Significant changes between target persons were found on the affect and rate dimensions of disclosure. Chelune (1976a, p. 262) concludes that "coding verbal behavior in terms of the basic parameters of self-disclosure permits a more meaningful and systematic explanation of the effects of independent variables upon self-disclosing behavior than previous single dimensional approaches."

Summary

It is clear that many diverse and interesting techniques have been designed to assess self-disclosing behavior. This variability is both a strength and a weakness. The creativity of researchers in developing these new assessment techniques has led to a better understanding of the complex nature of self-disclosure and the variables affecting it. However, this same diversity of assessment techniques makes rigorous cross-study comparisons of data difficult, and is a probable factor in some of the contradictory findings reported in the literature. Whatever the strengths and weaknesses of these various techniques, one must be impressed by the interest and ingenuity stimulated by the concept of self-disclosure.

In the preceding pages we have attempted not only to highlight some of the major approaches currently used to assess self-disclosure but also to point up several key conceptual issues and their implications for future research. The first of these is the multidimensional nature of self-disclosing behavior and the need for assessment procedures that are explicitly designed to assess the various parameters of disclosure. A second key issue that affects the interpretation of results is that judgments about disclosing behavior differ depending on whose perspective is taken. If investigators are to generalize from their results, they must be cautioned about discussing self-disclosure beyond the perspective from which it was measured. Finally, there is a need for new research methodologies that examine the contextual influences of various social-situational factors on self-disclosure as an ongoing behavioral process. This is especially important in research that attempts to examine the role of self-disclosure in personality adjustment.

References

Altman, I., and Taylor, D. A. *Social Penetration: The Development of Interpersonal Relationships.* New York: Holt, Rinehart and Winston, 1973.

Anchor, K. N., Vojtisek, J. E., and Berger, S. E. "Social Desirability as a Predictor of Self-Disclosure in Groups." *Psychotherapy: Theory, Research and Practice,* 1972, 9, 262-264.

Argyle, M., and Little, B. "Do Personality Traits Apply to Social Behavior?" *Journal for the Study of Social Behavior,* 1972, 2, 1-35.

Axtell, B., and Cole, C. W. "Repression-Sensitization Response Mode and Verbal Avoidance." *Journal of Personality and Social Psychology,* 1971, 18, 133-137.

Bath, K. E., and Daly, D. L. "Self-Disclosure: Relationships to Self-Described Personality and Sex Differences." *Psychological Reports,* 1972, 31, 623-628.

Block, E. L., and Goodstein, L. D. "Comment on 'Influence of an Interviewer's Disclosure on the Self-Disclosing Behavior of Interviewees.' " *Journal of Counseling Psychology,* 1971, *18,* 595-597.

Brooks, L. "Interactive Effects of Sex and Status on Self-Disclosure." *Journal of Counseling Psychology,* 1974, *21,* 469-474.

Burhenne, D., and Mirels, H. "Self-Disclosure in Self-Descriptive Essays." *Journal of Consulting and Clinical Psychology,* 1970, *35,* 409-413.

Campbell, D. T., and Fiske, D. W. "Convergent and Discriminant Validation by the Multitrait-Multimethod Matrix." *Psychological Bulletin,* 1959, *56,* 81-105.

Carroll, D. "Repression-Sensitization and the Verbal Elaborations of Experience." *Journal of Consulting and Clinical Psychology,* 1972, *38,* 147.

Certner, B. C. "Exchange of Self-Disclosures in Same-Sexed Groups of Strangers." *Journal of Consulting and Clinical Psychology,* 1973, *40,* 292-297.

Chaikin, A. L., and Derlega, V. J. "Liking for the Norm-Breaker in Self-Disclosure." *Journal of Personality,* 1974a, *42,* 117-129.

Chaikin, A. L., and Derlega, V. J. "Variables Affecting the Appropriateness of Self-Disclosure." *Journal of Consulting and Clinical Psychology,* 1974b, *42,* 588-593.

Chaikin, A. L., Derlega, V. J., Bayma, B., and Shaw, J. "Neuroticism and Disclosure Reciprocity." *Journal of Consulting and Clinical Psychology,* 1975, *43,* 13-19.

Chelune, G. J. "Self-Disclosure: An Elaboration of Its Basic Dimensions." *Psychological Reports,* 1975a, *36,* 79-85.

Chelune, G. J. "Sex Differences and the Relationship Between Repression-Sensitization and Self-Disclosure." *Psychological Reports,* 1975b, *37,* 920.

Chelune, G. J. "Studies in the Behavioral and Self-Report Assessment of Self-Disclosure." Unpublished doctoral dissertation, University of Nevada at Reno, 1975c.

Chelune, G. J. "A Multidimensional Look at Sex and Target Differences in Disclosure." *Psychological Reports,* 1976a, *39,* 259-263.

Chelune, G. J. "Reactions to Male and Female Disclosure at

Two Levels." *Journal of Personality and Social Psychology*, 1976b, *34*, 1000-1003.

Chelune, G. J. "The Self-Disclosure Situations Survey: A New Approach to Measuring Self-Disclosure." *Catalog of Selected Documents in Psychology*, 1976c, *6*, 111-112. (Order Ms. 1367)

Chittick, E. V., and Himelstein, P. "The Manipulation of Self-Disclosure." *Journal of Psychology*, 1967, *65*, 117-121.

Cozby, P. "Self-Disclosure: A Literature Review." *Psychological Bulletin*, 1973, *79*, 73-91.

Davis, J. D., and Sloan, M. "The Basis of Interviewee Matching of Interviewer Self-Disclosure." *British Journal of Social and Clinical Psychology*, 1974, *13*, 359-367.

Dimond, R. E., and Hellkamp, D. T. "Race, Sex, Ordinal Position of Birth and Self-Disclosure in High School Students." *Psychological Reports*, 1969, *25*, 235-238.

Dimond, R. E., and Munz, D. C. "Ordinal Position of Birth and Self-Disclosure in High School Students." *Psychological Reports*, 1967, *21*, 829-833.

Dollard, J., and Mowrer, O. H. "A Method of Measuring Tension in Written Documents." *Journal of Abnormal and Social Psychology*, 1947, *42*, 3-32.

Doster, J. A. "The Disclosure Rating Scale." Unpublished rating manual, University of Missouri, 1971.

Doster, J. A. "Effects of Instructions, Modeling, and Role Rehearsal on Interview Verbal Behavior." *Journal of Consulting and Clinical Psychology*, 1972, *39*, 202-209.

Doster, J. A. "Individual Differences Affecting Interviewee Expectancies and Perceptions of Self-Disclosure." *Journal of Counseling Psychology*, 1975, *22*, 192-198.

Doster, J. A., and Brooks, S. J. "Interviewer Disclosure Modeling, Information Revealed, and Interviewee Verbal Behavior." *Journal of Consulting and Clinical Psychology*, 1974, *42*, 420-426.

Doster, J. A., and Slaymaker, J. "Need Approval, Uncertainty, Anxiety, and Expectations of Interview Behavior." *Journal of Counseling Psychology*, 1972, *19*, 522-528.

Doster, J. A., and Strickland, B. R. "Individual Difference Variables Affecting Reported Self-Disclosure and Observed Verbal Behavior." Paper presented at the meeting of the Southeastern Psychological Association, New Orleans, 1969.

Doster, J. A., and Strickland, B. R. "Disclosing of Verbal Material as a Function of Information Requested, Information About the Interviewer, and Interviewee Differences." *Journal of Consulting and Clinical Psychology,* 1971, *37,* 187-194.

Ellis, A. "Rationalism and Its Therapeutic Applications." *Annual of Psychotherapy,* 1959, *1,* 55-64.

Epting, F. R., Suchman, D. I., and Barker, E. N. "Some Aspects of Revealingness and Disclosure: A Review." Unpublished manuscript, University of Florida, 1969.

Fischer, M., and Apostal, R. "Selected Vocal Cues and Counselor's Perceptions of Genuineness, Self-Disclosure, and Anxiety." *Journal of Counseling Psychology,* 1975, *22,* 92-96.

Fiske, D. W. "Some Hypotheses Concerning Test Adequacy." *Educational and Psychological Measurement,* 1966, *26,* 69-88.

Fitzgerald, M. P. "Self-Disclosure and Expressed Self-Esteem, Social Distance and Areas of Self Revealed." *Journal of Psychology,* 1963, *56,* 405-412.

Frankel, A., and Powers, B. "An S-R Inventory of Self-Disclosure." Paper presented at the meeting of the Western Psychological Association, San Francisco, 1971.

Fromm, E. *The Sane Society.* New York: Holt, Rinehart and Winston, 1955.

Gary, A. L., and Hammond, R. "Self-Disclosures of Alcoholics and Drug Addicts." *Psychotherapy: Theory, Research and Practice,* 1970, *7,* 142-143.

Goldman-Eisler, F. "The Distribution of Pause Durations in Speech." *Language and Speech,* 1961, *4,* 232-237.

Goodstein, L. D., Goldstein, J. J., D'Orta, C. W., and Goodman, M. A. "Measurement of Self-Disclosure in Encounter Groups: A Methodological Study." *Journal of Counseling Psychology,* 1976, *23,* 142-146.

Goodstein, L. D., and Reinecker, V. M. "Factors Affecting Self-

Disclosure: A Review of the Literature." In B. A. Maher (Ed.), *Progress in Experimental Personality Research.* Vol. 7. New York: Academic Press, 1974.

Graham, S. "Level of Self-Disclosure as a Variable of Death Attitudes." Unpublished master's thesis, University of Florida, 1970.

Green, R. "Sentence Completion Test for Measuring Self-Disclosure." Unpublished master's thesis, Ohio State University, 1964.

Halverson, C., and Shore, R. "Self-Disclosure and Interpersonal Functioning." *Journal of Consulting and Clinical Psychology,* 1969, *33,* 213-217.

Hamshire, J. H., and Farina, A. "Openness as a Dimension of Projective Test Responses." *Journal of Consulting Psychology,* 1967, *31,* 525-528.

Haymes, M. "Self-Disclosure and the Acquaintance Process." Unpublished manuscript, Cornell University, 1969.

Himelstein, P., and Kimbrough, W. "A Study of Self-Disclosure in the Classroom." *Journal of Psychology,* 1963, *55,* 437-440.

Himelstein, P., and Lubin, B. "Attempted Validation of the Self-Disclosure Inventory by the Peer-Nomination Technique." *Journal of Psychology,* 1965, *61,* 13-16.

Hurley, J. R., and Hurley, S. J. "Toward Authenticity in Measuring Self-Disclosure." *Journal of Counseling Psychology,* 1969, *16,* 271-274.

Janofsky, A. I. "Affective Self-Disclosure in Telephone Versus Face-to-Face Interviews." *Journal of Humanistic Psychology,* 1971, *11,* 93-103.

Jourard, S. M. "Self-Disclosure and Other Cathexis." *Journal of Abnormal and Social Psychology,* 1959, *59,* 428-431.

Jourard, S. M. "Age Trends in Self-Disclosure." *Merrill Palmer Quarterly,* 1961a, *7,* 191-197.

Jourard, S. M. "Self-Disclosure and Rorschach Productivity." *Perceptual and Motor Skills,* 1961b, *13,* 232.

Jourard, S. M. "Self-Disclosure Scores and Grades in Nursing College." *Journal of Applied Psychology,* 1961c, *7,* 244-247.

Jourard, S. M. "Self-Disclosure in British and American College

Females." *Journal of Social Psychology*, 1961d, *54*, 315-320.

Jourard, S. M. *The Transparent Self*. New York: D. Van Nostrand, 1964.

Jourard, S. M. *Disclosing Man to Himself*. New York: D. Van Nostrand, 1968.

Jourard, S. M. *Self-Disclosure: An Experimental Analysis of the Transparent Self*. New York: Wiley-Interscience, 1971.

Jourard, S. M., and Jaffe, P. E. "Influence of an Interviewer's Behavior on the Self-Disclosing Behavior of Interviewees." *Journal of Counseling Psychology*, 1970, *17*, 252-257.

Jourard, S. M., and Lasakow, P. "Some Factors in Self-Disclosure." *Journal of Abnormal and Social Psychology*, 1958, *56*, 91-98.

Jourard, S. M., and Resnick, J. "Some Effects of Self-Disclosure Among College Women." *Journal of Humanistic Psychology*, 1970, *10*, 84-93.

Jourard, S. M., and Richman, P. "Factors in the Self-Disclosure Inputs of College Students." *Merrill Palmer Quarterly*, 1963, *9*, 141-148.

Kaplan, M. F. "Interviewer Interaction of Repressors and Sensitizers." *Journal of Consulting Psychology*, 1967, *31*, 513-516.

Kipnis, D., and Goodstadt, B. "Character Structure and Friendship Relations." *British Journal of Social and Clinical Psychology*, 1970, *9*, 201-211.

Knecht, L., Lippman, D., and Swap, W. "Similarity, Attraction and Self-Disclosure." *Proceedings of the 81st Annual Convention of the American Psychological Association*, 1973, *8*, 205-206.

Kohen, J. "The Development of Reciprocal Self-Disclosure in Opposite Sex Interaction." *Journal of Counseling Psychology*, 1975, *22*, 404-410.

Kraft, L. W., and Vraa, C. W. "Sex Composition of Groups and Pattern of Self-Disclosure by High School Females." *Psychological Reports*, 1975, *37*, 733-734.

Levinger, G., and Senn, D. J. "Disclosure of Feelings in Marriage." *Merrill Palmer Quarterly*, 1967, *13*, 237-249.

Lubin, B., and Harrison, R. L. "Predicting Small Group Behavior with the Self-Disclosure Inventory." *Psychological Reports*, 1964, *15*, 77-78.

McGuire, D., Thelen, M. H., and Amolsch, T. "Interview Self-Disclosure as a Function of Length of Modeling and Descriptive Instructions." *Journal of Consulting and Clinical Psychology*, 1975, *43*, 356-362.

Mann, B., and Murphy, K. C. "Timing of Self-Disclosure, Reciprocity of Self-Disclosure, and Reactions to an Initial Interview." *Journal of Counseling Psychology*, 1975, *22*, 304-308.

Marsden, G. "Content-Analysis Studies of Psychotherapy: 1954 Through 1968." In A. Bergin and S. Garfield (Eds.), *Handbook of Psychotherapy and Behavior Change*. New York: Wiley, 1971.

Marshall, M. J. "The Effects of Two Interviewer Variables on Self-Disclosure in an Experimental Interview Situation." Unpublished master's thesis, Pennsylvania State University, 1970.

Matarazzo, J. D., Wiens, A. M., and Saslow, G. "Studies of Interview Speech Behavior." In L. Krasner and L. P. Ullmann (Eds.), *Research in Behavior Modification: New Developments and Their Clinical Implications*. New York: Holt, Rinehart and Winston, 1965.

Mayer, J. E. "Disclosing Marital Problems." *Social Casework*, 1967, *48*, 342-351.

Mehrabian, A. "Verbal and Nonverbal Interaction of Strangers in a Waiting Situation." *Journal of Experimental Research in Personality*, 1971, *5*, 127-138.

Melikian, L. "Self-Disclosure Among University Students in the Middle East." *Journal of Social Psychology*, 1962, *57*, 259-263.

Mowrer, O. H. *The Crisis in Psychiatry and Religion*. New York: D. Van Nostrand, 1961.

Mulcahy, G. A. "Sex Differences in Patterns of Self-Disclosure Among Adolescents: A Developmental Prospective." *Journal of Youth and Adolescence*, 1973, *2*, 343-356.

Panyard, C. "A Method to Improve the Reliability of the Jourard Self-Disclosure Questionnaire." *Journal of Counseling Psychology,* 1971, *18,* 606.

Panyard, C. "Self-Disclosure Between Friends: A Validity Study." *Journal of Counseling Psychology,* 1973, *20,* 66-68.

Pedersen, D. M. "Self-Disclosure, Body-Accessibility and Personal Space." *Psychological Reports,* 1973, *33,* 975-980.

Pedersen, D. M., and Breglio, V. J. "The Correlation of Two Self-Disclosure Inventories with Actual Self-Disclosure: A Validity Study." *Journal of Psychology,* 1968a, *68,* 291-298.

Pedersen, D. M., and Breglio, V. J. "Personality Correlates of Actual Self-Disclosure." *Psychological Reports,* 1968b, *22,* 495-501.

Pedersen, D. M., and Higbee, K. "An Evaluation of the Equivalence and Construct Validity of Various Measures of Self-Disclosure." *Educational and Psychological Measurement,* 1968, *28,* 511-523.

Pedersen, D. M., and Higbee, K. "Self-Disclosure and Relationship to the Target Person." *Merrill Palmer Quarterly,* 1969, *15,* 213-220.

Plog, S. C. "The Disclosure of Self in the United States and Germany." *Journal of Social Psychology,* 1965, *65,* 193-203.

Powell, W. J. "Differential Effectiveness of Interviewer Interventions in an Experimental Interview." *Journal of Consulting and Clinical Psychology,* 1968, *32,* 210-215.

Rappaport, J., Gross, T., and Lepper, C. "Modeling, Sensitivity Training and Instructions: Implications for Training of College Student Volunteers and for Outcome Research." *Journal of Consulting and Clinical Psychology,* 1973, *40,* 99-107.

Ribner, N. G. "Effects of an Explicit Group Contract on Self-Disclosure and Group Cohesiveness." *Journal of Counseling Psychology,* 1974, *21,* 116-120.

Rivenbark, W. H. "Self-Disclosure and Sociometric Choice in the Adolescent Period." Ann Arbor, Mich.: University Microfilms, 1967. (No. 67-13157)

Rivenbark, W. H. "Self-Disclosure Patterns Among Adolescents." *Psychological Reports,* 1971, *28,* 35-42.

Rogers, C. *On Becoming a Person.* Boston: Houghton Mifflin, 1961.

Rogers, J. M. "Operant Conditioning in a Quasi-Therapy Setting." *Journal of Abnormal and Social Psychology,* 1960, *60,* 247-252.

Ryckman, R. M., Sherman, M. F., and Burgess, G. D. "Locus of Control and Self-Disclosure of Public and Private Information by College Men and Women: A Brief Note." *Journal of Psychology,* 1973, *84,* 317-318.

Salzinger, K., and Pisoni, S. "Reinforcement of Affect Responses of Schizophrenics During the Clinical Interview." *Journal of Abnormal and Social Psychology,* 1958, *57,* 84-90.

Shapiro, J. G., Krauss, H. H., and Truax, C. B. "Therapeutic Conditions and Disclosure Beyond the Therapeutic Encounter." *Journal of Counseling Psychology,* 1969, *16,* 290-294.

Shimkunas, A. M. "Demand for Intimate Self-Disclosure and Pathological Verbalizations in Schizophrenia." *Journal of Abnormal Psychology,* 1972, *80,* 197-205.

Simonson, N. R., and Bahr, S. "Self-Disclosure by the Professional and Paraprofessional Therapist." *Journal of Consulting and Clinical Psychology,* 1974, *42,* 359-363.

Skypeck, G. "Self-Disclosure in Children Ages Six Through Twelve." Unpublished master's thesis, University of Florida, 1967.

Sote, G. A., and Good, L. R. "Similarity of Self-Disclosure and Interpersonal Attraction." *Psychological Reports,* 1974, *34,* 491-494.

Sousa-Poza, J. F., and Rohrberg, R. "Communicational and Interactional Aspects of Self-Disclosure in Psychotherapy: Differences Related to Cognitive Style." *Psychiatry,* 1976, *39,* 81-91.

Sousa-Poza, J. F., Shulman, E., and Rohrberg, R. "Field Dependence and Self-Disclosure." *Perceptual and Motor Skills,* 1973, *36,* 735-738.

Stone, G. L., and Gotlib, I. "Effect of Instructions and Modeling on Self-Disclosure." *Journal of Counseling Psychology,* 1975, *22,* 288-293.

Strassberg, D. S., and Anchor, K. N. "Rating Intimacy of Self-Disclosure." *Psychological Reports,* 1975, *37,* 562.

Suchman, D. I. "A Scale for the Measurement of Revealingness in Spoken Behavior." Unpublished master's thesis, Ohio State University, 1965.

Suchman, D. I. "Responses of Subjects to Two Types of Interviews." (Doctoral dissertation, Ohio State University) Ann Arbor, Mich.: University Microfilms, 1966. (No. 67-2548)

Sullivan, H. S. *The Psychiatric Interview.* New York: Norton, 1954.

Taylor, D. A. "The Development of Interpersonal Relationships: Social Penetration Processes." *Journal of Social Psychology,* 1968, *75,* 79-90.

Taylor, D. A., and Altman, I. "Intimacy-Scaled Stimuli for Use in Studies of Interpersonal Relations." *Psychological Reports,* 1966, *19,* 729-730.

Taylor, D. A., Altman, I., and Sorrentino, R. "Interpersonal Exchange as a Function of Rewards and Costs and Situational Factors: Expectancy Confirmation-Disconfirmation." *Journal of Experimental Social Psychology,* 1969, *5,* 324-339.

Taylor, D. A., Altman, I., and Wheeler, L. "Self-Disclosure in Isolated Groups." *Journal of Personality and Social Psychology,* 1973, *26,* 39-47.

Taylor, D. A., and Oberlander, L. "Person-Perception and Self-Disclosure: Motivational Mechanisms in Interpersonal Processes." *Journal of Experimental Research in Personality,* 1969, *4,* 14-28.

Thurstone, L. L., and Chave, E. J. *The Measurement of Attitude.* Chicago: University of Chicago Press, 1929.

Truax, C. B. "Therapeutic Conditions." Discussion Paper No. 13. Wisconsin Psychiatric Institute, Madison, 1961.

Truax, C. B. "Depth of Patient Intrapersonal Exploration in Psychotherapy and Case Outcome." Research report. Wisconsin Psychiatric Institute, Madison, 1962a.

Truax, C. B. "A Tentative Scale for the Measurement of Depth of Intrapersonal Exploration (DX)." Discussion Paper No. 29. Wisconsin Psychiatric Institute, Madison, 1962b.

Truax, C. B., and Carkhuff, R. R. "Concreteness: A Neglected Variable in Research in Psychotherapy." *Journal of Clinical Psychology*, 1964, *20*, 264-267.

Truax, C. B., and Carkhuff, R. R. "Client and Therapist Transparency in the Psychotherapeutic Encounter." *Journal of Counseling Psychology*, 1965, *12*, 3-9.

Truax, C. B., and Whittmer, J. "Self-Disclosure and Personality Adjustment." *Journal of Clinical Psychology*, 1971, *27*, 535-537.

Tulkin, S. R. "Author's Reply: Environmental Influences on Intellectual Achievement." *Representative Research in Social Psychology*, 1970, *1*, 29-32.

Vondracek, F. W. "Behavioral Measurement of Self-Disclosure." *Psychological Reports*, 1969a, *25*, 914.

Vondracek, F. W. "The Study of Self-Disclosure in Experimental Interviews." *Journal of Psychology*, 1969b, *72*, 55-59.

Vondracek, F. W., and Marshall, M. J. "Self-Disclosure and Interpersonal Trust: An Exploratory Study." *Psychological Reports*, 1971, *28*, 235-240.

Vondracek, S., and Vondracek, F. W. "The Manipulation and Measurement of Self-Disclosure in Preadolescents." *Merrill Palmer Quarterly*, 1971, *17*, 51-58.

Walker, A. M., Rablen, R. A., and Rogers, C. R. "Development of a Scale to Measure Process Changes in Psychotherapy." *Journal of Clinical Psychology*, 1960, *16*, 79-85.

Weintraub, W., and Aronson, H. "The Application of Verbal Behavior Analysis to the Study of Psychological Defense Mechanisms: Methodology and Preliminary Report." *Journal of Nervous and Mental Disease*, 1962, *134*, 169-181.

West, L. W. "A Study of the Validity of the Self-Disclosure Inventory for Adolescents." *Perceptual and Motor Skills*, 1971, *33*, 91-100.

West, L. W., and Zingle, H. W. "A Self-Disclosure Inventory for Adolescents." *Psychological Reports*, 1969, *24*, 439-445.

Whalen, C. "Effects of a Model and Instructions on Group Behavior." *Journal of Consulting and Clinical Psychology*, 1969, *33*, 509-521.

Wilson, M. N., and Rappaport, J. "Personal Self-Disclosure: Expectancy and Situational Effects." *Journal of Consulting and Clinical Psychology,* 1974, *42,* 901-908.

Worthy, M., Gary, A. L., and Kahn, G. M. "Self-Disclosure as an Exchange Process." *Journal of Personality and Social Psychology,* 1969, *13,* 59-63.

Yalom I. D. *The Theory and Practice of Group Psychotherapy.* New York: Basic Books, 1970.

VIII

Assessment of Assertiveness

JAMES R. HALL

The study and modification of assertive behavior is a recently developed but rapidly expanding area in psychology. Although much of the impetus for the interest in assertion has come from behaviorally oriented psychologists, the area is also of concern to therapists from widely divergent schools. A strong popular interest has also been generated in the topic, as evidenced by a plethora of self-improvement books currently available (for example, Alberti and Emmons, 1974; Fensterheim and Baer, 1975; Phelps and Austin, 1975).

The increased professional interest in assertive behavior has produced a great deal of research directed toward comparing the effectiveness of one approach for treating nonassertiveness with another. In order to judge the effectiveness of therapy, it has been necessary to develop mechanisms to assess assertiveness. The assessment approaches that have been utilized include self-report inventories, self-ratings, and behavioral measures. Due to the relative newness of the area and the divergent conceptualizations present in the field, no one approach has come to dominate the assessment of assertiveness. In this chapter the various techniques used will be surveyed and evaluated.

Concept of Assertiveness

Assertive behavior in its broadest sense refers to "all socially acceptable expressions of rights and feelings" (Wolpe and Lazarus, 1966, p. 39). The equivocal nature of this and most definitions of assertive behavior or assertiveness has produced conceptual difficulties that have direct implications for assessment. The first major difficulty relates to determining the parameters of assertive behavior. A great deal of research has focused on what Wolpe (1973) has called "hostile" assertiveness. This kind of assertive behavior refers to the appropriate expression of demands and legitimate opposition, such as "I insist that you come to work on time" and "I'm sorry, but it won't be possible."

Lazarus (1971) and Jakubowski-Spector (1973) have argued that the inclusion of aspects other than the expression of legitimate rights stretches the term beyond its lexical boundaries and makes the concept so broad as to become meaningless. A number of assessment approaches have emphasized hostile assertion and developed mechanisms to measure this specific aspect (Bates and Zimmerman, 1971; McFall and Marston, 1970). However, there is no general agreement on what behaviors make up hostile assertion or on whether these components are independent. This situation has led to the development of overall measures of negative assertion as well as approaches focusing on a single aspect, such as refusal behavior (for example, McFall and Lillesand's Conflict Resolution Inventory, 1971).

Wolpe (1969) takes the view that assertive behavior is not limited to hostile assertion but includes the expression of positive feelings and praise. The inclusion of positive or commendatory assertion requires the development of multidimensional assessment instruments. Issues relating to the additivity of negative and positive components have had an influence on the assessment strategy and scoring systems that have been developed. Galassi, Delo, Galassi, and Bastien's (1974) College Self-Expression Scale and Eisler, Hersen, Miller, and Blanchard's (1975) roleplaying battery are examples of divergent assessment approaches attempting to measure both positive and negative assertion.

Lazarus (1973), in a more recent discussion, has argued that four relatively distinct areas of assertiveness have become apparent from his clinical work. These areas are: the expression of both positive and negative feelings, refusal behavior, the ability to ask for favors and make demands, and the ability to initiate and continue conversations. This classification, however, adds little to an already confused picture of a wide range of assessment approaches all purporting to measure assertiveness. Throughout this review we will point out the various interpretive viewpoints with respect to assertiveness and the assessment difficulties associated with each.

A second conceptual difficulty that affects assessment is the problem of defining assertiveness either as a personality trait or as a situation-specific response. This problem is present even in the title of the present review. The word *assertiveness* implies a unidimensional, transsituational tendency or trait. Although it is not the purpose of this chapter to argue this conceptual issue, the problem points up a significant difficulty. The translation of this difficulty into assessment approaches produces both situationally specific measures and instruments that disregard the importance of situations and emphasize global personality measures (for example, Rathus' Assertiveness scale, 1973b).

With this brief introduction to the conceptual difficulties involved in the assessment of assertiveness, we will first discuss self-report approaches and then turn to the behaviorally oriented assessment methods.

Self-Rating and Self-Report Inventories

The issues surrounding the validity of self-report data have been widely discussed (Walsh, 1967, 1968; Thomas, 1974; Eisler, 1976), with many questions relating to reliability, social desirability factors, and the usefulness of self-report methods as measures of social skills still remaining unclear. Despite these unanswered questions, however, the economy and quantifiability of self-ratings and self-report inventories have made this form of assessment a major approach in the assessment of assertiveness.

Wolpe-Lazarus Assertiveness Questionnaire. One of the earliest self-report measures in the area of assertiveness was a series of thirty questions with a yes-no response format developed by Wolpe and Lazarus (1966). This questionnaire was a loosely constructed series of questions that Wolpe and Lazarus saw as a useful clinical tool for gaining information on specific areas of assertive and nonassertive behavior. It included questions relating to a variety of specific situations (for example, "Do you avoid complaining about the poor service in a restaurant or elsewhere?" and "If a policeman should forbid you to enter premises that you are in fact entitled to enter, would you argue with him?") and also questions relating to general behavioral tendencies ("Are you inclined to be overapologetic?" and "Is it difficult for you to compliment and praise others?"). Questions from the Wolpe and Lazarus questionnaire, along with additional assertive questions developed by Wolpe (1969) and Lazarus (1971), have served as a major source of items for a number of assertiveness inventories (for example, Galassi, Delo, Galassi, and Bastien, 1974; Rathus, 1973b; Callner and Ross, 1976).

Wolpe and Lazarus (1966) considered their questionnaire to be best used for facilitating the gathering of information in clinical settings, as reflected in the statement that "more information may be gleaned from discussing each question with the patient than from constructing a quantitative scale or insisting on 'yes/no' answers" (p. 42). Nevertheless, the Wolpe-Lazarus Assertiveness Questionnaire has been used in a number of assertiveness-training studies to gather pre- and postdata (Eisler, Miller, and Hersen, 1973; Hersen, Eisler, and Miller, 1973; McFall and Marston, 1970; Kazdin, 1976). These studies have produced few data directly relevant to the validity of the questionnaire.

McFall and Marston (1970), in a study of assertive training, reported that the Wolpe-Lazarus questionnaire showed significant differences between treatment and control groups.
Eisler, Miller, and Hersen (1973) found the questionnaire able
to differentiate highly from low assertive psychiatric patients as
determined by their responses to fourteen assertiveness situations. Kazdin (1974, 1975, 1976), in a series of studies, obtained significant differences between treatment groups and
controls on the Wolpe-Lazarus questionnaire immediately after
treatment and also in a four-month follow-up. These studies
suggest that the Wolpe-Lazarus Assertiveness Questionnaire has
some utility and validity. However, the lack of any research specifically oriented toward clarifying the instrument's psychometric properties makes an adequate evaluation of its worth as
an assessment instrument impossible. It is unfortunate that the
many studies utilizing the questionnaire have not provided data
on the instrument itself. Until more information is available it
would seem prudent to use other, better-developed inventories
in assertiveness-training research. Perhaps the Wolpe-Lazarus
work is best viewed as an important first step in the assessment
of assertiveness and a source of conceptualization of assertiveness rather than as a useful assessment tool.

College Self-Expression Scale (CSES). This instrument,
developed by Galassi and his colleagues (Galassi, Delo, Galassi,
and Bastien, 1974) is one of the most widely used devices for
assessing assertiveness. The scale is a fifty-item self-report
test developed specifically for use with college students. Items
used in the scale were derived and elaborated from the work by
Lazarus (1971) and Wolpe (1969), along with modified items
from the early Wolpe and Lazarus (1966) scale. Utilizing a
Likert format, the scale presents stimulus situations related to
assertive situations with strangers, authority figures (primarily
college professors), business relations, family, like and opposite
sex peers, and nonspecific situations. Respondents mark the frequency with which they engage in each behavior on a 0-4 scale.

The CSES presents twenty-one positively worded and
twenty-nine negatively worded items and attempts to measure
positive, negative, and self-denial aspects of assertiveness. Ga-

lassi, Delo, Galassi, and Bastien (1974) have defined positive assertiveness as consisting of the expression of feelings of love, affection, admiration, approval, and agreement. Negative assertiveness, on the other hand, is defined as consisting of justified feelings of anger, annoyance, disagreement, and dissatisfaction. All of these characteristics are compared with the theme of self-denial, which represents a set of nonassertive behaviors such as excessive interpersonal anxiety, overapologizing, and an exaggerated concern for the feelings of others. Some empirical support (Galassi and Galassi, 1974a) has been found for Galassi's categorization of items into these behavioral and situational dimensions in preliminary factor-analytic studies, which are currently being extended.

No subscales are available for the CSES, and the validation research has utilized a total scale score based on summing all items and reverse-scored items, the maximum score being 200. Higher scores indicate greater frequencies in engaging in assertive behavior. Galassi has suggested that since assertiveness is "considered to be learned and situation specific," attention to the individual items may be more profitable for the clinician than the total score (Galassi and Galassi, 1974a).

Initial reliability data gathered on ninety-one introductory psychology students and forty-seven upper-division students indicated two-week test-retest reliability coefficients of 0.89 and 0.90, respectively (Galassi, Delo, Galassi, and Bastien, 1974). Normative data are available on over three thousand students given the CSES by Galassi and his colleagues (Galassi and Galassi, 1974a).

Validation of the CSES has been based primarily on correlations with the Gough and Heilbrun (1965) Adjective Check List (ACL), observer ratings (Galassi, Delo, Galassi, and Bastien, 1974) and peer ratings (Galassi and Galassi, 1974b), and through the method of contrasted groups (Galassi and Galassi, 1974b). Construct validity was demonstrated through significant correlations with ACL scales that were conceived as typifying assertiveness (Self-Confidence, Dominance, and Autonomy). Further, significant negative correlations were found with ACL Scales that were considered characteristic of nonassertiveness (Succorance, Abasement, Deference, and Counseling Readiness).

Galassi found no significant correlation between the CSES and the ACL Aggression Scale (Galassi, Delo, Galassi, and Bastien, 1974) or between the CSES and Buss-Durkee Aggression Inventory (Galassi and Galassi, 1975). Galassi suggested that this lack of signficant relationships is an indication that the CSES is in fact tapping assertiveness rather than less socially valued aggression, which is often confused with assertiveness.

Concurrent validity was established through the correlation of student teachers' CSES scores and the assertiveness ratings made by their supervisors on the CSES Behavioral Rating Form. A low ($r = 0.19$) but significant correlation was obtained between the two measures. Galassi (Galassi, Delo, Galassi, and Bastien, 1974) again suggested that the correlation may be somewhat depressed by the use of observers with no special training in the use of rating scales and by limited interaction opportunities.

The construct and concurrent validity of the CSES has been bolstered by further validation research using peer ratings and contrasted-group studies (Galassi and Galassi, 1974b). A moderate but significant correlation was found between the ratings by dormitory counselors and the dormitory residents' scores on the CSES. Galassi again suggested that the correlation may have been somewhat depressed by untrained observers and limited interaction opportunities. The contrasted-group studies used student legislators and various criterion groups, such as non-person-oriented college majors (math and engineering) and dormitory residents for the male sample and majors in traditionally female-oriented areas (child development and family relations) and dormitory students for the female sample. The consistent finding for both males and females was that, as predicted, student legislators scored higher than the criterion groups, although differences between the criterion groups were not all in the predicted directions. More clear-cut findings emerged when personal adjustment counselees were compared with vocational-educational counselees and noncounselees. As had been expected, the adjustment counselees scored significantly lower on the CSES than the two comparison groups (Galassi and Galassi, 1974b).

Further support for the validity of the CSES was provided by a study of the CSES against behavioral performance criteria (Galassi, Hollandsworth, Radecki, Gay, Howe, and Evans, 1976). Low, moderate, and high assertive groups were selected on the basis of their scores on the CSES, and they then enacted roleplaying scenes. Observer ratings were made on eye contact, response latency, and assertive content of verbalizations along with self-report of subjective anxiety. The results indicated that a linear combination of the dependent variables showed significant differences between low assertives and combined moderate and high assertives, and between low and high assertives. Galassi states that "assertiveness as measured by the CSES reflects a combination of verbal and nonverbal behaviors including eye contact, assertive content of verbal responses, and subjectively experienced anxiety" (Galassi and others, 1976, p. 451).

Scores on the CSES have been used as a dependent variable in a number of studies of assertiveness training (Galassi, Galassi, and Litz, 1974; Galassi, Kostka, and Galassi, 1975; Winship and Kelley, 1976). Posttraining scores have shown increases toward greater assertiveness for groups given assertiveness training, suggesting that the CSES is measuring, at least to some extent, the behaviors that are being modified in assertiveness training.

The research discussed above indicates that the CSES possesses a high degree of construct validity in that it has a positive relationship with ACL scales viewed as representing assertive responses and a negative relationship with ACL scales seen as tapping nonassertive responses. The lack of relationship with scales measuring aggression also supports high construct validity. The concurrent validity studies add little to the validation of the scale. This may be due to the lack of trained observers or the use of a rater form that is relatively insensitive and not based on measuring all the aspects of assertiveness that are assessed by the CSES.

The contrasted-group studies—especially the counselee research—provide some additional support for the validity of the CSES. However, these studies suffer from the conceptual problem that haunts much of the research on assertiveness: Is assertiveness a situational response or a personality trait? Predicting, as Galassi (Galassi and Galassi, 1974b) does, that certain groups (college majors) will differ in assertiveness suggests a traitlike notion that is opposed to his conceptualization of assertiveness used in developing the CSES. This problem points up the need to develop more fully the situational and behavioral dimensions of the CSES, rather than simply emphasizing the global score measure. A recent study by the author (Hall and Beil-Warner, 1977) compared a sample of Mexican-American male college students with Anglo male college students on the CSES. Overall scores indicated significantly higher assertiveness for the Anglos. However, an analysis of the items categorized by situations revealed that the difference was due primarily to responses on three of the seven situations involved, each of which was related to specific socialization practices in the Mexican-American culture. This study underscores the need to develop more fully the situational and behavioral aspects of the CSES and to use these when making screening decisions for assertiveness training.

The strongest support for the validity of the CSES comes from the research utilizing behavioral measures (Galassi and others, 1976). Insofar as the behaviors rated are important components of assertiveness, the CSES is shown to be a good measure of assertive behavior. The evidence presented suggests that the CSES possesses strong construct validity as a measure of assertiveness. Further studies using other validation instruments and research directed toward clarifying the factor structure of the CSES will greatly enhance its value as both a research and screening instrument for use with college populations.

Adult Self-Expression Scale (ASES). Galassi's CSES, along with the majority of assertiveness inventories to be discussed, has been developed for and validated on relatively homogenous samples of college students. Gay, Hollandsworth, and Galassi (1975), drawing on Galassi's work, have developed an inventory to assess assertiveness in adults: The Adult Self-Expression Scale (ASES). In developing the scale Gay and others made use of a two-dimensional descriptive model of assertive behavior based on six interaction situations similar to Galassi's (Galassi, Delo, Galassi, and Bastien, 1974) and seven types of assertive behaviors that might occur in these situations. The assertive behaviors included expressing personal opinions, refusing unreasonable requests, taking initiative in conversations and in dealing with others, expressing positive feelings, standing up for legitimate rights, expressing negative feelings, and asking for favors from others. The ASES contains four of the original CSES items, twenty-nine rewritten CSES items, and fifteen new items that were selected for inclusion on the basis of discriminative power, correlation with total score, and test-retest reliability. Items were retained in forty of the forty-two cells of the descriptive model. The ASES utilized the same format and scoring procedure as Galassi's CSES. For a sample of 194 subjects (mean age of 24.5 years) the ASES correlated highly with the CSES ($r = 0.88$), although for subjects over thirty and married the correlation fell to 0.79 (Gay and others, 1975). Two- and five-week test-retest reliability correlations were 0.88 and 0.91, respectively.

Initial validation research (Gay and others, 1975) produced correlations with the ACL scales that were similar to those found by Galassi (Galassi, Delo, Galassi, and Bastien, 1974). This study and the discriminant-analysis validation studies (Hollandsworth, Galassi, and Gay, 1977) used community college students with a mean age of twenty-five years as subjects. High and low assertives, as defined by ASES scores, were found to be significantly different on Taylor's (1953) Manifest Anxiety Scale and the ACL Self-Confidence scale, but not on Rotter's (1966) Locus of Control (IE) scale. This result is somewhat in contrast to the findings by Bates and Zimmerman (1971), who reported the IE scale to be related to their Constriction scale, a measure of assertiveness to be discussed shortly. Significantly lower ASES scores were found for students seeking counseling than for students in general. The factor structure revealed for the ASES (Gay and others, 1975) provided general support for the two-dimensional model used to construct the scale.

Subsequent validation studies (Hollandsworth and others, 1977) used the multitrait-multimethod procedure to investigate the relationship between the ASES and Aggression, Dominance, and Abasement. Self-reports, peer ratings, and unobtrusive measures were obtained on samples drawn from an avocational interest class at a technical-vocational institute, from psychiatric inpatients, from convicted male felons, and from adults in a graduate evening psychology course.

Hollandsworth and others (1977) suggest that these studies indicate that the ASES has "relatively strong and consistent convergent validity" in its relationship with self-report measures of Abasement and Dominance (ACL scales) and in its correlation with another measure of assertiveness (Rathus Assertiveness scale, which is discussed later). Convergent validity, as determined by peer ratings, is seen as "moderately strong and relatively consistent." Discriminant validity as determined both by common and different assessment methods of assertion and aggressiveness is described as "moderate."

The validation studies on the ASES represent the most complete and stringent validation research carried out on any measure of assertiveness. The picture that emerges from this research is that the ASES is a scale with moderate discriminant validity and relatively strong convergent and construct validity. These qualities, along with the availability of a self-scoring answer sheet and the ASES's applicability to a variety of populations, make it an extremely useful research tool. As is the case with the CSES, the development of subscales based on situational and behavioral dimensions, along with research on older populations, would greatly enhance the value of the ASES.

Rathus Assertiveness Scale (RAS). The RAS (Rathus, 1973b) has been widely used in correlational studies of assertiveness (Morgan, 1974; Orenstein, Orenstein, and Carr, 1975; Hollandsworth, 1976), in validation studies of other assertiveness measures (Hollandsworth and others, 1977), and as a pretest-posttest measure in research on assertiveness training (Holmes and Horan, 1976; Kazdin, 1975; Rathus, 1973a). The RAS is a thirty-item scale with items based on the work of Wolpe (1969) and Wolpe and Lazarus (1966), and on rewritten items from Allport's (1949) A-S Reaction Study and Guilford and Zimmerman's (1956) social scale of the Temperament Survey. Respondents mark each item in terms of how characteristic the behavior is of the individual from +3 ("very characteristic") to −3 ("very uncharacteristic") with no 0, or center point. A total score is derived from summing numerical responses to each item after changing signs of the reverse-scored items. The scale was developed as a global measure of trait assertiveness and is not intended to assess situational or behavioral dimensions of assertive behavior.

Rathus (1973b) presents a two-month test-retest correlation of 0.78 and a split-half Pearson product moment correlation of 0.77 between total odd and total even item scores. These coefficients indicate moderately high stability and moderate to high homogeneity for the RAS.

Construct validity for the RAS was established by comparing RAS scores with peer ratings on a seventeen-item semantic differential constructed by Rathus (1973b). Total RAS scores correlated positively with each of the items comprising the peer-rating scale's assertiveness factor. The RAS scores did not covary with items that Rathus suggested were measuring social desirability.

An item analysis of the RAS items in terms of their correlation with the assertiveness factor revealed significant positive correlations for nineteen of the thirty RAS items. The remaining items did not correlate significantly with any of the assertiveness items. Rathus (1973b) stated that the nineteen-item version of the RAS can be used with acceptable results but that the other items do not detract from the scale's validity and do provide some additional information to the therapist.

Concurrent validity of the RAS was established by determining the relationship between RAS scores and observer ratings of verbal behavior in response to five questions asking for assertive behavior. A significant correlation between the RAS and observer ratings of 0.705 was reported by Rathus (1973b), providing evidence for moderate concurrent validity. MacDonald (1974) lends support to the concurrent validity of the RAS in his findings of a moderate relationship between RAS scores and behavioral measures of assertiveness.

Indirect support for the construct validity of the RAS came from a study investigating the relationship between anxiety and assertiveness (Orenstein and others, 1975). Scores on the RAS were found to be significantly related to interpersonal fears as measured by the social factors from the Wolpe-Lang (1964) Fear Survey, with correlations ranging from −0.60 to −0.75. These findings conform to Wolpe's (1973) argument of an inverse relationship between trait anxiety and assertiveness, and support the construct validity of the RAS. However, some contradictory evidence for the relationship between interpersonal fears and the RAS is given by Morgan (1974), who found low but significant correlations between RAS scores and an abbreviated fear survey (r's = 0.172 to −0.239). Hollandsworth (1976), who, like Morgan, used a sample of college students, found a significantly higher correlation (−0.436) between the RAS and Morgan's (1974) Social Fear Survey. Hollandsworth provides no explanation for these differences, although when taken together these studies appear to provide at least some support for the construct validity of the RAS.

Viewed in its entirety, the research on the RAS suggests that the scale possesses high test-retest reliability, moderate-to-high test homogeneity, and moderate construct and concurrent validity. Evidence for convergent validity for the RAS with other self-report measures is provided by the high positive correlations between the RAS and the ASES found by Gay and others (1975) (r = 0.78) and Hollandsworth (1976) (r = 0.846), and between the RAS and CSES (Norton and Warnick, 1976) (r = 0.84). The validation of the RAS would be further enhanced by research utilizing more generally accepted behavioral measures of assertive behavior in additional construct validity studies. The scoring system currently employed is somewhat difficult to deal with and makes intuitive interpretation of the scores ambiguous. This problem could be alleviated by changing the scoring system to allow only positive scores or through additional norming research on larger and more varied samples.

The usefulness of the RAS depends to a great degree on the interpretation of the construct of assertiveness held by the user. As with the summation score of the CSES and the ASES, the RAS appears to measure a global trait that may not reflect the situational characteristic of assertive responses. Morgan

(1974) argues that the low correlations found in his study are due to the lack of "behavioral specificity" as assessed by the global score. Hollandsworth (1976), on the other hand, suggests that the global score does not represent a response set or behavioral trait, but rather indicates that "scores from these instruments perhaps should be interpreted in terms of an individual's self-report of himself as being . . . unassertive in more situations than another individual" (p. 87). Hollandsworth's argument does not appear to deal with the issue, especially in the absence of adequate norming studies that would allow for comparisons or knowledge of the individual's subjective comparison group. The RAS does not seem to have the potential for use as an instrument that allows for situational and behavioral specificity and hence may be less useful for the clinician interested in the assessment of specific nonassertive situations and responses than for the clinician interested in trait measures. The test does appear to be a very adequate general screening instrument for research on assertiveness training with college students.

Other Assertiveness Inventories. A number of assertiveness inventories that have been reported less frequently in the assertiveness literature than those considered above are nevertheless important for discussion because of their specific approach, their theoretical conceptualization, or their applicability to specific populations.

The Bates and Zimmerman (1971) Constriction scale was developed as an inventory of nonassertion to screen individuals for assertive training. The authors utilized the term *constriction* to indicate inappropriate nonassertion. A twenty-nine item scale (CS2) with a forced yes-no response format requiring respondents to state whether they tend to react in the manner described by the stimulus items was developed. The scale is scored in the constricted direction with a high score indicating less assertiveness.

Research on the CS2 showed moderately high one-month test-retest reliabilities (male sample $r = 0.79$ and female sample $r = 0.91$) and moderate internal-consistency reliabilities (Kuder-Richardson 20 = 0.80 for both males and females; Bates and Zimmerman, 1971). Construct validity studies reported by the authors presented significant relationships in the expected direction with the ACL scales of Affiliation, Dominance, Autonomy, Exhibitionism, Deference, and Abasement. The correlations with these scales differed for males and females and produced distinctly different regression equations for CS2 scores for the sexes. Sex differences were also found in the factor structure of CS2 scores for males and females.

Significant relationships were found between CS2 scores and measures of neuroticism and fear. Bates and Zimmerman (1971) also found a significant correlation between locus of control and constriction. These relationships suggest that the CS2 has at least moderate construct validity and may have some utility as a measure of assertiveness. Necessary additional research on the scale in terms of validation and normative studies is still lacking.

The Conflict Resolution Inventory (CRI) developed by McFall and Lillesand (1971) is a self-report inventory of refusal behavior. Part I of the CRI consists of an eight-item face sheet asking for the respondent's self-ratings of assertiveness on a 100-point scale ranging from 0 ("not much of a problem") to 100 ("a very significant problem"), and self-ratings of the extent to which he or she sees nonassertiveness as a significant problem. The second part of the scale contains a thirty-five-item inventory of specific refusal situations for which the respondent chooses one of five responses ranging from complete refusal to acquiescence.

The CRI has been used primarily as a screening device in assertive training studies, with various levels of problem ratings on Part I being used as one screening criterion and responses to the thirty-five situations in Part II as a second criterion (Aiduk and Karoly, 1975; Kazdin, 1975, 1976; McFall and Lillesand, 1971; McFall and Twentyman, 1973). No standardized screening criteria have been adopted nor is there a standardized scoring system for the CRI. With the exception of the Aiduk and Karoly (1975) study, research with the CRI has utilized the actual number of assertive responses as the dependent measure. Aiduk and Karoly used a transposed score based on difference scores (assertive minus nonassertive responses), with 50 as a

base indicating equal numbers of assertive and nonassertive responses. Scores above 50 indicated a greater number of assertive
responses, and scores below 50 a greater number of nonassertive
responses. In order for the CRI to be a useful instrument, some
standardized scoring system needs to be developed and studies
gathering normative data need to be conducted using the standardized system.

There have been no direct validation studies on the CRI
reported in the literature. However, the research on various
assertiveness-training techniques provides some indirect evidence for the validity of the CRI. Studies by McFall and his
colleagues (McFall and Lillesand, 1971; McFall and Twentyman, 1973) on various aspects of assertive training found that
the self-report global ratings in Part I of the CRI were not sensitive to treatment effects. However, Aiduk and Karoly (1975)
and Kazdin (1976) report significant changes in global ratings
for treatment groups but not for controls, suggesting that the
global ratings of the CRI may be a sensitive measure of assertiveness problems. Additional research on these self-report
global ratings is necessary to determine if these short and easily
completed ratings are adequate measures of assertiveness.

Evidence supporting the validity of the thirty-five-item
CRI inventory is also indirect. McFall and Twentyman (1973)
found that the CRI scores showed significant treatment effects,
although in a four-month follow-up no significant treatment differences were revealed by the CRI. This finding has been supported by Kazdin (1976) in comparing treatment groups with
controls. McFall and Twentyman classified subjects into high
and low assertive groups on the basis of CRI scores and found
significant differences between the groups on a roleplaying
assertion test. These data provide some support for the validity
of the CRI. However, without significant validation research,
the CRI retains only the potential for being a good measure of
the "refusal" aspect of assertion.

Gambrill and Richey (1975) have developed an assertion
inventory that reports the respondents' probability of engaging
in assertive behavior and the level of discomfort experienced in
each assertion situation, along with information on situations

that the respondents would like to handle more assertively. The Assertion Inventory (AI) includes forty items presenting a variety of assertive behaviors in a number of interpersonal relationships. Respondents indicate the degree of discomfort felt in each situation and the likelihood of engaging in the assertive behavior described in each item. Items that present situations that the respondent would like to handle more assertively are then circled. Discomfort and response-probability scores are determined by summing the responses on each discussion.

Reliability data on the AI reported by the authors show five-week test-retest correlations of 0.87 for the discomfort score and 0.81 for the response-probability score. A comparison between an assertive-training sample and samples of undergraduates indicated the ability of the inventory to discriminate between the groups. Significant differences for pre- and posttraining scores were reported for both the discomfort and response-probability dimensions. A significant relationship was also found between changes in observer ratings of discomfort and changes in the discomfort inventory scores pre- and posttraining. A factor analysis of the discomfort scores yielded eleven factors including thirty-seven of the forty items. These factors provide the basis for subscales that could provide behaviorally specific information on various types of assertive deficits.

The Gambrill and Richey (1975) scale provides a great deal of information to the user and allows for the development of profiles based on assertiveness and felt anxiety. However, the inventory requires additional validation research in terms of behavioral measures in order to increase its value. The nature of the inventory and the information provided by it suggest its great potential as a research and clinical instrument for use with college students and relatively well-educated adults.

An assertion inventory for use with a male drug addict population has been developed by Callner and Ross (1976). This inventory contains forty items sampling assertive behavior in content areas felt to be important for male subjects. These areas include the general areas of heterosexual interactions, interactions with authority figures, situations in which the expression and receiving of praise is appropriate, and the expres-

sion of and response to negative feedback. A fifth area specifically related to drug-related assertive situations (for example,
turning down drug offers) is also included. A four-alternative
Likert format is used requiring the respondent to mark how
self-descriptive each statement is.

A one-week test-retest reliability figure of 0.86 was obtained by the authors. Correlations of inventory scores with
self-ratings and behavioral ratings indicate that the inventory
possesses a fairly high degree of convergent validity. The discriminate validity of the inventory appears to be poor, a fact
that may be a function of the small and unique samples used in
the research. The inventory is very limited in its applicability,
although Callner and Ross (1976) suggested that various content areas other than drugs could be substituted on the inventory, thus making it applicable to different clinical populations.

A number of other self-report inventories have been discussed in the literature, although few validation data have been
reported. Lawrence's (1970) assertion inventory is a 112-item
inventory that presents various assertion situations that are responded to by choosing from one of three nonassertive
responses or one assertive response. Percell, Berwick, and Beigel
(1974), using a clinical population, and Kirschner (1976), using
a college population, found that the Lawrence measure was sensitive to treatment effects in studies of assertion training. Although both studies utilized a number of measures of assertive
behavior, no relationships that would reflect on the value of the
Lawrence inventory were reported.

Cautela and Upper (1976) have incorporated a short
assertive-behavior survey in their Behavioral Inventory Battery.
The survey includes a six-situation inventory with assertive and
nonassertive response choices and sections asking for the patient's perception of the consequences of being assertive with a
variety of stimulus persons and situations. The Assertive Behavior Survey Schedule (ABSS) was developed to provide the therapist with information for developing appropriate treatment
approaches. Although the ABSS appears to have some face
validity and may be a useful adjunct to clinical data gathering,

there has been no research directed toward determining its psychometric properties or validity.

With the exception of the CSES, ASES, and RAS, there are insufficient data available to provide definitive evaluations of asscrtiveness inventories. A decision to use any of the assertiveness inventories discussed should be based not only on the psychometric properties of the instrument but also on the specific nature of the information desired and the use to which that information will be put.

Behavioral Assessment of Assertiveness

A number of researchers have attempted to avoid the difficulties usually associated with self-report methods through the use of behavioral tasks and roleplaying tests of asscrtiveness. There is strong support in the behaviorally oriented literature for the use of roleplaying as both an assessment and therapeutic approach (Corsini, 1966; Mischel, 1973; Rimm and Masters, 1974), along with a long-standing orientation in assessment to make assessment samples as close to "real life" situations as possible (Anastasi, 1968; Cronbach, 1970).

A major problem in the behavioral assessment of assertiveness has been that of developing a clear delineation of the components of assertive behaviors in order to allow observers to focus on its essential components. This problem is compounded by the influence of varying social contexts on the nature and appropriateness of assertive behavior and by the varying types of behavioral expression that have been called assertive. With these problems in mind, this section will review the behavioral assessment techniques that have been developed to measure assertive behavior.

Behavioral Roleplaying Assertion Test. McFall and Marston (1970), in a study of the effectiveness of various treatment techniques on college students, developed a behavioral test employing sixteen roleplaying situations requiring asscrtive responses. The situations were presented to each subject on audiotape. A bell sounded as the cue for the subject's response. The subject was instructed to respond to each situation as if he or she were actually experiencing it. The situations presented included interpersonal interactions with friends, employers, and strangers. The example presented below (McFall and Marston, pp. 297-298) illustrates the format of the situations.

> Narrator: In this scene, picture yourself standing in a ticket line outside of a theater. You've been in line for at least ten minutes, and it's getting close to show time. . . . There you are, waiting patiently, when two people walk up to the person in front of you and begin talking. . . . One of the newcomers says to his friend in line:
>
> Newcomer: "Hey, the line's a mile long. How 'bout if we cut in here with you?"
>
> Person in line: "Sure, come on. A couple won't make any difference."
>
> Narrator: And as the two people squeeze in line between you and your friend, one of them looks at you and says:
>
> Newcomer: "Excuse me. You don't mind if we cut in do you?"
>
> (Bell sounds as cue for S to respond).

The taped pre- and posttreatment responses were rated by five "blind" judges on a global basis as to which response was more assertive. No data were presented to indicate inter-judge reliabilities or the specific criteria used by the judges to determine assertiveness. McFall and Marston (1970) found that there was a significant difference between experimental and control groups in terms of the judges' preference for posttreatment responses. These findings indicate that the measurements were to some extent accurate indices of assertiveness levels.

McFall and Marston (1970) also made use of an interesting follow-up measure that was found to correlate highly ($r = 0.76$) with the behavioral index, which consisted of a magazine-sales telephone call made to the subjects two weeks after treatment. The subjects' responses to the sales pitch were rated by four judges on sales resistance, activity level, and social poise in handling the call. Adequate interjudge reliabilities were found only for the dimension of sales resistance. Measurements based on elapsed time before the first sign of "assertive resistance" and total time of the call indicated significant treatment-control group differences. Although the performance measures for the follow-up did not consistently provide useful assessment data, McFall and Marston point up the possibility of using real-life situations in the assessment of assertive behavior. The research by McFall and his colleagues (McFall and Marston, 1970; McFall and Lillesand, 1971; McFall and Twentyman, 1973) has provided the basis for the development of a standardized role-playing test of assertiveness.

Behavioral Assertiveness Test (BAT). Eisler, Miller, and Hersen (1973) extended the work of McFall and Marston (1970) in a study of male psychiatric patients. They developed a series of fourteen standard roleplaying situations called the Behavioral Assertiveness Test (BAT). Unlike the research by McFall and Marston, Eisler, Miller, and Hersen used a live role model in each of the situations. The fourteen situations were developed to simulate real-life assertiveness situations and include interactions with a female enacting the roles of the patient's wife, sales clerk, a stranger, and a waitress. The subjects are instructed to respond as if they were in these situations in real life. A short narration (1973, p. 296) is presented, followed by a line from the role model that serves as the cue for the subject's response.

> Narrator: "You're in a drug store, and you buy something that costs 75 cents. You go to the cashier to pay for it and hand her a five-dollar bill. She rings up the sale and hands you 25 cents, change for only a dollar."
>
> Role model cashier: "Here's your change sir."

In the Hersen and others (1973) study two trained judges rated each scene in terms of nonverbal (duration of looking at model, frequency of smiles), speech (response duration and latency, loudness and fluency of speech), content (compliance content, content requesting new behavior), and affect components. An overall rating was made on each subject utilizing descriptions of assertive behavior adapted from Wolpe and Lazarus (1966) as the criteria. Interjudge reliabilities of 100 percent and 99.3 percent were reported for the content and affect measures, respectively. Reliability of the other measures was reported in terms of correlations between each measure and the overall assertiveness rating. These correlations ranged from 0.96 to 0.99. High and low assertive subjects, as determined by overall ratings, were differentiated on five of the behavioral measures (response latency, loudness of speech, duration of response, compliance, and requests for new behaviors), as well as by scores on a modified Wolpe-Lazarus Assertiveness Questionnaire. This research and a subsequent study (Eisler, Hersen, and Miller, 1973) utilizing five of the BAT situations has begun to isolate some of the key components of assertiveness that are amenable to behavioral assessment.

Other studies utilizing various roleplaying situations in the study of assertive behavior have produced support for the use of overall ratings (Kazdin, 1976; Kirschner, 1976; Rathus, 1973a), nonverbal measures of response duration (Kazdin, 1975), and eye contact (Galassi and others, 1976) as indices of assertiveness. There has been little support for the use of response latency as a component of assertiveness (Galassi and others, 1976; Galassi, Galassi, and Litz, 1974; McFall and Marston, 1970; McFall and Lillesand, 1971) with the exception of a study by Arkowitz, Lichtenstein, McGovern, and Hines (1975) on the social competence of college males. These various studies suggest that both verbal and nonverbal components of assertiveness can be reliably measured through the use of roleplaying situations.

Although the studies discussed above were carried out in research settings with relatively large samples, Serber (1972) has argued that roleplaying can be used by the clinician as both an assessment and a therapeutic tool to teach the nonverbal components of assertive behavior. Serber used a single three-minute roleplaying situation in which a male patient was required to deny some unjust charges. This investigation focused on the extraverbal components of assertiveness involving voice loudness, facial expression, body expression, eye contact, interaction distance, and fluency in order to assess the specific nonverbal behaviors to be taught. Serber viewed the behavioral assessment of these components of assertiveness as quite possible and as a necessary process in assertiveness training.

Behavioral Assessment of Situational Factors. The research discussed thus far provides some indications of the observable components of assertiveness that can be assessed behaviorally. However, these studies did not investigate the situational factors that influence the manifestation and assessment of assertiveness. Weinman, Gelbart, Wallace, and Post (1972) have developed a series of four behavioral tasks to investigate the effects of various treatments on the assertiveness of psychiatric patients. Their Behavior in Critical Situations Scale (BCSS) score is composed of the sum of the ratings of observations in each of four situations. Situation 1 (Affiliation) involves observing and rating the patient's interactions with a confederate in a waiting room. Situation 2 (Failure) presents the patient with a series of sorting tasks and insoluble puzzles, with mild criticism of the patient's performance expressed by an experimenter. Situation 3 (Disagreement) involves an experimenter disagreeing with a statement made by the patient. Situation 4 (Default) involves the patient in a situation in which he or she is shortchanged. The five-day test-retest reliability for the BCSS was 0.72 and the interjudge agreement for total score was 98 percent. None of the four subtests were found to be sensitive enough to reflect treatment changes, although total score did show treatment differences. The Affiliation and Failure subtests were not associated with total BCSS score; however, the Default and Disagreement subtests were significantly related to the total score. The value of the subscales of the BCSS is limited by the small number of items for each, although the total score appears useful in the assessment of change in psychiatric patients undergoing assertive training. The BCSS attempts, but is unable to adequately assess, specific situational factors in assertive behavior.

Eisler, Hersen, Miller, and Blanchard (1975) have developed a roleplaying assessment strategy that attempts to deal with the influence of various social-interpersonal contexts on assertive behavior. They point out that it is necessary, in order to adequately specify difficulties in assertiveness, to assess both positive and negative expressions of assertiveness. They also emphasize the importance of varying situational factors, such as the sex of the interactant and the subject's familiarity with the interactant. Using the variables of positive-negative, male-female, and familiar-unfamiliar, Eisler and others developed a roleplaying battery comprising thirty-two scenes with four scenes for each of the eight categories of stimuli for research on male psychiatric patients.

Subjects were instructed to respond to each scene as if they were in that situation and to express their true feelings as fully as possible. The narration for each scene was read and a live model enacted the cue line.

Male-Positive-Familiar Scene

Narrator: "You have been working on a difficult job all week, your boss comes over with a smile on his face."

Your boss says (enacted by male model): "That's a very good job you have done; I'm going to give you a raise next week."

Female-Negative-Unfamiliar-Scene

Narrator: "You are in a crowded grocery store and are in a hurry because you are already late for an appointment. You pick up one small item and get in line to pay for it. Then a woman with a shopping cart full of groceries cuts in line in front of you."

She says (enacted by female model): "You don't mind if I cut in here, do you?" [Eisler and others, 1975, p. 332].

Videotapes of the scene enactments were rated by two experienced judges in terms of nonverbal behavior (eye contact, smiles, duration, response latency, loudness of speech, appropriate affect, and speech fluency), negative content (compliance and requests for new behavior), and positive content (praise, appreciation, and spontaneous positive behavior), along with a rating of overall assertiveness. Eisler and others (1975) reported interjudge agreement of 95 percent on measures of speech content, speech fluency, and smiles. The reliabilities of the other observations were determined by Pearson product moment correlations with the overall ratings. All the coefficients exceeded 0.94. These high reliability figures were seen by Eisler and others as being due to the specificity of the criteria for each measure, the rating of only one measure on each videotape playback, and the use of very experienced raters.

The results of this study support the view that situational factors are functionally related to the expression and nature of assertive behavior. Responses to negative and positive situations were found to differ not only in speech content but also on six of the seven nonverbal variables measured. Differences on the variables studied were also found for the sex of interactant and the familiarity dimensions. The research by Eisler and others (1975) on psychiatric patients and by Edinberg, Karoly, and Gleser (in press) on elderly subjects (discussed later) point up an important consideration in the behavioral assessment of assertiveness. In order to adequately assess assertiveness, variations in the nature of the assertiveness behavior and the situational factors that may be important to its expression must be considered. The number of these factors may be quite large and may include such things as relations with various types of people (subordinates or supervisors), types of relational situations (intimate or casual), and types of sociocultural contexts. Attempting to take all possible situations into account would produce an immense assessment battery. It is essential that the nature of the construct "assertiveness" be clearly delineated in order to focus on those situational factors that primarily influence assertive behavior.

Instructional Set. Another important issue in the behavioral assessment of assertiveness is the question of whether the instructions for roleplaying lead to the measurement of acquisition or of performance deficits in the nonassertive individual.

Most current roleplaying techniques instruct the subjects to respond as they "normally would" or as they would in "everyday life."

Nietzel and Bernstein (1976) investigated this issue by varying the demand level of the instructions for roleplaying. In the low-demand condition subjects were instructed to react as they would in "real life," whereas in the high-demand condition subjects were instructed to respond as they believed the "most assertive person" would. Nietzel and Bernstein's results demonstrate the effects of demand characteristics on behavioral measures of assertiveness. They argue for the use of sequential low- and high-demand versions of roleplaying tests and draw implications for therapy from their research.

> The sequential use of low- and high-demand versions . . . could clarify the usually neglected learning-performance dimension by allowing the researcher/clinician to assess not only what the client will do in assertion situations but also what she or he *can* do under maximal demand for assertion in the same situations. Clients who display appropriate assertion only under high-demand could then be assigned to treatment oriented toward removal of inhibitory factors. . . . Those whose assertion remains inadequate under both demand conditions could be exposed to skill-building experiences [Nietzel and Bernstein, p. 500].

The issue raised by Nietzel and Bernstein (1976) has important implications for the behavioral assessment of assertiveness. For example, the situationally based roleplaying battery of Eisler and others (1975) would require a minimum of sixteen scenes to take into account variations in instructional demands and the situational variables if only one scene were used for each situation. This number would greatly extend the time involved in assessment and could introduce complicating secondary factors such as fatigue. The value of the information gathered from such variations in instructions may, however, offset the problems attendant with additional scenes. Significant additional research focusing on the variations in performance due to instructions and on the effectiveness of therapeutic approaches derived from this variation would help to clarify the need for changes in the assessment process.

Improvisation Test for Individuals (IMPRO-I). The Improvisation Test for Individuals developed by McReynolds, De Voge, Osborne, Pither, and Nordin (1976, 1977) provides an interesting contrast in approach to the McFall and Marston (1970) or Eisler and others (1975) based roleplaying batteries. This instrument, which is discussed more completely in Chapter Six of this volume, is a measure of interpersonal behavioral style. The test assesses behavior in twelve different roleplaying situations, of which three concern assertiveness. The IMPRO-I differs from other batteries in its approach to the roleplaying scenes and its rating strategy. The test makes use of live actors and expert observers (judges) and presents to the subject brief narratives, along with lines to be read by the actor and the subject. The expression of assertiveness scenes include one involving a person of the same sex as the subject, one a person of the opposite sex, and one involving both parents. The subject is instructed to imagine that the situation is happening to him or her and to deal with it as well as possible (McReynolds and others, 1976, p. 23).

Expression of Assertiveness, Same Sex Scene

You took an expensive suede coat to the cleaners. When you pick it up, you notice some spots on the back that weren't there when you brought the coat in.

Business person (read by actor): "Does it look okay, sir/ma'am?"

Subject: "No, there are two white spots here on the back."

Business person: "Oh, yes. Those look like bleach spots. I'm afraid we can't do anything about those."

Subject: "But they weren't here when I brought the coat in."

Business person: "Well, it certainly couldn't have happened here, I'm sure of that. You must have spilled some bleach without noticing it. It's a real shame, that was a nice coat."

Subject: "No, I couldn't have done it. There isn't any bleach in the house."

Business person: "Well I don't know how you did it, but you must have gotten bleach on this coat somehow. There's nothing I can do about it now."

(Subject responds:)

The actors are instructed to respond to the subject in a standardized way and to continue the improvisation in a specified manner. The interaction is terminated by the administrator when the subject has exhibited sufficient behavior for adequate rating and when the termination would not leave the subject with "unfinished feelings." McReynolds and others (1976) have found that each interaction lasts about two minutes or less. The use of these extended interactions appears to allow longer and more interactionally based responses than do other approaches.

The rating approach used in the IMPRO-I reflects the interest in assessing interpersonal styles. Each of the scenes in the battery is rated on a 7-point scale, with the extremes representing "too much" or "too little" of the improvisation theme and the middle of the scale representing levels of appropriate behavior. The ratings are made on the "entire gestalt" of the individual's performance, taking into account both nonverbal and verbal behaviors. In the rating of the assertiveness situation presented above, the "too little" extreme is described as "accepts explanation without question; withdraws." The "too much" extreme is described as "immediately explodes; quickly resorts to threatening, demanding, name calling." Since the scale is still new, definitive reliability and validity data are not yet available, though preliminary reliability estimations are encouraging.

The IMPRO-I includes a participant-rating scale that provides important information not tapped by other behavioral batteries. At the completion of each scene subjects rate themselves on the level of satisfaction experienced in the way they handled the scene. This provides the assessor with additional information on the subjects' perception of performance and may give information on those areas that subjects would like to deal with in a better manner. Subjects also rate the extent to which their performance is similar to the way the situation would be handled in real life. This rating can be used as a check on the role involvement of the subject and may reflect the validity of the test for that individual.

Assessment of the Elderly. A behavioral assessment device to measure assertiveness for older adults has been developed by Edinberg, Karoly, and Gleser (in press), who made use of Goldfried and D'Zurilla's (1969) behavior-analytic model for assessing competence in developing the instrument. This approach emphasizes a detailed analysis of both environmental situations related to assertiveness and potential responses to the situations. Applying this method, Edinberg and others arrived at twenty situations applicable to older adults, involving a range of situations and requiring a variety of assertive behaviors. Through the use of response categorizations and appropriateness ratings, four situations were selected for inclusion in the final behavioral assessment battery. Half of the scenes were presented on audiotape and half were role played.

The responses of thirty-three subjects (mean age of 70.4 years) were recorded and judged by two trained observers on response assertiveness and assertive content. Interjudge reliabilities for the two ratings were 0.89 and 0.91, respectively. A five-week test-retest reliability coefficient of 0.81 for twelve other elderly subjects was obtained.

Moderate concurrent validity for the instrument was demonstrated by a significant correlation ($r = 0.45, p < 0.055$) between rankings by assertiveness-training group leaders and scores on the assessment instrument. Attempts to demonstrate construct validity through correlations with a geriatric morale scale (Lawton, 1975) and an anxiety measure yielded no significant correlations.

The reliability and concurrent validity findings of Edinberg and others (in press) suggest that their instrument may be of great value in the assessment of assertiveness in the elderly. Further construct validity studies utilizing instruments more closely related to the conceptualization of assertiveness are needed to provide adequate validation for the assessment battery. The application of the behavior-analytic model in the construction of assertiveness batteries is an important step and should be emulated, especially in the development of assessment devices for well-defined populations.

The use of roleplaying approaches in the assessment of assertiveness provides an opportunity to gain precise and complete information about the individual in situations that approximate real life. The ideal assessment battery would utilize highly specific behavioral measures, allow for the assessment of assertiveness under varying situations, require the expression of different types of assertive behavior, include variations in instructional demands, and measure the role involvement of the subject. At this stage in the development of the behavioral assessment of assertiveness no one battery has all the qualities of the ideal battery. It may be impractical to include all these elements in an economical and workable assessment approach.

Conclusion

In light of the problems involved in both self-report and roleplaying assessment, the most useful research may be in the continued specification and refinement of the behavioral components of assertion and their assessment. Rather than emphasizing the development of a standard battery of situations, it appears preferable to standardize the observational measures. If empirically valid and reliable measures were available, the clinician-researcher, using information gained from interview and self-report inventories, could assess a limited number of roleplaying situations that appear to be problem areas for the subject. The specific skill deficits or inhibiting factors revealed could then become the focus of assertiveness training and research.

A number of areas remain to be investigated in the assessment of assertiveness. There has been relatively little attention paid to assessing the physiological correlates of assertiveness. The research utilizing pulse rate as a measure (Kazdin, 1975; McFall and Marston, 1970) provides little insight into the value or use of physiological measures in the assessment of assertiveness. Another area that remains relatively unexplored is the assessment of assertiveness in children. To date only a few studies have attempted to measure and modify assertive behavior in children (Chittenden, 1942; Dorman, 1973; Patterson, 1972). No specific or well-defined assessment strategy has emerged from this research.

The present status of the assessment of assertiveness can best be described as unsettled. Although many advances have been made in a relatively short span of time, the lack of a clear conceptualization of assertiveness greatly constrains progress in assessment.

References

Aiduk, R., and Karoly, P. "Self-Regulatory Techniques in the Modification of Nonassertive Behavior." *Psychological Reports,* 1975, *36,* 895-905.

Alberti, R., and Emmons, M. *Your Perfect Right: A Guide to Assertive Behavior.* (2nd ed.) San Luis Obispo, Calif.: Impact, 1974.

Allport, G. W., and Allport, F. H. *A-S Reaction Study.* Boston: Houghton Mifflin, 1949.

Anastasi, A. *Psychological Testing.* (3rd ed.) New York: Macmillan, 1968.

Arkowitz, H., Lichtenstein, E., McGovern, K., and Hines, P. "The Behavioral Assessment of Social Competence in Males." *Behavior Therapy,* 1975, *6,* 3-13.

Bates, H., and Zimmerman, S. "Toward the Development of a Screening Scale for Assertive Training." *Psychological Reports,* 1971, *28,* 99-107.

Callner, D. A., and Ross, S. M. "The Reliability and Validity of Three Measures of Assertion in a Drug Addict Population." *Behavior Therapy,* 1976, *7,* 659-667.

Cautela, J. R., and Upper, D. "The Behavioral Inventory Battery: The Use of Self-Report Measures in Behavioral Analysis and Therapy." In M. Hersen and A. S. Bellack (Eds.), *Behavioral Assessment: A Practical Handbook.* Elmsford, N.Y.: Pergamon Press, 1976.

Chittenden, G. E. "An Experimental Study in Measuring and Modifying Assertive Behavior in Young Children." *Monographs of the Society for Research in Child Development,* 1942, 7 (1), No. 31.

Corsini, R. J. *Roleplaying in Psychotherapy: A Manual.* Chicago: Aldine, 1966.

Cronbach, L. *Essentials of Psychological Testing.* New York: Harper & Row, 1970.

Dorman, L. "Assertive Behavior and Cognitive Performance in Preschool Children." *Journal of Genetic Psychology,* 1973, *123,* 155-162.

Edinberg, M. A., Karoly, P., and Gleser, G. "Assessing Assertion in the Elderly: An Application of the Behavior Analytic Model of Competence." *Journal of Clinical Psychology,* in press.

Eisler, R. M. "The Behavioral Assessment of Social Skills." In M. Hersen and A. S. Bellack (Eds.), *Behavioral Assessment: A Practical Handbook.* Elmsford, N.Y.: Pergamon Press, 1976.

Eisler, R. M., Hersen, M., and Agras, W. S. "Videotape: A Method for the Controlled Observation of Nonverbal Interpersonal Behavior." *Behavior Therapy,* 1973, *4,* 420-425.

Eisler, R. M., Hersen, M., and Miller, P. M. "Effects of Modeling on Components of Assertive Behavior." *Journal of Behavior Therapy and Experimental Psychiatry,* 1973, *4,* 1-6.

Eisler, R., Hersen, M., Miller, P. M., and Blanchard, E. "Situational Determinants of Assertive Behavior." *Journal of Consulting and Clinical Psychology,* 1975, *43,* 330-340.

Eisler, R. M., Miller, P. M., and Hersen, M. "Components of Assertive Behavior." *Journal of Clinical Psychology,* 1973, *29,* 295-299.

Fensterheim H., and Baer, J. *Don't Say Yes When You Want To Say No.* New York: Dell, 1975.

Galassi, J. P., Delo, J. S., Galassi, M. D., and Bastien, S. "The College Self-Expression Scale: A Measure of Assertiveness." *Behavior Therapy,* 1974, *5,* 165-171.

Galassi, J. P., and Galassi, M. D. *Instructions for Administering and Scoring the College Self-Expression Scale.* Chapel Hill: University of North Carolina, 1974a.

Galassi, J. P., and Galassi, M. D. "Validity of a Measure of Assertiveness." *Journal of Counseling Psychology,* 1974b, *21,* 248-250.

Galassi, J. P., and Galassi, M. D. "The Relationship Between Assertiveness and Aggressiveness." *Psychological Reports,* 1975, *36,* 352-354.

Galassi, J. P., Galassi, M. D., and Litz, M. D. "Assertive Training in Groups Using Video Feedback." *Journal of Counseling Psychology,* 1974, *21,* 390-394.

Galassi, J. P., Hollandsworth, J. G., Jr., Radecki, J. C., Gay, M. L., Howe, M. R., and Evans, C. L. "Behavioral Performance in the Validation of an Assertiveness Scale." *Behavior Therapy,* 1976, *7,* 447-452.

Galassi, J. P., Kostka, M. P., and Galassi, M. D. "Assertive Training: A One Year Follow-Up." *Journal of Counseling Psychology,* 1975, *22,* 451-452.

Galassi, M. D., and Galassi, J. P. "The Effects of Role Playing Variations on the Assessment of Assertive Behavior." *Behavior Therapy,* 1976, *7,* 343-347.

Gambrill, E., and Richey, C. "An Assertion Inventory for Use in Assessment Research." *Behavior Therapy,* 1975, *6,* 550-561.

Gay, M. L., Hollandsworth, J. G., Jr., and Galassi, J. P. "An Assertiveness Inventory for Adults." *Journal of Counseling Psychology,* 1975, *22,* 340-344.

Goldfried, M. R., and D'Zurilla, T. J. "A Behavior-Analytic Model for Assessing Competence." In C. D. Speilberger (Ed.), *Current Topics in Clinical and Community Psychology.* New York: Academic Press, 1969.

Gough, H. G., and Heilbrun, A. B., Jr. *The Adjective Check List Manual.* Palo Alto, Calif.: Consulting Psychologists Press, 1965.

Guilford, J. P., and Zimmerman, W. S. "Fourteen Dimensions of Temperament." *Psychological Monographs,* 1956, *70* (10), No. 417.

Hall, J. R., and Beil-Warner, D. "Assertiveness of Male Anglo and Mexican-American College Students." Paper presented at 24th annual meeting of Southwestern Psychological Association, Fort Worth, Tex., April 1977.

Hedquist, F., and Weinhold, B. "Behavioral Counseling with Socially Anxious and Unassertive College Students." *Journal of Counseling Psychology,* 1970, *17,* 237-242.

Hersen, M., Eisler, R., and Miller, P. "Development of Assertive Responses: Clinical Measurement and Research Consideration." *Behavior Research and Therapy,* 1973, *2,* 505-521.

Hollandsworth, J. G. "Further Investigation of the Relationship Between Expressed Social Fear and Assertiveness." *Behavior Research and Therapy,* 1976, *14,* 85-87.

Hollandsworth, J. G., Galassi, J. P., and Gay, M. L. "The Adult Self Expression Scale: Validation Using the Multitrait-Multimethod Procedure." *Journal of Clinical Psychology,* 1977, *33,* 407-415.

Holmes, D., and Horan, J. "Anger Induction in Assertion Training." *Journal of Counseling Psychology,* 1976, *2,* 108-111.

Jakubowski-Spector, P. "Facilitating the Growth of Women Through Assertive Training." *Counseling Psychologist,* 1973, *4,* 75-86.

Kazdin, A. E. "Effects of Covert Modeling and Reinforcement on Assertive Behavior." *Journal of Abnormal Psychology,* 1974, *83,* 240-252.

Kazdin, A. E. "Covert Modeling, Imagery Assessment, and Assertive Behavior." *Journal of Consulting and Clinical Psychology,* 1975, *43,* 716-724.

Kazdin, A. E. "Assessment of Imagery During Covert Modeling of Assertive Behavior." *Journal of Behavior Therapy and Experimental Psychiatry,* 1976, *7,* 213-219.

Kirschner, N. "Generalization of Behaviorally Oriented Assertive Training." *Psychological Record,* 1976, *26,* 117-125.

Lawrence, P. "The Assessment and Modification of Assertive Behavior." Unpublished doctoral dissertation, Arizona State University, 1970.

Lawton, M. P. "The Philadelphia Geriatric Center Morale Scale: A Revision." *Journal of Gerontology*, 1975, *30*, 85-89.

Lazarus, A. A. *Behavior Therapy and Beyond*. New York: McGraw-Hill, 1971.

Lazarus, A. A. "Assertive Training: A Brief Note." *Behavior Therapy*, 1973, *4*, 697-699.

MacDonald, M. L. "A Behavioral Assessment Methodology Applied to the Measurement of Assertion." Unpublished doctoral dissertation, University of Illinois, 1974.

McFall, R., and Lillesand, D. "Behavior Rehearsal with Modeling and Coaching in Assertive Training." *Journal of Abnormal Psychology*, 1971, *77*, 313-323.

McFall, R., and Marston, A. "An Experimental Investigation of Behavior Rehearsal in Assertiveness Training." *Journal of Abnormal Psychology*, 1970, *76*, 295-303.

McFall, R., and Twentyman, C. "Four Experiments on the Relative Contributions of Rehearsal, Modeling and Coaching to Assertion Training." *Journal of Abnormal Psychology*, 1973, *81*, 199-218.

McReynolds, P., De Voge, S., Osborne, S. K., Pither, B., and Nordin, K. *Manual for the IMPRO-I*. Reno: University of Nevada, 1976.

McReynolds, P., De Voge, S., Osborne, S. K., Pither, B., and Nordin, K. "An Improvisational Technique for the Assessment of Individuals: A Preliminary Report." Unpublished manuscript, University of Nevada, Reno, 1977.

Mischel, W. "Implications of Behavior Therapy for Personality Assessment." In W. Mischel and H. Mischel (Eds.), *Readings in Personality*. New York: Holt, Rinehart and Winston, 1973.

Morgan, W. G. "The Relationship Between Expressed Social Fears and Assertiveness and Its Treatment Implications." *Behavior Research and Therapy*, 1974, *12*, 255-257.

Nietzel, M., and Bernstein, D. "Effects of Instructionally Mediated Demand on the Behavioral Assessment of Assertiveness." *Journal of Consulting and Clinical Psychology*, 1976, *44*, 500.

Norton, R., and Warnick, B. "Assertiveness as a Communication Construct." *Human Communication Research*, 1976, *3*, 62-66.

Orenstein, H., Orenstein, E., and Carr, J. "Assertiveness and Anxiety: A Correlational Study." *Journal of Behavior Therapy and Experimental Psychiatry*, 1975, *6*, 203-207.

Patterson, R. "Time-Out and Assertive Training for a Dependent Child." *Behavior Therapy*, 1972, *3*, 466-468.

Percell, L., Berwick, P., and Beigel, A. "The Effects of Assertive Training on Self-Concept and Anxiety." *Archives of General Psychiatry*, 1974, *31*, 502-504.

Phelps, S., and Austin, N. *The Assertive Woman*. San Luis Obispo, Calif.: Impact, 1975.

Rathus, S. A. "Instigation of Assertive Behavior Through Video-Tape Mediated Assertive Models and Directed Practice." *Behavior Research and Therapy*, 1973a, *11*, 57-65.

Rathus, S. A. "A 30-Item Schedule for Assessing Assertive Behavior." *Behavior Therapy*, 1973b, *4*, 398-406.

Rimm, D., and Masters, J. *Behavior Therapy: Techniques and Empirical Findings*. New York: Academic Press, 1974.

Rotter, J. B. "Generalized Expectancies for Internal Versus External Control of Reinforcement." *Psychological Monographs*, 1966, *80* (1), No. 609.

Serber, M. "Teaching the Nonverbal Components of Assertive Training." *Journal of Behavior Therapy and Experimental Psychiatry*, 1972, *3*, 179-183.

Taylor, J. A. "A Personality Scale of Manifest Anxiety." *Journal of Abnormal and Social Psychology*, 1953, *48*, 285-290.

Thomas, E. J. *Behavior Modification Procedure: A Sourcebook*. Chicago: Aldine, 1974.

Walsh, W. B. "Validity of Self-Report." *Journal of Counseling Psychology*, 1967, *14*, 18-23.

Walsh, W. B. "Validity of Self-Report: Another Look." *Journal of Counseling Psychology*, 1968, *15*, 180-186.

Weinman, B., Gelbart, P., Wallace, M., and Post, M. "Inducing

Assertive Behavior in Chronic Schizophrenics." *Journal of Consulting and Clinical Psychology,* 1972, *39,* 246-252.

Winship, B., and Kelley, J. "A Verbal Response Model of Assertiveness." *Journal of Counseling Psychology,* 1976, *23,* 215-220.

Wolpe, J. *The Practice of Behavior Therapy.* Elmsford, N.Y.: Pergamon Press, 1969.

Wolpe, J. "Supervision Transcript: V. Mainly About Assertive Training." *Journal of Behavior Therapy and Experimental Psychology,* 1973, *4,* 141-148.

Wolpe, J., and Lang, P. J. "A Fear Survey for Use in Behavior Therapy." *Behavior Research and Therapy,* 1964, *2,* 27-30.

Wolpe, J., and Lazarus, A. A. *Behavior Therapy Techniques.* Elmsford, N.Y.: Pergamon Press, 1966.

IX

Assessment of Depression

Johanna M. Mayer

The study of depression, sparked by the development of antidepressant drug therapies and biochemical theories, has undergone a strong resurgence of interest during the past twenty years. The high risks associated with undetected depression, particularly in medical patients, as well as the increasing volume of research in the area have highlighted the need for accurate identification and assessment of depressive symptomatology. Despite the availability of validated assessment techniques, many researchers continue to rely on unstandardized ad hoc measures, perhaps in part because of the lack of information for choosing a technique. The intent of this chapter is to provide a review of the literature on some techniques for detecting and quantifying depressive illness, symptomatology, or mood, irrespective of psychiatric diagnosis or type of depressive disorder.

To measure a phenomenon it must first be defined, a formidable problem in the case of depression because it involves subjective experience and because the term is used in a wide variety of ways. *Depression* may be used to describe an affect, emotion, mood, symptom, disease, or diagnostic label, and may refer to both normal and pathological events that can be transient or enduring. Although etiological significance has been given to both endogenous biochemical changes and environmental events, investigation of the relationships has not progressed to the point of refining the definition or of providing a new assessment mode. Depressed mood has been most commonly identified as the core of depression; however, there is considerable disagreement over the utility of mood assessment given the difficulties associated with the measurement of subjective states. Some authors contend that mood deviations are neither necessary nor sufficient for a diagnosis of depression (Popoff, 1969) and that the term *primary mood disorder* is misleading (Beck, 1970).

Attempts to define the dimensions of depression using factor analysis have consistently yielded several factors such as guilt, depressed mood, and somatic disturbance; however, many of the findings are discrepant, which may reflect the difficulty in identifying and distinguishing among symptoms. At present, factor-analytic studies have raised more questions about the nature of depression than they have answered. It appears that depression is more complex than existing nosological classifications would lead us to believe (Cropley and Weckowicz, 1966).

The lack of agreement concerning a measurable core or dimension of depression has resulted in the development of rating scales based on one aspect of depression over which there is considerably less controversy: the symptoms that characterize the disorder. Descriptive definitions, such as Hippocrates' clinical description of melancholia and the Old Testament's Book of Job, have proved to be stable and enduring. Despite variations in terminology, a high degree of consensus can be found concerning the symptomatology of depression among theorists with divergent orientations. But for the purposes of this review, depression is viewed as a general concept of illness that tends to be defined descriptively by the symptoms selected for inclusion in each measure. The assumption underlying this approach is that the greater the number, intensity, or frequency of symptoms, the greater the severity or depth of depression. Objective assessment techniques can be divided into two broad categories: self-report measures and interviewer or observer ratings. The distinction is simply who does the rating.

Two major types of self-report instruments will be considered. The first, generally called an *inventory,* consists of a series of graded scales on which the subject rates the presence, frequency, or intensity of a range of symptom complaints. Inventories have also been designed to measure a single symptom, such as mood. Instruments consisting of a series of ungraded items are known as *checklists* and comprise the second type of self-report instrument. The checklists to be discussed assess only one symptom, mood, or affect, and require subjects to check those adjectives on a list that apply to them during some specified time period. Observer ratings may or may not involve an interview. Interviewer rating scales require a skilled clinician to elicit information, observe behavior, and interpret the data before making a rating. Other observer ratings have been designed for use by nurses or trained aides to record behavior on hospital wards.

The choice of a scale and the criteria on which it is evaluated depend largely on the purpose of assessment. Scales are generally used for clinical or research purposes. Specific clinical tasks include detection of depression, assessment of its depth, measurement of changes in degree of depression, and classification of patients by diagnostic category. Scales designed primarily to differentiate depression from other diagnostic categories or for classifying types of depression will not be considered. Diagnostic-oriented rating systems, such as the Inpatient Multidimensional Psychiatric Scale (IMPS), and projective techniques, such as the Rorschach, will not be included. Only those instruments constructed to detect and quantify a general concept of depressive illness, symptomatology, or mood will be reviewed.

Self-Report Inventories

In his introduction to a volume devoted to measurement in psychopharmacological research, Pichot (1974) remarked that depression is unusual in that it can be evaluated about equally well by the patient and by an observer. In spite of disagreements about the accuracy of self-reports in psychological research, there has been tremendous interest in the self-report assessment of depressive symptomatology, perhaps because its large subjective component appears to make depression particularly amenable to self-report. The technique is attractive to researchers because the absence of raters and consequent rater bias provides ease of administration and economy with respect to staff time, as well as increased comparability of results by different investigators in various settings.

MMPI-D Scale. First published in 1942, the D scale of the Minnesota Multiphasic Personality Inventory (MMPI-D) (Hathaway and McKinley, 1951) has been widely used, its deficits have received considerable attention, and it has been subjected to numerous revisions. The frequent use of the MMPI-D to validate other scales reviewed herein makes its construct validity of particular relevance.

The MMPI-D consists of sixty statements to which the subject responds true or false. The items reflect various aspects of depressive illness and were selected on the basis of their ability to discriminate a psychiatric group showing relatively uncomplicated depressive patterns from a normal group (Dahlstrom, Welsh, and Dahlstrom, 1972).

The MMPI-D has been described as a measure of depressive mood and reaction independent of the underlying personality structure or adjustment status of the individual (Gravitz, 1968). However, the validity of the MMPI-D as a measure of the construct of depressive illness has been challenged on the grounds that it reflects personality factors rather than illness (Snaith, Ahmed, Mehta, and Hamilton, 1971). The multidimensionality of the scale, as demonstrated by factor-analytic studies (Comrey, 1957; O'Conner, Stefic, and Gresock, 1957), has also provided a basis for questioning its construct validity. McNair (1974) has raised questions about the sensitivity of the MMPI-D on the basis of a review that revealed the MMPI-D to be less sensitive to drug effects than other scales. He suggested that one problem with the MMPI-D is the lack of any clear time reference period in the instructions.

In an effort to improve the MMPI-D, McCall (1958) divided the sixty items into three categories according to their relevance to a description of known depressive symptomatology. He found the twenty-six "face valid" items to be most effective in discriminating between depressed and nondepressed psychotics, but not significantly better than the entire scale; the twelve "irrelevant" items failed to discriminate between the two groups; and the remaining twenty-two "congruent" items were moderately effective discriminators. Foulds and Caine (1959) obtained similar results using four groups of hospitalized women, except that neither the entire MMPI-D nor any part of it was able to discriminate nondepressed neurotics from either depressed neurotics or depressed psychotics.

Dempsey (1964) also attempted to revise the MMPI-D, using an empirical method designed to eliminate items that were not consistent with the major dimension underlying the scale. The resulting thirty-item scale, which was found to have higher test-retest reliability coefficients and more consistent interitem relationships than the full scale, was also found to share twenty-five items with Comrey's (1957) neuroticism factor, leaving unresolved the question of what is being measured by all or part of the MMPI-D.

Among the seven Tryon, Stein, and Chin (TSC) scales, which were derived from a cluster analysis of all 550 MMPI items, is a cluster labeled Depression and Apathy Versus Positive and Optimistic Outlook (Stein, 1968). The cluster shares only ten of its twenty-eight items with the MMPI-D; however, the two scales were found to be highly correlated (0.81). The MMPI-D also contributed a substantial number of items to the Body Complaints cluster and the Tension cluster.

Dahlstrom and others (1972) reviewed several revisions of the MMPI-D and concluded that there was little evidence that they have any clear advantage over the original scale. Rather than continue to rely on MMPI items, some researchers responded to the need for a mixture of symptoms and personality traits. In spite of the questions raised about the dimensionality and sensitivity of the MMPI-D, it has been used to help validate many of the scales to be reviewed in this chapter and is widely considered a measure of person characteristics that are consistent with, if not identical to, depressive illness.

Beck Depression Inventory (BDI). This scale, developed

by Beck, Ward, Mendelson, Mock, and Erbaugh (1961) to measure the depth or intensity of depression, became the first inventory for the self-assessment of depressive symptomatology to become widely used. The BDI consists of twenty-one categories of symptoms and attitudes that had been observed and recorded during the course of psychoanalytic psychotherapy with depressed patients. Those symptoms that appeared characteristic of as well as specific to depression and that were consistent with descriptions of depression in the psychiatric literature were selected.

For each of the twenty-one categories of symptoms, which are listed under the BDI in Table 1, there is a graded series of four or five alternatives, which range from neutral to a maximum level of severity and are scored from 0 to 3. The scale thus provides a multiple-choice situation for patients, who are asked to select the statement in each category that best fits them at the present time. The scores for each statement are then summed to obtain the total BDI score. Administration of the test is described as "interviewer-assisted," since trained interviewers read the statements to the patients and score the responses. If able to do so, patients read their own copies of the test at the same time. Revisions of the BDI that permit complete self-rating will be discussed shortly.

Based on a psychiatric sample totaling 409 patients drawn from the inpatient and outpatient services of two hospitals, Beck and others (1961) obtained a corrected split-half reliability coefficient of 0.93. Weckowicz, Muir, and Cropley (1967) reported a lower figure (0.53), which may have been a function of a narrow range of scores in their sample. However, their use of the Kuder-Richardson formula would also account for the difference if BDI items are heterogeneous. Using data on thirty-eight patients who were tested twice within two to six weeks, stability was inferred from the parallel between changes in BDI scores and clinical ratings (Beck and others, 1961). Miller and Seligman (1973) reported a test-retest reliability coefficient of 0.74 for thirty subjects tested at a three-month interval.

Compared with other depression assessment devices (see

Table 1. Item Content of Depression Measures.

Beck Depression Inventory (BDI)	Zung Self-Rating Depression Scale (SDS)	Hamilton Rating Scale (HRS)
Mood[a]	Depressed, sad and blue	Depressed mood[b]
Pessimism[a]	Hopelessness	Depressed mood[b]
Crying spells	Crying spells	Depressed mood[b]
Sense of failure[a]	Personal devaluation	Guilt
Lack of satisfaction[a]	Dissatisfaction	—
Guilt feeling[a]	—	Guilt[b]
Sense of punishment	—	Guilt[b]
Self-hate[a]	—	—
Self-accusations	—	Guilt[b]
Self-punitive wishes[a]	Suicidal rumination	Suicide
Irritability	Irritability	—
Indecisiveness[a]	Indecisiveness	Work and interests
Social withdrawal[a]	—	Work and interests[b]
Work inhibition[a]	—	Work and interests[b]
Body image[a]	—	—
—	—	Insomnia, initial
—	Sleep	Insomnia, middle
Sleep disturbance	—	Insomnia, delayed
Fatigability[a]	Masculoskeletal, fatigue	Somatic symptoms, general
Weight loss	Weight loss	Weight loss
Loss of appetite[a]	Appetite	Somatic symptoms, gastro-intestinal
—	Gastrointestinal, constipation	Somatic symptoms, gastro-intestinal[b]
—	Cardiovascular, tachycardia	Anxiety, somatic
Somatic preoccupation	—	Hypochondriasis
Loss of libido	Sex, decreased libido	Genital symptoms
—	Diurnal variation	—
—	Confusion	—
—	Emptiness	—
—	—	Loss of insight
—	Agitation	Agitation
—	Retardation	Retardation
—	—	Anxiety, psychic

[a]Item retained on Beck short form.

[b]Correspondence of item content for a single item on one scale with more than one item on another.

Table 1), the BDI contains fewer items related to anxiety, agitation, and specific somatic complaints, and appears to place a heavier emphasis on cognitive manifestations of depression, an emphasis that is consistent with Beck's (1970) theory of depression. The BDI has also been criticized for assessing only one of the variety of manifestations of sleep disturbance (Little and McPhail, 1973).

The basic assumption underlying the BDI is that the number, frequency, and intensity of the symptoms assessed are directly related to the depth of depression. In developing the scale, Beck and others (1961) chose to rely primarily on clinical ratings of the overall depth of depression as the criterion measure, and found BDI scores to successfully discriminate among four clinical rating categories of depth of depression. Cutting scores established from the first sample permitted discrimination between extreme ratings (none versus severe) with 91 percent accuracy. For less extreme but nonadjacent categories the accuracy fell to 83 percent. Possible bias resulting from the same research team both devising the test and providing the criterion ratings appears to have had a minimal influence on the data obtained by Beck and others (1961). Correlations in the same range of magnitude (0.62 to 0.73) have been reported for a hospitalized group (May, Urquhart, and Tarran, 1969), for a general practice sample (Salkind, 1969), and for repeated assessments of severely depressed patients (Metcalfe and Goldman, 1965). The higher estimates may have been somewhat inflated by a wide range of severity in the group tested.

The BDI has been found to be more highly related to other self-report symptom inventories, such as the MMPI-D, the Zung Self-Rating Depression Scale (SDS), and the Costello-Comprey Depression Scale (CC-D), and to interviewer rating scales, specifically the Hamilton Rating Scale (HRS), than to global clinical ratings, mood adjective checklists, or the Visual Analogue Scale (VAS) (Bailey and Coppen, 1976; Bloom and Brady, 1968; Davies, Burrows, and Poynton, 1975; Lubin, 1965; Mendels, Weinstein, and Cochrane, 1972; Schwab, Bialow, and Holzer, 1967; Williams, Barlow, and Agras, 1972; Zung, 1969). It appears that the BDI has more in common with measures that also assess a range of symptoms, regardless of whether the rater is the patient or a clinician, than it does with measures of affect alone or with ratings of a global concept of depression.

Concerning the criterion of sensitivity, Beck and others (1961) reported parallel changes in BDI scores and clinical ratings taken within a two- to five-week period in twenty-eight out of thirty-three patients. Little and McPhail (1973) found differing levels of depression for the BDI and a global rating made by both the psychiatrist and the patient; however, change tended to occur in the same direction and in similar amounts over a period of sixteen months, yielding high (0.76) overall correlations between the two measures. Great variation in correlations (0.21 to 0.93) for individual subjects suggested that the validity of one or both instruments varies across subjects. Johnson and Heather (1974) reported corresponding decreases in BDI scores with clinically rated improvement in seventy-three depressed outpatients. Changes in the BDI sometimes preceded changes in clinical ratings, leading the authors to suggest that the BDI is the more sensitive technique.

Using clinical ratings of anxiety and depression, Beck (1970) demonstrated discriminant validity for the entire inventory, as well as for all individual items except irritability. Similar findings for the total BDI have been reported using the Costello-Comprey Depression and Anxiety scales (Mendels and others, 1972). Beck also reported that in a mixed-diagnoses sample each individual BDI item was more highly related to the rated depth of depression than to the rated severity of illness.

Inconsistent findings regarding the relationship between BDI scores and subject variables have been reported. Metcalfe and Goldman (1965) found no significant correlations for age, sex, or intelligence with BDI scores. An analysis of the records of 606 patients revealed negligible correlations between race, age, and vocabulary scores and both BDI scores and clinical ratings (Beck, 1970). On the other hand, small but significant biserial correlations were found between sex and both measures (0.19 and 0.22), which corresponds to the view that depression is more frequent among females. The significant correlation (−0.16) between the BDI and educational level, which was used as an index of social class, appeared not to be a function of differences in verbal skills, since the correlation with vocabulary scores was nonsignificant.

In order to provide support for the construct validity of the BDI, Beck and Beamesderfer (1974) cited investigations that supported a variety of hypotheses concerning depression in which the BDI had been the criterion measure. Beck and Beck (1972) reported that the BDI had been used as the criterion measure in more than one hundred published studies. In drug trials, McNair (1974) found the BDI superior to any other measure of depression in detecting drug effects; however, the number of studies in which it had been used was small.

Beck and Beamesderfer (1974), citing the findings of several French studies, reported high item-total correlations on an item analysis of the BDI, and a factor analysis that yielded a general factor with significant positive loadings for every item. A comparison of the six factors obtained by Cropley and Weckowicz (1966), the four factors obtained by Weckowicz and others (1967), and the four factors labeled by Pichot and Lemperierè (cited in Beck, 1970) reveal that three of the factors appear consistently in analyses of other measures: guilty depression, retardation, and somatic disturbance. Three similar factors were described by Beck and Beamesderfer; however, they were labeled "negative view of self and future," "physiological," and "physical withdrawal." The labels seem to reflect a cognitive versus physical dichotomy, which may be an artifact of the test rather than a characteristic of depression. Schwab, Bialow, Brown, and Holzer (1967) commented that the BDI seems heavily weighted with items that refer to pessimism, sense of failure, punishment, and self-punitive wishes. The emphasis on these themes follows from Beck's (1970) theory of depression, in which disturbances in affect, behavior, and physiological functioning in depression are thought to be the consequence of cognitive patterns that lead to viewing oneself, one's experience, and one's future in a negative way.

For the purpose of identifying a group of "pure" depressives for research, Beck and Beamesderfer (1974) specified a score of 21 on the BDI. Where it is desirable to minimize false negatives, as in screening for depression in a psychiatric population, a score of 13 is recommended. A cut-off score of 10 has been suggested for detecting depression in normal and medical populations (Schwab, Bialow, Clemmons, Martin, and Holzer, 1967).

The BDI may be more sensitive to depression among lower socioeconomic groups than ordinary diagnosis by physicians. There is some evidence that the BDI is more sensitive to improvement than global ratings and that it is more sensitive to drug effects than many other measures. Factor-analytic studies suggest that the BDI does measure a concept of depression that resembles the generally accepted view. In addition, the data indicate that the BDI measures depression rather than anxiety or general severity of illness. While the validity of the BDI has been supported using a variety of approaches, users should consider potential problems with the technique.

The BDI is subject to the primary limitation common to almost all self-report measures: Its validity can be affected by the subject's literacy, cooperation, concentration, and degree of illness (in severe depression or psychosis). These limitations can be circumvented to some extent by using the interviewer-assisted method, though at greater cost in staff time. Data on the comparability of the two methods of administration are needed in order to justify this procedure, since the arrangement of the lengthy items in order of increasing severity in the original BDI creates a potential for response set bias as a function of the failure to consider every item. A major criticism of the BDI is concerned with its content. Hamilton (1972) has argued that all self-report measures of depression are inadequate because they cannot take into account nonverbal behavior, denial, and distortion and because they cannot assess insight, retardation, and agitation. The most important observation about content, however, seems to be that cognitive items predominate at the expense of items dealing with physiological and affective disturbance.

Further reliability data are needed, particularly since the BDI is frequently used for repeated assessments. It is important to know how often and at what intervals the test can be administered without bias from extraneous factors. While considerable evidence of validity has been offered, it would seem that further comparisons with other scales and more studies testing the sensitivity and predictive potential of the BDI are the next logical steps.

Two revisions of the BDI have been published. May and others (1969) suggested a change in the format of the BDI that would maximize attention to the item content while minimizing the effects of response set and memory factors by randomizing the order of each statement within a category and the order of presentation of each category. Using a procedure similar to the original validation, a correlation of approximately the same magnitude (0.65) was found between the revised scale and clinical rating of depth of depression.

Beck and Beck (1972) have developed a shorter version of the BDI that could be completely self-administered, primarily for use by family physicians in screening for depression. Selection of the item categories that maximized the correlation with clinical ratings of depression and that correlated better than 0.90 with the original BDI resulted in a thirteen-item inventory (see Table 1) that correlated 0.96 with the BDI and 0.61 with clinical ratings (a slight improvement over the original scale). The format of the new scale was changed to facilitate self-administration by arranging the items in order of decreasing rather than increasing severity. In a cross-validation of the short form of the BDI, correlations between the original BDI and the short form were found to be high (0.89 and 0.96) (Beck, Rial, and Rickels, 1974). Correlations between the short form and clinical ratings ranged from 0.55 to 0.67, comparing favorably to the longer version. No relationships between short-form scores and age, sex, or race were found.

Self-Rating Depression Scale (SDS). This instrument was designed to provide a short, self-administered instrument that would quantitatively describe depression in patients with a primary diagnosis of depressive disorder (Zung, 1965). Selection of the symptoms to be assessed was based on the common factors obtained by Grinker, Miller, Sabshin, Nunn, and Nunnally (1961), Overall (1962), and Friedman, Cowitz, Cohen, and Granik (1963). Zung (1965) classified these factors into three characteristic groups of symptoms: pervasive affect, physiological equivalents, and psychological concomitants. Verbatim records of patient interview material were used to provide statements that would be representative of each symptom. A list of the symptoms assessed by the SDS appears in Table 1.

The SDS consists of twenty statements, of which ten are worded symptomatically positive and ten symptomatically negative. Subjects are asked to rate themselves on each item according to the way in which it applies to them at the time of testing. The scale provides four anchor points: "a little of the time," "some of the time," "good part of the time," and "most of the time." The anchors were later modified (Zung, 1973) so that the extremes were: "none or a little of the time" and "most or all of the time." The items are scored from 1 to 4, with higher scores indicating increasing amounts of depression. A percentage index was devised, thus permitting easy handling of unanswered items. Two items have been altered since the scale was first published. "I still enjoy sex" was changed to "I enjoy looking at, talking to, and being with attractive women (or men)" in order to more accurately reflect libido. It was thought that the sleep disturbance that is typical of depressive illness was better represented by "I have trouble sleeping through the night" than by "I have trouble sleeping at night" (Zung, 1973).

The contention that the content of the SDS is free of theoretical bias (Zung, 1973) was challenged by Hunt, Singer, and Cobb (1967), who argued that the factor-analytic studies used to select items were based entirely on clinical ratings rather than self-report and on samples that included older patients and psychotic depressives. The absence of items pertaining to guilt, retardation, hypochrondriasis, and loss of insight were considered as serious omissions by Hamilton (1972), in spite of the fact that hypochondriasis and loss of insight cannot, by definition, be self-reported. Hamilton also stated that suicidal tendencies were inadequately assessed by the single item "I feel others would be better off if I were dead." Although the empirical basis for the choice of diagnostic categories was sound, the actual choice of items has been criticized, most often for the restriction of items to a single variety of a symptom that may appear in many forms (Carroll, Fielding, and Blashki, 1973). For example, somatic anxiety is assessed by a single item that relates only to tachycardia. Recently, the meaning of symptomatically negative items has been questioned, particularly in normal populations. Blumenthal (1975) pointed out that, for example, the absence of hopefulness may not be equivalent to hopelessness.

Using the split-half method based on odd versus even halves of the SDS, a reliability coefficient of 0.73 was obtained for a sample of psychiatric patients with mixed diagnoses (Zung, 1973).

The original validation study (Zung, 1965) was based on the SDS scores of one hundred staff and medical inpatients (control group) and fifty-seven patients admitted with a diagnosis of depression. The patients were divided into two groups on the basis of whether the diagnosis of depression had been retained at the time of discharge. The mean SDS score for the control group (33) was significantly lower than both the depressed group mean before treatment (74) and the mean for the "other diagnosis" group (53), but did not differ significantly from the mean for the depressed group after treatment (39). Additional validation studies (Zung, Richards, and Short, 1965; Zung, 1967b) demonstrated the ability of the SDS (as well as the MMPI-D) to differentiate a group of psychoneurotic depressive outpatients from three other diagnostic groups: psychoneurotic anxiety disorder, personality disorder, and transient situational reaction. Using samples of inpatients and outpatients representing a wide variety of diagnosis, Zung (1971b, 1972b) found the mean SDS index to be higher in depressed groups (58.7 and 65.0 than in other diagnostic groups (47.5 and 56.0).

Zung (1972a) has reported one attempt to classify individuals on the basis of their SDS scores. Applying a cut-off score of 50 to subjects used in previous studies, 88 percent of the 360 depressives and 88 percent of the 1,108 normals were correctly classified; however, the samples included only adults between the ages of twenty and sixty-four. Zung noted that because adolescents and aged normals tend to score considerably higher on the SDS, the use of a cut-off score of 50 classifies almost half of the subjects in these age groups as depressed. Using a sample of thirty-two general practice patients who had been diagnosed as suffering from depressive illness on the basis of a psychiatric interview, Popoff (1969) found that a cut-off score of 50 on the SDS classified only 53 percent of the patients as depressed. He concluded that the SDS was not sensitive to the milder, covert, and highly somaticized depressions that commonly confront the family physician, and so devised a test that included "covert" statements of depression that might be more readily endorsed by patients who were denying their illnesses. However, in a comparison of the two scales by Downing and Rickels (1972), the SDS was found to be more effective for differentiating between depressed and nondepressed individuals.

The SDS has also been criticized (Carroll and others, 1973) for its failure to differentiate levels of severity of depressive illness: Scores on an interviewer rating scale (the Hamilton Rating Scale) were significantly different for three treatment settings, whereas SDS scores were not. However, aside from the introduction of uncontrolled variance in HRS scores by using a different rater in each setting, the use of treatment setting as an indicator of severity may be questioned. Raters' assumptions about severity may have been influenced by the setting rather than the patient's condition at the time of testing. Setting may reflect socioeconomic status or other situational variables rather than severity of depression.

In a cross-cultural study using translated versions of the SDS, Zung (1969) obtained similar mean scores for depressives (61.4), other-diagnoses patients (53.7), and normals (37.0) in a combined sample of 613 inpatients, 430 outpatients, and 364 normals from six countries. The study illustrated the potential utility of the SDS in cross-cultural research and supported previous conclusions about the level of depression, as measured by the SDS, to be found in the diagnostic groups studied. In addition, Zung reported correlations ranging from 0.43 to 0.65 between the SDS and global ratings of severity of primary diagnosis in cross-cultural samples. Near-zero correlations were found for a sample of nondepressed patients. Investigations in a variety of populations (Brown and Zung, 1972; Carroll and others, 1973; Davies and others, 1975; Marone and Lubin, 1968; Marsella, Sanborn, Kameoka, Shizuru, and Brennan, 1975; Mendels and others, 1972; Zung, 1967b, 1969; Zung and others, 1965) indicate that the SDS tends to be more highly related to inventories that are specific to depressive symptomatology, such as the BDI, MMPI-D, and CC-D, than it is to interviewer rating scales or mood adjective checklists.

Another criterion against which the SDS has been validated is subsequent treatment (antidepressant drug or electroconvulsive therapy) for depression regardless of the primary diagnosis (Zung, 1969). In a large cross-cultural sample, the mean SDS scores for treated versus untreated patients in both depressed and other diagnostic groups were significantly different, while the mean global ratings were not.

One aspect of the validity of the SDS that has received considerable attention is the effect of demographic and personality variables and response sets on SDS scores. Interpretation of the relationships of age and socioeconomic class to SDS scores is complicated by the possibility that both are factors in the incidence of depression. Although age has been shown to be unrelated to SDS scores in studies where the population has consisted of adults between the ages of twenty and sixty-four (Zung, 1967b, 1971a), mean SDS scores have been found to be considerably higher in adolescent samples (Mikesell and Calhoun, 1969; Zung, 1972a) and in groups over sixty-five years of age. Zung suggested that a higher baseline of depressive symptomatology may be the norm in elderly and adolescent populations as a result of greater environmental stress at these life stages. This conclusion has been supported by reports of distinct symptom patterns in the elderly, which are characterized by loss of self-esteem and apathy rather than guilt (Zung, 1967a).

The findings with respect to other variables are even less definitive. In an investigation of the relationship between SDS scores and subject factors, Zung (1967b) reported that SDS scores were uninfluenced by age, financial status, literacy, sex, and marital status. Zung described the correlation between SDS scores and educational level (−0.28) as low and concluded that the test is unaffected by education; however, the correlation is significant at the 0.01 level and the degree of variance in SDS scores accounted for by education in this study merits further investigation. Blumenthal (1975) found education related to

Optimism, Depressed Mood, and Well-Being clusters but not to the Somatic Symptom cluster. Rickels, Downing, Lipman, Fisher, and Randall (1973) reported that the SDS was less sensitive to change in lower socioeconomic status (SES) patients than in private practice patients. The difference appeared to be a function of stability in response to symptomatically negative or "healthy" items, such as "Life is pretty full," compared with the symptomatically positive items that showed clinical improvement. Although Zung found no relationship between financial status and SDS scores, this may have been due to the restricted range of income in his sample (88 percent earning under $5,000 annually).

A personality variable that has been extensively studied with respect to its effect on SDS scores is repression-sensitization. Zung and Gianturco (1971) found depression scores to be significantly and positively related to the degree of sensitization in an outpatient sample. The results were interpreted as indicating that increasingly depressed individuals are less likely to repress or deny their illness and are more sensitive to their symptoms; however, it is possible that subjects who repress their symptoms are not identified as depressed by the SDS or that sensitizers are more likely than repressors to become depressed. The latter interpretation is supported by the finding that depressed patients tend to be sensitizers (Brown and Zung, 1972; Piorkowski, 1972). Marked sensitization and repression have both been associated with low correlations between self-report (SDS) and clinical ratings (HRS) (Brown and Zung, 1972), but it is not clear to what extent validity is impaired for either measure.

The susceptibility of the SDS to deliberate misrepresentation by the subject has been the topic of several investigations. Normal adolescents and college students were able to "fake bad" and obtain higher SDS scores than a control group but were unable to "fake good" (Mikesell and Calhoun, 1969), even when they were specifically instructed that the dimension being assessed was depression (Swanson and Anderson, 1972). One difficulty with both studies is that the control mean was much closer to the minimum SDS score than to the maximum score, thus limiting variability at the lower end of the scale.

As evidence for the construct validity of the SDS, Zung (1973) has cited several studies in which SDS scores were used to identify depressives or as indicators of change in depression. McNair (1974) reported that the SDS was used twice as often as any other scale and that it was more sensitive than most scales to antidepressant treatment effects. Rickels, Downing, Lipman, Fisher, and Randall (1973) found the SDS less sensitive than physician rating to drug-placebo differences, more sensitive to the effects of stimulatory agents on retarded depression than to the effects of tranquilizing drugs on anxious depression, and more sensitive to changes in less severely depressed patients.

Most of the factor-analytic studies of the SDS have involved comparisons of unrelated factor patterns obtained from different populations, for example, normals, depressives, and the aged (Zung, 1971a), or the generation of factor scores for the prediction of treatment success (Zung and Wonnacott, 1970). One analysis of the factor structure of the SDS, based on the SDS responses of 831 depressed outpatients, yielded three stable factors (retarded depression, anxious depression, and appetite disturbance) that nearly duplicate three of the four factors emerging from the Weckowicz and others (1967) analysis of the BDI (Rickles, Downing, Lipman, Fisher, and Randall, 1973). Morris, Wolf, and Klerman (1975) found two rotated factors: agitation and self-satisfaction. The possibility that symptomatically negative items reflect a distinct dimension in normal populations was supported by Blumenthal's (1975) finding of a well-being cluster made up of seven out of the ten healthy items.

In summary, it can be said that SDS is an easily administered and scored inventory that can be completed quickly and independently by most subjects. It includes a broad range of symptom categories that have been empirically identified as comprising the essential symptom clusters of depressive illness. Translations of the SDS have already provided considerable cross-cultural data. The availability of an interviewer rating scale version (Zung, 1972b) and a form that can be completed by a significant other (Zung, Coppedge, and Green, 1974) make possible comparisons of the same item content obtained from different sources. Validation studies provide considerable support for the use of the SDS in identifying depressives in an adult population. The little evidence that is available thus far tends to support the discriminant and factorial validity of the SDS. On the negative side, the reference to frequency in the anchors tends to produce higher ratings for mild, persistent symptoms than for severe, infrequent symptoms (Carroll and others, 1973). The requirement that patients compare their present condition to a previous state of well-being has been criticized for problems it presents to subjects with long-standing illnesses (Wang, Treul, and Alverno, 1975). Resistance to the SDS because of objectionable items has been reported for elderly subjects (Salzman, Kochansky, and Shader, 1972) and medical patients in a coronary care unit (Froese, Vasquez, Cassem, and Hackett, 1974). At present, there has been little research on repeated assessments using the SDS, and no data are available on the temporal stability of the method. Even internal consistency has not been adequately assessed. More research is also needed on discriminant validity, the effects of response sets, the meaning of scores for specific age groups, and the appropriateness of the SDS in nonpsychiatric settings.

   Wakefield Self-Assessment Depression Inventory. This device, a revision of the SDS, is made up of the ten SDS items that were found most sensitive in a study of electroconvulsive therapy (Zinkin and Birtchnell, 1968) and two items assessing the "psychic experience of anxiety" (Snaith and others, 1971). The authors contend that anxiety responds to treatment in a manner comparable to depression and that it is commonly experienced by depressives. Zung's frequency scale was abandoned in favor of the anchors used by Zinkin and Birtchnell: "yes, definitely," "yes, sometimes," "no, not much," and "no, not at all."

   Snaith and others (1971) took advantage of the memory impairment associated with electroconvulsive therapy (ECT) to estimate test-retest reliability. A correlation of 0.68 was obtained for twenty-five subjects tested before and after ECT, a value that provides less than impressive support for the temporal stability of the test. With respect to validity, significant differences between mean scores for depressed and normal samples have been reported (Snaith and others, 1971). The distributions of scores for the two samples overlapped only slightly, with 3 percent of the patients and 7.5 percent of the normals misclassified. A high correlation between Wakefield and HRS scores (0.87) for forty-six patients may have been inflated by the inclusion of scores for repeated assessments during the course of illness. No sex differences in mean scores were found; however, correlations of 0.48 and 0.23 between age and the total score were obtained for men and women, respectively. An age correction equation for males is provided.

Although the Wakefield fulfills the requirements of brevity and ease of administration and has shown the ability to identify depressives and reflect changes in their condition, too little data are available for a comparison with the SDS or other measures.

Costello-Comrey Depression Scale (CC-D). This fourteen-item inventory for the assessment of the "tendency to experience a depressive mood" was developed, along with a companion anxiety scale, to provide measures that could discriminate between the two states (Costello and Comrey, 1967). The authors had found that existing scales, particularly the MMPI-D, correlated with both anxiety and depression, reflected a general neuroticism factor, and were contaminated by response sets. Items for the CC-D were selected empirically on the basis of repeated factor analyses in large samples of normal subjects using hundreds of items from a variety of measures. The method was designed to create two distinct affective dimensions that were minimally related to subject variables and response set factors. The final version consisted of fourteen items reflecting the affective and cognitive aspects of depressive mood, which are worded so that some are scored positively and some negatively. The items are rated on a nine-point scale.

A split-half reliability coefficient of 0.90 was obtained for the normal sample. The correlation between the scores of patients tested at admission and their scores when asked at the time of discharge to rate their condition when admitted (0.79) provided evidence of satisfactory temporal stability to the extent that subjects were recalling their earlier condition rather than their previous responses.

The method of item selection and the large samples employed support the claim of content validity for the scales, but evidence of criterion-related validity is limited. In a study of electroconvulsive therapy, the CC-D and the BDI both reflected treatment effects and were found to be highly correlated (0.74 and 0.78) (Costello, Belton, Abra, and Dunn, 1970). High correlations (0.65 to 0.74) between the CC-D and other self-report measures of depression have been reported in a mixed psychiatric sample (Mendels and others, 1972). The primary purpose of the scale (and therefore the major criterion of its validity) is its ability to discriminate between anxiety and depression. The correlation between the two scales ranged from 0.40 to 0.51 in three samples (Costello and Comrey, 1967), representing a greater degree of independence between the scales than has been obtained for other mood scales. In the same study, the Taylor Manifest Anxiety Scale was more highly correlated with the MMPI-D (0.69) than it was with the CC-D (0.20). Mendels and others (1972) reported correlations of 0.59 between the CC-D and the CC-A and 0.58 between the CC-D and the Multiple Affect Adjective Check List Anxiety scale. The coefficients, which were higher than those reported by Costello and Comrey but lower than those found for the CC-D and other depression measures, may reflect a higher rate of simultaneously occurring depression and anxiety in the sample. Construct validity was supported by finding distinct patterns of response on a semantic differential task for high scorers on each of the scales and by the emergence of depression and anxiety factors from an analysis of patient responses, which had loadings similar to those obtained in the normal sample.

The CC-D was intended as a measure of one symptom of depression, depressive mood, and not as a substitute for measures of severity of depressive illness. The scale has demonstrated homogeneity, and there is some evidence of temporal stability as well. While more data are needed on reliability, validity, and the effects of extraneous variables, the evidence for the convergent and discriminant validity of the scale is promising. A mood inventory of this type may be most applicable to personality and nonclinical research purposes where the ability to detect depressive illness or assess change is less important.

Institute for Personality and Ability Testing (IPAT) Depression Scale. This forty-item inventory for the assessment of depression was developed (Krug and Laughlin, 1976) to provide a companion scale for the IPAT Anxiety Scale Questionnaire (ASQ) (Krug, Scheier, and Cattell, 1976). Items were drawn from the Clinical Analysis Questionnaire (CAQ) (Delhees and Cattell, 1975) based on a factor analysis of the responses of 965 normal adults and 950 inpatients and outpatients with various clinical diagnoses. The criteria for item selection were that the item be more highly correlated with the depression factor than with any other factor and that it significantly differentiate normals from depressives and depressives from patients with other clinical diagnoses. In addition, items showing significant sex differences in the strength of their relationship to the depression factor were excluded. Four negatively scored anxiety items were added to the thirty-six depression items in order to increase the discriminatory power of the test. Scoring of these items is optional and norms are provided for both the thirty-six-item form and the forty-item form. Item scores (standard scores on a ten-point scale) and percentiles are provided for males, females, and the combined sample. Cut-off scores can be determined from a graph of the accuracy of classification of depressives and normals using raw scores on the Depression Scale. Additional norms are available for alcoholics, narcotics addicts, depressives, college students, prisoners, and general clinical cases. The test employs a three-point scale with anchors specific to each item and takes ten to twenty minutes to complete.

The authors of the test report split-half reliability coefficients ranging from 0.89 to 0.95 and alpha coefficients ranging from 0.85 to 0.93, thus indicating satisfactory internal consistency for the Depression Scale. The thirty-six-item scale was found to be highly correlated (0.88) with the depression factor obtained from the large standardization sample described previously and to discriminate between depressives and normals in the same sample. Correlations between the Depression Scale and several measures (CAQ, MMPI, Tennessee Self-Concept Scale, and Motivation Analysis Test) were cited as support for the construct validity of the new test. However, the correlation between the Depression Scale and the MMPI-D (0.31) was lower than the correlations between the Depression Scale and five other subscales of the MMPI, suggesting the need for further investigation of concurrent validity.

Women tend to score only slightly higher on the Depression Scale and sex differences appear to have been minimized. The test appears to be insensitive to subtle attempts to fake. An evaluation of the test must await further evidence of validity using other criteria in other samples; nevertheless, it appears to be a carefully constructed instrument for which much of the preliminary work, for example, normative data and reliability studies, has been done.

Visual Analogue Scales (VAS). This measure, developed by Folstein and Luria (1973), is a 100-millimeter line, that represents a continuum from "best mood" to "worst mood" on which subjects mark the points reflecting their current state. The scale is based on a method described by Aitken (1969, 1970) as ideal for the repeated assessment of subjective states because it provides a sensitive language that can reflect any perceived change in the intensity of experience.

Temporal stability estimates based on the average correlation of scores for pairs of adjacent days for within and between subjects indicated, according to Folstein and Luria (1973), that individual differences in mood were greater than within-subject fluctuations during a twenty-four-hour period and that the VAS is sensitive to day-to-day mood changes.

These same investigators reported significant differences in mean VAS scores for several diagnostic groups. Significant correlations with the SDS and most of the Clyde mood scales indicated that the VAS, which does not specify the mood to be rated, reflects a number of feelings but is most highly related to depression. In the same study, performance on a digit-symbol test was found to parallel changes in VAS scores only in patients with affective disorders. A decrease in mood score was accompanied by better performance in manic patients and poorer performance in depressives.

Using a VAS that represented a continuum from normal

mood to extreme depression, Zealley and Aitken (1969) found scores to be highly related to HRS scores (0.79) and psychiatrist's global ratings (0.78) at admission. In the same report, the use of a VAS with depressed and happy extremes suggested that patients' VAS ratings reflect changes that are not detected by observers. Nurses' ratings tended to show less day-to-day variability and lagged several days behind patients' reports of change. Little and McPhail (1973) found patient VAS ratings to be more sensitive, compared with psychiatrists' ratings and BDI scores, but highly related to both measures. Davies and others (1975) also reported the VAS to be significantly correlated with the BDI, as well as the SDS.

Despite the limited data available, visual analogue procedures provide an individualized method of assessment that may prove particularly useful in longitudinal treatment studies and for clinical purposes. The suggestion that the VAS provides greater sensitivity at low levels of mood because the extremes are determined only by the rater's experience is an advantage for sensitivity to change but a liability for detection of depression for across-subjects comparisons.

Several other individualized self-report methods have been published. A Subjective Unit of Arousal (SUA) scale, which can be used to assess depression, anger, and sexual arousal, is constructed by clients assigning the value 10 to an event that they recall as being maximally arousing and 0 to an event by which they were not aroused with respect to the dimension being rated (McCullough and Montgomery, 1972). Shapiro and Post (1974) constructed an individualized inventory on the basis of the symptoms reported by a patient in the initial interview using the patient's own words and standards. A similar method reported by Park, Uhlenhuth, Lipman, Rickels, and Fisher (1965) involved selection of symptoms from an inventory that was identified as present by both the patient and the doctor.

Adjective Checklists

The need for easily administered, repeatable instruments has led to the development of various adjective checklists. The technique involves presenting subjects with a list of adjectives that they check or rate to provide a description of the variable under consideration. The major mood adjective checklists have employed a free response format in which subjects simply check the adjectives that they consider applicable. In addition to the advantages of brevity and ease of administration and scoring, adjective checklists elicit minimal resistance from subjects because the task with which they are presented is meaningful and not threatening. The simplicity of the response permits repeated administration even when the intervals between testings are brief.

Despite these virtues, the adjective checklist technique involves a number of difficult methodological problems, including such factors as social desirability of responses, response sets, and fakability. These and other issues have been reviewed by Masterson (1975).

Multiple Affect Adjective Check List (MAACL). This instrument was designed to provide a self-administered measure of negative affects that is flexible with respect to specification of a time referent, such as "now" or "during the experiment," and sufficiently brief to assure its completion before changes in the state being measured are likely to occur (Zuckerman, Lubin, Vogel, and Valerius, 1964). The earliest version of the MAACL was a measure of anxiety that was called the Affect Adjective Check List (Zuckerman, 1960). Later, scales for depression and hostility were added, bringing the total number of items from 61 to 132 (Zuckerman and others, 1964). Beginning with a pool of adjectives that had been gathered by using a thesaurus, the choice of items was based on their ability to discriminate groups of anxious and depressed patients from normals and on their selection by subjects experiencing hypnotically induced affective states. Depression items were chosen from the lists that comprise the Depression Adjective Check List (DACL) (Lubin, 1965), to be described shortly. No item above an eighth grade reading level was retained.

The MAACL consists of twenty-one anxiety items, forty depression items, twenty-eight hostility items, and forty filler items, all arranged in alphabetical order. Each scale contains an approximately equal number of plus (scored when checked) and minus (scored when not checked) items as a means of controlling for a checking response set while preserving a free response format. Subjects are asked to check those adjectives that describe their mood during the time period specified—today or generally. Normative data are available for both the Today and General forms, which are considered state and trait measures, respectively. Each subscale is scored by adding the number of plus items checked to the number of minus items not checked. The higher the score, the greater the intensity of the negative affect. Normative data have been presented for job applicants, college students, and psychiatric patients (Zuckerman and Lubin, 1965).

Moderate to high test-retest reliability estimates have been obtained for the General form (0.68) and for the Today form (0.34 to 0.84) (Pankratz, Glaudin, and Goodmonson, 1972; Zuckerman and Lubin, 1965) in psychiatric samples. The Today form in normal samples has yielded the lowest correlations (0.15 to 0.31), except when brief intervals (two hours) are employed, thereby increasing the reliability (0.88 to 0.90) and providing support for the explanation of low reliability in terms of mood fluctuation (Pankratz and others, 1972). Zuckerman and Lubin suggest that patients do not adequately discriminate between General and Today time sets, while Pankratz and others hypothesized less variation in mood levels and higher means for patient groups to account for the findings. An alternative explanation may be that mood fluctuations do occur in patients but that the MAACL is not sufficiently sensitive to detect change at higher levels of mood intensity.

Zuckerman and Lubin (1965) have suggested that measures of transitory states should have low test-retest reliability but high internal consistency. Split-half reliability coefficients have been much higher (0.60 to 0.92) for odd versus even halves than for plus and minus halves (−0.11 to 0.73) (Herron, Bernstein, and Rosen, 1968; Zuckerman and Lubin, 1965). The fact that plus-minus estimates of internal consistency were much lower than correlations between minus halves of different subscales (0.60 to 0.88) casts doubt on the discriminant validity of the MAACL. Herron and others suggest that odd-even correlations are inflated by response sets and that the true internal reliability is somewhere between the odd-even and plus-minus estimates.

Although scale items were selected empirically and cross-validated, the content validity of the MAACL has been challenged on the grounds that some words are not scored on the expected dimension (for example, *hostility, aggression,* and *incensed* are not scored for the hostility scale) because hypnotized subjects did not increase their responses to these words (Plutchik, Platman, and Fieve, 1971). In validation studies, the MAACL-D has reflected the expected differences in affect level between job applicants and psychiatric patients (Zuckerman and Lubin, 1965), between normal and neurotic males (Zuckerman, Persky, Eckman, and Hopkins, 1967), and among the phases of manic-depressive illness (Plutchik and others, 1971). On the other hand, student samples have not scored consistently lower than psychiatric patients and the MAACL failed to discriminate among diagnostic groups in one psychiatric sample (Zuckerman and Lubin, 1965).

Zuckerman and others (1967) reported moderate correlations (0.51 to 0.61) between MAACL-D Today scores and global clinical ratings for a sample of neurotic males. Correlations were considerably lower for the General form (0.16 to 0.32) and for a normal sample (0.06 to 0.21), thus raising the question of the MAACL's sensitivity at low levels of affect. Zuckerman and Lubin (1965) reported significant correlations between the MAACL-D and four MMPI scales. In subsequent research, higher correlations (0.57 to 0.66) were found between the MAACL-D and self-report scales (BDI, SDS, CC-D, and MMPI-D); however, correlations between the MAACL-D and the other two affect subscales of the MAACL were much higher (0.80 to 0.87) (Bloom and Brady, 1968; Mendels and others, 1972). In addition, the correlations of MAACL Anxiety and Hostility scales with various depression scales were only slightly lower than those reported for the MAACL-D.

Another method used to validate the MAACL (Zuckerman and Lubin, 1965) involved experimentally manipulating depressive affect (for example, returning false low exam grades to a college class and showing a documentary film about slaughterhouse procedures).

Considerable attention has been given to the effects of various subject characteristics and extraneous variables on MAACL scores. No significant sex differences have been found for the MAACL-D in normal samples (Pankratz and others, 1972; Zuckerman and Lubin, 1965), but in psychiatric samples females have tended to score higher than males, leading the authors of the test to suggest that data for normals may be combined but that sex comparisons should be made in psychiatric samples. Although Zuckerman and Lubin reported that age, educational level, and intellectual ability do not appear to be related to MAACL scores, most of the data were obtained from populations representing a narrow range of these variables, that is, adolescents, young adults, and college students. No significant differences were found among groups of psychiatric patients rated as below average, average, and above average in intelligence; however, further data are needed concerning the effect of education or intellectual ability on the validity of the MAACL.

Zuckerman and Lubin (1965) have concluded, based on data for the MAACL-A, that social desirability and acquiescence response sets are not important influences on the MAACL, particularly the Today form. However, other researchers (Herron, 1969; Herron and others, 1968) have differed with this conclusion and speculated about the effect of a checking response set, observing that scoring minus items on a blank MAACL will yield scores above the mean on all three subscales. They found minus scores to be highly related (0.70 to 0.97) to total scores for the same scales, as well as to total scores of other subscales with correlations the same order of magnitude as odd-even reliability coefficients. In fact, the only part or whole score that was not highly related to minus scores was the plus score for each scale. The results suggest that the plus and minus components of the MAACL are measuring different variables. It also seems that minus scores may be in part responsible for the high correlations among the three scales of the MAACL, since they were highly related to scores across scales. Although it has been suggested that the minus scores for all three scales represent a single variable of pleasant affect (Plutchik and others, 1971), Herron and others concluded that the high correlations between the number of adjectives checked and the minus scores (−0.71 to −0.84) were evidence of a response set operating through the minus items. The failure of the two-part scoring system to control for a checking response set was demonstrated by correlations ranging from −0.56 to −0.66 between MAACL scores and the number of adjectives checked.

It is apparent from the previous discussion that the problems of discriminant validity appear inseparable from questions concerning the operation of response sets, the role of minus scores, and the relationship among affects. Reported intercorrelations among scales have been quite high, in most cases higher than validity coefficients, and in many cases as high as split-half reliability coefficients (Herron, 1969; Herron and others, 1968; Pankratz and others, 1972; Zuckerman and Lubin, 1965; Zuckerman and others, 1967). While Zuckerman and Lubin conceded that the findings probably reflect a common factor of negative affect, they argued that since MAACL subscales independently reflected the effects of manipulations of specific affects, they are not invalidated by the high correlations among them. In contrast, Bloom and Brady (1968) failed to obtain correspondence between clinical rankings of affect and rank orderings of the three MAACL subscale scores (except for Depression). Zuckerman and others (1967) found higher correlations between MAACL-D scores and anxiety ratings than between MAACL-D scores and depression ratings.

Several explanations have been offered to account for the problems of discriminant validity. One involves the assumption of a true relationship among negative affects so that they generally occur in mixed forms and are difficult to arouse independently (Masterson, 1975; Plutchik and others, 1971; Zuckerman and others, 1967). An alternative explanation involves attributing the problem to method variance, most frequently to the operation of response sets. This view is supported by the observation that other types of adjective checklists are plagued by similar problems of high interscale correlations (Masterson). Another possibility is that negative affects are indeed distinct but are represented only by plus items. Minus items on all scales may actually assess pleasant affect, which may account for the shared variance in scale scores and the inflated interscale correlations. This interpretation is supported by the high correlations among minus scores of different scales and by the increase in the magnitude of the correlations between plus items and total scores when negative affect was aroused (Herron, 1969). In addition, a factor analysis of a smaller pool of depression and anxiety adjectives from the MAACL yielded "positive affect" and "negative affect" as the first two factors (McLachlan, 1976). The minus items from both scales loaded on the first factor and the plus items loaded on the second.

In an effort to improve the discriminative power of the MAACL, Zuckerman and Lubin (1965) developed a brief scale containing the items with the highest correlations with their respective subscales and the lowest correlations with the other subscales. Interscale correlations were substantially reduced between Hostility and each of the other subscales, but remained high between Anxiety and Depression, tending to support the view that the relationship reflects an actual clinical phenomenon (Mendels and others, 1972). It seems likely that a variety of factors contribute to the intercorrelations among MAACL scales, and further research is needed to separate true variance from method variance.

To sum up, the MAACL provides a brief, self-administered measure of negative affects with easily altered time set instructions that render the test suitable for a wide range of applications, particularly where repeated assessment of affect level is desired. Some evidence that the MAACL meets the essential requirements of stability and sensitivity to change is provided by the relationship between the General and Today forms; however, more data are needed. Like most self-report measures, the validity of MAACL scores depends on the verbal facility of subjects and their inclination to accurately report their affective states. Much of the validation of the MAACL has been accomplished through the use of the Anxiety scale and the

Today form. Separate validation of each form and all three sub-scales is needed because of the claimed distinctness of affects and the differentiation between state and trait.

Differing patterns of temporal stability in normal versus patient samples have cast doubt on the sensitivity of the MAACL at high levels of affect, while low correlations between MAACL scores and observer ratings of affect in normals have raised questions about the test's sensitivity at low levels of affect. Data supporting the MAACL's ability to differentiate among diagnostic groups and between patient and normal samples have been meager. Correlations with other measures of depression have been moderate for the MAACL-D, which might be expected, since affect is only one symptom among many related to depressive illness; however, the other scales of the MAACL also tend to have moderate correlations with other depression measures.

Depression Adjective Check List (DACL). This checklist (Lubin, 1967) was designed to provide a brief, self-administered measure of depressive mood. Seven equivalent forms of the list, each of which can be completed in approximately two and one-half minutes, are available for use in repeated-measurement designs. The test is printed in two equal columns providing fourteen brief checklists that facilitate checking split-half reliability (Lubin, 1966). Since the adjectives for the MAACL-D scale were taken from the original DACL lists, there is some overlap of items between the two scales.

Items for the DACL were selected from a pool of 171 adjectives on the basis of their ability to discriminate between depressed patients and normals. Four lists, each of which contains twenty-two plus and ten minus adjectives, were compiled from the responses of female subjects so that there were no overlapping items and the average discrimination power of each list was similar. Three additional lists, each containing twenty-two plus and eleven minus items, were constructed in the same manner, from the same item pool, using a male sample.

Subjects taking the DACL are typically instructed to rate "how you feel now—today"; however, the instructions can be altered to change the time set just as in the MAACL. A single stencil scores all lists. The total score is the number of plus adjectives checked added to the number of minus adjectives not checked. Increasing scores indicate greater depression. Normative data have been reported for samples of high school, college, and graduate students, senior citizens, adolescent delinquents, and psychiatric patients. Standard score equivalents based on the student sample are also available (Lubin, 1967).

No temporal stability estimates have been reported for the DACL. Internal-consistency estimates have been high, ranging from 0.79 to 0.90 from analysis of variance data and from 0.82 to 0.93 for split-half reliability coefficients. Lubin also reported that varying the sequence of administration of the lists produced no order effects. Demonstrating the comparability of the seven DACL lists in normal samples, Lubin (1967) reported no significant differences among mean scores for each list and correlations among lists ranging from 0.80 to 0.93. Even when affect level was varied in the sample by administering the lists before, during, and after sensitivity training, no differences were found among these lists (Lubin, Dupree, and Lubin, 1967).

Comparisons of mean DACL scores on all lists have generally yielded significant differences consistent with the expectation of increasing scores from normals through nondepressed patients to depressed patients (Lubin, 1965, 1966, 1967), while showing no significant differences as a function of treatment setting (Lubin, 1967). Although Lubin concluded that the DACL has utility with varying degrees of personality disorganization, and the data support the claim that the test is sensitive to the differing degrees of affect expected to be present in these groups, the large standard deviations in DACL scores indicate considerable overlap between groups. It seems unlikely that the DACL would be adequate for identification of depressed individuals even though it reflects group differences.

Efforts to demonstrate the concurrent validity of the DACL using other depression measures have generally yielded low to moderate correlation coefficients. Global self-report ratings have been more highly correlated (0.30 to 0.71) with the DACL than have global clinical ratings (0.32 to 0.53) (Fogel, Curtis, Kordasz, and Smith, 1966; Lubin, 1967). The correlations between the DACL and the MMPI-D, which range from 0.54 to 0.57, have been among the highest obtained for a standardized measure; however, coefficients were even higher for the MMPI-Pt (0.58 to 0.62) and were significant for most of the clinical scales of the MMPI (Lubin, 1967). The magnitude of correlations with other measures has varied considerably. Lubin (1965, 1966, 1967) reported coefficients ranging from 0.27 to 0.66 between the BDI and the DACL. Much lower correlations (0.27 to 0.38) were found for the SDS using the same sample (Lubin, 1967); however, in another study, Marone and Lubin (1968) found coefficients ranging from 0.51 to 0.64 between the SDS and the DACL. The failure to find higher correlations with other measures may reflect the fact that mood, the only aspect of depression measured by the DACL, is one of many symptoms assessed in most inventories. Support for this view was provided by Lubin (1967), who reported significant correlations between DACL scores and individual BDI items related to mood, pessimism, sense of failure, sense of punishment, and self-hate. The nonoverlapping items of the MAACL-D and the DACL have been shown to be highly related (0.76 to 0.85); however, the conclusion that the correlations were inflated by response set or other method variance was supported by the finding that Today and General DACL scores are more highly correlated with each other than with the MMPI-D (Lubin, 1967).

Lubin (1967) reported sex differences in mean DACL scores, which increased in magnitude with increasing depressive pathology. The finding was attributed to a greater tendency for female patients to admit depressive symptomatology, an interpretation supported by the finding that twice as many correlations between individual BDI items and DACL scores were significant for normal females than for normal males. Lubin found no systematic relationship between DACL scores and age or education; however, it is not clear that these groups were well represented in his samples.

In his discussion of response sets, Lubin (1967) reported low but significant relationships between DACL scores and both the need for social approval and MMPI validity scales. The findings were interpreted as consistent with the expectation that self-reports of depressive mood would be negatively related to the need for social approval and defensiveness, and positively related to an index of general psychopathology. Lubin demonstrated the potential effects of checking response sets, finding considerably lower mean scores when he altered the instructions for the DACL so that a forced-choice (true-false) format was imposed. Further evidence for a checking response set is the finding that plus or minus halves had higher intercorrelations across scales than plus and minus scores for the same scale (Fogel and others, 1966). The failure to find significant correlations between total scores and the number of adjectives checked suggested the possibility that plus and minus items reflect different phenomena.

The DACL shares many of the advantages, limitations, and applications of the MAACL; however, the DACL offers several advantages over the MAACL for repeated assessment. It requires less time to complete than the MAACL, a large number of parallel forms are available, and the sensitivity of the DACL to change in affect level has been demonstrated for both normal and psychiatric samples.

On the negative side, the temporal stability of the DACL has not been investigated, in spite of the emphasis on its utility for repeated assessments and the availability of equivalent forms. The DACL appears to have the same difficulties as the MAACL with respect to possible checking response sets and a lack of discriminant validity. Low correlations with observer ratings of affect suggest that self-reported affect may be a less well-differentiated phenomenon than observer affect.

Lubin (1967) suggested that further investigation of response sets, normative data, and utility for diagnostic screening is needed for the DACL. Even more important is the need to clarify just what dimensions are being measured by affect adjective checklists and what can be predicted from those dimensions. In spite of the fact that depressive affect is generally viewed as a single symptom, it appears to be a more vague and elusive construct than depressive illness or depressive symptomatology.

Interviewer Rating Scales

An interviewer rating scale is essentially a structured interview guide that provides an easily completed, quantitative method of recording and communicating information about patients. Its main advantage, as well as its primary disadvantage, is its use of an expert rater, who may introduce a source of error variance. Although rater reliability is usually assessed by calculating the proportion of agreement in assignments to categories or the correlation between the scores obtained by two raters, Gleser (1968) has argued that the reliability of not just the rater, but of the entire interview procedure, should be assessed. A major concern with respect to interviewer ratings has been the effects of theoretical bias on the rater's perception and interpretation of the patient's responses, and its effect on comparability of results across settings. Global ratings, which involve the rating of a single variable (for example, depression) on a single scale, are probably most susceptible to rater bias. However, McNair (1974) found single rating scales of global improvement to be most sensitive to treatment effects. Global ratings have also been used to validate other depression measures, particularly self-report. Unfortunately, global assessments, though they may be reliable and sensitive in any one study, are not readily comparable across studies and investigators. It is not clear just what they measure. Among the several systematic alternatives to global ratings that are available, the Hamilton Rating Scale is the most widely used.

Hamilton Rating Scale (HRS). This instrument (Hamilton, 1960) provides a systematic method for quantifying the results of an interview with an individual already diagnosed as suffering from a depressive disorder and for assessing the pattern and severity of illness. Hamilton (1967) stressed that the scale is not to be used as a diagnostic instrument, but suggested that it might eventually be used for such purposes as selection of treatment mode and prediction of outcome. Schwab, Bialow, Clemmons, and Holzer (1967) have described the use of the HRS for detecting depression in medical inpatients.

The HRS consists of seventeen variables that were chosen

to reflect the presence and severity of depression (see Table 1), apparently on the basis of the author's observations of symptoms (Lyerly and Abbott, 1966). Although no important affective or psychological symptoms appear to be absent, it has been noted (Carroll and others, 1973) that behavioral and somatic components of depression account for between 50 percent and 80 percent of the total HRS score. Schwab, Bialow, and Holzer (1967) have also noted that the HRS is heavily weighted toward somatic symptomatology.

The total HRS score, which may range from 0 to 100, is the sum of two independent ratings, one by the interviewer and the other by an observer who may ask supplemental questions at the end. When only one rater is available, the score obtained is doubled. The two-rater method provides a check on interrater reliability. Hamilton (1967) reported that training on about twelve patients is sufficient to produce close agreement, that is, no more than one point difference on any one item and less than four points difference in the total score. He also suggested that experienced raters can learn to give half points. Eight of the HRS items are rated on a five-point scale, the points of which are defined by a series of symptom descriptions that reflect increasing severity. No distinction is made between intensity and frequency of symptoms; this is left to the rater's judgment. The remaining nine items are rated absent (0), slight or doubtful (1), or clearly present (2), because, according to Hamilton (1960), the quantification of these variables is either difficult or impossible. The points are defined by lists of symptoms that make no reference to intensity.

Since Hamilton (1967) considered the value of the HRS to be entirely dependent on the skill of the interviewer in eliciting the necessary information, he provided extensive guidelines for rating, including general instructions on interviewing depressives. Each of the seventeen variables is discussed in detail with separate guidelines provided for rating male and female patients on certain items (for example, work and interests, and loss of libido). Many of the judgments involved are quite complex and require a high level of inference. Raters were instructed to allow at least one half hour for the interview and to direct their questions to the patient's condition during the week preceding the interview. The need for complete independence of repeated ratings is stressed. Raters are urged to obtain data from relatives, friends, and hospital personnel whenever in doubt as to the accuracy of a patient's responses.

Reported interrater reliability coefficients for two raters scoring the same interview range from 0.80 to 0.90, increasing as the raters become more experienced (Hamilton, 1960, 1969). Agreement to within two points for the total HRS score has been reported by Carroll and others (1973). These findings suggest that the reliability of the HRS is not diminished by rater differences, at least when careful training is provided. The only data relevant to internal consistency were provided by Schwab, Bialow, and Holzer (1967), who reported correlations between individual items and total scores ranging from 0.45 to 0.78, which were higher than those obtained for the BDI in the same study.

Although most of the scales discussed thus far have not had their reliability any more adequately demonstrated than has the HRS, the validity of most has been subjected to considerably finer scrutiny. For the most part, Hamilton (1967, 1969) confined his investigations of the HRS to factor analyses of the scale and the use of factor scores to identify clinical syndromes.

In failing to describe the basis for selection of items for the HRS, Hamilton provided no support for the content validity of the scale. A comparison of the items assessed by the HRS with those included in the SDS and BDI (see Table 1) reveals that the HRS includes most of the same symptom categories. Since the content of both the SDS and BDI are based on the psychiatric literature on factor analyses, the degree of correspondence lends support to content validity.

Although Hamilton has presented no data on the concurrent validity of HRS scores, the test has been described as sensitive to differences in severity in depression (Carroll and others, 1973; Mowbray, 1972). Unfortunately, the only criterion of severity in both studies was treatment setting, a variable that may be influenced by severity of illness in general or other factors related to the decision to hospitalize. In order to conclude that differences in mean scores across treatment settings actual-ly reflect differences in severity of depression, HRS scores of nondepressed hospitalized patients, nondepressed outpatients, and normals should be compared with the scores of depressed groups. Carroll and others also reported a relatively low correla-tion (0.41) between the HRS and the SDS, which was attrib-uted to the inadequacies of the SDS and self-report measures in general. In support of their conclusion, they cited two other studies in which low correlations (0.52 to 0.54) between the BDI and the HRS were found in depressed samples. However, lower correlations can be expected when the range of the vari-able measured is restricted. Schwab, Bialow, Clemmons, and Holzer (1967) have reported high correlations (0.75) between the HRS and self-report measures in a sample of 153 medical in-patients, a population likely to reflect a wide range of severity. A correlation of 0.82 between the BDI and the HRS, based on repeated assessments of ten severely depressed inpatients over a period of several weeks, was reported by Williams and others (1972). The high correlation may reflect a high degree of tem-poral consistency in the relationship of the two scales within subjects. The correlation between the HRS and a behavioral measure was somewhat lower (0.71). Unfortunately, the HRS has not been validated against global ratings or against other de-pression measures using large samples.

The bulk of the evidence for the construct validity of the HRS has come from factor-analytic studies. The factor analysis presented in the first published study on the HRS (Hamilton, 1960) was later described by Hamilton (1967) as containing sev-eral flaws that had resulted in mislabeling factors and other errors. He therefore reported new analyses performed on the scores of 152 men and 120 women that yielded four factors for each sample. In both groups, the first factor (Factor I) was iden-tified as a "General Factor of Depressive Illness," the second (Factor II) was labeled "Retarded vs. Agitated Depression," and the remaining factors failed to correspond to any established clinical syndrome. Mowbray (1972) cross-validated the study using the HRS scores of 213 females and 134 males from a vari-ety of settings. The wide range of severity in the sample produced an even clearer general factor (Factor III) that was highly correlated (0.93 and 0.96) with the total score. In addition, all but one item had a significant positive loading on Factor I, indicating a high degree of internal consistency for the scale and supporting its validity as a measure of a single dimension of depression. Although Factor II was bipolar, it differed from Hamilton's (1967) in that anxiety features formed the positive pole while different items loaded negatively for males and females. Although no other factors could be labeled, Mowbray calculated factor scores that successfully differentiated among patients in three treatment settings. General practice patients showed more anxiety features (Factor II) than day hospital patients and inpatients; day hospital patients, who showed a high incidence of social or personality disorders, scored high on Factor III. A factor that polarized psychological and somatic aspects of depression differentiated day hospital patients from inpatients. The near-zero correlations of these factors with the total score suggests that the aspects of the HRS associated with setting are unrelated to severity.

A comparison of the factor structure of the HRS to that of other scales requires an examination of rotated factors that were unavailable in the Mowbray (1972) study and were neither labeled nor discussed by Hamilton (1967). Nevertheless, a comparison of Hamilton's table of rotated factor loadings with factors obtained by other investigators (for example, Friedman and others, 1963; Overall, 1962; Rickels, Downing, and Spaeth, 1973; Weckowicz and others, 1967) reveals similarities in the first two factors, the major differences being the absence of items relating to guilt, failure, pessimism, and other features of cognitive and affective disturbance that are minimized in the item content of the HRS. This difference also emerged from an item-to-item correlation between the HRS and BDI (Schwab, Bialow, and Holzer, 1967). They found that one HRS item, suicide, correlated above 0.75 with five different BDI items, raising the question of whether self-devaluing thoughts and verbalizations are adequately assessed by a single rating of suicide. The remaining four factors appeared to reflect combinations of somatic symptomatology that tend to cluster together in a single factor on other measures. The failure to interpret the factors casts doubt on the utility of the heavy emphasis on somatic symptomatology, particularly when it comes at the expense of finer discrimination between negative self-evaluation and suicidal potential.

The relationship between HRS scores and subject factors or rater characteristics has not been systematically investigated. The available data indicate that male and female samples do not differ significantly on total HRS scores (Hamilton, 1967) and that the different factor patterns that emerged for the sexes have not been stable across studies (Hamilton, 1967; Mowbray, 1972). Schwab, Bialow, Brown, and Holzer (1967) found the BDI and the HRS to be more sensitive to depression in lower-class patients than the medical staff, whose diagnoses were based on the admission workup. Its emphasis on somatic symptomatology may account for the higher HRS scores in this group. Although no data are available, the same effect might be expected in elderly patients.

An expanded form of the HRS employing a seven-point scale with closely defined anchor points (Paykel, Klerman, and Prusoff, 1970; Paykel, Prusoff, Klerman, and DiMascio, 1973) and a self-rating version of the HRS (Carroll and others, 1973) have been proposed; however, sufficient data are not yet available on these revisions to support evaluative comments.

The HRS was designed to provide an easy to use, standardized interview and rating procedure for the quantification of the degree of depression present in depressed patients. It assumes a variety of symptoms, focusing on behavioral and somatic components in order to minimize inferences about subjective experiences. Extensive guidelines for rating are provided to assure standardized training of raters with respect to the judgments necessary to categorize self-reports and observed behaviors into symptom categories. Satisfactory interrater reliability for two ratings of the same interview have been obtained. Factor-analytic studies have provided support for the claim that the HRS reflects a single dimension of depression. In addition, the potential utility of factor scores for identifying subgroups of depressives has been demonstrated. Schwab, Bialow, Clem-

mons, and Holzer (1967) found the HRS useful with medical inpatients, because it drew the physician's attention to symptoms
not considered in a conventional history.

The advantages of the HRS, decreasing the effects of deception or denial by the patient and including observations that
are not available to the patient, are offset to some extent by the
expense of two professional raters for each half hour interview.
As a result, the HRS is not suited for repeated assessments at
brief time intervals. The item content of the HRS may not
allow for adequate sensitivity to the range of self-evaluative
ideas and feelings. This neglect of cognitive and affective manifestations in favor of somatic symptomatology may account for
the observation that investigators have found the HRS more
suitable for severely ill patients than for the milder depression
found in outpatients (Hamilton, 1972). In addition, the HRS
was not designed to detect depression and therefore is not suitable for use with groups not diagnosed as depressed. A major
drawback of any interviewer rating scale is the bias that may be
introduced by different raters with differing theoretical orientations and interviewing styles. Hamilton's (1967) guidelines for
rating are sufficiently detailed to overcome some of the difficulties of rater bias by providing standardized training; however,
no investigations of reliability of the test across raters and interviews have been reported. There have been no reports dealing
with issues of temporal stability and very little data on criterion-related validity and the influence of extraneous variables.
Carroll and others (1973) have argued that a demonstration of
discriminant validity is unnecessary since the scale is not a diagnostic tool; however, it is important to establish the validity of
the HRS as a measure of depression and not of general severity
of illness, psychosis, or some other variable.

Other Interviewer Rating Scales. A variety of other interviewer rating scales has been developed, particularly in psychopharmacological research, that provide alternatives to the HRS.
The Depression Rating Scale (DRS) is a twenty-eight-item scale
that is completed on the basis of a nondirective interview during
the usual mental status examination (Wechsler, Grosser, and
Busfield, 1963). The scale assesses patients' attitudes and feel-

ings, their comments about their physiological functioning, and the interviewers' observations in six areas of symptomatology: physical functioning, motor activity, motivation or drive, mood and affect, intellectual functioning, and self-devaluation and guilt. The scales on which the items are rated range from three to six points and are anchored by descriptions specific to each item. No reason for the variety of scale lengths was offered but it appears that the length is based on the number of meaningful differentiations considered possible.

The scale is unique among interviewer rating scales in its differentiation between information obtained from patients' self-reports and from observed data. Some items, such as concentration, are assessed by both methods and are therefore heavily weighted. The scale is also distinctive in its emphasis on intellectual functioning and various aspects of motivation, such as interest in surroundings, plans for the future, initiative, and persistence. The DRS also includes items on rate of speech, inflection of voice, and rapport with interviewer.

Interrater reliability estimates based on different interviews with the same patient ranged from 0.52 for interviews conducted on the same day to 0.78 for those held six to seven days apart. The authors suggested that the increase reflected diurnal variation in symptoms; however, the effects of training over time should also be considered. A higher estimate (0.88), which was much closer to those obtained for other scales, was found for the same interview for twenty-two subjects. This discrepancy indicates the need for reliability estimates of the former type for other scales. It is not sufficient to know that two raters can agree on ratings of identical information if they are unable to elicit the same information in separate interviews. Demonstrating validity in a patient sample, a cut-off score was used to correctly classify 80 percent of the subjects as depressed or nondepressed and significant differences in mean scores were found for groups based on severity and improvement ratings.

The Depression Status Inventory (DSI) is an interviewer rating scale version of the SDS (Zung, 1972b). The test was constructed by writing one question for each item on the SDS. The questions are to be asked in a semistructured interview and the

answers rated on a four-point scale of severity, which takes into
account intensity, frequency, and duration of symptoms.
Guidelines for rating are provided. The summed scores are con-
verted to a percentage index in the same way as SDS scores.
Zung (1972b) reported the split-half reliability coefficient for
odd-even halves of the DSI to be 0.81. Interrater reliability has
not been reported. Validity was demonstrated by significant differences between mean DSI scores for depressed and nondepressed groups of patients and by a correlation of 0.87 between the DSI and the SDS. Zung, Coppedge, and Green (1974)
have also developed a form of the SDS that is completed by a
significant other. Except for changes in pronouns, the scale is
also identical to the SDS. Aside from providing a means for
comparing data obtained from different sources and obtaining
comparable data when self-report is unavailable, neither of these
additional scales seems to offer any advantages over the already
widely used SDS.

The Physician Depression Scale (PDS) has been used extensively by Rickels and his associates in clinical drug trials. The
twenty-three items are rated on a four-point scale of intensity
on the basis of a standard twenty-minute psychiatric interview.
Although no data have been presented, the authors claimed that
"physicians can quickly reach substantial inter-rater reliability"
(Rickels, Downing, and Spaeth, 1973, p. 285). Sensitivity to
drug-placebo difference in treatment response has been demonstrated for total scores, cluster scores based on items with similar content, and factor scores obtained from an analysis of the
scores of 983 depressed outpatients (Rickels, Downing, and
Spaeth, 1973). PDS change scores were sufficiently sensitive to
differentiate between mild and marked improvement in depressed patients. Mean PDS scores were found to discriminate a
depressed group from a group of anxious patients. Correlations
with self-report, specifically the SDS, were moderate (0.58 to
0.75); however, correspondence for parallel items ranged from
0.35 to 0.64 on the SDS and from 0.66 to 0.85 on other interviewer rating scales. These figures seem unimpressive, since identical item content was being compared.

The item content of the PDS is fairly complete relative to

other interviewer rating scales; in addition, several unusual items also appear on the PDS: hostile attitude, paranoid thinking, irritability, and elation. It is interesting to note that these items load on the one factor obtained using this scale that has not been found in any other analysis. The factor seems to represent a psychotic, perhaps manic, dimension of depressive illness and may be responsible for the sensitivity of the PDS to drug treatment effects.

The use of very brief rating scales has been proposed for assessing depression in outpatient drug treatment (Simpson, Hackett, and Kline, 1966) and for international drug treatment studies (Asberg, Kragh-Sorensen, Mindham, and Tuck, 1973). The scales published by each group of researchers are similar in item content. Both contain nine items that are rated on a four-point scale of severity with descriptive anchors specific to each item. Evaluative data are not available for the Simpson and others scale. Asberg and others reported interrater reliability coefficients for the same interview ranging from 0.86 to 0.97 in samples of English, Swedish, and Danish patients. For individual items the correlations ranged from 0.51 for anxiety, which the authors contended is a difficult term to translate, to 1.00 for sleep disturbance. Support for the concurrent validity of the test was limited to its correlation with the BDI (0.63) and with a depression rating scale (0.87) completed by nurses.

Finally, two scales that were published in the early 1960s deserve mention for unique aspects of item content and format. Both were designed for repeated assessment and maximal sensitivity to changes in the severity of depression, and both employ dichotomous ratings.

Cutler and Kurland (1961) developed a twenty-seven-item checklist of symptoms of depression, which are rated either present or absent on the basis of an interview. Dichotomous items were used in order to minimize the need for subjective interpretation. The items, which are arranged in three sections, content of thought, agitated behavior, and retarded behavior, differ from those of other scales in that they refer to specific behaviors that are generally rated in a single item. In addition, there are many items that appear to reflect severe (psychotic) disturbances. In fact, two items are applicable only to hospitalized patients. Only preliminary data on a small number of subjects were published, but the attempt to quantify phenomena such as agitation by counting behavioral manifestations appears promising. Unfortunately, this scale appears to be limited to use with severely disturbed, hospitalized patients.

The Psychiatric Judgment Depression Scale (Overall, Hollister, Pokorny, Casey, and Katz, 1962) is a thirty-one-item scale that is completed on the basis of an interview. A nine-point continuum from "not at all" to "extremely" is used to rate sixteen of the items. The remaining fifteen are questions that are answered yes or no. Items are weighted in order to correct for disparity in variance. Approximately half of the items were derived from the Inpatient Multidimensional Psychiatric Scale (Lorr, 1974).

Overall and others (1962) found the scale to be more sensitive to drug treatment effects than self-report or nurses' ratings. On the other hand, McNair (1974) reported that the scale detected differential drug effects in only 15 percent of the thirteen statistical comparisons in which it has been used. An examination of the item content reveals only one major difference between Overall's scale and other similar rating scales: an emphasis on items relating to severe pathology, particularly to manic states. An examination of the factor loadings based on an analysis of scores for 204 patients (Overall, 1962) reveals that these items, which include euphoria, conceit, boisterousness, overtalkativeness, and dominance, all load on the same factor. While inclusion of agitation-related items is likely to increase the sensitivity of the scale to drug treatment effects in populations that include many psychotic patients who also exhibit manic behavior, discrimination among types of treatment effects (for example, antidepressant versus antipsychotic) and even among patient groups (depressed versus nondepressed) may be impaired.

Several interviewer rating scales have been presented. All share the advantages of the use of a skilled rater, as well as the problems of costliness and potential rater bias. They differ most with respect to length, content, and method of scaling items, and therefore vary in their suitability for specific applications. Some of the scales were designed to be more sensitive to changes during brief time intervals by focusing on behavior during the interview (Cutler and Kurland, 1961) or by requiring finer discriminations in ratings (Overall and others, 1962). On the other hand, the HRS is limited to infrequent assessments by specifying the week prior to the interview as the time-set. The methods used to minimize the level of rater judgment and interpretation required include: writing items in fairly specific behavioral terms (Cutler and Kurland; Overall and others), providing specificity in anchoring the scale points (Simpson and others, 1966), and including detailed rating guidelines for each item (Asberg and others, 1973; Hamilton, 1967). Unfortunately, the empirical comparisons necessary to determine the effects of varying levels of inference are not available.

Scales also tend to be directed to particular populations as a function of their content. Cutler and Kurland (1961) limited their scale to use with hospitalized patients, and the HRS seems most suitable for severely depressed individuals, while both the Simpson and others (1966) scale and the PDS have been used with outpatients. The inclusion of items that assess psychotic and manic symptoms may enhance sensitivity to drug effects in the PDS and in Overall's (1962) scale. The test designed by Asberg and others (1973) was intended for cross-cultural comparisons; Zung's (1972b) DSI provides for comparisons across types of raters; and the DRS permits differentiation between observed and self-reported data on the patient's physical, intellectual, and social functioning. Too little data are available on which to recommend a specific scale over any other for most purposes; however, the superiority of a standardized rating scale to global ratings should be apparent.

Behavioral Techniques

Behavioral observation of depressed behavior has been suggested as an alternative to time-consuming interviewer rating scales and possibly unreliable self-reports, particularly when repeated assessments are required in order to monitor change

(Bunney and Hamburg, 1963; Williams and others, 1972). A daily record allows a close examination of the course of illness and can aid in identifying factors associated with improvement. In addition to its potential for economy and reliability in frequent, repeated assessments, behavioral observation is considered to be a more objective method that may be less subject to theoretical biases or interpretations, particularly if the key behaviors are clearly specified. The validity of the method depends on the behaviors selected for observation, just as the validity of rating scales is affected by item content. Behavioral observations are even more limited than self-reports with respect to the range of classical depressive symptoms that can be assessed, because so much depressive symptomatology, as it has been traditionally defined, involves affective and cognitive states that are not directly observable. Although depressive behaviors have been rated in general psychiatric behavior rating scales (for example, Bunney and Hamburg, 1963; Wyatt and Kupfer, 1968), few behavioral measures designed solely for depression have appeared in the literature.

Williams, Barlow, and Agras Behavioral Measure. The technique employed by Williams and others (1972) was designed to provide an economical, precise, objective measure of severity of depression that is sensitive to changes during the course of the illness. The instrument was constructed by selecting overt depressive behaviors that are frequent and easily observed and excluding infrequent or highly subtle behavior not involving verbal content or estimations of affect. Based on preliminary observations of depressed patients, the behaviors selected were talking, smiling, motor activity, and time out of the room. Motor activity was further defined by ten subclasses. The behaviors observed are essentially nondepressed behaviors, the assumption being that the extent of the depression is reflected by the absence of these behaviors, therefore, a higher score reflects less severity.

The Williams and others (1972) study involved the use of a behavioral measure along with the BDI and the HRS for repeated assessment of ten severely depressed patients during the course of their hospitalization. Daily behavioral observations by trained psychiatric aides were made randomly within the sixteen half hour segments of the day shift. The BDI was administered by a psychiatric nurse, in the morning and evening, every three days. The HRS was completed by psychiatric residents every three days during the course of hospitalization.

An interrater reliability estimate based on approximately twenty of the observations on each patient indicated a high degree of agreement (96 percent). The four classes of behavior counted were highly related and therefore summed into a single index for further analysis. The correlation between the HRS scores and the behavioral scores for the corresponding three-day period was 0.71; for the BDI and the behavioral measure it was 0.67. The higher correlation between the BDI and the HRS (0.82), compared with findings from other studies using these scales, suggests that correlations in this study are somewhat inflated by the use of repeated observations on only ten subjects, and behavioral measures are more distinct from self-report and interviewer ratings than self-report and interviewer ratings are from each other. The longitudinal data for each patient suggested that the behavioral measures were often sensitive to extraneous environmental influences and to physical disabilities of patients (for example, a situational change unrelated to depression may produce social withdrawal or physical inactivity). On the other hand, the scale demonstrated potential utility for prediction of posthospitalization adjustment. In several cases the behavioral signs were more sensitive than the BDI and the HRS to symptoms late in the course of treatment (worsening of depression just prior to discharge) that appeared related to readmission. In addition, the HRS and BDI seemed to plateau fairly early in the course of hospitalization and were therefore less sensitive to further improvement than was the behavioral score. This difference may be a function of the orientation of the behavioral measure toward assessing the frequency of positive or nonpathological behaviors rather than the severity of symptoms. Presumably, positive change may continue after symptoms disappear and may be predictive of posttreatment adjustment.

No other published reports of the validity of the measure

have appeared, and conclusions based on data for only ten subjects must be considered highly tentative. Nevertheless, it is possible that the behavioral measure may be more sensitive to different aspects of depressive illness than self-report and
interviewer ratings, and that the difference may permit a more
accurate determination of prognosis and better evaluation of
the ongoing treatment process. In addition, a behavioral instrument of this type can in principle be used as frequently as desired to assess a single individual without becoming uneconomi-
cal or unreliable.

   Other Behavioral Approaches. Hargreaves (1972) suggested several methods of direct measurement of depressive
behavior—that is, measurements that eliminate the need for observer judgment. The proposed procedures involve counting the
frequencies of certain classes of behavior, for example, overall
word rate and rates within specific categories of words, and the
use of an apparatus to measure some aspect of behavior, such as
voice loudness. He suggested that voice loudness, utterance
length, latency of response, and word rate might be combined
to provide an index of vocal retardation. A direct measure of
overt behavior that can be used to assess psychomotor retardation and agitation in inpatient settings has been developed by
Kupfer, Detre, Foster, Tucker, and Delgado (1972) for research
on sleep and depression. The apparatus, which permits continuous telemetric recording of motor activity within a range of one
hundred feet by means of a small transmitter worn around the
wrist, has been used to assess changes in activity level in uni-
polar and bipolar depressives during the course of drug treatment (Kupfer, Weiss, Foster, Detre, Delgado, and McPartland,
1974).

   Several studies of treatment of depression by modifying
certain target behaviors have demonstrated the relationships of
these behaviors to improvement in depression and the feasibility
of assessing their frequency. Behaviors such as crying and smiling (Reisinger, 1972), "depressed talk" (Robinson and Lewinsohn, 1973b), and speech rate (Robinson and Lewinsohn,
1973a) have been reliably counted. The extent to which the frequency of certain behaviors can be used as an index of depres-

sion has not been determined. Since some depressed patients do not complain or cry and display anxiety or agitation rather than retardation, it is unlikely that a single behavior would adequately assess depression in every case. Although there is ample evidence that many behaviors that occur frequently, though not exclusively, in depression can be reliably counted by observers without the necessity of expert interpretation or judgment, it should be noted that there are exceptions. Weiss, McPartland, and Kupfer (1973) reported that nurses generally overestimated the duration and quality of sleep as compared with EEG measures of sleep.

The focus on the ability to obtain positive reinforcement from one's environment as an etiological factor in depressive illness has created an interest in assessment of social skills and activity level in depressed individuals. Lewinsohn (1968) developed a method for the observation of interpersonal behavior that has been used to assess social skill deficits among depressives (Libet and Lewinsohn, 1973). Behavior is classified as an action (for example, somatic complaint and information request), a positive reaction (for example, approval and laughter), or a negative reaction (for example, ignore and disagree). The technique has been expanded to include nineteen social skill variables for which reliability and validity have been assessed in the context of group and home observations (Libet, Lewinsohn, and Javorek, 1973). MacPhillamy and Lewinsohn (1974) have designed an instrument, the Pleasant Events Schedule, for the assessment of obtained pleasure, activity level, and potential for reinforcement by a variety of events.

A major difficulty with using these instruments as measures of depression is that it is unclear whether the variables assessed are related to severity of depression or simply indicate a more enduring behavior pattern. Reduced activity and inadequate social skills may be characteristic of people who have a tendency to become depressed but are not unique to them or limited to periods of depressive illness. A determination of the utility of such measures for quantifying or detecting depression awaits further research. In a review of behavioral assessment of depression, Pehm (1976) described the use of social skill and activity level measures in depression research and in clinical evaluation of target problems for therapeutic intervention.

Conclusions

Before selecting an instrument for a research problem or clinical use, the most appropriate approach for the situation must be determined. Among the factors to consider are: the requirements for administration of the instrument (for example, literacy of subject), the range and type of symptoms assessed, potential sources of bias, suitability for the population and setting, and applicability to the specific measurement problem. The choice between self-report measures and interviewer rating scales will be considered first, followed by a comparison of both of these approaches with behavioral approaches to techniques that rely on self-report of subjective experience or clinical interpretation of behavior. Finally, some overall generalizations on the selection of instruments will be offered.

The primary advantages of self-report methods in the assessment of depression are, first, that they sample the patients' own perceptions, and second, that they are convenient and relatively inexpensive to use. The main advantages of interviewer rating scales are that they permit in-depth, expert evaluation and include both self-report and observational data. Both approaches, however, have serious limitations.

With respect to self-report measures, a possible limitation concerns various response biases, such as social desirability response set and denial. Characteristic response styles for two types of depressives have even been identified: neurotic depressives tend to exaggerate their illness, while psychotics are more likely to minimize their symptoms (Paykel and others, 1973). However, the greatest problem for self-report measures is the subject's lack of skill and experience. Having no knowledge of the range of severity of symptoms in the population, subjects have only their experience on which to base quantification of intensity, frequency, or duration.

In interviewer rating scales, the greater the dependence on the rater's expertise in eliciting the relevant material, weighing the importance of various impressions and observations, and transforming the data into a numerical score, the greater the potential for rater bias. Training does not guarantee identical interpretation of events and, in fact, may lead to perceptions colored by a theoretical point of view. In addition, rater variance may be a function of halo effects, failures to independently rate symptoms that generally occur together, and central or extreme tendency response sets. In the case of pre- and post-assessment of treatment, awareness of the stage of illness may influence ratings. Many of the same rating errors can of course also be made by subjects who are rating themselves.

Paykel and others (1970) pointed out that the response styles associated with types of depression were also related to treatment setting. Exaggerators tended to appear more frequently in outpatient settings, while minimizers were more often inpatients. One implication of their findings is that the use of self-report for detection of depression in outpatient settings is likely to result in fewer false negatives. Another is that clinical ratings may be more appropriate for inpatients. An aspect of response that may also be related to setting is the degree to which the subject is willing and able to cooperate with the assessment procedure. Several investigators (Rickels, Downing, Lipman, Fisher, and Randall, 1973; Schwab, Bialow, Brown, and Holzer, 1967) have noted that self-report scores of lower-class subjects tend to reflect feelings of futility and a pessimistic outlook, and may lack sensitivity to improvement due to treatment because the patients' economic circumstances remain unchanged. Thus, it would appear that selection of an appropriate technique for use with lower socioeconomic groups depends upon the purpose of assessment: Self-report appears most suitable for detection of depression, but interviewer ratings may be superior for assessing treatment effects.

The major classes of applications of depression measures are detection of depressive symptomatology, description of the pattern of symptoms, and quantification or assessment of the severity of symptoms. Self-report has been found to be useful for detection of depression partly because it can be conveniently administered to large numbers of subjects, but also because self-report can reveal depressive symptoms that are concealed from physicians by the somatic complaints that demand their attention (Beck and Beck, 1972; Popoff, 1969).

Because depressive symptomatology is characterized by subjective experience, some researchers (Paykel and others, 1973) have suggested that a patient's symptomatology can be best described using self-report methods. This does not appear to be the case, however, when distinctions among affects are required. Although affective states are largely inaccessible to observers and must be rated on the basis of self-report, Pinard and Tetreault (1974) found greater discrimination among affects in interviewer than in patient ratings. The difference seemed to be a function of the different connotations attributed to affect terms by patients and professionals. Patients tended to associate more feelings with each word and did not make the distinctions among negative affects made by clinicians. The problems encountered in differentiating depression from anxiety in self-report have received considerable attention in the literature (Mendels and others, 1972; Raskin, Schulterbrandt, Reatig, and Rice, 1967) and may be an important factor to consider, for example, in studies comparing the effects of tranquilizing and energizing drugs.

According to Paykel and others (1973), the major discrepancy between self-report and clinical ratings is in the area of assessment of severity. They argued that because subjects lack knowledge of others' experiences, they cannot provide quantifications that can be compared to those of other subjects. However, they can accurately characterize the pattern of their symptoms. It has also been argued that this restriction applies only to comparisons of severity across subjects, and that for repeated assessments designed to detect changes in depth of depression, self-report is superior (Aitken, 1970).

In drug trials, a variety of assessment techniques have been utilized, with global clinical ratings detecting effects more frequently than any other criterion measure (McNair, 1974). Unfortunately, the extent to which bias as a function of expecting change is operating is unknown. When making a global rating, raters may respond to drug effects that are independent of changes in the severity or nature of depressive symptoms. McNair recommends the use of multiple methods: a seven-point global rating, a physician symptom checklist, and a self-report measure.

Behavioral Assessment Versus Self-Report and Clinical Inference. Although research in the area of behavioral assessment of depression is limited, there are a number of circumstances under which one might select behavioral observations over self-report or interview methods. Perhaps the major advantage is the greater objectivity of observation methods. Rater bias can be reduced and comparability of results across settings improved by clearly specifying the behaviors to be recorded. Because observers need not be professionally trained and require only basic instruction in observational procedures, the method can be economically utilized in hospital settings without disruption of the routine and even without the patient's awareness. Moreover, it can be utilized with patients who are illiterate or too ill to rate themselves.

Behavioral measures may be preferred to interviewer ratings not only because they are less costly but also because a clinician is less likely to detect day-to-day fluctuations in severity of illness from a brief interview, particularly at extremes of pathology. In addition, the sensitivity of behavioral measures to changes in each subject can be increased by individualizing the assessment. A longitudinal record of each subject's primary symptomatic behaviors may prove to be as sensitive to change as self-report, and at the same time is more objective and less subject to bias than self-report.

Selection Considerations. A summary description of the instruments reviewed in the present report is presented in Table 2; however, selection of the most appropriate assessment method may be difficult given the limited data available for many techniques. Most of the instruments have scant reliability data, particularly with respect to temporal stability; some show poor discriminant validity; and the generalizability of validity data for many scales is limited by the use of a single approach to validation or restricted populations. In the absence of more definitive data, few generalizations can be made. However,

Table 2. Summary of Available Techniques for Assessment of Depression.

Measure	Characteristics	Applications
Beck Depression Inventory (BDI) (Beck, Ward, Mendelson, Mock, and Erbaugh, 1961)	Self-report, interviewer-assisted symptom inventory, 21 categories, multiple-choice format, items contain specific referents. Emphasis on cognitive, not somatic or anxiety symptoms. (Short form: brief, self-administered.)	Assess severity, reflect change over time, treatment studies, drug trials. Detection of depression in low SES groups and medical patients.
Self-Rating Depression Scale (SDS) (Zung, 1965)	Self-report, symptom inventory, 20 items rated on a 4-point frequency scale. Samples wide range of symptom categories, restricted in content within categories. Translations and "other rater" versions available.	Group comparison, identifying depressives, epidemiological investigations, group administration, cross-cultural research, studies of age-related depression, comparisons of three types of ratings.
Wakefield Self-Assessment Depression Inventory (Snaith, Ahmed, Mehta, Hamilton, 1971)	Self-report, symptom inventory, 12 items (10 from SDS plus 2 "anxiety" items), 4-point scale, more general anchors. Brief, easy to administer.	Assess severity in depressed patients, reflect change.
Costello-Comrey Depression Scale (CC-D) (Costello and Comrey, 1967)	Self-report mood inventory, 14 items, 9-point scale, nonspecific anchors.	Assess relatively enduring depressed mood apart from anxiety.
IPAT Depression Scale (Krug and Laughlin, 1976)	Self-report inventory, 40 items rated on a 3-point scale, anchors specific to items, administered in 10 to 20 minutes. Manual with normative data available.	Assess a general depression factor apart from anxiety and with sex differences minimized. Norms for a variety of populations increase utility for detection.
Visual Analogue Scale (VAS) (Aitken, 1969)	100-mm line, rate any single variable, self-report or observer rating.	Continuous or frequent assessment of fluctuating states, intrasubject comparisons.
Multiple Affect Adjective Check List (MAACL) (Zuckerman and Lubin, 1965)	Self-report, 132 items (40 for depression), free response format checklist, flexible time set. Brief, easy to administer. Published with manual and normative data. Problems: high interscale correlations, possible	Assessment of transitory negative affect, preferable to ad hoc adjective checklists.

Table 2 (Continued)

Measure	Characteristics	Applications
	checking response set. (Brief MAACL-D: 24 items.)	
Depression Adjective Check List (DACL) (Lubin, 1967)	Self-report, free response format checklist, flexible time set. 7 lists, 32-34 items each. 14 brief lists, 16-17 items each, provide parallel forms. Very brief (2½ minutes to complete each list). Published with manual and normative data.	Assessment of transitory depressive affect, repeated assessments.
Hamilton Rating Scale (HRS) (Hamilton, 1960)	Psychiatrist rating scale, 17 categories of symptoms with detailed guidelines for rating, requires skilled rater, two raters recommended, rating based on interview. Emphasis on somatic symptoms.	Assess severity and pattern of symptoms in severely depressed inpatients.
Depression Rating Scale (DRS) (Wechsler, Grosser, and Busfield, 1963)	Psychiatrist rating scale, 28 items 3-6-point scale, nondirective interview. Separates rating of patients' feelings from interviewer's observations. Emphasis on intellectual functioning, motivation.	Assess change, group comparisons.
Depression Status Inventory (DSI) (Zung, 1972b)	Psychiatrist rating scale, 20 items parallel SDS in content, 4-point scale, rate frequency, intensity and duration. Like SDS, content restricted. Guidelines for rating, semistructured interview.	Comparisons with self-report and "significant other" ratings.
Physician Depression Scale (PDS) (Rickels, Downing, and Spaeth, 1973)	Psychiatrist rating scale, 23 items, 4-point scale, standard interview. Four clusters of items based on symptom types. Wide range of items, includes some psychotic or manic symptoms.	Drug trials, relationship of clusters to drug effects.
(Simpson, Hackett, and Kline, 1966)	Psychiatrist rating scale, 9 items, 4-point scale, moderately specific anchors. Brief, simple.	Designed for assessment in outpatient drug treatment.

(continued on next page)

Table 2 (Continued)

Measure	Characteristics	Applications
(Asberg, Kragh-Sorensen, Mindham, and Tuck, 1973)	Psychiatrist rating scale, 9 items, 7 point scale, detailed examples provide rating guidelines, translations available.	Cross-cultural research, especially drug trials.
(Cutler and Kurland, 1961)	Psychiatrist rating checklist, 27 dichotomous items. Emphasis on retarded and agitated behavior, focus on severe pathology.	Severely depressed, hospitalized patients, assess severity and change.
Psychiatric Judgment Depression Scale (Overall, Hollister, Pokorny, Casey, and Katz, 1962)	Psychiatrist rating scale, 31 items (16 rated on a 9-point scale, 15 dichotomous), wide range of symptoms assessed, includes psychotic and manic behavior.	Assessment of severity for drug trials.
Behavioral Technique (Williams, Barlow, and Agras, 1972)	Observer recording of frequency of behavior, 4 categories, nonpathological behaviors, time sampling method. Little training required, not disruptive of ward routine. Oversensitive to environmental events.	Daily assessments, correlations with other measures over time, hospitalized depressives, not medical patients.

certain general conclusions can be drawn concerning the best measurement approach for major categories of applications. Self-report is probably the best method for detection of symptoms in epidemiological research and in screening medical patients and large groups of subjects for depressive symptomatology. In addition, self-report seems to be the most accurate and convenient method of providing a description of the pattern of symptomatology. Interviewer rating scales are considered by many researchers to have the advantage where assessment of illness severity across subjects is the goal. Finally, a combination of self-report and behavioral observation appears to have the greatest potential for providing sensitive assessments of change over time, an application that may permit further investigation of physiological and biochemical correlates of depression and, perhaps, the development of new objective techniques.

References

Aitken, R. C. "Measurement of Feeling Using Visual Analogue Scales." *Proceedings of the Royal Society of Medicine,* 1969, *62,* 989-993.

Aitken, R. C. "Communication of Symptoms." *Psychotherapeutics and Psychosomatics,* 1970, *18,* 74-79.

Asberg, M., Kragh-Sorensen, P., Mindham, R. H. S., and Tuck, J. R. "International Reliability and Communicability of a Rating Scale for Depression." *Psychological Medicine,* 1973, *3,* 458-465.

Bailey, J., and Coppen, A. "A Comparison Between the Hamilton Rating Scale and the Beck Inventory in the Measurement of Depression." *British Journal of Psychiatry,* 1976, *128,* 486-489.

Beck, A. T. *Depression: Causes and Treatment.* Philadelphia: University of Pennsylvania Press, 1970.

Beck, A. T., and Beamesderfer, A. "Assessment of Depression: The Depression Inventory." *Modern Problems of Pharmacopsychiatry,* 1974, *7,* 151-169.

Beck, A. T., and Beck, R. W. "Screening Depressed Patients in Family Practice. A Rapid Technique." *Postgraduate Medicine,* 1972, *52,* 81-85.

Beck, A. T., Rial, W. Y., and Rickels, K. "Short Form of Depression Inventory: Crossvalidation." *Psychological Reports,* 1974, *34,* 1184-1186.

Beck, A. T., Ward, C. H., Mendelson, M., Mock, J., and Erbaugh, J. "An Inventory for Measuring Depression." *Archives of General Psychiatry,* 1961, *4,* 53-63.

Bloom, P. M., and Brady, J. P. "An Ipsative Validation of the Multiple Affect Adjective Check List." *Journal of Clinical Psychology,* 1968, *24,* 45-46.

Blumenthal, M. D. "Measuring Depressive Symptomatology in a General Population." *Archives of General Psychiatry,* 1975, *32,* 971-978.

Brown, G. L., and Zung, W. W. K. "Depression Scales: Self- or Physician-Rating?" *Comprehensive Psychiatry,* 1972, *13,* 361-367.

Bunney, W. E., Jr., and Hamburg, D. A. "Methods for Reliable

Longitudinal Observation of Behavior." *Archives of General Psychiatry*, 1963, *9*, 280-291.

Carroll, B. J., Fielding, J. M., and Blashki, T. G. "Depression Rating Scales: A Critical Review." *Archives of General Psychiatry*, 1973, *28* (3), 361-366.

Comrey, A. L. "A Factor Analysis of Items on the MMPI Depression Scale." *Educational and Psychological Measurement*, 1957, *18*, 578-585.

Costello, C. G., Belton, G. P., Abra, J. C., and Dunn, B. E. "The Amnesic and Therapeutic Effects of Bilateral and Unilateral ECT." *British Journal of Psychiatry*, 1970, *116*, 69-78.

Costello, C. G., and Comrey, A. L. "Scales for Measuring Depression and Anxiety." *Journal of Psychology*, 1967, *66*, 303-313.

Cropley, A. J., and Weckowicz, T. E. "The Dimensionality of Clinical Depression." *Australian Journal of Psychology*, 1966, *18*, 18-25.

Cutler, R. P., and Kurland, H. D. "Clinical Quantification of Depressive Reactions." *Archives of General Psychiatry*, 1961, *5*, 280-285.

Dahlstrom W. G., Welsh, G. S., and Dahlstrom, L. E. *An MMPI Handbook*. Vol. 1. *Clinical Interpretation*. Minneapolis: University of Minnesota Press, 1972.

Davies, B., Burrows, G., and Poynton, C. "A Comparative Study of Four Depression Rating Scales." *Australian and New Zealand Journal of Psychiatry*, 1975, *9*, 21-24.

Delhees, K. H., and Cattell, R. B. *Handbook for the Clinical Analysis Questionnaire*. Champaign, Ill.: Institute for Personality and Ability Testing, 1975.

Dempsey, P. "A Unidimensional Depression Scale for the MMPI." *Journal of Consulting Psychology*, 1964, *28*, 364-370.

Downing, R. D., and Rickels, K. "Some Properties of the Pop-off Index." *Clinical Medicine*, 1972, *79*, 11-18.

Fogel, M. L., Curtis, G. C., Kordasz, F., and Smith, W. G. "A Validation Study of Two Affect Check Lists." *Psychological Reports*, 1966, *19*, 299-307.

Folstein, M. F., and Luria, R. "Reliability, Validity, and Clinical Applications of the Visual Analogue Mood Scale." *Psychological Medicine,* 1973, *3* (4), 479-486.

Foulds, G. A., and Caine, T. M. "The Assessment of Some Symptoms and Signs of Depression in Women." *Journal of Mental Science,* 1959, *105,* 182-189.

Friedman, A., Cowitz, B., Cohen, H., and Granik, S. "Syndromes and Themes of Psychotic Depression: A Factor Analysis." *Archives of General Psychiatry,* 1963, *9,* 504-509.

Froese, A., Vasquez, E., Cassem, N. H., and Hackett, T. P. "Validation of Anxiety, Depression and Denial Scales in a Coronary Care Unit." *Journal of Psychosomatic Research,* 1974, *18,* 137-141.

Gleser, G. C. "Psychometric Contributions to the Assessment of Patients." In D. H. Efron (Ed.), *Psychopharmacology: A Review of the Progress, 1957-1967.* Washington: Public Health Service Publication No. 1836. Washington, D.C.: U.S. Government Printing Office, 1968.

Gravitz, M. A. "Self-Described Depression and Scores on the MMPI-D Scale in Normal Subjects." *Journal of Projective Techniques in Personality Assessment,* 1968, *32,* 88-91.

Grinker, R. R., Miller, J., Sabshin, M., Nunn, R., and Nunnally, J. C. *The Phenomena of Depressions.* New York: Harper & Row, 1961.

Hamilton, M. "A Rating Scale for Depression." *Journal of Neurology, Neurosurgery, and Psychiatry,* 1960, *23,* 56-62.

Hamilton, M. "Development of a Rating Scale for Primary Depressive Illness." *British Journal of Social and Clinical Psychology,* 1967, *6,* 278-296.

Hamilton, M. "Standardized Assessment and Recording of Depressive Symptoms." *Psychiatria Neurologia Neurochirurgia,* 1969, *72,* 201-205.

Hamilton, M. "Rating Scales in Depression." In P. Kielholz (Ed.), *Depressive Illness: Diagnosis, Assessment, Treatment.* Baltimore, Md.: Williams & Wilkins, 1972.

Hargreaves, W. A. "Longitudinal Measurement of Depressive Symptoms." In T. A. Williams, M. M. Katz, and J. A.

Shield, Jr. (Eds.), *Recent Advances in the Psychobiology of Depressive Illness.* Department of Health, Education and Welfare Publication No. (HSM) 70-9053. Washington, D.C.: Department of Health, Education and Welfare, 1972.

Hathaway, S. R., and McKinley, J. C. *The Minnesota Multiphasic Personality Inventory Manual.* (Rev. ed.) New York: Psychological Corporation, 1951.

Herron, E. W. "The Multiple Affect Adjective Check List: A Critical Analysis." *Journal of Clinical Psychology,* 1969, *25,* 46-53.

Herron, E. W., Bernstein, L., and Rosen, H. "Psychometric Analysis of the Multiple Affect Adjective Check List: MAACL — Today." *Journal of Clinical Psychology,* 1968, *24,* 448-450.

Hunt, S. M., Singer, K., and Cobb, S. "Components of Depression." *Archives of General Psychiatry,* 1967, *16,* 441-447.

Johnson, D. A. W., and Heather, B. B. "The Sensitivity of the Beck Depression Inventory to Changes of Symptomatology." *British Journal of Psychiatry,* 1974, *125,* 184-185.

Krug, S. E., and Laughlin, J. E. *Handbook for the IPAT Depression Scale.* Champaign, Ill.: Institute for Personality and Ability Testing, 1976.

Krug, S. E., Scheier, I. H., and Cattell, R. B. *Handbook for the IPAT Anxiety Scale.* Champaign, Ill.: Institute for Personality and Ability Testing, 1976.

Kupfer, D. J., Detre, T. P., Foster, F. G., Tucker, G. J., and Delgado, J. "The Application of Delgado's Telemetric Motility Recorder for Human Studies." *Behavioral Biology,* 1972, *7,* 585-590.

Kupfer, D. J., Weiss, B. L., Foster, F. G., Detre, T. P., Delgado, J., and McPartland, R. "Psychomotor Activity in Affective States." *Archives of General Psychiatry,* 1974, *30,* 765-768.

Lewinsohn, P. M. "Manual of Instruction for the Behavior Rating Used for the Observation of Interpersonal Behavior." Unpublished manuscript, University of Oregon, 1968.

Libet, J., and Lewinsohn, P. M. "The Concept of Social Skill with Special References to the Behavior of Depressed Persons." *Journal of Consulting and Clinical Psychology,* 1973, *40,* 304-312.

Libet, J. M., Lewinsohn, P. M., and Javorek, F. "The Construct of Social Skill: An Empirical Study of Several Measures on Temporal Stability, Internal Structure, Validity, and Situational Generalizability." Unpublished manuscript, University of Oregon, 1973.

Little, J. C., and McPhail, N. I. "Measures of Depressive Mood at Monthly Intervals." *British Journal of Psychiatry,* 1973, *122,* 447-452.

Lorr, M. "Assessing Psychotic Behavior by the IMPS." *Modern Problems of Pharmacopsychiatry,* 1974, 7, 50-63.

Lubin, B. "Adjective Check Lists for Measurement of Depression." *Archives of General Psychiatry,* 1965, *12,* 57-62.

Lubin, B. "Fourteen Brief Depression Adjective Checklists." *Archives of General Psychiatry,* 1966, *15,* 205-208.

Lubin, B. *Depression Adjective Check Lists: Manual.* San Diego, Calif.: Educational and Industrial Testing Service, 1967.

Lubin, B., Dupre, V. A., and Lubin, A. W. "Comparability and Sensitivity of Set 2 (Lists E, F, and G) of the Depression Adjective Check Lists." *Psychological Reports,* 1967, *20,* 756-758.

Lyerly, S. B., and Abbott, P. S. *Handbook of Psychiatric Rating Scales (1950-1964).* Public Health Service Publication No. 1495. Bethesda, Md.: National Institute of Mental Health, 1966.

McCall, R. J. "Face Validity in the D Scale of the MMPI." *Journal of Clinical Psychology,* 1958, *14,* 77-80.

McCullough, J. P., and Montgomery, L. E. "A Technique for Measuring Subjective Arousal in Therapy Clients." *Behavior Therapy,* 1972, *3,* 627-628.

McLachlan, J. F. "A Short Adjective Check List for the Evaluation of Anxiety and Depression." *Journal of Clinical Psychology,* 1976, *32,* 195-197.

McNair, D. M. "Self-Evaluations of Antidepressants." *Psychopharmacologia,* 1974, *37,* 281-302.

MacPhillamy, D. J., and Lewinsohn, P. M. "Depression as a Function of Levels of Desired and Obtained Pleasure." *Journal of Abnormal Psychology,* 1974, *83,* 651-657.

Marone, V. and Lubin, B. "Relationship Between Set 2 of the Depression Adjective Check Lists (DACL) and Zung Self-Rating Depression Scale (SDS)." *Psychological Reports,* 1968, *22,* 333-334.

Marsella, A. J., Sanborn, K. O., Kameoka, V., Shizuru, L., and Brennan, J. "Cross-Validation of Self-Report Measures of Depression Among Normal Populations of Japanese, Chinese, and Caucasian Ancestry." *Journal of Clinical Psychology,* 1975, *31,* 281-287.

Masterson, S. "The Adjective Checklist Technique: A Review and Critique." In P. McReynolds (Ed.), *Advances in Psychological Assessment.* Vol. 3. San Francisco: Jossey-Bass, 1975.

May, A. E., Urquhart, A., and Tarran, V. "Self-Evaluation of Depression in Various Diagnostic and Therapeutic Groups." *Archives of General Psychiatry,* 1969, *21,* 191-194.

Mendels, J., Weinstein, N., and Cochrane, C. "The Relationship Between Depression and Anxiety." *Archives of General Psychiatry,* 1972, *27,* 649-653.

Metcalfe, M., and Goldman, E. "Validation of an Inventory for Measuring Depression." *British Journal of Psychiatry,* 1965, *111,* 240-242.

Mikesell, R. H., and Calhoun, L. G. "Faking on the Zung Self-Rating Depression Scale." *Psychological Reports,* 1969, *25,* 173-174.

Miller, W. R., and Seligman, M. E. P. "Depression and Perceptions of Reinforcement." *Journal of Abnormal Psychology,* 1973, *82,* 62-73.

Morris, J. N., Wolf, R. S., and Klerman, L. V. "Common Themes Among Morale and Depression Scales." *Journal of Gerontology,* 1975, *30,* 209-215.

Mowbray, R. M. "The Hamilton Rating Scale for Depression. A Factor Analysis." *Psychological Medicine,* 1972, *2,* 272-280.

O'Connor, J., Stefic, E., and Gresock, C. "Some Patterns of Depression." *Journal of Clinical Psychology,* 1957, *13,* 122.

Overall, J. E. "Dimensions of Manifest Depression." *Journal of Psychiatric Research,* 1962, *1,* 239-245.

Overall, J. E., Hollister, L. E., Pokorny, A. D., Casey, J. F., and Katz, G. "Drug Therapy in Depressions." *Clinical Pharmacology and Therapeutics,* 1962, *3,* 16-22.

Pankratz, L., Glaudin, V., and Goodmonson, C. "Reliability of the Multiple Affect Adjective Check List." *Journal of Personality Assessment,* 1972, *36,* 371-373.

Park, L. C., Uhlenhuth, E. H., Lipman, R. S., Rickels, K., and Fisher, S. "A Comparison of Doctor and Patient Improvement Ratings in a Drug (Meprobamate) Trial." *British Journal of Psychiatry,* 1965, *111,* 535-540.

Paykel, E. S., Klerman, G. L., and Prusoff, B. A. "Treatment Set and Clinical Depression." *Archives of General Psychiatry,* 1970, *22,* 11-21.

Paykel, E. S., Prusoff, B. A., Klerman, G. D., and DiMascio, A. "Self-Report and Clinical Interview Ratings in Depression." *Journal of Nervous and Mental Disease,* 1973, *156,* 166-182.

Pehm, L. P. "Assessment of Depression." In M. Hersen and A. S. Bellack (Eds.), *Behavioral Assessment: A Practical Handbook.* Elmsford, N.Y.: Pergamon Press, 1976.

Pichot, P. "Introduction." *Modern Problems of Pharmacopsychiatry,* 1974, *7,* 1-7.

Pinard, G., and Tetreault, L. "Concerning Semantic Problems in Psychological Evaluation." *Modern Problems of Pharmacopsychiatry,* 1974, *7,* 8-22.

Piorkowski, G. K. "Relationship Between Repression-Sensitization and Psychiatric Symptoms." *Journal of Clinical Psychology,* 1972, *28,* 28-30.

Plutchik, R., Platman, S. R., and Fieve, R. R. "Evaluation of Manic-Depressive States with an Affect Adjective Check List." *Journal of Clinical Psychology,* 1971, *27,* 310-314.

Popoff, L. M. "A Simple Method for Diagnosis of Depression by the Family Physician." *Clinical Medicine,* 1969, *76,* 24-30.

Raskin, A., Schulterbrandt, J. G., Reatig, N., and Rice, C. E. "Factors of Psychopathology in Interivew, Ward Behavior, and Self-Report Ratings of Hospitalized Depressives." *Journal of Consulting Psychology*, 1967, *31*, 270-278.

Reisinger, J. J. "The Treatment of 'Anxiety-Depression' via Positive Reinforcement and Response Cost." *Journal of Applied Behavioral Analysis*, 1972, *5*, 125-130.

Rickels, K., Downing, R. W., Lipman, R. S., Fisher, E., and Randall, A. M. "The Self-Rating Depression Scale (SDS) as a Measure of Psychotropic Drug Response." *Diseases of the Nervous System*, 1973, *34*, 98-104.

Rickels, K., Downing, R. W., and Spaeth, H. "The Physician Depression Scale (PDS): A Factor Analytic Study." *Pharmakopsychiatrie/Neuro-Psychopharmakologie*, 1973, *6*, 280-286.

Robinson, J. C., and Lewinsohn, P. M. "Behavior Modification of Speech Characteristics in a Chronically Depressed Man." *Behavior Therapy*, 1973a, *4*, 150-152.

Robinson, J. C., and Lewinsohn, P. M. "Experimental Analysis of a Technique Based on the Premack Principle Changing Verbal Behavior of Depressed Individuals." *Psychological Reports*, 1973b, *32*, 199-210.

Salkind, M. R. "Beck Depression Inventory in General Practice." *Journal of the Royal College of General Practitioners*, 1969, *18*, 267.

Salzman, C., Kochansky, G. E., and Shader, R. I. "Rating Scales for Geriatric Psychopharmacology—A Review." *Psychopharmacology Bulletin*, 1972, *8*, 3-50.

Schwab, J. J., Bialow, M., Brown, J. M., and Holzer, C. E. "Diagnosing Depression in Medical Patients." *Annals of Internal Medicine*, 1967, *67*, 695-707.

Schwab, J. J., Bialow, M. R., Clemmons, R. S., and Holzer, C. E. "Hamilton Rating Scale for Depression with Medical In-Patients." *British Journal of Psychiatry*, 1967, *113*, 83-88.

Schwab, J., Bialow, M., Clemmons, R., Martin, P., and Holzer, C. "The Beck Depression Inventory with Medical Inpatients." *Acta Psychiatria Scandia*, 1967, *43*, 255-266.

Schwab, J. J., Bialow, M. R., and Holzer, C. E. "A Comparison of Rating Scales for Depression." *Journal of Clinical Psychology,* 1967, *23,* 94-96.

Shapiro, M. B., and Post, F. "Comparison of Self-Ratings of Psychiatric Patients with Ratings Made by a Psychiatrist." *British Journal of Psychiatry,* 1974, *125,* 36-41.

Simpson, G. M., Hackett, E., and Kline, N. S. "Difficulties in Systematic Rating of Depression During Out-Patient Drug Treatment." *Canadian Psychiatric Association Journal,* 1966, *11* (Suppl.), 116-122.

Snaith, R. P., Ahmed, S. N., Mehta, S., and Hamilton, M. "Assessment of the Severity of Primary Depressive Illness: Wakefield Self-Assessment Depression Inventory." *Psychological Medicine,* 1971, *1,* 143-149.

Stein, K. B. "The TSC Scales: The Outcome of a Cluster Analysis of the 550 MMPI Items." In P. McReynolds (Ed.), *Advances in Psychological Assessment.* Vol. 1. Palo Alto, Calif.: Science and Behavior Books, 1968.

Swanson, B. R., and Anderson, G. W. "Faking on the Zung Self-Rating Depression Scale: A Replication and Refinement." *Journal of Clinical Psychology,* 1972, *28* (2), 193-194.

Wang, R. I., Treul, S., and Alverno, L. "A Brief, Self-Assessing Depression Scale." *Journal of Clinical Pharmacology,* 1975, *15,* 163-167.

Wechsler, H., Grosser, G. H., and Busfield, B. L., Jr. "The Depression Rating Scale. A Quantitative Approach to the Assessment of Depressive Symptomatology." *Archives of General Psychiatry,* 1963, *9,* 334-343.

Weckowicz, T. E., Muir, W., and Cropley, A. J. "A Factor Analysis of the Beck Inventory of Depression." *Journal of Consulting Psychology,* 1967, *31,* 23-28.

Weiss, B. L., McPartland, R. J., and Kupfer, D. J. "Once More: The Inaccuracy of Non-EEG Estimations of Sleep." *American Journal of Psychiatry,* 1973, *130,* 1282-1285.

Williams, J. G., Barlow, D. H., and Agras, W. S. "Behavioral Measurement of Severe Depression." *Archives of General Psychiatry,* 1972, *27,* 330-337.

Wyatt, R., and Kupfer, D. J. "A Fourteen-Symptom Behavior and Mood Rating Scale for Longitudinal Patient Evaluation by Nurses." *Psychological Reports,* 1968, *23,* 1331-1334.

Zealley, A. K., and Aitken, R. C. "Measurement of Mood." *Proceedings of the Royal Society of Medicine,* 1969, *62,* 993-996.

Zinkin, S., and Birtchnell, J. "Unilateral Electroconvulsive Therapy: Its Effects on Memory and Its Therapeutic Efficacy." *British Journal of Psychiatry,* 1968, *114,* 973-988.

Zuckerman, M. "The Development of an Affect Adjective Check List for the Measurement of Anxiety." *Journal of Consulting Psychology,* 1960, *24,* 457-462.

Zuckerman, M., and Lubin, B. "Normative Data for the Multiple Affect Adjective Check List." *Psychological Reports,* 1965, *16,* 438.

Zuckerman, M., Lubin, B., Vogel, L., and Valerius, E. "Measurement of Experimentally Induced Affects." *Journal of Consulting Psychology,* 1964, *28,* 418-425.

Zuckerman, M., Persky, H., Eckman, K. M., and Hopkins, T. R. "A Multitrait Multimethod Measurement Approach to the Traits (or States) of Anxiety, Depression and Hostility." *Journal of Projective Techniques and Personality Assessment,* 1967, *31,* 39-48.

Zung, W. W. K. "A Self-Rating Depression Scale." *Archives of General Psychiatry,* 1965, *12,* 63-70.

Zung, W. W. K. "Depression in the Normal Aged." *Psychosomatics,* 1967a, *8,* 287-292.

Zung, W. W. K. "Factors Influencing the Self-Rating Depression Scale." *Archives of General Psychiatry,* 1967b, *16,* 543-547.

Zung, W. W. K. "A Cross-Cultural Survey of Symptoms in Depression." *American Journal of Psychiatry,* 1969, *126,* 116-121.

Zung, W. W. K. "Depression in the Normal Adult Population." *Psychosomatics,* 1971a, *12,* 164-167.

Zung, W. W. K. "The Differentiation of Anxiety and Depressive Disorders: A Biometric Approach." *Psychosomatics,* 1971b, *12,* 380-384.

Zung, W. W. K. "How Normal Is Depression?" *Psychosomatics,* 1972a, *13,* 174-178.

Zung, W. W. K. "The Depression Status Inventory: An Adjunct to the Self-Rating Depression Scale." *Journal of Clinical Psychology,* 1972b, *28,* 539-543.

Zung, W. W. K. "From Art to Science: The Diagnosis and Treatment of Depression." *Archives of General Psychiatry,* 1973, *29,* 328-337.

Zung, W. W. K., Coppedge, H. M., and Green, R. L., Jr. "The Evaluation of Depressive Symptomatology: A Triadic Approach." *Psychotherapeutics and Psychosomatics,* 1974, *24* (2), 170-174.

Zung, W. W. K., and Gianturco, J. "Personality Dimension and the Self-Rating Depression Scale." *Journal of Clinical Psychology,* 1971, *27,* 247-248.

Zung, W. W. K., Richards, C. B., and Short, M. J. "Self-Rating Depression Scale in an Outpatient Clinic: Further Validation of the SDS." *Archives of General Psychiatry,* 1965, *13,* 508-515.

Zung, W. W. K., and Wonnacott, T. H. "Treatment Prediction in Depression Using a Self-Rating Scale." *Biological Psychiatry,* 1970, *2,* 321-329.

X

Clinical Assessment of Memory

Moyra Williams

In a field as vast as memory an article must be selective. This one will be confined to the activities of man and will concentrate on problems found in the clinical setting. A full consideration of the organic basis of memory cannot, alas, be attempted, although some of the current theories, models, and arguments on memory will be mentioned. These have been greatly influenced in recent years by some of the clinical data, especially by studies of organic amnesic (Korsakov) states; so it is essential that the data be thoroughly scrutinized.

Reasons for assessing memory in the clinical field usually have a practical foundation. First, clinical diagnosis, with all its implications for treatment and prognosis, often rests on the nature and extent of memory disorders. In the past great emphasis was placed on distinguishing organic from functional memory impairment. Long and embittered wrangles raged over such questions, one particularly famous case, summarized by Zangwill (1967), being that of "B," about whom papers filled the

German literature and international congresses from 1926 (the year "B" was first described by Grünthal and Störrung) to 1958. Although Zangwill (p. 113) points out at the end of his account that "we appear to have reached the limits of usefulness of this particular dichotomy," it is still important to recognize the components of memory that may reflect either organic or psychogenic aspects of a disorder.

Second, changes in a patient's condition are often indicated by alterations of memory before they can be seen in other spheres; hence the assessment of these alterations may be an aid to diagnosis. Third, some forms of treatment, such as electroconvulsive therapy, which is given for depression, and agents in treatment, such as anesthesia, may have side effects influencing the mnemonic functions that can only be eliminated if carefully assessed.

Finally, it can be very helpful to a person to have evidence that his memory is not worse than other people's. With increasing age, as well as after debilitating illness, one becomes aware that events are recalled with less ease, certainty, and clarity than before. Everyday tasks, shopping lists, and administrative chores are more difficult to remember. The development of mnemonic systems to compensate for such defects is part of the adjustment to life that all must make.

Before discussing the assessment of memory, it is logical to consider the nature of memory itself. This, however, has its difficulties. There are many aspects of behavior that are best understood by first examining the conditions that influence them; this is particularly true of memory—an activity so complex and so intricately bound up with other aspects of behavior that its definition becomes harder as one discovers more about it. (For up-to-date reviews, see Baddeley's *The Psychology of Memory*, 1976; Pribram and Broadbent's *Biology of Memory*, 1970; Tulving and Donaldson's *Organization of Memory*, 1972.)

Memory is clearly not a single, simple entity. Even its classical division into three phases—registration, retention, and recall—is oversimplified. But some form of classification is essential, and the simplest form to use in the clinical setting is one based on the pattern of memory loss.

In the clinical field, one finds that disorders may occur almost independently in: (1) the recall of remote experiences, (2) the recall of recent experiences, (3) the recall of the contexts of experiences, (4) the acquisition of a new pattern of behavior (perceptual, motor, or verbal), (5) the performance of an acquired pattern, and (6) a sense of familiarity with acquired patterns.

The manner in which these disorders are assessed and examples of their occurrence will be discussed in the main section of this chapter. First some of the factors known to influence memory will be considered.

Factors Influencing Memory

Whatever form of measurements are used to assess memory, the results obtained will be influenced by a variety of factors for which allowance must be made. These are summarized as follows.

Events Between Presentation of Stimulus and Test

Not only the length of time lapse but also its content are important. Preceding and subsequent events affect the recall of target items (pro- and retroactive inhibition, respectively) in relation to the degree of similarity between them, a fact that was demonstrated in some of the very first psychological experiments. That this effect is enormously exaggerated in organic amnesic states has also been demonstrated by Luria (1971) and others. A period of mental rest, especially sleep, after learning is said to assist consolidation, but dreaming may hinder it (Stones, 1974; Ekstrand, 1972; Idzikowski, 1977).

The effect of time alone is less clear-cut. It is not disputed that recency plays a major role but exactly what the role is and how it works are unclear. By and large, it has been recognized ever since the days of Ebbinghaus (see Baddeley, 1976) that recent events are recalled more easily than remote ones, but if two sets of similar items (words or numbers) are learned one after the other, reconstruction of the second list often involves intrusions from the first. Moreover, after a certain time interval (the "middle distance") remote events are often remembered better than recent ones. The difference is not just quantitative but also qualitative, which will be detailed later. Again, in the retrograde amnesia caused by cerebral damages, remote memories are recalled before recent ones. In the classical organic amnesic state, events and stimuli can be described and recognized by the patients immediately after exposure but not after very short time lapses, while in the normal subject the effect of time lapse depends largely on rehearsal. Events that are rehearsed shortly after perception are remembered better than those that are not rehearsed until later (Williams, 1954). All these observations suggest that the manner in which stimuli are assimilated, processed, or "encoded" is the primary factor, rather than the passage of time.

The division of memory into two systems, short term and long term, was once popular and gained great support from studies that showed that amnesic patients are often able to recall strings of items immediately after a single hearing, even when quite unable to recall any of them after a short time lapse. However, the common findings that patterns of behavior may be reproduced in these patients even if they lack the sense of familiarity and that recall can often be instigated by partial reconstruction of the original stimulus (Williams, 1953; Warrington and Weiskrantz, 1971) contradict this simple dichotomy. The fact that traces retained after five or ten minutes fade no faster over the next twenty-four hours in amnesics than in normals (Huppert and Piercy, 1976) has been used as an argument that amnesia cannot be due to excessive speed of trace decay, though in the experiments demonstrating this so very little was retained by the patients after the initial period of forgetting that further losses would have been difficult to detect.

Even in academic and experimental psychology, further studies have contributed to the decline in popularity of distinguishing between short-term and long-term memory.

Context of Stimulus and Test

Even though a person may not consciously assimilate the original context with a stimulus, the presence or absence of the

original context at the time of recall influences performance
(Godden and Baddeley, 1975). How far this extends is again unclear. It is obvious that if the context is closely associated with
the stimulus—for example, the background to the figure in a
picture or, in the case of a word, a list of items from the same
category—the two may be assimilated as a single unit; but the
context of both place and time also has an effect. Thus, items
learned in one environment (for example, underwater or in a
particular room) are recalled better in that environment than in
another. Items learned in one period of the day (for example,
early morning or late evening) are recalled better at that period
twenty-four hours later than at a different stage of the diurnal
cycle, such as twelve hours later.

Sensory Modality of the Stimulus

Most of the experimental work on memory in the clinical
field has been confined to verbal and pictorial material, presented either visually or auditorily. Some experiments have
been reported on haptic (touch) senses (O'Connor and Hermalin, 1963) and olfactory sensation (Butters and others, 1973),
but the data available are few in comparison. Moreover, the
techniques for testing in these modalities have not yet been
clearly standardized.

In most experiments on normal subjects, visually presented material is recalled and recognized better than that
presented verbally (Paivio and Csapo, 1973), regardless of the
concreteness or abstractness of its content. Easily envisioned
words or stories are also better recalled than those that are not.
Yet contradicting this observation is the finding that verbal cues
are helpful in aiding the recall of visual material and that items
in recall are confused more readily with those bearing similar
names than with those of similar visual appearance (Williams,
1973).

Familiarity or Frequency of Stimulus

While strings of items are best retained if the items are
familiar, easily named, and readily assimilated, a single rare or

odd item will be better retained than a familiar one if it appears in a familiar surrounding (Von Restorff effect). Thus the frequency with which an event has been experienced is, like recency, a variable that can work both for and against retrieval, depending on other variables in the total situation.

Method of Assessment

The methods used in the assessment procedure have an important bearing on the scores obtained. Three basic methods are available: recall, recognition, and reproduction. In recall and reproduction, accuracy, certainty, and response latency must be considered. In recognition, the number and similarity of alternatives offered (if the task is one of choice) are important variables. Another method of assessment not in general use but which will be described in detail later is based on cued recall, where the score depends on the number of cues required to elicit an item.

Individual Variations Among Subjects

That attention and motivation are closely involved in the way a person retains material is obvious. Not quite so obvious is the fact that retention varies with chronological age, though whether this is due to the elaboration of strategies or due to biological factors is as yet unclear. Young individuals tend to recall material exactly as it was presented, item by item, each one in its own context. Older ones recall in a schematized system involving past experiences. Age is also related to the type of material that an individual remembers best. In early childhood perceptual experiences seem to be retained best; motor skills are developed most easily in the middle range of childhood, but verbal skills continue to be elaborated well into adult life.

Another important cause of individual variation in memory is the intellectual capacity of the subject (IQ), which may determine strategies for and the background against which new material is assimilated. IQ also enables retrieval methods to be developed and storage systems to be designed that may be involved in memory, although a direct connection between memory and intelligence is not always present. Luria (1969) described one subject who had an apparently limitless capacity to retain observations, which he made use of as a professional entertainer, but showed no other outstanding intellectual skills.

In summary, it appears that in contrast to past decades, when storage systems were emphasized, recent workers on memory are emphasizing how experiences are assimilated (or processed or encoded) as well as retrieval mechanisms. Both of these aspects of memory can be studied with cuing or probe techniques, in which the effects of variations in the retrieval situation are studied. It will be realized that in tests used to assess memory in the clinical field, full allowance must be made for the factors listed above. In particular, the culture in which the subject is raised, which determines perceptual and linguistic behavior patterns, must be considered—a point that has yet to be stressed.

Measurement of Memory

General Tests for Measurement

As mentioned above, most of the studies of memory have used visual or verbal stimuli that were tested for by reproduction, recall, or recognition. There are few batteries of tests available in which all the different forms of retention on all the different types of stimuli can be compared in the same individual, and even fewer in which allowance is made for age, culture, and IQ.

The most used and standardized scale is that published originally by Wechsler in 1945, available from the Psychological Corporation of New York. The scale involves seven subtests covering mental control (counting backwards, counting by 3s, and repetition of the alphabet), orientation, current events, logical memory, digit span, reproduction of designs, and word association learning. It does not include any measure of retention over time. One serious disadvantage of this scale is that different aspects of memory cannot be assessed individually and compared with one another. However, allowances for age and IQ are well worked out.

The Wells and Martin (1923) test contains twenty-six items covering all aspects of memory, including the naming of objects. Tables are given from which points scored on the different tests can be reduced to a percentage of norms; performance is thus read off as a profile as well as an overall memory quotient. This test takes a long time to administer, however, and is therefore unsuitable for patients who are severely ill or tire easily.

In 1968, Williams published a short battery of tests covering immediate memory span, delayed recall, memory for remote events, and two types of learning, verbal and nonverbal. Each section is scored individually, and emphasis is laid on the importance of the pattern rather than the overall score in making a diagnosis.

In Luria's system of memory assessment (see Christensen, 1974), the subject is given a series of tasks involving (1) learning (of verbal sequences, finger movements, and tapped rhythms), (2) retention and retrieval (of visual, verbal, and numerical items), and (3) logical memorizing (of words or phrases associated to visual stimuli). Interpretation is based on qualitative rather than quantitative aspects of performance, but there is no statistical support for the accuracy of these interpretations.

In addition to the above, which are designed to measure memory alone, many cognitive test batteries include some aspects of retention or learning. Thus, Digit Span is one of the subtests of the Wechsler Intelligence Scale; Digit Span and Sentence Repetition are included in the Terman-Merrill Scale. Several tests for deterioration are based largely on measuring a discrepancy between the performance of long-established skills (such as vocabulary) and the acquisition of new behavior patterns (for example, Hunt-Minnesota; see Hunt, 1943; Babcock, 1933). In all of these, however, interpretations are made in terms of general cognitive functions rather than in terms of memory. Tests for use in non-Western cultures will not be considered further here, although some have now been devised.

Retrieval of Established (Remote) Memories

It is the ability to retain impressions and to recall them at will that enables one to retain orientation for person, place, and time. If an experience is not repressed for emotional reasons, time and frequency of rehearsal appear to be the most important factors in remote memory performance. Recent events, although recalled most easily by the normal person, are the most readily forgotten by the brain-damaged person, who, it is commonly said, "lives further into the past" as damage progresses (Ribot, 1885). Ribot's law of regression has, however, been questioned. Warrington and Sanders (1971) and Sanders and Warrington (1971) studied memory in non-brain-damaged people between the ages of sixteen and eighty and in patients with organic amnesic syndromes. They used two different methods: the recollection of finite events of major significance and the recognition of "well-known faces." Neither method evidenced sparing of remote memories in organic amnesia. However, two more recent studies have shown the opposite. Seltzer and Benson (1974) tested memory with questionnaires; Marslen-Wilson and Teuber (1975) tested the ability (with and without prompts) to identify by name photographs of prominent people. Both groups of experimenters found that subjects with amnesia due to long-standing brain damage did better on the remote than on the recent items. The different findings may have been due to the slightly different techniques used and also to fluctuations that may occur in the day-to-day behavior of very amnesic patients. Illustrating this last point, Talland (1965) quotes several cases of patients who, when interviewed on three successive days, gave three completely different accounts of their own personal histories. One of the patients, Rose, on the first occasion "brought her uncle into almost every answer she gave about her circumstances. Next day her mother occupied the same central position, referred to as if alive, although she had been dead for some years. The patient did not mention her husband till the third day, but then everything she talked about led to him" (p. 48).

Not all aspects of orientation are necessarily affected to the same degree. Orientation for time is the first aspect to be lost, probably due to a person's inability to recall just the most recent events, such as what meal was just eaten or where he or she has just been. Keeping track of time is, however, probably not a simple skill. Although few studies have been made of how we do this, it is a common clinical experience that brain-damaged subjects, even with minimal disabilities, may find it difficult to give their age or the present year. Hence, if when asked for age a person gives the date of birth ("I know I was born in 1942; you work out how old I am") or the day of the week and month ("I know today is Tuesday—it's April, isn't it?"), brain damage should be suspected.

Orientation for place is next to be lost. The subject may retain a fixed, faulty orientation, believing himself in a familiar place from the distant past and then fitting this into the presently perceived environment. For example, if the subject has been hospitalized previously and recognizes the present environment as that of a hospital, he may equate it to the previous hospital experience. Alternatively, the subject may take his orientation from whatever environmental cues he is currently receiving. Thus, when his wife is with him, he may believe himself to be at home; but if he is asked to do simple intellectual tests, he will believe himself to be at school.

Orientation for person is the last aspect to be lost. Except for the question of age, a patient completely disoriented in time and place can often give his or her name, marital status, occupation, and even home address.

Questions to elicit orientation usually form the starting point of any clinical examination if there is doubt about a patient's mental state. These questions are also included in some standardized tests (for example, Wechsler, 1945; Babcock, 1933), although Babcock usually includes topics of an impersonal nature as well, such as the name of the president or prime minister. The difficulty about this type of question is that norms for such matters are difficult to ascertain, as was shown in the studies already mentioned. An attempt to assess memory for the past by questions relating to personal events (as opposed to public ones) was made by Williams (1968), but this was also found difficult because of the variability of individual life experiences.

Retrograde Amnesia. A special instance of the loss of established memory is retrograde amnesia (RA) following a sudden loss of consciousness, particularly when due to concussional head injuries. Because the length of RA is a fairly good indication of the severity of injury (Russell, 1959), it is important to establish its extent as accurately as possible. Two characteristics of RA are its close association with time (events closest to injury are lost first) and its "shrinkage" with recovery.

The facts that RA exists, that it is closely related with time, and that it only follows cerebral insults causing loss of consciousness, have important indications for model builders and theorists. Many models are based on animal work, particularly on experiments associated with electroconvulsive shock and the presence or absence of single-trial avoidance learning (McGeogh, 1974). The generalization of these findings to man must be made with caution. Avoidance learning in amnesic patients is commonly observed, as shown by the Grünthal-Störrung case (see Zangwill, 1967); but although patients may take steps to avoid what experience has proved to be painful, they may be apparently amnesic because of such avoidance, and even fabricate or rationalize excuses for their actions.

A classical example of this was featured in a clinical demonstration by the famous neurologist Claparède (see McCurdy, 1926). When meeting the professor, one severely amnesic patient always shook the professor's hand and said how delighted he was to make his acquaintance. One day Claparède hid a pin in his hand, which gave the patient a sharp jab as he clasped it. The next time the patient was ushered to the doctor, he started forward with his hand outstretched in the usual manner, but then withdrew it and sat down. Asked by Claparède why he had done so, the patient replied that he suddenly had a stupid feeling that the professor might have a pin in his hand.

The main problems of academic interest raised by RA concern its cause. Is it due to a failure to consolidate or an inability to retrieve? Clinical studies of patients during the course of RA shrinkage suggest that while both factors may play a part, two of the most important aspects in the recall of past events are their rehearsal and their intellectual reconstruction. A person's past experiences are not just recovered; they are "worked out." The cues and reminders a person receives from visitors, together with his or her understanding of "what must have happened," become fused into "knowledge." Williams (1969) demonstrated this by comparing the recollection of past events by several groups of hospitalized patients, comprising those admitted after head injuries of mild and moderate severity and those admitted for illnesses of sudden or gradual onset. Each subject was asked to describe events preceding specific events in his or her life: a very recent one, such as admission to the hospital; a moderately remote one, such as the same day a year ago; and a very remote one, such as the patient's twenty-first birthday. The difference was that whereas recent events were given in considerable detail and as isolated instances ("I got up when the alarm went off, put the dog out, collected the paper, . . ."), remote ones were given in schemata and as generalizations ("I expect I did what I always did at that time; that's to say I would wake up about 7:30, . . .").

Whether the very short (up to one minute) RA that almost invariably follows minor concussions should be interpreted on the basis of consolidation is a moot point. Although there is a tendency to feel that this must be so, Williams (1969) also discovered that even the recall of small events preceding an accident may depend on rehearsal as well as on continuity of consciousness. One patient interviewed had broken his leg falling off a motorcycle and was able to describe in detail the antecedent events. "I always mend my own punctures," he explained, "and had just mended one that day. I suppose I must have bungled it as going round a sharp corner, a tyre burst" (Williams, p. 80). Asked when he had mended the previous puncture to this and what had happened subsequently he looked quite offended and remarked, "How could I possibly remember that, nothing happened to fix it [in my memory] ."

When assessing RA, which is conventionally rated in terms of the time lapse between the subject's last memory and the cerebral insult, care must be taken to ensure that what the subject describes as his last memory is not an incident taken from a different era of his past (the dating and time sequencing of one's own personal experiences are extremely fallible), that the last memory is part of a continuous stream of experiences and not an isolated instance, and that further shrinkage may not occur as a result of reminders, reconstruction, and reconstitution (such as a return to the scene of the accident). Although the permanent RA seen after full recovery seldom covers more than a few hours, instances have been recorded of permanent residual gaps of many months. A common cause of these in the 1950s was tuberculous meningitis—an illness in which the patient might remain comparatively alert but extremely amnesic for many weeks, but from which full intellectual and physical recovery is often finally made. Some of these patients after recovery had apparently lost their memory for weeks preceding the onset of the illness. Thus, one soldier, who was interviewed two and a half years after making a good recovery, had little recollection of the two years preceding his illness except for one or two isolated events. He remembered that he had been posted to a regiment in the Ruhr where he took a clerk's course. He learned typewriting and apparently became very efficient, but he found that on recovery from his illness all he could recall of the course was a large plaque on the wall, the first letters of which were *q, w, e, r,* and *t.* Later he was shown a photograph of the men in the course. He found that he could name them all without difficulty, although he had no idea when or how he had met them (Williams and Smith, 1954).

Hysterical Fugue States. The classical loss of memory, in which an individual may be found wandering around without any knowledge of who he is or what he has done up to that moment, is now rare but does occur occasionally. Three characteristics distinguish this from organic conditions: (1) loss of personal orientation (especially for name), which is rare in organic cases except in the very early confusional state, (2) the all-embracing or global nature of the amnesia and its resistance to recovery by prompting, and (3) the persistence of the inability to recall past events even when retention of recent ones is good. Thus a global amnesia for the past and disorientation for person in the presence of good retention are strong indications of a hysterical amnesia.

A tendency to equate these conditions with malingering or to assume that the sufferer is trying to cover up a misdeed are seldom justified. Although there is always an element of the desire to escape from emotional stress, the mechanisms responsible for fugue states are not under conscious control; nor is the cause of stress necessarily due to conflict with society.

Performance of Established Skills

Although the performance of established skills could rightly be considered part of the memory function, the various defects that can occur as a result of injury or illness are normally considered separately under such terms as aphasia, apraxia, acalculia, amnesia, alexia, and agraphia. When assessing memory, the examiner should be sure that any defects in a person's performance are *not* attributable to any of the above. Thus if the patient is being asked to reproduce designs of figures from memory, one must be sure that he can correctly copy them when they are before him; if the patient is asked to repeat or recall words, one should be certain that he has no specific word-finding difficulties. Although gross disorders in these spheres are not difficult to detect, milder ones may be. Thus a person with mild dysphasia may show little sign of this in conditions where he is free to choose his own words (as in normal conversation), but if asked to give specific words (as when repeating a sentence or a string of numbers) or to recall the names of objects, he may have great difficulty. Similarly, one with mild visuospatial loss may be able to cope when the cues are constantly present, as in a copying task, but not when they are removed. For this reason it is always advisable to assess memory with both visual and verbal material. A big discrepancy between a subject's performance in the two spheres can suggest a mild, specific impairment.

Establishment of New Behavior Patterns (Learning)

The ease with which new patterns of behavior are established is closely related to age, as has already been mentioned. It is typical that the acquisition of learning, as opposed to memory, depends on repetition rather than on a single exposure, though single-trial learning does exist, mainly in the form of avoidance or association. Learning can be assessed in three overlapping spheres: the acquisition of motor patterns, the acquisition of new associations, and the acquisition of rote material. Performance is usually scored in terms of the number of exposures needed to elicit error-free performance, but different clinical conditions can also be recognized in the qualitative aspects of performance. Perseveration, failure to improve performance beyond a certain level, and rapid loss are characteristic of brain damage. Uneven gain, seen in a disjointed rather than smooth learning curve, is characteristic of anxiety (Zangwill, 1943). Retardation or slowness of response suggests depression. Retention in the learning situation can be assessed by "saving" scores, that is, the number of exposures needed the first time minus the number needed the second. A poor saving score often indicates an organic amnesic state.

Acquisition of Motor Patterns. Standardized tests suitable for use in a clinical setting are almost nonexistent. Existing visuomotor tracking tasks commonly used in laboratory studies with normal subjects are not suitable for general clinical use. Finger mazes have been used in some clinical studies (Milner, 1968) but are not available commercially.

There is good evidence that on tasks of this type even severely amnesic patients show steady improvement with practice at a rate similar to normals, even though every time they are shown the material they may deny having seen it or used it before. The finding not only has theoretical implications (which will be discussed later in this chapter) but also practical ones, which can be utilized in management and rehabilitation.

A useful test for measuring nonverbal learning is the Rey-Davis Form Board, a test first described by Rey (1941) and further elaborated by Davis and Zangwill (see Zangwill, 1946) on which much research has been carried out. The material consists of four square boards each having nine holes containing pegs in three columns and three rows. Eight of the pegs are inserted loosely in the holes, the ninth is fixed. The patient's task is to find the position of the fixed peg by trial and error and to remember it on subsequent trials. A good deal of data is available concerning performance on this test by different clinical and age groups (Zangwill, 1946; Williams, 1968; Smith and Humphrey, 1973), indicating that it can be a useful tool for assessing nonverbal behavior, although it appears that verbalization can be, and often is, involved. Thus by saying to himself "top right-hand corner," for instance, the subject can retain spatial information as well as, if not better than, by perceptual means.

Acquisition of New Associations. The materials for testing the acquisition of new associations usually involve word pairs, the examiner reading over the list of word pairs first, then in the test giving the first member of the pair and asking the subject to provide the second, as in the association learning section of the Wechsler scale.

A novel and highly imaginative test of word learning was described by Walton and Black (see Walton, 1959). Because performance on this test is implicitly related to verbal IQ, no special allowance for this variable need be made. Walton and Black took the first nine words that the subject was unable to define correctly in a vocabulary test, told the subject the true definitions of the words, and then tested his ability to recall these definitions. The Walton and Black New Word Learning Test was modified by Williams (1968) for inclusion in a battery of memory tests. Inability to acquire "difficult" (that is, distantly associated) word pairs is usually found in organic amnesic states, and learning such pairs is less stable in the organic than in the nonorganic patient, but it is also found in functional disorders. The strategy used by subjects to acquire the definitions or associations appears to be an important factor, and hence performance on this type of task is closely related to IQ.

As in the learning of motor patterns, the qualitative as well as the quantitative aspects of performance are important diagnostically. Inability to correct faulty responses (perseveration) indicates organic conditions, whereas unevenness is characteristic of functional conditions.

Acquisition of Rote Learning. Tests to measure a subject's ability to reproduce sequences consisting of words (whether connected, as in a sentence, or unconnected, as in a word list), numbers (as in the conventional Digit Span test), tapped rhythms, or designs are commonly used. Zangwill was one of the first to point out that the immediate repetition span of patients with brain injury could remain unimpaired, although if asked to learn a sequence one or two items longer than this span, the patient might be unable to do so despite repeated trials (see also Drachman and Arbit, 1966). Zangwill claimed that the inability to give a perfect reproduction of Babcock's (1933) sentence "One thing a nation must have to become rich and great is a large secure supply of wood" after ten trials indicated cerebral pathology.

Visuoperceptual learning is harder to assess, but an attempt to do this was first described by Rey (1941) and elaborated by Osterreith (1944). A very complex but meaningless design is shown to the subject for ten seconds, after which he is asked to reproduce as much of it as he can. It is then exposed for another ten-second period, after which he can correct or elaborate his first attempt. The score is based on the total number of exposures required by the subject to make a perfect reproduction.

Immediate Reproduction

The ability to recall or reproduce a single experience immediately after perceiving it is associated with the development and maintenance of special skills (for example, language, comprehension, perception, and praxis). The amount or complexity of material that can be correctly reproduced—the memory span —is also closely related to general intellectual ability (IQ). The verbal memory span is usually *un*impaired in amnesic patients who show no other sign of intellectual deterioration, but the ability to reproduce visual material (in the form of designs) tends to be disturbed by any cerebral pathology. Benton (1955) and Graham and Kendall (1973) have published tests consisting of the reproduction of designs, in which a clear distinction has been shown between the performance of brain-damaged and non-brain-damaged patients. It is, however, general brain damage rather than specific memory impairment that is diagnosed by these tests. Tests of the ability to reproduce designs immediately after a single ten-second exposure are also included in the Wechsler Memory Scale and in Babcock's test for organic disorder, of which a shortened form suitable for general clinical use has been described by Brody (1948).

The reproduction of a short story or a news paragraph after a single hearing is another form of assessment commonly used in clinical practice (for example, the cowboy story). Paragraphs of news items are included in the Wechsler Memory Scale, but interpretation of the performance on these can again only be made in conjunction with all other subtests of the scale.

Retention (Delayed Recall or Recognition)

This is clinically the most important aspect of the memory function—indeed, it is what most people equate with memory—but it is also the hardest to assess. Recall or recognition after a time lapse depends largely on the length of the time lapse, but it also involves the presence or absence of cues, the degree of overlearning and/or length of exposure of the target, the number and nature of intervening rehearsals, and events occurring between exposure and test. In order to make an accurate assessment of retention, therefore, it is necessary to control (1) the nature of the target stimulus, (2) the number and length of stimulus exposures, (3) the length of time between exposure and test, (4) events occurring in this time interval, and (5) the cues present at the test. As already mentioned in the introduction to this chapter, the manner in which the test is carried out, whether by recall, reproduction, multiple choice, or single (yes/no) recognition, is also important. But how accurate does recall or recognition have to be to show evidence of retention? It is well-known that with the lapse of time, memories become distorted, displaced, and condensed (Bartlett, 1932). Hence, the quality of a subject's response should also be examined. The speed and certainty with which it is given are other characteristics that should be considered. In other words, standardization of the tests is essential, and this is just what is lacking in most tests in common clinical use.

A common form of measuring retention in the clinical

setting is to compare a patient's immediate reproduction of a story or design with that demanded some time later. The difference between the two scores (immediate and delayed) is taken as a measure of loss over time. So far no tests are available with published norms against which a subject's performance can be compared. A method commonly advocated in clinical use is the "name, address, and flower test" ("Will you try to remember the name, Joseph Spencer, of 15 Mills Drive, Dartford, and the flower bluebell?"), but this, like the cowboy story, is one for which standards for comparison are not available.

Luria (1971) suggests that a measure of retention can be based on the difference between a subject's ability to recall three numbers (or names) after ten seconds of unfilled time compared with his or her performance after ten seconds filled with either an unlike or a like task. Standards for this could quite easily be established but have not yet been published.

It is a familiar clinical finding that memory defects seldom come in a clear, all-or-none dichotomy. One particular aspect of memory that is important to recognize, especially for practical purposes and management, is the improvement in recall that may follow slight prompts. There is a great deal of difference between the subject who has been shown a picture and denies any recollection of it, even when confronted with the same picture again, and the one who may at first deny having seen a picture but will recognize it as soon as he hears any cue relating to its nature. In order to take this into account, Williams's (1974) test of delayed recall uses a scoring procedure based on both free and prompted recall of pictures after a ten-minute interval filled by fairly standard verbal tests.

The procedure consists of showing the subject a page containing nine pictures of common objects, which he is asked to name (so that dysphasic and perceptual difficulties will be recognized) and try to remember, since his memory for them will be tested later. He is then occupied in vocabulary or other verbal tests for eight to ten minutes, after which he is instructed to "tell me as many of the items which were shown to you as you can recall." If he asks about it, he is assured that the order in which he names them is not important.

For every item not recalled, he is then given a standard cue or prompt. If after this he still fails to recall some of the items, he is shown a sheet of pictures containing the original nine pictures and nine others and is asked to point to all the ones he saw before. Three parallel sets of material are available, so that repeated testing can be carried out without the practice effects being too pronounced.

The total raw scores (consisting of two points for each item not recalled immediately, three additional points for each item not recalled after its prompt, and four additional points for each one not recognized) vary not only with the presence but also with the locale of cerebral pathology (see Figure 1). Thus lesions involving the cerebral cortex cause a far greater disturbance than subcortical ones involving the basal ganglia and cerebellum. The performances of normal people and of psychi-

Figure 1. Sample Score Sheet for Delayed Recall Test.

Object	Prompt	Unaided (2 points each)	Recall Prompt (3 points each)	Recognition (4 points each)
Apple	A common fruit	✓		
Axe	You use it when you want some wood for the fire	✓		
Dressing table	You find it in ladies' bedrooms	✗	✓	
Violin	You would see it at a concert	✓		
Fish	Cats like eating it	✗	✓	
Jug	You'd look for it if you were thirsty	✓		
Squirrel	It lives in woods	✓		
Spoon	You see it on a well-laid table	✗	✗	✗
Spectacles	We see through them	✓		
		3 × 2 = 6	1 × 3 = 3	1 × 4 = 4

Total Raw Score = 13

atric patients are very similar and show little variation between the ages of twenty and sixty (see Figure 2; Williams, 1974).

Figure 2. Performance by Normal and Psychiatric People on Williams's Test of Delayed Recall.

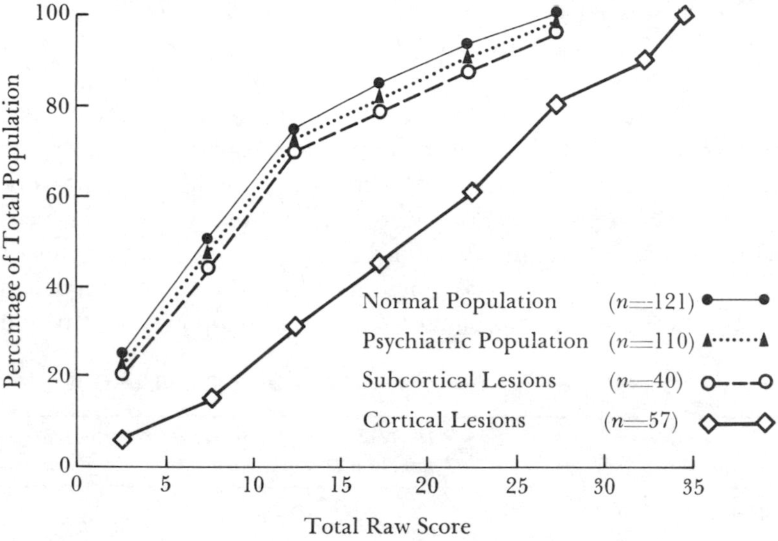

This test has been used in a number of research projects. One of its main values is that patients do not find it tiring or distressing.

Subjective Impairments (Loss of the Sense of Familiarity)

Although the gross changes in memory function obvious to an outsider can be measured by many of the techniques described in the main sections of this paper, there remain subtle alterations of the memory function that are frequently complained about but are extremely difficult to demonstrate objectively. These characteristically occur as side effects of otherwise valuable forms of treatment (such as electroconvulsive therapy), or of anesthesia, and can nullify the beneficial effects of treatment.

Since most attempts to quantify or measure these disturbances are unsuccessful, there is a tendency to write them off as superficial or to attribute them to hysterical elaborations, but the fact remains that they are seen as serious handicaps by the sufferers, and their occurrence is so common as to indicate that they constitute a problem that should be investigated further.

As long as the measurement of memory concentrates on changes in behavior, as it tends to at the moment, rather than on the subjective sense of familiarity, these problems will probably not be solved; but there is encouraging evidence of a swing away from the purely behavioral slant of modern experimental psychology back to a consideration of sensation. Thus the sense of familiarity associated with repeated events is now considered a subject worthy of experimental investigation (Gaffan, 1974; Owen and Williams, in press), and the application to the clinical field of some of the laboratory techniques by which familiarity is studied gives promise for the future.

Assessment of Memory in Children

In children memory is so intimately concerned with the development of skills that it is usually measured in terms of mental age on motor, speech, or perceptual tests, and often separation of memory from IQ is impossible. The immediate memory span and the ability to acquire new skills increases with age in childhood, so that mental age can be assessed by the amount and complexity of material a child can reproduce immediately after a single hearing. Retention of visual and non-visual skills also increases with age; in contrast, the ability to localize and recognize discrete visual stimuli possibly reaches its optimum at the ages of eleven to fourteen, and begins to deteriorate at the same time that the reproduction of discrete experiences tends to be confused by "sets" and expectancies derived from past experience.

Therefore, it is particularly in its effect on the recollection of discrete visual stimuli that amnesia in childhood can best be recognized. The responses of children to the test situation are, however, somewhat different from those of adults. Children, having fewer past experiences and established habits or skills to fall back on, are less inclined to confabulate when pressed for recall than adults. They tend instead to remain mute. If given a prompt or a cue, children respond in a less related way than adults, and if forced to make a response they may repeat what they have just done or heard instead of falling back on personal idiosyncrasies.

Practical Applications of Memory Assessment

Four of the most important practical reasons for assessing memory have already been mentioned briefly at the beginning of the chapter. The methods most suitable for fulfilling two of these functions will now be discussed.

Diagnosis

Diagnosis in medicine carries many implications for treatment, management, and prognosis; any methods leading to increased accuracy are therefore welcomed. The elicitation of specific memory impairments is an especially valuable diagnostic aid in patients of late middle age, who may show behavior changes after a variety of illnesses, such as depression, cortical atrophy, space-occupying cerebral lesions, toxic states, heart disease, and respiratory failure. The majority of these can be diagnosed more accurately by physical than by mental examination, but the psychological picture is also valuable.

Many critical points and situations in which they become evident have been mentioned. Of special interest is a patient's behavior on tests of retention, especially those involving cuing (see Table 1). Depression is characterized by retardation but little loss of retention. Cortical atrophy is characterized by a strong tendency for the subject to respond to the cue itself and to treat this as the target, rather than using it as a signpost for a particular search field. The patient suffering from a cerebral vascular accident is likely to have specific losses of skills (cerebral, visual, or motor) depending on the location of the vessels af-

Table 1. Main Characteristics of Different Diagnostic Groups in Different Memory Situations.

Diagnostic Group	Memory Situation				
	Established Skills	Immediate Reproduction	Retention of Incidental Events	Cued Recall	Learning
General cerebral deterioration	Patchy losses	Normal	Variable, but usually poor	Response to cue as if it is a new stimulus—no memory search	Perseveration of faulty response
General physical illness	Normal	Usually poor	Depends on attention and arousal at time of experience	Normal	Poor due to lack of effort
Organic amnesic (Korsakov) state	Normal	Normal	Very poor	Claim familiarity with response first aroused	Much perseveration, but motor skills can be retained
Depression	Normal	Normal	Normal	Normal	Poor due to unwillingness to make effort
Anxiety	Normal	Tend to be poor and uneven	Normal	Normal	Uneven, often fluctuating performance

fected, while the patient suffering from concussional head injuries (often caused by falls and possibly complicated by intracranial hematoma) may well show a transient RA and/or the retention defect of the organic amnesic syndrome. This latter is characterized by a good immediate memory span but very poor retention, and a close relationship between the cues or prompts provided and the sense of familiarity associated with the memories evoked. (Those memories most readily evoked by the cue, whether actually experienced at the time under consideration or in a previous context, will be accepted as the target items).

In general physical illness, a retention defect is usually accompanied by general intellectual impoverishment that may be seen on a poor immediate memory span (see Table 1).

Practical Management

How can one deal with or compensate for loss of memory function? Cases in which this is the sole behavior abnormality are extremely rare, even in the classic chronic alcoholic (perhaps because of the improved nutritional state of the population), but when they do occur they present considerable problems to both the sufferer and his or her relatives. Such patients are usually comparatively young and may have many years of life before them. Moreover, in recent years their dwindling number has been made up by patients recovering from encephalitic illness that may leave the sufferers with a permanent problem of retention similar to that originally described by Wernicke and by Korsakov.

When vitamins and other forms of chemotherapy have failed to produce improvement, attempts to retrain the subjects either by practice or by the development of new strategies have been attempted but without great success. Based on the suggestion (which will be discussed in the next section) that in these conditions the main defect is in the method of encoding or assimilating the material to be remembered, attempts have been described in which patients have been actively encouraged to form new schemata. The results have not been spectacularly successful. The amnesic subject remains very dependent on the total situation at the moment of recall and tends to recall only what this situation arouses. An alternative method of management, in which a subject's environment is altered to accommodate for his disability (instead of vice versa) might be more profitable. The success of such treatment would, however, depend on the environmental manipulations being individually tailored to the subject's deficiencies, which in turn depends on a fairly detailed assessment of the patient's main deficits and the cues to which he responds best.

In the majority of subjects showing memory impairment, amnesia is just one aspect of deranged behavior among many abnormalities and can only be treated as part of the total picture. There is one condition, however, in which memory change can not only be anticipated but can be quite satisfactorily compensated for if new strategies are developed in advance to cope with it. This is the change that occurs with aging in all living beings and that many individuals anticipate and train themselves to overcome by the use of diaries, notebooks, memo pads, and so on. The important point is to establish reliable habits of storage while it is still comparatively easy, for once these habits are established they can be used with a minimum of residual function. Knowing where to look for information (both physically and mentally) constitutes half the job of finding it. Indeed, usually the people who complain of poor memory as they grow older are the ones whose life habits have always lacked organization.

The Nature of Memory

The mechanism whereby the aftereffects of experiences are retained and affect alterations of behavior are still largely unknown. The construction of mechanical models able to store information and use it in relevant situations is not difficult, but whether the human race carries out the functions of memory in the same manner (and indeed whether all persons remember by the same method) is difficult to establish. There seems little doubt that specific areas of the brain known as the limbic system (see Figure 3) must be intact for all normal memory func-

Figure 3. Limbic System of the Brain.

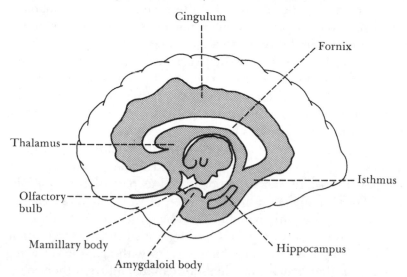

tions to be carried out, but exactly what aspect of memory is impaired by disruption of these areas is still unknown.

As has already been mentioned in the section on learning, patients with classical organic amnesia (that is, those with destruction in some areas within the limbic system) are still able to profit from repeated experience and to show some development of what might be called motor skills, as well as the more mechanical responses to repeated stimulation such as conditioning and habituation. Possibly this sort of behavior (which is also evident in invertebrate animals) is mediated by different systems than the conscious awareness of previous experience or the sense of familiarity, which appears to be the specific impairment in amnesia.

Some of the hypotheses that account for this lack of familiarity have been considered recently by Baddeley (1975) and Piercy (1977). These hypotheses can be divided into three groups, depending on whether they attribute lack of familiarity to disorders of storage, retrieval, or encoding.

Storage-Deficit Hypotheses

The consolidation hypothesis (Milner, 1968) was based on the observation that patients with lesions affecting the limbic system (in Milner's patient it affected the bilateral ablation of the hippocampus) were able to repeat items immediately after hearing them but not after short time lapses. The suggestion arose that there might be two separate memory systems, short term and long term, and that material which would normally be transferred automatically from the former to the latter for "storage," was not transferred in the amnesic subject. The idea that a certain time period was necessary for this consolidation to occur was also used to explain RA (McGeogh, 1970). The finding that animals treated with protein-synthesis inhibitors appeared unable to "learn" provided physiological support for the theory (Deutsch, 1971).

The theory came under criticism when it was realized that although retrieval of previous experiences might be difficult for the amnesic, partial reconstructions of the original situation (or target) in the form of prompts often elicited a fair degree of recall, indicating the presence of some long-term memory.

Studying more closely the nature of the prompts eliciting recall in amnesics, and particularly those eliciting false recognition (that is, a sense of familiarity connected with previously unpresented items), Owen and Williams (in press) have recently elaborated a hypothesis of consolidation based on the idea of a "threshold of arousal" in the storage system If this is low, only those items most easily aroused by the recall situation (for example, the cues or prompts presented) would reach conscious awareness, or the "output phase," and would be accepted as the targets.

Another elaboration of consolidation envisages normal memories being integrated into cognitive maps—a process which amnesic subjects may be unable to do. O'Keefe and Nadel (see Baddeley, 1975) have argued from evidence based on the behavior of rats with hippocampal lesions that this rather than failure of storage is responsible for amnesic behavior.

Retrieval-Failure Hypotheses

According to some theorists, memory failure in amnesics is due not to lack of storage but to lack of retrieval; the subjects have the information but cannot reach it. Evidence for this is based on two well-known observations: Subjects often behave as if they remember past experiences, even though they deny them; and prompts and cues can elicit a great deal of information that subjects thought they had forgotten.

Retrieval failure can be explained on the basis of a raised-threshold hypothesis, but an alternative explanation has been put forward by Warrington and Weiskrantz (1971), generally known as the interference hypothesis. To explain not only the presence of prompted recall in amnesics but also the familiar observation of intrusions, in addition to retroactive interference, it was argued that traces of past experiences were not readily recalled because of competition from other experiences, and that the effectiveness of prompts was due to elimination of response competition and narrowing of the search field. In dynamic terms, this hypothesis is the exact opposite of the consolidation, or threshold-reduction, hypothesis: It envisages over-arousal of all responses rather than underarousal.

Encoding-Failure Hypotheses

It is often suggested that past experiences cannot be retrieved by amnesic subjects mainly because these experiences have not been assimilated (encoded) normally. Evidence for this is largely based on two things: the difference between the ability to recall (or recognize) verbal experiences and the ability to recall visual (nonverbal) and/or motor (haptic) or olfactory experiences, and the response to semantic category cues. This hypothesis has been advocated most forcibly by Butters and Cermak (1975).

The evidence for a significant difference between amnesic subjects' ability to remember verbal as opposed to pictorial material is conflicting. Butters and others (1973) claim that verbal material is as well remembered as visual, but some observers have found the opposite. Owen and Williams (in press) found that amnesics, like most nonaphasic subjects (normal or brain damaged), tend to remember stimuli by their names rather than by their visual appearances, indicating the use of verbalization in encoding and rehearsal when possible.

There seems to be no doubt that amnesics are less efficient than control subjects in responding to a category cue for the recall of an object name in that category, but Owen and Williams (in press) have shown that, in general, the response of amnesics to cues and prompts of all types is more superficial than that of nonamnesic subjects. Amnesics show a greatly increased tendency to treat as familiar the response first aroused by a cue, instead of holding this in store and comparing it with other possible responses. To paraphrase Talland (1965), search is prematurely closed. This can be explained as well by a storage hypothesis as by a hypothesis of encoding or retrieval failure.

Is it necessary to choose between these theories or may each be right in certain situations? For example, in the case of RA, especially that seen in the early stages following concussional head injury, retrieval seems to be the major deficit; for as this improves, memories are regained. In the case of the learning deficits of the senile, however, an encoding deficit seems to be present, as evidenced by perceptual defects.

In conclusion, it has been pointed out by Piercy (1977) that since the nature of normal forgetting is still clothed in ignorance, it is not surprising that the cause of amnesia is subject to controversy. However, further studies of the latter might well improve the former, and when we know more about the causes of forgetting, we may be a little nearer to understanding the mechanism of remembering. In particular, our division of memory into three phases—encoding, storage, and retrieval (or as they used to be called, assimilation, retention, and recall)—may be artificial. All three phases are closely interdependent, and it may turn out that there are as many different mechanisms for achieving the same end in remembering as there are in flying, swimming, breathing, and communicating.

Summary and Conclusion

The two points to be stressed here are (1) that *memory* is a word used loosely to cover a multiple of acts and feelings, of which the only common attribute is that they are influenced by previous individual experiences, and (2) that in the clinical field, different illnesses can affect different aspects of this phenomenon.

One of the values of clinical study is that it teaches us much about the mechanisms of normal healthy behavior. Another, of course, is that knowledge can sometimes enable the failures caused by sickness to be remedied or overcome. If memory failings are to be remedied, however, they must be carefully delineated in each case. This measurement can often provide an invaluable aid to diagnosis, and by establishing the conditions that aid recall, recognition, and reproduction, steps can sometimes be taken to minimize their inconvenience.

Clinically caused disorders of memory can be accurately measured by means of psychological tests, but care must be taken when using these tests: It is important (1) to use them only on the population for which they have been standardized, (2) to always score them both qualitatively and quantitatively, and (3) never to generalize further than the tests themselves warrant. For example, if a verbal learning deficit has been established, this does not imply a deficit in all other aspects of retention or reproduction.

One of the aspects of memory most commonly affected by cerebral dysfunction (especially if this involves either large areas of the cerebral cortex or small areas of that special circuit, the limbic system) is an alteration in the sense of familiarity normally associated with events when they are repeated. Thus in amnesic patients, events that have occurred recently may not seem to have done so, while those that have not occurred for many years may seem quite recent. As yet there are no standardized tests for measuring this sense of familiarity, and experimental work in the field has only begun recently; but the factors on which a sense of familiarity depend may become clearer as study proceeds.

References

Babcock, H. *The Examination for Mental Deterioration.* Chicago: Stoelting, 1933.

Baddeley, A. D. "Theories of Amnesia." In A. Kennedy and A. Weekes (Eds.), *Studies in Long-Term Memory.* New York: Wiley, 1975.

Baddeley, A. D. *The Psychology of Memory.* New York: Harper & Row, Open University Set Books, 1976.

Baddeley, A. D. and Warrington, E. K. "Memory Coding and Amnesia." *Neuropsychologia,* 1973, *11,* 159.

Bartlett, F. C. *Remembering.* London: Cambridge University Press, 1932.

Benton, A. L. *The Revised Visual Retention Test.* New York: Psychological Corporation, 1955.

Brierley, J. B. "The Neuropathology of Amnesic States." In C. W. M. Whitty and O. L. Zangwill (Eds.), *Amnesia.* (2nd ed.) Woburn, Mass.: Butterworths, 1977.

Brion, S. "Korsakoff's Syndrome." In G. A. Talland and N. C. Waugh (Eds.), *The Pathology of Memory.* New York: Academic Press, 1969.

Brody, M. B. "A Test for the Measurement of Dementia." *Journal of Abnormal and Social Psychology,* 1948, *43,* 102.

Brooks, D. N. and Baddeley, A. D. "What Can Amnesic Patients Learn?" *Neuropsychologia,* 1975, *14,* 111-122.

Butters, N., and Cermak, L. S. "The Memory Disorders of Alcoholic Patients with the Korsakoff Syndrome." *Annals of the New York Academy of Sciences,* 1975, *233,* 61-75.

Butters, N., Levil, R., Cermak, L. S., and Goodglass, H. "Memory Deficits in Alcoholic Korsakov Patients." *Neuropsychologia,* 1973, *11,* 291.

Cermak, L. S. "Imagery in Korsakov Patients." *Cortex,* 1975, *2,* 163.

Cermak, L. S., Butters, N., and Gerrain, J. "Verbal Encoding Ability in Korsakov Patients." *Neuropsychologia,* 1973, *11,* 85.

Cermak, L. S., Butters, N., and Goodglass, H. "The Extent of

Memory Loss in Korsakov Patients." *Neuropsychologia,* 1971, *9,* 307-315.

Christensen, A.-L. *Luria's Neuropsychological Investigation.* Copenhagen: Munksgaard, 1974.

Dawson, R. G., and McGaugh, J. L. "Drug Facilitation of Learning and Memory." In J. R. Deutsch (Ed.), *The Physiological Basis of Memory.* New York: Academic Press, 1973.

Deutsch, J. A. "The Cholinergic Synapse and the Site of Memory." *Science,* 1971, *174,* 788-794.

Drachman, D. A. and Arbit, J. "Memory and the Hippocampal Complex." *Archives of Neurology,* 1966, *15,* 52-61.

Ekstrand, B. R. "To Sleep, Perchance to Dream." In C. P. Duncan, L. Sechrist, and A. W. Helton (Eds.), *Human Memory.* New York: Appleton-Century-Crofts, 1972.

Farnsworth, P. R. "Examination in Familiar and Unfamiliar Surroundings." *Journal of Social Psychology,* 1934, *5,* 128-129.

Gaffan, D. "Fornix Transection and Memory." *Journal of Comparative and Physiological Psychology,* 1974, *86,* 1100.

Godden, D. R. and Baddeley, A. D. "Content Dependent Memory in Two Natural Environments." *British Journal of Psychology,* 1975, *66,* 325-331.

Graham, F. K. and Kendall, B. G. "Memory for Designs Test." *Perceptual and Motor Skills.* Monograph Supplement 2. Missoula, Mont.: Psychological Test Specialists, 1973, p. vii.

Hunt, H. F. "A Practical Clinical Test for Organic Brain Damage." *Journal of Applied Psychology,* 1943, *27,* 375-386.

Huppert, F. A., and Piercy, M. F. "Recognition Memory in Amnesia Patients." *Cortex,* 1976, *12,* 3-20.

Idzikowski, C. J. "Memory and Sleep." Paper read at the Experimental Psychology Society, Bedford College, London, January 1977.

Jones, B. P., Moskowitz, H. R., and Butters, N. "Olfactory Discrimination in Alcoholic Korsakov Patients." *Neuropsychologia,* 1975, *13,* 173.

Kennedy, A. and Wilkes, A. *Studies in Long Term Memory.* New York: Wiley, 1975.

Luria, A. R. *The Mind of a Mnemonist.* London: Jonathan Cape, 1969.

Luria, A. R. "Memory Disturbances in Local Brain Lesions." *Neuropsychologia,* 1971, *9,* 367-378.

McCurdy, J. T. *Common Principles in Psychology and Physiology.* London: Cambridge University Press, 1926.

McGeogh, J. L. "Memory Storage Processes." In K. H. Pribram and D. E. Broadbent (Eds.), *Biology of Memory.* New York: Academic Press, 1970.

McGeogh, J. L. "ECS Effects on Learning and Memory in Animals." In M. Fink (Ed.), *The Psychobiology of E.C.T.* New York: Wiley, 1974.

Marslen-Wilson, W. D. and Teuber, H.-L. "Memory for Remote Events in Anterograde Amnesia: Recognition of Public Figures from Newsphotographs." *Neuropsychologia,* 1975, *13,* 347.

Milner, B. "Preface: Material Specific and Generalized Memory Loss." *Neuropsychologia,* 1968, *6,* 175-179.

O'Connor, N. and Hermalin, B. *Speech and Thought in Severe Subnormality.* Oxford, England: Pergamon Press, 1963.

Osterreith, P. "Le test de copie d'une figures complexe." *Archives de Psychologie,* 1944, *30,* 206.

Owen, G. M. and Williams, M. In press.

Paivio, A. and Csapo, K. "Picture Superiority in Free Recall." *Cognitive Psychology,* 1973, *5,* 176.

Piercy, M. In C. W. M. Whitty and O. L. Zangwill (Eds.), *Amnesia.* (2nd ed.) Woburn Mass.: Butterworths, 1977.

Pribram, K. H. and Broadbent, D. E. *Biology of Memory.* New York: Academic Press, 1970.

Rey, A. "L'examin psychologique dans les cas d'encephal pathie traumatique." *Archives de Psychologie. Suisse romande.* 1941, *28,* 215.

Ribot, T. *Diseases of Memory.* London: Routledge & Kegan Paul, 1885.

Russell, W. R. *Brain, Memory and Learning.* Oxford, England: Clarendon Press, 1959.

Sanders, H. I. and Warrington, E. K. "Memory for Remote Events in Amnesic Patients." *Brain,* 1971, *94,* 661.

Seltzer, B. and Benson, D. F. "Temporal Patterns of Retrograde Amnesia in Korsakov Disease." *Neuropsychologia,* 1974, *14,* 527.

Smith, E. and Humphrey, M. "Non-verbal Learning after Right and Left Cerebral Hemisphere Lesions." Paper presented at the annual winter conference of the British Psychological Society, London, January 1973.

Stones, M. "Sleep and the Storage and Retrieval Processes in Humans." Unpublished doctoral dissertation, University of Sheffield, England, 1974.

Talland, G. *Deranged Memory.* New York: Academic Press, 1965.

Tulving, E. and Donaldson, W. *Organization of Memory.* New York: Academic Press, 1972.

Walton, D. "The Modified Word-Learning Test." *British Journal of Medical Psychology,* 1959, *32,* 213.

Warrington, E. K. "Deficient Recognition in Organic Amnesia Patients." *Cortex,* 1971, *3,* 289.

Warrington, E. K. and Baddeley, A. D. "Amnesia and Memory for Visual Location." *Neuropsychologia,* 1974, *12,* 257.

Warrington, E. K. and Sanders, H. "The Fate of Old Memories." *Quarterly Journal of Experimental Psychology,* 1971, *23.*

Warrington, E. K. and Weiskrantz, L. "Organisational Aspects of Amnesic Patients." *Neuropsychologia,* 1971, *9,* 67.

Wechsler, D. "A Standardised Memory Scale for Clinical Use." *Journal of Psychology,* 1945, *19,* 87.

Weiskrantz, L. and Warrington, E. K. "Learning and Retention in Amnesic Patients Using Partial Information." *Psychonomic Science,* 1970, *20,* 210.

Wells, F. L. and Martin, H. A. A. "A Method of Memory Examination." *American Journal of Psychiatry,* 1923, *3,* 243.

Williams, M. "The Effect of Progressive Prompting on Memory After Head Injuries." *Journal of Neurology, Neurosurgery, and Psychiatry,* 1953, *16,* 14.

Williams, M. "Memory Defects Associated with Cerebral Lesions." Doctoral dissertation, Oxford University, 1954.

Williams, M. "The Measurement of Memory in Clinical Practice." *British Journal of Sociological and Clinical Psychology,* 1968, *7,* 19-34.

Williams, M. "Traumatic Retrograde Amnesia and Normal For-
    getting." In G. A. Talland and N. C. Waugh (Eds.), *The
    Pathology of Memory*. New York: Academic Press, 1969.
Williams, M. "Errors in Picture Recognition after ECT." *Neuro-
    psychologia*, 1973, *11*, 429.
Williams, M. "A Test for the Measurement of Delayed Recall."
    Unpublished manuscript, 1974. Available privately from
    the author c/o Department of Clinical Psychology, 2
    Bene't Place, Cambridge CB2 1 EL, England.
Williams, M. and Smith, H. V. "Memory Defects in Tuberculous
    Meningitis." *Journal of Neurology, Neurosurgery, and
    Psychiatry*, 1954, *17*, 173.
Zangwill, O. L. "Clinical Tests of Memory Impairment." *Pro-
    ceedings of the Royal Society of Medicine*, 1943, *36*,
    576.
Zangwill, O. L. "Clinical Applications of the Rey-Davis Per-
    formance Test." *Journal of Mental Science*, 1946, *92*, 19.
Zangwill, O. L. "The Grünthal-Störrung Case." *British Journal
    of Psychiatry*, 1967, *113*, 113-128.

XI

Assessment of Cognitive Style

KENNETH M. GOLDSTEIN, SHELDON BLACKMAN

Cognitive psychology continues to increase in importance (Mahoney, 1977; McKeachie, 1976). One manifestation of this trend is the attention being paid to the area of cognitive style, as evidenced in recent publications (Kogan, 1976; Landfield, 1977; Messick and associates, 1976). In this chapter we will first present a brief overview of various approaches to the study of cognitive style. The main portion of the chapter will present a more detailed review of five approaches that vary in their emphasis on the content of thought.

Nature and Definition of Cognitive Style

Cognitive style is a hypothetical construct that is posited to explain the mediation between stimuli and responses. The term *cognitive style* refers to how individuals conceptually organize the environment. Representative of this use of the term is Harvey's (1963) view that cognitive style refers to the way an individual filters and processes stimuli so that the environment takes on psychological meaning. Bieri (1971) maintains that individuals learn "strategies, programs, or other transformation operations" in order to translate "objective" stimuli into meaningful dimensions. Bieri terms these strategies *cognitive structures*. Messick and associates (1976) similarly define cognitive style in terms of consistencies in "organizing and processing information." The point of view that cognitive structures serve as mediators between environmental input and the organism's output is also evident in the writing of Zajonc (1968). Zajonc adds the idea that cognitive structures organize output as well as input.

In contrast, Coop and Sigel (1971) maintain that cognitive style is a term generally used "to denote consistencies in individual modes of functioning in a variety of behavioral situations." This definition equates cognitive style with behavior rather than with mediating processes. The definition advanced by Coop and Sigel is, as they point out, similar to Allport's (1937) use of the term *style* to describe consistencies in behavior.

While the contruct of cognitive style is relatively new, it has its roots in earlier work. Coop and Sigel (1971) noted the similarity of the construct of cognitive style to the Gestalt concept of silent organization, a term used to describe processes that are not tied to specific content but are cognitive structures that guide behavior (Scheerer, 1954).

The common thread in all research on cognitive style is a concern with the structure of thinking rather than its content (for example, Suedfeld, 1971). Structure refers to how thinking is organized; content refers to what information is available. In this chapter we will use *cognitive style* as a generic term to refer to the ways in which thought is structured. Consistencies in behavior are viewed as the expression of this structure.

Over the years, many approaches to the study of cognitive style have been made. Messick (1970) originally delineated nine approaches. The first four are products of the work of Gardner, Klein, and their colleagues (for example, Gardner, Holzman, Klein, Linton, and Spence, 1959): scanning, leveling-sharpening, constricted-flexible control, and tolerance for incongruous or unrealistic experience. A fifth approach investigated by these researchers, field articulation, was originated by Witkin and his coworkers (for example, Witkin, Lewis, Hertzman, Machover, Meissner, and Wapner, 1954), who used the term *field-dependence-independence*. A sixth approach noted by Messick is that of cognitive complexity, represented by the work of Bieri, Atkins, Briar, Leaman, Miller, and Tripodi (1966) and Harvey, Hunt, and Schroder (1961). The final three approaches are reflection-impulsivity (Kagan, Rosman, Day, Albert, and Phillips, 1964), styles of categorization (Pettigrew, 1958), and styles of conceptualization (Kagan, Moss, and Sigel, 1963). More recently, Messick and associates (1976) modified the previous categories, added new ones, and listed nineteen approaches to the study of cognitive style. This reflects increasing research interest in cognitive style, as well as Messick's attempt to organize and integrate work in widely differing areas.

In his book *Cognitive Styles in Infancy and Early Childhood,* Kogan (1976) classifies cognitive styles in three ways. Type I relates to an ability to perform, measured against some standard. For example, in the measurement of field dependence, the field-independent person is superior in locating figures embedded in a surrounding context. A person is judged field-independent to the extent that he makes correct responses. Type II refers to approaches to cognitive style in which the investigator places greater value on one of the categories. For example, in the work of Kelly (1955) and Bieri and others (1966), the cognitively complex person is seen to have an advantage in processing information about his environment. Type III measures of cognitive style do not relate to ability, nor does the investigator attribute superiority to any particular pole or category. Kogan considers Pettigrew's (1958) category-width approach to be an example of Type III.

Approaches to the Study of Cognitive Style

In this section we briefly consider a number of approaches to cognitive style that will not be reviewed in detail in this chapter. The approaches to be surveyed here are cognitive controls, category width, conceptual styles, and reflection-impulsivity.

Cognitive Controls. In an early paper, Klein (1954) introduced the term *cognitive control,* one that has been used interchangeably with the terms *cognitive style* and *cognitive attitude.* According to Klein, cognitive controls are hypothetical constructs that channel the expression of need in socially acceptable ways according to the requirements of the situation. Gardner (1962) provided a historical overview of some of the terminology used. In the initial work, Klein and his associates used the term *perceptual attitudes.* Later the terms *cognitive attitudes* and *cognitive system principles* were used. Because a delaying, controlling function was involved in these processes, the terms *cognitive controls* and *cognitive control principles* were adopted.

Gardner, Jackson, and Messick (1960) distinguished cognitive controls from cognitive style. According to these authors, the former term refers to the specific dimensions investigated in the Perception Project at the Menninger Foundation (Gardner, 1962). These dimensions include leveling-sharpening, scanning, field articulation, conceptual differentiation, and constricted-flexible control. Cognitive style is conceived of as the pattern or organization of these dimensions within an individual. However, as Kagan and Kogan (1970) have noted, this distinction between cognitive control and cognitive style has not been strictly maintained by researchers in the area of cognitive controls.

A number of dimensions of cognitive control have been explored:

1. Tolerance for Unrealistic Experiences. Klein and Schlesinger (1951) found that individuals who tended to give literal, concrete, and unelaborated responses to Rorschach inkblot stimuli also tended to have difficulty perceiving movement in the phi phenomenon. This behavior was termed *intolerance for instability.* In later research, Klein, Gardner, and Schlesinger (1962) posited that this behavior was an aspect of broader cognitive control, a dimension that they labeled *intolerance for unrealistic experiences.* They (1962, p. 41) defined this dimension as "the subject's readiness to accept and report experiences at variance with conventional reality or with what they [sic]

knew to be true." The perception of movement on the phi phenomenon is used as the measure of tolerance for unrealistic
experiences (Segal and Barr, 1969).

2. Conceptual Differentiation. The cognitive control dimension of conceptual differentiation, first termed *equivalence
range,* was developed by Gardner (1953, p. 229) who hypothesized that individuals would be consistent in "what they will
accept as similar or identical in a variety of adaptive tasks." In a
later paper, Gardner and others (1960, p. 122) referred to
equivalence range as "the degree of differentiation in individuals' experiencing of similarity and difference." In their monograph, Gardner and Schoen (1962) extended the concept of
equivalence range to that of *conceptual differentiation,* the
term that is in current usage (Gardner and Moriarty, 1968). An
individual who is high in conceptual differentiation is one who
has a narrow equivalence range; in a free-sorting task, such an
individual utilizes many categories.

To measure equivalence range, Gardner (1953) used an
Object Sorting Test, requiring the subject to sort seventy-three
objects into as many categories as the subject felt the objects
warranted. A fifty-item form of the Object Sorting Test was developed by Clayton and Jackson (1961). A second instrument
for assessing equivalence range is the Size Constancy Test,
which requires the subject to match a stimulus with standards
on the basis of retinal image size. Good performance requires
that the subject retain a set developed in previous training for
distinguishing between real and apparent size (Gardner and
others, 1960).

3. Constricted-Flexible Control. The first report of the
constricted-flexible dimension of cognitive control is that by
Smith and Klein (1953). The early work leading to the study of
this dimension was reported by Klein (1954). The dimension
allows an ordering of individuals in terms of their susceptibility
to distraction.

The major instrument for the assessment of constricted-
flexible control is the Color-Word Test (Gardner and others,
1960), which is Thurstone's (1944) modification of a test developed by Stroop (1935). The task presents the subject with

four color names—*red, green, blue,* and *yellow*—each of which is printed many times. The color of the ink with which these names are printed may be red, green, blue, or yellow. For example, the word *red* may be printed with yellow ink. The subject's task is to name the color of the ink with which the word was printed. In effect, the subject must disregard one of the two conflicting cues. The flexible individual is one who is able to disregard the conflicting cue and perform the task quickly and accurately.

Broverman (1960a, 1960b) derived indices from the Stroop test to measure two dimensions of cognitive style: perceptual-motor versus conceptual dominance, and automatization. Golden (1975a) developed a group-administered version of the Stroop test that relates well with an individually administered version. Santostefano and Paley (1964) reported a measure of constricted-flexible control, the Fruit-Distraction Test, that is suitable for use with children. Jensen (1965) has considered some of the psychometric properties of the Stroop test, finding satisfactory reliability for the more common indices. Jensen and Rohwer (1966) have presented a comprehensive review of the literature on the Stroop Color-Word Test, while Dyer (1973) has presented a review of more recent research.

4. Leveling-Sharpening. Another dimension of cognitive control is leveling-sharpening, which was defined by Gardner and others (1960, p. 122) as "the characteristic degree to which current percepts and relevant memory traces interact or assimilate in the course of registration of the current percepts and memories." That is, in the course of the perception of events there is an interaction between events already perceived and stored in memory, and the new event that is being perceived. This interaction is termed *assimilation,* a coming together of memory traces and the new perception. Holzman and Klein (1954) noted that leveling results in the maximum simplification of the cognitive field; sharpening results in maximum complexity and differentiation. Holzman and Klein were interested in individual consistency in assimilation (Gardner and Moriarty, 1968). They termed individuals who showed great assimilation *levelers*; those who did not, *sharpeners.*

The principal measure of leveling-sharpening is the Schematizing Test, which is based on a procedure developed by Hollingworth (1913). Subjects are placed in a dark room following a period of dark adaptation and are required to judge the size of a series of squares of light of increasing size. Subjects tend to underestimate the size of the squares as new squares of light of increasing size are added. The major reason for errors on the test is "assimilation among percepts of new squares and the trace aggregate of smaller squares seen earlier" (Gardner and others, 1960, p. 72). Levelers are defined as those who perform poorly on this task by making large underestimates. Several scores have been derived to measure performance on this test, with Pritchard (1975) recommending the use of a ranking-accuracy score rather than a lag score.

Santostefano (1964) developed three instruments, all involving the use of a memory drum, for the measurement of leveling-sharpening in children. He also developed another instrument, the House Test (Santostefano, Rutledge, and Randall, 1965), for use with children.

5. Scanning. Scanning is defined in terms of the extent to which an individual checks the judgments that he makes (Gardner and Moriarty, 1968). The dimension of scanning is assessed with two Size Estimation Tests. In one, the subject is presented with three standard disks and is instructed to match a projected circle of light to each of the standards. In the second, a variable light circle is adjusted to each of two projected discs. To the extent that the subject is continually comparing the stimulus with the standard, he is scanning, and his performance should be better (Gardner and others, 1960). Several highly intercorrelated scores (Gardner and Long, 1962a, 1962b) may be derived as measures of scanning from these tests. Santostefano and Paley (1964) developed a measure of scanning for use with children, the Circles Test, which is a size estimation task in somewhat different format.

6. Contrast Reactivity. In a paper on cognitive control and differentiation, Gardner, Lohrenz, and Schoen (1968) introduced the cognitive control dimension of contrast reactivity. They define this control as "concerning reactivity to con-

trast." This dimension is measured with the Lines Contrast Test, in which the subject estimates the lengths of pairs of lines; the ratio of these estimates is used as an index of contrast reactivity. Gardner (1973) presented data on the reliability of the measure and suggested that the test be lengthened.

7. Field Articulation. One of the dimensions of cognitive control that is identical with one of the areas that we will review in detail is that of field articulation. Gardner and Long (1960a) based their construct on Witkin's work on field dependence (Witkin and others, 1954). Gardner and Long argued that field articulation is a more general concept, since the field-independent individual was evidencing selectivity of attention and could attend to the embedding context if it contained relevant cues. In another paper, Gardner and others (1960, p. 121) referred to field articulation in terms of "selective attention to relevant versus compelling irrelevant stimuli." The operational distinction between the two dimensions is unclear, a fact that troubles Gardner (1962).

The major instruments for the assessment of field articulation are also derived from the work of Witkin and consist of the Embedded Figures Test (EFT) and the Rod-and-Frame Test (RFT) (Gardner and others, 1960). These instruments are considered in detail later in this chapter. Essentially, the EFT requires the subject to recognize a geometric figure located within an embedding context. The RFT requires the subject to bring a rod into a true vertical position under a variety of conditions providing disorienting cues. On occasion, Gardner has used a size estimation test as a measure of field articulation (Gardner and Moriarty, 1968).

Category Width. Pettigrew (1958) cited the work of Bruner and his coworkers (compare Bruner, Goodnow, and Austin, 1956) as having shown that there are intraindividual consistencies in the range in which individuals consider events likely to occur. That is, individuals who estimate a wide range for the brightness of an overcast sky are likely to estimate wide ranges for other phenomena, such as the pitch of a female singer's voice. Pettigrew proposed that this was a stylistic phenomenon and developed a paper-and-pencil measure of category width, the C-W Scale. The final form of the instrument is a twenty-item test in which, for each item, the subject is presented with a central measure and required to select one of four alternatives as the highest end of the range and one of four as the lowest. For example, the average width of windows is given as thirty-four inches. The subject is asked to choose the width of the narrowest window and of the widest window.

In his original paper, Pettigrew (1958) posited two explanations for the observed consistency in category-width judgments. One involves risk taking; that is, broad categorizers are willing to risk being overinclusive. The second explanation involves the concept of equivalence range, one of the cognitive controls studied by Gardner (1953) and Gardner and Schoen (1962) that deals with the number of differentiations an individual tends to make. Research on these two explanations of category-width consistency has been reviewed by Bieri (1969) and Touhey (1973).

Conceptual Styles. Kagan and others (1963, p. 74) defined cognitive style as reflecting "stable individual preferences in mode of perceptual organization and conceptual categorization of the external environment." They developed an approach to the study of cognitive style through an analysis of how individuals group objects. The investigators were interested in the principles underlying the basis for the groupings. They (1963, p. 74) postulated that individuals could be ordered on the basis of their proclivity "to analyze and to differentiate the stimulus environment." The development of this position has also been discussed by Kagan and others (1964).

The Conceptual Style Test (CST) developed by Kagan and others (1963) initially consisted of forty-four triads of pictures; shorter versions are more commonly used. The subject is asked to select the two pictures that go together in some way. Responses are then scored for analytic, relational, and inferential styles. The analytic-descriptive style involves combinations based on common elements; for example, the pictures may be grouped on the basis of people without shoes. The relational style involves concepts utilizing functional, thematic relationships; for example, two people are grouped together because they are married. The inferential-categorical style involves groupings on the basis of a more abstract similarity; for example, two individuals may be seen as poor. This category is observed infrequently, possibly owing to the simplicity of the stimuli (Stanes, 1973).

There have been a number of modifications of the CST. One by Sigel (1967) is the Sigel Conceptual Styles Test (SCST), another is the Sigel Object Categorization Task (SOCT), which uses three-dimensional objects (Sigel and Olmsted, 1970). The SOCT has been reviewed by Lindstrom and Shipman (1972), and the use of the instruments with young children has been reviewed by Kogan (1976).

Later in the present chapter the approach by Kelly (1955) and Bieri and others (1966) will be reviewed in some detail. The CST and its variants are similar in concept to the instruments used by Kelly and by Bieri. In the latter approaches, however, the investigators have focused on the measurement of cognitive complexity through a study of the number of different ways in which objects are grouped, rather than on the rationale for the groupings. In Kogan's (1976) typology, the CST is a Type III approach, while cognitive complexity is a Type II approach.

Reflection-Impulsivity. One approach to the study of cognitive style that is receiving considerable attention is that of reflection-impulsivity. This dimension was originally introduced by Kagan and others (1964) to describe differences in the speed with which decisions are made under conditions of uncertainty. A second major statement on reflection-impulsivity was made by Kagan and Kogan (1970).

Reflection-impulsivity is most often assessed with the Matching Familiar Figures (MFF) Test (Kagan and others, 1964). On each of the test's twelve items the subject is presented with a picture and asked to indicate which of several almost identical alternatives precisely matches the stimulus picture. Subjects responding quickly and with errors were identified as impulsive; those responding slowly and accurately were designated reflective. A number of investigators have been concerned with the adequacy of the MFF Test. Block, Block, and Harrington (1974) noted that the definition of reflection-impulsivity involves the time taken to reach a decision, while the MFF Test measures both time and accuracy. Kagan and Messer (1975) replied that both speed and accuracy are involved in reflection-impulsivity, but Block, Block, and Harrington (1975) remained unconvinced. More recent criticisms of the psychometric properties of the MFF Test were advanced by Ault, Mitchell, and Hartmann (1976) and Egeland and Weinberg (1976). An important, recent overview of research on reflection-impulsivity was presented by Messer (1976), while Kogan (1976) presented a review focusing on the literature on reflection-impulsivity in the first years of life.

Approaches To Be Reviewed in Detail

The material that follows was selected to represent other approaches to studying cognitive style. It should be recognized that, as noted above, there are a number of investigators, whose work falls outside the scope of this review, who have made major contributions to the field. It is our aim to present five approaches representing a continuum from emphasis on content to increasing emphasis on structure.

The first of the five approaches to be considered is authoritarianism. Research on authoritarianism represents the most content-laden approach to the study of cognitive style. The major concern of Adorno, Frenkel-Brunswik, Levinson, and Sanford (1950) was with the individual whose structure of thinking would make him especially susceptible to antidemocratic propaganda. These authors began with a study of attitude content—anti-Semitism, ethnocentrism, and political-economic conservatism—and then focused on the personality variables underlying these attitudes. Finally, they were interested in the behavioral correlates of authoritarianism, especially rigidity and intolerance of ambiguity, two classes of behavior that are manifestations of an underlying cognitive style.

The next approach that we will examine is Rokeach's (1960) work on dogmatism. Rokeach attempted to devise a structurally based measure of authoritarianism to replace the content-based measure of rightist authoritarianism that had been developed by Adorno and his colleagues.

The work of Kelly (1955) and his students, to which we will next turn, emphasizes the psychological dimensions that individuals use to structure their environments. Kelly's Role Construct Repertory Test provides us with a measure of cognitive style that is less content laden than the preceding measures.

The next approach to the assessment of cognitive style that we will review is that of Harvey, Hunt, and Schroder (1961). These investigators attempted to divorce the measurement of cognitive style from content still further through the use of a sentence completion method to measure differentiation and integration involved in the individual's processing of information.

Finally, the theory and research of Witkin and his associates (Witkin, Dyk, Faterson, Goodenough, and Karp, 1962; Witkin and others, 1954) will be reviewed. Witkin's approach is to measure cognitive style via the perceptual domain, devoid of content.

Warr and Coffman (1970) noted an expected similarity in functioning among authoritarian, dogmatic, and cognitively simple individuals. Klein, Barr, and Wolitzky (1967) also commented on the similarities among various approaches to the study of cognitive style. They noted that Bieri and others (1966), Witkin and others (1954), and Harvey and others (1961) were all concerned with the degree to which experience and judgment are differentiated. They point out the need for additional research to determine the common aspects of the various positions. These authors have commented, as have Coop and Sigel (1971), on the difficulties that arise when similar terms are used with different meanings and different measures are used to evaluate similar concepts.

Authoritarianism

Research on authoritarianism began in the 1940s with an interest in the dynamics underlying the anti-Semitism that existed in Nazi Germany. A series of studies was conducted at the University of California in Berkeley, California, culminating in the publication of *The Authoritarian Personality* (Adorno and others, 1950). One aim of the research was to develop objective scales to measure prejudice. Another aim of the research was to analyze clinically individuals with extreme scores on these scales.

As the research effort evolved, the investigators moved from their specific concern with anti-Semitic attitudes to measurement of the personality of fascist individuals. The major product of this endeavor was the thirty-item F Scale (Form 40/45) (Adorno and others, 1950). The F Scale was designed to provide an indirect measure of prejudice. None of the items mention ethnic minority groups. Items were derived from clinical interview material and objective test data, as well as from fascist writings and speeches. The instrument was designed to tap underlying fears, anxieties, values, and impulses. For example, Item 1, "Obedience and respect for authority are the most important virtues children should learn," is intended to measure rigid adherence to conventional middle-class values.

The F Scale is not itself a measure of cognitive style (Scott, 1963a). However, in the detailed clinical study of persons scoring high on the F Scale, it was noted that there was a tendency for these individuals to exhibit high levels of rigidity and intolerance of ambiguity. These behaviors are expected from individuals who have a simple cognitive style. Thus, while the F Scale was not designed as a measure of cognitive style, studies have shown that F Scale scores correlate with behavior that presumably reflects an underlying disposition to process information in a characteristic way. The F Scale is also an important forerunner of the Dogmatism Scale (Rokeach, 1960), a more direct measure of cognitive style that we will examine shortly. Messick and associates (1976) note the stylistic component that characterizes the functioning of the authoritarian individual.

Structure of the F Scale. F Scale items are responded to in Likert-type categories, ranging from strong support/agreement to strong opposition/disagreement. The items are grouped into nine categories, some items appearing in more than one category. Factor-analytic studies have replicated some of these dimensions (Christie and Cook, 1958), but virtually all research investigators use a single total score.

All F Scale items are written so that agreement with the item contributes to a higher authoritarianism score. This fact led to the criticism that the test is confounded with acquiescence response bias, that is, the tendency of a respondent to agree with an item, regardless of its content. Since the initial work by Cohn (1953, 1956), the problem of acquiescence response bias has been the object of considerable research. Investigators have attempted to study the effects of acquiescence by correlating F Scale scores with independent measures of acquiescence by reversing items of the F Scale and by using a forced-choice format. There is now some agreement that a small portion of the variance of F Scale scores is due to acquiescence. However, acquiescent individuals are likely to be authoritarian, so that the effects of the bias do not invalidate the instrument (for example, Messick and Frederiksen, 1958).

Reliability. The originally reported split-half reliability of 0.90 for the F Scale has generally not been found in subsequent research (Christie and Cook, 1958). For an instrument as widely used as the F Scale, there are surprisingly few data on reliability. In many studies, abbreviated forms of the instrument are used, reducing the reliability (and hence the validity) of the test. Christie, Havel, and Seidenberg (1958) report reliabilities from 0.34 to 0.78 for various samples for a ten-item F Scale.

Variations of the F Scale. Robinson and Shaver (1973) have reviewed a variety of instruments that were developed to measure authoritarianism. Gough, Harris, Martin, and Edwards (1950) developed the Children's Antidemocratic Scale. The F Scale has been translated into a number of languages, including German (Cohn and Carsch, 1954), Arabic (Melikian, 1956), Swedish (Rubenowitz, 1963), Hindi (Bhushan, 1971), and Italian (Gough and Lazzari, 1974). Christie and other's (1958) reversed form to control for acquiescence has been translated into Japanese (Niyekawa, 1960).

Rigidity and Intolerance of Ambiguity. We will now turn to a consideration of the relationship of authoritarianism to two measures of behavior that reflect cognitive style with which authoritarianism has often been associated in the literature, namely, rigidity and intolerance of ambiguity.

Rigidity may be understood as the persistence of a given behavior when a change in the situation requires a change in that behavior for more efficient functioning. A number of studies have tested the hypothesis that rigidity is associated with high levels of authoritarianism. The Einstellung water jug test (Luchins, 1942) is the measure of rigidity that has been most frequently employed in these studies. In the Einstellung water jug test a problem solving set is established. The subject's ability to overcome the set and choose a direct solution to a problem is assessed.

Since the first study in this area by Rokeach (1948), the relationship between authoritarianism and rigidity has been unclear. While Rokeach's study supported the existence of a positive relationship, a replication by Brown (1953) did not. Brown attributed the disparate findings to different conditions of test administration, since he found that greater rigidity by high authoritarian subjects was evidenced only under conditions of stress. This interpretation led to a series of research studies (for example, Applezweig, 1954; French, 1955; Levitt and Zelen, 1953) on the relationship between authoritarianism and rigidity under conditions of stress. The research, however, has failed to consistently replicate either the general finding or the finding with regard to stress.

It must be pointed out that the validity of the Einstellung task as a measure of rigidity has been seriously questioned (Levitt, 1956; Levitt and Zelen, 1953, 1955; Luchins, 1949). Because of this criticism and the general desirability of a multi-method approach, it is necessary to consider the relationship of authoritarianism to other measures of rigidity. However, various paper-and-pencil measures of rigidity often do not correlate well with each other (Applezweig, 1954; Baer, 1964; Cattell and Tiner, 1949; Chown, 1959; Fisher, 1950; Forster, Vinacke, and Digman, 1955). One of the other measures of rigidity that has received considerable attention is a procedure in which a subject is shown a series of pictures that depict stages in the transition of one object to another (for example, dog to cat). The measure of rigidity is the point in the series at which the subject recognizes the transition. In the initial report using this technique, Frenkel-Brunswik (1949) found that ethnocentric children evidenced greater rigidity. However, French (1955) failed to find this relationship between authoritarianism and a similar measure of rigidity for his adult subjects, while Kidd and Kidd (1972) found a very strong relationship between the two measures.

A second cognitive style variable that has been related to authoritarianism is intolerance of ambiguity, which involves the tendency to oversimplify and to prefer definiteness and regularity. A popular vehicle for the study of intolerance of ambiguity has been the development of movement norms in the auto-kinetic situation. The autokinetic phenomenon (Sherif, 1936) is the perception of movement of a stationary pinpoint of light in a dark room. Some subjects have been observed to establish norms, that is, to stabilize their perceptions regarding the amount of movement. Block and Block (1951) found that subjects who established norms regarding the movement were more authoritarian than those who did not. Similar findings were obtained by Taft (1956) and Zacker (1973). Millon (1957), studying subjects who established norms, found that high authoritarian individuals formed norms more quickly than did low authoritarians.

Other studies indicating a relationship between authoritarianism and intolerance of ambiguity have involved the reported frequency of fluctuation of the Necker Cube (Jones, 1955) and the Decision-Location test (Levitt, 1953). In the latter test the subject is presented with a series of pictures that increase in detail. A subject who seeks to identify the picture early in the series is considered to be intolerant of ambiguity. A number of studies using paper-and-pencil tests of intolerance of ambiguity have also indicated a positive relationship between authoritarianism and intolerance of ambiguity (MacDonald, 1970; Muuss, 1959; Siegel, 1954; Vannoy, 1965), despite the fact that such paper-and-pencil measures are generally independent of one another (Kenny and Ginsberg, 1958). In addition, a number of studies have shown that Walk's (1950) scale of intolerance of ambiguity relates significantly to authoritarianism (Kates and Diab, 1955; Kelman and Barclay, 1963; Kenny and Ginsberg, 1958; O'Connor, 1952; Pilisuk, 1963).

Summary. Beginning with an interest in the psychology of prejudice, Adorno and others (1950) eventually developed the F Scale, an attitude instrument designed to differentiate the fascist individual from the nonfascist individual. Once this differentiation was made, it was observed that the fascist individual tends to be rigid and intolerant of ambiguity. This led to research on the relationship of F Scale scores to performance on measures of rigidity and intolerance of ambiguity. Despite some concern over the adequacy of the F Scale because of an acquiescence response bias, the expected relationships were often obtained, particularly with regard to intolerance of ambiguity. Thus, a content-laden instrument—the F Scale—that was developed out of an interest in the study of anti-Semitism was shown to differentiate subjects who differed in behavior reflecting cognitive style.

Dogmatism

Theory and Tests. The Dogmatism Scale (Rokeach, 1960) was developed in response to the criticism that the F Scale measured only authoritarianism of the political right. Summarizing research that had begun almost a decade earlier, Rokeach presented the construct of dogmatism as an approach to the study of cognitive style. Central to this position is the notion that beliefs may be held in an open or closed system, independent of the content of those beliefs. Rokeach hypothesized that an individual who is dogmatic, or closed-minded, in one area is likely to be closed-minded in other areas. Further, the dogmatic individual glorifies authority figures supporting his beliefs and is intolerant toward those opposing his beliefs.

Structure of the Dogmatism Scale. The final forty-item version of the Dogmatism Scale (Form E) (Rokeach, 1960) is, like the F Scale, a Likert-type instrument with response categories ranging from "I Agree Very Much" to "I Disagree Very Much." An example of an item is "A person who gets enthusiastic about too many causes is likely to be a pretty 'wishy-washy' sort of person." It was intended that the items on the scale would not measure the content of beliefs. However, the preponderance of evidence indicates that high dogmatism is related to political conservatism (Barker, 1963; Hanson, 1973; Kirtley and Harkless, 1969), although to a lesser extent than authoritarianism. Items for the Dogmatism Scale were written to reflect various aspects of Rokeach's complex theory. Because of this, it is important to consider the results of factor-analytic studies on the dimensionality of the instrument. These studies indicate that the Dogmatism Scale is factorially complex. Some of the studies (Pedhazur, 1971; Vacchiano, Schiffman, and Strauss, 1967) have yielded factors that have been interpreted as supporting Rokeach's conceptualization, while other studies have yielded factors that have not (Gulo and Lynch, 1973; Parrott, 1971). It thus appears to be appropriate to use factor scores rather than a single total score.

Like the F Scale, the Dogmatism Scale is worded so that agreement with an item contributes to a high score, again raising the question of acquiescence response bias. The studies that have been done (for example, Couch and Keniston, 1960; Peabody, 1961) indicate that the Dogmatism Scale, like the F Scale, is subject to some acquiescence response bias, but that the bias does not adversely affect the validity of the instrument.

There is also some possibility that the Dogmatism Scale is biased by social desirability factors, the results of several studies yielding inconsistent data on the relationship between dogmatism and the tendency to respond in a socially desirable manner (Becker and Dileo, 1967; MacDonald, 1970; Stanley and Martin, 1964). Wolfer (1967) provided some evidence that the instrument is subject to faking.

Reliability. Most studies on the reliability of the Dogmatism Scale have indicated satisfactorily high reliability for the instrument, for both adult and high school samples. Vacchiano, Strauss, and Hochman (1969) have reviewed many of these studies.

Variations of the Dogmatism Scale. Peabody (1962) and Korn and Giddan (1964) showed that scoring the Dogmatism Scale on the basis of a simple agree-disagree dichotomy yielded results similar to those obtained from the conventional 6-point scoring. Shupe and Wolfer (1966) showed that such a scoring system yielded data that were satisfactorily reliable.

Steininger (1973) developed an eleven-item, open-ended version of the Dogmatism Scale that correlated significantly with the original. Other investigators have also been interested in shortening the Dogmatism Scale, with Troldahl and Powell (1965) and Schulze (1962) reporting success. Figert (1968) developed an elementary school version of the Dogmatism Scale, which Murray (1974) successfully shortened to twenty items. The scale has been translated into Italian (DiRenzo, 1967) and German (Gaensslen, May, and Wolpert, 1973).

Norms. There is a strong tendency to ignore the question of norms in the measurement of cognitive style. One exception to this is a paper by Alter and White (1966), in which the authors present means and standard deviations of Dogmatism Scale scores for thirty-seven samples totaling almost thirteen thousand subjects. They reported a grand mean of 159.2 and a standard deviation of 31.38. The means ranged widely from one sample to another. Thus, subjects selected as highly dogmatic in one study might not be considered highly dogmatic in another sample, a design flaw that is characteristic of almost all research on cognitive style.

Rigidity and Intolerance of Ambiguity. Data on the relationship of dogmatism to rigidity (Korn and Giddan, 1964; MacDonald, 1970; Riley and Armlin, 1965; Schroder and Streufert, 1962; White and Alter, 1965) and to intolerance of ambiguity (Barker, 1963; Chabassol and Thomas, 1975; Day, 1966; Feather, 1969b, 1971; MacDonald, 1970) indicate that dogmatic subjects tend to evidence rigidity and intolerance of ambiguity. Correlations between Dogmatism Scale scores and measures of rigidity and intolerance of ambiguity cluster in the 0.30-0.40 range.

Analysis and Synthesis. While rigidity and intolerance of ambiguity were the major cognitive style concerns in research on authoritarianism, for dogmatism the major concern has been with the concepts of analysis and synthesis. Analysis refers to the replacement of old beliefs with new beliefs, a process that is, in some aspects, the opposite of rigidity. Synthesis refers to the integration of the new beliefs into a belief system (Rokeach, McGovney, and Denny, 1955, 1960). Rokeach hypothesized that both high and low dogmatic subjects would perform similarly with regard to analysis but that subjects high on dogmatism would perform more poorly with regard to synthesis than subjects low on dogmatism. With regard to analysis, this prediction is inconsistent with the hypothesized relationship between authoritarianism and rigidity. The nonauthoritarian individual should be superior in analyzing ability, since he should be better able to break sets.

The major vehicle for the study of analyzing and synthesizing abilities was the Denny Doodlebug Problem (Rokeach and others, 1955), a problem that requires the subject to overcome several implicit sets (or beliefs) in order to reach a solution. At intervals, the experimenter provides hints to help the subject to overcome each of the sets. Analyzing ability is reflected in the adoption of the new beliefs; synthesizing ability is reflected by the speed of solution once the new beliefs have been adopted. Rokeach's hypotheses, noted above, were supported in a number of early studies (Rokeach, 1960; Rokeach and others, 1955; Rokeach and Vidulich, 1960).

In the perceptual area, Levy and Rokeach (1960) used a hidden figures test as a measure of analyzing ability and a block design test as a measure of synthesizing ability. There were no statistically significant differences in performance on these measures between extremely high and low dogmatic subjects. However, Iverson and Schwab (1967) provided some evidence of the superior synthesizing ability of low dogmatic subjects in a perceptual fusion task. Similar results were reported by Kaplan and Singer (1963) for performance on sensory acuity tasks.

Ability to Reject the Irrelevant. Rokeach (1960) posited that subjects high in dogmatism would have difficulties in distinguishing a message from the source of the message and in evaluating one of these independently of the other. Studies of this have generally supported Rokeach's hypothesis (Becker, 1967; Bettinghaus, Miller, and Steinfatt, 1970; Harvey and Hays, 1972; Mouw, 1969; Powell, 1962; Rosenman, 1967; Vidulich and Kaiman, 1961). Representative of these studies is one by Schultz and DiVesta (1972), in which high dogmatic subjects were found to be more uncritically accepting of expert-endorsed beliefs in the doodlebug situation than were low dogmatic subjects.

Consistency. A number of investigators have hypothesized that individuals high in dogmatism would be less likely to seek out and accept information that was inconsistent with their beliefs than would subjects low in dogmatism. The results of studies in this area are mixed, some supporting the hypothesis (Durand and Lambert, 1975; Feather, 1969b; Hunt and Miller, 1968; Osborn, 1973), and others failing to support it (Feather, 1969a; Gormly and Clore, 1969; Rosnow, Gitter, and Holz, 1969; Snoek and Dobbs, 1967); still other studies have provided partial support for the hypothesis (Clarke and James, 1967; Kleck and Wheaton, 1967; Smith, 1968). Similarly, it has been hypothesized that high dogmatic subjects would be less receptive to novel stimuli than low dogmatic subjects. Again, the results of some studies support the hypothesis (Miller and Bacon, 1971; Zagona and Kelly, 1966), whereas others do not (Day, 1966; Leckart and Wagner, 1967). The results of a study by Mikol (1960) provide mixed support.

Creativity. Since creativity requires synthesizing ability and openness to new information, a number of investigators have hypothesized that individuals high in dogmatism would score low on measures of creativity. Data from a study by Uhes and Shaver (1970) support this prediction; however, Williams, Harlow, and Borgen (1971) found only partial support for the hypothesis. Jacoby (1967) found no relationship between dogmatism and creativity.

Summary. Unlike the F Scale, which is a measure of rightist orientation, the Dogmatism Scale was intended as a measure of authoritarianism independent of political orientation. Rokeach's intent, to develop a measure of cognitive style that would not be bound to content, was only partially successful. Findings indicate that dogmatism as assessed by this scale is related to rightist political orientation. The evidence also suggests that high dogmatic individuals are rigid and intolerant of ambiguity. In Rokeach's study of analysis and synthesis, he approached the study of differentiation and integration, a conceptualization of cognitive style that will be developed more intensively in the sections to follow. There is some evidence that highly dogmatic subjects are poorer in synthesizing ability and have difficulty distinguishing the relevant aspects of a message.

Cognitive Complexity

Theory and Tests. Another stage in the development of cognitive style as a measure independent of the content of thought is represented by Kelly's (1955) work on personal constructs. Kelly viewed man as an information processor who is actively engaged in organizing the stimuli impinging on him. He believed that individuals vary in the way they organize, or represent, the environment. These representations were termed *constructs,* and they are the basis of the organization of behavior. At the heart of Kelly's theory is the notion that people are free to develop alternate constructs and choose among them. The theory has been developed in detail by Kelly (1955, 1970) and others (Bannister and Fransella, 1971; Bannister and Mair, 1968; Hinkle, 1970).

In order to measure an individual's personal constructs, Kelly developed several variations of the Role Construct Repertory Test (Rep Test). In the most popular version of the Rep Test, the grid, the subject is presented with a list of role types (for example, mother, friend) and asked to note how two are similar to each other and different from a third. In this way bipolar constructs are generated for various combinations of the role types, taken three at a time. Kelly derived a number of indices from this procedure. The number of different constructs used by an individual is the index of cognitive complexity. The more dimensions used by the person, the more differentiated his cognitive system and the greater his cognitive complexity.

Because the administration and scoring of the various

Rep Tests is complex, a modification developed by Bieri (1955) and again modified by Bieri and others (1966) is often used. The essential difference between the Bieri modification and the original Rep Test is that the former provides the constructs that are to be used in judging the role types; in Kelly's version, the constructs are elicited from the subject. Crockett (1965) has also developed a measure of cognitive complexity derived from elicited constructs. Miller (1969) and Little (1969) failed to find significant correlations between the Bieri and Crockett measures.

Structure of the Bieri Modification of the Rep Test. The subject is presented with a 10 X 10 grid, ten role types listed along the top of the grid and ten pairs of bipolar constructs (for example, outgoing-shy, adjusted-maladjusted) listed along the side of the grid. The subject rates each role type on each of the bipolar constructs, using a 6-point scale from +3 to −3. The more that the ratings assigned to the role types differ from one another, the higher the cognitive complexity score.

An important issue has been the similarity between cognitive complexity scores obtained from instruments in which the constructs are elicited from the subjects and those obtained from the Bieri modification, in which the constructs are provided by the examiner. While some researchers (Kuusinen and Nystedt, 1975a, 1975b; Leitner, Landfield, and Barr, 1974; Metcalfe, 1974) have questioned the equivalence of the two procedures, the bulk of the evidence (Adams-Webber, 1970; Bieri and others, 1966; Stringer, 1972) indicates that the two techniques yield similar results.

There is some indication that measures of cognitive complexity are moderately related to social desirability (Bieri, 1965) and to acquiescence response set (Goldstein and Blackman, 1976).

Reliability. Reliability data are available for cognitive complexity scores derived from different versions of the Rep Test (Epting, 1972; Meyers, 1964; Tripodi and Bieri, 1963, 1964). The test-retest reliabilities reported are often in the range of 0.45-0.80, somewhat below accepted levels. It may be possible to improve reliability by lengthening the instrument through the use of additional role-type stimuli.

Variations. Aside from the major modification made by Bieri and his associates as described above, most modifications of the Rep Test have involved the use of different types of stimuli to be judged. These include social issues (Epting, 1972), automobiles (Mazis, 1973), group therapy patients (Fransella and Joyston-Bechal (1971), universities (Reid and Holley, 1972), friendship groups (Duck, 1972; Duck and Spencer, 1972), and acquaintances (Landfield, 1977), as well as films, paintings, inanimate objects, emotions, problem situations in a person's life, and types of bread (compare Bannister and Mair, 1968; Slater, 1969). Variations suitable for use with children have also been reported by Reker (1974) and by Vacc and Vacc (1973). The latter appears to have satisfactory test-retest reliability and correlates at a statistically significant level with a modified Bieri version.

Perception of Others. As a test of Kelly's hypothesis that cognitively complex individuals are more accurate predictors of events, a number of investigators hypothesized that cognitively complex individuals would be more accurate predictors of the behavior of others. Some of these studies clearly support the hypothesized relationship (Adams-Webber, 1969; Adams-Webber, Schwenker, and Barbeau, 1972), some yield marginal support (Bieri, 1955; Sechrest and Jackson, 1961), while others fail to confirm the hypothesis (Leventhal, 1957; Macrae, 1969; Vacc, 1974). These various studies involved the ability of judges differing in level of cognitive complexity to predict such aspects of behavior as responses on a paper-and-pencil situations test, academic achievement, how a subject would complete a scale of the Eysenck Personality Inventory, and measures of cognitive complexity itself. Leitner and others (1974) reviewed the literature and concluded that cognitively complex individuals can more accurately predict differences, but not similarities, between themselves and others.

Consistency. As was noted in a previous section of this chapter, subjects high in dogmatism were hypothesized to be less tolerant of inconsistent information than are subjects low in dogmatism. In the area of cognitive complexity, tolerance for inconsistency has been most often studied with regard to the ability to integrate contrasting personality descriptions. The majority of studies (Campbell, 1960; Mayo and Crockett, 1964; Nidorf, 1961; Supnick, 1964; Tripodi and Bieri, 1966) indicated that cognitively complex individuals are better able to integrate contrasting personality descriptions than are cognitively simple individuals. However, Rosenkrantz and Crockett (1965), as well as Fertig and Mayo (1970), failed to obtain the anticipated results. In a study more closely related to those done in the investigation of dogmatism, Lundy and Berkowitz (1957) provided evidence that individuals high in cognitive complexity are less likely to modify their attitudes as a function of irrelevant communications from peers or authority figures.

Generality Across Stimulus Domains. One of the recurring questions in the literature is whether the complexity of an individual's cognitive style can be generalized across a variety of stimulus domains. Because the stimuli used to derive Rep Test scores of cognitive complexity can be varied, this test is particularly suited to the study of the question of generalizability. A number of investigators (Allard and Carlson, 1963; Bodden, 1970; Epting, 1972) have shown that cognitive complexity scores derived from different types of stimuli are significantly related. Correlations have generally been in the 0.50-0.60 range. Koenig and Seaman (1974), however, found that higher cognitive complexity scores were generated when male role types were used as stimuli than when female role types were used.

It has also been shown (Baldwin, 1972; Miller and Bieri, 1965; Supnick, 1964) that higher cognitive complexity scores are obtained when the role types are socially distant (for example, person you dislike) rather than socially close (for example, mother). Similarly, higher cognitive complexity scores are obtained when the role types are negatively evaluated than when they are positively evaluated (Carr, 1969; Irwin, Tripodi, and Bieri, 1967; Koenig and Seaman, 1974; Soucar, 1971; Soucar and Du Cette, 1971; Turner and Tripodi, 1968; Wilkins, Epting, and Van De Riet, 1972). Similar results obtained when Koenig and Edmonds (1972) contrasted positively and negatively evaluated literary works and when Bodden and Klein (1973) compared liked and disliked vocations.

Thus it appears that differences in the evaluative dimension of the stimuli being judged affect cognitive complexity scores, negatively evaluated stimuli generating greater complexity.

Summary. Unlike the work on authoritarianism and dogmatism, which attempted to move from content-bound approaches to a structural approach to cognitive style, in the work of Kelly and Bieri we have examples of a structural orientation as the theoretical basis. From his clinical interests, Kelly developed a measure of personality that Bieri later modified into a direct measure of cognitive style. Bieri's measure assesses differentiation in the sense of the number of dimensions that an individual uses to make comparisons among stimuli. In this system a cognitively complex individual is one who uses many dimensions. There is some evidence that this direct structural measure of cognitive style is consistent across stimulus domains and that it relates to accuracy in one's perception of others and to one's ability to tolerate inconsistency.

Integrative Complexity

Theory and Tests. The work of Harvey and others (1961) and Schroder, Driver, and Streufert (1967) represents another approach to the content-free measurement of cognitive style. Following Schroder, Driver, and Streufert, the term *integrative complexity* will be used to refer to this work. Central to this position is the view of man as an information processor. The two aspects of information processing that are of concern in this approach are differentiation and integration, aspects of cognitive structure that have also been considered by Scott (1962, 1963b). Differentiation refers to the number of dimensions and the number of categories within dimensions that are used by individuals in the perception of the physical and social environment. In this regard, differentiation is similar to the cognitive complexity aspect of Kelly's construct theory and to the Bieri measure of cognitive complexity. However, the approach that we are considering in this section expands on the Kelly and Bieri approaches by adding the concept of integration, which refers to the ability of persons to organize the differentiated dimensions within a hierarchical system. Based on their ability to differentiate and integrate information, individuals may be ordered along a dimension varying from concrete to abstract. Individuals differing in concreteness-abstractness are posited to behave differently in environments differing in informational complexity. For example, it is hypothesized that abstract individuals will perform more effectively than concrete individuals in complex situations.

The major approach to the assessment of integrative complexity has involved the projective technique of stem completion. The first of the instruments developed to measure what was then termed the complexity of conceptual systems was the Sentence Completion Test (Schroder and Streufert, 1962), an instrument that was later modified into the Paragraph Completion Test (Schroder and others, 1967). A similar measure, used in research on integrative complexity by Harvey and his associates, is the "This I Believe" Test (Harvey, 1963, 1964).

Structure of the Stem Completion Tests. The Sentence Completion Test presents the subject with eight stems and instructs him to complete the sentence and to write an additional one or two sentences on the topic. Concreteness-abstractness was rated on a five-point scale on the basis of a global rating of the underlying differentiating and integrating structure. The total score was often obtained by summing concreteness-abstractness scores for the individual stems.

The Paragraph Completion Test presents the subject with only five stems. Three sentences are to be written for each stem within the allotted ninety seconds. The integrative complexity score is the mean of the two most abstract responses after each stem has been scored on a 7-point scale that ranges from concrete to abstract. An example of a stem is "When I Am Criticized . . . ." An example of an extremely concrete response to this stem is "I feel unhappy. Anyway, I don't listen too carefully to criticism. I guess I'm occupied with my own little world, so outside criticism isn't very important to me" (Schroder and others, 1967, p. 192). An example of an extremely abstract response to this stem is "I listen carefully. Criticism tells me much about the criticizer—how he thinks, what he believes in, what he expects of others, etc. It also tells me how others see me. After that, I usually find myself changing my way of acting or thinking in order to take this into account" (Schroder and others, p. 193).

The Paragraph Completion Test and its scoring manual are presented in Schroder and others (1967). In addition to providing the scoring manual, the authors have conducted seminars intended to train researchers in the use of the scoring system. Based on the experience of the present authors, attendance at such seminars is invaluable preparation for the use of the instrument.

The third major stem completion approach, the "This I Believe" Test (Harvey, 1963, 1964), is similar in format to the Sentence Completion Test and the Paragraph Completion Test. The major differences concern scoring. Unlike the other two tests, the "This I Believe" Test is scored by assigning a single global score based on responses to all the stems and is scored partly on the basis of content (for example, a statement of high positive dependence on external authority is scored for concreteness).

There is some evidence (Bottenberg, 1969) that acquiescence is not related to performance on the Paragraph Completion Test or on the Interperson Topical Inventory or the Conceptual Systems Test (Stewin and Anderson, 1974), two tests that will be discussed below. There is also some evidence (Schroder and Streufert, 1962) that the Sentence Completion Test is not subject to social desirability bias. Suedfeld (1968) found that responses on the Impression Formation Test and the Paragraph Completion Test could be modified by verbal instructions. A recurrent problem in the use of the Paragraph Completion Test has been the difficulty in locating highly abstract subjects.

Reliability. When there is proper training, interjudge reliability for the scoring of the stem completion tests is generally satisfactory (Harvey and Felknor, 1970; Schroder and others, 1967). Further, limited data (Greaves, 1971; Harvey and Felknor, 1970) on test-retest reliability suggest that the instruments are satisfactorily stable over time. However, before a study using these instruments is undertaken, the investigator should attain a satisfactory level of interjudge reliability in the scoring of these tests.

Variations. There exist several versions of the stem completion procedures as well as of other techniques employed to assess integrative complexity. Included in the former category are Hunt and Halverson's (1964) Conceptual Levels Questionnaire, an instrument designed for children, and Bottenberg's (1969) German adaptation of the Paragraph Completion Test. An early measure of integrative complexity, designed specifically to provide an index of integrating ability, was the Impression Formation Test (Streufert and Driver, 1967; Streufert and Schroder, 1962). This task involves writing an integrated description of an individual based on inconsistent sets of adjectives. There are some data (Streufert and Driver, 1967) to indicate satisfactory test-retest reliability for this measure.

There have also been some attempts to use multidimensional scaling methods in order to provide measures of differentiation and integration (Blackman, 1966; Warr, Schroder, and Blackman, 1969a, 1969b), but the relationship between the scaling procedures and integrative complexity is not yet clear. Tuckman (1966) developed a forced-choice instrument, the Interpersonal Topical Inventory, based on responses to the stem completion procedures. An objectively scored version of the "This I Believe" Test, the Conceptual Systems Test, developed by Harvey (1967), has not been widely used.

Intercorrelations Among the Measures. Studies relating measures of integrative complexity with one another have often shown that the instruments do not interrelate well. Research has shown that the Paragraph Completion Test and "This I Believe" Test are not significantly related statistically (Cox, 1974; Epting and Wilkins, 1974). The Impression Formation Test generally correlates significantly, at about the 0.50 level, with the Sentence Completion Test and the Paragraph Completion Test (Schroder and others, 1967; Streufert and Driver, 1967). The correlations between the Interpersonal Topical Inventory and either the Sentence Completion Test or the Paragraph Completion Test, while statistically significant, are usually less than

0.20 (Jacobson, 1973; Russell and Sandilands, 1973; Suedfeld, Tomkins, and Tucker, 1969).

Consistency. On the basis of integrative complexity as assessed by the "This I Believe" Test, concrete subjects have been shown to be more likely to modify their beliefs when required to argue against them (Harvey, 1965), to do poorly in role-playing situations where they are required to perform contrary to their own positions (Harvey, 1963; Miller and Harvey, 1973), and to be uncomfortable with trait inconsistency (Harvey and Ware, 1967; Ware and Harvey, 1967). Crano and Schroder (1967) showed that low complexity subjects are more consistent in their reaction to attitude-discrepant information than are high complexity subjects.

Articulation of Environmental and Individual Complexity. A number of studies, cited below, have been conducted by Schroder and his associates on the way individuals varying in level of integrative complexity perform in environments differing in level of informational complexity. It was hypothesized that the optimal level of performance for abstract subjects would take place in more complex environments than would the optimal performance of concrete subjects. It was also maintained that at any given level of environmental complexity the performance of abstract subjects would be superior to that of concrete subjects, with the performance of all subjects being optimal at intermediate levels of environmental complexity.

Two major situations have been used to create environments of unusual complexity. Simulation games, because of the ability to overload information, can create environments of high complexity; sensory deprivation, because of reduced sensory input, creates an environment in which the effects of low information load can be studied. In simulation situations, the predicted superior functioning of abstract subjects in high complexity environments has generally been demonstrated (Karlins, 1967; Karlins, Coffman, Lamm, and Schroder, 1967; Karlins and Lamm, 1967; Stager, 1967; Streufert and Driver, 1965; Streufert and Schroder, 1965; Streufert, Suedfeld, and Driver, 1965; Suedfeld and Streufert, 1966). For example, Streufert and Driver (1965) used a war-simulation procedure and had subjects answer questions about their tactics and about the enemy's tactics. The responses were scored for differentiation and integration. It was shown that when information load was intermediate, the complexity of the perceptions of the environment was greatest. Also, concrete subjects tended to view the situation more simply than did abstract subjects. These results are consistent with theoretical expectations.

Research involving the sensory deprivation situation has also supported the theoretical expectations (Hewitt, 1972; MacNeil and Rule, 1970; Suedfeld, 1963, 1964; Suedfeld and Vernon, 1966). For example, it was shown that in sensory deprivation, concrete subjects request less information than do abstract subjects (Suedfeld and Vernon, 1966).

Summary. The measurement of cognitive style represented in the approach of Harvey and others (1961) includes the dimension of integration as well as that of differentiation. Like cognitive complexity, integrative complexity provides a direct measure of cognitive style. In the approach of Kelly and Bieri, the number of dimensions is the index of complexity. In the integrative complexity approach, the manner in which the dimensions are hierarchically organized, or integrated, is also important. The more complex individual is one who uses more dimensions, makes more discriminations along the dimensions, and organizes these dimensions in a more complex way. However, the relative contributions of differentiation and integration to the integrative complexity score is not made explicit.

The most noteworthy contribution of the Harvey, Hunt, and Schroder approach has been the attempt to study the performance of individuals varying in level of integrative complexity in environments varying in level of informational complexity. Superior performance by high complex individuals in highly complex environments and in low complex environments has generally been substantiated.

Field Dependence

Theory and Tests. Research on field dependence (Witkin and others, 1962; Witkin and others, 1954) presents an entirely different approach to the study of cognitive style from those we have considered so far in that it is content free and it began with a study of perception. Witkin began his research by studying factors associated with the perception of the upright and found large differences between individuals in their errors of perception. He also noted a tendency for individuals to be consistent in how they erred. Witkin then postulated that individual differences in perception were reflections of cognitive style, which in turn would be correlated with behavior (Witkin, Oltman, Raskin, and Karp, 1971).

Subjects who were accurate perceivers of the upright, despite extraneous environmental cures, were termed *field-independent*. Subjects who performed poorly on the task were termed *field-dependent* and were generally shown to be passive and have low self-esteem, poor impulse control, and a primitive and undifferentiated body image (Witkin and others, 1954). In later years the construct was broadened to a dimension of differentiation, including a variety of cognitive and personality functions.

A number of instruments were developed to assess field dependence. Some of the initial techniques were quite elaborate. The room-adjustment test required suspending a chair in a room, with both the chair and room capable of being tilted right or left. With the chair tilted, the subject's task was to instruct the examiner to reorient the room in an upright position. In the body-adjustment test, it was the subject who was brought to the upright. The major assessment instruments, however, have been the Rod-and-Frame Test (RFT) (Witkin and others, 1954) and the Embedded Figures Test (EFT) (Witkin and others, 1971).

Structure of the RFT and EFT. In the RFT a luminous rod is placed in a luminous frame. The subject is seated in complete darkness. The experimenter may tilt the subject's chair, the rod, or the frame, instructing the subject to bring the rod to the vertical. The subject's score is based on the deviation of his errors from errors made by others of his age and sex. Witkin and others (1962) suggested using the series of eight trials in which the frame is tilted twenty-eight degrees to the left or right and the subject's task is to bring the rod to the upright.

In the EFT the subject is required to find a simple figure

within a complex context. The standard test consists of two forms, each with twelve figures. The test is scored on the basis of the time taken to locate all twelve figures, with a limit of three minutes per figure (Witkin and others, 1971). The subject's score is the mean amount of time taken to find all the hidden figures. Various versions of the EFT are available from Consulting Psychologists Press, Palo Alto, California.

There appears to be no relationship between field dependence and measures of the social desirability response set (Evans, 1969; Farley, 1974).

Reliability of the RFT and EFT. Over a one-week interval, test-retest reliabilities for the RFT and EFT cluster between 0.85 and 0.95 (Witkin and others, 1962). Reliabilities for the RFT have also been high over periods of several years (Adevai and McGough, 1968; Bauman, 1951; Witkin and others, 1962).

Other Versions. Both the RFT and the EFT have been subject to considerable modification. Oltman (1968) has developed a widely used portable RFT that correlated well with the standard method. Handel (1972) and Long (1973) have discussed other modifications in RFT instrumentation and procedure. Two versions of the portable RFT are available from the Stoelting Company of Chicago; the instrument manufactured by the Polymetric Company is preferred. Busch and Simon (1972) presented a children's version of a portable RFT; this test, however, was shown to have a two-month test-retest reliability of only 0.57 for the seventy children in their study.

Group forms of the EFT were developed by Jackson, Messick, and Myers (1962, 1964) and by Witkin and others (1971). The magnitude of the correlation coefficients obtained in comparing performance on individually administered and group-administered EFTs varies considerably, and Witkin and others (1971) have recognized the need for additional validation of their Group Embedded Figures Test. An early children's version (Goodenough and Eagle, 1963) was modified by Karp and Konstadt (1963) into the Children's Embedded Figures Test (CEFT). Witkin and others (1971), in their manual for the CEFT, recommend the test for children aged five through nine years; for older children (nine through twelve years) who are able to complete an EFT the correlation between the CEFT and EFT is high. Other children's versions have been developed by Banta (1970), Herkowitz (1972), and Coates (1972), the latter published by Consulting Psychologists Press as the Preschool EFT. Instructions for the CEFT have been translated into a number of foreign languages, including Spanish (Mebane and Johnson, 1970), Italian (Pizzamiglio and Pizzamiglio, 1974), and Ibo (Okonji, 1969). Evans (1969) developed a fifty-item questionnaire measure of field dependence that correlates moderately with the EFT.

Intercorrelations Among the Measures. When the various versions of the RFT are intercorrelated and the various versions of the EFT are intercorrelated, the correlation coefficients generally fall between 0.60 and 0.80. Correlations between the RFT and EFT, however, are generally lower, ranging between 0.30 and 0.60. In light of the magnitude of these correlations, the unidimensionality of the construct field dependence must be questioned.

Rigidity and Intolerance of Ambiguity. With regard to the relationships of field dependence to rigidity and to intolerance of ambiguity, the data are mixed. Early studies tended to confirm a positive relationship between field dependence and rigidity (Fenchel, 1958; Goodman, 1960; Guetzkow, 1951), while later studies did not obtain this result (Breskin and Gorman, 1969; Hritzuk and Taylor, 1973; however, compare Busse, 1968).

Discrimination and Synthesis. There are some data (Blasi, Cross, and Hebert, 1972; Ehri and Muzio, 1974; Fine, 1973; Kessler and Kronenberger, 1967; Messick and Damarin, 1964; Vaught and Auguston, 1967a, 1967b; Vaught and Ellinger, 1966; Vaught and Roodin, 1973) that suggest that field-dependent subjects are poor in their ability to discriminate and synthesize. Fine, for example, used the Gottschaldt Hidden Figures Test as a measure of field dependence and found that for the fifty-six soldiers who were his subjects, field-dependent individuals were poorer discriminators of color, but were equal to field-independent individuals in the ability to discriminate among weights.

Conformity. Several investigators have been interested in

the relationship between field dependence and conformity. Studies have yielded mixed results. Linton (1955) and Solar, Davenport, and Bruehl (1969) found greater conformity by field-dependent subjects, while Rosner (1957) and Busch and DeRidder (1973) found no differences in conforming behavior between field-dependent and field-independent individuals.

Creativity. There is little evidence that field-dependence is related to creativity. While Moore, Gleser, and Warm (1970) found that field-independent subjects gave responses to ambiguous stimuli that indicated greater creativity, Bieri, Bradburn, and Galinsky (1958), Spotts and Mackler (1967), Busse (1968), and Ohnmacht and McMorris (1971) failed to find this relationship for a variety of measures of creativity.

Summary. Witkin's research on field dependence approaches the study of cognitive style by comparing individuals on the basis of their performance on perceptual tasks. The field-independent, or well-differentiated, individual is able to discriminate figure from ground or a stimulus from distracting cues. With regard to the relationship of field dependence to rigidity and intolerance of ambiguity, data are inconsistent; however, there is evidence that field-dependent subjects perform more poorly on tasks requiring discrimination and synthesis.

Conclusion and Integration

Five approaches to the study of cognitive style have been presented in a sequence that reflects a transition from an emphasis on content to an increasing emphasis on structure. In research on authoritarianism the initial interest was on an understanding of the personality dynamics involved in anti-Semitism. This content-laden research interest eventually broadened to encompass the study of authoritarianism of the political right. Research on cognitive style was a collateral interest, represented in the work on the relationship of authoritarianism to rigidity and intolerance of ambiguity. The next section of the chapter was devoted to a consideration of Rokeach's attempt to deemphasize content by developing a measure of authoritarianism that would be independent of rightist or leftist orientation.

The work of Kelly and Bieri on personal constructs and cognitive complexity, reviewed next, was yet another step in the direction of a content-free measure of cognitive style. The instruments of these investigators were designed to measure the number of dimensions underlying the individual's perceptions. The approach of Harvey, Hunt, and Schroder, unlike the previous work, began with an interest in cognitive style. Their measuring instruments were designed to tap both the number of dimensions underlying the subject's perceptions and the hierarchical organization of these dimensions. Witkin began his research with the measurement of the perception of the upright. Intraindividual consistencies in perceptual errors led him to study individual styles of thinking.

Intercorrelations Among the Measures of Cognitive Style. While the F Scale and the Dogmatism Scale are factorially discriminable (Kerlinger and Rokeach, 1966; Warr, Lee, and Jöreskog, 1969), all studies that we have been able to locate (Goldstein and Blackman, forthcoming) indicate significant positive relationships between the two measures. The correlations are generally between 0.50 and 0.80. The two instruments, both Likert-type measures, share method variance. The F Scale is also moderately correlated with measures used to assess the other three major approaches to the study of cognitive style reviewed here, although the Dogmatism Scale is not. The measures of cognitive complexity, integrative complexity, and field dependence generally do not correlate well with each other (for example, Elliot, 1961; Streufert, 1970; Wolfe, Egelston, and Powers, 1972).

For the purpose of this summary, we will use the phrase "differentiated cognitive style" in referring to the individual who is nonauthoritarian, nondogmatic, cognitively complex, integratively complex, or field-independent. As discussed above, the various measures of cognitive style, both within and across the various areas reviewed, are not always significantly related. On the other hand, the measures examined in this chapter were selected specifically because they represent different approaches to the study of cognitive style. As such, one would not necessarily expect a high degree of interrelatedness. Despite this evidence of lack of unidimensionality, we believe there is sufficient commonality of relationships to dependent variables to warrant the use of the phrase "differentiated cognitive style."

Stability. Regarding the question of stability over time, the measures of cognitive style are satisfactorily reliable over short intervals (Goldstein and Blackman, forthcoming), the correlations clustering between 0.70 and 0.90, with somewhat lower correlations obtained for cognitive complexity. There is also considerable evidence of developmental changes, with an increase in differentiation of cognitive style at least through the college years; there is some evidence that with old age and infirmity there is a decrease in differentiation.

Intelligence. There has been some concern as to whether different measures of cognitive style are independent of measures of intelligence. This issue has been extensively studied with regard to field dependence. Positive relationships in the range of 0.40 to 0.60 have been obtained between measures of field dependence and a variety of measures of intelligence (Blackman and Goldstein, 1976). There are fewer data regarding the relationship of intelligence to the other measures of cognitive style. The data that do exist generally indicate either independence of intelligence from cognitive style or a low level of relationship. When relationships are found, high intelligence is related to a more differentiated cognitive style.

Overview. There are many problems with the research that we have reviewed that make generalizations across studies difficult. For example, the instruments used to measure cognitive style are often modified from one investigation to another. Also, the methods used for measuring dependent variables often differ. Further, the actual level of subjects on any particular dimension of cognitive style differs from study to study; for example, a subject defined as high dogmatic in one study may be defined as low dogmatic in another. This contributes to inconsistent findings across studies. Finally, the relationship between measures of cognitive style and measures of performance has not been consistently explored in the various approaches to the study of cognitive style.

Despite these problems we believe there is sufficient evidence to conclude that certain behaviors are related to a less differentiated cognitive style. Individuals so characterized tend to be rigid and intolerant of ambiguity, are poorer synthesizers and integrators of information, and tend to conform. There is less evidence to support the existence of consistent relationships between cognitive style and accuracy of judgment and between cognitive style and the tendency to be consistent.

In summary, there are various approaches to the measurement of cognitive style. Investigators differ in the aspects, or dimensions, that they use to study this concept. However, each of the five approaches reviewed here has made substantial contributions to the prediction of behavior in one or another setting. Additional development of instruments and the use of multivariate research procedures should further clarify the relationships between cognitive style and behavior. Study of the interaction between environmental complexity and cognitive style seems to us to be an especially important area for further research.

References

Adams-Webber, J. R. "Cognitive Complexity and Sociality." *British Journal of Social and Clinical Psychology,* 1969, *8,* 211-216.

Adams-Webber, J. R. "Elicited Versus Provided Constructs in Repertory Grid Technique: A Review." *British Journal of Medical Psychology,* 1970, *43,* 349-354.

Adams-Webber, J. R., Schwenker, B., and Barbeau, D. "Personal Constructs and the Perception of Individual Differences." *Canadian Journal of Behavioural Science,* 1972, *4,* 218-224.

Adevai, G., and McGough, W. E. "Retest Reliability of Rod-and-Frame Scores During Early Adulthood." *Perceptual and Motor Skills,* 1968, *26,* 1306.

Adorno, T. W., Frenkel-Brunswik, E., Levinson, D. J., and Sanford, R. N. *The Authoritarian Personality.* New York: Harper & Row, 1950.

Allard, M., and Carlson, E. R. "The Generality of Cognitive

Complexity." *Journal of Social Psychology,* 1963, *59,* 73-75.

Allport, G. W. *Personality: A Psychological Interpretation.* New York: Holt, Rinehart and Winston, 1937.

Alter, R. D., and White, B. J. "Some Norms for the Dogmatism Scale." *Psychological Reports,* 1966, *19,* 967-969.

Applezweig, D. G. "Some Determinants of Behavioral Rigidity." *Journal of Abnormal and Social Psychology,* 1954, *49,* 224-228.

Ault, R. L., Mitchell, C., and Hartmann, D. P. "Some Methodological Problems in Reflection-Impulsivity Research." *Child Development,* 1976, *47,* 227-231.

Baer, D. J. "Factors in Perception and Rigidity." *Perceptual and Motor Skills,* 1964, *19,* 563-570.

Baldwin, B. A. "Autonomic Stress Resolution in Repressors and Sensitizers Following Microcounseling." *Psychological Reports,* 1972, *31,* 743-749.

Bannister, D., and Fransella, F. *Inquiring Man.* New York: Penguin, 1971.

Bannister, D., and Mair, J. M. M. *The Evaluation of Personal Constructs.* New York: Academic Press, 1968.

Banta, T. J. "Tests for the Evaluation of Early Childhood Education: The Cincinnati Autonomy Test Battery (CATB)." In J. Hellmuth (Ed.), *Cognitive Studies.* Vol. 1. New York: Brunner/Mazel, 1970.

Barker, E. N. "Authoritarianism of the Political Right, Center, and Left." *Journal of Social Issues,* 1963, *19,* 63-74.

Bauman, G. "The Stability of the Individual's Mode of Perception, and Perception-Personality Relationships." Unpublished doctoral dissertation, New York University, 1951.

Becker, G. "Ability to Differentiate Message from Source as a Curvilinear Function of Scores on Rokeach's Dogmatism Scale." *Journal of Social Psychology,* 1967, *72,* 265-273.

Becker, G., and Dileo, D. T. "Scores on Rokeach's Dogmatism Scale and the Response Set to Present a Positive Social and Personal Image." *Journal of Social Psychology,* 1967, *71,* 287-293.

Bettinghaus, E., Miller, G., and Steinfatt, T. "Source Evaluation, Syllogistic Content, and Judgments of Logical Validity by High- and Low-Dogmatic Persons." *Journal of Personality and Social Psychology,* 1970, *16,* 238-244.

Bhushan, L. I. "A Study of Leadership Preference in Relation to Authoritarianism and Intolerance of Ambiguity." *Journal of the Indian Academy of Applied Psychology,* 1971, *8,* 34-38.

Bieri, J. "Cognitive Complexity-Simplicity and Predictive Behavior." *Journal of Abnormal and Social Psychology,* 1955, *51,* 263-268.

Bieri, J. "Cognitive Complexity: Assessment Issues in the Study of Cognitive Structure." Paper presented at meeting of the American Psychological Association, Chicago, September 1965.

Bieri, J. "Category Width as a Measure of Discrimination." *Journal of Personality,* 1969, *37,* 513-521.

Bieri, J. "Cognitive Structures in Personality." In H. M. Schroder and P. Suedfeld (Eds.), *Personality Theory and Information Processing.* New York: Ronald Press, 1971.

Bieri, J., Atkins, A. L., Briar, S., Leaman, R. L., Miller, H., and Tripodi, T. *Clinical and Social Judgment: The Discrimination of Behavioral Information.* New York: Wiley, 1966.

Bieri, J., Bradburn, W., and Galinsky, M. D. "Sex Differences in Perceptual Behavior." *Journal of Personality,* 1958, *26,* 1-12.

Blackman, S. "The Application of Multidimensional Scaling to the Measurement of Cognitive Patterning." In J. L. Kennedy and others, "Cognitive Patterning of Complex Stimuli: A Symposium." *Journal of General Psychology,* 1966, *74,* 25-49.

Blackman, S., and Goldstein, K. M. "Five Approaches to the Study of Cognitive Style." In T. Tomaszewski (Chair), *Cognitive Processes in Social Psychology.* Symposium presented at the 21st International Congress of Psychology, Paris, July 1976.

Blasi, E. R., Cross, H. A., and Hebert, J. A. "Effects of Field-Dependency on Weight Comparisons." *Perceptual and Motor Skills,* 1972, *35,* 111-114.

Block, J., and Block, J. "An Investigation of the Relationship Between Intolerance of Ambiguity and Ethnocentrism." *Journal of Personality,* 1951, *19,* 303-311.

Block, J., Block, J. H., and Harrington, D. M. "Some Misgivings about the Matching Familiar Figures Test as a Measure of Reflection-Impulsivity." *Developmental Psychology,* 1974, *10,* 611-632.

Block, J., Block, J. H., and Harrington, D. M. "Comment on the Kagan-Messer Reply." *Developmental Psychology,* 1975, *11,* 249-252.

Bodden, J. L. "Cognitive Complexity as a Factor in Appropriate Vocational Choice." *Journal of Counseling Psychology,* 1970, *17,* 364-368.

Bodden, J. L., and Klein, A. J. "Cognitive Differentiation and Affective Stimulus Value in Vocational Judgments." *Journal of Vocational Behavior,* 1973, *3,* 75-79.

Bottenberg, E. H. "Instrumental Characteristics and Validity of the Paragraph Completion Test (PCT) as a Measure of Integrative Complexity." *Psychological Reports,* 1969, *24,* 437-438.

Breskin, S., and Gorman, B. S. "On Rigidity and Field Dependence." *Perceptual and Motor Skills,* 1969, *29,* 541-542.

Broverman, D. M. "Cognitive Style and Intra-Individual Variation in Abilities." *Journal of Personality,* 1960a, *28,* 240-256.

Broverman, D. M. "Dimensions of Cognitive Style." *Journal of Personality,* 1960b, *28,* 167-185.

Brown, R. W. "A Determinant of the Relationship Between Rigidity and Authoritarianism." *Journal of Abnormal and Social Psychology,* 1953, *48,* 469-476.

Bruner, J. S., Goodnow, J., and Austin, G. A. *A Study of Thinking.* New York: Wiley, 1956.

Busch, J. C., and DeRidder, L. M. "Conformity in Preschool Disadvantaged Children as Related to Field-Dependence, Sex, and Verbal Reinforcement." *Psychological Reports,* 1973, *32,* 667-673.

Busch, J. C., and Simon, L. H. "Methodological Variables in the Study of Field Dependent Behavior of Young Children."

Paper presented at the annual meeting of the American Educational Research Association, Chicago, April 1972.

Busse, T. V. "Establishment of the Flexible Thinking Factor in Fifth-Grade Boys." *Journal of Psychology,* 1968, *69,* 93-100.

Campbell, V. N. "Assumed Similarity, Perceived Sociometric Balance, and Social Influence." Unpublished doctoral dissertation, University of Colorado, 1960.

Carr, J. E. "Differentiation as a Function of Source Characteristics and Judge's Conceptual Structure." *Journal of Personality,* 1969, *37,* 378-386.

Cattell, R. B., and Tiner, L. G. "The Varieties of Structural Rigidity." *Journal of Personality,* 1949, *17,* 321-341.

Chabassol, D. J., and Thomas, D. "Needs for Structure, Tolerance of Ambiguity and Dogmatism in Adolescents." *Psychological Reports,* 1975, *37,* 507-510.

Chown, S. M. "Rigidity: A Flexible Concept." *Psychological Bulletin,* 1959, *56,* 195-223.

Christie, R., and Cook, P. "A Guide to Published Literature Relating to the Authoritarian Personality Through 1956." *Journal of Psychology,* 1958, *45,* 171-199.

Christie, R., Havel, J., and Seidenberg, B. "Is the F Scale Irreversible?" *Journal of Abnormal and Social Psychology,* 1958, *56,* 143-159.

Clarke, P., and James, J. "The Effects of Situation, Attitude Intensity and Personality on Information-Seeking." *Sociometry,* 1967, *30,* 235-245.

Clayton, M. B., and Jackson, D. N. "Equivalence Range, Acquiescence, and Overgeneralization." *Educational and Psychological Measurement,* 1961, *21,* 371-382.

Coates, S. W. *The Preschool Embedded Figures Test Manual.* Palo Alto, Calif.: Consulting Psychologists Press, 1972.

Cohn, T. S. "The Relation of the F Scale to a Response Set to Answer Positively." *American Psychologist,* 1953, *8,* 335.

Cohn, T. S. "Relation of the F Scale to a Response Set to Answer Positively." *Journal of Social Psychology,* 1956, *44,* 129-133.

Cohn, T. S., and Carsch, H. "Administration of the F Scale to a

Sample of Germans." *Journal of Abnormal and Social Psychology,* 1954, *49,* 471.

Coop, R. H., and Sigel, I. E. "Cognitive Style: Implications for Learning and Instruction." *Psychology in the Schools,* 1971, *2,* 152-161.

Couch, H., and Keniston, K. "Yeasayers and Naysayers: Agreeing Response Set as a Personality Variable." *Journal of Abnormal and Social Psychology,* 1960, *60,* 151-174.

Cox, G. B. "A Comparison of Two Measures of Cognitive Complexity and Their Relationships with Intelligence, Sex, Age, and Race." JSAS *Catalog of Selected Documents in Psychology,* 1974, *4,* 80.

Crano, W. D., and Schroder, H. M. "Complexity of Attitude Structure and Processes of Conflict Resolution." *Journal of Personality and Social Psychology,* 1967, *5,* 110-114.

Crockett, W. H. "Cognitive Complexity and Impression Formation." In B. A. Maher (Ed.), *Progress in Experimental Personality Research.* Vol. 2. New York: Academic Press, 1965.

Day, H. "Looking Time as a Function of Stimulus Variables and Individual Differences." *Perceptual and Motor Skills,* 1966, *22,* 423-428.

DiRenzo, G. J. "Professional Politicians and Personality Structures." *American Journal of Sociology,* 1967, *73,* 217-225.

Duck, S. W. "Friendship, Similarity and the Reptest." *Psychological Reports,* 1972, *31,* 231-234.

Duck, S. W., and Spencer, C. "Personal Constructs and Friendship Formation." *Journal of Personality and Social Psychology,* 1972, *23,* 40-45.

Durand, R. M., and Lambert, Z. V. "Dogmatism and Exposure to Political Candidates." *Psychological Reports,* 1975, *36,* 423-429.

Dyer, R. N. "The Stroop Phenomenon and Its Use in the Study of Perceptual, Cognitive, and Response Processes." *Memory and Cognition,* 1973, *1,* 106-120.

Egeland, B., and Weinberg, R. A. "The Matching Familiar Figures Test: A Look at Its Psychometric Credibility." *Child Development,* 1976, *47,* 483-491.

Ehri, L. C., and Muzio, I. M. "Cognitive Style and Reasoning About Speed." *Journal of Educational Psychology,* 1974, *66,* 569-571.

Elliot, R. "Interrelationships Among Measures of Field Dependence, Ability, and Personality Traits." *Journal of Abnormal and Social Psychology,* 1961, *63,* 27-36.

Epting, F. R. "The Stability of Cognitive Complexity in Construing Social Issues." *British Journal of Social and Clinical Psychology,* 1972, *11,* 122-125.

Epting, F. R., and Wilkins, G. "Comparison of Cognitive Structural Measures for Predicting Person Perception." *Perceptual and Motor Skills,* 1974, *38,* 727-730.

Evans, F. J. "Effects of Practice on the Validity of a Group-Administered Embedded Figures Test." *Acta Psychologica* (Amsterdam), 1969, *29,* 172-180.

Farley, F. H. "Sensation-Seeking Motive and Field Independence." *Perceptual and Motor Skills,* 1974, *38,* 330.

Feather, N. T. "Cognitive Differentiation, Attitude Strength, and Dogmatism." *Journal of Personality,* 1969a, *37,* 111-126.

Feather, N. T. "Preference for Information in Relation to Consistency, Novelty, Intolerance of Ambiguity, and Dogmatism." *Australian Journal of Psychology,* 1969b, *21,* 235-249.

Feather, N. T. "Value Differences in Relation to Ethnocentrism, Intolerance of Ambiguity, and Dogmatism." *Personality,* 1971, *2,* 349-366.

Fenchel, C. H. "Cognitive Rigidity as a Behavioral Variable Manifested in Intellectual and Perceptual Tasks by an Outpatient Population." Unpublished doctoral dissertation, New York University, 1958.

Fertig, E. S., and Mayo, C. "Impression Formation as a Function of Trait Consistency and Cognitive Complexity." *Journal of Experimental Research in Personality,* 1970, *4,* 190-197.

Figert, R. S., Jr. "An Elementary School Form of the Dogmatism Scale." *Journal of Experimental Education,* 1968, *37,* 19-23.

Fine, B. J. "Field-Dependence—Independence as 'Sensitivity' of the Nervous System: Supportive Evidence with Color and Weight Discrimination." *Perceptual and Motor Skills,* 1973, *37,* 287-295.

Fisher, S. "Patterns of Personality Rigidity and Some of Their Determinants." *Psychological Monographs,* 1950, *64* (1) (entire issue).

Forster, N. C., Vinacke, W. E., and Digman, J. M. "Flexibility and Rigidity in a Variety of Problem Situations." *Journal of Abnormal and Social Psychology,* 1955, *50,* 211-216.

Fransella, F., and Joyston-Bechal, M. P. "An Investigation of Conceptual Process and Pattern Change in a Psychotherapy Group over One Year." *British Journal of Psychiatry,* 1971, *119,* 199-206.

French, E. G. "Interrelation Among Some Measures of Rigidity Under Stress and Nonstress Conditions." *Journal of Abnormal and Social Psychology,* 1955, *51,* 114-118.

Frenkel-Brunswik, E. "Intolerance of Ambiguity as an Emotional and Perceptual Personality Variable." *Journal of Personality,* 1949, *18,* 108-143.

Gaensslen, H., May, F., and Wolpert, F. "Relation Between Dogmatism and Anxiety." *Psychological Reports,* 1973, *33,* 955-958.

Gardner, R. W. "Cognitive Styles in Categorizing Behavior." *Journal of Personality,* 1953, *22,* 214-233.

Gardner, R. W. "Cognitive Controls in Adaptation: Research and Measurement." In S. Messick and J. Ross (Eds.), *Measurement in Personality and Cognition.* New York: Wiley, 1962.

Gardner, R. W. "Contrast Reactivity: Situational and Temporal Stability of Cognitive Control." *Perceptual and Motor Skills,* 1973, *36,* 617-618.

Gardner, R. W., Holzman, P. S., Klein, G. S., Linton, H. B., and Spence, D. P. "Cognitive Control: A Study of Individual Consistencies in Cognitive Behavior." *Psychological Issues,* 1959, *1* (entire issue).

Gardner, R. W., Jackson, D. N., and Messick, S. "Personality Organization in Cognitive Controls and Intellectual Abilities." *Psychological Issues,* 1960, *2* (4) (entire issue).

Gardner, R. W., Lohrenz, L., and Schoen, R. "Cognitive Control of Differentiation in the Perception of Persons and Objects." *Perceptual and Motor Skills,* 1968, *26,* 311-330.

Gardner, R. W., and Long, R. I. "Cognitive Controls as Determinants of Learning and Remembering." *Psychologia,* 1960a, *3,* 165-171.

Gardner, R. W., and Long, R. I. "Leveling-Sharpening and Serial Learning." *Perceptual and Motor Skills,* 1960b, *10,* 179-185.

Gardner, R. W., and Long, R. I. "Cognitive Controls of Attention and Inhibition: A Study of Individual Consistencies." *British Journal of Psychology,* 1962a, *53,* 381-388.

Gardner, R. W., and Long, R. I. "Control, Defense and Centration Effect: A Study of Scanning Behavior." *British Journal of Psychology,* 1962b, *53,* 129-140.

Gardner, R. W., and Moriarty, A. "Dimensions of Cognitive Control at Preadolescence." In R. Gardner (Ed.), *Personality Development at Preadolescence.* Seattle: University of Washington Press, 1968.

Gardner, R. W., and Schoen, R. A. "Differentiation and Abstraction in Concept Formation." *Psychological Monographs,* 1962, *76,* 1-21.

Golden, C. J. "A Group Version of the Stroop Color and Word Test." *Journal of Personality Assessment,* 1975a, *39,* 386-388.

Golden, C. J. "The Measurement of Creativity by the Stroop Color and Word Test." *Journal of Personality Assessment,* 1975b, *39,* 502-506.

Goldstein, K. M., and Blackman, S. "Cognitive Complexity, Maternal Child Rearing, and Acquiescence." *Social Behavior and Personality,* 1976, *4,* 97-103.

Goldstein, K. M., and Blackman, S. *Cognitive Style: Five Approaches to Theory and Research.* New York: Wiley, forthcoming.

Goodenough, D. R., and Eagle, C. J. "A Modification of the Embedded-Figures Test for Use with Young Children." *Journal of Genetic Psychology,* 1963, *103,* 67-74.

Goodman, B. "Field Dependence and Closure Factors." Unpublished manuscript, 1960.

Gormly, M. V., and Clore, C. L. "Attraction Dogmatism, and Attitude Similarity-Dissimilarity." *Journal of Experimental Research in Personality,* 1969, *4,* 9-13.

Gough, H. G., Harris, D. B., Martin, W. E., and Edwards, M. "Children's Ethnic Attitudes: I. Relationship to Certain Personality Factors." *Child Development,* 1950, *21,* 83-91.

Gough, H. G., and Lazzari, R. "A 15-item Form of the F Scale and a Cross-Cultural Application." *Journal of Psychology,* 1974, *88,* 39-46.

Greaves, G. "Harvey's 'This I Believe' Test: Studies of Reliability." *Psychological Reports,* 1971, *28,* 387-390.

Guetzkow, H. "An Analysis of the Operation of Set in Problem-Solving Behavior." *Journal of General Psychology,* 1951, *45,* 219-244.

Gulo, E. V., and Lynch, M. D. "Evidence on the Validity of Rokeach Dogmatism Scale (DS) Form E." *College Student Journal,* 1973, *7,* 62-67.

Handel, A. "Perception of Verticality of a Modified Portable Rod-and-Frame Test." *Perceptual and Motor Skills,* 1972, *34,* 459-468.

Hanson, D. J. "Dogmatism and Attitude Extremity." *Journal of Social Psychology,* 1973, *89,* 155-156.

Harvey, J., and Hays, D. G. "Effect of Dogmatism and Authority of the Source of Communication upon Persuasion." *Psychological Reports,* 1972, *30,* 119-122.

Harvey, O. J. "Cognitive Determinants of Role Playing." Technical Report No. 3, Contract Nonr 1147(07), University of Colorado, 1963.

Harvey, O. J. "Some Cognitive Determinants of Influencibility." *Sociometry,* 1964, *27,* 208-221.

Harvey, O. J. "Some Situational and Cognitive Determinants of Dissonance Resolution." *Journal of Personality and Social Psychology,* 1965, *1,* 349-355.

Harvey, O. J. "Conceptual Systems and Attitude Change." In C. Sherif and M. Sherif (Eds.), *Attitude, Ego-Involvement and Change.* New York: Wiley, 1967.

Harvey, O. J., and Felknor, C. "Parent-Child Relations as an Antecedent to Conceptual Functioning." In R. A. Hoppe,

G. A. Milton, and E. C. Simmel (Eds.), *Early Experiences and the Processes of Socialization.* New York: Academic Press, 1970.

Harvey, O. J., Hunt, D. E., and Schroder, H. M. *Conceptual Systems and Personality Organization.* New York: Wiley, 1961.

Harvey, O. J., and Ware, R. "Personality Differences in Dissonance Resolution." *Journal of Personality and Social Psychology,* 1967, *7,* 227-230.

Herkowitz, J. "Moving Embedded Figures Test." *Research Quarterly,* 1972, *43,* 479-488.

Hewitt, D. "Conceptual Complexity, Environment Complexity, Communication Salience and Attitude Change." *European Journal of Social Psychology,* 1972, *2,* 285-305.

Hinkle, D. N. "The Game of Personal Constructs." In D. Bannister (Ed.), *Perspectives in Personal Construct Theory.* New York: Academic Press, 1970.

Hollingworth, H. "The Central Tendency of Judgment in Experimental Studies of Judgment." *Archives of Psychology,* 1913, *29,* 44-52.

Holzman, P. S., and Klein, G. S. "Cognitive System—Principles of Leveling and Sharpening: Individual Differences in Assimilation Effects in Visual Time-Error." *Journal of Psychology,* 1954, *37,* 105-122.

Hritzuk, J., and Taylor, L. "A Relationship Between Field-Dependency-Independency and Set: A Western and Soviet View." *Social Behavior and Personality,* 1973, *1,* 23-28.

Hunt, D. E., and Halverson, C. "Manual for Scoring Sentence Completion Responses for Adolescents." Unpublished manuscript, Syracuse University, 1964.

Hunt, M. F., and Miller, G. R. "Open- and Closed-Mindedness, Belief-Discrepant Communication Behavior, and Tolerance for Cognitive Inconsistency." *Journal of Personality and Social Psychology,* 1968, *8,* 35-37.

Irwin, M., Tripodi, T., and Bieri, J. "Affective Stimulus Value and Cognitive Complexity." *Journal of Personality and Social Psychology,* 1967, *5,* 444-448.

Iverson, M., and Schwab, H. G. "Ethnocentric Dogmatism and

Binocular Fusion of Sexually and Radically Discrepant Stimuli." *Journal of Personality and Social Psychology,* 1967, *7,* 73-81.

Jackson, D. N., Messick, S., and Myers, C. T. *The Role of Memory and Color in Group and Individual Embedded-Figures Measures of Field-Independence.* Princeton, N.J.: Educational Testing Service, 1962.

Jackson, D. N., Messick, S., and Myers, C. T. "Evaluation of Group and Individual Forms of Embedded-Figures Measures of Field-Independence." *Educational and Psychological Measurement,* 1964, *24,* 177-192.

Jacobson, G. H. "An Examination of Possible Changes in Authoritarianism, Values, and Cognitive Complexity, with Their Implications for Business." Unpublished doctoral dissertation, University of Southern California, 1973.

Jacoby, J. "Open-Mindedness and Creativity." *Psychological Reports,* 1967, *20,* 822.

Jensen, A. R. "Scoring the Stroop Test." *Acta Psychologica,* 1965, *24,* 398-408.

Jensen, A. R., and Rowher, W. D., Jr. "The Stroop Color-Word Test: A Review." *Acta Psychologica,* 1966, *25,* 36-93.

Jones, M. B. "Authoritarianism and Intolerance of Fluctuation." *Journal of Abnormal and Social Psychology,* 1955, *50,* 125-126.

Kagan, J., and Kogan, N. "Individual Variation in Cognitive Processes." In P. H. Mussen (Ed.), *Carmichael's Manual of Child Psychology.* Vol. 1. New York: Wiley, 1970.

Kagan, J., and Messer, S. B. "A Reply to 'Some Misgivings About the Matching Familiar Figures Test as a Measure of Reflection-Impulsivity.'" *Developmental Psychology,* 1975, *11,* 244-248.

Kagan, J., Moss, H. A., and Sigel, I. E. "Psychological Significance of Styles of Conceptualization." In J. C. Wright and J. Kagan (Eds.), "Basic Cognitive Process in Children." *Monographs of the Society for Research in Child Development,* 1963, *28,* 73-112.

Kagan, J., Rosman, B., Day, D., Albert, J., and Phillips, W. "Information Processing in the Child: Significance of Analytic and Reflective Attitudes." *Psychological Monographs,* 1964, *78* (entire issue).

Kaplan, M. F., and Singer, E. "Dogmatism and Sensory Alienation: An Empirical Investigation." *Journal of Consulting Psychology,* 1963, *27,* 486-491.

Karlins, M. "Conceptual Complexity and Remote-Associative Proficiency as Creativity Variables in a Complex Problem-Solving Task." *Journal of Personality and Social Psychology,* 1967, *6,* 264-278.

Karlins, M., Coffman, T., Lamm, H., and Schroder, H. M. "The Effect of Conceptual Complexity on Information Search in a Complex Problem-Solving Task." *Psychonomic Science,* 1967, *7,* 137-138.

Karlins, M., and Lamm H. "Information Search as a Function of Conceptual Structure in a Complex Problem-Solving Task." *Journal of Personality and Social Psychology,* 1967, *5,* 456-459.

Karp, S. A., and Konstadt, N. "Manual for the Children's Embedded-Figures Test: Cognitive Tests." Unpublished manuscript, 1963.

Kates, S. L., and Diab, L. N. "Authoritarian Ideology and Attitudes on Parent-Child Relationships." *Journal of Abnormal and Social Psychology,* 1955, *51,* 13-16.

Kelly, G. A. *The Psychology of Personal Constructs.* New York: Norton, 1955.

Kelly, G. A. "A Brief Introduction to Personal Construct Theory." In D. Bannister (Ed.), *Perspectives in Personal Construct Theory.* New York: Academic Press, 1970.

Kelman, H. C., and Barclay, J. "The F Scale as a Measure of Breadth of Perspective." *Journal of Abnormal and Social Psychology,* 1963, *67,* 608-615.

Kenny, D. T., and Ginsberg, R. "Authoritarian Submission, Intolerance of Ambiguity and Aggression." *Canadian Journal of Psychology,* 1958, *21,* 121-126.

Kerlinger, F., and Rokeach, M. "The Factorial Nature of the F and D Scales." *Journal of Personality and Social Psychology,* 1966, *4,* 391-399.

Kessler, M. R., and Kronenberger, E. J. "Dogmatism and Perceptual Synthesis." *Perceptual and Motor Skills,* 1967, *24,* 179-182.

Kidd, A. H., and Kidd, R. M. "Relation of F-test Scores to Rigidity." *Perceptual and Motor Skills,* 1972, *34,* 239-243.

Kirtley, D., and Harkless, R. "Some Personality and Attitudinal Correlates of Dogmatism." *Psychological Reports,* 1969, *24,* 851-854.

Kleck, R. E., and Wheaton, J. "Dogmatism and Responses to Opinion-Consistent and Opinion-Inconsistent Information." *Journal of Personality and Social Psychology,* 1967, *5,* 249-252.

Klein, G. S. "Need and Regulation." In M. R. Jones (Ed.), *Nebraska Symposium on Motivation.* Lincoln: University of Nebraska Press, 1954.

Klein, G. S., Barr, H. L., and Wolitzky, D. L. "Personality." *Annual Review of Psychology,* 1967, *18,* 467-560.

Klein, G. S., Gardner, R. W., and Schlesinger, H. J. "Tolerance of Unrealistic Experiences: A Study of the Generality of a Cognitive Control." *British Journal of Psychology,* 1962, *53,* 41-55.

Klein, G. S., and Schlesinger, H. J. "Perceptual Attitudes Toward Instability: I. Prediction of Apparent Movement Experiences from Rorschach Responses." *Journal of Personality,* 1951, *19,* 289-302.

Koenig, F., and Edmonds, D. "Cognitive Complexity and Affective Value of Literary Stimuli." *Perceptual and Motor Skills,* 1972, *33,* 947-948.

Koenig, F., and Seaman, J. "Comparison of Cognitive Complexity of Male and Female Subjects Responding to Male and Female Stimuli." *Perceptual and Motor Skills,* 1974, *38,* 1345-1346.

Kogan, N. *Cognitive Styles in Infancy and Early Childhood.* Hillsdale, N.J.: Lawrence Erlbaum Associates, 1976.

Korn, H. A., and Giddan, N. S. "Scoring Methods and Construct Validity of the Dogmatism Scale." *Educational and Psychological Measurement,* 1964, *24,* 867-874.

Kuusinen, J., and Nystedt, L. "The Convergent Validity of Four

Indices of Cognitive Complexity in Person Perception: A Multiindex Multimethod and Factor Analytical Approach." *Scandinavian Journal of Psychology,* 1975a, *16,* 131-136.

Kuusinen, J., and Nystedt, L. "Individual Versus Provided Constructs, Cognitive Complexity and Extremity of Ratings in Person Perception." *Scandinavian Journal of Psychology,* 1975b, *16,* 137-148.

Landfield, A. W. "Interpretive Man: The Enlarged Self-Image." In A. W. Landfield (Ed.), *Nebraska Symposium on Motivation, 1976.* Vol. 24. Lincoln: University of Nebraska Press, 1977.

Leckart, B. T., and Wagner, J. F. "Stimulus Familiarity, Dogmatism and the Duration of Attention." *Perception and Psychophysics,* 1967, *2,* 268-270.

Leitner, L. M., Landfield, A. W., and Barr, M. A. "Cognitive Complexity: A Review and Elaboration Within Personal Construct Theory." Unpublished manuscript, University of Nebraska, 1974.

Leventhal, H. "Cognitive Processes and Interpersonal Predictions." *Journal of Abnormal Social Psychology,* 1957, *55,* 176-180.

Levitt, E. E. "Studies in Intolerance of Ambiguity: I. The Decision-Location Test with Grade School Children." *Child Development,* 1953, *24,* 263-268.

Levitt, E. E. "The Water Jar Einstellung Test as a Measure of Rigidity." *Psychological Bulletin,* 1956, *53,* 347-370.

Levitt, E. E., and Zelen, S. L. "The Validity of the Einstellung Test as a Measure of Rigidity." *Journal of Abnormal and Social Psychology,* 1953, *48,* 573-580.

Levitt, E. E., and Zelen, S. L. "An Investigation of the Water-Jar Extinction Problem as a Measure of Rigidity." *Psychological Reports,* 1955, *1,* 331-334.

Levy, J. M., and Rokeach, M. "The Formation of New Perceptual Systems." In M. Rokeach, *The Open and Closed Mind.* New York: Basic Books, 1960.

Lindstrom, D. R., and Shipman, V. C. "Sigel Object Categorization Test." In V. C. Shipman (Ed.), *Disadvantaged Chil-*

dren and Their First School Experiences. Princeton, N.J.: Educational Testing Service, 1972.

Linton, H. "Dependence on External Influence: Correlates in Perception, Attitudes, and Judgment." *Journal of Abnormal and Social Psychology,* 1955, *51,* 502-507.

Little, B. R. "Sex Differences and Comparability of Three Measures of Cognitive Complexity." *Psychological Reports,* 1969, *24,* 607-609.

Long, G. M. "The Rod-and-Frame Test: Further Comments on Methodology." *Perceptual and Motor Skills,* 1973, *36,* 624-626.

Luchins, A. S. "Mechanization in Problem-Solving." *Psychological Monographs,* 1942, *54* (6) (entire issue).

Luchins, A. S. "Rigidity and Ethnocentrism: A Critique." *Journal of Personality,* 1949, *17,* 449-466.

Lundy, R. M., and Berkowitz, L. "Cognitive Complexity and Assimilative Projection in Attitude Change." *Journal of Abnormal and Social Psychology,* 1957, *55,* 34-37.

MacDonald, A. P., Jr. "Revised Scale for Ambiguity Tolerance: Reliability and Validity." *Psychological Reports,* 1970, *26,* 791-798.

McKeachie, W. J. "Psychology in America's Bicentennial Year." *American Psychologist,* 1976, *31,* 819-833.

MacNeil, L. W., and Rule, B. G. "Effects of Conceptual Structure on Information Preference under Sensory-Deprivation Conditions." *Journal of Personality and Social Psychology,* 1970, *16,* 530-535.

Macrae, J. A. "Interpersonal Perception—Some Determinants and Variables." *Papers in Psychology,* 1969, *3,* 39-40.

Mahoney, M. J. "Reflections on the Cognitive-Learning Trend in Psychotherapy." *American Psychologist,* 1977, *32,* 5-13.

Mayo, C. W., and Crockett, W. H. "Cognitive Complexity and Primacy-Recency Effects in Impression Formation." *Journal of Abnormal and Social Psychology,* 1964, *68,* 335-338.

Mazis, M. B. "Cognitive Tuning and Receptivity to Novel Information." *Journal of Experimental Social Psychology,* 1973, *9,* 307-319.

Mebane, D., and Johnson, D. L. "A Comparison of the Performance of Mexican Boys and Girls on Witkin's Cognitive Tasks." *Interamerican Journal of Psychology*, 1970, *4*, 3-4.

Melikian, L. H. "Some Correlates of Authoritarianism in Two Cultural Groups." *Journal of Psychology*, 1956, *42*, 237-248.

Messer, S. B. "Reflection-Impulsivity: A Review." *Psychological Bulletin*, 1976, *83*, 1026-1052.

Messick, S. "The Criterion Problem in the Evaluation of Instruction: Assessing Possible, Not Just Intended, Outcomes." In M. C. Wittrock and D. Wiley (Eds.), *The Evaluation of Instruction: Issues and Problems*. New York: Holt, Rinehart and Winston, 1970.

Messick, S., and associates. *Individuality in Learning*. San Francisco: Jossey-Bass, 1976.

Messick, S., and Damarin, F. "Cognitive Styles and Memory for Faces." *Journal of Abnormal and Social Psychology*, 1964, *69*, 313-318.

Messick, S., and Frederiksen, N. "Ability, Acquiescence, and Authoritarianism." *Psychological Reports*, 1958, *4*, 687-697.

Metcalfe, R. J. "Own vs. Provided Constructs in a Reptest Measure of Cognitive Complexity." *Psychological Reports*, 1974, *35*, 1305-1306.

Meyers, B. "An Analysis of Factors Relating to Cognitive Complexity in Three High School Groups." Progress report, Grant MH-08334-02, September 1964.

Mikol, B. "The Enjoyment of New Musical Systems." In M. Rokeach, *The Open and Closed Mind*. New York: Basic Books, 1960.

Miller, A. G. "Amount of Information and Stimulus Valence as Determinants of Cognitive Complexity." *Journal of Personality*, 1969, *37*, 141-157.

Miller, A. G., and Harvey, O. J. "Effects of Concreteness-Abstractness and Anxiety on Intellectual and Motor Performance." *Journal of Consulting and Clinical Psychology*, 1973, *40*, 444-451.

Miller, G. R., and Bacon, P. "Open- and Closed-Mindedness and

Recognition of Visual Humor." *Journal of Communication,* 1971, *21,* 150-159.

Miller, H., and Bieri, J. "Cognitive Complexity as a Function of the Significance of the Stimulus Objects Being Judged." *Psychological Reports,* 1965, *16,* 1203-1204.

Millon, T. "Authoritarianism, Intolerance of Ambiguity, and Rigidity Under Ego- and Task-Involving Conditions." *Journal of Abnormal and Social Psychology,* 1957, *55,* 29-33.

Moore, S. F., Gleser, G. C., and Warm, J. S. "Cognitive Style in the Organization and Articulation of Ambiguous Stimuli." *Psychonomic Science,* 1970, *21,* 243-244.

Mouw, J. T. "Effect of Dogmatism on Levels of Cognitive Processes." *Journal of Educational Psychology,* 1969, *60,* 363-369.

Murray, C. "Item Analysis of the Elementary School Form of the Dogmatism Scale." *Journal of Experimental Education,* 1974, *42,* 50-54.

Muuss, R. E. "A Comparison of 'High Causally' and 'Low Causally' Oriented Sixth Grade Children on Personality Variables Indicative of Mental Health." *Proceedings of the Iowa Academy of Science,* 1959, *66,* 388-394.

Nidorf, L. J. "Individual Differences in Impression Formation." Unpublished doctoral dissertation, Clark University, 1961.

Niyekawa, A. M. "Factors Associated with Authoritarianism in Japan." Unpublished doctoral dissertation, New York University, 1960.

O'Connor, P. "Ethnocentrism, Intolerance of Ambiguity and Abstract Reasoning Ability." *Journal of Abnormal and Social Psychology,* 1952, *47,* 526-530.

Ohnmacht, F. W., and McMorris, R. F. "Creativity as a Function of Field Independence and Dogmatism." *Journal of Psychology,* 1971, *79,* 165-168.

Okonji, M. O. "The Differential Effects of Rural and Urban Upbringing on the Development of Cognitive Styles." *International Journal of Psychology,* 1969, *4,* 293-305.

Oltman, P. "A Portable Rod-and-Frame Apparatus." *Perceptual and Motor Skills,* 1968, *26,* 503-506.

Osborn, W. P. "Dogmatism, Tolerance for Cognitive Inconsistency, and Persuasibility Under Three Conditions of Message Involvements." *Proceedings of the 81st Annual Convention of the American Psychological Association,* 1973, *8,* 365-366.

Parrott, G. "Dogmatism and Rigidity: A Factor Analysis." *Psychological Reports,* 1971, *29,* 135-140.

Peabody, D. "Attitude Content and Agreement Set in Scales of Authoritarianism, Dogmatism, Anti-Semitism, and Economic Conservatism." *Journal of Abnormal and Social Psychology,* 1961, *63,* 1-11.

Peabody, D. "Two Components in Bipolar Scales: Direction and Extremeness." *Psychological Review,* 1962, *69,* 65-73.

Pedhazur, E. J. "Factor Structure of the Dogmatism Scale." *Psychological Reports,* 1971, *28,* 735-740.

Pettigrew, T. F. "The Measurements and Correlates of Category Width as a Cognitive Variable." *Journal of Personality,* 1958, *26,* 532-544.

Pilisuk, M. "Anxiety, Self-Acceptance, and Open-Mindedness." *Journal of Clinical Psychology,* 1963, *19,* 387-391.

Pizzamiglio, C. L., and Pizzamiglio, L. ["Psychometric Data of Some Tests of Field Dependence Related to an Italian Population of Children Four and a Half to Ten and a Half Years Old."] *Archivio di Psicologia Neurologia e Psichiatria,* 1974, *35,* 127-143.

Powell, F. A. "Open- and Closed-Mindedness and the Ability to Differentiate Message from Source." *Journal of Abnormal and Social Psychology,* 1962, *65,* 61-64.

Pritchard, D. A. "Leveling-Sharpening Revisited." *Perceptual and Motor Skills,* 1975, *40,* 111-117.

Reid, W. A., and Holley, B. J. "An Application of Repertory Grid Techniques to the Study of Choice of University." *British Journal of Educational Psychology,* 1972, *42,* 52-59.

Reker, G. T. "Interpersonal Conceptual Structures of Emotionally Disturbed and Normal Boys." *Journal of Abnormal Psychology,* 1974, *83,* 380-386.

Riley, J., and Armlin, N. J. "The Dogmatism Scale and Flexibility in Maze Performance." *Perceptual and Motor Skills,* 1965, *21,* 914.

Robinson, J. P., and Shaver, P. R. *Measures of Social Psychological Attitudes.* (Rev. ed.) Ann Arbor, Mich.: Survey Research Center, Institute for Social Research, 1973.

Rokeach, M. "Generalized Mental Rigidity as a Factor in Ethnocentrism." *Journal of Abnormal and Social Psychology,* 1948, *43,* 259-278.

Rokeach, M. *The Open and Closed Mind.* New York: Basic Books, 1960.

Rokeach, M., McGovney, W. C., and Denny, M. R. "A Distinction Between Dogmatic and Rigid Thinking." *Journal of Abnormal and Social Psychology,* 1955, *51,* 87-93.

Rokeach, M., McGovney, W. C., and Denny, M. R. "Dogmatic Thinking Versus Rigid Thinking." In M. Rokeach, *The Open and Closed Mind.* New York: Basic Books, 1960.

Rokeach, M., and Vidulich, R. N. "The Formation of New Belief Systems: The Roles of Memory and the Capacity to Entertain." In M. Rokeach, *The Open and Closed Mind.* New York: Basic Books, 1960.

Rosenkrantz, P. S., and Crockett, W. H. "Some Factors Influencing the Assimilation of Disparate Information in Impression Formation." *Journal of Personality and Social Psychology,* 1965, *2,* 397-402.

Rosenman, M. F. "Dogmatism and the Movie 'Dr. Strangelove.'" *Psychological Reports,* 1967, *20,* 942.

Rosner, S. "Consistency in Response to Group Pressure." *Journal of Abnormal and Social Psychology,* 1957, *55,* 145-146.

Rosnow, R. L., Gitter, A. G., and Holz, R. F. "Some Determinants of Postdecisional Information Preferences." *Journal of Social Psychology,* 1969, *79,* 235-245.

Rubenowitz, S. *Emotional Flexibility-Rigidity as a Comprehensive Dimension of Mind.* Stockholm: Almqvist and Wiksell, 1963.

Russell, G. W., and Sandilands, M. L. "Some Correlates of Conceptual Complexity." *Psychological Reports,* 1973, *33,* 587-593.

Santostefano, S. "A Developmental Study of the Cognitive Control 'Leveling—Sharpening.' " *Merrill-Palmer Quarterly of Behavior and Development*, 1964, *10*, 343-360.

Santostefano, S., and Paley, E. "Development of Cognitive Controls in Children." *Child Development*, 1964, *35*, 939-949.

Santostefano, S., Rutledge, L., and Randall, D. "Cognitive Styles and Reading Disability." *Psychology in the Schools*, 1965, *2*, 57-62.

Scheerer, M. "Cognitive Theory." In G. Lindzey (Ed.), *Handbook of Social Psychology*. Vol. 1. Reading, Mass.: Addison-Wesley, 1954.

Schroder, H. M., Driver, M. J., and Streufert, S. *Human Information Processing*. New York: Holt, Rinehart and Winston, 1967.

Schroder, H. M., and Streufert, S. "The Measurement of Four Systems of Personality Structure Varying in Level of Abstractness (Sentence Completion Method)." Technical Report No. 11, Office of Naval Research, Princeton University, 1962.

Schultz, C. B., and DiVesta, F. J. "Effects of Expert Endorsement of Beliefs on Problem Solving Behavior of High and Low Dogmatics." *Journal of Educational Psychology*, 1972, *63*, 194-201.

Schulze, R. H. K. "A Shortened Version of the Rokeach Dogmatism Scale." *Journal of Psychological Studies*, 1962, *13*, 93-97.

Scott, W. A. "Cognitive Structure and Social Structure: Some Concepts and Relationships." In N. F. Washburne (Ed.), *Decisions, Values, and Groups*. Vol. 2. Elmsford, N.Y.: Pergamon Press, 1962.

Scott, W. A. "Cognitive Complexity and Cognitive Balance." *Sociometry*, 1963a, *26*, 66-74.

Scott, W. A. "Conceptualizing and Measuring Structural Properties of Cognition." In O. J. Harvey (Ed.), *Motivation and Social Interaction: Cognitive Determinants*. New York: Ronald Press, 1963b.

Sechrest, L., and Jackson, D. N. "Social Intelligence and Accuracy of Interpersonal Predictions." *Journal of Personality*, 1961, *29*, 167-182.

Segal, S. J., and Barr, H. L. "Effect of Instructions on Phi Phenomenon, Criterion Task of 'Tolerance for Unrealistic Experiences.' " *Perceptual and Motor Skills*, 1969, *29*, 483-486.

Sherif, M. *The Psychology of Social Norms.* New York: Harper & Row, 1936.

Shupe, D. R., and Wolfer, J. A. "Comparative Reliability of the Dogmatism Scale with 2 and 6 Scale Points." *Psychological Reports*, 1966, *19*, 284-286.

Siegel, S. "Certain Determinants and Correlates of Authoritarianism." *Genetic Psychology Monographs*, 1954, *49*, 187-230.

Sigel, I. E. *SCST Manual: Instructions and Scoring Guide.* Detroit: Merrill-Palmer Institute, 1967.

Sigel, I. E., and Olmsted, P. "Modification of Cognitive Skills Among Lower-Class Black Children." In J. Hellmuth (Ed.), *The Disadvantaged Child,* Vol. 3. New York: Brunner/Mazel, 1970.

Slater, P. "Theory and Technique of the Repertory Grid." *British Journal of Psychiatry*, 1969, *115*, 1287-1296.

Smith, D. D. "Dogmatism, Cognitive Consistency, and Knowledge of Conflicting Facts." *Sociometry*, 1968, *31*, 259-277.

Smith, G. J. W., and Klein, G. S. "Cognitive Controls in Serial Behavior Patterns." *Journal of Personality*, 1953, *22*, 188-213.

Snoek, J., and Dobbs, M. F. "Galvanic Skin Responses to Agreement and Disagreement in Relation to Dogmatism." *Psychological Reports*, 1967, *20*, 195-198.

Solar, D., Davenport, G., and Bruehl, D. "Social Compliance as a Function of Field Dependence." *Perceptual and Motor Skills*, 1969, *29*, 299-306.

Soucar, E. "Vigilance and the Perceptions of Teachers and Students." *Perceptual and Motor Skills*, 1971, *32*, 83-86.

Soucar, E., and Du Cette, J. "Cognitive Complexity and Political Preferences." *Psychological Reports*, 1971, *29*, 373-374.

Spotts, J. V., and Mackler, B. "Relationships of Field-Dependent and Field-Independent Cognitive Styles to Creative Test Performance." *Perceptual and Motor Skills,* 1967, *24,* 239-268.

Stager, D. P. "Conceptual Level as a Composition Variable in Small-Group Decision Making." *Journal of Personality and Social Psychology,* 1967, *5,* 152-161.

Stanes, D. "Analytic Responses to Conceptual Style Test as a Function of Instructions." *Child Development,* 1973, *44,* 389-391.

Stanley, G., and Martin, J. "How Sincere Is the Dogmatist?" *Psychological Review,* 1964, *71,* 331-334.

Steininger, M. "A Comparison of Two Kinds of Dogmatism Scores: Rokeach Categories *Versus* Open-Ended Responses." *Journal of Psychology,* 1973, *83,* 11-15.

Stewin, L., and Anderson, C. C. "Cognitive Complexity as a Determinant of Information Processing." *Alberta Journal of Educational Research,* 1974, *20,* 233-243.

Streufert, S. "Complexity and Complex Decision Making." *Journal of Experimental Social Psychology,* 1970, *6,* 494-509.

Streufert, S., and Driver, M. J. "Conceptual Structure, Information, Load and Perceptual Complexity." *Psychonomic Science,* 1965, *3,* 249-250.

Streufert, S., and Driver, M. J. "Impression Formation as a Measure of the Complexity of Conceptual Structure." *Educational and Psychological Measurement,* 1967, *27,* 1025-1039.

Streufert, S., and Schroder, H. M. "The Measurement of Varying Levels of Abstractness in Personality Structure (Impression Formation Method)." Unpublished manuscript, Princeton University, 1962.

Streufert, S., and Schroder, H. M. "Conceptual Structure, Environmental Complexity and Task Performance." *Journal of Experimental Research in Personality,* 1965, *1,* 132-137.

Streufert, S., Suedfeld, P., and Driver, M. J. "Conceptual Structure, Information Search, and Information Utilization." *Journal of Personality and Social Psychology,* 1965, *2,* 736-740.

Stringer, P. "Psychological Significance in Personal and Supplied Construct Systems: A Defining Experiment." *European Journal of Social Psychology,* 1972, *2,* 437-447.

Stroop, J. R. "Studies of Interference in Serial Verbal Reactions." *Journal of Experimental Psychology,* 1935, *18,* 643-662.

Suedfeld, P. "Conceptual and Environmental Complexity as Factors in Attitude Change." Unpublished doctoral dissertation, Princeton University, 1963.

Suedfeld, P. "Attitude Manipulation in Restricted Environments: I. Conceptual Structure and Response to Propaganda." *Journal of Abnormal and Social Psychology,* 1964, *68,* 242-246.

Suedfeld, P. "Verbal Indices of Conceptual Complexity: Manipulation by Instructions." *Psychonomic Science,* 1968, *12,* 377.

Suedfeld, P. "Information Processing as a Personality Model." In H. M. Schroder and P. Suedfeld (Eds.), *Personality Theory and Information Processing.* New York: Ronald Press, 1971.

Suedfeld, P., and Streufert, S. "Information Search as a Function of Conceptual and Environmental Complexity." *Psychonomic Science,* 1966, *4,* 351-353.

Suedfeld, P., Tomkins, S. S., and Tucker, W. H. "On Relations Among Perceptual and Cognitive Measures of Information Processing." *Perception and Psychophysics,* 1969, *6,* 45-46.

Suedfeld, P., and Vernon, J. "Attitude Manipulation in Restricted Environments: II. Conceptual Structure and the Internationalization of Propaganda Received as a Reward for Compliance." *Journal of Personality and Social Psychology,* 1966, *3,* 586-589.

Supnick, J. Unpublished manuscript, Clark University, 1964.

Taft, R. "Intolerance of Ambiguity and Ethnocentrism." *Journal of Consulting Psychology,* 1956, *20,* 153-154.

Thurstone, L. L. "A Factorial Study of Perception." In *Psychometric Monographs,* No. 4. Chicago: University of Chicago Press, 1944.

Touhey, J. C. "Category Width and Expectancies: Risk Conservatism or Generalization?" *Journal of Research in Personality*, 1973, *7*, 173-178.

Tripodi, T., and Bieri, J. "Cognitive Complexity as a Function of Own and Provided Constructs." *Psychological Reports*, 1963, *13*, 26.

Tripodi, T., and Bieri, J. "Information Transmission in Clinical Judgments as a Function of Stimulus Dimensionality and Cognitive Complexity." *Journal of Personality*, 1964, *32*, 119-137.

Tripodi, T., and Bieri, J. "Cognitive Complexity, Perceived Conflict, and Certainty." *Journal of Personality*, 1966, *34*, 144-153.

Troldahl, V. C., and Powell, F. A. "A Short-Term Dogmatism Scale for Use in Field Studies." *Social Forces*, 1965, *44*, 211-214.

Tuckman, B. W. "Integrative Complexity: Its Measurement and Relation to Creativity." *Educational and Psychological Measurement*, 1966, *26*, 369-382.

Turner, R., and Tripodi, T. "Cognitive Complexity as a Function of Type of Stimulus Object and Affective Stimulus Value." *Journal of Consulting and Clinical Psychology*, 1968, *32*, 182-185.

Uhes, M. J., and Shaver, J. P. "Dogmatism and Divergent-Convergent Abilities." *Journal of Psychology*, 1970, *75*, 3-11.

Vacc, N. A. "Cognitive Complexity in Resident Assistants and Their Accuracy in Predicting Student Academic Performance." *Journal of College Student Personnel*, 1974, *15*, 194-197.

Vacc, N. A., and Vacc, N. E. "An Adaptation for Children of the Modified Role Repertory Test—A Measure of Cognitive Complexity." *Psychological Reports*, 1973, *33*, 771-776.

Vacchiano, R. B., Schiffman, D. C., and Strauss, P. S. "Factor Structure of the Dogmatism Scale." *Psychological Reports*, 1967, *20*, 847-852.

Vacchiano, R. B., Strauss, P. S., and Hochman, L. "The Open and Closed Mind: A Review of Dogmatism." *Psychological Bulletin*, 1969, *71*, 261-273.

Vannoy, J. S. "Generality of Cognitive Complexity-Simplicity as a Personality Construct." *Journal of Personality and Social Psychology,* 1965, *2,* 385-396.

Vaught, G. M., and Augustson, B. "Field Dependence and Form Discrimination in Females." *Psychonomic Science,* 1967a, *7,* 333-334.

Vaught, G. M., and Augustson, B. "Field Dependence and Form Discrimination in Males." *Psychonomic Science,* 1967b, *8,* 233-234.

Vaught, G. M., and Ellinger, J. "Field Dependence and Form Discrimination." *Psychonomic Science,* 1966, *6,* 357-358.

Vaught, G. M., and Roodin, P. A. "Cognitive Style Performance and Form Discrimination." *Social Behavior and Personality,* 1973, *1,* 17-22.

Vidulich, R. N., and Kaiman, I. P. "The Effects of Information Source Status and Dogmatism upon Conformity Behavior." *Journal of Abnormal and Social Psychology,* 1961, *63,* 639-642.

Walk, R. D. "Perception and Personality: A Pretest." Unpublished manuscript, Social Relations Library, Harvard University, 1950.

Ware, R., and Harvey, O. J. "A Cognitive Determinant of Impression Formation." *Journal of Personality and Social Psychology,* 1967, *5,* 38-44.

Warr, P. B., and Coffman, T. L. "Personality, Involvement and Extremity of Judgment." *British Journal of Social and Clinical Psychology,* 1970, *9,* 108-121.

Warr, P. B., Lee, R. E., and Jöreskog, K. G. "A Note on the Factorial Nature of the F and D Scales." *British Journal of Psychology,* 1969, *60,* 119-123.

Warr, P. B., Schroder, H. M., and Blackman, S. "A Comparison of Two Techniques for the Measurement of International Judgment." *International Journal of Psychology,* 1969a, *4,* 135-140.

Warr, P. B., Schroder, H. M., and Blackman, S. "The Structure of Political Judgment." *British Journal of Social and Clinical Psychology,* 1969b, *8,* 32-43.

White, B. J., and Alter, R. D. "Dogmatism, Authoritarianism, and Contrast Effects in Judgment." *Perceptual and Motor Skills,* 1965, *20,* 99-101.

Wilkins, G., Epting, F., and Van De Riet, H. "Relationship Between Repression-Sensitization and Interpersonal Cognitive Complexity." *Journal of Consulting and Clinical Psychology,* 1972, *39,* 448-450.

Williams, J. D., Harlow, S. D., and Borgen, J. S. "Creativity, Dogmatism, and Arithmetic Achievement." *Journal of Psychology,* 1971, *78,* 217-222.

Witkin, H. A., Dyk, R. B., Faterson, H. F., Goodenough, D. R., and Karp, S. A. *Psychological Differentiation.* New York: Wiley, 1962.

Witkin, H. A., Lewis, H. B., Hertzman, M., Machover, K., Meissner, P. B., and Wapner, S. *Personality Through Perception.* New York: Harper & Row, 1954.

Witkin, H. A., Oltman, P. K., Raskin, E., and Karp, S. A. *A Manual for the Embedded Figures Tests.* Palo Alto, Calif.: Consulting Psychologists Press, 1971.

Wolfe, R., Egelston, R., and Powers, J. "Conceptual Structure and Conceptual Tempo." *Perceptual and Motor Skills,* 1972, *35,* 331-337.

Wolfer, J. A. "Changes in Dogmatism Scores of High and Low Dogmatics as a Function of Instructions." *Psychological Reports,* 1967, *20,* 947-950.

Zacker, J. "Authoritarian Avoidance of Ambiguity." *Psychological Reports,* 1973, *33,* 901-902.

Zagona, S. V., and Kelly, M. A. "The Resistance of the Closed Mind to a Novel and Complex Audio-Visual Experience." *Journal of Social Psychology,* 1966, *70,* 123-131.

Zajonc, R. B. "Cognitive Theories in Social Psychology." In G. Lindzey and E. Aronson (Eds.), *The Handbook of Social Psychology.* Vol. 1. Reading, Mass.: Addison-Wesley, 1968.

XII

Nature and Assessment of Human Curiosity

Wallace H. Maw, Ethel W. Maw

The volume of research in the area of human curiosity is increasing rapidly. As late as 1964, the authors wrote that "the nature of human curiosity has only recently been studied to any extent" (Maw and Maw, 1964, p. 23). Since that date, more than 350 references on curiosity have become available from ERIC, some thirty-five doctoral dissertations on the topic have been completed, and *curiosity* has become a major heading in *Psychological Abstracts*.

The growth of publications in this area was recently commented on by Beswick of Melbourne University, a scholar who has devoted much of his professional life to developing a cognitive theory of curiosity. Beswick, in a personal letter to the authors, wrote in 1976 that "there are a number of interesting approaches to the topic now and a surprising amount of work on measurement. There was a time when I felt in the forefront, in fact almost on my own, in some aspects of this work but things have changed very considerably since 1960."

Two of the interesting facets of research in curiosity are the many ways of looking at the subject, and as a result, the development of several theories to account for behavior that can be classified as resulting from curiosity.

Multiple Nature of Curiosity

Although many earlier writers had suggested that curiosity is not a unitary concept, it was Langevin (1970) who explored the question in depth in his dissertation research. He discussed his findings in a paper entitled "Is Curiosity a Unitary Construct?": his answer was no (Langevin, 1971).

As early as 1954, Berlyne (1954b) had hypothesized at least two kinds of curiosity—perceptual and epistemic. He summarized them succinctly when he later wrote, "Uncertainty can generate the kind of motivational condition that we call 'curiosity.' It may be termed 'perceptual curiosity' if uncertainty stems from nonsymbolic stimulation and 'epistemic curiosity' if it is produced by symbolic structures" (Berlyne, 1971, p. 100).

Berlyne (1960, p. 80) also distinguished between specific and diversive exploration. One of his students, Day (1971), building on this distinction, developed tests of specific and diversive curiosity. According to Day (p. 101), specific curiosity is a state of arousal brought on by stimuli high in ambiguity, complexity, incongruity, or novelty for the person involved; diversive curiosity is arousal induced by monotony or boredom.

In these definitions, both Berlyne and Day were speaking about curiosity as a state. A person becomes curious when confronted by a particular kind of situation. It also appears that some persons are curious more often than others and are curious in a greater variety of situations. Educators often speak with regret of children's having "lost" their curiosity or with hope of fostering children's curiosity. Therefore, it might be conjectured that some persons have within themselves certain conditions that contribute to curiosity behavior; that is, they may be said to have a curiosity trait. Thus, there is a need to consider both state and trait aspects of curiosity. The assessment of state curiosity (Leherissey, 1971) is different from the measurement of trait curiosity.

Explorations of the multidimensional nature of curiosity

were undertaken by Kreitler, Zigler, and Kreitler (1975) in a factor-analytic study of a range of behavior that could be regarded as manifestations of curiosity. Five factors were found: manipulatory curiosity, perceptual curiosity, conceptual curiosity, curiosity about the complex, and adjustive-reactive curiosity.

Theories of Curiosity

Different theories of curiosity lend themselves to different approaches in its assessment. Therefore, several theories will be reviewed here. These are the optimal arousal theory, the cognitive theory, and the social learning theory. In addition, the self-conceptual and the transactional emphases will be discussed in connection with the most appropriate theory.

To accept the optimal arousal theory, one must posit that the organism functions on a homeostatic principle when confronted by arousing stimuli. If the organism has too little stimulation, it will seek more or become curious. If the organism has too much stimulation, it will suffer anxiety and retreat. Berlyne (1960, 1967) and Day (1969) hypothesized that curiosity and anxiety are continuous in an inverted U-shaped curve when plotted against arousal potential. Spielberger and Butler (1971), however, contend that curiosity and anxiety are not continuous, but are different drive states activated by separate reward and aversion systems. In other words, curiosity and anxiety are only phenomenologically related. Leherissey (1971) suggests a new model that includes three separate motivational states— diversive curiosity, specific curiosity, and anxiety—which are differentially related to each other and to performance.

Cognitive theorists take issue with the tension-reduction aspects of arousal theory, believing that although arousal may be induced by stimuli with collative properties, it is not a mediator of behavior. Instead, they generally choose to focus on discrepancy or mismatch between incoming stimulation and the "storage" or cognitive structures of the individual as the springs of curiosity behavior (Diament, 1972). A number of writers have developed the cognitive approach including Beswick

(1971), Bieri (1955, 1961, 1971), Bruner (1951), Hunt (1963, 1971), Lanzetta (1971), McReynolds (1971b), and Suchman (1971), all of whom set forth their positions in a symposium held in Toronto in 1970.

Hunt (1971) restated his position that there must be some mechanism of motivation "inherent within information processing and action." This he calls "intrinsic motivation." He replaces the "reflex arc" with the "feedback loop" and uses the idea of standards developing through repeated encounters with input to explain self-concept, learning-set-like expectations, and the instigation of action.

Beswick's (1964, 1971) theory may be referred to as a cognitive strategy theory. He assumes a category system or cognitive map to which incoming information (an external stimulus or a covert event) is referred and within which it is encoded. He sees individual differences in curiosity to be a function of characteristics of the category system and differences in coding operation. He maintains that there is an inherent tendency toward systematic integration of the cognitive map. This map is in disorder whenever uncertain signals are perceived or whenever other causes are operative such as deprivation of stimuli. A new ordering, or structure, always results in the integration of new signals. For every state of disorder there is a signal or class of signals that is necessary for reintegration. This procedure of assimilation and accommodation is all that is necessary for learning to take place. One characteristic of this system is that individuals are seen to differ in mode or strategy of coding.

Similar to Beswick, McReynolds (1971b) deals with alteration and development of cognitive structures to accommodate inputs that do not fit existing cognitive structures, a process that he calls "cognitive innovation." He also suggests that some inputs may remain unassimilated. Unassimilated data are kept at a minimum by the selective avoidance of inputs that are incongruent with existing structures and by the development of new structures with which the data are congruent. His theory differs from others in that the individual is thought to attempt to keep rate of cognitive structural change at an optimal level. Each individual tends to set up programmatic cognitive structures and to become committed to their completion. Such programmatic structures are termed *cognitive commitments*. Since one's self-image is in part defined by such commitments, the McReynolds theory points directly to the relationship of curiosity and the nature of the self-concept.

Several investigators have developed what might be called a social theory of curiosity. There seem to be two aspects of the theory. First, in terms of social learning theory an individual's curiosity behavior is a function of whether it was reinforced in the past (Miller, 1971b). Second, there is evidence that the social setting at the time that arousing stimuli are present will influence the level of curiosity behavior. Among such influences Hutt (1970) includes objects, the nature of the environment, and what she calls "conspecifics," or others of the same species.

In commenting on the social model, Gross (1975) pointed out that for "curiosity to grow in a healthy way, it must be rooted . . . in values. The key lies in the relationship between a growing child and significant adults in his life" (p. 243). Saxe (1968) identified mothers who showed curiosity behavior and found that their children also were high in curiosity. Using another approach, Hess (1967) had similar findings.

Not only is curiosity by the parent significant, but other characteristics of parents were found to be related to curiosity in offspring. In a study of intolerance in young children, Harrington, Block, and Block (1975) found that intolerant children were low in curiosity. The parents of boys in the study were hostile, impatient, and rejecting; the parents of the girls unusually supportive. In an earlier study, Maw and Maw (1966) found that fathers of high-curiosity boys were more equalitarian, while fathers of low-curiosity boys tended to foster dependency and seclusiveness and to suppress sexuality. The fathers of low-curiosity boys also believed in harsh punishment and in their own ascendency in the family. The results with girls were ambiguous. While the role of parents is not entirely clear, Weisler and McCall (1976) conclude that poor homes give the child fewer schemata for assimilating data.

Bijou (1975) speaks of the ecological stimuli as a setting factor for exploratory behavior, emphasizing the physical, both

natural and man-made; social and biological, including the ana-
tomical structure of others; biological functions; and own actions. Rabinowitz, Moely, and Finkel (1975) found that prekindergarten children in a social condition engaged in more
specific exploration, while Eckerman and Rheingold (1974) concluded that amount of looking and smiling at persons present in
the environment was a good measure of curiosity in ten-month-
old infants. Passman and Weisberg (1975) found that the approach to novelty by two- and three-year-olds was a function of
the nature of the environment.

Earlier, Weintraub (1968) had found that boys identified
as lacking curiosity in school were found to be highly curious in
the home environment. It is likely that some school environments may have too few stimuli to arouse curiosity while others
may have too many. Corlis and Weiss (1973) raised questions
about the open classroom and suggested that a moderate program of openness with guidance might provide the best stimulation for curiosity arousal.

Haywood (1971), using the Picture Motivation Scale,
found that the scores vary significantly as a function of chronological age, sex, urban-rural residence, and socioeconomic
status. However, Nicki and Shea (1971), using a series of questions and manipulating the uncertainty of correct responses,
found that learning by middle- and lower-class children tended
to converge as the uncertainty increased beyond a very low
value.

The role of ethnic background has not been researched to
any extent. Peterson (1975) and Peterson and Lowery (1970,
1972) reported that black children in kindergarten through
grade six seemed to be more sensory exploratory oriented than
white children of the same age. At the college age, however,
Maw, Maw, and Laskaris (1976) found that black students
showed a significantly lower acceptance of curiosity-related behavior than did white students.

Although the evidence in many areas is limited, it seems
to be sufficient to indicate that environmental conditions can
affect the manifestation of curiosity. Peters (1976) explored
this question with college classes and found that threatening

instructors could inhibit information seeking on the part of students.

As stated earlier, McReynolds (1971b), in his cognitive theory of curiosity, pointed out that cognitive commitment is intimately related to the self-concept. Maw and Maw (1970) administered several instruments to high- and low-curiosity boys. The instruments measured self-reliance, sense of personal worth, sense of personal freedom, feeling of belonging, strong self-sentiment, high ergic tension, lack of withdrawing tendencies, and ego strength. All except high ergic tension discriminated between the groups. Minuchin (1971b) reported that "more exploratory and vigorous children tend to be more confident of the support and effectiveness of adults, more differentiated in their self-image and have a stronger sense of their own worth" (p. 7).

Although a self-concept theory of curiosity cannot be set forth separately from social and cognitive theories, it is necessary to keep the affective as well as the cognitive sphere in mind. Litt (1973) reported on the work of McClelland (1962), finding that "truly creative scientists are distinguished from their colleagues not by a greater degree of achievement motivation as McClelland had originally expected, but by the simple possession of curiosity. Internal reinforcement, therefore, is more vital than any concern for external reward" (p. 71).

Reviewing the major theories of curiosity, one is impressed by their many areas of agreement. Perhaps one of the problems of measuring and assessing curiosity is that all of the theories make significant contributions to our understanding of the problem, but none can be clearly distinguished from the others. Towell (1972) emphasized the complexity of the problem when he wrote "it may be assumed that curiosity is a transactional function of the biological organism and the environment of which it takes its subsistence" (p. 2). Piaget (1972, p. 19), making the same point, stated "On the one hand, knowledge arises neither from a self-conscious subject, nor from objects already constituted (from point of view of the subject) which would impress themselves on him; it arises from interactions which take place midway between the two and thus involve both at the same time."

The transactional nature of curiosity has indicated a need for more multivariate approaches to its study. Such studies must include the qualitative as well as the quantitative, and should include the sequence of events in which the behavior occurs, from the inception of the act to its end (Riegel, 1976; Weisler and McCall, 1976). Perhaps a theory will emerge that incorporates what are now considered separate theories of curiosity.

The Validation Problem

One of the major problems in the assessment of curiosity is the establishment of validity. Minton (1963), who replicated Berlyne's studies, questioned whether individuals who are rated as curious because they press buttons to extend viewing time are curious in other situations. In fact, Weintraub (1968) has presented evidence that children who show curiosity behavior in one situation may not show it in other situations. C. F. Miller (1971) studied the effects of different kinds of instructions under frustrating and neutral conditions on looking time for materials differing in ambiguity, complexity, and incongruity. She concluded that preference for collative stimuli does not seem to be a measure of curiosity and that factors other than curiosity account for exploratory behavior.

She proposed frustration to account for exploration of incongruous stimuli, and "structure building" to determine exploration in the case of three collative variables—ambiguity, complexity, and incongruity.

Other questions have been raised regarding Berlyne's formulations. There are those who ask if the arousal experienced in the presence of collative variables should be called curiosity. Greenberger and Entwisle (1968) believe need for achievement (n-Ach) as well as need for sense of control may increase the time needed to view collative stimuli. They consider n-Ach, sense of control, and curiosity to be unrelated and to stem from different socialization processes. Frick (1971), drawing upon the work of Rappaport (1960), thinks curiosity, structure building, and n-Ach have been confused by some investigators. She believes that only incongruous stimuli arouse curiosity. Reactions to complex and ambiguous stimuli, she claims, are related to structure building and achievement striving. Schultz (1974) raises the question of the relationship between cognitive dissonance and epistemic curiosity, suggesting that whatever creates one may create the other.

In Berlyne's early studies of curiosity, he made no attempt at validation. He assumed that looking at a display indicated curiosity (Berlyne, 1958a, 1958b). In later studies, he asked for ratings of interestingness and pleasingness of the displays (Berlyne, 1963a). More recently, he has extended these ratings and compared his Canadian findings with data obtained in Uganda (Berlyne, Robbins, and Thompson, 1974) and in India (Berlyne, 1975). The results support the notion that his measure does tap the motive curiosity. Similar findings by Eisenman (1966), Greenberger, Woldman, and Yourshaw (1967), and Frick (1971) give further support to Berlyne's assumptions.

In order to validate paper-and-pencil measures of curiosity, Maw and Maw (1961) had teachers and peers establish groups of high- and low-curiosity children on the basis of a definition of curiosity. They proposed that a person is curious to the extent that he "(1) reacts positively to new, strange, incongruous, or mysterious elements in his environment by moving toward them, by exploring them or by manipulating them, (2) exhibits a need or a desire to know more about himself and/or his environment, (3) scans his surroundings seeking new experiences, (4) persists in examining and exploring stimuli in order to know more about them" (p. 299).

The use of teachers' ratings to determine the curiosity of their pupils can be criticized on three fronts. First, too often teachers confuse curiosity with other traits, such as intelligence. Some of these influences, however, can be handled statistically. Second, some teachers find it difficult to evaluate sharply twenty-five or more pupils in their classrooms. Several techniques have been devised to counter this problem. Both Snyder (1971) and Schwartz (1963) used teacher rating scales with items describing student behavior indicating curiosity and also asked teachers to rank each pupil relative to other children their age. Saxe and Stollak (1971) had the teachers select two children for each of nineteen categories derived from a definition of curiosity. Towell (1972) had the teachers use a Q-sort technique in which they sorted names of their pupils into stanines, while Minuchin (1971a) employed the ratings of teachers along with the ratings of other observers. Another criticism of the use of teacher and peer ratings is simply that of situational influences —thus, children may display different behaviors in school than elsewhere (Snyder, 1971). It may be necessary to separate curiosity exhibited in school from curiosity displayed outside of school in much the same way that general anxiety has been distinguished from test anxiety (Sarason, 1957).

Vidler and Levine (1976), in validating a scale of academic curiosity, found correlations between instructor and self-ratings of curiosity ranging between 0.23 and 0.52 with a correlation of 0.47 for the total group of 110 students. These values were obtained in a college setting where there was extensive interaction between faculty and students. In another college where instructor ratings and self-ratings of curiosity were obtained in undergraduate introductory courses, the correlations ranged from 0.10 to 0.51, with a correlation of 0.41 for the total group of 185 students. The authors attributed the lower correlations between teacher ratings and self-ratings of curiosity found by Maw and Maw (1961) to the immaturity and lack of self-awareness of the fifth grade sample used in the latter study.

The major criticism of the Maw and Maw definition of curiosity was put forward by Berlyne (1963a, 1963b, 1965, 1966) and Day (1971) and discussed again by Diament (1972). They pointed out that on the basis of Berlyne's definition of specific and diversive exploration (Berlyne, 1965), the Maw and Maw definition includes both and therefore may confuse raters. Part 3 and aspects of part 2 of the quoted definition above describe diversive curiosity, whereas parts 1 and 4 seem to describe specific curiosity. Day incorporated parts 1 and 4 in his definition of specific curiosity on which his test, the Ontario Test of Intrinsic Motivation, was based.

Validity is an important topic in assessment of any kind. It is a particularly important and difficult consideration when the construct to be measured is as complex as curiosity. Each attempt to assess curiosity must concern itself with the questions "What is curiosity?" and "Is this procedure a measure of it?"

Use of Questions in the Assessment of Curiosity

On the assumption that question asking is meaningfully related to curiosity, investigators have used question asking as a way of measuring curiosity, as a source of stimuli to elicit curiosity, and as a means of identifying what it is that arouses curiosity. One of the most comprehensive studies of the use of questions was completed at the University of Southhamptom (Robinson, 1974). The resulting book indicates the extent to which researchers throughout the world have used this technique.

Several earlier investigators have used the question-asking procedure (Gatto, 1929; Smith, 1933; Conn, 1940; Fahey and Corey, 1941; Davis, 1932). Davis analyzed 3,650 questions asked by seventy-three children. It was discovered that children are not curious about anything that has not been encountered in some form in their own experiences. She reported that only 1.4 percent of the questions appeared not to have an experiential base. In fact, 88 percent of the questions resulted from the immediate situation. Davis also found that boys more often asked for explanations of the physical environment, while girls more often asked for explanations of social relationships.

Meyer and Shane (1973) repeated the Davis study, with similar results. They interpreted their findings in terms of the functional category system developed by Piaget (1955), "which was sufficiently clear to permit objective categorizing of the questions" (Meyer and Shane, 1973, p. 295). Ross and Balzer (1975) replicated the study, again with similar results.

Efforts have been made to validate the use of questions (Peterson, 1975; Peterson and Lowery, 1972; Evans, 1971). Peterson and Lowery found a significant correlation with teacher rating of curiosity; Evans found a significant correlation with the Ontario Test of Intrinsic Motivation.

It has been discovered that the way children are stimulated to ask questions has a bearing on the results obtained. When several stories and pictures selected to arouse curiosity by the presence of collative variables were presented together in groups of three, there were no significant differences in quantity and quality of questions between high- and low-curiosity groups. However, when the same stories and pictures were presented individually there were significant differences between high- and low-curiosity children (Maw and Maw, 1964).

Berlyne (1954b) designed an experiment to test epistemic curiosity, which he defined as a drive reducible by knowledge rehearsal. The experiment included the following elements: a pretest of questions about invertebrate animals, statements that included answers to these questions, and a posttest similar to the first test. The findings indicated that: (1) Prequestioning arouses curiosity; (2) statements recognized as answers to questions from the pretest are more likely to be recalled in the posttest; (3) questions about more familiar animals and those involving incompatible concepts increase curiosity; and (4) statements containing an element of surprise are recalled more frequently than other statements.

Since Berlyne's work was published, many other researchers have used questions to study epistemic curiosity. Frick and Cofer (1972), in their study of epistemic curiosity, found support for Berlyne's concepts by using both relevant and irrelevant questions. They found that the level of curiosity is relatively specific to the content of the questions used to arouse it. Bull (1971) and Bull and Dizney (1973), also using questions, found that general prequestions are ineffective in facilitating retention, but that prequestions high in epistemic-curiosity arousal potential are effective. Frase and Schwartz (1975) found that recall by high school and college students was greater when they engaged in question production than when they only studied the material. Seeking correlates of achievement from among forty-five variables in developmental histories, Shmidheiser (1970) found curiosity (question asking) to be the best predictor of achievement for kindergarten children.

Other researchers also have used questions in creative

ways to measure curiosity. Jenkins (1969), after asking children to select the questions they wanted to know about at different times during a course of eighteen lessons, found additional verification for Berlyne's theory. Inagaki and Hatano (1974) in Japan developed eight stories as stimulus material based on novelty, surprise, contradiction, and perplexity. Each included degrees of mismatch similar to the absurdities used by Maw and Maw (1972) in their verbal absurdities test, which will be discussed later. Inagaki and Hatano had 143 ten- to eleven-year-old children ask questions about the stories and rated them on their ability to identify words that did not fit the context or their ability to judge whether the inferences were valid.

Some researchers have investigated the possibility of raising curiosity by training pupils to ask questions. Adkisson (1970), working with first and second grade children, showed increases in scores on several curiosity tests by using questioning procedures devised by Bradley and Earp (1967). Mays (1969) was able to increase both curiosity and reading comprehension of fifth grade children by training them to ask questions based on making interpretations, drawing inferences, and predicting consequences.

One of the problems Susskind (1969) sees in utilizing questions to stimulate curiosity in the classroom is that teachers ask too many rote memorization questions at an incredible rate. Students have too little opportunity to raise curiosity-laden questions or to make curiosity declaratives.

Fry (1972), working with 192 college students, studied the inquiry dimension that was derived from a battery of six tests by Schulman, Loupe, and Piper (1968). Fry found students scoring high on the inquiry process to be high in cognitive complexity, preferring the ambiguous, asymmetrical, and unexpected to the regular, articulated, and predictable.

Approaches to Assessment

This section deals mainly with approaches to assessment of curiosity that have appeared in the literature since McReynolds wrote his comprehensive review for the second volume of this series (1971a). Its organization was intended to follow that of McReynolds's review as nearly as possible. One notable difference is the omission of a section on projectives. To our knowledge no new techniques have appeared since that review. A related study by Todd (1972) found support for imagery content as an approach to assessing curiosity. She did not, however, ask her subjects to produce imagery content, but had them indicate preference on a five-point scale for stories varying in imagery content. Another difference in the present review is treating the assessment of the curiosity of children and adults together rather than reserving a special category for children. Finally, a special section has been developed in order to examine curiosity assessment in the school situation. Instruments and techniques to assess curiosity are grouped, roughly, as self-description techniques, stimulus preference techniques, and performance measures. Effort is made not to duplicate studies reported by McReynolds. However, where instruments and techniques first mentioned in the earlier report have a bearing on those mentioned in this report, they may be briefly described.

Self-Description Techniques. The use of self-description techniques to assess curiosity has continued. In several cases, there have been attempts to improve earlier instruments, further validate them, or use them as points of departure for the development of new instruments. For example, Leherissey (1971) developed the State Epistemic Curiosity Scale by using items from Day's Ontario Test of Intrinsic Motivation and adding some of her own. The OTIM (Day, 1971) itself has been used to validate other instruments. Evans (1971) validated questioning with the OTIM. Maw and Maw (1975, 1976) found that their contrasting proverbs test correlated 0.39 with ambiguity, 0.35 with complexity, 0.35 with novelty, and 0.39 with specific curiosity of the OTIM.

The Sensation Seeking Scale (SSS) (Zuckerman, Kolin, Price, and Zoob, 1964) has continued to be a useful instrument. Norman and Fenson (1970) found it negatively correlated with depressive tendencies as measured by the MMPI, and positively related to the Barron-Welsh Art Scale (Barron and Welsh, 1952). Gorman (1970) found several significant correlations with Cattell's sixteen personality factors (Cattell and Eber, 1967, p. 742), which were summarized as follows: "Correlates indicate an impulsive cognitive style which may underlie psychopathic functioning but which, in itself, is not necessarily psychopathic." Farley has made several studies of the SSS with his coworkers (Farley and Cox, 1971; Farley and Farley, 1972; Farley and Haubrich, 1974). Their findings indicate a significant relationship between delinquent behavior and stimulus seeking and suggest possible sex differences after adolescence. Farley and Farley suggest that those high on the SSS might be low in physiological arousal. Zuckerman (1971) factor analyzed the scale and found four factors: thrill and adventure seeking, experience seeking, disinhibition, and boredom susceptibility. He also reported that Kish (1970) had found a correlation of 0.43 between the SSS and the Obscure Figures Tests in a large sample of alcoholics and schizophrenics. However, when intelligence was partialed out (Acker and McReynolds, 1965), the correlation was reduced to 0.23, which corresponded to a correlation of 0.25 found by Acker and McReynolds (1967) in a large sample of undergraduates. Zuckerman and his coworkers (Zuckerman, Bone, Neary, Mangelsdorff, and Brustman, 1972) found the SSS to be related to locus of control as measured by Rotter's (1966) I-E Scale. Segal (1973) found a negative correlation between the SSS and anxiety.

Adkisson (1970) reports on a parallel form of the Maw and Maw (1961, 1968) Self-Judgment of Curiosity Scale developed by Bradley (1969), which correlated significantly with the Maw and Maw scale. Adkisson used these tests, together with others that were downward extensions of tests developed by Maw and Maw, to predict academic achievement of first and second grade pupils. Both of the forms of the Self-Judgment of Curiosity scales consisted of forty-one items, such as "I like to explore strange places," which pupils were directed to mark "never," "sometimes," "often," or "always." The reliabilities were 0.91 for the Maw and Maw test, determined by the Spearman-Brown split-half technique, and 0.61 for the Bradley test using the test-retest method. Neither of the tests showed a significant relation to academic achievement. The lack of relationship between the variables was confirmed by Weintraub (1968), who pointed out that the Maw and Maw Self-Judgment of Curiosity Scale was more related to nonschool curiosity behavior than to academic curiosity.

In her study of curiosity as information seeking, Berman (1972) found the What Would You Do Test, developed by Maw and Maw (1964), to be one of four curiosity tests that predicted directed and incidental verbal learning of fifth grade children. In evaluating the items of the test, Berman found them to be "especially consistent in measuring the extent of a child's willingness to be involved in the learning process, and to initiate and sustain his own information search."

Vidler and associates (Vidler, 1972; Vidler and Karan, 1975; Vidler and Rawan, 1974, 1975) have been developing a scale of academic curiosity that they have used with students in grades nine through twelve and with college undergraduates. They found a significant relationship with convergent thinking, as measured by the Guilford (1956) Associations III Test ($r = 0.36, p < 0.001$), and a somewhat weaker relationship ($r = 0.23, p < 0.01$) with a digit-symbol test similar to the one used in the Wechsler Adult Intelligence Scale (Wechsler, 1955). Vidler and Karan used Guilford's Alternate Uses and Possible Jobs tests to measure the relationship between curiosity and divergent thinking in three groups of students: ninth and tenth graders, eleventh and twelfth graders, and college undergraduates. All correlations were significant, about half at the 0.05 level, the balance at the 0.01 level.

The Academic Curiosity scale is composed of items from the Test-Anxiety scale developed by Sarason (1971) from a factor-analytic study by Chiu (1967) of academic motivation and from the Rokeach (1960) Dogmatism Scale. The authors believe that their scale is measuring at least five factors. The items were judged for content validity and for the elimination of a social desirability trend. The test yielded a distribution of scores that was normal or of slightly positive skewness, and a split-half reliability estimate of 0.88. Vidler and Rawan (1975), in a validation study using a sample of 611 college students, had teachers rate the curiosity of their students on a seven-point scale. They found a significant correlation ($r = 0.47$, $p < 0.01$) between teacher ratings and the scale of academic curiosity.

Beswick and Tallmadge (1971) devised two measures of curiosity, using items from the Kuder Vocational Preference Record and from a biographical inventory, which they named Kuder Curiosity and Biographical Curiosity, respectively. Items were examined by three judges for presence or absence of curiosity imagery as defined by Beswick (1964). The correlation between the two tests of 0.33 indicates considerable independence —the tests appear to measure different aspects of curiosity. Internal-consistency reliabilities of 0.83 for Kuder Curiosity and of 0.75 for Biographical Curiosity were obtained, using Kuder Richardson Formula 20 on data from 580 young men.

Langevin (1971) had concluded earlier that curiosity is not a unitary construct. In his work, he developed the Experiential Curiosity Measure (ECM). This instrument consists of forty "most-want-to-experience" items and seven "least-want-to-experience" items. The latter are intended to serve as validity or "catch" items. Students score "wish to experience very much" as 3, "wish to experience somewhat" as 2, and "do not wish to experience" as 1. If more than four "least-want-to-experience" items are selected by a pupil, this pupil's test is considered invalid. The test-retest reliability was found to be 0.57 for a sample of 269 children between eleven and twelve years of age. Langevin explains the lower-than-expected reliability estimate as due to the long interval between testings, during which the children discussed the items of the ECM.

Rosendorn (1976) also began her work by assuming that curiosity is a multidimensional construct. Her items were selected to measure mechanical exploratory behavior, academic curiosity, risk taking, observation, and persistence in ten- and eleven-year-old children. The content of the items was judged by teachers. The split-half reliabilities of the subparts ranged from 0.90 to 0.96. In order to determine the independence of the dimensions, the subparts were added together, thus creating a single scale. The correlation computed between the odd-even items of this scale was $r = 0.09$, which was not significant. The test correlated positively with achievement in arts, English, and mathematics. One of the unusual features of the test is the use of pictures of smiling and frowning faces for agreement and disagreement with the items.

Leherissey (1971) developed a test of specific curiosity concerned with motivation for a particular learning experience, which she calls the State Epistemic Curiosity Scale (SECS), and for which she claims "high internal consistency and substantial concurrent and construct validity." There are three forms of the test, two long forms consisting of twenty items and a short form of seven items. Two items from the short form are: "I found it difficult to concentrate on this material" and "I thought it was fun to increase my understanding about the subject matter." Alpha reliabilities of the SECS ranged from 0.81 to 0.96 for both long forms, indicating high internal consistency. Correlations with the OTIM, SSS, and Anxiety scales were as predicted in both magnitude and direction. A validation study of the SECS using 441 undergraduate students in a course in educational psychology was undertaken by Judd, McCombs, and O'Neil (1973). They report that the SECS appears to be a particularly reliable instrument. Their study tended to support the negative relationship between anxiety and curiosity hypothesized by Leherissey, but did not support her finding of correlation between curiosity and performance. They believed, however, that the latter was a function of the low difficulty level of the materials and tests.

Spielberger developed a State-Trait Curiosity Inventory (STCI), which he states is "more directly related to Berlyne's epistemic curiosity." In early testing, Spielberger has found his test unrelated to the Sensation Seeking Scale and has concluded that cognitive information seeking as measured by his test and physical sensation seeking as measured by the SSS are very different concepts. At the time of this writing (November 1976) a test manual for the STCI was being developed.

Several investigators have developed self-description techniques to measure curiosity as it relates to other variables. For example, Kahoe (1974) was concerned with intrinsic and extrinsic religious orientation. Working with Polk, he used true-false items to evaluate several motivational variables, of which curiosity was one (Kahoe and Polk, 1971). Schiffer (1970) studied the relationship of curiosity and homosexuality with a thirteen-item questionnaire, which included such items as "I would like to get beyond the world of logic and reason and experience something new and different." The items had been evaluated by a jury. Rothburd (1970) developed a Cynosural Narcissism-Scoptic Curiosity Scale, which was used with college and mental hospital samples to study the relation of curiosity and voyeurism. No support was found for the psychoanalytic interpretation that curiosity behaviors are underlain with voyeurism.

Stimulus-Preference Techniques. Several investigators have presented two or more stimuli to children or adults and measured either their choice of such stimuli or the differences in looking time given to each. From the data thus obtained, the level of curiosity has been inferred. Much of the monumental work of Berlyne was based on this procedure. Berlyne's work is now classic and does not need to be thoroughly reviewed in this chapter. Two examples suffice to give the flavor of his recent work.

In 1970, Berlyne looked at the relationships among novelty, complexity, and hedonic value. In the study, subjects who differed in exposure to sequences of colored shapes rated the shapes on pleasingness and interestingness. The results indicated that pleasingness and interestingness were positively related to novelty. Further study indicated that homogeneous sequences declined in judged pleasantness more than sequences in which several stimuli were interspersed, and simple stimuli became less pleasant as they became less novel, while complex stimuli declined less or became more pleasant. In 1976, Berlyne and Ditkofsky investigated the effects of novelty on selective attention through tachistoscopic recognition. Subjects habituated to dots of one color identified letters of a different color more often than letters of the same color on a following exposure.

The value of Berlyne's approach is attested to by the continued acceptance of his paradigm for studying curiosity (for example, Frick and Cofer, 1972; Snyder, 1971; Rahman, 1970).

Skidgell, Witryol, and Wirzbicki (1976), employing this procedure, gave children repeated choices between two incentives. Their selections were influenced both by material reward and by novelty-familiarity sequences.

Recently there has been a trend, especially in working with young children, toward utilizing three-dimensional polygons as curiosity stimuli. Switzky, Haywood, and Isett (1974) observed eight two-year-olds and thirty-two four- to seven-year-olds as they explored and played with three-dimensional polygons, varying from four to forty sides. Wohlwill (1975) measured curiosity in grades one, three, and six using similar material.

Adding to the variety of preference materials, Kirkland (1976) used cartoon preference to investigate curiosity of college students. Cartoons were presented with labels removed. Half of the cartoons were of physical objects, half were of human beings. Half of the subjects were art majors; the others were science majors. Art majors were more people oriented. Kirkland suggests that established interests can direct previously aroused epistemic curiosity. This finding tends to support the relationship between curiosity and interest suggested by Maw (1971).

Connolly and Harris (1971) used both looking time and facial expression of children five to eleven years old to indicate curiosity. In this study of incongruity, fifteen congruous and fifteen incongruous pictures were presented. The incongruous pictures were a combination of congruous parts of the pictures assembled incongruously. The investigators found that looking time and picture naming are valid indices of recognition of stimulus incongruity and that recognition and responsiveness to incongruity increase with chronological age.

Hutt, Forrest, and Newton (1976) used three types of colored pictures, which were judged to be nice, nasty, or neutral. These were presented to five- to seven-year-old children. These investigators reported that visual attention appears to reflect primarily cognitive dimensions; preference may reflect affective dimensions. It is suggested by this study that assessment of curiosity by preference techniques may be influenced

by interdependence of the developmental processes of attention, preference, and semantics.

One of the problems encountered in use of the preference
technique is that it is difficult to adapt to groups. Most of the
work requires the assessment of individuals in one-to-one sessions. However, one major attempt has been made to develop a
group technique. Miller and Geller (Miller, 1971a; Miller and
Geller, 1972) developed a Group Visual Exploratory Technique
(GVET) consisting of booklets in which there are thirty-three
pairs of items, three of which are for practice. The pairs differ
in irregularity of arrangement, amount of material, heterogeneity of elements, irregularity of shape, incongruity, and incongruous juxtaposition. The pairs in the booklets are covered
with tapes. The same pairs are projected on the screen for three
seconds. The child selects the one to look at again by removing
the tape. The split-half reliability estimate for the instrument
was 0.865. The GVET and teacher rating of curiosity correlated
0.273 for third graders and 0.621 for fourth graders. Berman
(1972), using the GVET and three other measures of curiosity
in a study of information seeking in fifth grade children, found
the GVET to be correlated with only one of the other measures,
the Which to Discuss Test (Maw and Maw, 1964). The relationship was a modest one ($r = 0.40$).

Harter devised a curiosity task, Pictorial Curiosity, as one
component of a battery to assess effectance motivation (Harter,
personal communication, 1976; Harter and Zigler, 1971, 1974;
Snyder, 1971). The task consists of twenty-three poster board
houses. The front of each house represents two separate doors.
On one door is a picture and behind it an identical picture. The
other door is blank and behind it is an unknown or novel picture. The child is told that only one door can be opened and is
given ample opportunity to realize that the door with a picture
will always have the same picture behind it. The task is followed
by verbal inquiry to find out how the child decides which door
to pick generally and why specific doors are chosen. The author
reports that the verbal data mirror the choice data and lend
credence to the validity of the measure.

Snyder (1971) developed a Preference-for-the-Incongruous-Picture task consisting of twenty-one pairs of drawings (one demonstration plate and twenty test items) with each pair on a separate page. Each page presents a whole (congruous) picture paired with a combination (incongruous) picture, for example, a picture of a duck with a picture formed from the lower half of a telephone and a duck's head. The measure of curiosity is the number of incongruous pictures chosen. In a study of children's curiosity, Snyder combined this score with other preference scores to obtain a Composite Preference Score, which he judged to be the most adequate representation of curiosity among the various means of assessment he employed.

Innes (1974) exposed his subjects to nonsense syllables for a fixed period for a number of trials and then rated the words for affect or allowed the subjects to explore them for as long as they wanted. The words were obtained from Zajonc (1968) and Harrison (1968), and included "iktitof," "afwordu," "saracik," "biwogini," and "cividra." Innes found that novel stimuli are explored longer. He also concluded that providing incentive increases amount of exploration and decreases amount of liking for novel stimuli.

Bradley and Adkisson (Adkisson, 1970) developed a form of the Memory for Stories technique that is appropriate for first and second grade children, and two parallel forms of the Which-to-Discuss test; both of these tests had originally been developed by Maw and Maw (1964) for use with fifth grade children. The Story Memory technique yields a measure of memory for the novel or unusual. The Which-to-Discuss tests, as developed by Bradley and Adkisson, consist of forty-one sets of three figures varying in degree of balance, complexity, or congruity. The children are asked which of the three figures in each set they would choose to hear a story about. A reliability estimate of 0.47 was reported for Story Memory; no estimate was reported for the two forms of the Which-to-Discuss tests. The reliability of the Maw and Maw version of the Which-to-Discuss test was 0.91, as computed by the split-half technique with 720 fifth grade children (Maw and Maw, 1964, p. 97).

A verbal absurdities test was designed by Maw and Maw (1964, 1972) to identify high- and low-curiosity children by measuring how many absurd statements children could select from among normal, straightforward statements. This test significantly separated high- and low-curiosity children. It did not significantly separate boys and girls. The reliability estimate was 0.85.

Kreitler, Kreitler, and Zigler (1974), in a study of cognitive orientation and curiosity in first grade children, used a measure based upon the theory of Kreitler and Kreitler (1968, 1972). It was called the Cognitive Orientation Questionnaire of Curiosity and was designed for the assessment of beliefs that may orient a child toward curiosity behavior. The belief types are four: beliefs about norms ("A child should not bother grown-ups with questions"), general beliefs ("The kids like better children who ask many questions"), beliefs about self ("I like new games"), and beliefs about goals ("I want to know many things"). The questionnaire included seventy-three questions that were distributed around ten core themes and that referred to the four belief types. Each core theme was in the form of a story. The authors give the following example: "Tim and Johnny (Jane and Linda) see their friends do something strange. They don't understand what's going on. Tim goes over to them and asks what they are doing. Johnny also wants to know but he doesn't go over and ask." The child hears the story and is asked, "Who is the better boy? Is Tim, who asks, a better boy or is Johnny, who does not ask, a better boy?" The answers were scored 2, 1, or 0 for procuriosity orientation, indeterminate position (for example, wanting to be like the curious child but unsure that it is good), and anticuriosity orientation, respectively. The scores were summed so that each child had a score for each type of belief. Each of these scores was then scored 1 or 0 depending upon whether it was above or below the group median for that belief. The sum of these scores, ranging from zero to four, constituted the Cognitive Orientation score. The authors report that these scores relate to a wide range of curiosity behaviors.

Performance-Situations Techniques. Next to paper-and-pencil techniques, performance techniques have been used by researchers more often than any other procedure for the assessment of curiosity. In some cases, curiosity is inferred from the performance alone; in others, performance is combined with other techniques intended to affect degree of curiosity exhibited.

Efforts to assess curiosity through observation of behavior have taken numerous forms and have involved subjects ranging from infancy to adulthood. Perhaps the youngest subjects were those of Eckerman and Rheingold (1974). They studied ten-month-old infants' exploratory responses to unfamiliar toys and persons in the presence of their mothers. They found that toys evoked approach and sustained physical contact; persons evoked regard and smiling but little contact. The authors conclude that looking and smiling at persons serve an exploratory function similar to the touching and manipulating of inanimate objects.

Toys have been used extensively as curiosity stimuli with young children. Sometimes the toys are in curiosity boxes; at other times they are presented in an open setting. Basing their work on social learning theory, Saxe (1968) and Saxe and Stollak (1971) studied the curiosity behavior of first grade boys in the presence of their mothers. The children's approach and exploration of novel toys was found to be related to the mothers' curiosity behavior and the mothers' expression of positive feeling toward exploration. They reported a correlation of 0.72 between curiosity ratings of the mothers' and the children's novelty seeking.

A study using older subjects attempts to measure epistemic curiosity of adults outside of the typical laboratory situation (Heckel, 1969). He mailed empty envelopes and envelopes containing only the second page of a letter to general and clinical psychologists. He found no difference between general and clinical psychologists in the amount of curiosity behavior evoked.

One of the most studied assessment procedures for use with preschool children, the Cincinnati Autonomy Test Battery (CATB), was developed by Banta (1970). He defined autonomy as self-regulating behaviors that facilitate effective problem solving. The CATB measures curiosity, exploratory behavior, persistence, resistance to distraction, control of impulse, reflectivity, analytic perceptual processes, and innovative behavior. The test is administered individually, and verbal demands on the child are minimized. The total test battery can be administered in about one hour. For curiosity assessment, Banta uses a Task Initiation Test for two or three minutes, depending upon whether initiative occurs, and a Curiosity Box for four to five minutes, depending upon whether the child explores the box immediately or after prompting. The Task Initiation Test consists of small wooden figures arranged on a table. The child is observed and scored as "no initiation," "minimal contact," "initiation with minimal involvement," or "initiation with a high degree of involvement." The curiosity box furnishes five scores: manipulatory exploration, tactual exploration, visual exploration, movement by the subject, and the subject's movement of the box. The measures of curiosity correlated well with one another (convergent validity) and relatively low with other measures (discriminant validity). Banta reports reliability coefficients of 0.76 (test-retest) and of 0.96 (interrater) for the Task Initiation Test and of 0.91 (internal consistency) for the Curiosity Box. Boger and Knight (1969) confirmed many of the findings of Banta with Head Start pupils. They also replicated some of the work of Minuchin (1971a).

One of the devices used by Minuchin was a kaleidoscope. The child was observed and scored using techniques employed earlier by others (Lucco, 1965; McReynolds, Acker, and Pietila, 1961; Pangrac, 1963). The relationship between such observations made in a new school situation and those made when the child explored the kaleidoscope was 0.70 ($p < 0.01$). Later Minuchin, who was using a discovery board (a large picture stimulus), asked children to tell what they saw in the picture. A score is obtained by counting responses with repetition eliminated. A test-retest rank-order correlation of 0.70 was reported after a two-month interval. The discovery board scores correlated 0.37 ($p < 0.01$) with teacher ratings and 0.25 ($p < 0.01$) with scores from the kaleidoscope test mentioned above.

The curiosity box has been designed in several ways and used somewhat differently by different researchers. Schiltz and

Burchett (1975) designed a sensory box in which the feet instead of the hands were used. Walls and Rude (1972) used a wooden box resembling a puppet theatre. In this case, the preschoolers looked for prizes under cups, especially under novel cups. G. Miller (1971), working with children three to five years of age, used a box with lights. He observed the children and measured curiosity by the times the child manipulated any or all of the dimmer switches, turned the cranks, operated an electronic metronome, made noises to activate a lamp, and activated a ball that was in a rack. His work was similar to that carried out by Hutt (Hutt, 1970; Hutt and others, 1976).

Hutt designed an elaborate box with an external lever. She found that children reacted first by examining the object and then by playing with it. She was able to diagram clearly the difference in approach for examining or exhibiting curiosity about an object and playing with the object. She obtained clear-cut sex differences with her curiosity box.

Cripps (1976) designed a box for kindergarten children that consisted of several drawers. She also designed an elaborate recording sheet to be used with her surprise box.

Hess (1967) combined a viewing box with a choice of stimuli techniques. This box contained eight complex and eight simple pictures, which four-year-old children could select to view by pushing their heads against the box. This action activated the light and permitted the child to look at chosen pictures.

Coie (1973, 1974) studied cross-situational stability of children's curiosity and the motivation of exploration strategies. He used a curiosity-box task, a pigeon display, a chemical task, and an inclined plane task. He classified the conflict caused by the inclined plane task in terms of Piaget's developmental stages. The inclined plane was used to generate cognitive conflict and surprise (Coie, 1973). The apparatus consists of two 5½-inch wheels. The placement of steel weights in the wheels causes them to roll either up or down the inclined plane depending upon the placement of the wheel on the plane relative to the placement of the weight. The quality of the boys' subsequent exploratory behavior was rated. Using teachers' ratings of curiosity, Coie found that teachers were better able to distinguish the curiosity of girls than boys. Teachers seemed to confuse distractibility in boys with curiosity. Coie reports high interrater reliability for all tasks.

Several researchers have inferred curiosity from children's approach and exploration of objects. Kreitler and others (1975) examined the extent to which first grade children explored the structure of ordinary objects. Peterson and Lowery (1972) watched children five to thirteen years of age manipulate objects in a waiting room. Minuchin (1971a) observed children approach objects in a classroom. Richman, Kahle, and Rutland (1972), after defining curiosity as information seeking, used twelve "junk" items for assessing curiosity. After the child was allowed to play with an item, it was taken away and the child was given the choice of having it returned or of receiving an unknown item from a box.

Adkisson (1970) measured persistence "in examining and exploring stimuli in order to know more about them" with three small tests, including pictures in which items that were hidden had to be found, simple mazes, and a Christmas tree triangle in which there were a number of triangles that the child was asked to find. Another of his tests consisted of words and pictures that the child connected. It had a test-retest reliability of 0.48 ($p < 0.01$) and contributed to the prediction of achievement of second grade children. Since there were only eight items, the low reliability coefficient could be expected.

Rabinowitz and others (1975) used familiar and novel toys with prekindergarten children. The children spent 68 percent of their time with familiar toys and 28 percent with novel toys. They found that children in a social condition engaged in more specific exploration and played more with familiar toys than did children not in a social condition. Boys spent more time than girls in diversive but not in specific exploration.

In a study of the effects of a curiosity incentive on children's discrimination learning, Snyder (1971) used a set of fourteen rebus puzzles as the curiosity incentive. Children in the high-curiosity incentive condition (those not presented with the complete rebus before the learning task) learned faster than children in the low curiosity incentive condition (those presented with the complete rebus before undertaking the learning task).

Curiosity Assessment and School Subjects

There has been an increasing amount of work directed at understanding various aspects of the relationship between curiosity and school subjects. Sometimes subject matter itself has been used to develop instruments for the assessment of curiosity. At other times, the study of the relationship between curiosity and educational growth has had the development of assessment techniques as a secondary feature.

Where the development of techniques to evaluate state curiosity is the primary purpose, there is a need to consider the role of subject matter in determining the states. Leherissey (1971) studied computer-assisted learning of science materials and developed the State Epistemic Curiosity Scale described above. Jenkins (1969) explored the effect of number of structured science experiences on curiosity of fourth grade children for the particular concepts stressed in the structured experiences. He developed a Curiosity Inventory composed of questions in sets of three and asked pupils to select the questions from each set they wanted to know about. The author reports establishing content and construct validity and sufficient test-retest reliability for his inventory. Brown (1972) used prose material directly to elicit epistemic curiosity and found that subjects' prechoice exploration of alternatives offered for further reading may predict reading choice. He claimed that reading, broadly speaking, is the exploration of written material.

Curiosity assessment has been used in multimeasurements of aspects of school programs other than academic achievement. Beswick and Rao (1975), using a modified proverbs test of curiosity together with other instruments, studied career choices of Australian and Indian secondary school students. Torrance (1969) related curiosity and creativity in gifted children. However, Towell (1972), using teacher and self-judgment as measures of curiosity and the Torrance Creativity Tests, did not find the expected relationship with an average group of children.

Whitsitt (1975) developed the Curiosity-Arousing Instructional Model (CAIM) for teaching art in the elementary school. The model uses devices incorporating novelty, incongruity, and change, and questions such as "What color is water?" and "Skies are always blue?" which the author terms "search and compare" questions. The model was tested with a group of ninety-nine fourth grade children (two experimental and two control classes) and was found to be effective in eliciting exploratory behavior and learning.

Persons concerned with science teaching have been the most prolific in designing curiosity assessment instruments. Campbell (1971, 1972) developed the Scientific Curiosity Inventory (Forms A and B) for use with junior and senior high school students. The instrument was constructed to measure depth of curiosity in terms of the first three levels of the Krathwohl, Bloom, and Masia (1964) five-level taxonomy of affective behaviors. Level 1 requires a student only to attend, Level 2 requires attention and response, while Level 3 requires attention, response, and the development of values. The inventory was intended to measure indirectly how far along the hierarchy of behaviors a student would go to satisfy curiosity about science questions. The hierarchy of behaviors used in construction of the items was validated by a jury of researchers. Only items that showed 80 percent or better agreement among jurors were retained in the final forms of the inventory. Using scores of 251 students from urban and suburban settings, the author obtained a reliability coefficient of 0.89.

Richardson (1971) designed an instrument composed of multiple-choice and Likert-type items for use in grades six to nine. This assessment tool, the Scientific Curiosity and Interest Test, was validated through interviews with students for whom test scores were available. In development, the test was tried in several forms. The reliability estimates of the final form were 0.94 (Kuder-Richardson) and 0.72 (test-retest). In two-factor analysis studies, using two separate and independent samples, fairly stable dimensions were found.

A forty-item chemistry-based test of cognitive preference was developed by Kempa and Dubé (1973) and administered to 284 male students of chemistry. The results were analyzed and two major cognitive scales formulated: one a measure of scientific curiosity, the other a measure of orientation toward pure or applied science.

Stothart (1972) attempted to measure curiosity for high school biology with a seventeen-item test. He used judges to determine validity of his instrument and reported a test-retest reliability coefficient of 0.74.

There is a conspicuous absence of the use of curiosity assessment in the social studies. We found no instance where a social science was utilized in the development of a curiosity-measuring instrument or where curiosity was considered a fundamental variable in teaching or in achievement in social studies. In light of the seriousness of problems in the social sciences, this lack of curiosity is surprising. We hope to see work in this direction very soon.

Summary and Conclusions

Perhaps the most significant and satisfying conclusion to be reached regarding the assessment of human curiosity is that increasing numbers of students are being attracted to the subject and are seriously engaged in trying to find answers to the many difficulties involved. This augurs well for future developments in curiosity assessment.

Among the major needs in curiosity assessment is better understanding of the issues considered earlier in this chapter. Study is needed to more sharply delineate different kinds of curiosity, as well as to reveal the similarities among the various theories of curiosity. To do this, better ways of validating assessment techniques and instruments must be developed. We need to have more confidence that what we are measuring is indeed curiosity.

If curiosity is specific to a given person in relation to a specific situation, then researchers must investigate this transactional relationship. Those studying curiosity may see a need for more idiographic analysis in which one looks at the curiosity reactions of an individual in several distinct situations. Few studies have attempted case study approaches. The one doctoral study we found that used this technique gave evidence of the fruitfulness of the approach (Weintraub, 1968).

Weisler and McCall (1976) argue for studying the qualitative as well as the quantitative aspects of exploratory behavior. They ask for more multivariate approaches, more study of the sequence of events in the approach toward any stimuli, and more studies of the behavioral responses—facial expression, physiological responses, degree of vacillation, and reactions to the environment after exploration.

Most of the approaches to assessment of curiosity have been quantitative. If we take seriously what Weisler and McCall are saying, we need to approach the topic with qualitative measures as well. Is it possible that what is needed is a marriage of behavioristic psychology and phenomenology? In 1968 Berlyne expressed the opinion that in some ways it is a great pity that phenomenology has not had a greater hearing in the United States. He doubted, however, that a fruitful merger was possible. Perhaps in curiosity assessment it can be brought about.

Finally, the work in the field of curiosity must eventually be utilized in school situations. The work in this field to date is limited. A review of the material points up serious voids. While the role of curiosity in learning and teaching has been studied to some extent, the work in this area up to this time constitutes only a beginning. Efforts in curiosity assessment need to be oriented more specifically in this direction. It may be one of the most exciting and valuable areas of study in the near future.

References

Acker, M., and McReynolds, P. "The Obscure Figures Test: An Instrument for Measuring 'Cognitive Innovation.' " *Perceptual and Motor Skills,* 1965, *21,* 815-821.

Acker, M., and McReynolds, P. "The Need for Novelty." *Psychological Reports,* 1967, *17,* 177-182.

Adkisson, J. "A Study of the Value of Selected Curiosity Tests for Predicting Academic Achievement in First and Second Grades." Unpublished doctoral dissertation, North Texas University, 1970.

Banta, T. J. "Tests for the Evaluation of Early Childhood Education: The Cincinnati Autonomy Test Battery (CATB)." In J. Hellmuth (Ed.), *Cognitive Studies*. Vol. 1. New York: Brunner/Mazel, 1970.

Barron, F., and Welsh, G. S. "Artistic Perception as a Possible Factor in Personality Style: Its Measurement by a Figure Preference Test." *Journal of Psychology*, 1952, *33*, 199-203.

Berlyne, D. E. "An Experimental Study of Human Curiosity." *British Journal of Psychology*, 1954a, *45*, 256-265.

Berlyne, D. E. "A Theory of Human Curiosity." *British Journal of Psychology*, 1954b, *45*, 180-191.

Berlyne, D. E. "Influences of Complexity and Novelty in Visual Figures on Orienting Responses." *Journal of Experimental Psychology*, 1958a, *55*, 289-296.

Berlyne, D. E. "Supplementary Report: Complexity and Orientating Responses with Longer Exposures." *Journal of Experimental Psychology*, 1958b, *56*, 183.

Berlyne, D. E. *Conflict, Arousal, and Curiosity*. New York: McGraw-Hill, 1960.

Berlyne, D. E. "Complexity and Incongruity Variables as Determinants of Exploratory Choice and Evaluation Ratings." *Canadian Journal of Psychology*, 1963a, *17*, 274-290.

Berlyne, D. E. "Exploratory and Epistemic Behavior." In S. Koch (Ed.), *Psychology: A Study of Science*. Vol. 5. New York: McGraw-Hill, 1963b.

Berlyne, D. E. *Structure and Direction of Thinking*. New York: Wiley, 1965.

Berlyne, D. E. "Curiosity and Exploration." *Science*, 1966, *153*, 25-33.

Berlyne, D. E. "Arousal and Reinforcement." In D. Levine (Ed.), *Nebraska Symposium on Motivation*. Lincoln: University of Nebraska Press, 1967.

Berlyne, D. E. "American and European Psychology." *American Psychologist,* 1968, *23,* 447-452.

Berlyne, D. E. "Novelty, Complexity, and Hedonic Value." *Perception and Psychophysics,* 1970, *8,* 279-286.

Berlyne, D. E. *Aesthetics and Psychobiology.* New York: Appleton-Century-Crofts, 1971.

Berlyne, D. E. "Extension to Indian Subjects of a Study of Exploratory and Verbal Responses in Visual Patterns." *Journal of Cross-Cultural Psychology,* 1975, *6,* 316-330.

Berlyne, D. E., and Ditkofsky, J. "Effects of Novelty and Oddity on Visual Selective Attention." *British Journal of Psychology,* 1976, *67,* 175-180.

Berlyne, D. E., Robbins, M. C., and Thompson, R. "A Cross-Cultural Study of Exploratory and Verbal Responses to Visual Patterns Varying in Complexity." In D. E. Berlyne (Ed.), *Studies in the New Experimental Aesthetics: Steps Toward an Objective Psychology of Aesthetic Appreciation.* Washington, D.C.: Hemisphere, 1974.

Berman, P. "Curiosity as Information Seeking in Fifth Grade Children." Unpublished doctoral dissertation, Yeshiva University, 1972.

Beswick, D. G. "Theory and Measurement of Human Curiosity." Unpublished doctoral dissertation, Harvard University, 1964.

Beswick, D. G. "Cognitive Process Theory of Individual Differences in Curiosity." In H. I. Day, D. E. Berlyne, and D. E. Hunt (Eds.), *Intrinsic Motivation: A New Direction in Education.* Toronto: Holt, Rinehart and Winston of Canada, 1971.

Beswick, D. G., and Rao, G. L. "Cultural Differences and Similarities in Academic Motivation: A Comparison of Indian and Australian Student Abilities." Unpublished document, the Australian National University, Canberra, 1975.

Beswick, D. G., and Tallmadge, G. K. "Reexamination of Two Learning Style Studies in the Light of the Cognitive Process Theory of Curiosity." *Journal of Educational Psychology,* 1971, *42,* 456-462.

Bieri, J. "Cognitive Complexity-Simplicity and Predictive Behavior." *Journal of Abnormal and Social Psychology,* 1955, *51,* 263-268.

Bieri, J. "Complexity-Simplicity as a Personality Variable in Cognitive and Perceptual Behavior." In D. W. Fiske and S. R. Maddi (Eds.), *Functions of Varied Experience.* Homewood, Ill.: Dorsey Press, 1961.

Bieri, J. "Intrinsic Motivation, Memory and Personality." In H. I. Day, D. E. Berlyne, and D. E. Hunt (Eds.), *Intrinsic Motivation: A New Direction in Education.* Toronto: Holt, Rinehart and Winston of Canada, 1971.

Bijou, S. W. "Exploratory Behavior." Paper presented at the Society for Research in Child Development Conference, Denver, April 1975.

Boger, R. P., and Knight, S. S. *Social-Emotional Task Force: Final Report.* ERIC No. ED033744/PS002106. East Lansing: Michigan State University, 1969.

Bradley, R. C. "Do Current Reading Practices Stifle Curiosity?" *The Reading Teacher,* 1969, *22,* 448-452.

Bradley, R. C., and Earp, N. W. *Exemplars of the Teachers' Cognitive Domain.* Dubuque, Iowa: William C. Brown, 1967.

Brown, L. T. "A Behavioral Index of the Exploratory Value of Prose Materials." *Journal of Educational Psychology,* 1972, *63,* 437-445.

Bruner, J. S. "Personality Dynamics and the Process of Perceiving." In R. R. Blake and G. V. Ramsey (Eds.), *Perception: An Approach to Personality.* New York: Ronald Press, 1951.

Bull, S. G. H. "The Effect of Pre-Questions That Arouse Epistemic Curiosity in Long Term Retention." Unpublished doctoral thesis, University of Oregon, 1971.

Bull, S. G. H., and Dizney, H. F. "Epistemic-Curiosity-Arousing Prequestions: Their Effect on Long-Term Retention." *Journal of Educational Psychology,* 1973, *65,* 45-49.

Campbell, J. R. "Cognitive and Affective Process Development and Its Relation to a Teacher's Interaction Ratio." *Journal of Research in Science Teaching,* 1971, *8,* 317-323.

Campbell, J. R. "Is Scientific Curiosity a Viable Outcome in Today's Secondary School Science Program?" *School Science and Mathematics,* 1972, *72,* 139-147.

Cattell, R. B., and Eber, H. W. *Handbook for the Sixteen Personality Factor Questionnaire.* Champaign, Ill.: Institute for Personality and Ability Testing, 1967.

Chiu, L. H. "A Factorial Study of Academic Motivation." Unpublished doctoral dissertation, Columbia University, 1967.

Coie, J. D. "The Motivation of Exploration Strategies in Young Children." *Genetic Psychology Monographs,* 1973, *87,* 177-196.

Coie, J. E. "An Evaluation of the Cross-Situational Stability of Children's Curiosity." *Journal of Personality,* 1974, *42,* 93-116.

Conn, J. H. "Sexual Curiosity of Children." *American Journal of Diseases of Children,* 1940, *60,* 1110-1119.

Connolly, M. R., and Harris, L. "Effects of Stimulus Incongruity on Children's Curiosity as Measured by Looking Time and Expression Change." *Psychonomic Science,* 1971, *25,* 232-234.

Corlis, C., and Weiss, J. "Curiosity and Openness: Empirical Testing of a Basic Assumption." Paper presented at the American Education Research Association Meeting, New Orleans, February/March 1973.

Cripps, J. H. "Measurement of Quality, Cost, and Staff Use in Day Care Environments for Research and Self-Analysis Purposes." Unpublished master's thesis, University of Delaware, 1976.

Davis, E. A. "The Form and Function of Children's Questions." *Child Development,* 1932, *3,* 57-74.

Day, H. I. "Are Activation and Cue Functions Really Separate?" Paper presented at a conference on arousal, University of Vermont, September 1969.

Day, H. I. "The Measurement of Specific Curiosity." In H. I. Day, D. E. Berlyne, and D. E. Hunt (Eds.), *Intrinsic Motivation: A New Direction in Education.* Toronto: Holt, Rinehart and Winston of Canada, 1971.

Diament, B. "A Study of Specific Curiosity in Third and Fourth

Grade Children." Unpublished doctoral dissertation, Yeshiva University, 1972.

Eckerman, C. O., and Rheingold, H. L. "Infant's Exploratory Responses to Toys and People." *Developmental Psychology,* 1974, *10,* 255-259.

Eisenman, R. "Pleasing and Interesting Visual Complexity: Support for Berlyne." *Perceptual and Motor Skills,* 1966, *23,* 1167-1170.

Evans, D. R. "The OTIM, Question Asking and Autistic Thinking." *Psychological Reports,* 1971, *29,* 154.

Fahey, G. L., and Corey, S. M. "Inferring Level of Mental Activity from Pupils' Classroom Questions." *Journal of Educational Research,* 1941, *35,* 193-200.

Farley, F. H., and Cox, O. "Stimulus-Seeking Motivation in Adolescents as a Function of Age and Sex." *Adolescence,* 1971, *6,* 207-218.

Farley, F. H., and Farley, S. V. "Stimulus-Seeking Motivation and Delinquent Behavior Among Institutionalized Delinquent Girls." *Journal of Consulting and Clinical Psychology,* 1972, *39,* 94-97.

Farley, F. H., and Haubrich, A. S. "Response Set in the Measurement of Stimulation Seeking." *Educational and Psychological Measurements,* 1974, *34,* 631-637.

Frase, L. T., and Schwartz, B. J. "Effect of Question Production and Answering on Prose Recall." *Journal of Educational Psychology,* 1975, *67,* 628-635.

Frick, J. "Curiosity and Need Achievement: The Effects of Two Motives on Exploratory Behavior." Unpublished doctoral dissertation, Pennsylvania State University, 1971.

Frick, J. W., and Cofer, C. N. "Berlyne's Demonstration of Epistemic Curiosity: An Experimental Re-Evaluation." *British Journal of Psychology,* 1972, *63,* 221-228.

Fry, J. P. "Interactive Relationship Between Inquisitiveness and Student Control of Instruction." *Journal of Educational Psychology,* 1972, *63,* 459-465.

Gatto, J. L. "Pupils' Questions: Their Nature and Their Relationship to the Study Process." *University of Pittsburgh Bulletin,* 1929, *26,* 65-71.

Gorman, B. S. "16 PF Correlates of Sensation-Seeking." *Psychological Reports,* 1970, *26,* 741-742.

Greenberger, E., and Entwisle, D. R. *Need for Achievement, Curiosity and Sense of Control: A Pilot Study for a Large-Scale Investigation.* U.S. Office of Education, Dept. of Health, Education and Welfare Project 61610-03-01. Baltimore: Johns Hopkins University, 1968.

Greenberger, E., Woldman, J., and Yourshaw, S. "Components of Curiosity: Berlyne Reconsidered." *British Journal of Psychology,* 1967, *58,* 375-386.

Gross, D. W. "Curiosity in Context." *Childhood Education,* 1975, *51,* 242-243.

Guilford, J. P. "The Structure of Intellect." *Psychological Bulletin,* 1956, *53,* 267-293.

Harrington, D. M., Block, J. H., and Block, J. "Behavioral Manifestations and Parental Correlates of Intolerance of Ambiguity in Young Children." Paper presented at the Society for Research in Child Development Conference, Denver, April 1975.

Harrison, A. A. "Response Competition, Frequency, Exploratory Behavior, and Liking." *Journal of Personal and Social Psychology,* 1968, *9,* 363-368.

Harter, S., and Zigler, E. "Effectance and Mastery Motivation in the Performance of Normal and Retarded Children." Unpublished manuscript, Yale University, 1971.

Harter, S., and Zigler, E. "The Assessment of Effectance Motivation in Normal and Retarded Children." *Developmental Psychology,* 1974, *10,* 169-180.

Haywood, H. C. "Individual Differences in Motivational Orientation: A Trait Approach." In H. I. Day, D. E. Berlyne, and D. E. Hunt (Eds.), *Intrinsic Motivation: A New Direction in Education.* Toronto: Holt, Rinehart and Winston of Canada, 1971.

Heckel, R. V. "Curiosity in Young Psychologists." *American Psychologist,* 1969, *24,* 754-756.

Hess, R. D. *The Cognitive Environments of Urban-Preschool Children.* Chicago: Social Science Research Committee, Division of Social Sciences, University of Chicago, 1967.

Hunt, J. M. "Information Processing and Motivation." In O. J. Harvey (Ed.), *Motivation and Social Interaction.* New York: Ronald Press, 1963.

Hunt, J. M. "Toward a History of Intrinsic Motivation." In H. I. Day, D. E. Berlyne, and D. E. Hunt (Eds.), *Intrinsic Motivation: A New Direction in Education.* Toronto: Holt, Rinehart and Winston of Canada, 1971.

Hutt, C. "Curiosity in Young Children." *Science Journal,* 1970, *6,* 69-71.

Hutt, C., Forrest, B., and Newton, J. "The Visual Preference of Children." *Journal of Child Psychology and Psychiatry,* 1976, *17,* 63-68.

Inagaki, K., and Hatano, G. "Correlates of Induced Question-Asking Behavior." *Japanese Psychological Research,* 1974, *16,* 50-57.

Innes, J. M. "The Effect of Familiarity on Liking and Exploration." *European Journal of Social Psychology,* 1974, *4,* 489-494.

Jenkins, J. A. "An Experimental Investigation of the Effects of Structured Science Experience on Curiosity Among Fourth Grade Children." *Journal of Research in Science Teaching,* 1969, *6,* 128-135.

Judd, W. A., McCombs, B. L., and O'Neil, H. F., Jr. "Further Validation of a State Epistemic Curiosity Measure in Computer-Managed Instruction." Paper presented at the 81st annual convention of the American Psychological Association, Montreal, September 1973.

Kahoe, R. D. "Personality and Achievement Correlates of Intrinsic and Extrinsic Religious Orientations." *Journal of Personality and Social Psychology,* 1974, *29,* 812-818.

Kahoe, R. D., and Polk, J. D., Jr. "Personality Scales Assessing Intrinsic and Extrinsic Motivational Variables." *Faculties Studies Bulletin Southwest Baptist College,* 1971, *2,* 38-42.

Kempa, R. F., and Dubé, G. E. "Cognitive Preference Orientations in Students of Chemistry." *British Journal of Educational Psychology,* 1973, *43,* 279-288.

Kirkland, J. "Epistemic Curiosity and Cartoon Preference." *Psychological Reports,* 1976, *38,* 354.

Kish, G. B. "Cognitive Innovation and Stimulus Seeking: A Study of the Correlates of the Obscure Figures Test." *Perceptual and Motor Skills,* 1970, *30,* 95-101.

Krathwohl, D. R., Bloom B. S., and Masia, B. B. *Taxonomy of Educational Objectives: The Classification of Educational Goals.* Handbook 2. *Affective Domain.* New York: McKay, 1964.

Kreitler, S., and Kreitler, H. "Dimensions of Meaning and Their Measurement." *Psychological Reports,* 1968, *23,* 1307-1329.

Kreitler, S., and Kreitler, H. "The Model of Cognitive Orientation: Towards a Theory of Human Behaviour." *British Journal of Psychology,* 1972, *63,* 9-30.

Kreitler, S., Kreitler, H., and Zigler, E. "Cognitive Orientation and Curiosity." *British Journal of Psychology,* 1974, *65,* 43-52.

Kreitler, S., Zigler, E., and Kreitler, H. "The Nature of Curiosity in Children." *Journal of School Psychology,* 1975, *13,* 185-200.

Langevin, R. "A Study of Curiosity, Intelligence and Creativity." Unpublished doctoral dissertation, University of Toronto, 1970.

Langevin, R. "Is Curiosity a Unitary Construct?" *Canadian Journal of Psychology/Review of Canadian Psychology,* 1971, *25,* 360-373.

Lanzetta, J. T. "The Motivational Properties of Uncertainty." In H. I. Day, D. E. Berlyne, and D. E. Hunt (Eds.), *Intrinsic Motivation: A New Direction in Education.* Toronto: Holt, Rinehart and Winston of Canada, 1971.

Leherissey, B. L. "The Effects of Stimulating State Epistemic Curiosity on State Anxiety and Performance in a Complex Computer-Assisted Learning Task." Unpublished doctoral dissertation, Florida State University, 1971.

Litt, S. "Shaping Up or Self-Shaping: A Look at Modern Educational Theory." *Journal of Humanistic Psychology,* 1973, *13,* 69-73.

Lucco, A. "The Curiosity Behavior of Four-Year-Old Children: An Exploratory Study." Unpublished doctoral dissertation, University of Chicago, 1965.

McClelland, D. "The Psychodynamics of Creative Physical Scientists." In H. Gruber, G. Terrell, and M. Wertheimer (Eds.), *Contemporary Approaches to Creative Thinking.* New York: Atherton, 1962.

McReynolds, P. "The Nature and Assessment of Intrinsic Motivation." In P. McReynolds (Ed.), *Advances in Psychological Assessment.* Vol. 2. Palo Alto, Calif.: Science and Behavior Books, 1971a.

McReynolds, P. "The Three Faces of Cognitive Motivation." In H. I. Day, D. E. Berlyne, and D. E. Hunt (Eds.), *Intrinsic Motivation: A New Direction in Education.* Toronto: Holt, Rinehart and Winston of Canada, 1971b.

McReynolds, P., Acker, M., and Pietila, C. "Relation of Object Curiosity to Psychological Adjustment in Children." *Child Development,* 1961, *32,* 393-400.

Maw, W. H. "Differences in the Personalities of Children Differing in Curiosity." In H. I. Day, D. E. Berlyne, and D. E. Hunt (Eds.), *Intrinsic Motivation: A New Direction in Education.* Toronto: Holt, Rinehart and Winston of Canada, 1971.

Maw, W. H., and Maw, E. W. "Establishing Criterion Groups for Evaluating Measures of Curiosity." *Journal of Experimental Education,* 1961, *29,* 299-306.

Maw, W. H., and Maw, E. W. "An Exploratory Investigation into the Measurement of Curiosity in Elementary School Children." U.S. Office of Education, Cooperative Research Report No. 801. University of Delaware, 1964.

Maw, W. H., and Maw, E. W. "Children's Curiosity and Parental Attitudes." *Journal of Marriage and the Family,* 1966, *28,* 343-345.

Maw, W. H., and Maw, E. W. "Self-Appraisal of Curiosity." *Journal of Educational Research,* 1968, *41,* 462-465.

Maw, W. H., and Maw, E. W. "Self-Concepts of High- and Low-Curiosity Boys." *Child Development,* 1970, *41,* 123-129.

Maw, W. H., and Maw, E. W. "Differences Between High- and Low-Curiosity Fifth-Grade Children in Their Recognition of Verbal Absurdities." *Journal of Educational Psychology,* 1972, *63,* 558-562.

Maw, W. H., and Maw, E. W. "Contrasting Proverbs as a Measure of Attitudes of College Students Toward Curiosity-Related Behaviors." *Psychological Reports,* 1975, *37,* 1085-1086.

Maw, W. H., Maw, E. W., and Laskaris, J. B. "Contrasting Proverbs as a Measure of Attitudes Toward Curiosity-Related Behavior of Black and White College Students." *Psychological Reports,* 1976, *39,* 1229-1230.

Mays, G. S. C. "Curiosity in the Reading Encounter: An Experimental Study of the Effect of Selected Questioning Procedures on Curiosity and on Reading Comprehension." Unpublished doctoral dissertation, North Texas State University, 1969.

Meyer, W. J., and Shane, J. "The Form and Function of Children's Questions." *Journal of Genetic Psychology,* 1973, *123,* 285-296.

Miller, C. F. "Frustration and Curiosity in Exploratory Behavior." Unpublished doctoral dissertation, Pennsylvania State University, 1971.

Miller, G. *Measuring Children's Curiosity.* Charleston, W. Va.: Appalachia Educational Laboratory, 1971.

Miller, M. B. "A Group Visual Exploratory Technique." *Perceptual and Motor Skills,* 1971a, *33,* 51-54.

Miller, M. B. "Intrinsic Motivation, Unlearned, Learned, and Modifiable." In H. I. Day, D. E. Berlyne, and D. E. Hunt (Eds.), *Intrinsic Motivation: A New Direction in Education.* Toronto: Holt, Rinehart and Winston of Canada, 1971b.

Miller, M. B., and Geller, D. "Curiosity in Retarded Children: Sensitivity to Intrinsic and Extrinsic Reinforcement." *American Journal of Mental Deficiency,* 1972, *76,* 668-679.

Minton, H. "A Replication of Perceptual Curiosity as a Function of Stimulus Complexity." *Journal of Experimental Psychology,* 1963, *66,* 522-524.

Minuchin, P. "Correlates of Curiosity and Exploratory Behavior in Preschool Disadvantaged Children." *Child Development,* 1971a, *42,* 939-950.

Minuchin, P. "Curiosity and Exploratory Behavior in Disadvantaged Children: A Follow-Up." Paper presented at the Society for Research in Child Development Conference, Minneapolis, April 1971b.

Nicki, R. W., and Shea, J. F. "Learning Curiosity and Social Group Membership." *Journal of Experimental Child Psychology*, 1971, *11*, 124-132.

Norman, R. D., and Fenson, J. S. "Further Aspects of Construct Validity of the Zuckerman Sensation-Seeking Scale." *Journal of Psychology*, 1970, *74*, 131-140.

Pangrac, I. "The Relationship of Curiosity in Children to the Child's Perception of Selected Dimensions of Parental Behavior." Unpublished doctoral dissertation, Purdue University, 1963.

Passman, R. H., and Weisberg, P. "Mothers and Blankets as Agents for Promoting Play and Exploration in a Novel Environment: The Effects of Social and Nonsocial Attachment Objects." *Developmental Psychology*, 1975, *11*, 170-177.

Peters, R. A. "The Effects of Anxiety, Curiosity, and Instructor Threat on Student Verbal Behavior in the College Classroom." Unpublished doctoral dissertation, University of South Florida, 1976.

Peterson, R. W. "The Differential Effect of an Adult's Presence on the Curiosity Behavior of Children." *Journal of Research in Science Teaching*, 1975, *12*, 199-208.

Peterson, R. W., and Lowery, L. F. "Curiosity, Persistence, and Problem Solving Behaviors Among Elementary School Children." Bureau of Research, U.S. Office of Education, Dept. of Health, Education and Welfare No. OEG-9-9-140012-0055(057). University of California, 1970.

Peterson, R. W., and Lowery, L. F. "The Use of Motor Activity as an Index of Curiosity in Children." *Journal of Research in Science Teaching*, 1972, *9*, 193-200.

Piaget, J. *The Language and Thought of the Child.* New York: World, 1955.

Piaget, J. *The Principles of Genetic Epistemology.* (W. Mays, Trans.) London: Routledge and Kegan Paul, 1972.

Rabinowitz, F. M., Moely, B. E., and Finkel, N. "The Effects of

Toy Novelty and Social Interaction on the Exploratory Behavior of Preschool Children." *Child Development,* 1975, *46,* 286-289.

Rahman, M. M. "Effects of Pre-Exposure on Perceptual Curiosity for Stimulus and Novelty." Unpublished doctoral dissertation, University of New Mexico, 1970.

Rappaport, D. "Psychoanalytic Theory of Motivation." *Nebraska Symposium of Motivation,* 1960, *8,* 173-247.

Richardson, R. P. "Development and Use of SCI Inventory to Measure Upper Elementary School Children's Scientific Curiosity and Interest." Unpublished doctoral dissertation, Ohio State University, 1971.

Richman, C. L., Kahle, D., and Rutland, S. "Curiosity Behavior in Normal and Mentally Retarded Children." *Psychonomic Science,* 1972, *29,* 212.

Riegel, K. F. "The Dialectics of Human Development." *American Psychologist,* 1976, *31,* 689-700.

Robinson, W. P. (Ed.). *Education, Curiosity and Questioning.* Southhampton, England: University of Southhampton, 1974.

Rokeach, M. *The Open and Closed Mind.* New York: Basic Books, 1960.

Rosendorn, A. "Relationship Between Curiosity and School Performance." Unpublished master's thesis, Institute of Education, University of London, 1976.

Ross, H. S., and Balzer, R. B. "Determinants and Consequences of Children's Questions." *Child Development,* 1975, *46,* 536-539.

Rothburd, M. I. "Behaviors Related to Scores on the Cynosural Narcissism—Scoptic Curiosity Scale in College and Mental Hospital Populations." Unpublished doctoral dissertation, Ohio University, 1970.

Rotter, J. B. "Generalized Expectancies for Internal vs. External Control of Reinforcement." *Psychological Monographs,* 1966, *80,* 1 (entire issue).

Sarason, I. G. "Test Anxiety, General Anxiety and Intellectual Performance." *Journal of Consulting Psychology,* 1957, *21,* 485-490.

Sarason, I. G. "Experimental Approaches to Test-Anxiety: Attention and the Uses of Information." In C. D. Spielberger (Ed.), *Anxiety and Behavior.* Vol. 2. New York: Academic Press, 1971.

Saxe, R. M. "The Relationship Between Maternal Behaviors and a Child's Curiosity and Play Behavior." Unpublished doctoral dissertation, Michigan State University, 1968.

Saxe, R. M., and Stollak, G. E. "Curiosity and the Parent-Child Relationship." *Child Development,* 1971, *42,* 373-384.

Schiffer, D. "Relation of Inhibition of Curiosity to Homosexuality." *Psychological Reports,* 1970, *27,* 771-776.

Schiltz, J. M., and Burchett, B. "Sensory Boxes." *Science and Children,* 1975, *12,* 7-9.

Schulman, L. S., Loupe, M. J., and Piper, R. M. "Studies of the Inquiry Process: Inquiry Patterns of Students in Teacher-Training Programs." U.S. Office of Education, Cooperative Research Report No. 5-0597. Michigan State University, 1968.

Schultz, C. B. "Information Seeking Following the Confirmation or Contradiction of Beliefs." *Journal of Educational Psychology,* 1974, *66,* 903-910.

Schwartz, L. L. "Relationships Among Curiosity, Anxiety, and Risk-Taking in Fifth-Grade Children." Unpublished doctoral dissertation, Bryn Mawr College, 1963.

Segal, B. "Sensation Seeking and Anxiety: Assessment of Responses to Specific Stimulus Situations." *Journal of Consulting and Clinical Psychology,* 1973, *41,* 135-138.

Shmidheiser, N. "An Investigation of the Relationships Between Developmental History and Adjustment and Achievement in Kindergarten." Unpublished master's thesis, Bryn Mawr College, 1970.

Skidgell, A. C., Witryol, S. L., and Wirzbicki, P. J. "The Effect of Novelty-Familiarity Levels on Material Reward Preference of First-Grade Children." *Journal of Genetic Psychology,* 1976, *128,* 291-297.

Smith, M. E. "The Influence of Age, Sex, and Situation on the Frequency, Form, and the Function of Questions Asked by Pre-School Children." *Child Development,* 1933, *4,* 201-213.

Snyder, S. S. "The Effects of a Curiosity Incentive on Children's Discrimination Learning." Unpublished master's thesis, Yale University, 1971.

Spielberger, C. D., and Butler, T. F. "On the Relationship Between Anxiety, Curiosity and Arousal: A Working Paper." Unpublished manuscript, Florida State University, 1971.

Stothart, J. R. "Teacher Characteristics, Student Curiosity, and Problem Selection in High School Biology." Unpublished doctoral dissertation, University of Houston, 1972.

Suchman, J. R. "Motivation Inherent in the Pursuit of Meaning: Or the Desire to Inquire." In H. I. Day, D. E. Berlyne, and D. E. Hunt (Eds.), *Intrinsic Motivation: A New Direction in Education.* Toronto: Holt, Rinehart and Winston of Canada, 1971.

Susskind, E. C. "Questioning and Curiosity in the Elementary School Classroom." Unpublished doctoral dissertation, Yale University, 1969.

Switzky, H. N., Haywood, H. C., and Isett, R. "Exploration, Curiosity and Play in Young Children: Effects of Stimulus Complexity." *Developmental Psychology,* 1974, *10,* 321-329.

Todd, S. R. "Story Preferences: A Technique for Assessing Children's Curiosity." Unpublished doctoral dissertation, Arizona State University, 1972.

Torrance, E. P. "Curiosity of Gifted Children and Performance of Timed and Untimed Tests of Creativity." *Gifted Child Quarterly,* 1969, *13,* 155-158.

Towell, R. D. "Test Performance of High and Low Curiosity Subjects on Timed and Untimed Verbal Tests of Creativity." Unpublished doctoral dissertation, University of Georgia, 1972.

Vidler, D. C. "The Relationship Between Convergent and Divergent Thinking, Test Anxiety and Curiosity." Unpublished doctoral dissertation, Columbia University, 1972.

Vidler, D. C., and Karan, V. E. "A Study of Curiosity, Divergent Thinking and Test-Anxiety." *Journal of Psychology,* 1975, *90,* 237-243.

Vidler, D. C., and Levine, J. "Teachers' Ratings and Self-Ratings of Curiosity." *Psychological Reports,* 1976, *39,* 149-150.

Vidler, D. C., and Rawan, H. R. "Construct Validation of a Scale of Academic Curiosity." *Psychological Reports,* 1974, *35,* 263-266.

Vidler, D. C., and Rawan, H. R. "Further Validation of a Scale of Academic Curiosity." *Psychological Reports,* 1975, *37,* 115-118.

Walls, R. T., and Rude, S. H. *Exploration and Learning-to-Learn in Disadvantaged Pre-Schoolers.* Social and Rehabilitation Service, Dept. of Health, Education and Welfare, ERIC No. ED073847/PS006385. West Virginia University, 1972.

Wechsler, D. *Wechsler Adult Intelligence Scale Manual.* New York: Psychological Corporation, 1955.

Weintraub, H. "Case Studies of Boys Identified as High or Low in Curiosity." Unpublished doctoral dissertation, Rutgers —The State University, 1968.

Weisler, A., and McCall, R. B. "Exploration and Play: Résumé and Redirection." *American Psychologist,* 1976, *31,* 492-508.

Whitsitt, M. E. "A Model of Elementary Art Instruction Based upon Curiosity as Motivation." Unpublished doctoral dissertation, University of Wisconsin, 1975.

Wohlwill, J. F. "Children's Voluntary Exploration and Preference for Tactually Presented Nonsense Shapes Differing in Complexity." *Journal of Experimental Child Psychology,* 1975, *20,* 159-167.

Zajonc, R. B. "The Attitudinal Effects of Mere Exposure." *Journal of Personal and Social Psychology,* 1968, *9* (2, Monograph suppl.) 1-27.

Zuckerman, M. "Dimensions of Sensation Seeking." *Journal of Consulting and Clinical Psychology,* 1971, *36,* 45-52.

Zuckerman, M., Bone, R. N., Neary, R., Mangelsdorff, D., and Brustman, B. "What Is the Sensation Seeker? Personality Trait and Experience Correlates of the Sensation-Seeking Scales." *Journal of Consulting and Clinical Psychology,* 1972, *39,* 308-321.

Zuckerman, M., Kolin, E. A., Price, L., and Zoob, I. "Development of a Sensation-Seeking Scale." *Journal of Consulting Psychology,* 1964, *28,* 477-482.

Name Index

Abbott, P. S., 393, 419
Abra, J. C., 378, 416
Acker, M., 540, 550, 556, 565
Adair, J. G., 182, 219
Adams, H. E., 3, 9
Adams-Webber, J. R., 484, 485, 499
Adevai, G., 494, 499
Adinolfi, A. A., 247, 267
Adkisson, J., 538, 540, 547, 552
Adorno, T. W., 472, 474, 478, 499
Agras, W. S., 365, 395, 404-406, 414, 423
Ahmed, S. M., 361, 376, 412, 423
Aiduk, R., 335, 336, 351
Aitken, R. C., 380, 381, 410, 412, 415, 424
Albee, E., 132
Albert, J., 464, 470, 471, 510-511
Alberti, R., 321, 351
Alexander, S., 41, 46
Allard, M., 486, 499-500
Allen, V. L., 265, 275
Allport, F. H., 181, 219, 331, 351
Allport, G. W., 331, 351, 463, 500
Alperson, B. L., 113, 135
Alperson, E. D., 113, 135
Alter, R. D., 480, 500, 525
Altman, I., 280, 282, 284, 291, 292, 295, 300, 309, 318

Altrocchi, J., 40, 43
Alverno, L., 376, 423
Amolsch, T., 285, 300, 305, 307
Anastasi, A., 339, 351
Anchor, K. N., 284, 300, 303, 309
Anderson, C. C., 489, 521
Anderson, G. W., 374, 423
Anderson, W., 225, 267
Angel, T., 105, 138
Apfeldorf, M., 32, 33, 43
Apostal, R., 285, 306, 312
Applebaum, M., 18, 54
Applezweig, D. G., 476, 500
Arbit, J., 442, 458
Archer, D., 6, 179-221
Argyle, M., 191, 192, 219, 247, 267, 295, 309
Arkowitz, H., 252-253, 267, 342
Armlin, N. J., 480, 517-518
Armor, D. J., 197, 219
Arnaud, S. H., 237, 269
Aronson, H., 284, 319
Asberg, M., 401, 403, 414, 415
Asch, S. E., 67, 97
Ashton, S. G., 59, 61, 97
Atkins, A. L., 464, 471, 473, 484
Atkinson, R. E., 115, 136
Auguston, B., 495, 524
Ault, R. L., 472, 500

573

Austin, G. A., 469, 502
Austin, N., 321, 356
Auvenshine, D., 33, 46
Axtell, B., 283, 309
Ayers, J., 32, 33, 51

Babcock, H., 433, 435, 442, 443
Bach, G. R., 106, 135
Bachelard, G., 143, 149, 173
Bacon, P., 482, 515-516
Baddeley, A. D., 427, 428, 430, 452,
    453, 457, 458, 460
Baer, D. J., 476, 500
Baer, J., 321, 352
Bahr, S., 288, 290, 298, 317
Bailey, D. E., 19, 53, 157, 177
Bailey, J., 365, 415
Baldwin, B. A., 42, 43, 486, 500
Bales, R. F., 241, 267
Balint, M., 143, 149, 173
Balzer, R. B., 536, 568
Banmen, J., 113, 135
Bannister, D., 483, 485, 500
Banta, T. J., 113, 495, 549-550
Barbeau, D., 485, 499
Barclay, J., 478, 511
Barker, E. N., 299, 312, 479, 480
Barlow, D. H., 365, 395, 404-406,
    414, 423
Barr, H. L., 466, 473, 512, 520
Barr, M. A., 484, 485, 513
Barron, F., 34-36, 43, 66, 67-68, 97,
    130, 539, 557
Barry, J., 40, 44
Barry, W. A., 257-259, 261-262, 275
Bartlett, F. C., 443, 457
Bastien, S., 323, 324, 325-327,
    329-330, 353
Bates, H., 222, 330, 334-335, 351
Bath, K. E., 284, 290, 303, 305
Bauman, G., 494, 500
Bayma, B., 298, 310
Beamesderfer, A., 366-367, 415
Bebout, J., 113, 135
Beck, A. T., 359, 363, 364, 365,
    366-367, 369, 410, 412, 415
Beck, R. W., 367, 369, 410, 415
Becker, G., 479, 482, 500
Beigel, A., 338, 356
Beil-Warner, D., 329, 354

Bell, P. A., 41, 43
Bellack, A. S., 3, 10, 254, 270-271
Belton, G. P., 378, 416
Benson, D. F., 434, 459-460
Bentler, P. M., 65n, 86, 98, 121
Benton, A. L., 442, 457
Berger, S. E., 303, 309
Berkowitz, L., 486, 514
Berlyne, D. E., 527, 528, 533, 534,
    535, 537, 543, 544, 556, 557-558
Berman, P., 541, 546, 558
Bernhardson, C. S., 40, 43
Bernstein, D., 346, 355-356
Bernstein, L., 383-384, 385, 386
Berwick, P., 338, 356
Beswick, D. G., 526, 528, 529, 542,
    553, 558
Bettinghaus, E., 482, 500-501
Bhushan, L. I., 475, 501
Bialow, M. R., 365, 367, 392, 393,
    394, 395, 396, 397-398, 409
Bieri, J., 463, 464, 470, 471, 473,
    484, 485, 486, 487, 492, 496,
    497, 501, 509, 516, 523, 529,
    559
Bijou, S. W., 3, 8, 530-531, 559
Birtchnell, J., 376, 424
Blackburn, R., 38, 44
Blackman, S., 8, 462-525
Blake, R. R., 248, 268
Blanchard, E. B., 251, 269, 323,
    344-345, 346, 347, 352
Blashki, T. G., 370, 372, 376, 393,
    394, 395, 397, 398, 416
Blasi, E. R., 495, 501
Blatner, H. A., 247, 267
Block, E. L., 284, 305, 309-310
Block, J., 24, 44, 171, 173, 471-472,
    477, 502, 530, 562
Block, J. H., 471-472, 477, 530
Bloom, B. S., 61, 102, 554, 564
Bloom, P. M., 365, 384, 386, 415
Blumenthal, M. D., 371, 373-374,
    375, 415
Bobele, H. K., 113, 136
Bodden, J. L., 486, 502
Boerger, A. R., 18, 20, 44
Boger, R. P., 550, 559
Boies, K. G., 246, 267
Bonarius, J. C. P., 247, 268

Bone, R. N., 540, 571
Bonk, E. C., 109, 136-137
Borgatta, E. F., 236, 239, 240-241, 242, 268
Borgen, J. S., 482, 525
Borkovec, T. D., 253, 268
Bottenberg, E. H., 489, 490, 502
Bovard, E. W., 257, 274
Bradburn, W., 496, 501
Bradley, R. C., 538, 540, 547, 559
Brady, J. P., 365, 384, 386, 415
Breglio, V. J., 283, 284, 288, 297-298, 301, 316
Brennan, J., 372, 420
Breskin, S., 495, 502
Briar, S., 464, 471, 473, 484, 501
Broadbent, D. E., 427, 459
Brockman, C. G., 147, 175
Brody, M. B., 443, 457
Bronfenbrenner, U., 229, 230, 231, 232, 268
Brookhart, D., 38, 49
Brooks, L., 285, 299, 310
Brooks, S. J., 284, 300, 305, 306, 307, 311
Broverman, D. M., 467, 502
Brown, E. C., 2, 8-9
Brown, G. L., 372, 374, 415
Brown, J. M., 367, 397, 409, 422
Brown, L. T., 553, 559
Brown, R. W., 476, 502
Bruehl, D., 496, 520
Bruner, J. S., 39, 237, 469, 529
Brustman, B., 540, 571
Bryant, B., 247, 267
Buchan, L. G., 248, 268
Buck, R., 194, 219
Buckspan, B., 80, 99
Bull, S. G. H., 537, 559
Bunney, W. E., Jr., 404, 415-416
Burch, W. R., Jr., 155, 173
Burchett, B., 551, 569
Burgess, G. D., 282, 317
Burhenne, D., 283, 288, 297, 298, 301, 310
Burrows, G., 365, 372, 381, 416
Busch, J. C., 494, 496, 502-503
Busfield, B. L., Jr., 398, 413, 423
Buss, A. H., 242, 243, 268
Busse, T. V., 495, 496, 503

Bustanoby, A., 127, 135
Butcher, J. N., 17, 49
Butler, T. F., 528, 570
Butters, N., 430, 454-455, 457-458
Byrd, R. E., 113, 135
Byrne, D., 24, 25, 39-42, 43, 44

Caine, T. M., 362, 417
Caldwell, A. B., 32, 45
Calhoun, K. S., 3, 9
Calhoun, L. G., 373, 374, 420
Callner, D. A., 324, 337-338, 351
Calvin, J., 14, 15, 44
Cameron, N., 23, 44
Campbell, D. T., 164, 173, 288, 310
Campbell, J. F., 554, 559
Campbell, R. J., 181, 219
Campbell, V. N., 486, 503
Canon, L. K., 80, 98
Cantor, J., 32, 54
Capelle, R., 113, 135
Carithers, M., 18, 53
Carkhuff, R. R., 279, 284, 299, 319
Carlson, E. R., 486, 499-500
Carr, J., 331, 333, 356, 486, 503
Carroll, B. J., 370, 372, 376, 393, 394, 395, 397, 398, 416
Carroll, D., 283, 310
Carsch, H., 475, 503-504
Casey, G. A., 247, 268
Casey, J. F., 402, 403, 414, 421
Cassem, N. H., 376, 417
Cattell, R. B., 148, 379, 476, 540
Catton, W. R., Jr., 147, 175
Cautela, J. R., 3, 9, 338, 352
Cermak, L. S., 430, 454-455, 457-458
Certner, B. C., 280, 281, 293, 310
Chabassol, D. J., 480, 503
Chabot, J. A., 41, 44
Chaikin, A. L., 286, 298, 310
Chang, A. F., 32, 45
Charns, H., 167, 173
Charter, S. P. R., 149, 173
Chave, E. J., 291, 318
Chelune, G. J., 7, 278-320
Chesler, M., 248, 268
Chittenden, G. E., 351, 352
Chittick, E. V., 283, 302, 311
Chiu, L. H., 541, 560

Chown, S. M., 476, 503
Christensen, A. L., 433, 458
Christiansen, C., 14, 47
Christie, R., 78, 80, 98, 475, 503
Chu, C., 19-21, 45
Ciminero, A. R., 3, 9
Clark, J. V., 113, 136
Clarke, P., 482, 503
Clawson, M., 155, 173
Clayton, M. B., 466, 503
Clemmons, R., 367, 392, 395, 397-398, 422
Cline, V. B., 181, 219
Clore, C. L., 482, 508
Coan, R. W., 123, 136
Coates, S. W., 495, 503
Cobb, S., 370, 418
Cochrane, C., 365, 366, 372, 378, 384, 387, 410, 420
Cofer, C. N., 537, 544, 561
Coffman, T. L., 473, 491, 511, 524
Cohen, H., 369, 396, 417
Cohen, J., 197, 214, 219
Cohler, B. J., 17, 18, 45
Cohn, T. S., 475, 503-504
Coei, J., 551-552, 560
Cole, C. W., 283, 309
Comrey, A. L., 14, 45, 115, 136, 137, 361, 362, 377, 378, 412, 416
Cone, J. D., 3, 9
Conn, J. H., 536, 560
Conn, L. K., 182, 219
Connolly, M. R., 545, 560
Cook, M., 191, 192, 193, 219
Cook, P. E., 36-39, 50, 475, 503
Coop, R. H., 463, 473, 504
Coopersmith, S., 75, 98
Coppedge, H. M., 375, 400, 425
Coppen, A., 365, 415
Corey, S. M., 536, 561
Corlis, C., 531, 560
Corsini, R. J., 224, 238-239, 245, 246, 248, 268, 339, 352
Costello, C. G., 377, 378, 412, 416
Couch, H., 479, 504
Cowitz, B., 369, 396, 417
Cox, G. B., 490, 504
Cox, O., 540, 561
Coyle, F. A., 18, 46

Coyne, L., 18, 53
Cozby, P., 279, 280, 282, 283, 295
Craddick, R. A., 2, 9
Craik, K. H., 4, 9, 141, 142, 144, 145, 146, 147, 149, 173-174
Crano, W. D., 491, 504
Cripps, J. H., 551, 560
Crockett, W. H., 484, 486, 504
Cronbach, L. J., 148, 174, 339, 352
Cropley, A. J., 359, 363, 367, 375, 396, 416, 423
Cross, H. A., 495, 501
Crosson, S., 117, 136
Crowne, D., 182, 219
Crutchfield, R. S., 67-68, 98, 117
Csapo, K., 430, 459
Culbert, S. A., 113, 136
Curran, J. P., 253, 269
Curry, N. E., 237, 269
Curtis, G. C., 389, 391, 416
Cutler, R. P., 401-402, 403, 414

Dahlstrom, L. E., 11, 13, 14, 17, 19, 21, 22, 23, 24, 26, 27, 28-29, 30, 32, 34, 35, 37, 40, 42, 45, 361, 362, 416
Dahlstrom, W. G., 11, 13, 14, 17, 19, 21, 22, 23, 24, 26, 27, 28-29, 30, 32, 34, 35, 37, 40, 42, 45, 361, 362, 416
Daly, D. L., 284, 290, 303, 305, 309
Damarin, F. L., 18, 50, 495, 515
Danahy, S., 32, 48
Davenport, G., 496, 520
Davies, B., 365, 372, 381, 416
Davis, E. A., 536, 560
Davis, H., 32, 51
Davis, J. D., 283, 298, 305, 311
Day, D., 464, 470, 471, 510-511
Day, H. I., 480, 482, 504, 527, 528, 535, 539, 560
DeFrank, J. A., 193, 195n, 213, 221
Deiker, T. E., 38, 45-46
Delgado, J., 406, 418
Delhees, K. H., 379, 416
Delo, J. S., 323, 324, 325-327, 329-330, 353
Dempsey, P., 362, 416
Denny, M. R., 481, 518
Denny, R., 105, 138

DeRidder, L. M., 496, 502
Derlega, V. J., 286, 298, 310
Detre, T. P., 406, 418
Deutsch, J. A., 453, 458
DeVoge, S., 6-7, 222-277, 347-348
Diab, L. N., 478, 511
Diament, B., 528, 535, 560-561
Dickoff, H., 40, 43
Dickson, C. R., 3, 9
Digman, J. M., 476, 506
Dileo, D. T., 479, 500
DiMascio, A., 397, 408, 409, 410
DiMatteo, M. R., 6, 179-221
Dimond, R. E., 282, 287, 311
DiRenzo, G. J., 480, 504
Distler, L. S., 35, 46
Ditkofsky, J., 544, 558
DiVesta, F. J., 482, 519
Dizney, H. F., 537, 559
Dobbs, M. F., 482, 520
Dollard, J., 304, 311
Donaldson, W., 427, 460
Dorman, L., 351, 352
D'Orta, C. W., 284, 286, 296, 297, 305, 312
Doster, J. A., 284, 287, 300, 304, 305, 306, 307, 311-312
Downing, R. W., 372, 374, 375, 396, 400, 409, 413, 416, 422
Doyle, J. A., 118, 136
Drachman, D. A., 442, 458
Driver, M. J., 487, 488, 489, 490, 491-492, 519, 521
Dubé, G. E., 555, 563
Du Cette, J., 486, 520
Duck, S. W., 485, 504
Duncan, S., 182, 219-220
Dunn, B. E., 378, 416
Dunnette, M. D., 248, 269
Dunning, G. B., 250-251, 264
Dupre, V. A., 389, 419
Durand, R. M., 482, 504
Durkee, A., 243, 268
Dyer, R. N., 467, 504
Dyk, R. B., 473, 492-493, 494, 525
D'Zurilla, T. J., 349, 353

Eagle, C. J., 494, 507

Earp, N. W., 538, 559
Eber, H. W., 540, 560
Eckart, C., 88, 98
Eckerman, C. O., 531, 549, 561
Eckman, K. M., 384, 386, 424
Edinberg, M. A., 251, 269, 345, 349-350, 352
Edmonds, D., 486, 512
Edwards, A. L., 23, 46, 65, 98
Edwards, C. N., 182, 219
Edwards, M., 475, 508
Efran, J. S., 254-255, 269
Egeland, B., 472, 504
Egelston, R., 497, 525
Ehri, L. C., 495, 505
Eisenman, R., 534, 561
Eisler, R. M., 251, 254, 323, 324, 325, 341-342, 344-345, 346, 347
Ekman, P., 192, 220
Ekstrand, B. R., 428, 458
Ellenberger, H., 105, 138, 236, 269
Ellinger, J., 495, 524
Elliot, R., 497, 505
Ellis, A., 279, 312
Ellsworth, P., 192, 220
Emmons, M., 321, 351
Entwisle, D. R., 533, 562
Epstein, J. S., 182, 219
Epting, F. R., 299, 312, 484, 485, 486, 490, 505, 525
Erbaugh, J., 363, 365, 412, 415
Erickson, J. R., 18, 50
Evans, C. L., 328, 329, 342, 353
Evans, D., 41, 46, 536, 539, 561
Evans, F. J., 494, 495, 505
Eysenck, H. J., 115, 136
Eysenck, S., 115, 136

Fagan, J., 247, 269
Fahey, G. L., 536, 561
Farber, I. E., 24, 46
Farina, A., 297, 313
Farley, F. H., 494, 505, 540, 561
Farley, S. V., 540, 561
Faterson, H. F., 473, 492-493, 494
Fawcett, J. T., 164, 174
Feather, N. T., 480, 482, 505
Felknor, C., 489, 508-509
Fenchel, C. H., 495, 505
Fenson, J. S., 539, 567

Fensterheim, H., 321, 352
Fertig, E. S., 486, 505
Field, G. D., 247, 269
Fielding, J. M., 370, 372, 376, 393, 394, 395, 397, 398, 416
Fieve, R. R., 384, 386, 421
Figert, R. S., Jr., 480, 505
Fine, B. J., 495, 505-506
Finkel, N., 531, 552, 567-568
Finney, J., 33, 46
Fischer, M., 285, 306, 312
Fisher, E., 374, 375, 409, 422
Fisher, G., 38, 40, 41, 46, 121
Fisher, S., 381, 421, 476, 506
Fiske, D. W., 164, 173, 228, 231, 232, 271, 288, 310, 312
Fitzgerald, M. P., 288, 290, 312
Fitzgerald, O. R., 113, 137
Fode, K. L., 182, 221
Fogel, M. L., 389, 391, 416
Foley, J. M., 181, 221
Folstein, M. F., 380, 417
Forrest, B., 545, 551, 563
Forster, N. C., 476, 506
Foster, F. G., 406, 418
Foulds, G. A., 362, 417
Foulds, M. L., 111, 113, 134, 136
Fouraker, L. E., 80, 98, 101
Fowler, R. D., 13, 32, 33, 46
Fox, J., 107, 136
Fox, R., 248, 268
Frankel, A., 281, 295, 312
Fransella, F., 483, 485, 500, 506
Frase, L. T., 537, 561
Fredericksen, S. J., 38, 46
Frederiksen, N., 475, 515
Freedman, J. L., 244, 269
French, E. G., 476, 477, 506
Frenkel-Brunswik, E., 472, 474, 477, 478, 499, 506
Freud, S., 131, 142
Frick, J. W., 533-534, 537, 544
Fricke, L., 113, 139
Friedman, A., 369, 396, 417
Friedman, H., 197, 220
Friend, R., 71, 98
Friesen, D. D., 250-251, 264
Friesen, W. V., 192, 220
Frijda, N. H., 192, 220
Froese, A., 376, 417
Fromm, E., 124, 143, 279, 312

Fruchter, B., 81, 101
Fry, J. P., 538, 561
Furness, P., 248, 270

Gaensslen, H., 480, 506
Gaffan, D., 447, 458
Galassi, J. P., 323, 324, 325-327, 328, 329-331, 333, 342, 353, 354
Galassi, M. D., 323, 324, 325-327, 328, 329, 330, 353
Galinsky, M. D., 496, 501
Gambrill, E. D., 3, 9, 336-337, 353
Gardner, R. C., 82-83, 98
Gardner, R. W., 463, 465-466, 467, 468, 469, 470, 506-507, 512
Garlington, W. K., 146, 174
Garvey, C., 237, 270
Garvey, F. J., 109, 136-137
Gary, A. L., 280, 281, 282, 293
Gatto, J. L., 536, 561
Gay, M. L., 328, 329-331, 333, 342
Geis, F., 78, 80, 98
Gelbart, P., 343, 356-357
Geller, D., 546, 566
Gelso, C. J., 113, 137
Geoghegan, S., 247, 267
Getter, H., 35, 46
Gianturco, J., 374, 425
Giddan, N. S., 480, 512
Ginsberg, R., 478, 511
Ginsburg, G. P., $222n$, 244, 270
Gitter, A. G., 482, 518
Glacken, C. J., 149, 174
Glaudin, V., 383, 385, 386, 421
Glazer, N., 105, 138
Gleser, G. C., 148, 174, 251, 269, 345, 349-350, 352, 392, 417, 496
Gocka, E., 13, 14, 15, 21, 24, 30, 34, 47
Godden, D. R., 430, 458
Goffman, E., 236, 270
Goldberg, H., 106, 135
Goldberg, L. R., 17, 18, 47, 54, 59, 61, 97, 148, 174
Golden, C. J., 467, 507
Goldfried, M. R., 3, 9, 349, 353
Goldman, E., 365, 366, 420
Goldman-Eisler, F., 306, 312
Goldsmith, J. B., 247, 270
Goldstein, J. J., 284, 286, 296, 297, 305, 312

Goldstein, K. M., 8, 462-525
Good, L. R., 290, 317
Goodenough, D. R., 473, 492-493, 494, 507, 525
Goodglass, H., 430, 454-455, 457-458
Goodman, B., 495, 507
Goodman, M. A., 284, 286, 296, 297, 305, 312
Goodman, P., 105, 138
Goodmonson, C., 383, 385, 386, 421
Goodnow, J., 469, 502
Goodrich, D. W., 258, 270
Goodstadt, B., 282, 284, 291, 314
Goodstein, L. D., 280, 281, 284, 286, 296, 297, 305, 309-310
Gordon, B., 113, 135
Gorman, B. S., 495, 502, 539-540
Gormly, M. V., 482, 508
Gotlib, I., 304, 317
Gottesman, I. I., 35, 47
Gough, H. G., 56, 66, 98, 146, 148, 164, 165, 174, 326, 353, 475, 508
Graham, F. D., 442, 458
Graham, J. R., 5, 11-55
Graham, S., 297, 313
Granik, S., 369, 396, 417
Gravitz, M. A., 361, 417
Greaves, G., 489, 508
Greeley, A., 135
Green, R., 297, 313, 375, 400, 425
Greenberg, I. A., 247, 270
Greenberger, E., 533, 534, 562
Greenwald, H., 4, 9
Gresock, C., 361, 421
Griffin, C., 18, 53
Grinker, R. R., 369, 417
Gross, D. W., 530, 562
Gross, T., 302, 316
Grosser, G. H., 398, 413, 423
Grunebaum, H. V., 17, 18, 45
Guetzkow, H., 495, 508
Guilford, J. P., 331, 354, 541, 562
Guinan, J. F., 113, 136
Gulo, E. V., 479, 508

Hackett, E., 401, 403, 423
Hackett, T. P., 376, 417
Hall, C. S., 61, 98

Hall, J. A., 6, 179-221
Hall, J. R., 7, 321-357
Halverson, C., 290, 297, 313, 490
Hamburg, D. A., 404, 415-416
Hamilton, M., 361, 368, 370, 376, 392-398, 403, 412, 413, 417, 423
Hamilton, V. L., 244, 270
Hammond, R., 293, 312
Hamshire, J. H., 297, 313
Handel, A., 494, 508
Hannigan, P. S., 111, 113, 134, 136
Hanson, D. J., 479, 508
Hanvik, L. J., 29-31, 47
Hargreaves, W. A., 406, 417-418
Harkless, R., 479, 512
Harlow, S. D., 482, 525
Harmeling, P. C., 236, 270
Harrington, D. M., 472, 502, 530
Harris, D. B., 475, 508
Harris, L., 545, 560
Harris, R., 12-15, 47
Harrison, A. A., 547, 562
Harrison, R. L., 288, 298, 315
Harrow, G. S., 233-234, 270
Harter, S., 546, 562
Hartlage, L. C., 155, 176
Hartmann, D. P., 472, 500
Harvey, J., 482, 508
Harvey, O. J., 462-463, 464, 473, 487, 488, 489, 490, 491, 492, 497, 508-509, 515, 524
Hase, H. D., 17, 47
Hatano, G., 538, 563
Hathaway, S. R., 11, 17, 47, 361
Haubrich, A. S., 540, 561
Havel, J., 475, 503
Haven, H. J., 38, 48
Hawkins, R. P., 3, 9
Hawkinson, J. R., 35, 48
Hawley, R. C., 248, 270
Haymes, M., 283, 304, 308, 313
Hays, D. G., 482, 508
Haywood, H. C., 531, 545, 562, 570
Heather, B. B., 366, 418
Hebert, J. A., 495, 501
Heckel, R. V., 549, 562
Hefferline, R., 105, 138
Heilbrun, A. B., Jr., 146, 326
Hekmat, H., 115, 117, 136
Hellkamp, D. T., 282, 287, 311
Hempel, C. G., 87, 99

Hendee, J. C., 147, 157, 176
Hendricks, C., 244, 270
Herkowitz, J., 495, 509
Hermalin, B., 430, 459
Herron, E., 383-384, 385, 386, 387
Hersen, M., 3, 10, 251, 254, 323, 324, 325, 341-342, 344-345, 346, 347
Hertel, R. K., 247-249, 261-262
Hertzman, M., 464, 469, 473, 492-493
Hess, R. D., 530, 551, 562
Hewitt, D., 492, 509
Higbee, K., 281, 288, 289, 316
Hilgard, E. R., 115, 136
Himelstein, P., 35, 48, 283, 288, 297, 301-302, 305, 311, 313
Hines, P., 252-253, 267, 342, 351
Hinkle, D. D., 483, 509
Hochman, L., 479, 523
Hoffman, H., 18, 32, 33, 86, 87
Hollandsworth, J. G., Jr., 328, 329-331, 333, 334, 342, 353, 354
Holley, B. J., 485, 517
Hollingworth, H., 468, 509
Hollister, L. E., 402, 403, 414, 421
Holloway, H., 14, 15, 47
Holmes, D. S., 35, 48, 331, 354
Holz, R. F., 482, 518
Holzer, C. E., 365, 367, 392, 393, 394, 395, 396, 397-398, 409
Holzman, P. S., 463, 467, 506, 509
Hopkins, T. R., 384, 386, 424
Horan, J., 331, 354
Horney, K., 143
Hourany, L., 74, 99
Howard, K. I., 146, 176
Howe, M. R., 328, 329, 342, 353
Hritzuk, J., 495, 509
Huber, J. W., 128, 136
Huber, N., 32, 48
Humphrey, M., 441, 460
Hunt, D. E., 464, 473, 487, 490, 492, 497, 509
Hunt, H. F., 433, 458
Hunt, J. M., 529, 563
Hunt, M. F., 482, 509
Hunt, S. M., 370, 418
Huntington, E., 149, 175
Huntley, P., 32, 33, 43

Huppert, F. A., 429, 458
Hurley, J. R., 288, 313
Hurley, S. J., 288, 313
Hutt, C., 530, 545, 551, 563
Huxley, T. H., 58

Ibsen, H., 131
Idzikowski, C. J., 428, 458
Inagaki, K., 538, 563
Innes, J. M., 547, 563
Insel, P. M., 4, 10
Irwin, M., 486, 509
Isett, R., 545, 570
Ittelson, W. H., 142, 177
Iverson, M., 481, 509-510

Jackson, D. D., 130, 137
Jackson, D. N., 5-6, 17, 56-102, 465-466, 467, 468, 469, 485, 494, 503
Jacobson, G. H., 491, 510
Jacobson, L. I., 113, 140, 182, 221
Jacoby, J., 482, 510
Jaffe, P. E., 281, 284, 314
Jakubowski, P. A., 250, 276
Jakubowski-Spector, P., 322, 354
James, J., 482, 503
Janis, I. L., 75, 99
Janofsky, A. I., 285, 313
Jansen, D. G., 109, 124, 136-137
Javorek, J., 407, 419
Jenkins, J. A., 538, 553, 563
Jensen, A. R., 467, 510
Jew, C. C., 115, 138
Johnson, D. A. W., 366, 418
Johnson, D. L., 495, 515
Johnson, F. G., 87, 101
Jolly, A., 237, 268
Jones, M. B., 477, 510
Jöreskog, K. G., 497, 524
Jourard, S. M., 279, 280, 281, 282, 283, 284, 286, 287-290, 291, 292, 293, 294, 297, 298, 304, 313-314
Joyston-Bechal, M. P., 485, 506
Judd, W. A., 543, 563

Kagan, J., 464, 465, 470, 471
Kagan, N., 181, 219
Kahle, D., 552, 568

Kahn, G. M., 280, 281, 282, 293, 320
Kahoe, R. D., 543-544, 563
Kaiman, I. P., 482, 524
Kaloupek, D. G., 253, 268
Kameoka, V., 372, 420
Kammeier, M. L., 18, 32, 33, 48, 49
Kaplan, M. F., 283, 314, 481, 511
Karan, V. E., 541, 570
Karlins, M., 491, 511
Karoly, P., 251, 269, 335, 336, 345, 349-350, 351, 352
Karp, S. A., 473, 492-493, 494, 511
Kates, S. L., 478, 511
Katz, G., 402, 403, 414, 421
Kay, L. W., 234, 271
Kazdin, A. E., 324, 325, 331, 335, 336, 342, 351, 354
Kegel-Flom, P., 164, 175
Kelley, J., 328, 357
Kelley, R. K., 126, 137
Kelly, E. L., 231, 232, 271
Kelly, G. A., 66, 100, 247, 271, 464, 471, 473, 483, 484, 485, 487, 492, 497, 511
Kelly, M. A., 482, 525
Kelman, H. C., 244, 271, 478, 511
Kelz, J. W., 250, 271
Kempa, R. F., 555, 563
Kendall, B. G., 442, 458
Keniston, K., 479, 504
Kenny, D. T., 478, 511
Kent, R. N., 3, 9
Kerlinger, F., 497, 511
Kerstetter, L., 234, 271
Kessler, M. R., 495, 511-512
Kidd, A. H., 477, 512
Kidd, R. M., 477, 512
Kimball, R., 113, 137
Kimbrough, W., 283, 288, 301-302, 305, 313
Kipnis, D., 282, 284, 291, 314
Kirkland, J., 545, 563
Kirschner, N., 338, 342, 354
Kirtley, D., 479, 512
Kish, G. B., 540, 564
Kissinger, J. R., 38, 48
Kleck, R. E., 482, 512
Kleijunas, P., 82, 101
Klein, A. J., 486, 502

Klein, G. S., 143, 463, 465-466, 467, 473, 506, 509, 512, 520
Kleinmuntz, B., 26-28, 35, 48-49
Klerman, G. L., 397, 408, 409, 410
Klerman, L. V., 375, 420
Klett, C. J., 34, 35, 53
Kline, N. S., 401, 403, 423
Kluckhohn, F. R., 147, 149, 175
Knapp, L., 2, 6, 103-140
Knapp, M., 192, 220
Knapp, R. R., 2, 6, 103-140
Knecht, L., 282, 314
Knight, S. S., 550, 559
Knoblochova, F., 247, 271
Knoblochova, J., 247, 271
Kochansky, G. E., 376, 422
Koenig, F., 486, 512
Kogan, N., 74, 96, 100, 462, 464, 465, 471, 472, 510, 512
Kohen, J., 302, 314
Koivumaki, J. H. See Hall, J. A.
Kolin, E. A., 146, 149, 177, 539
Konstadt, N., 494, 511
Kordasz, F., 389, 391, 416
Korn, H. A., 480, 512
Korn, P. R., 254-255, 269
Koss, M. P., 17, 49
Kostka, M. P., 328, 353
Kraft, L. W., 303, 314
Kragh-Sorensen, P., 401, 403, 414, 415
Kramer, J. A., 254, 264, 272, 275
Kranitz, L., 32, 33, 49
Krasner, L., 246, 271
Krathwohl, D. R., 181, 219, 554, 564
Krauss, H. H., 281, 317
Kreitler, H., 241-242, 271, 528, 548, 552, 564
Kreitler, S., 241-242, 271, 528, 548, 552, 564
Kronenberger, E. J., 495, 511-512
Krug, S. E., 379, 412, 418
Kupfer, D. J., 404, 406, 407, 418
Kurland, H. D., 401-402, 403, 414
Kuusinen, J., 484, 512-513

Lambert, Z. V., 482, 504
Lamm H., 491, 511
Landfield, A. W., 462, 484, 485

Lane, P. J., 37, 38, 49
Lang, P. J., 333, 357
Langer, T. S., 28, 49
Langevin, R., 527, 542, 564
Lanzetta, J. T., 529, 564
Lasakow, P., 281, 282, 283, 287-290, 291, 298, 314
Laskaris, J. B., 531, 566
Laughlin, J. E., 379, 412, 418
Lawrence, P., 338, 355
Lawton, M. P., 349, 355
Lazarus, A. A., 247, 271, 322, 323, 324-325, 331, 342, 355, 357
Lazzari, R., 475, 508
League, B. J., 77, 100
Leaman, R. L., 464, 471, 473, 484
Leary, T., 35, 43, 130, 137
Leckart, B. T., 482, 513
Lederer, W. J., 130, 137
Lee, R. E., 497, 524
Leherissey, B. L., 527, 528, 539, 543, 553, 564
Lehman, R. S., 182, 221
Leib, J. W., 119, 137
Leibowitz, G., 242-243, 264, 271-272
Leitner, L. M., 484, 485, 513
Le Maistre, J., 166
Lepper, C., 302, 316
Lester, D., 38, 49
Leventhal, H., 485, 513
Levil, R., 430, 454-455, 457
Levine, H. G., 248-249, 272
Levine, J., 535, 570
Levine, R., 113, 135
Levinger, G., 280, 281, 314
Levinson, D. J., 472, 477, 478, 499
Levitt, E. E., 476, 477, 513
Levy, J. M., 481, 513
Lewin, K., 143, 175, 228, 236, 272
Lewinsohn, P. M., 22, 30, 35, 49, 406, 407, 418, 419, 420, 422
Lewis, C. S., 124, 132
Lewis, H. B., 464, 469, 473, 492-493, 525
Libet, J., 407, 419
Lichtenstein, E., 252-253, 342, 351
Lillesand, D. B., 247, 251, 272, 322, 335-336, 341, 342, 355
Lilly, R. S., 15, 47

Lindquist, C. U., 254, 264, 272
Lindstrom, D. R., 471, 513-514
Lindzey, G., 61, 98
Lingoes, J., 12-15, 47, 49
Linton, H. B., 67, 100, 463, 496
Lipman, R. S., 374, 375, 381, 409
Lippa, R., 242, 272
Lippman, D., 282, 314
Litt, S., 532, 564
Little, B. R., 147, 152, 161, 175, 295, 309, 484, 514
Little, J. C., 365, 366, 381, 419
Littmann, S. K., 42, 50
Litwak, E., 243, 265, 276
Litz, M. D., 328, 342, 353
Loevinger, J., 59, 100
Lohrenz, L., 468-469, 507
Long, G. M., 494, 514
Long, R. I., 468, 469, 507
Loper, R. G., 18, 32, 33, 48, 49
Lopez, F. M., 248, 272
Lorr, M., 88, 100, 121, 137, 402
Loupe, M. J., 538, 569
Lowery, L. F., 531, 536, 552, 567
Lubin, A. W., 389, 419
Lubin, B., 288, 297, 298, 313, 315, 365, 372, 382, 383, 384-385, 386, 387, 388-391, 412, 413, 419, 420
Lucco, A., 550, 564
Luchins, A. S., 476, 514
Lundy, R. M., 486, 514
Luria, A. R., 428, 432, 433, 444
Luria, R., 380, 417
Lyerly, S. B., 393, 419
Lynch, M. D., 479, 508

McAdoo, W. G., 38, 54
MacAndrew, C., 31-34, 49
McCall, R. B., 530, 533, 556, 571
McCall, R. J., 361-362, 419
McClain, E. W., 109, 137-138
McClelland, D., 532, 565
McCombs, B. L., 543, 563
McCourt, W. F., 32, 33, 55, 247
McCreary, C. P., 38, 50
McCullough, J. P., 381, 419
McCurdy, J. T., 436, 459
MacDonald, A. P., Jr., 477, 479, 480, 514

MacDonald, M. L., 254, 264, 332
McFall, R. M., 247, 251, 253, 270, 272, 276, 322, 324, 325, 335-336, 339-341, 342, 347, 351, 355
McGeogh, J. L., 436, 453, 459
McGough, W. E., 494, 499
McGovern, K., 252-253, 342, 351
McGovney, W. C., 481, 518
McGrath, R. A., 254, 264, 272, 275
McGuire, C., 248-249, 272
McGuire, D., 285, 300, 305, 307
Machiavelli, N., 78
Machover, K., 464, 469, 473, 492-493, 525
McKeachie, W. J., 462, 514
McKechnie, G. E., 6, 141-177
McKinley, J. C., 11, 17, 47, 361
MacKinnon, D. W., 61, 100, 130, 228
Mackler, B., 496, 521
McLachlan, J. F., 387, 419
McMorris, R. F., 496, 516
McNair, D. M., 361, 367, 375, 392, 402, 410-411, 419
MacNeil, L. W., 492, 514
McPartland, R., 406, 407, 418, 423
McPhail, N. I., 365, 366, 381, 419
MacPhillamy, D. J., 407, 420
Macrae, J. A., 485, 514
McReynolds, P., 1-10, 64, 100, 222-277, 347-348, 355, 529-530, 532, 538-539, 540, 550, 556, 565
Mahoney, M. J., 462, 514
Maier, A. A., 248, 273
Maier, N. R. F., 243, 273
Mair, J. M. M., 483, 485, 500
Mallory, C. H., 38, 50
Maloney, M. P., 3, 10
Mangelsdorff, D., 540, 571
Mann, B., 303, 315
Mann, J. H., 246, 273
Margraff, W., 14, 45
Marlow, L. D., 147, 175
Marone, V., 372, 390, 420
Marsden, G., 302, 315
Marsella, A. J., 372, 420
Marshall, M. J., 282, 284, 291-292
Marshall, N., 147, 152, 176
Marslen-Wilson, W. D., 434, 459
Marston, A. R., 247, 251, 252-253, 272, 275, 322, 324, 325, 339-341, 342, 347, 351, 355
Martin, A., 155, 176
Martin, H. A. A., 433, 460
Martin, J., 479, 521
Martin, P., 367, 422
Martin, W. E., 475, 508
Marx, L., 149, 176
Mash, E. J., 3, 10
Masia, B. B., 554, 564
Maslow, A. H., 105, 106, 112, 115, 117, 118-119, 121, 124, 134, 138
Masters, J., 339, 356
Masterson, S., 382, 386, 387, 420
Matarazzo, J. D., 306, 315
Mattocks, A. L., 115, 138
Maw, E. W., 8, 526-571
Maw, W. H., 8, 526-571
Maxwell, G. M., 247, 273
May, A. E., 365, 369, 420
May, F., 480, 506
May, P. R., 35, 46
May, R., 105, 138
Mayer, J. E., 282, 315
Mayer, J. M., 7, 358-425
Mayo, C. W., 486, 505, 514
Mayo, P. R., 42, 50
Mays, G. S. C., 538, 566
Mazis, M. B., 485, 514
Mebane, D., 495, 515
Medley, D. N., 96, 100
Megargee, E. I., 36-39, 255
Mehrabian, A., 146, 147, 284, 305
Mehta, S., 361, 376, 412, 423
Meissner, P. B., 464, 469, 473, 492-493, 525
Melikian, L. H., 282, 287, 291, 315, 475, 515
Melnick, J., 252, 273
Mendels, J., 365, 366, 372, 378, 384, 387, 410, 420
Mendelsohn, G. A., 36-39, 50
Mendelson, M., 363, 365, 412, 415
Menzies, E. S., 255, 273
Merrens, M. R., 3, 10
Messer, S. B., 472, 510, 515
Messick, S., 65, 68, 87, 99, 102, 462, 463, 464, 465-466, 467, 468, 469, 474, 475, 494, 495, 506, 510, 515

Metcalfe, M., 365, 366, 420
Metcalfe, R. J., 484, 515
Meyer, W. J., 536, 566
Meyers, B., 484, 515
Mezzich, J. E., 18, 50
Michael, W. B., 107, 136
Middleton, P., 242, 273
Mikesell, R. H., 373, 374, 420
Mikol, B., 482, 515
Miller, A. G., 484, 491, 515
Miller, C. F., 533, 566
Miller, G., 482, 500-501, 509, 551, 566
Miller, H., 464, 471, 473, 484, 486, 501, 516
Miller, J., 369, 417
Miller, M. B., 530, 546, 566
Miller, P. M., 251, 269, 323, 324, 325, 341-342, 344-345, 346, 347
Miller, R., 247, 277
Miller, W. R., 363, 420
Millon, T., 477, 516
Mills, R. B., 249, 273
Milner, B., 440, 453, 459
Mindham, R. H. S., 401, 403, 414
Minton, H., 533, 566
Minuchin, P., 532, 535, 550, 552
Mirels, H., 283, 288, 297, 298, 301, 310
Mischel, W., 339, 355
Mitchell, C., 472, 500
Mitzel, H. E., 96, 100
Mixon, D., 224, 244, 273
Mock, J., 363, 365, 412, 415
Moely, B. E., 531, 552, 567-568
Moldawsky, S., 233, 273
Montgomery, L. E., 381, 419
Moore, S. F., 496, 516
Moos, R. H., 4, 10
Moreno, J. L., 224-228, 273-274
Moreno, A. T., 224, 274
Morgan, W. G., 331, 333-334, 355
Moriarty, A., 466, 467, 468, 469
Morris, J. N., 375, 420
Moss, H. A., 464, 470, 510
Moss, T., 32, 45
Mouw, J. T., 482, 516
Mowbray, R. M., 394, 395-396, 397
Mowrer, O. H., 228, 279, 304, 311
Muir, W., 363, 367, 375, 396, 423

Mulcahy, G. A., 287, 294, 315
Munz, D. C., 282, 287, 311
Murphy, K. C., 303, 315
Murray, C., 480, 516
Murray, H. A., 60-61, 66, 72, 100, 143, 148, 176, 228
Muuss, R. E., 477, 516
Muzio, I. M., 495, 505
Myers, C. T., 494, 510
Myers, I. B., 146, 176

Neary, R., 540, 571
Neill, J. A., 60, 68, 69, 76
Nelson, D., 40, 44
Newcomb, T. M., 229, 230, 231, 232
Newton, G., 257, 274
Newton, J., 24, 50, 545, 551, 563
Nicki, R. W., 531, 567
Nidick, S., 113, 138
Nidorf, L. J., 486, 516
Nietzel, M., 346, 355-356
Niyekawa, A. M., 475, 516
Nordin, K., 222n, 259-261, 264, 272-273, 275, 347-348, 355
Norman, R. D., 539, 567
Norton, R., 333, 356
Novaco, R. W., 256-257, 274
Nunn, R., 369, 417
Nunnally, J. C., 369, 417
Nystedt, L., 484, 512-513

Oberlander, L., 282, 318
O'Brien, G. T., 253, 268
O'Connell, W. E., 247, 274
O'Connor, J., 361, 421
O'Connor, N., 430, 459
O'Connor, P., 478, 516
Ohnmacht, F. W., 496, 516
Okonji, M. O., 495, 516
Olmsted, P., 471, 520
Oltman, P. K., 493, 494, 516, 525
O'Neil, H. F., Jr., 543, 563
Orenstein, E., 331, 333, 356
Orenstein, H., 331, 333, 356
O'Riordan, T., 167, 176
Osborn, W. P., 482, 517
Osborne, D., 24, 30, 52
Osborne, S. K., 222n, 259-263, 264, 272-273, 274, 275, 347-348, 355

Osterreith, P., 442, 459
Overall, J. E., 369, 396, 402, 403, 414, 421
Owen, G. M., 447, 453, 455, 459

Paivio, A., 430, 459
Paley, E., 467, 468, 519
Pangrac, I., 550, 567
Pankratz, L., 383, 385, 386, 421
Panton, J., 15, 50
Panyard, C., 281, 283, 288, 290
Paquin, M. J., 95, 101
Park, L. C., 381, 421
Parker, C. A., 27, 50
Parrott, G., 479, 517
Parsons, O. A., 40, 43
Partington, J. T., 87, 101
Passman, R. H., 531, 567
Patterson, R., 351, 356
Paul, J., 257, 274
Paykel, E. S., 397, 408, 409, 410
Payne, F. D., 18, 50-51
Payne, I. R., 71, 99
Peabody, D., 479, 480, 517
Pearson, J. S., 24, 30, 52
Pearson, O., 119, 138
Pedersen, D. M., 118, 281, 283, 284, 287, 288, 289, 297-298, 301
Pedhazur, E. J., 479, 517
Pehm, L. P., 407-408, 421
Pellegrine, R. J., 42, 51
Pengel, J. E., 42, 51
Penny, R. K., 146, 176
Percell, L., 338, 356
Perdue, W. C., 38, 49
Perls, F. S., 105, 106, 123, 124, 138, 247, 274-275
Persky, H., 384, 386, 424
Peters, R. A., 531-532, 567
Peterson, R. F., 3, 8
Peterson, R. W., 531, 536, 552, 567
Pettigrew, T. F., 464, 469-470, 517
Phelps, S., 321, 356
Phillips, W., 464, 470, 471, 510
Piaget, J., 532, 536, 551, 567
Pichot, P., 360, 367, 421
Piercy, M. F., 429, 452, 455, 458
Pietila, C., 550, 565
Pilisuk, M., 478, 517
Pinard, G., 410, 421

Piorkowski, G. K., 374, 421
Piper, R. M., 538, 569
Pisoni, S., 285, 317
Pither, B. F., 222n, 259-263, 264, 272-273, 274, 275, 347-348, 355
Pizzamiglio, C. L., 495, 517
Pizzamiglio, L., 495, 517
Platman, S. R., 384, 386, 421
Plog, S. C., 282, 290, 291, 316
Plutchik, R., 384, 386, 421
Pokorny, A. D., 402, 403, 414, 421
Polanyi, M., 180, 220
Polk, J. D., Jr., 544, 563
Pomeranz, D. M., 3, 9
Popoff, L. M., 359, 371-372, 410
Post, F., 381, 423
Post, M., 343, 356-357
Postman, L., 39, 44
Powell, F. A., 480, 482, 517, 523
Powell, W. J., 283, 303, 316
Powers, B., 281, 295, 312
Powers, J., 497, 525
Poynton, C., 365, 372, 381, 416
Pribham, K. H., 427, 459
Price, L., 146, 149, 177, 539, 571
Pritchard, D. A., 468, 517
Proshansky, H. M., 142, 177
Prusoff, B. A., 397, 408, 409, 410
Ptacek, M., 18, 53

Quay, H., 35, 51

Rabinowitz, F. M., 531, 552
Rablen, R. A., 285, 298, 319
Radecki, J. C., 328, 329, 342, 353
Rahman, M. M., 544, 568
Rampton, G. M., 96, 102
Randall, A. M., 374, 375, 409, 422
Randall, D., 468, 519
Rao, G. L., 553, 558
Rappaport, D., 533, 568
Rappaport, J., 288, 290, 302, 316
Raskin, A., 410, 422
Raskin, E., 493, 494, 525
Rathus, S. A., 323, 324, 331-334, 342, 356
Raush, H. L., 257-259, 261-262
Rawan, H. R., 541, 571
Rawlings, M. L., 38, 51
Reatig, N., 410, 422

Reddy, W. B., 113, 138
Reed, P. L., 86, 95, 101, 102
Rehm, L. P., 252-253, 275
Reichenbach, H., 145, 176-177
Reid, W. A., 485, 517
Reinecker, V. M., 280, 281, 312-313
Reinehr, R. C., 146, 176
Reisinger, J. J., 406, 422
Reissman, F., 266, 275
Reker, G. T., 485, 517
Resnick, J., 284, 292, 293, 314
Rettig, S., 74, 101
Rey, A., 440, 442, 459
Rheingold, H. L., 531, 549, 561
Rhodes, R., 32, 51
Rhyne, L. D., 254, 264, 272, 275
Rial, W. Y., 369, 415
Ribner, N. G., 298, 316
Ribot, T., 434, 459
Rice, C. E., 410, 422
Rich, C., 32, 51
Richards, C. B., 371, 372, 425
Richardson, R. P., 554, 568
Richey, C., 336-337, 353
Richman, C. L., 552, 568
Richman, P., 280, 289, 314
Rickels, K., 369, 372, 374, 375, 381,
    396, 400, 409, 413, 415
Riegel, K. F., 533, 568
Riesman, D., 105, 106, 138
Riley, J., 480, 517-518
Rimm, D., 339, 356
Rivenbark, W. H., 280, 282, 294,
    316
Rivlin, L. G., 142, 176
Robbins, M. C., 534, 558
Robinson, J. C., 405, 422
Robinson, J. P., 475, 518
Robinson, W. P., 536, 568
Rofsky, M., 124, 138
Rogers, C. R., 106, 119, 138, 279,
    285, 298, 317, 319
Rogers, J. M., 303, 317
Rogers, P. L., 6, 179-221
Rohan, W., 32, 51
Rohrberg, R., 282, 287, 302-303
Rokeach, M., 81-82, 472-473, 474,
    476, 478, 481-483, 496, 497, 541
Roodin, P. A., 495, 524
Rosen, A., 35, 51

Rosen, H., 383-384, 385, 386, 418
Rosenberg, N., 32, 51
Rosendorn, A., 542-543, 568
Rosenkrantz, P. S., 486, 518
Rosenman, M. F., 482, 518
Rosenthal, R., 6, 80, 101, 179-221
Rosman, B., 464, 470, 471, 510-511
Rosner, S., 496, 518
Rosnow, R. L., 482, 518
Ross, H. S., 536, 568
Ross, S. M., 324, 337-338, 351
Rothburd, M. I., 544, 568
Rotman, S., 32, 51
Rotter, J. B., 232-233, 330, 540
Rowher, W. D., Jr., 467, 510
Rubenowitz, S., 475, 518
Rude, S. H., 551, 571
Ruff, C., 32, 33, 51
Rule, B. G., 492, 514
Russell, G. W., 491, 518
Russell, J. A., 146, 147, 176
Russell, W. R., 436, 459
Rutland, S., 552, 568
Rutledge, L., 468, 519
Ryckman, R. M., 282, 317
Ryder, R. G., 258, 270

Sabshin, M., 369, 417
Salkind, M. R., 365, 422
Salzinger, K., 285, 317
Salzman, C., 376, 422
Sanborn, K. O., 372, 420
Sanders, H., 434, 459, 460
Sandilands, M. L., 491, 518
Sanford, N., 472, 474, 478, 499
Santostefano, S., 467, 468, 519
Sapir, E. A., 180, 221
Sarason, B. R., 248, 275
Sarason, I. G., 248, 275, 535, 541
Sarbin, T. R., 265, 275
Saslow, G., 306, 315
Satir, V., 247, 275
Saxe, R. M., 530, 535, 549, 569
Scheerer, M., 463, 519
Scheier, I. H., 379, 418
Scherer, K. R., 186, 220, 221
Schiffer, D., 544, 569
Schiffman, D. C., 479, 523
Schiltz, J. M., 550-551, 569
Schlesinger, H. J., 465-466, 512

Schneider, L., 32, 33, 55
Schoen, R. A., 466, 468-469, 470
Schroder, H. M., 464, 473, 480, 487, 488, 489, 490, 491, 492, 497
Schulman, L. S., 538, 569
Schulterbrandt, J. G., 410, 422
Schultz, C. B., 482, 519, 534, 569
Schulze, R. H. K., 480, 519
Schwab, H. G., 481, 509-510
Schwab, J. J., 365, 367, 392, 393, 394, 395, 396, 397-398, 409
Schwartz, B. J., 537, 561
Schwartz, L. L., 534, 569
Schwartz, M. S., 40, 41, 51
Schwendiman, G., 117, 136
Schwenker, B., 485, 499
Scott, W. A., 474, 487, 519
Seaman, J., 486, 512
Searles, H. F., 142, 143, 149, 178
Sechrest, L., 66, 78, 101, 485
Seeman, W., 113, 138
Segal, B., 42, 51-52, 540, 569
Segal, S. J., 466, 520
Seidenberg, B., 475, 503
Seligman, M. E. P., 363, 420
Seltzer, B., 434, 459-460
Senn, D. J., 280, 281, 314
Serber, M., 342-343, 356
Serkownek, K., 15, 16, 52
Sewell, W. R. D., 167, 177
Shader, R. I., 376, 422
Shane, J., 536, 566
Shapiro, J. G., 281, 317
Shapiro, M. B., 381, 423
Shaver, J. P., 482, 523
Shaver, P. R., 475, 518
Shaw, G. B., 132
Shaw, J., 298, 310
Shaw, M. E., 248, 268
Shea, J. F., 531, 567
Shepherd, I., 247, 269
Sherif, M., 477, 520
Sherman, M. F., 282, 317
Shimkunas, A. M., 300, 317
Shimota, H. E., 146, 174
Shipman, V. C., 471, 513-514
Shizuru, L., 372, 420
Shmidheiser, N., 537, 569
Shoobs, N. E., 247, 275-276
Shore, R., 290, 297, 313

Short, M. J., 371, 372, 425
Shostrom, E. L., 2, 6, 10, 103-140
Shostrom F. L., 132, 139
Shroeder, H. E., 15, 47
Shulman, E., 282, 287, 317
Shupe, D. R., 480, 520
Siegel, S., 80, 98, 101, 477, 520
Siess, T. F., 95, 101-102
Sigel, I. E., 463, 464, 470, 471, 473, 504, 510, 520
Silverstein, A. B., 121, 139
Simon, L. H., 494, 502-503
Simonson, N. R., 288, 290, 298, 317
Simpson, G. M., 401, 403, 413, 423
Singer, E., 481, 511
Singer, J. E., 78, 102
Singer, J. L., 237, 276
Singer, K., 370, 418
Skeeters, D., 33, 46
Skidgell, A. C., 545, 569
Skinner, H. A., 86, 87, 88, 89, 96, 99, 102
Skypeck, G., 282, 294, 317
Slater, P., 485, 520
Slaymaker, J., 300, 311
Sloan, M., 283, 298, 305, 311
Slovic, P., 74, 102
Smith, D., 33, 46, 159, 177, 482, 520
Smith, E., 441, 460
Smith, G. J. W., 466, 520
Smith, H. V., 438, 461
Smith, K. H., 118, 140
Smith, M. E., 536, 569
Smith, W. G., 389, 391, 416
Snaith, R. P., 361, 376, 412, 423
Snock, J., 482, 520
Snyder, S. S., 534, 535, 544, 546-547, 552-553, 569-570
Snyder, W. U., 119, 137
Solar, D., 496, 520
Solem, A. R., 248, 273
Sommer, R., 149, 177
Sonnenfeld, J., 147, 177
Sorrentino, R., 280, 284, 318
Soskin, W. F., 232, 276
Sote, G. A., 290, 317
Soucar, E., 486, 520
Sousa-Poza, J. F., 282, 287, 302-303
Spaeth, H., 396, 400, 413, 422

Speigel, D. E., 35, 52
Spence, D. P., 463, 506
Spence, J. T., 24, 52
Spence, K. W., 24, 52
Spencer, C., 485, 504
Spielberger, C. D., 24-25, 52, 64, 102, 527, 528, 543, 570
Spotts, J. V., 496, 521
Sprafkin, J. N., 3, 9
Stager, D. P., 491, 521
Stanes, D., 471, 521
Stanley, G., 479, 521
Stanton, H. R., 243, 265, 276
Stefic, E., 361, 421
Stein, K. B., 19-21, 52, 362, 423
Stein, M. I., 61, 102
Steinfatt, T., 482, 500-501
Steininger, M., 480, 521
Stern, G. C., 4, 10, 61, 102
Stewin, L., 489, 521
Stollak, G. E., 535, 549, 569
Stone, G. L., 304, 317
Stone, N. M., 253, 268
Stones, M., 428, 460
Stothart, J. R., 555, 570
Strasburger, E. L., 95, 102
Strassberg, D. S., 284, 300, 318
Strauss, P. S., 479, 523
Streufert, S., 480, 487, 488, 489, 490, 491-492, 497, 519, 521, 522
Stricker, L. J., 68, 102
Strickland, B. R., 287, 300, 304, 305, 306, 307, 311-312
Stringer, P., 484, 522
Strodtbeck, F. L., 147, 149, 175
Stroop, J. R., 466-467, 522
Suchman, D. I., 284, 285, 299, 312
Suchman, J. R., 529, 570
Suedfeld, P., 463, 491, 492, 521
Suinn, R. M., 24, 52
Sullivan, H. S., 143, 279, 318
Sundberg, D., 121
Sundberg, N. D., 3, 10
Sundland, D. M., 35, 46
Supnick, J., 486, 522
Susskind, E. C., 538, 570
Swain, M. A., 257-259, 261-262, 275
Swanson, B. R., 374, 423
Swap, W., 282, 314

Swenson, W. M., 24, 30, 52
Switzky, H. N., 545, 570
Sylva, K., 237, 268
Symonds, P. M., 228, 229, 230, 276

Taft, R., 35, 52, 477, 522
Tagiuri, R., 181, 221
Talland, G., 434, 455, 460
Tallmadge, G. K., 542, 558
Tamkin, A. S., 34, 35, 53
Tanley, J. C., 42, 53
Tarran, V., 365, 369, 420
Tart, C. T., 182, 221
Taylor, D. A., 280, 282, 284, 291, 292, 295, 300, 309, 318
Taylor, J. A., 22-26, 53, 330, 356
Taylor, J. B., 18, 53
Taylor, L., 495, 509
Templer, D., 32, 33, 51
Terdal, L. G., 3, 10
Test, M. A., 247, 269
Tetreault, L., 410, 421
Tetro, R., 32, 51
Teuber, H.-L., 434, 459
Theiss, M., 115, 117, 136
Thelen, M. H., 42, 53, 285, 300, 305, 307, 315
Thomas, D., 480, 503
Thomas, E. J., 323, 356
Thompson, R., 534, 558
Thurber, J., 131
Thurstone, L. L., 291, 318, 466
Tiner, L. G., 476, 503
Todd, S. R., 539, 570
Tolman, E., 228
Tomkins, S. S., 71, 102, 491, 522
Torrance, E. P., 553, 570
Touhey, J. C., 470, 523
Towell, R. D., 532, 535, 553-554
Travis, P. Y., 127
Travis, R. P., 127
Treppa, J. A., 113, 139
Treul, S., 376, 423
Tripodi, T., 464, 471, 473, 484, 486, 501, 509, 523
Troffer, S. A., 182, 221
Troldahl, V. C., 480, 523
Trower, P., 247, 267
Truax, C. B., 279, 281, 284, 287, 290, 298, 299, 317, 318-319

Tryon, R. C., 19-21, 53, 157, 228
Tuck, J. R., 401, 403, 414, 415
Tucker, G. J., 406, 418
Tucker, W. H., 491, 522
Tuckman, B. W., 490, 523
Tulkin, S. R., 282, 319
Tulving, E., 427, 460
Tuma, A. H., 35, 46
Turner, R., 486, 523
Twentyman, C., 251, 253, 272, 276,
    335, 336, 341, 355

Uecker, A. E., 32, 53
Uhes, M. J., 482, 523
Uhlenhuth, E. H., 381, 421
Upper, D., 338, 352
Urquhart, A., 365, 369, 420

Vacc, N. A., 485, 523
Vacc, N. E., 485, 523
Vacchiano, R. B., 479, 523
Valerius, E., 382, 424
Vanderbeck, D. J., 38, 53
Van De Riet, H., 486, 525
Vannoy, J. S., 477, 524
Vasquez, E., 376, 417
Vaught, G. M., 495, 524
Vega, A., 32, 54
Verden, P., 84n
Vernon, J., 492, 522
Vidler, D. C., 535, 541, 570-571
Vidmar, N. J., 74, 99
Vidulich, R. N., 481, 482, 518, 524
Vinacke, W. E., 476, 506
Vogel, L., 382, 424
Vojtisek, J. E., 303, 309
Vondracek, F. W., 284, 288, 292,
    301, 305, 319
Vondracek, S., 301, 319
Vraa, C. W., 303, 314

Wagner, J. F., 482, 513
Wagner, M. K., 255-256, 276
Walk, R. D., 478, 524
Walker, A. M., 285, 298, 319
Walker, E. C., 38, 50
Walker, R. E., 181, 221
Wallace, M., 343, 356-357
Wallach, M. A., 74, 96, 100
Walls, R. T., 551, 571

Walsh, W. B., 323, 356
Walton, D., 113, 139, 441, 460
Walton, H. J., 42, 50
Wang, R. I., 376, 423
Wapner, S., 464, 469, 473, 492-493
Ward, C. H., 363, 365, 412, 415
Ward, M. P., 3, 10
Ware, R., 491, 509, 524
Warm, J. S., 496, 516
Warnick, B., 333, 356
Warr, P. B., 473, 490, 497, 524
Warrington, E. K., 429, 434, 454
Wechsler, D., 432, 435, 443, 541
Wechsler, H., 398, 413, 423
Weckowicz, T. E., 359, 363, 367,
    375, 396, 416, 423
Weinberg, R. A., 472, 504
Weiner, H., 224, 276
Weinman, B., 343, 356-357
Weinstein, N., 365, 366, 372, 378,
    384, 387, 410, 420
Weintraub, H., 531, 533, 541, 556
Weintraub, W., 284, 319
Weisberg, P., 531, 567
Weiskrantz, L., 429, 454, 460
Weisler, A., 530, 533, 556, 571
Weiss, B. L., 406, 407, 418, 423
Weiss, J. L., 17, 18, 45, 531, 560
Weiss, R. L., 3, 10, 252, 276
Wells, F. L., 433, 460
Welsh, G. S., 11, 13, 14, 17, 19,
    21-22, 23, 24, 26, 27, 28-29, 30,
    32, 34, 35, 37, 40, 42, 45, 54,
    361, 362, 416, 539, 557
West, L. W., 281, 293-294, 319
Whalen, C., 302, 319
Wheaton, J., 482, 512
Wheeler, C. A., 38, 54
Wheeler, L., 291, 318
Whisler, R., 32, 54
White, B. J., 480, 500, 525
White, L., 149, 177
White, M., 149, 177
White, W. C., 38, 54
Whiteley, J. M., 250, 276
Whitsitt, M. E., 554, 571
Whittmer, J., 287, 290, 319
Wickens, D. D., 232-233, 275
Wiener, D. W., 14, 54
Wiens, A. M., 306, 315

Wiggins, J. S., 16-19, 61, 102, 166
Wilkins, G., 486, 490, 505, 525
Williams, A., 32, 33, 55
Williams, D. R., 86, 88, 99
Williams, J. D., 482, 525
Williams, J. G., 365, 395, 404-406,
    414, 423
Williams, M., 7-8, 426-461
Wilson, G. D., 84n, 102
Wilson, M. N., 288, 290, 302, 320
Winch, R. F., 130, 131, 140
Winship, B., 328, 357
Wirt, R. D., 34, 55
Wirzbicki, P. J., 545, 569
Witkin, H. A., 118, 464, 469, 473,
    492-493, 494, 496, 497, 525
Witryol, S. L., 545, 569
Wohlking, W., 224, 276
Wohlwill, J. F., 545, 571
Woldman, J., 534, 562
Wolf, R. S., 375, 420
Wolf, W., 155, 177
Wolfe, R., 497, 525
Wolfer, J. A., 479, 480, 520, 525
Wolff, W. T., 3, 10
Wolitzky, D. L., 473, 512
Wolpe, J., 247, 276, 322, 324-325,
    331, 333, 342, 357
Wolpert, F., 480, 506
Wonnacott, T. H., 375, 425
Worthy, M., 280, 281, 282, 293, 320

Wyatt, R., 404, 424

Yablonsky, L., 247, 276
Yalom, I. D., 279, 320
Young, E. R., 113, 140
Young, G., 88, 98
Yourshaw, S., 534, 562

Zacker, J., 477, 525
Zagona, S. V., 482, 525
Zajonc, R. B., 463, 525, 547, 571
Zangwill, O. L., 426-427, 436, 440,
    441, 442, 461
Zealley, A. K., 381, 424
Zelen, S. L., 476, 513
Zigler, E., 528, 546, 548, 552
Zimmerman, S. F., 118, 140, 222,
    330, 334-335, 351
Zimmerman, W. S., 331, 354
Zingle, H. W., 281, 293-294, 319
Zinkin, S., 376, 424
Zoble, E. J., 182, 221
Zoob, I., 146, 149, 177, 539, 571
Zuckerman, M., 146, 149, 177, 193,
    194n, 213, 221, 382, 383,
    384-385, 386, 387, 412, 424,
    539, 540, 571
Zung, W. W. K., 365, 369-375,
    399-400, 403, 412, 413, 415
Zweben, J., 247, 277
Zytowski, D. G., 248, 277

Subject Index

Academic Curiosity scale, 541-542
Acceptance of Aggression (A) scale, 107, 108, 112, 113, 114
Actualizing: defined, 103; interpersonal actualizing, 124-133; intrapersonal actualizing, 105-124
Actualizing Assessment Battery (AAB), 103, 104, 119, 133-135
Actualizing person, assessment of, 103-140
Adjective Check List (ACL): and assertiveness, 326-327, 328, 330, 335; and environmental dispositions, 146, 159; and Wiggins content scales, 18
Adult Self-Expression Scale (ASES), 329-331
Affection (or Agape) (A) scale, 125, 129
Alternate Uses Test, 541
Ambiguity, intolerance of, 477-478, 480, 495
Analysis and synthesis, 480-481
Anger Expressiveness Test (AE-Test), 255-256
Anger scale, 120, 122
Antiquarianism (AN) scale, 151, 153-154, 169, 171
Anxiety (Anx) scale, 63-66, 91-94, 543

Assertion Inventory (AI), 337
Assertive Behavior Survey Schedule (ABSS), 338
Assertiveness: assessment of, 321-357; behavioral assessment of, 339-350; concept of, 322-323; of the elderly, 349-350; and instructional set, 345-347; inventories for, 334-339; self-reports on, 323-339; situational factors in, 343-345
Assessment: action-based methods in, 4, 5; behavioral techniques in, 3, 4-5; in clinical psychology, role of, 1-3, 4
Associations III Test, 541
Authoritarianism, 472, 473-478
Awareness scales, 120-121

Barron-Welsh Art Judgment scale, 66, 539
Beck Depression Inventory (BDI): analysis of, 363-369, 412; item content of, 364; and other depression measures, 375, 378, 381, 384, 390, 394, 395, 396, 397, 399, 401, 404-405
Behavior, levels of, 234-236
Behavior in Critical Situations Scale (BCSS), 343

591

Behavior modification, 2-3, 4-5
Behavioral Assertiveness Test (BAT), 251, 341-343
Behavioral Inventory Battery, 338
Behavioral Role-Playing Assertion Test, 251, 339-341
Behavioral Technique, 404-406, 414
Being Love (BL) scale, 125, 126, 129, 130
Being scale, 120-121, 122
Bentler Interactive Psychological Inventory (BIPI), 65n, 67, 70, 71-72, 73, 74, 75, 76, 77, 81, 85
Bentler Psychological Inventory (BPI), 65, 66, 68, 72, 73, 75, 76, 81, 84-85
Biographical Curiosity test, 542
Body Symptoms scale, 19, 20
Breadth of Interest (Bdi) scale, 66, 91-94
Buss aggression machine (BAM), 242-243
Buss-Durkee Aggression Inventory, 327

California Psychological Inventory (CPI), 18, 155
Capacity for Intimate Contact (C) scale, 107, 108, 112, 113, 114
Caring Relationship Inventory (CRI), 104, 105, 124-130, 133, 134
Category width, 469-470
Children's Anti-democratic Scale, 475
Children's Embedded Figures Test (CEFT), 494-495
Cincinnati Autonomy Test Battery (CATB), 549-550
Circles Test, 468
Clinical Analysis Questionnaire (CAQ), 379
Cognitive complexity, 483-487, 497
Cognitive controls, 465-469
Cognitive Orientation Questionnaire of Curiosity, 548
Cognitive style: assessment of, 462-525; differentiated, 497-498; intercorrelated measures of, 497-498; nature of, 462-464; study of, 464-472

College Maladjustment (MT) scale, 26-28
College Self-Expression Scale (CSES), 323, 325-329, 333
Color-Word Test, 466-467
Communality (CO) scale, 151-152, 153
Complexity (Cpx) scale, 66-67, 91-94
Comrey Personality Scale, 115
Conceptual differentiation, 466
Conceptual Levels Questionnaire, 490
Conceptual Style Test (CST), 470-471
Conceptual styles, 470-471
Conceptual Systems Test, 489, 490
Conflict Resolution Inventory (CRI), 335-336
Conformity, 495-496
Conformity (Cny) scale, 67-69, 91-94
Consistency, 482, 485-486, 491
Constricted-flexible control, 466-467
Constriction scale (CS2), 334-335
Contrast reactivity, 468-469
Core Centeredness scale, 120, 122
Costello-Comrey Depression Scale (CC-D): analysis of, 377-379, 412; and other depression measures, 365, 366, 373, 384
Crafts (CR) scale, 157, 158, 159, 161
Creative Living scale, 120, 121, 122
Creativity, 482, 496
Curiosity: assessment of, 526-571; measures of, 538-553; nature of, 527-528; performance-situations measures of, 548-553; question asking and, 536-538; and school subjects, 553-555; self-description measures of, 539-544; stimulus-preference measures of, 544-548; theories of, 528-533
Curiosity-Arousing Instructional Model (CAIM), 554
Curiosity Inventory, 553
Cynosural Narcissism-Sceptic Curiosity Scale, 544

Decision-Location test, 477
Decision making, 166-171
Deficiency Love (DL) scale, 125, 126, 129, 130
Denny Doodlebug Problem, 481
Depression: adjective checklists for, 381-391; assessment of, 358-425; behavioral observation of, 403-408, 411; concept of, 358-359; Harris and Lingoes Subscale for, 13, 29; interviewer rating scales for, 392-403, 408-409, 410; self-report inventories for, 360-381, 408-414; Wiggins content scale for, 17
Depression Adjective Check List (DACL), 388-391, 413
Depression and Apathy scale, 19, 20
Depression Rating Scale (DRS), 398-399, 403, 413
Depression Status Inventory (DSI), 399-400, 403, 413
Depth of Intrapersonal Exploration Scale, 298-299
Discrimination and synthesis, 495
Dogmatism, 472-473, 478-483
Dogmatism Scale, 474, 478-480, 482-483, 497

Edwards Personal Preference Schedule, 18, 20
Ego Strength (Es) scale, 34-36
Embedded Figures Test (EFT), 469, 493-495
Emotional Disorder (Ed) scale, 28-29
Empathy (Em) scale, 125, 129, 130
Energy Level (Enl) scale, 69, 91-94
Environment: assessment of, 3-4, 5; integrative complexity related to, 491-492; and personality, 145-148
Environmental Adaptation (EA) scale, 149, 150, 169, 171
Environmental dispositions: applications of, 163-171; assessment of, 141-177; and personality research, 142-145
Environmental Response Inventory (ERI), 148-155, 163-171

Environmental Trust (ET) scale, 151, 162, 169, 171
Eros (Er) scale, 125, 129, 130
Existentiality (Ex) scale, 106, 108, 112, 113, 114
Experiential Curiosity Measure (ECM), 542
Eysenck Personality Inventory, 115

Fear Survey, 333
Feeling Reactivity (Fr) scale, 106, 108, 113, 114
Field articulation, 469
Field dependence, 492-496, 497
Friendship (F) scale, 125, 126-127, 129, 130
Fruit-Distraction Test, 467
F Scale, 474-475, 478, 497

Generality, 486-487
Glamour Sports (GS) scale, 157, 158, 162
Group Embedded Figures Test, 205
Group Visual Exploratory Technique (GVET), 546

Hamilton Rating Scale (HRS): analysis of, 392-398, 413; item content of, 364; and other depression measures, 365, 372, 374, 377-381, 403, 404-405
Harris and Lingoes subscales, 12-15
Health Opinion Survey (HOS), 28
House Test, 468
Humanistic psychology, 2
Hypomania (HY) scales, 13, 17, 29
Hysteria scale, 13

Impression Formation Test, 489, 490
Improvisation Test for Couples (IMPRO-C), 261-263, 264
Improvisation Test for Individuals (IMPRO-I), 259-261, 264, 347-349
Improvisational assessment: advantages of, 266-267; and anger, expression of, 255-257; assertiveness and, 251; current developments in, 246-263; described, 223-224; history of, 224-234; in-

formal applications in, 246-248; interpersonal conflict and, 257-258, 259-261; logic of, 237-240; nature of, 234-246; personnel evaluation through, 248-251; problems of, 264-266; psychodrama and, 224-228; real-life behavior similar to, 240-246; and social skills, 252-255; standardization in, 264; studies of, 232-234; techniques in, 222-277
Improvisations test, 228-229
Infrequency (Inf) scale, 85-86
Inner-Direction (I) scale, 106, 107, 108, 112, 113, 114, 117, 118
Innovation (Inv) scale, 69-70, 91-94
Institute for Personality and Ability Testing (IPAT) Depression Scale, 379-380, 412
Integration scales, 120
Integrative complexity, 487-492, 497
Intellectual (IN) scale, 157, 158, 161
Interperson Topical Inventory, 489, 490
Interpersonal affect (Iaf) scale, 70-72, 91-94
Intimacy Rating Scale (IRS), 300-301
Irrelevancy, rejection of, and dogmatism, 481-482

Jackson Personality Inventory (JPI): interpretation of, 56-102; modal profiles for, 86-97; norms for, 57-58; scale construction for, 58-60; scales for, concepts underlying, 60-62; scales for, described, 62-86
Jackson Vocational Interest Survey, 66, 73

Kuder Curiosity test, 542

Leisure Activities Blank (LAB), 156-163
Leveling-sharpening, 467-468
Lines Contrast Test, 469
Locus of Control (IE) scale, 330
Love scale, 120, 122
Low Back Pain (Lb) scale, 29-31

MacAndrew Alcoholism scale, 31-34
Machiavellianism, 78
Maladjustment (MT) scale, 26-28
Manifest Anxiety scale, 22-26, 330
Manipulation Awareness scale, 120, 121, 123
Marriage, mate choices in, 131-132
Masculinity-femininity (Mf) subscale, 15-16
Matching Familiar Figures (MFF) Test, 471-472
Mechanical Orientation (MO) scale, 151, 152, 153
Mechanics (ME) scale, 157, 158, 159, 161
Memory: applications of assessment of, 448-451; in children, 447-448; clinical assessment of, 426-461; encoding failure in, 454-455; factors influencing, 428-432; and hysterical fugue states, 438-439; and learning, 439-442; measurement of, 432-448; nature of, 451-455; and performance of skills, 439; and reproduction, immediate, 442-443; and retention, 443-446; retrieval failure in, 454; retrieval of established memory, 433-439; and retrograde amnesia, 435-438; storage deficits in, 453; and subjective impairments, 446-447
Memory for Stories test, 547
Migration, 145-146, 163-164
Minnesota Multiphasic Personality Inventory (MMPI): and curiosity measures, 539; depression scale of, 361-362, 365, 371, 373, 378, 379, 380, 384, 390; and other measures, 67, 69, 76, 81, 95, 109-110, 115; special scales of, 11-55
Mission scale, 120, 121, 122
Motivation Analysis Test, 380
Multiple Affect Adjective Check List (MAACL), 378, 382-388, 390, 391, 412
Myers-Briggs Type Indicator, 146, 162

Nature of Man (Constructive) (Nc) scale, 107, 108, 113, 114

Necker Cube, 477
Need for Privacy (NP) scale, 151, 152, 153
Nonverbal communication: expectations related to, 182, 212-214; measures of, 181-184; study of, 179-181
Norms: of Dogmatism Scale, 480; of Jackson Personality Inventory, 57-58; of Minnesota Multiphasic Personality Inventory scales, 14, 16, 18, 20, 21-22, 24, 27, 28-29, 30, 32, 34-35, 37, 40-41

Object Sorting Test, 466
Obscure Figures Tests, 540
Office of Strategic Services (OSS), 228-230
Omnibus Personality Inventory, 20
Ontario Test of Intrinsic Motivation (OTIM), 535, 536, 539, 543
Organization (Org) scale, 72-73, 91-94
Orientation scales, 120
Overcontrolled-Hostility scale, 36-39

Pair Attraction Inventory (PAI), 104, 105, 130-133, 134
Paragraph Completion Test, 488-489, 490
Paranoia scale, 13
Pastoralism (PA) scale, 150, 153-154, 162, 169, 171
Perception of others, 485
Personal Orientation Dimensions (POD), 103, 105, 112, 119-124, 134
Personal Orientation Inventory (POI): and actualizing, 103, 105, 120, 121, 123, 124, 133, 134; applications of, 107-112; constructs of, 112, 115-119; and intrapersonal actualizing, 105-119; and therapy, 109-114
Personality: assessment of, through improvisation, 222-277; domains of, 144-145; environment related to, 141-177; inventories of, 11-102
Personality Research Form (PRF),

57, 65, 66, 68, 69, 70, 72, 76, 77, 81
Physician Depression Scale (PDS), 400-401, 403, 413
Pictorial Curiosity test, 546
Picture Motivation Scale, 531
Pleasant Events Schedule, 407
Polarities scales, 120
Possible Jobs Test, 541
Potentiation scale, 120, 122
Preference-for-the-Incongruous Picture task, 546-547
Pretending behavior, 235, 236-237
Process Scale, 298-299
Profile of Nonverbal Sensitivity (PONS): analysis of, 179-221; data-analytic model of, 189-190; design and development of, 184-189; findings of, 196-214; grouping samples in, 198-200; and impaired groups, 207-209; and individual differences, 214-217; limitations and advantages of, 190-196; and practice and training, 211-212; and roles and relationships, 209-211; short tests for, 217-219
Psychiatric Judgment Depression Scale, 402, 414
Psychodrama: applications of, 246-247; development of, 224-228
Psychology: clinical psychology, assessment in, 1-3, 4; interpersonal, 142-143, 144; intrapsychic, 142, 144
Psychopathic Deviate scale, 13, 29

Rathus Assertiveness Scale (RAS), 331-334
Real-life behavior, 235, 239-240
Recreation, 145, 155-163
Reflection-impulsivity, 471-472
Reliability: of assertiveness measures, 326, 330, 333, 334, 337, 338, 340-341, 342, 343, 345, 349; of cognitive-style measures, 475, 479, 484, 489-490, 494; of curiosity measures, 541, 542, 543, 546, 547, 548, 550, 552, 553, 554, 555; of depression mea-

sures, 362, 363, 368, 371, 377, 379, 383, 385, 386, 392, 394, 397, 398, 399, 400, 404, 405; of environmental dispositions measures, 155, 162-163; of improvisational assessment, 232-233, 241, 243, 249, 252, 253, 254, 255, 258, 263, 264; of Minnesota Multiphasic Personality Inventory scales, 16, 17, 20, 21, 24, 26-27, 30, 32, 34, 37, 40; of Profile of Nonverbal Sensitivity, 197-198; of self-disclosure measures, 288, 289, 290, 291, 294, 295-296, 297, 299, 300, 301, 302, 303, 307

Repression-Sensitization scale, 39-42

Responsibility (Rsy) scale, 73-74, 91-94

Revealingness (REV) scale, 299-300

Rey-Davis Form Board, 440-441

Rigidity: and cognitive style, 476-477, 480, 495; and improvisational assessment, 233

Risk Taking scale, 74-75, 91-94

Rod-and-Frame Test (RFT), 469, 493-495

Role Construct Repertory Test (Rep Test), 473, 483-485

Role-Played Dating Interactions (RPDI) test, 254, 264

Role Test, 228, 234

Scanning, 468

Schematizing Test, 468

Schizophrenia scale, 13, 29

Scholastic Aptitude Test (SAT), 202, 204, 205

Scientific Curiosity and Interest Test, 554

Scientific Curiosity Inventory, 554

Self-Acceptance (Sa) scale, 106-107, 108, 112, 113, 114

Self-Actualizing Value (SAV) scale, 106, 108, 112, 113, 114

Self-descriptive essays, 297-298

Self-disclosure: affective manner of, 285; amount of, 283, 287-290, 301-304; assessment of, 278-320;

assessment techniques in, 286-306; child and adolescent measures of, 293-294; concept of, 278-280; dimensions of, 283-286; and discloser's characteristics, 282-283; factors affecting, 280-283; flexibility of, 285-286, 296; intimacy of, 284, 291-293, 300-301; multidimensional assessment of, 306-308; objective measures of, 301-306; observational measures of, 296-301; peer nominations and, 297; and projective techniques, 296-297; rate and duration of, 284-285, 304-306; rating systems in, 298-301; self-report measures in, 287-296; situational inventories of, 294-296

Self-Disclosure Coding System (SDCS), 307-308

Self-Disclosure Inventory for Adolescents (SDIA), 293-294

Self-Disclosure Questionnaire: Jourard's, 287-290, 291, 294, 297-298; Pedersen and Breglio's, 297-298

Self-Disclosure Rating Scale, 300

Self-Disclosure Sentence Blank (SDSB), 297

Self-Disclosure Situations Survey (SDSS), 286, 295-296

Self-Esteem (Ses) scale, 75-78, 91-94

Self-Judgment of Curiosity Scale, 540-541

Self-Love (SL) scale, 125, 126, 129, 130

Self-Rating Depression Scale (SDS): analysis of, 369-376, 412; item content of, 364; and other depression measures, 365, 380, 381, 384, 390, 394, 395, 399-400

Self-Regard (Sr) scale, 106, 108, 113, 114

Sensation Seeking Scale (SSS), 539-540, 543

Sentence Completion Test, 488, 489, 490

Sigel Conceptual Styles Test (SCST), 471

Sigel Object Categorization Task (SOCT), 471
Situation Test (ST), 252
Size Constancy Test, 466
Size Estimation Tests, 468
Slow Living (SL) scale, 157, 158, 159, 161-162
Social Adroitness (Sca) scale, 78-81, 91-94
Social Fear Survey, 333
Social Introversion scale, 19, 20
Social Introversion (Si) subscale, 15-16
Social Participation (Spt) scale, 81, 91-94
Spontaneity (S) scale, 106, 108, 112, 113, 114, 118
Spontaneity Test, 226-227, 233
Sports (SP) scale, 157, 158, 162
S-R Inventory of Self-Disclosure (SRISD), 295
State Epistemic Curiosity Scale (SECS), 539, 543, 553
State-Trait Curiosity Inventory (STCI), 543
Stem Completion tests, 488-491
Stimulus Seeking (SS) scale, 149, 150, 162, 169
Strength scale, 120, 122
Strong Vocational Interest Blank, 18, 20, 154
Subject Unit of Arousal (SUA), 381
Suspicion and Mistrust scale, 19, 20
Synergistic Integration scale, 120, 122
Synergy (Sy) scale, 107, 108, 113, 114

Taped Situation Test (TST), 252-253
Taylor Manifest Anxiety scale, 65, 378
Tennessee Self-Concept Scale, 379
"This I Believe" Test, 488, 489, 490, 491
Time Competence (Tc) scale, 106, 107, 108, 113, 114
Time Orientation scale, 120, 122
Tolerance (Tol) scale, 81-83, 91-94

Trust in Humanity scale, 120, 121, 122
Tryon, Stein, and Chu (TSC) cluster scales, 19-21, 362

Urbanism (UR) scale, 150, 154, 155, 164, 169, 171

Validity: of actualizing measures, 107-112, 124, 126-130, 132-133; of assertiveness measures, 325, 326-328, 330-331, 332-333, 334-335, 336, 337, 338, 349-350; of curiosity measures, 533-536, 541-542, 543, 550, 553, 554; of depression measures, 361, 366-367, 368, 369, 371, 373, 375-376, 378, 383-384, 386, 387-388, 389-390, 391, 394-396, 398, 399, 400, 401, 404, 405; of environmental dispositions measures, 146-147, 154, 162; of improvisational assessment, 249, 253-254, 264; of Minnesota Multiphasic Personality Inventory scales, 14-15, 16, 18, 20-21, 22, 24-25, 27-28, 29, 30, 32-33, 35, 37-38, 41-42; of Profile of Nonverbal Sensitivity, 214; of self-disclosure measures, 288-289, 294, 300-301
Value Orthodoxy scale, 83-85, 91-94
Veterans Administration, 231-232
Visual Analogue Scales (VAS), 365, 380-381, 412

Wakefield Self-Assessment Depression Inventory, 376-377, 412
Weakness scale, 120, 122
Wechsler Adult Intelligence Scale, 541
Welsh Anxiety (A) scale, 21-22
What Would You Do Test, 541
Which to Discuss Test, 546, 547
Wiggins Content Scales, 16-19
Wolpe-Lazarus Assertiveness Questionnaire, 324-325, 342